A History of Norwegian Literature

A History of Scandinavian Literatures

Sven H. Rossel, General Editor

VOLUME 2

A History of Norwegian Literature

Edited by Harald S. Naess

Published by
the University of
Nebraska Press,
Lincoln & London,
in cooperation
with The American-
Scandinavian
Foundation

Manufactured in the United
States of America
The paper in this book
meets the minimum
requirements of American
National Standard for
Information Sciences –
Permanence of Paper for
Printed Library Materials,
ANSI Z 39.48 – 1984
Library of Congress
Cataloging-in-
Publication Data
A History of Norwegian
literature / edited by Harald
S. Naess. p.   cm. –
(A History of Scandinavian
Literatures; v. 2) Includes
bibliographical references
and index.
ISBN 0-8032-3317-5 (cl.:
alk. paper) 1. Norwegian
literature – History and
criticism. I. Naess, Harald
S. II. Series.
PT8363.H57   1993
839.8'209 – dc20
92-20990 CIP

Contents

7. Norwegian Literature since 1950

Jan I. Sjåvik

8. Norwegian Children's Literature

Margaret Hayford O'Leary

9. Norwegian Women Writers

Faith Ingwersen

General Editor's Preface

This book is part of a five-volume work on the histories of the Scandinavian literatures. Its first objective is to satisfy a deep need in Anglo-American scholarship. Various studies dealing with individual Scandinavian literatures have been published in English. Most of them, however, are outdated, out of print, or cover only limited chronological periods, and only few match contemporary expectations of stringent research; furthermore, most of these works have viewed their subject in isolation.

The five volumes of the present work attempt to view Danish, Faroese, Norwegian, Swedish, Icelandic, and Finnish literature as part of both a continuous interrelationship and world literature at large. For the first time, women's and children's literature have been included, and in addition to a comparatist approach, it has been a major editorial wish to incorporate social and cultural history in the discussion.

Almost fifty internationally recognized scholars from the United States, England, and Scandinavia have contributed to the project. It is aimed at students, comparatists, and a general readership interested in familiarizing themselves with a literary tradition that has produced fifteen Nobel laureates. Since the Middle Ages Scandinavian writers and works have been immensely influential in the development of world literature. They are being introduced and discussed here with the hope that an even larger public will find them attractive, exciting, and entertaining.

Preface

Literary histories of Norway and other Scandinavian countries have existed in English for more than a hundred years. They have either been written by English or American scholars and travelers or translated from Scandinavian and other languages. Some of them have mainly provided a listing of the best-known authors and works, whereas others have attempted more consciously to place the authors and their works within a historical framework. Here the aim has been to combine the two methods, making the volume at the same time a handbook of major names and titles in Norwegian letters and a history of the political, social, and cultural conditions that shaped literary currents in Norway. We have emphasized whatever is specific to the Norwegian situation, while trying to show connections with general European trends. Finally, since the book is part of a multivolume work devoted to Scandinavian literatures, we have referred to literature in the other Nordic countries whenever it has been possible and appropriate. We believe that these aims have been generally realized, though naturally in varying degrees, depending on the literary period in question and on the personal priorities of each of the eight contributors to the book. All unattributed translations are by the individual contributors.

My coauthors have all been exceptionally cooperative, and I want to take this opportunity to show my appreciation. Among many others to whom I owe gratitude, let me mention my wife, Ann Mari; the University of Wisconsin Scandinavian Department program assistant, Judy Anderson; my friends and colleagues Dick Ringler, Mary Kay Norseng, Øystein Rottem, and—particularly—Niels Ingwersen. Finally, I wish to thank Sven H. Rossel, general editor of *A History of Scandinavian Literatures,* for his support and understanding throughout.

Introduction

With its emphasis on historical and social context, *A History of Norwegian Literature* does not differ radically in method from most Norwegian treatments of the country's national literature, which have traditionally relied heavily on social history. Over the years, Norwegian literary historians have been criticized for stressing their nationalism, for concentrating their attention too much on the nineteenth century, and for being too "positivistic" in their approach. It is difficult to see, however, how literary history in Norway could have developed differently. Norwegian civilization is a product of the country's history, which is one of unions with more powerful neighbors, and deep-rooted nationalism is a natural result.

Nationalism is not the same as provincialism. Next to Iceland, Norway is probably the most peripheral of European nations, but since Viking times the people there have been travelers, some even becoming cosmopolitans, and it is possible to see in the development of Norwegian literature a periodic interaction of nationalism and internationalism. Writers and critics in Norway have regularly visited foreign shores, from which they have returned with renewed energy, fresh ideas, and (sometimes) a deep appreciation of their home background. Typical examples are Holberg and Ibsen, both of whom spent years outside Scandinavia. From our own century are several writers who, though they resided in Norway, were fully aware of international currents: Sigurd Hoel, whose "Yellow Series" of books introduced the most recent work of contemporary European and American writers, and Tarjei Vesaas, a Norwegian modernist from the remote village of Vinje in Telemark.

The nineteenth century must be central in any history of modern Norway. That history began with Norway's declaration of independence on

May 17, 1814, and, after the country's defeat by Bernadotte's forces the same summer, continued with the nation's struggle to free itself, politically from Sweden, culturally from Denmark. The result was a remarkable burst of energy in the fields of music, literature, and the arts, by such people of note as Edvard Grieg, Henrik Ibsen, and Edvard Munch. From its beginnings, with Lorentz Dietrichson's *Omrids af den norske poesis historie* (1866–69; History of Norwegian Poetry in Outline), Norwegian literary history had the goal of explicating and fostering whatever the author in question considered the spirit of true Norwegianness, and that goal, though modified, continued to inspire the large histories of Norwegian literature published before and after the dissolution of the union with Sweden in 1905. The general emphasis on "positivism" in Norwegian literary histories—that is, on facts of history and biography, on content rather than form—could also be explained as resulting from special conditions in Norwegian history. Because of Norway's inferior position as a partner in Scandinavian unions, Norway's poets have been preoccupied not only with political freedom but also with social equality, and with a few famous exceptions (preeminent among them Knut Hamsun) there has been little emphasis on the doctrine of "art for art's sake" in Norwegian letters. Also influential has been the literary criticism of French positivists such as Hippolyte Taine and Charles Sainte-Beuve, which was channeled to Scandinavia through the work of Georg Brandes and inspired Henrik Jæger's important two-volume *Illustreret norsk litteraturhistorie* (1896; Illustrated History of Norwegian Literature). Though Norway has had schools of French and English New Criticism, some form of historical or biographical approach has dominated Norwegian literary research to the present day. The central name in this development is that of Francis Bull (1887–1974), professor of Scandinavian literature at the University of Oslo, whose approach to literature was a blend of nationalism (the historical "line") and positivism (the biographical emphasis), in some ways a synthesis of Dietrichson's and Jæger's manner. With Fredrik Paasche, A. H. Winsnes, and Philip Houm, Bull authored the magisterial six-volume *Norsk litteraturhistorie* between 1924 and 1955. Also generally within this "Norwegian school" of literary history is Harald Beyer's *Norsk litteraturhistorie* (1952; Eng. tr. *History of Norwegian Literature,* 1956), now available in a fourth edition revised by Edvard Beyer, who also edited the six-volume *Norges litteraturhistorie* (1974–75). A systematic analysis of works on the exclusive bases of historical and social background is found in Willy Dahl's three-volume *Norges litteratur: Tid og tekst* (1981–90; Norway's Literature: Time and Text). Most recent among Norwegian literary histories is the three-volume *Norsk kvinnelitteraturhistorie* (1988–90; History of Norwegian Women's Literature), edited by Irene Engelstad and others.

A History of Norwegian Literature is indebted to all these works; indeed, the basic teachings of the Norwegian school, with its emphasis on national movements and the relevance of history and biography, have been preserved, as have the national reputations of certain internationally unknown writers (Kinck, Uppdal, and others). In the present volume, the nineteenth century is still central, though balanced by a fuller presentation of the literature of the eighteenth and twentieth centuries. As in Beyer's six-volume history, there is a separate chapter on children's literature, and—for the first time in a work meant to encompass Norwegian literary history as a whole—a separate chapter on Norwegian women's literature.

In the planning of this book, some questions connected with the very word "Norwegian" had to be answered right from the beginning. Does the great medieval writer and historian Snorri Sturluson belong to Norwegian literature? Was the eighteenth-century historian and writer of comedies Ludvig Holberg Norwegian? Did Ibsen write Norwegian or Danish?

The history of the five Scandinavian nations is a history of the establishment and dissolution of unions. Sweden was united with (and under) Denmark until 1521. Norway was under Denmark until 1814 and under Sweden until 1905, Finland was under Sweden until 1809 and under Russia until 1917, Iceland was under Norway until 1398 and under Denmark until 1944. During Norway's four-hundred-year union with Denmark, Norwegian literature—defined as literature written in "Norway's official language" by people born or living in Norway—was actually written in the Danish language and sometimes even referred to as Danish. William and Mary Howitt, in their two-volume *Literature and Romance of Northern Europe* (1852), treated the literatures of Denmark, Sweden, and medieval Iceland separately, with the literature of Norway "being classed with that of Denmark, their language and their history being for the most part the same" (Howitt 1: 256). Wergeland and Welhaven are not mentioned by the Howitts; neither are Asbjørnsen and Moe, even though the tales referred to in a chapter called "The Folk Sagas" are taken from the Asbjørnsen and Moe collections. The literary historians of Denmark and Norway have sorted out the problem more democratically by referring to Danish and Norwegian letters 1600–1814 as *felleslitteraturen,* "the common literature." The Danes have also traditionally given equal space to Danish and Norwegian members of *felleslitteraturen,* whereas Norwegian literary historians of the last hundred years have confined themselves to writers born and raised in Norway and Danish-born writers who lived and wrote in Norway; that practice (with its many inconsistencies) has been followed in the present history. The system makes both Peter Frimann (born in Norway, lived in Denmark) and Christiane Koren (born in Denmark, lived in Norway) Norwegian. In the treatment of Danish and Norwegian literature in *A History of Scandinavian Literatures,* an attempt has been made to show different approaches to writers claimed by both countries, as in the case of Holberg, whose Norwegian background and liberal views have traditionally been emphasized by Norwegian literary historians.

About the relationship of Norwegian literature to Icelandic literature, James Knirk writes in Chapter 1:

> The preservation of the Norwegian poetic production of the period is due chiefly to Icelanders, especially through their activity of producing and preserving manuscripts. During the years 870–930, Iceland was settled, for the most part, by Norwegians. Thus the two peoples had the same language in the Viking Age, and although minor dialectal differences allow for a distinction to be made between Old Norwegian and Old Icelandic during the subsequent period of 1050 to 1350, the common term for them is Old Norse. Norwegians and Icelanders had approximately the same background and had basically the same storehouse of tales about legendary heroes and heathen gods. But although the Norwegians apparently held their own in literary production during the Viking Age, they for some reason had to play second fiddle to the gifted poets and storytellers of Iceland thereafter. Nevertheless, the two countries constituted one cultural region, and they enjoy a common heritage in the literary genres that they shared.

Partly because of this complicated situation, older Norwegian literary histories, as well as the most recent English-language history of Norwegian literature (1956), have included a treatment of the Eddas and sagas, even though it is recognized that most, if not all, of this material is of Icelandic origin. In *A History of Scandinavian Literatures,* this material is covered in the Icelandic volume, with the Norwegian volume concentrating on material actually produced by Norwegians. The change in attitude is reflected in the names used over the years to describe this early stage of written Scandinavian literature: *Gammelnorsk* (Old Norwegian), *Oldnordisk* (Old Scandinavian), and *Gammelislandsk* (Old Icelandic). The adjective *norrøn* (Old Norse) has been widely used to describe Old Norwegian *and* Old Icelandic. Of most recent date is the term "Old Norse-Icelandic," now generally accepted in English-language publications.

A semantic conflict has also affected the debate over modern Norwegian. A well-known anthology, *Norske dikt frå Edda til idag* (1960; Norwegian Poems from the Edda to the Present Day), contains only poems written in Norway's second language, *nynorsk,* and the title invites the interpretation that poetry written in the Norwegian language of the majority, *bokmål,* is not Norwegian in the true sense of the word, but rather Dano-Norwegian. Today less than 20 percent of Norwegians use nynorsk in their daily lives, but throughout the last hundred years the percentage has been higher among creative writers, particularly among poets. Nynorsk is not very different from bokmål, and though we discuss in some detail in Chapter 4 the origin of the nynorsk movement, we have seen no reason to write a separate chapter on the history of Norwegian literature written in nynorsk. In recent years some authors have written books in their home dialects, and it is sometimes difficult to decide whether the language in question can best be characterized as bokmål or nynorsk. Nevertheless, we have tried to point out all cases in which the writer clearly uses nynorsk.

More complicated is the case of Sami literature, since it appears in one of two entirely different language families—a Scandinavian language or Sami—and because the area populated by the Sami crosses national borders. Of a total number of some 40,000 Sami, more than half live in Norway. Sweden has a Sami population of some 10,000; Finland 3,000; and Russia, about 2,000. Norway's first Sami novelist, Matti Aikio (1872–1924), wrote in Norwegian, as did the first Sami poet from Norway, Ailo Gaup (1936–). In 1973 a committee was established with the aim of furthering Sami literature. There is now a Sami author's union, which nominates candidates for the Nordic Literary Prize. Among the nominees have been the poet Rauni Magga Lukkari (1943–), originally from Finnish Lappland, but now a Norwegian citizen, and the prose writer and illustrator Nils Aslak Valkeapää, who won the prize for 1990. Valkeapää lives in Finland.

In selecting the authors to be included and deciding the amount of space to devote to each name, we let ourselves be guided by convention, personal taste, and some of the simpler methods of literary sociology. Using the annual bibliographies of *Norsk litterær årbok,* we have tried to measure the critical attention given to more than five hundred Norwegian writers in scholarly books and journals since 1965. There are many sources of error here. Gunnar Reiss-Andersen (1896–1964)—not mentioned once in the years 1965 to 1985—was recently (October 1990) honored with the epithet "most underrated Norwegian poet of the century." In other cases the method has proved useful and helps explain why Dag Solstad (more than sixty entries) received a prominent place in our survey, while Einar Solstad (five entries) had to be excluded. We have paid less attention to such statistics in the section on women's literature, part of the aim of which has been to bring in names not mentioned elsewhere.

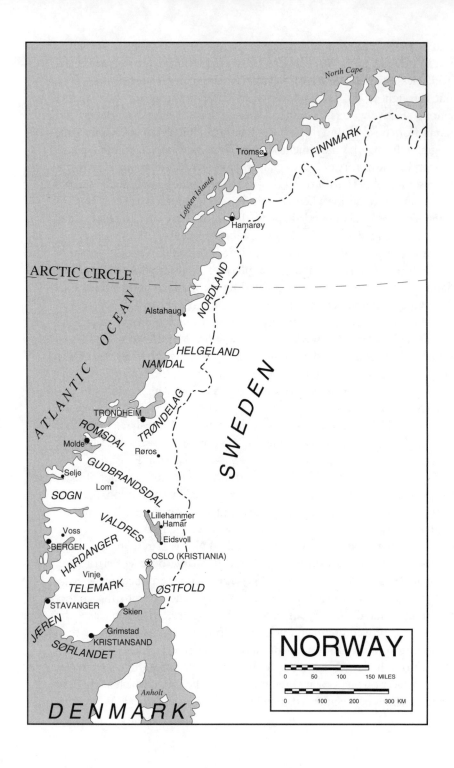

NORWAY

0   50   100   150 MILES

0   100   200   300 KM

Old Norwegian Literature

James E. Knirk

1

When the giant glacier of the most recent Ice Age melted and contracted, the coastal areas of Norway gradually became fit for habitation by plants and animals, and in their wake came humans, ca. 10,000 B.C. It is not known who these first Norwegians were or what their language was like, only that they were hunters, fishermen, and gatherers, who used stone tools. New immigrations followed and cultural impulses were transmitted from the Continent, and by 4000 B.C. agriculture and animal husbandry had been introduced, and the nomads were becoming settled. Cultural upheaval marked northern Europe around 2800 B.C., and a new implement appeared, the so-called battleax. This tool has traditionally, although not necessarily correctly, been interpreted as signaling the arrival of the Indo-Europeans.

The thoughts and intellectual endeavors of these early Norwegians are best revealed in their rock carvings, which date largely to 3000–400 B.C. These drawings are found on broad sloping surfaces and divide into two more or less chronological groups: hunting art and agrarian art. The former includes sticklike figures of wild animals presumably intended to ensure good luck while hunting, while the latter probably reflects sun worship and fertility rites and encompasses cup-shaped hollows and line drawings of ships, carts or plows and tame animals, the sun, and people, often with strong sexual marking. As indicated by this group of pictures, farming and cattle herding were now well established. Metal working with casting of bronze was practiced ca. 1800–500 B.C., and forging of iron began ca. 500 B.C.

By the beginning of the Iron Age, the inhabitants of southern and central Norway had most likely been speaking a Germanic tongue for at least two millennia, but they had no written language. Their rock carvings were pictorial representations, which perhaps communicated symbolically, but were at any rate not pictographic writing like Egyptian hieroglyphics. The system of letters known as the alphabet, with symbols representing individual sounds, not entire words, was an ingenious invention of the Phoenicians in the eastern Mediterranean some one thousand years B.C. This boon was transmitted westward to the Greeks and later from them to the Romans, and with time also to the Germanic tribes in northern Europe. The first prolonged contacts between Germanic peoples and the Mediterranean world came only after the Romans had broken the might of the Celts some two hundred years B.C. and extended their sphere of influence toward the north and west.

Inscriptions with the Older Runes

After being exposed to literacy, some gifted members of a Germanic tribe created a native alphabet, the individual letters of which are known as *runes*. The runic alphabet, called the *futhark* (*fuþark* = the first six individual runes, *þ* = th), is attested in an older version about A.D. 150–750, and the invention of runes has traditionally been fixed to around the birth of Christ. The Latin capitals appear to have been the most immediate model.

The runic forms have appropriate characteristics for incised letters, consisting basically of straight lines, such as vertical staves and slanting branches. The older futhark encompassed twenty-four letters in a special order, a standardized representation of which, with Latin-letter equivalents, follows.

ᚠᚢᚦᚨᚱᚲᚷᚹᚺᚾᛁᛃᛈᛇᛩᛊᛏᛒᛖᛗᛚᛜᛞᛟ

f u th a r k g w h n i j p ë R s t b e m l ng d o

Each rune had a name, the initial sound of which was in principle the sound the rune represented: for example, **fehu*[1] "cattle, wealth" for *f*. The alphabet had its own graphic and orthographic conventions, which were typical of early stages of literacy: for instance, freedom of direction in writing—right to left, left to right, or alternating from line to line.

There are nearly two hundred known inscriptions in this alphabet, not including most of the garbled runic legends found on numerous stamped

---

[1]. The asterisk indicates a reconstructed word form, i.e., a word not actually found in inscriptions.

gold medallions, called *bracteates*, chiefly from Denmark. (The corpus of inscriptions in the older futhark was published in 1966.*)[2] Most of them are short, consisting of only one or a few words, and many defy interpretation. There are often doubts concerning the reading, the meaning, and the purpose of these inscriptions. The majority are found in Scandinavia, especially Norway, and are in the Proto-Scandinavian language. They occur mainly on weapons, jewelry, tools, and stones.

The earliest archaeologically datable Norwegian runic text is on an iron spearhead found among burial goods in a man's grave at Øvre Stabu in Toten, which is dated with the help of weapons of Roman origin found in the same mound to A.D. 150–200. The inscription consists of the word "Tester," a good description of the weapon and one that might bring luck in battle. On precious, military, or everyday items one typically finds names: of the owner, of the person who crafted the object, or of the object itself.

Raised on a grave mound from A.D. 350–400, with which it may be contemporary, the slate monument at Einang in Valdres reads (after a few lost letters have been supplied): "[I, Go]dagastiR, wrote the rune [i.e., the inscription]." The verb translated "wrote" probably originally meant "colored" and thus may indicate that inscriptions could also be painted, probably with a natural red. In later inscriptions, the statement "*X* wrote the runes" is a stereotyped formula of little import. At this time, though, writing was an art not mastered by many, and one could be proud of simply having the ability, as was a man at Reistad on Hidra, who, after hewing the name "IuthingaR" into a boulder, wrote: "I, WakraR, have learned to write."

The Einang text says nothing about a grave mound or any burial, but other inscriptions do. The stone from Bø states simply, "HnabdaR's grave," whereas the one from Kjølevik relates poignantly: "HadulaikaR; I, HagustaldaR, buried my son." HadulaikaR has been variously identified as the name of the son or of the runic master. Such monuments were commemorative stones but not necessarily grave markers, and as memorials they were apparently as much or more for the survivors as for the deceased. Often a text begins with the self-aggrandizing "I" of the one responsible for the inscription.

From Tune in Østfold comes a tall granite monument inscribed with two lines on one side, here called *A*, and three on the opposite. The very end of the text on side *A* has been lost, at the top, and the text on side *B*, which has

---

2. Here the asterisk indicates an anthologized source, listed separately in the Bibliography under Chapter 1.

some damaged runes initially, may also have lost words at both the top and the bottom. Side *A* reads: "I, WiwaR, in memory of WoduridaR, the bread-warden [=lord], wrought [the runes]." This elevated prose, with alliteration (words repeatedly beginning with *w*) and the poetic circumlocution "bread-warden" for "lord," verges on being poetry. Side *B*, which is more prosaic and more difficult to interpret, begins with information about the stone's being for WoduridaR, introduces three daughters as his heirs, and tells something apparently about the funeral feast.

Relationships between two people are stated on a cliff face at Valsfjord, where one can read, "I, HagustaldaR, GodagaR's servant," and on the boulder from Rosseland, which is inscribed, "I, WagigaR, Agilamundo's 'iri-laR'" (Agilamundo is, by the way, a woman). The term *erilaR* or *irilaR* recurs in three other Norwegian inscriptions. It is most likely related to English "earl" but was at that time perhaps a designation for the runic master or for the pagan priest who knew runes. Cult celebrations using beer (for instance, wakes) might be reflected in the word *alu* (literally, "ale"), written on a large granite slab found in a grave mound at Elgesem. This word also occurs on the Bjørnerud bracteate, where it most likely is simply a protective word.

The words "linen" and "leek" on the meat scraper found in a grave urn at Fløksand and dated to 300–400 can be connected with concepts of fertility and have been compared with a medieval story told about St. Olav and known as *Vǫlsa Þáttr* (The Tale of Volsi). Here a disguised St. Olav visits a Norwegian farm where the housewife wraps the penis of a slaughtered horse with leeks in linen; then at dinner everyone takes a turn making poetry in honor of the phallos, called Volsi. St. Olav, however, throws it to the dog and instructs the family in Christian ways. The single upside-down *f* following the two words might stand for its rune-name, "wealth," or may be a shortened form of the entire futhark and an invocation of alphabet magic. The role of magic in runic inscriptions has, however, been exaggerated.

Germanic Traditions and Poetry

GodagastiR at Einang and WiwaR at Tune did not participate directly in the Germanic tribal migrations on the Continent, but indirectly they were a part of it. The ancient Germanic world constituted a cultural community having more in common than only language and alphabet. Also shared were, for instance, laws and organization and even concepts of decorative and verbal art. One verse type was used throughout the Germanic area: the long-line, constructed by joining together by means of alliteration two half-lines with two stresses each.

Alliteration, or initial rhyme, means that words commence with the same sound, for instance, "*prince—power*." Any consonant alliterates with itself, while the combinations *sp-, st-,* and *sk-* rhyme only individually with themselves. All vowels alliterate with each other, but there is a marked preference for variation. The inscription on the stone from Tune already illustrated alliteration in a runic text. A whetstone found in a cairn at Straum in Trøndelag and dated to 550–600 has a runic text, whose two lines with recurring initial *h*'s may be long-lines and the earliest example of an alliterative work song: *wate hali hino horna / haha skapi hapu ligi* ["May the horn wet this stone! / May the second mowing (?) be harmed! May that which has been mown down, lie!"]. The whetstone was apparently kept in water in a horn and used for sharpening a sickle employed in harvesting hay.

Religion and myths were also shared among the Germanic peoples. The Latin historian Tacitus tells in his *Germania* from A.D. 98 of a group of Germanic tribes that in concert worshiped the fertility goddess Nerthus, or Mother Earth. Their ceremonies included processions from a holy grove on an island with an image of the deity in a cart, and embraced the rite of human sacrifice. Archaeological finds in Denmark can be seen to confirm much of the report, and Nerthus is clearly related to the Scandinavian god Njord, who in later tradition is a leading fertility deity.

A war between the peaceful fertility gods, the Vanir, and a more martial group, the Aesir, is mentioned in the mythology recorded in the Middle Ages and may reflect an earlier shift of religion. The Aesir included two well-known gods: Odin (or Woden, as he is known in English), a great god of wisdom and war, who dwelled in the hall of the slain, Valhalla; and Thor, a mighty warrior who traveled around killing giants and creating thunder with his hammer. The tales of heathen gods and their exploits are the stuff of mythic poetry. Such stories lived a viable and functional life for centuries in oral transmission, perhaps partially as cult dramas, before finally being recorded.

The Germanic cultural community experienced mass movements of large groups, some of the leading tribes probably originally coming from Scandinavia, including the Goths. The two centuries of great Germanic tribal migrations on the Continent and the fall of Rome in 476 were precipitated by the encroachment of the Huns. That began around 375, and one of the first casualties was the Ostrogothic king Ermanaric, who committed suicide after being defeated. The greatest of the Hunnic kings was Attila, who led his people from 433 until he was defeated in 451. He died of a nosebleed on the night of his wedding with a Germanic woman two years later, after which the Hunnic empire crumbled. In succession various Germanic tribes conquered and politically controlled parts of the old Roman Empire.

Combined with the ancient Germanic belief in fate and the ethical principles of blood revenge and honorable military conduct, the stories of these turbulent times provided the stuff of heroic lays and legends. They were told and retold, modeled and remodeled, usually for many centuries, before being recorded. As early as the sixth century the Gothic historian Jordanes tells a different tale of Ermanaric's fate, based perhaps on a Gothic poem. The king had supposedly commanded that a woman, Sunilda, be torn apart by horses because her father had betrayed him, whereupon her brothers, Ammius and Sarus, attacked and wounded the king. A similar account, with further fictional accretions, is later recorded in Scandinavian heroic poetry, specifically in the Eddic *Hamðismál* (The Lay of Hamdir), in which the king is called Jormunrekk and the siblings are known as Svanhild, Hamdir, and Sorli, with an added half-brother, Erp.

Transitional Runic Inscriptions

In the time after the great Germanic tribal migrations on the Continent, radical linguistic changes occurred in Scandinavia when many unstressed vowels, and hence syllables, were lost in a process known as *syncope*. This process is demonstrated by the personal message on the reverse side of the Eikeland clasp, dated to about 600, which in a very literal translation might read: "I, WiR, for Wiwio, incised the runes, for the loved [?] one." The name WiR here corresponds to WiwaR on the Tune stone. These and other phonological changes led to a new language stage and left the older futhark less well suited to render the current speech-sounds. A transitional period followed, characterized by some alterations of the alphabet and by orthographic experimentation.

The linguistic development to Common Scandinavian is witnessed on the last known record in the older futhark from Norway, which, with its nearly two hundred runes, is also the longest. The inscription on the stone slab that covered a shallow grave or cenotaph from about 700 at Eggja in Sogn is an enigmatic necrology. The first reading saw the inscription as the relation of ritual acts performed at the funeral, specifically the preparation of the stone and its placement over the grave, its consecration by blood and transportation on a sled. According to this reading, the inscription closed with a riddle concealing the name of an avenger for the deceased and consisting of a question and then statements about a fish and a bird. In the next major interpretation, the preparation of the stone became a curse on grave robbers, and the sled was correctly replaced by a boat. Yet another understanding brought Odin into the riddle as the one who transports souls to the realm of the dead. And recently, the text was read as the tale of a shipwreck, including lines of poetry, and the name-riddle disappeared. There is not enough common ground to attempt a reconciliation of the various interpretations.

THE VIKING AGE (800–1066)

The Viking Age was a period of expansion for all Scandinavia, with Norway concentrating its efforts on the North Atlantic, including especially the northern British Isles, the Faroe Islands, and Iceland. A prerequisite for the Nordic conquests of the time was the viking longship, an engineering feat whose many innovations permitted both swift attacks and the safe transportation of heavy cargoes over long distances. The Scandinavians, however, did more than wreak havoc and loot their way to luxury during the more than two hundred fifty years known as the Viking Age, and their accomplishments in exploration, colonization, and commercial endeavors are patent. During this age the individual Scandinavian kingdoms took shape, and by the end of the period Christianity was established in the Scandinavian North.

Harald Fairhair was the first king to rule over all of coastal Norway, finally achieving sole sovereignty sometime before 900. After his death around 930 came a time of turbulence, as his many sons and grandsons vied for sovereignty under a system of shared kingship. The process of unification, consolidation, and organization of Norway initiated by Harald Fairhair was continued by his great-grandson Olav Tryggvason, who, after youthful years as a viking in Russia and England, was hailed king in his homeland on returning in 995. Having been previously baptized, he began the systematic Christianization of the Norwegians. In 1000 he fell in a sea battle at Svolder, the victim of a conspiracy of Danes, Swedes, and the earls of Lade (near Trondheim).

After an interregnum of fifteen years, Olav Haraldsson, a great-great-grandson of Harald Fairhair, ascended to kingship and became the first really effective ruler of all Norway. He had spent his youth on viking adventures in Russia and England, like Olav Tryggvason, and in his native land continued the process of Christianization begun by this namesake relative. After initial success he suffered both military and political setbacks and in 1028 was forced to flee to Russia. Attempting a comeback, the deposed king fell on July 29, 1030, at the battle of Stiklestad. His death was soon interpreted as a martyrdom, and the martyred monarch thereafter became the patron saint of the country. During political conflicts one hundred fifty to two hundred years later he came to embody the concept of a sole sovereign for the entire land and was hailed the "perpetual king of Norway."

In 1035 St. Olav's illegitimate son Magnus the Good was recalled from exile in Russia and then ruled Norway for twelve years, during the last two sharing power with his uncle Harald the Hardruler, St. Olav's half-brother. As sole sovereign after 1047, Harald pursued an aggressive political and cultural course. The death of King Knut (Canute) the Great of Denmark and England in 1035 had led to the disintegration of his North Sea empire, and when King Edward the Confessor died in 1066, Harald sailed with three hundred ships to England to assert claim to the throne there. King Harold Godwinson and the English army surprised them at Stamford Bridge, however, and with Harald the Hardruler's death the Viking Age in Norway was definitively over.

Runic Inscriptions

After the great linguistic changes that led to Common Scandinavian, a deliberate reform of the runic alphabet ensued, and sometime before the year 800 the younger futhark with only sixteen runes emerged. The paucity of signs and their resultant ambiguity made the reader's task more difficult, whereas the carver's work was made easier, since the characters generally took less room and were easier to form. There were two initial variants of the alphabet, which later became somewhat mixed. The standard Norwegian runic alphabet of the tenth and early eleventh centuries is as follows (the primary sound-value of each rune is listed):

ᚠᚢᚦᛆᚱᚴ ᚼᚾᛁᛆᛋ ᛏᛒ ᛘᛚ ᛦ

f u tha/o r k h n i a s t b m l R/y

Runestones are a hallmark of the Viking Age. As a rule they commemorate someone's death, although they were not necessarily erected on a grave, but could be put up in public places. The memorial epigraphs state who commissioned or sponsored the monument and who was honored by it, usually indicate the relationship between the two, and often contain a description of the deceased or other additions. In spite of their stereotyped nature, these texts are invaluable sources of knowledge about various aspects of the period. Hundreds of runestones from mainly the tenth and early eleventh centuries have been found in Denmark and southern Sweden, and this fashion accelerated in central Sweden, near Stockholm and Uppsala, reaching its apex there during the eleventh century when thousands of inscribed stones were erected.

It does not appear that there ever was a runestone fad in Norway, since the preserved native Norwegian runestones from 800 until 1050–1100 number only around sixty-five, the great majority of them from the mid-tenth century or later. (The Norwegian corpus of inscriptions in the younger futhark known at that time was published in 1941–60.*)[1] The inscriptions reflect the times, with a surprisingly large number commemorating men who died young, surely many of whom were victims of their own viking exploits. The stone from Galteland in Setesdal must date to ca. 1015, for it reads: "Arnstein raised this stone in memory of Bjor, his son; he died in the army when Knut [the Great] attacked England." Eleventh-century stones may have Christian additions to the stereotyped memorial formulation, such as, "May God help his soul."

Some stones include reference to persons otherwise known in history. Erling Skjalgsson, for example, whose death by deceit in 1028 precipitated King Olav Haraldsson's flight to Russia, is commemorated on a stone cross raised in Stavanger. The gneiss monument more than eleven feet tall at Oddernes (Kristiansand) was first raised in connection with a pagan death, probably in the tenth century, as can be inferred from the weathered dedication on the broad side. An inscription added along the small side, perhaps around 1040, reads: "Eyvind built this church, the godson of St. Olav, on his ancestral land." This Eyvind may be identical with the man who erected a monument at nearby Søgne in memory of his son, and he has perhaps correctly been identified as the Eyvind Aurochs-horn of later kings' sagas.

Two of the finest monuments from the early eleventh century come from eastern Norway. Both are of red-brown sandstone, were put up by women in memory of relatives, were ornamented with drawings, and apparently close with lines of poetry. The Alstad stone, which is adorned with stylized horses and a bird on one broad side and intertwining tendrils on the other, was transported more than sixty miles by a certain Jorunn and put up to commemorate her husband. It was reused some fifty years later by a man who wanted to remember his son who had perished in Russia. The text on the Dynna stone, whose drawings from the Nativity are more naturalistic and may indicate that it is somewhat younger than the Alstad stone, reads: "Gunnvor made a bridge, Thrydrik's daughter, in memory of Astrid, her daughter: She was the handiest / maiden in Hadeland."

---

1. The asterisk indicates an anthologized source, listed separately in the Bibliography under Chapter 1.

Inscriptions from the Viking Age on movable objects are considerably fewer than those on stones and tell usually much less. Remarkable, however, is the poem on a silver neck-ring from Senja in northern Norway, dated to 1000–1025 (the alliteration that binds lines together in pairs is here marked): *Fórum drengja / Fríslands á vit, / ok vígs fǫtum / vér skiptum* ["We traveled to an encounter with the young lads from Frisia, and we it was who split spoils of war"].

Eddic Poetry

Runes were apparently not used for fixing long literary or historical texts, but tales were told and poetry proliferated during the Viking Age, if only or mainly by word of mouth. A good deal of the traditional stuff of heroic poetry, based on historical happenings during the great Germanic tribal migrations and transmitted orally through centuries, probably found fairly final expression during this time, although it was not written down until several centuries later. Also much of the mythic poetry about the old Germanic gods in their special Scandinavian shape could have been put into somewhat final form.

The preservation of the Norwegian poetic production of the period is due chiefly to Icelanders, especially through their activity of producing and preserving manuscripts. During the years 870–930 Iceland was settled, for the most part, by Norwegians. Thus the two peoples had the same language in the Viking Age, and although minor dialectal differences allow for a distinction to be made between Old Norwegian and Old Icelandic during the subsequent period of 1050 to 1350, the common term for them is Old Norse. Norwegians and Icelanders had approximately the same background and basically the same storehouse of tales about legendary heroes and heathen gods. But although the Norwegians apparently held their own in literary production during the Viking Age, they for some reason had to play second fiddle to the gifted poets and storytellers of Iceland thereafter. Nevertheless, the two countries constituted one cultural region, and they enjoy a common heritage in the literary genres that they shared. Icelanders, however, developed in addition specifically Icelandic literary genres.

In old Germanic poetry, alliteration had to occur on stressed syllables, and normally the first stress of the concluding half-line had to alliterate with either one or both of the stressed syllables in the preceding half-line. In most old Germanic poetry, the long-lines could go on and on freely recounting an epic story without any obvious breaks. A specifically Scandinavian contribution to Germanic versification was the development of stanzaic structure.

Groups of half-lines, usually eight (but also six or ten), constitute distinct, self-contained building blocks in the story.

Old Norse verse can be divided into two general types: Eddic poetry and skaldic poetry. Eddic poems contain traditional material about heroes or gods and are related objectively by anonymous singers and later recorders whose roles were apparently not considered especially creative. The timeless tales were told simply, and the presentation was fairly straightforward. Skaldic poems, in contrast, are subjective verses composed by named authors whose main task was the snapshot presentation of occasional material in a complicated form, stylistically as well as metrically. The skaldic lyrics that have been preserved are often in honor of a prince. Although the basic subject matter of Eddic poetry is much older than the incidental events that evoked skaldic poetry, the two existed generally side by side. The distinctions between the two categories are not even always that sharp.

The term "Eddic" is derived from *Edda,* the name of an Icelandic treatise containing mythical stories and concerning poetic composition. This work, whose title should perhaps be translated "Poetics," is attributed in a manuscript from the early fourteenth century to Snorri Sturluson (died 1241). Many verses are cited or retold in Snorri's *Edda* (Eng. tr. 1987), and in the Renaissance it was assumed that they were quoted and referred to from an older collection, the author of which could have been none other than the almost legendary Icelandic scholar Sæmund Sigfusson the Learned, who flourished a century before Snorri. Therefore, when a medieval manuscript containing the majority of these poems was found in Iceland in the mid-seventeenth century and sent to the king of Denmark, it was dubbed *Sæmund's Edda.* It has also been termed the *Elder Edda,* or in English the *Poetic Edda,* as against Snorri's younger or prose *Edda*; it should, however, simply be called the Codex Regius of Eddic poetry. Almost the entire corpus of this category of poetry is preserved in this royal manuscript, and in manuscripts of Snorri's *Edda,* with only a few additional poems or fragments recorded elsewhere. (Eddic poetry is translated in *The Poetic Edda,* 1962, or *Poems of the Vikings,* 1969.)

Eddic poems were composed at different times, and some of the oldest ones are at best irregularly strophic, but regular stanzaic structure developed with time under the influence of skaldic poetry. The most common Eddic meter is called old lore meter (*fornyrðislag*), which consists of a simple stanza typically with four pairs of half-lines, and in general with two to three unstressed syllables per half-line in addition to the two stressed. It is an epic meter usually used in narrating action. An example follows from the cosmological poem *Vǫluspá* (The Sibyl's Prophecy), with alliteration marked in bold and also attempted in English, and stress otherwise indicated by roman script (note that Ymir was the giant from whose body the world was created):

Ár vas alda,	Early was the age
þat er Ymir byggði,	when Ymir lived;
vara sandr né sær	there was no sand, nor sea,
né svalar unnir;	nor surges cool;
jǫrð fannsk æva	earth existed never,
né upphiminn,	nor above-heaven,
gap var ginnunga,	the gap was of the great void,
en gras hvergi.	and grass nowhere.

The other basic Eddic meter, called song meter (*ljóðaháttr*), is mainly found in poems consisting of direct quotation, either dialogue or monologue, or of gnomic statements. Here each half-stanza consists of a normal pair of half-lines followed by a single line, often called a full line, with three (or sometimes two) stresses, two of which alliterate. An example follows from the wisdom poem *Hávamál* (Sayings of the High One), with alliteration marked in bold and attempted in English, and stress otherwise indicated by roman script:

Deyr fé,	Cattle die,
deyja frændr,	kinsmen die,
deyr sjálfr it sama;	one dies oneself also;
enn orðstírr	but word-esteem
deyr aldregi	dies ever not
hveim er sér góðan getr.	for him who gains good fame.

The Eddic poem that occupies the most significant position in the Norwegian cultural heritage is *Hávamál*. Although the work is recorded only in Icelandic manuscripts, some formulations reveal a Norwegian background, especially the description of Norwegian, not Icelandic, nature, including herons, wolves, reindeer, pine trees, and oaks. Additional Norwegian elements are the rule by kings and the Viking Age burial custom of cremation. The High One in the title is a poetic name for Odin, and the 164 stanzas grouped as his sayings represent various poems and fragments not originally found together. The first half, approximately, concerns manners and practical morality and encompasses a collection of aphorisms and ancient proverbs covering such topics as hospitality, trust, friendship, human interaction, and honor, including, for example, "Hail to hosts! A guest has come in; where shall he sit? He has haste who at the entrance must try to make his case," and "A fool who comes together with other people ought best be quiet; no one knows that he knows nothing, if he does not speak too much." Additional gnomic verses and further advice follow, and then a section of heathen religious mysticism, specifically Odin's acquisition of wisdom, and runic magic. The conglomerate poem closes with a list of magic songs, which are partially in an expansion of song meter called magic meter (*galdralag*). Here the last line of song meter is repeated and varied as a parallel seventh line.

Vǫlundarkvida (The Lay of Volund) likewise reveals a clear Norwegian connection, beginning in Lappland. It relates first the fairy tale of three swan-maidens who married three brothers, one of whom was the smith Volund, in English known as Wayland the Smith. Volund is later captured by a greedy king, hamstrung at the behest of his malicious queen, and forced to live on an island and produce fine objects for the ruler. The rest of the work concerns his ruthless revenge, which encompasses killing the monarch's sons and fashioning goblets out of their skulls, getting the monarch's daughter pregnant, and then informing the despot of his doings before flying away on wings he must have crafted.

Rígsþula (The Lay of Rig), preserved in a manuscript of Snorri's *Edda*, also reveals a connection to Norway through its presentation of more Norwegian than Icelandic social structure. Rig, a name of Celtic background which is said to be a cover for the god Heimdall, is presented as the progenitor of the human race. He visits successively three couples from different social classes, and their homes, activities, dress, and eating customs are each in turn described. Rig's intercourse with the respective wives results in three offspring—Thrall, Karl (churl), and Earl—whose physical characteristics, lifestyle, work, and so forth are vividly and often amusingly presented. These three proceed to have children, whose names are likewise descriptive of their station in society as slaves, farmers, or chieftains. Earl's youngest is called Kon the Young, which as a play on words, *Kon-* plus *ungr* (young), renders the Old Norse for king. Unfortunately not complete, this poem is likely from Christian times and may have been composed to honor a Norwegian ruler.

The second-best-known Eddic poem in Norway today is *Vǫluspá*, a cosmology and history of the world from the beginning of time through Ragnarok, the doomsday of the gods, after which the world will arise anew and cleansed. The work, which presents a philosophy of life with vivid pictures, is couched as answers to Odin put in the mouth of a female seer. It reflects the Viking Age and its meeting with Christianity and was probably composed toward the end of the tenth century, possibly by an Icelander who had personally experienced this confrontation and attempted to view the heathen myths in a Christian light. The death of the innocent Balder, before the doom of the gods, and his second coming after Ragnarok show the Christian remodeling.

The individual poems in the Codex Regius of Eddic poetry are arranged according to a plan: first mythic poetry about the gods and then heroic legends. For good reason it begins with the cosmological *Vǫluspá* and proceeds to three gnomic poems with Odin as the main character, starting with *Hávamál*. In *Vafþrúðnismál* (The Lay of Vafthrudnir), Odin proves himself the master of mythical lore in a contest with the giant Vafthrudnir, and in *Grímnismál* (The Lay of Grimnir), disguised as Grimnir and a captive, he instructs a king's son. After a dramatic interlude about the fertility god Frey's love for a giant maiden in *Fǫr Skírnis* (Skirnir's Journey) comes *Harbarðsljóð* (The Lay of Harbard), a humorous matching of wits between Odin, disguised as the ferryman Harbard, and Thor. This poem is followed by three more about the exploits of Thor, the foe of the forces of evil. In *Hymiskviða* (The Lay of Hymir), Thor goes fishing for the World Serpent with the giant Hymir and defeats the giant in contests of strength, whereas in *Lokasenna* (Loki's Mocking), Thor must act as a bouncer after a name-calling dispute in which the trickster Loki derides the gods. Then in the hilarious poem *Þrymskviða* (The Lay of Thrym), often considered a late work, Thor is forced to dress as a goddess to retrieve his hammer from the giants. This part closes with *Vǫlundarkviða*, on the turning point to heroic legend, followed by *Alvíssmál* (The Lay of Alvis), a poem in which Thor matches wits with an elf whose name means all-wise.

The section with heroic legend begins with the Helgi poems, which include *Helgakviða Hundingsbana in fyrra* (The First Lay of Helgi Hundingsbani) and what modern editors have determined to be two separate works: *Helgakviða Hjǫrvarðssonar* (The Lay of Helgi Hjorvardsson) and *Helgakviða Hundingsbana ǫnnur* (The Second Lay of Helgi Hundingsbani). They concern the Norwegian viking king Helgi Hjorvardsson and his beloved Svava, a valkyrie (that is, one of Odin's female helpers who decide who dies in battle), both of whom are reincarnated as lovers, he as Helgi the slayer of Hunding and she as the valkyrie Sigrun. The tragic element that characterizes genuine heroic poetry is missing from the first poem, which could well have been composed sometime during the eleventh century. The other two are probably correspondingly late conglomerations of prose and perhaps older poetry. The Helgi poems are connected with the following poems since Helgi Hundingsbani is supposedly a half-brother of the hero of the subsequent cycle.

The next poems, some of them consisting of a combination of interstitial prose and poetry, concern the legend of Sigurd the Dragon-slayer, who corresponds to the Siegfrid of the German *Nibelungenlied* (The Lay of the Nibelungs). The entire fateful plot is first plainly sketched in *Grípisspá* (The Prophecy of Gripir), and then the tale of the youthful exploits that won Sigurd his byname are told in detail in *Reginsmál* (The Lay of Regin) and *Fáfnismál* (The Lay of Fafnir [the dragon's name]). An intermezzo consisting of the valkyrie Sigrdrifa's instruction of Sigurd (in, among other things, runes), *Sigrdrífumál,* has lost its ending, since eight sheets are missing from the manuscript. The lacuna contained material connecting Sigurd, as in old Germanic tradition, with the Burgundian tribe, called the Gjukungs in Old Norse, including his wooing of the sometime valkyrie Brynhild for the leader of the Gjukungs and his own marriage to that prince's sister, Gudrun. Thus the fateful love triangle was established which led to the hero's tragic downfall. The manuscript resumes with the final part of a dramatic account of Sigurd's death by the deceit of his brothers-in-law, *Brot af Sigurðarkviða* (Fragment of a Sigurd Lay), followed by a poignant lament, *Guðrúnarkviða in fyrsta* (The First Lay of Gudrun). The tragic story is again told, mainly from Brynhild's point of view, in *Sigurðarkviða in skamma* (The Short Lay of Sigurd), after which follows Brynhild's self-justification for her part in Sigurd's murder in *Helreið Brynhildar* (Brynhild's Journey to Hel).

Gudrun vents her grief again in *Guðrúnarkviða in forna* (The Old Lay of Gudrun), another elegy in which her marriage to Atli (Attila) is also explained, whereas in *Guðrúnarkviða in þriðja* (The Third Lay of Gudrun), she clears herself by ordeal of a charge of infidelity to Atli. Reason for Hunnic animosity toward the Gjukungs is established in another elegy, *Oddrúnargrátr* (Oddrun's Lament), after which Gudrun becomes the connecting thread, playing first an unwilling part in the destruction of the Gjukungs by the Huns in *Atlakviða* (The Lay of Atli) and in the rather late literary reworking of the same material known as *Atlamál in grænlendsku* (The Greenlandic Lay of Atli). After Atli's death Gudrun remarries and is connected through her children with the tale of the Gothic king Ermanarik. In *Guðrúnarhvǫt* (The Egging of Gudrun), she first incites her sons Hamdir (Ammius) and Sorli (Sarus) to take revenge on Jormunrekk (Ermanarik) for the death of their sister, Svanhild (Sunilda), who was trampled by horses, and then tells her personal tale of woes. *Hamðismál,* the last poem in the collection, relates the slaying of Jormunrekk. Hamdir and Sorli, who are unaffected by metal weapons, avenge themselves on the ruler, cutting off his feet and hands. But since Erp, their half-brother whom they recently quarreled with and killed, is no longer around to cut off his head, the king, before expiring, succeeds in instructing his men to stone the attackers to death. *Atlakviða* and *Hamðismál* are considered to be among the oldest Eddic poems.

Skaldic Poetry

Snorri's *Edda*, although it quotes Eddic poetry initially and retells it generously, has as its main thrust skaldic poetry. The word *skáld* means simply "poet," but it most correctly applies to those who created original, occasional compositions, not the anonymous editors or adapters who in essence only recorded traditional mythical and heroic stories.

In addition to content, skaldic poetry reveals striking deviations from Eddic poetry in its complexity and artificiality, the differences embracing meter, structure, vocabulary, style, and word order. Skaldic poetry usually employs as a structural embellishment a type of rhyme and also counts syllables. The rhyme is not end rhyme, although that occurs, but two types of internal syllabic assonance, whose nature and position in the lines are strictly regulated. Full rhyme consists of the chiming of two stressed syllables with identical vowel and following consonant sounds (e.g., in English, "*gales*" and "*sails*ships"), whereas in half-rhyme the vowels in the two stressed syllables vary while the following consonants are the same (e.g., "*bold*" or "*bold*ly" and "*held*"). The skaldic meter above all others is court meter (*dróttkvæðr háttr*, or simply *dróttkvætt*). The stanza here, which usually divides naturally into two half-stanzas, consists of eight half-lines, each with six syllables and three stresses; every half-line ends with a trochaic foot, whose stressed syllable must participate in the scheme of internal assonance, with half-rhyme in the odd-numbered lines alternating with full rhyme in the even-numbered ones. In addition, the main alliterating stave must be on the first syllable of the even-numbered lines, and there have to be two so-called props alliterating with it in the preceding odd-numbered line.

The following is an example of court meter taken from Thorbjorn Horncleaver's *Glymdrápa* (The Din Poem). To demonstrate the metrical structure, alliteration is marked with boldface, internal rhyme with underlining, and stress otherwise with roman script; a simpler rephrasing with some explanations follows the quite literal translation:

Há<u>ði</u> **g**ramr, þars **g**n<u>uð</u>u,	Held the leader, there where roared,
geira hr<u>egg</u> við s<u>egg</u>i,	spears' storm with men,
(r<u>auð</u> f**n**ýsti **b**en **b**l<u>óð</u>i)	(red wounds sneezed blood)
bryng<u>ogl</u> í dyn Sk<u>ogl</u>ar,	mailcoat-geese in the din of Skogul,

þás á rausn fyr ræsi	when in the forecastle before the chieftain
(*réð egglituðr*) *seggir*	(ruled/won the cutting-edge-dyer) men
—*æfr gall hjǫrr við hlífar*—	—the eager sword resounded on shields—
hnigu fjǫrvanir (*sigri*).	stooped life-lacking (victory).

That is to say: "The leader held spears' storm [i.e., battle] with men where mailcoat-geese [arrows] roared in the din of Skogul [a valkyrie; her din is battle]—red wounds sneezed blood—, when in the forecastle, before the chieftain, men stooped dead; the eager sword resounded on shields; the cutting-edge-dyer [warrior] won victory."

A *drápa,* or stately poem consisting of several stanzas, was to have one or more refrains of at least one pair of half-lines set at fixed intervals. A shorter poem without a refrain (*flokkr*) was neither as solemn nor as respected, while an occasional stanza was referred to as a loose verse (*lausavísa*). Both the stanzaic structure of court meter and the architechtonic form of the *drápa* are almost fully developed in the earliest skaldic poetry, the beginnings of the art being lost in the dark of prehistoric times in Norway.

Many additional skaldic meters occur, though less frequently. The one called chant meter (*kviðuháttr*) is much simpler. Metrically, the lines resemble Eddic old lore meter, with only two stresses per half-line and alliteration binding the half-lines together in pairs, but the number of syllables per half-line is fixed, alternating between three and four; none of the rest of the skaldic metrical paraphernalia is present. An example from Thjodolf of Hvinir's *Ynglingatal* (List of the Ynglings) is:

Varð framgengt,	It was fulfilled,
þars Fróði bjó,	there where Frodi dwelled,
freigðar orð,	the fateful word,
es at Fjǫlni kom.	which to Fjolnir came.
Siklingi	On the prince
svigðis geira	of pikes of the ox [i.e., horns]
vágr vindlauss	the windless wave [i.e., drink]
of viða skyldi.	should work death.

The "wave of [drinking] horns" is "drink," and the drunken Fjolnir is said to have drowned in a vat of alcoholic beverage while partying at Frodi's.

The most conspicuous characteristic of skaldic poetry, besides meter and structure, is its language, both vocabulary and style. Skaldic verse is a poetry of nouns, secondarily of adjectives, much of its content consisting of substitutions, reworkings, and rephrasings of designations for gods, men, ships, weapons, horses, women, and so on. Its peculiar treasure of words encompasses poetic names called appellations (*heiti*), either simple synonyms, such as "steed" for "horse," or statement-of-fact periphrases, such as "Sif's husband" for "Thor" (which he was), or "ring-breaker" for "a generous man, usually a prince," since bits of precious rings were used for payment. As much as half of the entire vocabulary of a poem can be specifically poetic.

The style of skaldic poetry is metaphorical, and a device called a *kenning* abounds. This system of circumlocution consists of two nouns, a base word and a qualifier in the genitive case (or its equivalent), which together metaphorically render a new concept. For instance, a "ship" may be termed the "horse of the sea." The compound noun mentioned above, "ring-breaker" ("breaker of rings") for "prince," is another example. In skaldic poetry, substitution is allowed for each of the elements of the kenning, with either synonymous appellations or further kennings. Thus "the moon of the ship" as a kenning for "shield" (since round shields were mounted on the gunwales of viking ships) could be extended and expressed as "the moon of the horse of the sea" or "the moon of the steed of waves." This freedom can lead to chains of intricate periphrasis in which almost nothing is called by its own name.

The relatively free word order of Old Norse was employed to the extreme by the skalds in their elaborate art; in fact, the word order in skaldic verse often bears little relation to that in ordinary prose. A further complicating factor for the understanding of their poems is the possibility of sentence division. Skaldic stanzas sometimes consisted of two or three segmented sentences with their parts intricately intertwined, as in the metrical example of court meter quoted above. The art is ornamental and formal, rather than natural and realistic, as is also obvious in the laudatory contents, in which generalities abound: the din of battle, the beauty of women, the bravery of men. More effort obviously goes into the form, and less into the content.

The names of some 250 skalds from about 800 to 1300 are known, but most of their poems are lost, and those that are preserved, embedded in historical, semihistorical, or pseudohistorical prose sagas or quoted in Snorri's *Edda,* are frequently fragmentary, jumbled, or otherwise corrupted. No collection like the Codex Regius of Eddic poetry was made. Few examples of skaldic poetry exist in Sweden, and none in Denmark, save in some Icelandic prose tales of later centuries in which skaldic verse is put into the mouths of Danes. Works by about twenty Norwegian skalds, including a few women, plus some five Icelandic settlers who were born in Norway, are recorded from the ninth and tenth centuries. Many are, however, represented by only a few lines or stanzas. (English translations are found in *The Skalds,* 1968, and in *Corpus Poeticum Boreale,* vol. 2, 1883.)

The earliest skald whose poetry has been transmitted is Bragi Boddason the Old, who flourished in southwestern Norway in the early ninth century. His only preserved work of any length is a shield-poem, that is, a work describing four scenes painted on a shield given to the poet. It was composed to honor the donor, whom Snorri identifies as Ragnar Lodbrok (Shaggy-breeches), a figure also known from legend. Two of the stories are mythical and two are heroic, including the one in which Hamdir and Sorli slay Jormunrekk but perish themselves. The refrain in *Ragnarsdrápa* (Ragnar's Poem) reads: "Ragnar gave me the moon of the vehicle of Ræ and a multitude of stories"; Ræ is a viking chieftain, his vehicle would therefore be a ship, and the ship's "moon" is a shield.

Another ninth-century skald from southern Norway, Thjodolf of Hvinir (Kvinesdal), also composed a shield-poem in court meter, for some reason entitled *Haustlǫng* (Autumn-long). The first stanza from Thjodolf's other major poem, the genealogical *Ynglingatal*, was quoted above. The Ynglings were an ancient branch of the royal house of Sweden and the ancestors of Harald Fairhair. Supposedly composed for Harald's cousin, King Rognvald, the poem consists basically of information about the fates of some twenty-six generations of forefathers.

Harald Fairhair was himself a skald, but only the first stanza from his long poem of mourning over his beloved and bewitching Lapp wife Snefrid is preserved, plus a few lines of an offhand verse. Harald, perhaps using Charlemagne as a model, introduced into Norway the practice of entertaining court poets, sharing his table with a number of Norwegian skalds.

One of Harald's skalds was Thorbjorn Horn-cleaver, the author of *Glymdrápa* (quoted above), which preserves for posterity the din of battle during the king's youthful exploits. Thorbjorn's other poem about the monarch, in the Eddic old lore meter and called *Haraldskvæði* (The Lay of Harald), commemorates the great sea battle of Hafrsfjord, traditionally dated to 872, in which the king finally crushed the opposition to his rule in Norway. Structured as the conversation between a valkyrie and a raven who is returning from the battle with his beak and claws red with carrion, this work is also known as *Hrafnsmál* (The Lay of the Raven). Some of the verses assigned to *Haraldskvæði* are ascribed in sources to Thjodolf, so the group of stanzas known by this name may well represent the confusion of two poems.

When Harald's eldest living son and initial successor, Eirik Bloodaxe, died on a viking expedition in 954, his widow commissioned an encomium, known as *Eiríksmál* (The Lay of Eirik). This poem, like *Haraldskvæði*, is in old lore meter, but the skald here is unknown. Eirik's reception when he arrives at Valhalla is the material of the work, Odin awakening the troops and bidding the hall be made ready, informing the legendary father and half-brother of Sigurd the Dragon-slayer that he had chosen to let the best warrior die so that he might be able to fight by their side at Ragnarok. The preserved fragment ends before the king meets Odin.

The situation of *Eiríksmál* is roughly imitated by Eyvind Finnsson from northern Norway in his panegyric to commemorate Håkon the Good, Harald's youngest son (also Athelstan's foster son and an apostate Christian), who died in 961. *Hákonarmál* (The Lay of Håkon) begins: "The god of the Gauts [Odin] sent Gondul and Skogul [two valkyries] to choose between kings, which one of Yngvi's family [i.e., one of the Ynglings] should travel with Odin and be in Valhalla" and ends with a direct borrowing from *Hávamál*: "Cattle die, kinsmen die, the land and country are destroyed, since Håkon went with the heathen gods, many people are enslaved." Eyvind's poetic ability is obvious, especially in descriptions of battle, for instance, in the same poem: "Thus did the sword in the king's hand bite the clothing of Vafud [Odin "the roamer," whose clothing is war apparel] as if it were stuck in water; spikes cracked, shields broke, swords clashed on men's heads." In spite of the originality in his own expression, Eyvind's tendency to imitate others in ideas and structures apparently earned him the dishonorable byname Skald-despoiler (plagiarist?). He also imitated *Ynglingatal*, even employing its chant meter, in his *Háleygjatal* (List of the Håleygs), a presentation of the mythical and prehistoric ancestory of the earls of Lade.

For whatever reason, Eyvind Skald-despoiler was one of the last known Norwegian court poets, and from the close of the tenth century it appears that basically only Icelanders had the honor of being paid to sing the praises of the kings of Norway.

THE EARLY MIDDLE AGES (1030–1150)

The conversion to Christianity was a great event in Scandinavian history and marks the transition there to the Middle Ages. The vikings had first come into contact with Christians in the British Isles, and because of forceful impulses from the Ottonian rulers of the Holy Roman Empire, the new religion was accepted in Denmark as early as ca. 960. Missionaries from England, Denmark, and Germany played important roles in the Christianization of Norway, which was advanced and finally effected by the kings Olav Tryggvason and Olav Haraldsson. With Christianity came the Latin language, Roman letters, and the entire apparatus of the Church.

Initially, traveling bishops taught the new faith, and crosses were erected to mark sites for Christian assembly. Soon, however, the building of churches was under way and the Church became organized. Permanent bishoprics were established during the second half of the eleventh century in Nidaros (Trondheim), Selja (later transferred to Bergen), and Oslo, with an archbishopric for all Scandinavia being founded in the (at that time Danish) city of Lund in 1104. Stavanger and Hamar became sees in the twelfth century, and in 1152 Nidaros was elevated to the status of archbishopric for Norway and the Norse colonies in the British Isles and the North Atlantic, including Iceland and Greenland. Also during the twelfth century, monastic orders established cloisters, and the Church became the official educator, with both cathedral and monastery schools. Students also studied on the Continent, in France and Germany. By 1200 there were as many as nine hundred churches in the country, the great majority of them wooden stave churches, so named because of their supporting structure of timber columns, called "staves."

Literature in the Service of the Church

Although the Latin alphabet basically came to Scandinavia from the Continent in the form of the Carolingian miniscule script, in Norway the Anglo-Saxon insular script was of greater import. Thus the þ of runic origin in Old English writing was also used in the Latin alphabet in Norway and Iceland, as well as in Sweden. The literate used quill and ink, with a knife to scrape out mistakes, and wrote on parchment made of prepared calfskin, their final product often being bound as a book. Manuscripts were copied in scriptoria (writing rooms), where the clerks were clerics, and during the process of copying, both the language and the contents of works were revised to greater or lesser degrees.

In the very beginning the only types of literary writing were religious, that is, Latin missals and other texts useful in the church service. Probably because of English influence, scribes soon began writing the vernacular with Latin letters, and by about 1050 translations were being made of edifying devotional literature, both saints' legends and sermons. Gradually, codifications of oral material, primarily laws, and then original works in the vernacular, including property and tax lists and erudite scientific treatises, were added to the literary production. Most of this material no longer survives, and then only in copies; the earliest original Norwegian manuscripts preserved date to about 1150 and encompass fragments of translations of saints' lives and a fragment of the codification of the Older Gulathing Law.

On the publicly observed feast days of major saints, legends about them were read aloud in church. These were exciting tales that were meant to be both entertaining and informative. In the legends, ecclesiastical writing attained literary heights, and through them the Church undoubtedly contributed to storytelling in the vernacular. It is customary to divide the Latin works about saintly men and women into the following groups: *vita* concerning their lives, especially the exemplary life of a confessor; *passio* describing their suffering and death while defending Christian beliefs; and *miracula* retelling the religious miracles with which they are credited.

Tales of two native saints, other than St. Olav, were told and recorded in Latin, in the *Acta sanctorum in Selio* (publ. 1880*; Deeds of the Saints at Selja)[1] and the *Acta sancti Halvardi* (publ. 1880*; Deeds of St. Hallvard). St. Sunniva was the daughter of an Irish king who fled her native country with a group of believers in order to avoid marriage to a pagan and was miraculously buried alive on the island refuge on the western coast of Norway when pagans again threatened persecution in the late tenth century. The entire community of saints at Selja played a part during the conversion, but with time interest concentrated on Sunniva, who became the patron saint for western Norway. St. Hallvard is the patron saint of Oslo, who during the early eleventh century tried to save a woman falsely accused of being a thief by rowing her over a fjord, but was caught, killed with an arrow, and his body sunk with a stone, although it floated back to the surface.

Latin texts about St. Olav and their vernacular retellings illustrate the range of hagiographic literature of the early Middle Ages in Norway. A Latin *officium*, or order of worship, from ca. 1050 for his feast day, July 29, is preserved in England but contains only biblical quotations and provides no historical information. A *Translatio sancti Olavi* concerning the transferral of his earthly remains is lost, whereas a *vita* and a collection of *miracula* from the middle of the twelfth century have been preserved, but only in a later vernacular translation in the Old Norwegian Book of Homilies (see below) and as a source for a recounting by Archbishop Eystein Erlendsson. The archbishop's account exists in two versions, an older and shorter one known throughout Europe as the *Acta sancti Olavi regis et martyris* (publ. 1880*; Deeds of St. Olav, King and Martyr) and a younger and expanded version called *Passio et miracula beati Olavi* (Martyrdom and Miracles of St. Olav), known only from a manuscript in England and surely composed during the prelate's exile there in 1180–83. The prose panegyric among the homilies, "In die sancti Olavi regis et martyris" (For the Day of St. Olav, King and Martyr), presents a synopsis of St. Olav's acts as a good and just king and especially his death as a martyr, followed by twenty miracles performed by the saint.

---

1. The asterisk indicates an anthologized source, listed separately in the Bibliography under Chapter 1.

Sermons in the vernacular were used for instruction in church. The religious messages of the Church fathers, especially Gregory the Great's homilies and dialogues, are preserved both in fragments of Latin and in translation. The manuscript known as the Old Norwegian Book of Homilies (Norwegian: *Gammelnorsk homiliebok*), a handbook for preachers and a summit of religious literary endeavors in the country, was written in Bergen ca. 1200, but some of the sermons were composed and collected by 1150. It is the earliest preserved Norwegian book. (A parallel and approximately contemporary Icelandic manuscript, known as the Old Icelandic Book of Homilies, or *Homiliubók,* contains about one-third of the same texts.) The collection includes mainly homilies proper, that is, interpretations of the Gospels, such as the last lesson, an allegorical exegesis of the Lord's Prayer. It begins, however, with a translation of the ninth-century *De virtutibus et vitiis* (Concerning Virtues and Vices), a philosophical treatise by the English theologian Alcuin, Charlemagne's teacher and adviser.

Foreign sources or parallels have been identified for some of the preachings, but not all. Each homily has, however, received a clearly Old Norse form, indicating individual Norse authorship within the universal ecclesiastical tradition. One of them, in spite of the fact that foreign impulses and models lurk in the background, is considered quite indigenous: namely, the first of the two addresses used at the yearly celebration of the dedication of a church, "In dedicatione templi." This so-called Stave Church Sermon (Norwegian: *stavkirkepreken)* contains a twofold allegorical interpretation of the church building itself, including elements peculiar to structures with a wooden framework. First, each detail is seen as symbolizing a part of the entire Christian community: the chancel represents the blessed in heaven; the altar, Christ; the altar cloth, saints; the sill beams, the apostles; the doorway, the true belief; and so on. Then the same details are interpreted from the perspective of each individual Christian: the chancel is one's prayers and psalms; the altar, love; the altar cloth, one's good deeds; and so forth. There follows a plea to support the church with contributions, although saving souls by helping one's neighbors is mentioned as more important.

The style of the early translations and paraphrases of Latin texts is fairly simple and straightforward, although it can sometimes be colored by linguistic constructions in the original. Infrequently, however, as in the "In die sancti Olavi," the language becomes more rhythmic and alliterative. The Church continued to produce literature through the following centuries, especially pious expansions and reworkings of translations of saints' lives. Stylistically, these later texts were refurbished with ornate diction and rhetorical mannerisms.

Runic Inscriptions with Ecclesiastical Associations

The arrival of the Latin alphabet did not sound the death knell for runic inscriptions in Scandinavia, as it had centuries earlier on the Continent. Runes were apparently so well established that they continued to be used concurrently with Roman letters, the two, however, proving usually to be functional variants: temporal or occasional messages were communicated in runes cut on wood, whereas official or literary texts were preserved for posterity in Latin letters penned on parchment. Either could be used for epigraphy on stones, though runes were generally preferred, at least in the early Middle Ages.

More than fifty medieval gravestones with runic inscriptions are known from Norway, some with epitaphs reminiscent of Viking Age memorials, others with simple pious prayers ("May God help the soul of . . .") or a translation of the Latin *hic iacet*, "Here lies. . . ." Most are horizontal slabs rather than erected monuments, for instance, the large tablet from St. Mary's Church in Oslo from the 1100s inscribed: "Ogmund Squint-eyed had this stone laid over Gunna Gudulf's daughter, and the anniversary of her death [is] the mass of St. Luke [Oct. 18]."

Most runic inscriptions with ecclesiastical association are carved into the church buildings themselves. Of the about three hundred such inscriptions, more than two-thirds are in stave churches and the rest are in stone churches. Only a few are monumental and commemorate the structure itself, as in, for instance, the statements by a twelfth-century Thorolf at both Torpo and Ål naming himself as the master builder and listing others in his crew, or the one preserved from the stave church in Atrå in Telemark concerning the dedication of the church in ca. 1180 by Bishop Ragnar of Hamar. The great majority of messages carved into the woodwork or stonework are plain graffiti, scribblings consisting simply of signatures or short prayers; names are often found in the standard carver's formula, "*X* carved these runes." The stave church at Borgund in Sogn, for example, boasts more than thirty-five such graffiti inscriptions, including the statement, "This is the church at Kirkevoll," and the request, "May God support whoever supports me on a pilgrimage." The stone walls of the Nidaros Cathedral in Trondheim bear even somewhat more graffiti than the church walls at Borgund.

Various church furnishings carry runic inscriptions. In the case of church bells, the inscriptions often state who cast or commissioned the bells and include a prayer for them or quote a religious text such as the Hail Mary. Messages with runes also appear on crucifixes, baptismal fonts, wooden chests, and keys, rings, and mounting irons for doors. Loose finds from churches include runic amulets of wood or lead, invariably with Latin or apparently Latin texts. More than twenty lead amulets have turned up, frequently in some type of ecclesiastical context. Whereas the folded sheet from Ulstad has a good Latin rendering of the Lord's Prayer plus the names of the Evangelists, many texts on lead are quite corrupt, and several are inscribed with meaningless runes or only runelike signs.

Secular Texts: Laws and Skaldic Poetry

The regional laws of Norway were orally composed rules of justice initially formulated at popular assemblies where cases were decided and decisions promulgated, memorized, and proclaimed for the general public. Tradition claims that the laws for the Frostathing judicial district in central Norway were written down as early as the reign of St. Olav's son Magnus the Good, and that is possible. If not then, the codification of regional laws was certainly begun toward the end of the eleventh century during the peaceful and prosperous rule of Harald the Hardruler's son Olav the Quiet. The Older Gulathing Law for the legal district in western Norway (Eng. tr. *The Earliest Norwegian Laws*, 1935) is the best preserved and exists in an almost complete manuscript from ca. 1250. From the Eidsivathing district and the younger Borgarthing district in eastern Norway, only fragments of the Christian code have been transmitted. An old town law also exists.

The laws consist basically of case decisions, often in simple conditional statements of the type, "If a man does X, then he shall forfeit Y." They include pithy sayings and are expressed in straightforward language, with alliteration sometimes employed as an aid to memory. One ancient proclamation, *Tryggðamál* (Truce Formula), is especially poetic and although preserved completely only in Icelandic laws, it is no doubt of Norwegian origin. Here it is stated that whoever breaks the truce shall be banished and expelled as far as "men chase the wolf, Christians go to church, heathens worship temples, fire burns up, the earth grows, child calls for mother and mother nurtures child, people kindle fires, ships sail, shields gleam, the sun shines, snow falls, Lapps ski, pines grow. . . ."

Although Norwegians apparently no longer served as court poets, they continued to compose skaldic poetry, if maybe on a more modest scale. Many of the kings in the royal line of Harald Fairhair were known as skalds, but judging from what is preserved, only St. Olav, who supposedly composed stanzas about his battles, and especially Harald the Hardruler were poets of any stature. Harald's sixteen loose verses collectively called *gamanvísur* (amusement verses), only five of which survive, boast of various youthful exploits in a jocular fashion, each stanza closing with a refrain mentioning the princess Ellisiv in Novgorod, his later wife, who "still spurns my suit." A half-stanza from one of them has been found in a defective quotation on a rune-stick from the early fourteenth century uncovered during archaeological excavations in Bergen: "I was born where the men of Oppland flexed their bows, but now I [let my warships, loathed by the farmers, hover by the skerries]."

Skaldic poetry itself, as practiced mainly by Icelanders, underwent great changes as a result of the conversion. During the early eleventh century, pagan kennings were replaced by Christian recastings, and the use of kennings was greatly limited, although later they were again widely employed. Some new meters were even modeled on Latin verse-forms. Christian themes were introduced, and a platform was prepared for the extensive religious poetry of later centuries. An example of religious skaldic poetry is *Geisli* (Ray, or Beam), a *drápa* by the Icelander Einar Skulason, which was first delivered in the cathedral at Nidaros in 1153 just after the town had been made a metropolitan see. The work concerns St. Olav, who in it is referred to as a "ray of the sun of mercy" and a "ray of God's hall."

The only other Norwegian skald of note from the early Middle Ages is Kali Kolsson from Agder, who became earl of the Orkneys in 1136, changing his name to Rognvald. The Orkneys had been subjugated to Norway shortly before 1100 during the reign of Olav the Quiet's son Magnus Bareleg. More than thirty occasional stanzas attributed to Rognvald are preserved, many composed while he participated in a crusade in 1151–53. In collaboration with the Icelander Hall Thorarinsson and following foreign models, Rognvald composed a *Háttalykill* (Key of Meters), the contents of which concern legendary and historical battles, although more emphasis is placed on the range of meters and the knowledge of skaldic poetry being demonstrated. In the same colony but somewhat later, Bjarni Kolbeinsson, whose father was a Norwegian immigrant and who himself became bishop of the Orkneys in 1190, wrote a poem called *Jómsvíkingadrápa* (Poem of the Jomsvikings) about the legendary defeat in Norway of the vikings from Jom in the Baltic, and probably also *Málsháttakvæði* (The Proverb Poem); both poems are influenced by French love lyrics with their bemoaning of unrequited love. From the Orkneys come also Latin hymns about Earl Magnus the saint (died ca. 1115), whose life story is told in a *vita* written ca. 1135 by a Master Robert. The hagiographic text is partially preserved in Old Icelandic translation in the later, longer version of *Magnúss saga eyjajarls* (The Saga of Magnus, Earl of the Islands) and as a source for other biographies of the saint, such as in *Orkneyinga saga*.

Initially, a symbiotic relationship existed between the monarchy and the Church: the king protected the Church, and the Church legitimized the king. Discrepancies between national and international interests eventually led, however, to conflicts. Especially after the introduction of the tithe around 1100 and the establishment of the archbishopric in Nidaros in 1152, the Church became a powerful political factor in the country and organizationally, legally, and economically less dependent on secular powers.

The death in 1130 of Magnus Bareleg's most long-lived son, Sigurd the Crusader (whose byname comes from a holy campaign to Palestine in 1108–11), ushered in more than one hundred years of intermittent civil war in Norway. Sigurd had designated his son Magnus as heir to the throne, breaking the tradition of coregency. The first phase of the civil war initially pitted Magnus (who was blinded in 1135) against his half-brother Harald Gilchrist (who was killed in 1136), and then another half-brother, Sigurd Slembe, against Harald's sons. This phase ended with the deaths of Magnus the Blind and Sigurd Slembe in 1139 and a new coregency of half-brothers, namely, the sons of Harald Gilchrist, Inge Hunchback and Sigurd Mouth, who were a few years later joined by another half-brother, Eystein. Political factions eventually developed, and in 1159 the second phase of the civil war began. When Inge Hunchback fell in 1161, Earl Erling Crook-neck's young son Magnus, whose mother was a daughter of Sigurd the Crusader, succeeded him as king of one faction. This arrangement was supported by Archbishop Eystein Erlendsson in return for various concessions from the earl as regent for his son, including the introduction of canon law for the Church.

In 1177 Sverre Sigurdsson, who was raised in the Faroe Islands but claimed to be a son of Sigurd Mouth, became leader of a band of ragged partisans known as the Birchleg party. Earl Erling soon died in battle against Sverre, as did King Magnus Erlingsson in 1184, but the peace was short-lived, since after various minor uprisings the Church supported the major revolt of a new faction known as the Crosiers (named after the bishop's staff). The fighting between the Birchlegs and the Crosiers continued intermittently after Sverre's death in 1202 until his grandson Håkon Håkonsson became king in 1217. Even then new uprisings marred his rule, including finally Duke Skule Bårdsson's attempt to usurp power, which ended with the duke's death in 1240. During Håkon's subsequent reign of peace and prosperity, the Norwegian empire reached its greatest extent, culminating in the subjugation of Iceland and Greenland shortly before Håkon's death in 1263.

Succession was now legally based on primogeniture and legitimacy, and Håkon's son Magnus ascended to the throne.

Historical Literature: Kings' Sagas

With the Icelander Ari Thorgilsson's short *Íslendingabók* (Eng. tr. *The Book of the Icelanders,* 1930) from ca. 1130 begins the tradition of native historical writing in the Old Norse vernacular. A section on kings' lives, whose extent is debated but which probably was only a tracing of pedigrees and just the most basic information about the reigns of kings, was omitted from the extant version, which records largely Icelandic ecclesiastical history. Ari, who was called "the Learned," had a contemporary but somewhat older colleague, Sæmund Sigfusson the Learned, who also wrote about the kings of Norway, but he must have composed in Latin. It appears that the main service rendered by these scholars was the establishment of a chronological framework for historical lore, the collection and assignment of small bits to that framework, and the exercise of critical judgment.

Foreign stories of holy men and women had already been translated from Latin for some time. Apparently, the first real native saga, or lengthy historical recounting in Old Norse prose, was *Hryggjarstykki* (Backbone Piece) by the Icelander Eirik Oddsson, who in the mid-twelfth century wrote about events from the first phase of the Norwegian civil wars, especially 1136–39. The work is not preserved as such, and information about it can only be extrapolated from quotations in later kings' sagas. It may have been in particular a biography of Sigurd Slembe, whose death was presented as a martyrdom. The text was based on the oral accounts of Norwegian and Icelandic eyewitnesses and surely demonstrated Icelandic narrative skill, which like Norwegian storytelling must have been indebted to the written legends of the Church. The work apparently combined secular and hagiographic elements.

The next stage of native historical composition encompasses the three so-called Norwegian synoptics. The anonymous *Historia Norvegiae* (publ. 1880*),[1] found in Scotland in a late manuscript with connections to the Orkneys but composed by a Norwegian, may date to around 1170, thereby constituting the oldest preserved history of Norway. Geographical preliminaries are followed by stories of the kings of Norway from the legendary Ynglings to Olav Haraldsson, during whose arrival in Norway the flowery prose breaks off. Nikolas Arnason, the later Crosier bishop, has been sug-

---

1. The asterisk indicates an anthologized source, listed separately in the Bibliography under Chapter 1.

gested as the possible author, writing while he was a student in Denmark. Dedicated to Archbishop Eystein Erlendsson, the *Historia de antiquitate regum Norvagiensium* (publ. 1880*; History of the Norwegian Kings of Antiquity) by an otherwise unknown Theodoric the Monk may be some ten years younger. The author, who refers to Icelanders and their historical poems, claims to be the first to write Norwegian history, but he mentions an otherwise unknown and undoubtedly Norwegian *Catalogus regum Norvagiensium* (Catalog of the Norwegian Kings), which, like his own work, probably encompassed the rulers from Harald Fairhair to Sigurd the Crusader. Theodoric refused to recount the bloodshed of the civil-war period that followed. His composition is characterized by learned digressions and quotations showing both first- and secondhand scholarly knowledge. *Ágrip af Nóregs konunga sǫgum* (Compendium of the Sagas of the Kings of Norway), a nineteenth-century misnomer resulting from the belief that the work was an extract based on individual sagas of each king, dates to about 1190 and is thus the oldest survey of this kind in Old Norse. Written probably in Nidaros and preserved only in an early and defective Icelandic manuscript, the overview most likely began with Harald Fairhair's father and continued to 1177. Much scholarly debate has centered on the interdependence of these three preserved chronicles and their written and oral sources. If the textual history of all three is indebted to Icelandic learned tradition, there may be no independent Norwegian historical tradition. (During this time historical writing in Denmark was only in Latin, most notably Saxo Grammaticus's *Gesta Danorum* [History of the Danes], based also to a great extent on material from Icelandic informants; writing of history began somewhat later in Sweden.)

Ágrip introduced skaldic poetry and wove it into the fabric of the tale. Quotations of skaldic poetry quickly became one of the pillars in the composition of kings' sagas, complementing the learned chronological framework and providing supposedly reliable firsthand information about past happenings. In addition to skaldic verses and any accompanying explanatory prose, the sources of historical writing must encompass Norwegian and Icelandic oral traditions. Fictional motifs were also borrowed from the great storehouse of religious works translated from Latin or known in the original.

Literature was taken into the service of the monarchy with the composition of the first part of *Sverris saga* (Eng. tr. *Sverrissaga: The Saga of King Sverri of Norway,* 1899), which is called *Grýla* (Bugbear) and probably treated only the first few years of Sverre's reign. In the preface to the saga, it is told that the king himself, who was educated as a priest, supervised the composition of the first part by the Icelander Karl Jonsson, sometime abbot of the monastery at Thingeyrar, presumably in 1185–88 when the prelate was in Norway. The work is thus a fairly contemporary saga, not one of past times. *Sverris saga,* distinguished particularly by the use of long speeches, especially ones by the king himself, is a somewhat uneven text, though it may in its entirety still be the work of Karl Jonsson, with irregularities reflecting composition in three to four stages during which the author had varying access to sources. A harangue known as "A Speech against the Bishops" is preserved in a manuscript from the early fourteenth century but must date to the last decade of the twelfth century. This allegorical oration contains tendentious translations of canon law and was clearly written for King Sverre as an argument of his case against the prelates who supported the Crosiers. A concise text from earlier in the same decade, *Historia de profectione Danorum in Hierosolymam* (History of the Departure of Danes for Jerusalem), concerns mainly the preparations in Denmark and Norway for a crusade and is written in pompous and convoluted Latin by a Norwegian monk who at the time was perhaps living in Denmark.

The writing of contemporary national history continued under subsequent rulers, and two versions exist of what is known as *Bǫglunga sǫgur* (Sagas of the Crosiers [and the Birchlegs]). The shorter, Crosier version of this work is preserved in two manuscripts plus one fragment in Old Icelandic, whereas the longer, Birchleg version is best preserved in Peder Claussøn Friis's translation into Danish from around 1600, as well as in some Old Norse fragments.

Although kings' sagas are almost entirely a specifically Icelandic genre, they concern mainly Norwegian royal history. Many Icelandic manuscripts of kings' sagas were also found in Norway, and most of them were probably originally written for export. Among the more "Norwegian" texts of kings' sagas is the so-called *Fagrskinna* (Fair Vellum, so named to reflect its appearance at the time by the seventeenth-century Icelandic national historian for Norway, Thormodus Torfæus); in manuscripts it is called *Nóregs konungatal* (List of the Kings of Norway). This sober and somewhat skeletal version of kings' sagas up to 1177 was apparently written in Norway by an Icelander, perhaps specifically for Håkon Håkonsson, as it is probably the work he had read aloud to him on his deathbed. The so-called Legendary *Óláfs saga helga* ("Legendary" Saga of St. Olav), an expansion of an Icelandic text from around 1200 known as the "Oldest" saga of the saint, is preserved in a manuscript from Trøndelag dating to about 1250. The work is legendary since it contains a section on St. Olav's miracles and in addition more or less presents the king as a saint-in-making during his lifetime. It demonstrates the hagiographic interests connected with the two great missionary kings of

Norway. For Olav Tryggvason, this interest is represented in Iceland by two separate biographies written toward the end of the twelfth century by Odd Snorrason and Gunnlaug Leifsson, monks at Thingeyrar cloister. They composed in Latin following foreign models, but their works were translated into Old Icelandic.

The zenith of the composition of kings' sagas is reached in Snorri Sturluson's "Separate" *Óláfs saga helga* and especially in his *Heimskringla* (Eng. tr. *Heimskringla: History of the Kings of Norway,* 1964), in which a slightly revised version of the "Separate" saga is incorporated as the middle third. In *Heimskringla,* the author's critical historical judgment of cause and effect and sparkling literary skills at structuring a story and modeling dramatic dialogue are everywhere evident. Most of the information provided in scholarly histories of the Viking Age and the medieval kings of Norway up to 1177 derive from the individual sagas included in *Heimskringla.* Even tales of the prehistoric kings of Norway as recorded in the poem *Ynglingatal* are presented in the first section, known as *Ynglinga saga* (The Saga of the Ynglings). The modern title, *Heimskringla,* literally means "orb of the world" and is taken from the first two words of *Ynglinga saga* in the oldest manuscript. For some reason this manuscript lacks the prologue Snorri had written to the work.

Saga structure is episodic, with individual scenes often based mainly on direct discourse. In most cases the authorial stance appears objective. Other saga genres developed in Iceland during the thirteenth century, foremost among them the anonymously recorded sagas of Icelanders, or family sagas, brilliant narratives about the (to some extent historical) feudings of local chieftains in the early commonwealth period ca. 930–1030, for instance, *Egils saga Skallagrímssonar, Njáls saga,* and *Laxdæla saga.*

Another saga genre is comprised of legendary or mythical-heroic tales about prehistoric and pseudohistoric warriors. These stories are known as the sagas of ancient times (*fornaldarsǫgur*) and constitute what could be called native romances. This genre, too, was apparently mainly Icelandic but was popular in Norway as well. King Sverre, for example, is quoted in an Icelandic historical saga as stating that he found such "lying sagas" most amusing. They seem to have existed only as oral literature until the mid-thirteenth century, when the introduction of foreign romances helped legitimize wholly fictional literature. Best among the sagas of ancient times, and the first to be written down, is *Vǫlsunga saga* (Eng. tr. *The Saga of the Volsungs,* 1990), the prose tale of Sigurd the Dragon-slayer based on much of the corpus of heroic Eddic poetry. The work can be used to reconstruct partially the material lost in the lacuna of the Codex Regius. *Hervarar saga ok*

Heiðreks konungs (Eng. tr. *Saga Heiðreks:The Saga of King Heidrek the Wise,* 1960), which concerns strife through four generations of heroes and heroines, quotes many stanzas from several ancient Eddic poems not otherwise preserved, most notably remnants of *Hlǫðskviða* (The Lay of Hlod), about the battle between the Goths and the Huns.

Runic Inscriptions from an Urban Environment; Skaldic Poetry

During the Middle Ages, towns and cities developed in Scandinavia. The largest urban centers in Norway were, in order of their founding, Tønsberg, Nidaros (Trondheim), Oslo, and Bergen. In 1955 a fire destroyed part of Bryggen (the old German wharf) in Bergen, and subsequent archaeological excavations brought to light about six hundred runic inscriptions, mostly dating from 1150 to 1350 (publ. 1980–*).[1] These finds more than doubled the known medieval corpus. One-quarter of them are, unfortunately, now unreadable or entirely uninterpretable. The great majority of the inscriptions are on wood, including wooden utensils, with a large number on small sticks whittled flat on four sides to serve specifically as runic writing material. It was not previously known how general the knowledge of runes was on various social levels, nor how widespread their use for written communication. Medieval expansions of the runic alphabet had gradually remedied phonetic inadequacies.

The largest group of runic inscriptions from Bryggen is from the sphere of mercantile activity and includes some 110 ownership tags, usually with a statement such as "Einar owns (me)" or simply a personal name like "Eirik," which were tied or otherwise attached to merchants' wares. An additional fifteen commercial texts are letters and notes, including accounting records. Among them is a long letter dating to the end of the twelfth century and written or dictated by Sigurd Lavard, King Sverre's son. Employing standard formulaic expressions for medieval correspondence, the missive on this rune-stick is addressed to a smith and states specifications for the fabrication of spearheads.

The some-sixty alphabet inscriptions consisting of the medieval futhork (as the runic alphabet after a sound change now may be called) or portions thereof, and sometimes combined with names or other inscriptions, are probably on the whole simply examples of writing practice. Stereotyped runic declarations occur, such as ownership statements or carver's formulas, but various messages go beyond such commonplaces and provide rare in-

---

1. The asterisk indicates an anthologized source, listed separately in the Bibliography under Chapter 1.

sights into private lives; for instance, "Gyda says that you should go home," perhaps a note to a carousing husband, and "Ingibjorg made love with me while I was in Stavanger." Some 10 percent of the inscriptions are in Latin, including everything from truncated quotations of liturgical texts such as the Lord's Prayer or the Hail Mary used as protective formulas, to charms for stopping blood, protecting eyes against blindness, and helping during difficult childbirth, and finally Latin-like gibberish on magical sticks. Some recurring international formulas are AGLA (a protective word, actually an anagram for a Hebrew sentence) and the more or less meaningless palindrome *sator arepo tenet opera rotas*. An example is preserved of goliardic poetry (i.e., Latin verses recited by wandering, high-spirited students), namely, fragments of two poems transmitted in the *Carmina Burana*. The following well-known quotation from Vergil occurs a few times, once in conjunction with a skaldic verse: *Omnia vincit Amor, et nos cedamus Amori* ["Love conquers all, let us too yield to Love"].

More than thirty pieces of poetry, many fragmentary, were unearthed at Bryggen, including both skaldic stanzas and Eddic lines. Many of these verses are erotic, in contrast to most of the poetry otherwise preserved. A skaldic strophe is also found in the inscription cut into the stave church at Vinje in Telemark by Hallvard Grenske, clearly an opponent of King Sverre; it is political and concerns Hallvard's inability to make peace with the king. These instances demonstrate that the art of skaldic composition and recitation had not disappeared from Norway, as had previously been assumed. The preponderance of erotic skaldic verses from Bryggen probably gives an indication of the amount of that type of poetry that has been lost. The verses in Eddic meter from Bryggen include, "Hail to you and be of good cheer; may Thor accept you, may Odin own you," perhaps a quotation from an otherwise unknown old poem, rather than a reflection of genuine pagan feelings. Also preserved are instances of simple folk poetry, such as the ditty, "My Honey! I love you / with all my heart / and with all my mind."

The Court of Håkon Håkonsson and Magnus the Lawmender (1225–80)
Literary production flowered under King Håkon Håkonsson, and the mid-thirteenth century can be considered the golden age of medieval Norwegian literature. As the king's political perspective was European, so too was his taste in literature, and during his rule foreign influence reached new heights. This time, though, literature was shaped mainly by vernacular works from other lands, although some were still in Latin.

During the twelfth century a new literature was cultivated at the feudal courts in France and the Anglo-Norman royal court in England. This courtly literature encompassed verse romances describing the martial exploits and amorous adventures of knights, including the Celtic traditions of King Arthur and his knights of the Round Table. What was apparently the first of these sagas of chivalry or knights' sagas (*riddarasǫgur*) to be retold in Old Norse, the story of Tristan and Isolde by an unknown Norman poet called Thomas, is said to have been translated by a Brother Robert in 1226 as *Tristrams saga ok Ísǫndar* (Eng. tr. *The Saga of Tristram and Isönd*, 1973). Only fragments of the Anglo-Norman original exist now, and Robert's is the only complete translation extant. *Elis saga ok Rósamundu* (The Saga of Elis and Rosamunda) renders the incomplete French chanson de geste, or heroic song, *Elie de Saint Gille* in Old Norse and is said to have been translated by an Abbot Robert, surely the same person as Brother Robert, though after promotion within his order. Both works were done at the behest of Håkon Håkonsson. King Håkon also commissioned the reworking of the Arthurian verse romance *Yvain* or *Le chevalier au lyon* (The Knight of the Lion) by Chrétien de Troyes as *Ívens saga* (Eng. tr. in *Erex Saga and Ívens Saga*, 1977); the translation of twenty-one erotic short stories termed *Strengleikar* by modern editors (literally, "stringed instruments," i.e., ballads sung to stringed music; Eng. tr. 1979), eighteen of them based on songs or *lais* ascribed to Marie de France; and the retelling of the anonymous French parodic fable *Le mantel mautaillé* (The Poorly Fitting Mantle) as *Mǫttuls saga* (The Saga of the Mantle). This last work concerns tests of chastity by means of a magic cloak, tests that were miserably failed at King Arthur's court.

Tradition stresses Håkon Håkonsson's role in importing this literature to Norway, and several other works should most likely also be connected with his court, among them translations of Chrétien de Troyes's *Erec et Enide* as *Erex saga* (Eng. tr., 1977) and of his incomplete romance *Perceval* (or *Le conte du Graal*, The Story of the Grail) as *Parcevals saga* and *Valvens Páttr* (The Tale of Valven [Gawain]). *Karlamagnús saga* (Eng. tr. *Karlamagnús Saga: The Saga of Charlemagne and His Heroes*, 1975–80) is a compilation of probably separately translated tales dealing with Charlemagne and his twelve paladins; the sources for the cycle embrace both chansons de geste and Latin historiographical material. Most notable among its parts is the story of the Battle of Runzival (Roncevaux/Roncesvalles), a retelling of the *Chanson de Roland* (The Song of Roland). From the German, and perhaps translated about 1250 in Bergen, comes *Piðreks saga af Bern* (Eng. tr. *The Saga of Thidrek of Bern*, 1988), a patchwork of heroic material including the tale of Sigurd the Dragon-slayer in conjunction with the story of Theodoric the Great, the Ostrogothic king who subdued the Roman Empire in 493 and reigned until his death in 526 with Verona (Bern) as his chief residence.

A new style characterizes the prose retellings of French verse. This courtly style embraces alliteration, synonymous variation, rhythmic word placement, and syntactic parallelism, all elements of embellishment which could have been introduced by way of compensation for the poetic form of the originals. The Old Norse renderings are often considered inferior to the originals, since psychological details, monologues, and long exchanges of direct speech usually have been excised or severely cut. It is, however, difficult to judge the courtly translations into Old Norse. Many are preserved only in late Icelandic manuscripts, and in one of the few early, Norwegian manuscripts that exist—dating from ca. 1260 and containing *Strengleikar, Elis saga ok Rósamundu,* and *Pamphilus* (a rendering of the Latin love dialogue *Pamphilus de amore*)—scribal alterations are already evident. This literature became very popular in Iceland, where extensive revisions were usually undertaken. The Icelandic version of the story of Tristan and Isolde is so altered both in details, such as forms of names, and in story line that it is considered a separate work, *Tristrams saga ok Ísoddar.* The style for translations of this kind developed further in fourteenth-century Iceland into what is called florid style. Fictional literature became so popular in Iceland that indigenous romances were composed, first viking sagas and then purely fantastic adventure stories.

Religious literature translated in the thirteenth century includes *Barlaams ok Jósaphats saga* (The Saga of Barlaam and Josaphat), which is preserved in various Norwegian manuscripts. In this story of the monk Barlaam's conversion of the Indic prince Josaphat, a didactic account of Christianity is offered, mainly as long-winded dialogue, while much of the content is actually taken from legends of the life of Buddha. This popular piece of edification may have been translated by Håkon Håkonsson's son Håkon the Young (died 1257). From medieval visionary literature, the *Visio Tnugdali* (Tnugdal's Vision), written in Latin by an Irish monk in southern Germany around 1150, was masterfully translated as *Duggals leiðsla* (The Vision of Duggal; Eng. tr. 1983).

The crowning work of Norwegian thirteenth-century literature is *Konungs skuggsjá* (Eng. tr. *The King's Mirror,* 1917), a so-called *speculum regale* (royal mirror). As the title indicates, the book is meant as a pedagogical mirror of good manners and pious conduct for royalty, usually a royal heir. This didactic work is couched in the customary colloquy fashion as questions and answers, in this case questions by a son to his father. The first part, which concerns the merchant class, functions as a repository for much scientific and geographic knowledge, whereas the second section is more sociological and concerns courtly behavior and the duties of the king's retainers. The work concludes with a section describing the king and telling how the monarchy itself should function. The author, who came from central Norway and wrote in the 1250s in a very refined courtly style, gained his inspiration from foreign books but tailored his work to mirror Old Norwegian social conditions in the mid-thirteenth century. An Icelandic version of *Konungs skuggsjá* also exists, to which a prologue is attached that makes the work appear incomplete, since it does not include sections the prologue promises on priests and farmers.

Håkon Håkonsson died in 1263 during a campaign against Scotland, and his son Magnus succeeded him. First Magnus commissioned his father's saga to be written by the Icelander Sturla Thordarson, Snorri Sturluson's nephew. *Hákonar saga Hákonarsonar* (Eng. tr. *The Saga of Hacon, Hacon's Son,* 1894) was completed quickly, and perhaps because it was based on written historical sources and much detailed documentary material—including more than one hundred letters, lists of participants at meetings and formal gatherings, rolls from ships and itineraries, obituaries, and maybe even minutes from meetings—it lacks the warmth and narrative power of earlier kings' sagas. Sturla's task was also a delicate one, since he had to relate the altercations between King Håkon and Duke Skule Bårdsson, Magnus's father and maternal grandfather, respectively.

King Magnus supported and initiated other literary endeavors, and it is told that he asked the Icelandic cleric and bishop Brand Jonsson to translate *Gyðinga saga* (The Saga of Jews), a vernacular rendering mainly of 1 Maccabees. Brand is said in addition to have translated *Alexanders saga,* based on Walter of Châtillon's Latin poem in hexameter about Alexander the Great, *Alexandreis.* Other pseudohistorical works translated from Latin, possibly under the auspices of the Norwegian court of the mid- or later thirteenth century, are *Trójumanna saga* (The Saga of the Men of Troy), an Old Norse rendition mainly of the particular version of the tale of Troy falsely attributed to Dares of Phrygia, and *Breta sǫgur* (Sagas of the Britons), from Geoffrey of Monmouth's dubious *Historia regum Britanniae* (History of the Kings of Britain), written ca. 1135 and containing Arthurian material.

King Magnus is best known for his revision of the laws of Norway, a task that earned him the byname Lawmender. Legal scholars were convened, and the old regional laws were updated, expanded, harmonized, and ultimately replaced by national codes. In 1274 the new National Laws were promulgated, which among other things made crimes a public matter and replaced the custom of personal revenge with public adjudication. This more Christian and humane code was in effect for more than four hundred years, after 1604 in Danish translation. In 1276 new Municipal Laws were instituted, which established a city council form of government for Norwegian urban centers. Likewise, a special law for the king's retainers, *Hirðskrá* (The Retainers' Scroll), was proclaimed, and new laws, first *Járnsiða* (Ironside) and then in 1281 *Jónsbók* (Jon's Book), were imposed on Iceland.

After Magnus died in 1280, Sturla Thordarson wrote his saga, too, *Magnúss saga lagabœtis* (The Saga of Magnus the Lawmender; Eng. tr. *Fragments of the Saga of Magnus, Hacon's Son*, 1894), only two partly illegible fragments of which remain, in addition to various short interpolations from the lost text into Icelandic annals. This text, like the saga of his father, is quite dry. It was the last kings' saga to be composed.

About this time the manuscript known as *Morkinskinna* (Rotten or Dark Vellum, so named by Thormodus Torfæus) was copied in Iceland; its text was probably compiled only shortly beforehand. The version of kings' sagas between St. Olav and King Sverre preserved here is distinguished by the piecemeal inclusion of numerous short stories (*þættir*, sg. *þáttr*), chiefly about Icelanders. This work heralds the advent of the encyclopedic conflations and compilations of kings' sagas which dominate the fourteenth century and culminate in *Flateyjarbók* (The Book of Flatey, ca. 1390).

The Waning of the High Middle Ages (1280–1370)
Magnus Lawmender's sons succeeded him, first Eirik and then Håkon V Magnusson. Literary production was mainly religious, notably the translation of Genesis and Exodus 1–18 commissioned by Håkon V, with extensive interpolations from medieval biblical commentaries. This work is preserved only as part of an Icelandic Old Testament paraphrase from the Middle Ages called *Stjórn* (Governance). The religious literature also included several miracles of the Virgin Mary and various collections of Christian exempla, entertaining short stories with a pious lesson. Scholars usually group the miracles of the Virgin with similar Old Icelandic accounts and a short life history of St. Mary and term the entire collection *Maríu saga* (The Saga of Mary). Christian exempla were composed or recorded by, among others, Jon Halldorsson, one of the bishops of Iceland in the first half of the fourteenth century and apparently a Norwegian. Jon Halldorsson is also said to be responsible for *Klári saga* (The Saga of Klarus), which he supposedly translated from an unknown Latin romance. This saga is the fairy-tale story of Klarus's winning of the hand of a maiden warrior. Courtly literature was introduced into Sweden by Håkon V's Swedish queen, the German-born

Eufemia, for whom the three so-called Eufemia Songs (Swedish: *Eufemiavisorna*) were composed ca. 1300. They are long narrative poems in simple rhymed verse which were translated into Swedish from Old Norse renditions, probably in Norway, and perhaps in part from French or German originals. After Håkon's death in 1319 the court relocated to Sweden, and literary activities in Norway more or less ceased.

One form of writing activity remained throughout the Middle Ages, though: the composition of letters and charters, that is, legal, public documents such as deeds, affidavits, and true copies. Only infrequently are more private letters preserved; for example, in the first half of the fourteenth century the correspondence of the bishops of Bergen was recorded in a copy book. It reveals a highly learned environment.

The plague in 1349 had a profound effect on the cultural life of the country by decimating the intelligentsia. By about 1370, language changes that characterize the gradual transition to Middle Norwegian, especially the loss of case endings, generally prevailed in written texts over traditional forms.

Oral Tradition, Humanism, and the Baroque

Kathleen Stokker

2

THE FOURTEENTH AND FIFTEENTH CENTURIES: ORAL TRADITION

During the fourteenth century the combined effects of politics and the bubonic plague (the "Black Death") brought Norwegian literary activity to a standstill, and for the next two hundred years the country produced no significant literature. After the death of Håkon V in 1319 the royal court relocated in Sweden, an event that deprived Norway of the normal venue for literary activity and historical writing. Beginning in 1349 the Black Death and subsequent epidemics destroyed one-third of Norway's population, leaving numerous farms abandoned, entire communities uninhabited, and land values at a fraction of previous levels. A worsening climate exacerbated the plague's damage, and the resulting economic crisis destroyed the Norwegian aristocracy. As tender of the sick, the clergy also died in inordinately high numbers, and the severe effects on these two classes—essentially the only bearers of literary activity—hastened the process by which the Norwegian written language fell into disuse. Worse yet, Norway failed to recover from the plague's devastation for at least two hundred years and in this way suffered more severely than other Scandinavian countries.

The absence of a written culture at this time made the contribution of oral narrative tradition all the more prominent, though oral tradition is actually alive at all times and continually influences all other forms of culture. Unlike written texts, items of oral tradition have no single, fixed form. Instead, they exist in numerous, equally significant variants, since it is more the basic story line than its particular expression that is passed along. (This principle may apply somewhat less to ballads, whose rhythm and rhyme suggest that some memorization may be involved.) The largely unfixed form of transmission allows the material to be readily adapted and made relevant to new situations.

Given the malleable nature of oral tradition and the fact that systematic recording of the Norwegian material did not begin until the nineteenth century, it is impossible to be certain about the nature of oral tradition in the period under discussion. We can only make extrapolations from contemporary Icelandic written materials and from later-recorded ballads and narrative prose.

The Ballad

The ballad is a narrative verse with a lyrical refrain. Though scholars debate the date of its arrival in Scandinavia—suggesting times ranging from 1100 to 1500 and even later—most agree that its initial impulses came from France; various themes, formulas, plot elements, and moods from the chivalric culture of Provence moved northward, merged with the more narrative and less chivalric native traditions, and resulted in the ballad type now known as Scandinavian.

Fewer than ten ballad fragments of less than one strophe each are preserved in medieval Scandinavian manuscripts, and the first complete ballad texts are from the sixteenth-century songbooks of Danish and Swedish nobility. The exact nature of the medieval ballad thus remains a mystery. Nevertheless, the existence in Norway of pictorial representations of chain dancing and ring dancing suggests that ballads with refrains referring to dancing ("Step not too close to me, partner," "My lady dances on the greensward") reflect an authentic medieval tradition. The association of the ballad with dancing is also suggested by the etymology of its name, from the late Latin *ballare*, "to dance."

The ballads as they are now preserved reflect a medieval milieu. Their verse form differs from that of skaldic poetry by having end rhyme rather than assonance and being determined by syllable stress without consideration of length. A verse might consist of either a quatrain plus an end refrain or a couplet with a single-line refrain following each line. Couplets contain four stresses per line, while quatrains have three in the rhymed, even lines and four in the unrhymed, odd lines. In telling its story, the ballad employs a language rich in formulas (e.g., "maiden proud and fair," "both strong and true," "warriors bold") and uses the techniques of drama, rapidly shifting from scene to scene, making extensive use of dialogue, and showing rather than evaluating the action. Parallel verses and repetition also characterize ballad style and may have originated in the performance situation as an aid to comprehension.

Scholars have traditionally distinguished between an eastern (Danish and Swedish) and western (Norwegian, Icelandic, and Faroese) ballad area within Scandinavia. In the eastern area, chivalric and historical themes abound, while the western area (lacking a landed aristocracy and being outside the arena of contemporary historical events) has few ballads of these types. Instead, supernatural and heroic ballads dominate here. The former include ballads about witchcraft and magic (the so-called troll ballads, e.g., "Liten Lavrans" [Little Lavrans]) and those describing encounters with supernatural beings like *alver* (elves) and the *nøkk* (water sprite), as in "Olav Liljekrans" and "Villemann og Magnill" (Villemand and Magnhild). Related to the thirteenth and fourteenth-century Icelandic sagas of ancient times (*fornaldarsǫgur*), the heroic ballads depict battles among humans or between humans and fantastic monsters or giants, as in "Sigurd Svein" (i.e., Sigurd the Dragon-slayer) and "Ormålen unge" (Young Ormålen).

In recent years scholars have tended to ignore traditional ballad typology: rather than concentrating on the differences between ballads with regard to action and milieu, they have tried to reveal some of their significant similarities. Villy Sørensen, for example, has shown the striking ubiquity of conflict-filled courtship situations.

Unique to the Norwegian tradition is the visionary poem "Draumkvede" (Eng. tr. "The Dream Ballad," 1946), which portrays the journey of the hero to the realm of the dead, where he learns the contrasting fates of the virtuous and the sinful. The poem contains striking imagery and a rhetoric generally reminiscent of the Sermon on the Mount:

> I came to some men in the other world
> They were carrying red-hot mold.
> May God have mercy on their souls;
> They had moved the landmarks old.

> Blessed is he who to the poor
> Gives bed and shelter here.
> He need not fear the howl of wolves
> In the spirit world o'er there.

Only fragmentary texts exist, and scholars vigorously disagree about the work's date of composition, placing it as early as the thirteenth, and as late as the eighteenth, century (some scholars, who regard the poem as a compilation of related single stanzas of the kind called *gammelstev*, even reject the use of the term "ballad" in this case and claim that no one can know for sure whether a single, defined "Draumkvede" ever existed). Comparable in epic scope to Dante's *Inferno,* Norway's visionary poem may be the nation's most memorable literary monument from the Middle Ages and has inspired generations of Norwegian artists.

The Legend (Sagn)

The *sagn* (legend) is a short, usually single-episodic, narrative told as a true account and often mentioning a specific place, time, and person, all of which strengthens the impression of veracity. In saga literature, particularly in the *fornaldarsǫgur* and the kings' sagas of Olav Tryggvason and Olav Haraldsson, much material is based on legends, and Snorri Sturluson's *Edda* also includes several legends. Some scholars divide legends into three main types—etiological, historical, and supernatural—reflecting the views of the German folklorist Kurt Ranke, who held that legends result from three human needs: (a) to explain (e.g., how unusual natural formations came to be), (b) to remember cultural events (like St. Olav's conversion of Norway or the ravages of the bubonic plague), and (c) to share beliefs expressed by encounters with such supernatural beings as the *havfrue* (mermaid), the *draug* (sea ghost), and the *nøkk* (water sprite). (This last type of folk belief also underlies many ballads.) Recent legend studies have attempted to define situations that predispose an individual to explain unexpected phenomena as supernatural encounters. Other studies have analyzed discrepancies between historical documentation and legendary accounts of events, concluding that differences between the factual and legendary accounts offer accurate insights into people's attitudes toward the events. Since these studies can examine only those legends collected in more recent times, however, their conclusions may have no relevance to the period under discussion here. An indispensable aid to the comparative analysis of the later narratives is the catalog provided by Norwegian folklorist Reidar Christiansen in *The Migratory Legends.*

The Tale (Eventyr)

The tale, unlike the legend, is told as fiction, and one of the oldest Scandinavian references to the tale derides it for just this reason. In the foreword to his saga of Olav Tryggvason (ca. 1200), Odd Snorrason boasts of the greater virtue of his work over the "stepmother stories told by shepherds, about which no one knows what is true." Meanwhile, *Sverris saga* (also ca. 1200) likens King Sverre's arduous journey through dense forest to those of "old folktales in which the king's children are subjected to their stepmother's cruelty," showing how the wicked stepmother motif, so characteristic of folktales collected at a later time, must also have had currency in medieval Norwegian tales. The social conditions reflected in most of the later folktales, however, indicate that they developed their present form in the period after the Reformation, especially during the seventeenth century. Since the tales remained unrecorded until the nineteenth century, no conclusions can be drawn concerning the range of tale types and motives before that time.

Nineteenth-century international folklore scholarship (to which Scandinavians contributed significantly) advanced several theories concerning the origin of folktales, regarding them as remnants of myths, survivals of primitive initiation rites, derivations of Buddhist tales, and allegories of astronomical occurrences or fertility rituals. Later researchers have preferred to concentrate on the text of the tale itself, attempting to clarify its unique style (Axel Olrik) and its structure (Vladimir Propp). Others focus on the differences between folktales and legends, attempting a more precise definition of genres (Carl Wilhelm von Sydow) and pointing to their different functions. They contrast, for example, a legend's emphasis on human vulnerability with the folktales' suggestion of an overall plan for coping with existence (Max Lüthi).

Most scholars agree that oral tradition functions to confirm the tradition bearers and their audience in a particular outlook on life and experience. The concepts of fate, limited good (one person's gain means another's loss), and accepting one's lot in life underlie much of the extant Norwegian legend and ballad material. Since a particular item remains in oral tradition only as long as it has significance for its teller/singer and audience, however, we cannot attain any certainty about the content and world view of the unrecorded tradition from earlier times.

THE SIXTEENTH CENTURY: REFORMATION AND HUMANISM

During the early sixteenth century Norway fell to the lowest point in its history—economically, culturally, and politically. On October 30, 1536, the Danish King, Christian III, declared Norway a province of Denmark and the following year instituted Lutheranism as the official religion of the realm. In Denmark, as in Sweden and Germany, this religious transition arose out of popular debate and had been prepared for by authors and preachers who were enthusiastic champions or staunch opponents. Norway, in contrast, had neither sufficient warning of the change nor appreciable acquaintance with the pertinent issues, and lacking the universities, the middle class, and the printing presses that facilitated the Lutheran Reformation elsewhere, the country produced no counterpart to the religious publications appearing in Denmark and Sweden during the first part of the sixteenth century. In fact, almost a hundred years would pass before the reforms stipulated in the Church Ordinance of 1537 were generally instituted in Norway. Legends of a stupefied population helplessly watching beloved altars thrown into the river and taking revenge on the first Lutheran ministers reflect Norway's lack of preparation for the religious change. Linguistically, the Reformation also disfavored the Norwegian population, for while other countries produced vernacular editions of the sermon books and hymnals so characteristic of the Lutheran movement, in Norway these works, as well as the Bible (translated by Christiern Pedersen ca. 1550), appeared only in Danish. The Lutheran principle of vernacular Bible translation helped to normalize the national languages of other Protestant countries, but in Norway it only provided the conclusive step in establishing Danish as the country's official written language, a circumstance that raised yet another barrier against popular reception of the new theology.

The later sixteenth century did see marked economic and social growth as well as an eventual literary awakening. Farms that had lain fallow since the Black Death were recleared and communities repopulated, the fishing industry was revived, and mining and lumbering opened new economic prospects. Toward the end of the century, when committed Lutheran superintendents finally took charge of the dioceses, the cathedral schools were revived as centers of learning and nurtured the new impulses from humanism, a movement that arose in Italy during the fourteenth and fifteenth centuries and first manifested itself as an interest in the Greek and Roman past. In Norway this renaissance of classical scholarship occurred after the Lutheran Reformation, rather than, as in other lands, before. Like its continental European counterpart, this Humanism focused its efforts on a study of Greek and Roman antiquity, but it is particularly characterized by a resurgent interest in the country's own past as well as in pedagogy. Humanists in the dioceses of Bergen and Stavanger excelled in historical and topographical writing, while those in the Oslo diocese specialized in the composition of Latin verse. All were encouraged and financially supported by the local Danish governors.

Bergen Diocese

After the Reformation Bergen replaced Trondheim as Norway's ecclesiastical center, and the former Catholic bishop of Bergen, Geble Pederssøn (ca. 1490–1557), became the country's first Lutheran superintendent. In his youth Geble had studied humanities in the Netherlands, and after converting to Lutheranism he created a significant scholastic center at the Bergen Cathedral School. A favored student was Absalon Pederssøn Beyer (1528–

75), who was fostered by Geble Pederssøn and later developed into one of Norway's foremost humanists. Absalon studied in Copenhagen and Wittenberg under Philipp Melanchthon, Peder Palladius, and other influential scholars and then returned to Bergen to become an instructor at the cathedral school. During the years 1552–72 he kept a diary, *Liber capituli bergensis,* known as *Bergens kapitelsbog* (The Bergen Chapter Book), in which he recorded—first in Latin but after 1571 in his native tongue—episodes from the Seven Years' War as well as from Bergen daily life and gave glimpses of himself as a family man and a Lutheran minister. He also mentioned the dramas—probably Norway's first—that he and his students produced in accordance with Luther's recommendation that theater be used as a medium of biblical instruction.

Absalon's most significant work is *Om Norgis rige* (1780; On the Kingdom of Norway, written in 1567 and widely circulated in handwritten copies before its publication). It has counterparts in German and Italian humanistic literature and demonstrates Absalon's acquaintance not only with Norwegian sources but also with Danish (Saxo) and Swedish (Olaus Magnus), as well as with French, Scottish, Italian, and German chronicles. The work's commissioner, City Governor Erik Rosenkrantz, had a political rather than scholarly purpose in mind: by acquainting the citizens with their history, he hoped to see their native pride aroused. Thus *Om Norgis rige* would be a potent weapon in his battle against foreign domination by the Hanseatic League, a powerful federation of north German cities which had developed in the latter part of the twelfth century and monopolized trade throughout the North for more than four hundred years. In his work Absalon likens Norway's history to human life, portraying its progress from glorious youth (the Viking Age), when "she was honored and respected and wore a golden crown," to the present sad plight of old age, in which "Norway resembles an old widow who supports herself with a cane and can hardly walk." According to Absalon, it was Norway's subordination to Denmark that caused the country "to lose its virility," and it was this enfeebled state that allowed the Hansa to prevail. Absalon listed the country's material and cultural resources and postulated that Norway could recapture its past splendor, if only its rulers would take an active interest in realizing the country's potential.

Stavanger Diocese

Indicative of the slow progress Lutheranism initially made in Norway is the fact that Jørgen Erikssøn (1535–1604), who became superintendent of Stavanger diocese in 1571, was the first fully committed Lutheran to hold that position, and his *Jonæ prophetis skiøne historia udi 24 predicken begreben* (1592; Twenty-four Sermons on the Prophet Jonah) provided sorely needed guidelines in Lutheran theology and in the art of preaching. Jørgen Erikssøn's younger colleague Peder Claussøn Friis (1545–1614), though neither university-educated nor widely traveled, became the foremost representative of Renaissance humanism in the Stavanger diocese and possibly in all of Norway. The depth and breadth of his knowledge and his accuracy and skill in character portrayals made him one of the most popular writers of the sixteenth century. Peder Claussøn was born in Eigersund, attended the cathedral school in Stavanger, and spent his life as parish minister in Audnedal. He never left Norway and did not move extensively within its borders, but his book *Norriges oc omliggende øers sandfærdige bescriffuelse* (1632; A True Description of Norway and Surrounding Islands) treats its subject realistically and thoroughly and became a model for later topographers. Peder Claussøn demonstrates his familiarity with the Scandinavian medieval and humanistic sources, as well as with those in German, English, and Latin, but also builds on his own observations. His characterization of Norwegian peasants as hard, contrary, disobedient, obstinate, restless, rebellious, and bloodthirsty cannot conceal an underlying pride in country and people.

Most important among Peder Claussøn's works is his *Norske kongers chronica* (1633; Chronicle of the Norwegian Kings). It is based on several medieval kings' sagas and provided Scandinavians with their first complete and coherent account of Norway's ancient and medieval history. The work consists mainly of a translation of Snorri Sturluson's *Heimskringla*, completed by Claussøn in 1599 at the behest of Norway's governor, Aksel Gyldenstjerne. It served to revive the awareness of Snorri's work, which had fallen into obscurity when Old Norse ceased to be used in Norway, and Danish, rather than Modern Norwegian, became the country's written language. Especially the 1757 edition of *Norske kongers chronica* made the sagas widely known and cherished among the general Norwegian public.

Oslo Diocese
After the Seven Years' War (1563–70), Oslo became the political and religious center of Norway. Though smaller than Bergen, Oslo surpassed that city as a seat of learning, partly because of the support of the Danish governors Povel Huitfeld and Aksel Gyldenstjerne. Jens Nilssøn (1538–1600), perhaps the period's most prominent churchman, had studied theology in Copenhagen and became the superintendent of the Oslo diocese in 1580. Tirelessly traveling to enforce Lutheran doctrine and practice, he kept diaries—*Visitatsbøger og reiseoptegnelser* 1574–1597 (publ. 1880–85; Visita-

tion Books and Travel Memoirs, 1574–1597)—whose detailed record of destinations, travel difficulties, routes, and ecclesiastical conditions make them particularly valuable as a primary source on Norway's Reformation period. Nilssøn's most important poetic work is a Latin elegy, "Elegidion" (1591; Elegy), occasioned by the death of his three-year-old daughter. It uses conventional classical allusions to express the grief not of a theologian but of a believer comforted by his faith, and it gives a portrait of the daughter as well as a description of Telemark, where Nilssøn was traveling when he received the news of her death. Jens Nilssøn's work distinguishes itself from the majority of contemporary Latin poems by its personal tone and depth of emotion.

Most prolific of the Oslo humanists was Hallvard Gunnarssøn (1545–1608). A student of Jens Nilssøn, he became a lecturer at the cathedral school in 1577 and wrote several pedagogical works in verse—in Latin, Greek, Hebrew, and Danish—to aid rote memorization of various school subjects. Important and original is his "Achrostichis de inauguratione Christiani quarti" (Acrostic about the Inauguration of Christian IV), an acrostic (poem in which the first letters of each line constitute words) composed in honor of King Christian IV, whose inauguration in Oslo on June 8, 1591, provides the poem's subject. The poem, written in Latin hexameter and modeled on Vergil's pastorals, is narrated by two shepherds observing the festivities from the banks of the Aker River. They give a wealth of realistic detail concerning the exact arrangement of the observers' galleries and the contrasting dress and appearance of onlookers drawn by the occasion from all parts of the kingdom. They also provide an enthusiastic description of the king's arrival and of the riot afterward when the crowd breaks through the barriers and engages in a drunken brawl. In his versified *Chronicon regum Norvegiæ* (1606; Chronicle of Norwegian Kings), which also includes much realistic description of folk types and places, Gunnarssøn offered learned circles in Europe their first Norwegian history. In Norway, however, his most popular work was a rendering of the German pastor Michael Saxe's biblical quiz book of 1593. It was published as *Aandelige spørgsmaalsbog* (1602; Book of Spiritual Questions), but its popular name was *Preste piina* (The Pastor's Torture), suggesting the image of parishioners who use tricky questions to outwit their minister and making the book attractive to many readers at a time when the Church seemed to gain increasing authority over their lives. It was reprinted fourteen times (most recently in 1870), and some of its questions (which resemble those in the folktale "The Minister and the Sexton") are imitated by Ludvig Holberg's Per Degn in *Erasmus Montanus* (1722–23).

Hamar came under the supervision of Oslo after the Reformation but had formerly been an independent diocese, and *Hamarkrøniken* (The Hamar Chronicle) gives a nostalgic description of the city in pre-Reformation times. It tells of the 1522 sighting of a sea serpent in Lake Mjøsa, which was then interpreted as an omen of Norway's decline, and suggests that the warning was fulfilled in 1537 when Lutheranism replaced Catholicism and Hamar's bishop was arrested. The date and author of *Hamarkrøniken* are unknown; scholars date it as early as 1550 and as late as 1624. It was first published in 1774.

The Oslo humanists had their books printed in Copenhagen and Rostock. By the end of the sixteenth century a printed book was no longer a rarity in Norway, though the country still lacked a printing press of its own.

THE SEVENTEENTH CENTURY:
DEVELOPMENT OF VERNACULAR POETRY

The economic growth that began in the sixteenth century continued and expanded during the seventeenth. At the same time, the distance between the illiterate masses and the educated elite widened in Norway, as elsewhere in Europe. Calvinistic and Roman Catholic impulses manifested themselves increasingly after the 1600s, and in response, the Lutheran Church began instituting rules and ordinances aimed at achieving maximum uniformity in religious thought and behavior. Concurrently, the minister's role developed into that of a disciplinarian who was urged by the Church Ordinance of 1629 to use excommunication as a means of moral enforcement. The same ordinance significantly elevated the clergy's educational level by requiring a university degree for ordination.

While Sweden and Denmark developed closer ties with the rest of Europe, Norway continued to remain on the periphery. In 1643 the first printing press was established in the country, but no work of lasting literary significance appeared on a Norwegian press until 1678 (*Sjælens sang-offer*, by Dorothe Engelbretsdatter). Superstition flourished as a result of a growing emphasis on human sinfulness and on the empirical reality of the Devil and also because people became more aware of the implications of Lutheran dogma: its "justification by faith alone" (or, under orthodoxy, by correct belief) seemed more threatening than the old Catholic doctrine of salvation by good works and penance. Fear of damnation increased, and people—illiterate and learned alike—sought and found omens from God in comets and misshapen creatures and stood in awe of magic and witchcraft. Legends preserve the superstition of the age in the accounts of the Black Book ministers, wise folk, and witches, all of whom could harness supernatural powers to perform magical feats both helpful and harmful to those around them. The depth of the belief underlying these imaginative accounts is seen in the so-called witch craze that lasted from 1500 to 1700. In Norway 870 individuals were tried for witchcraft during this period, and 277 of them received the death sentence. Among them was Absalon Pederssøn Beyer's wife, Anne Pedersdotter, who was burned as a witch despite the Bergen clergy's efforts to save her (the event inspired H. Wiers-Jensen's play *Anne Pedersdotter* from 1908 [Eng. tr. *The Witch,* 1917] and, through the play, Carl Dreyer's famous film *Day of Wrath* from 1943). A reflection of the period's feverish superstition is found in *Et forfærdeligt huuskaars i Kjøge* (1678; A Terrible Visitation in Kjøge), by Johan Brunsman (1637–1707), an account of the hysteria caused by people's belief that the Devil had taken possession of a certain household in Køge (Denmark).

While poetry in Norway before the 1630s had mostly been in Latin, poets in Italy, France, the Netherlands, and Germany had long been trying to create vernacular verse based on classical Greco-Roman models. This movement arrived belatedly in Norway, brought by the Danish bishop of Trondheim, Anders Arrebo (1587–1637). Arrebo had encountered the new metric principles in Martin Opitz's *Buch von der deutschen Poeterey* (1624; Book on German Poetry), which called for a more firmly structured poetic line. While medieval poets had counted only the stressed syllables and allowed a varying number of unstressed ones, Opitz advocated a more regular relationship between the stressed and unstressed syllables to achieve lines of uniform length and stress. Arrebo applied these principles in his translation of the poem "La première Semaine" (1578; The First Week) by the French Huguenot Guillaume du Bartas, and the resulting work, *Hexaëmeron* (1661; The Six Days of Creation), which was written around 1630 and widely circulated in handwritten copies before publication, exerted a strong influence on the poetic language and style of the 1660s. In rendering his day-to-day presentation of creation, Arrebo, as the first among Danish poets, showed how to apply classical meters—the hexameter and its French derivate, the alexandrine—to his Danish vernacular. *Hexaëmeron* also makes frequent allusions to the period's new discoveries in physics, astronomy, and global navigation, and sees (in true orthodox Lutheran spirit) the wonders of creation as a proof of God's grace. Since it is a reworking, rather than a translation, of the French original, the poem draws on local scenery, including that of North Norway, for its natural descriptions. Arrebo also borrowed from Peder Claussøn's topography, telling of Norway's waterways, climate, fish, and wildlife, and in this way *Hexaëmeron* anticipates the topographical poetry of Petter Dass. Though it lacks the latter poet's immediacy and personal involvement, in its own time Arrebo's poem achieved considerable fame and conferred respectability on vernacular poetry.

Socially and politically, the date 1660 marks a decisive turning point in Denmark-Norway since in that year Frederik III (1648–70) instituted absolute monarchy, whereby the king and his order superseded all human laws and criticism, and praise became the only permissible form of social commentary. Society grew increasingly class-conscious, and position in the social hierarchy determined a person's overall importance. In Norway an urban upper class developed among the Danish-immigrant civil servants. Lutheran orthodoxy became firmly established with Jesper Brochmand's *Systema universæ theologiæ* (1633; System of Universal Theology), which demanded strict conformity in religious expression.

Beyond the influence of *Hexaëmeron*, the year 1661 marks a turning point for Danish and Norwegian poetry, instigated once more by a Dane indebted to German schools of poetry. In his *Nogle betænkninger om det cimbriske sprog* (1661; Some Reflections on the Cimbrian Language), Peder Pedersen Syv (1631–1702) claims that the subject matter of poetry should elevate the reader and that the poet himself should be an artist manipulating the reader's emotions by skillful use of rhetoric. Elaborate imagery, fondness for allegory, wordplays, and extremes of expression characterize the resultant poetry, now referred to as baroque. Corresponding well to the period's unquestioned ecclesiastical authority and absolute monarchial power, the highly structured poetry of the baroque strives to put everything into a fixed framework as it celebrates the supreme order of the Creation and supports the established social and political system.

Most successful in following the period's poetic form was Dorothe Engelbretsdatter (1634–1716). Though her works have lost much of their interest today, in her own time and for more than a century thereafter her poetry enjoyed unrivaled popularity. She was respected by her fellow poets, met the Danish hymnist Thomas Kingo (1643–1703), corresponded with Petter Dass, and was called by Ludvig Holberg (1648–1754) "the greatest poetess the Northern kingdoms have had." Martin Luther had advocated hymns as an important means of religious instruction, and Engelbretsdatter, daughter of a clergyman as well as the wife of one, is best known for her hymns, which include her most important work, *Sielens sang-offer* (1678; Song Offering of the Soul). She typically emphasizes the Lutheran doctrine of sincere repentance as the only way to salvation and frequently uses the relationship between father and daughter or bridegroom and bride as an allegory for the bond between God and humans. By portraying a constant tension between the allure of sin and the painful regret of having sinned, she often expresses a longing to escape this tearful world of suffering and temptation in order to be with God in Paradise. Engelbretsdatter thus employed the typical baroque effects of allegory, exaggeration, and contrast, though her poetry distinguishes itself from that of her contemporaries by her choice of typically feminine images such as motherhood and household chores and by her highly personal tone and the frequent mention of her gender. Considering that vernacular poetry was a recently acquired art, Engelbretsdatter's mastery of rhythm and rhyme is impressive. The appearance of *Sialens sang-offer* in seven editions before the poet's death and seventeen more afterward demonstrates her popular appeal.

Like Dorothe Engelbretsdatter, Petter Dass (1647–1707) employed concrete, everyday images and a personal tone in his religious poetry, but his work surpasses hers in its liveliness and ability to convey theology in a pedagogically effective manner. To modern taste, Dass seems by far the greater artist and indeed a poet who can still be read with enjoyment; during his lifetime, however, he managed to get only one of his many works into print.

Petter Dass was born at Alstahaug on the North Norwegian coast, attended Bergen Cathedral School, studied theology at the University of Copenhagen, and returned in 1669 to North Norway, where for twenty years he suffered economic hardship before finally becoming pastor of the prosperous Alstahaug parish. After his death Dass attained a reputation accorded only to the most admired and capable of ministers: he is celebrated in legends as having possessed the Black Book, with which he could conjure up the Devil and harness his mighty power to perform fantastic feats.

Because he had lived among the farmers and fishermen for whom he wrote, Dass learned to communicate his message with refreshing directness and could give even abstract theological principles a relevant and comprehensible form. In *Katechismus-sange* (1714; Catechism Songs, completed in 1698), for example, he related the Lord's Prayer and Ten Commandments to the peasant's daily concern: don't beat the horse, make honest measurements, give the hired hand Sunday off, and so on. Dass thus managed to bridge the growing gap between the civil-servant and peasant classes and exerted a powerful influence on his time by helping parishioners meet the increasing demands on their biblical understanding. His style conforms with the baroque in its frequent use of allegory, wordplay, artificial expressions, antitheses, and excessive words and images. Nevertheless, his natural exuberance comes through, and though he remained realistic about the difficulties of eking out a living in a harsh climate and a rugged terrain, he did not emphasize sin and sinfulness and expressed none of the period's longing to escape this life. Dass's religious poetry further distinguishes itself from that of Dorothe Engelbretsdatter by its variety, close-textured content, and lack of sentimentality.

Dass was also a writer of copious secular verse. He based his "Den norske dalevise" (1683; The Norwegian Dale Song, written around 1674) on an existing Danish poem of peasant life, but with his intimate familiarity with the landscape and people of Helgeland as described in the poem, he improved on his model. The poem consists of brief, loosely joined scenes from everyday life which give a detailed, unromanticized, and sometimes humorous view of the Norwegian peasant's quarrelsome nature, obstinacy, and casual concern for hygiene.

Dass further developed the subject of the "Dalevise," but warmed his tone, in *Nordlands trompet* (1739; Eng. tr. *The Trumpet of Nordland*, 1954), a topographical poem in fourteen songs, with preface and introduction—all in all, some three thousand lines, on which he worked during the years 1678 –92. Like its classical predecessors (e.g., Tacitus's *Germania*), Dass's topographical work begins with an overview of the entire region, Norway's three northernmost counties, before describing each district in detail. Though he builds on classical models, Dass in his preface declares that his work employs no mythological images or exotica: he will serve purely domestic fare at the feast to which he welcomes his audience. Taking them on a boat journey along the northern coast, he enlivens the description by conversing with his readers, pointing out features of the landscape as well as instructing, admonishing, consoling, and advising. As in oral tradition, Dass shows action rather than describing it, and he focuses particularly on the way in which the landscape affects the people who work and live in it, especially the fishermen. He does acknowledge that God's rewards and punishments often disappoint by their arbitrary nature, but he maintains an undiminished orthodox faith and frequently makes moralizing parables of individual incidents. *Nordlands trompet* has a vitality that derives partly from its rhythm, partly from its popular sayings, dialect words, and striking images. Except for its preface and introductions, the poem is composed in lines of 4(3) anapests, *x—xx—xx—x (x—)*, a meter that gives the text its distinctive mixture of festivity and reserved dignity. Unlike topographers of the previous century, Petter Dass expresses no longing for Norway's past greatness but instead sees abundant evidence of the country's strength and vitality in his own time. With those earlier topographers, however, Dass shared his love for the native land, a love that strikingly characterizes the majority of works from Norway's Renaissance literature.

Holberg and the Age of Enlightenment

Harald Naess

3

EIGHTEENTH-CENTURY NORWAY

The years 1715 and 1815—the first, the date of the death of Louis XIV; the second, of Napoleon's banishment to Saint Helena—both mark the end of a period of French military domination of Europe. But the two dates also stake out a century in which France dominated Europe intellectually, an era commonly known as the Age of Enlightenment. The term indicates light after a period of darkness, the darkness being the intolerance and superstition that inspired the religious wars of the two earlier centuries. Unfortunately, enlightenment did not mean the end of military aggression. Louis XIV himself had waged a series of wars in the fifty years of his government; at mid-century Frederick of Prussia, the typical enlightened despot, was not above imitating the Sun King in his attack on Austria; and at the end of the period there were the American and French revolutions, followed by protracted military operations, beginning at Lexington and ending at Waterloo.

In Scandinavia—very much the periphery of Europe—people watched the war theater with the excitement of safe bystanders, contemplating the successes and failures of its major players, the field marshals: from Condé, Prince Eugene, and Marlborough, to Napoleon, Bluecher, and Wellington. And for a short period between 1700 and 1709, Sweden, by then the most powerful of the Scandinavian nations, tried to play along: its warrior king Charles XII, called by Voltaire "half Don Quixote, half Alexander," was a brilliant military leader, who before his twentieth year had defeated the kings of Russia, Saxony-Poland, and Denmark in a series of battles.

There are certain instructive parallels between the situations in France and Scandinavia. As Louis XIV reduced the strength of the nobility in France, so, at the same time (1660), King Frederik III of Denmark assumed absolute power and made public offices available to the bourgeoisie. Charles XII of Sweden, like Louis XIV, made his country the most powerful among neighbors, but—again like Louis XIV—he left at his death a country with a devastated economy. Nevertheless, in the aftermath of its war years, Sweden still produced a brilliant culture, with names like Linnaeus, Swedenborg, and Bellman. The enlightened despots of Europe—Frederick of Prussia, Catherine of Russia, Joseph/Leopold of Austria—also had their counterparts in Scandinavia: Sweden's artist king Gustavus III and Denmark-Norway's liberal usurper, Count Struensee. Finally, the common people of Norway, who like their French counterparts had fought an unconspicuous battle against tax collectors and the ravages of nature, suddenly took up arms against oppressors in two uprisings; unlike the French Revolution, however, these revolts were local and transient.

During the years following the Scandinavian Kalmar Union under the Danish crown (1397–1520), Denmark gradually saw its leading position taken over by the larger, more populous, and more powerful Sweden. A series of wars between the two nations also resulted in loss of Danish lands on the Swedish continent, though the borders between the two countries remained the same after 1660. That year also saw the final transfer of power from Denmark's nobility to its new class of burghers and to the new absolutist king, Frederik III of Oldenburgh, who was followed by his son, Christian V, then by his grandson, Frederik IV, and so on. There are obvious differences between absolutist France and absolutist Denmark-Norway, a small nation of 2.4 million people, less than one-tenth the population of France. None of the Oldenburghers could have claimed, with Louis XIV of France, "the State—that's me": they were all ungifted men without a vision; though, with the exception of the philandering simpleton Frederik V and his demented son, Christian VII, they were honest and hardworking rulers who left most important decisions to a growing and powerful bureaucracy.

There were also differences, though less obvious, between Denmark and Norway. After the establishment of the absolute monarchy in 1660, Norway, which had earlier been little more than a Danish province, became Denmark's full partner in the union. Norway's distance from the center of political activity in the capital of Copenhagen was of some importance, leading in 1626 to the establishment of a Norwegian army, which was based democratically on conscription among the farmers and which in the following century and a half helped to build up a sense of Norwegian nationalism. This nationalism was bolstered by the development of a degree of prosperity, as fisheries, lumbering, and mining supported a new export industry and, with it, gradually a considerable merchant fleet. Norway's population doubled between the years 1660 and 1800 (882,000) and almost equaled that of Denmark. Ludvig Holberg could claim with some right that Norwegian export alone was responsible for the positive trade balance of the two countries.

The major dissimilarity between the two sister countries sprang from the contrast in topography: unlike the fertile and largely tillable Danish lands, mountainous Norway had never been suitable for the development of a landed nobility. While in Denmark the little landholder (such as Holberg's Jeppe of the Hill) suffered under the rule of a landed gentry, farms in Norway were small but independent, owned by a class of free landowners, whom Holberg referred to as "noblemen in miniature." Norway's taxpaying farmers, being the state's best milking cows, were generally aided by friendly legislation (except where competing with the growing merchant class) and, unlike the situation in Denmark, were even members of the local school boards. "The Norwegian Farmer" was an honorific epithet, used as a name of ships, compared to Rousseau's ideal citizen, and functioning as an inspiration for poets from Holberg to Zetlitz. Even so, eighteenth-century farmers in Norway, as elsewhere, lived in a backward society. Women were oppressed and persecuted: between the years 1560 and 1700 there were no fewer than 850 accusations of witchcraft. Violent crime was common, and once again women suffered more than men: the criminal most often punished was the unmarried mother who, because of social pressure, had killed her newborn baby. Norwegian farmers generally were conservative, loyal to the king (despite occasional uprisings against his civil servants), but suspicious of all innovators and those who, like the reformer Struensee, tried to improve their lots. Indeed, whatever progress can be found in the areas of industry, society, and general culture during the Norwegian Age of Enlightenment came from Norway's two other classes, the merchants and the civil servants, whose members often belonged to immigrant families of German, Danish, and sometimes British origin. They fought against superstition, administered justice, and tried to channel European culture into their adopted homeland. That this was a come-late culture is best seen by the fact that no book was printed in Norway before 1643.

The school law of 1741 had provided for general instruction in reading, but with the lack of suitable reading materials the ability to read was soon unlearned among the farmers. Thus, with few exceptions, the civil servants continued to be the only carriers of Norwegian national culture well into the nineteenth century. They set up musical societies and science academies: Bergen's Harmonien (said to be the oldest still-existing orchestra in Europe) was established in 1765 and the Royal Science Academy of

Trondheim in 1760. Writers in the eighteenth century were mostly ministers of the church. Holberg was a university professor; Nordahl Brun, a bishop; P. H. Frimann, a diplomat. Only Christian Tullin belonged to the merchant class (though he was educated as a theologian). Merchants often differed from the university-trained bureaucrats in being citizens of the world—men who knew foreign countries and their languages and beyond that had a sense of the direction of history. Mary Wollstonecraft, on her visit to Norway in 1799, found that many merchants shared her enthusiasm for the French Revolution and even intimated the desirability of the separation of Denmark and Norway. That was not only the opinion of practical businessmen who longed for freer trade, but the result of a new literary nationalism. Unlike the situation in Denmark, where the Reformation in 1537 had given rise to a rich development of hymn writing in the vernacular, in Norway the Reformation did not produce a separate poetic tradition. But in the wake of the Reformation came European humanism with its passion for the past, and when it reached Norway it gradually inspired a similar interest in history and topography among Norwegian writers and readers. Typically, of Holberg's rich production, his historical works and his moral philosophy were more often read than his comedies. After Holberg's death some historical works appeared that emphasized the glories of medieval Norway and, in the following century, inspired Norwegian nationalism and romantic poetry.

Otherwise, the general trends of the European Enlightenment were reflected in Norway, as elsewhere in Scandinavia, though the manifestations are weaker and later. There is no better guide to these European influences than Ludvig Holberg's numerous essays on matters historical, political, and philosophical, works that often refer to the major names in early English, French, and German Enlightenment. The Age of Reason was prepared by such English empiricists as Francis Bacon, John Locke, and Isaac Newton. Though they remained believers in conventional Christianity, the English, with their suspicion of the purely speculative and the general tolerance of the times, soon favored a *Christianity not mysterious,* to quote a title by English deist John Toland. The French rationalists, though they admired Locke and Newton, went beyond the English deists in their pursuit of pure reason. The heliocentric system of Copernicus—whose effect was to reduce the uniqueness of the planet Earth—as well as other scientific discoveries were made available in a popular and attractive form by François Fenelon, while Pierre Bayle, the name most often referred to by Holberg, demonstrated the need for historians to treat their sources critically. Although the infamous *L'Homme machine* (1747; Eng. tr. *Man a Machine,* 1749) by Julien Offray de La Mettrie, denying the existence of a soul, was publicly repudiated by Holberg, it is clear that its author's radical materialism held a strong fascination for this voracious reader. More directly appealing to him was Montesquieu, whose criticism of contemporary society in the *Les Lettres persanes* (1721; Eng. tr. *Persian Letters,* 1722) was later copied by Holberg and whose attempt to create a synthetic history, explaining social conditions on the basis of climate, was of some importance for the development of Norwegian nationalism. Holberg did not live to see the influence of the French encyclopedists, but he would have identified with their efforts to create a synoptic presentation of a modern world, as we know from his own attempts to make his private enlightenment public in more than six hundred essays. These works, together with journals, papers, and books in the major languages, helped to spread European Enlightenment among members of the merchant and civil-servant class in mountainous Norway.

Curiously, the writers of the Enlightenment, so revolutionary as thinkers, were lacking in striking stylistic innovation: the early eighteenth century is not rich in poetry. That is perhaps so because the message of the philosophes depended for its successful transmission on logic and a clear style. The classical ideal of clarity became an obsession, however, and was not improved by the added requirement of taste. Even though Holberg reacted against some of its exaggerated demands, he accepted the rules of French classicism. At midcentury, however, and partly promoted by the new Selskab til de skiønne og nyttige Videnskabers Forfremmelse (Society for the Advancement of the Beautiful and Useful Sciences, 1759), there was in Norway, as elsewhere in Europe, an orientation toward nature poetry of a type unknown to Holberg. Albrecht Haller's *Die Alpen* (1729; The Alps) and such English works as Alexander Pope's "Windsor Forest" (1713), James Thomson's *The Seasons* (1730), and Edward Young's *Night Thoughts* (1742–44) were important for the poetry of Holberg's successor, Christian Tullin. In the poets of the following generation this somewhat more "English" and more "modern" taste vied with a lingering and counterproductive French classicism so that the Norwegian Age of Enlightenment, which had begun with the truly radical ideas of Ludvig Holberg, ended in his hometown of Bergen with the antirevolutionary plays and sermons of Bishop Nordahl Brun. Brun's conservatism, however, contained within it a fiery nationalism that helped inspire the Norwegian political revolution of 1814 and, afterward, a belated romantic movement.

LUDVIG HOLBERG

Ludvig Holberg was born in Bergen in 1684. His father, Christian Holberg, had risen to the rank of lieutenant colonel in the Norwegian army.

Holberg's mother, Karen, was the granddaughter of Bishop Ludvig Munthe of Bergen and named her twelfth and youngest child after this distinguished forebear. Christian Holberg died in 1686, and that same year a fire in Bergen destroyed most of the Holberg property. Karen Holberg, however, was an industrious woman who managed to provide a good home for her surviving six children. When she died in 1695, her three boys had been started on educational careers that would eventually give all of them university degrees in theology. Ludvig Holberg attended Bergen High School, whose curriculum included no practical subjects but four hours of Latin per day and, in the top grade, disputations (in Latin) on metaphysical topics. He visited Copenhagen for the first time in 1702, when he passed his university entrance exam. The University of Copenhagen (founded in 1479) was a school with some three hundred students, seventeen professors distributed over four faculties, or schools—of theology, law, philosophy, and medicine. In most European seats of learning Scholasticism by this time had been replaced by the new ideals of rationalism and empiricism; Scholasticism survived at universities north of the Alps, however, where the one important subject was still theology, with philosophy regarded as nothing more than its handmaid (*ancilla theologiae*), that is, an instrumental science (*philosophia instrumentalis*) designed to prove logically the old verities of theology. Holberg's repeated plea for educational reform must be seen against the background of his personal experience of an antiquated educational system in Bergen and Copenhagen. Holberg spent the year 1702–03 as a tutor in the countryside near Bergen and began studying at Copenhagen in the fall of 1703. After one year as a student he received degrees in philosophy and theology and then spent the summer of 1704 tutoring the children of (the later) Bishop Niels Smed. In the fall of 1704, when Holberg was in his twentieth year, he left Bergen, never to return.

Memories of Bergen and of Norway stayed with Holberg throughout his life. Forty-three years later, when, as a newly created baron, he was to select his coat of arms, he chose one that incorporates a mountain and a spruce tree, both typical symbols of his home country. He always referred to his father with considerable pride but otherwise did not have much direct connection with his family. His special respect for women, though, may have something to do with his mother, who taught her youngest son to write and who singlehandedly brought up six successful children.

Growing up in the city of Bergen—largest in Norway, a city of commerce with ships from all over Europe—naturally added fire to Holberg's wanderlust, which he inherited from a father who had traveled on foot through Italy. That, and the reading of Niels Smed's diary of his travels in

Germany, Italy, France, and the Netherlands, finally made the young man collect his small inheritance and set out into the world, much like a schoolboy running away to sea, and against the advice of his two older brothers.

What special reasons Holberg may have had for visiting the Netherlands is not known (though a friend from Bergen had recently settled in Amsterdam); Colonel Holberg's son may simply have wanted to be where the action was: the Netherlands were important in the European war theater, as the forces were gathering in the final attack on Louis XIV. Marlborough and Prince Eugene had defeated the French at Blenheim that same year. Later Marlborough would conquer the Spanish Netherlands, and all the intricacies of the War of the Spanish Succession would have a central place in Holberg's first historical writings. Amsterdam was also a haven for freethinking philosophers such as Pierre Bayle, with journals published in French and English. Even so, the journey was unsuccessful. Holberg ran out of money, tried to run away from his hotel without paying, and finally had to borrow to get home—not to Bergen, where his family would be bound to laugh at him, but to Kristiansand in South Norway, where he had distant relatives. Here he earned enough from tutoring in foreign languages and music to pay his debts and put aside some money for his next journey abroad, taking him in the spring of 1706 to England, where he remained for two and a half years and where, like Montesquieu later, he acquired many of his enlightened views.

Holberg stayed at Oxford and worked in the Bodleian Library, copying books that would later be of importance for him as a writer. He was well liked by his fellow students, who admired his facility with Latin as well as his musical gifts and who generally treated him in a way that made him remember England and its people with respect and gratitude. Among the great philosophes of the Enlightenment, England was generally looked up to because of its critical attitude to traditional ways of thinking, and Holberg often expressed his admiration for the Royal Society and its motto *Nullius in verba [magisteri adjurare]*: "Never swear by the words of an authority," with the conclusion, "but find out for yourself." In Bergen, Holberg had been told by one of his progressive teachers to study the press, and England was a country blessed with newspapers, journals, and essays describing and commenting on recent events and ideas in a popular form. Holberg's stay in England helped consolidate his own natural skepticism and gave him a sense of the present, which stood him in good stead as he set out to present modern Europe to Scandinavians.

In the summer of 1708 Holberg, now twenty-three, arrived in Copenhagen, which became his home for the rest of his life. Copenhagen, a city of seventy thousand, was close to five times the size of Bergen. It was the capital of Denmark-Norway, home of its state administration and its only university. Holberg immediately set himself up as a private tutor for students and others who wished to receive information on foreign affairs. He made the acquaintance of important people who, in 1709, helped him get a fellowship at Borch's College, where he stayed for the next four and a half years. Here Holberg presented popular lectures on such modern subjects as the importance of studies abroad, the use of history, the pleasures of music, and the value of learning foreign language. His progress from medieval to modern education was begun at Oxford and continued in Copenhagen under the guidance of law professor Christian Reitzer, who introduced his young friend to the work of such luminaries as Hugo Grotius, Samuel Pufendorf, and Christian Thomasius. Pufendorf in particular was important for Holberg's first work in the field of history and natural law; indeed, much of Holberg's early work was little more than a translation of Pufendorf's writings. In 1711 he published his *Introduction til de fornemste europæiske rigers historie* (Introduction to European History) and two years later his *Anhang* (1713; Appendix), which treated the human geography of Germany, England, and the Netherlands. Holberg, bringing Pufendorf's similar work (1682) up-to-date, understood his readers' need for current information and, in addition, served his facts and arguments in a lively style ("Marlborough . . . gave the French monarchy such an unexpected slap in the face that it is still on its knees"). Holberg's European history, the first of its kind in Danish, was very successful, and the author was mentioned as a potential candidate for a professorship. In 1712 he received a four-year travel grant but did not leave Copenhagen until his academic situation was clear. In 1714 he was made adjunct professor, without salary or teaching duties, but with the promise of a chair as soon as one was vacant. Somewhat earlier, in his application for a chair, Holberg had mentioned his concern about "improving the Danish language," and before leaving for his great European journey, he submitted the manuscript of his *Introduction til natur-og folke-rettens kundskab* (Introduction to Natural Law). Once more Pufendorf is the inspiration, but Holberg's book (published in 1716) has many examples from Danish and Norwegian law. It defends absolutism over other forms of government and gives a good overview of Holberg's religion, a form of deism, with God as creator and nonintervener, a religion that rejects the concept of original sin and emphasizes man's reason, or "natural light," and his basically free will.

Holberg's European journey began in May 1714. He first visited friends in Amsterdam and then continued to Paris, where he stayed for one year. In the summer of 1715 he traveled through Marseilles and Genoa to Rome, spending the winter there, and then proceeded on foot through Italy, across the Alps at the Savoy, and all the way back to Paris. From Paris he traveled to Amsterdam, continued by boat to Hamburg, and from Hamburg set out on foot to Copenhagen, where he arrived in the late summer of 1716. If Holberg's stay in England influenced his critical mind and his journalism, the European journey was of similar or even greater importance for his creative writing, his satires and comedies. He continued his critical education by visiting libraries and looking for prohibited books. In the Biliothèke Mazarine in Paris, for instance, he studied Bayle's *Dictionnaire* and the father of modern Bible criticism, Richard Simon; he also enjoyed attending public discussions of religion in the Sainte Sulpice Church. In his memoirs, Holberg does not mention the Paris theater, and yet his stay in Paris and in Italy was an artistic experience: all around him was a colorful and exuberant life, such as he had never seen at home. In Rome a theatrical group moved into his pension, and he was able to observe the famous Italian pantomime theater (commedia dell'arte) in action, with members practicing their parts at night and performing during the day. In Paris the old discussion of the merits of classical versus modern literature (Boileau versus Perrault and Fontenelle) was revived, and Holberg, who felt that modern history was more important than ancient, may have sided with those who emphasized contemporary literature over the classics. He read widely and for fun and later claimed that "all I know I have from French books; from reading them I have developed my taste."

The practice of giving a candidate for a professorship whatever chair happened to be vacant never seemed more curious than in the case of Holberg, who in 1717 was made professor of metaphysics, a subject he claimed to know nothing about and despised. Luckily, in 1720 he was made instead professor of Latin poetry, a subject somewhat closer to his heart, particularly since at this time, at age thirty-four, he tried his hand at poetry and liked it. To a colleague who, Holberg felt, had criticized his European history, he addressed two parodic dissertations in Latin, which, though they were mean and inelegant, inspired him to take up satirical poetry after classical and neoclassical models. Then, in 1719–20, he published *Peder Paars,* a satirical poem in four books, which, through a veritable succèss de scandale, turned the university professor into a poet of the first rank. *Peder Paars* is a parody, on the one hand of such classical heroic poems as *The Odyssey* and *The Aeneid,* and on the other of the street ballads circulating among the common people. It describes in some six thousand six-footed iambs (alexandrines) the voyage of Peder Paars, a worthy citizen of Kallundborg who wishes to visit his fiancée in Århus but is driven off course and shipwrecked on the island of Anholt. Ever since the Renaissance, parodies of classical literature had been common, and Holberg had no difficulty finding useful models. A humorously violent scene from a University of Copenhagen disputation is clearly inspired by Boileau's *Le Lutrin* (1672–83; The Lectern), while Peder Paars and his servant Peder Ruus have much in common with Miguel de Cervantes' pair Don Quixote and Sancho Panza. The island of Anholt, with its greedy and ignorant citizens, is often seen as a symbol of late seventeenth-century Denmark, and certainly when the book first appeared it was treated as a roman à clef. The owner of Anholt, Frederik Rostgaard, appealed to the king to confiscate the book and was supported by Holberg's colleague and former friend, the historian Hans Gram, who resented the ridiculing of Copenhagen university life. Gram even pointed out that, with the revolutionary tone in Peder Ruus's speech to the landless farmers, Holberg had outmolesworthed Molesworth (an Englishman who, in 1693, had criticized absolutist Denmark as being an exceptionally oppressive country). The king is said to have stated: "We have read *Peder Paars* and We have found it amusing." There was no case, and Holberg emerged triumphant in the battle over his "heroic-comic poem, which is now read and committed to memory even by Swedes and Germans, whom its popularity has induced to learn the Danish language," as he recalled in his memoirs.

Peder Paars, like all Holberg's works from the 1720s, was published under the pseudonym of Hans Mickelsen, ostensibly a brewer in Kallundborg (though in one line Holberg reveals at least his true nationality: "I am from Norway, hence / no countryman of Paars'"). He also supplied the text with learned notes by one Just Justesen, presumably another pseudonym. In the text, as well as in Just Justeson's notes, the attitude is clearly pro-women. Men (and the male gods) are presented as simpleminded and afraid that women will take over if they are allowed to read books and newspapers, to which Just Justesen remarks: "In this digression the poet makes fun of those alarmed by women taking up reading." Some of the women in the poem are described as being particularly gifted: Jens Poulson's wife is eloquent, wise, and sexy; Gertrude is learned; Sophie is intelligent and wise; and Martha is the earliest version of Holberg's many later Pernillas: amoral, cunning, intellectually superior, and with a feminist program. And the author supports her, claiming, like Ibsen later, that he is no special friend of women, but rather a friend of truth and freedom for all. This same line of thinking is pursued in the poem "Zille Hansdotters gynaicologia eller forsvarsskrift for qvinde-kiønnet" (Zille Hansdotter's Defense of Womanhood), written probably in the aftermath of the Peder Paars discussion and published in

1722, along with four satires in verse. Zille is against men who glorify women as innocent and virtuous. Men also claim that women are ruled by feeling and prone to gossip, but if this is true, says Zille, it is nothing more than the result of a sexist education. Zille does not intend to take up arms against her male competitors; she merely wishes to show them that women's low position in society is not a result of their intellectual inferiority. If women were given more responsibility, they would also achieve more.

After his appointment to the chair of Latin poetry, Holberg read classical literature, including comedies by Plautus, but also modern comedies, particularly by Molière, who, he said (in Just Justesen's commentary in *Peder Paars*), "has done more to improve the world through his comedies than all philosophers with their morality." In a letter dated January 1722, he also speaks of many qualities in himself "that could be turned into nice comedies." During his childhood in Bergen, on travels throughout Europe, and especially on his endless walks in and around the city of Copenhagen, Holberg had been able to practice and develop his instinct for the ridiculous in human nature. The opportunity to put it all into actual plays came in the summer of 1722, when a member of a French theater company in Copenhagen, René Magnong de Montaigu, decided to open a Danish theater. Molière's *L'Avare* (1668; *The Miser*) was played on September 23 and Holberg's first comedy, *Den politiske kandestøber* (Eng. tr. *The Political Tinker*, 1915 and others), two days later.

In the fall of 1722 Holberg wrote another four comedies and ten more in the spring of 1723. Eleven additional plays followed in the next couple of years, so that by February 1727, when the theater closed, Holberg had written in all twenty-six comedies. All of them have been performed many times in Denmark and Norway, most right down to the present day, some with more than six hundred performances. Though Holberg has a just claim to fame as a poet, novelist, and moral philosopher, today he is remembered first and foremost as a playwright, and the widespread and lasting popularity of his plays is again what has earned for him such epithets as the father of the Danish language, of Danish and Norwegian literature, and of Danish and Norwegian theater.

Holberg's comedies can be divided into two basic categories. In one he explores some human quality, often explained in the title or subtitle of the play: *The Weathercock, The Fussy Man, The Talkative Barber* (*Den vægelsindede, Den stundesløse, Den meget talende barbeer*), which bring to mind the plays of Molière, with such titles as *The Miser, The Hypochondriac, The Misanthrope*. To the other category belong plays that emphasize intrigue more than character, and the intrigue (actually found in most Holberg plays) concerns a young couple whose union, though opposed by members of the older generation, is achieved through the help of the servants of the household. Many of the types in these comedies are the same as in the commedia dell'arte: Holberg's Jeronimus is related to the old fool Pantalone, the servant Henrik to Pedrolino or Arlecchino, and the maid Pernille to Columbine. Holberg's lovers Leander and Leonora correspond to Lelio and Isabella in the Italian pantomime. Holberg, writing about comedies, always admired Molière, but not his successors, whose "deprived taste" he often deplored. He made a distinction between plays that "are for the eyes only," meaning comedies in which visual effects—costume and processions— played a major part, and comedies like Molière's, "which are for the ear" and which contain a clearly defined moral. Though Holberg claimed to have a low opinion of the former, some of his merriest plays undeniably belong in that category, such as *Henrik og Pernille* (Eng. tr. *Henry and Pernilla,* 1912) and *Mascarade* (Eng. tr. *Masquerades,* 1946), later turned into a festively frivolous opera by Denmark's Carl Nielsen. It should also be emphasized that what has sustained our interest in those of Holberg's plays with a clearly defined moral is, in the final analysis, his marvelous sense of the absurd.

Among Holberg's most popular plays are *Den politiske kandestøber, Erasmus Montanus* (Eng. tr. 1915 and others), and *Jeppe paa bierget* (Eng. tr. *Jeppe of the Hill,* 1915 and others). They are also examples of a "higher" humor, a humor with tragic elements, which Holberg shares with such famous predecessors and successors as Cervantes and Ibsen. *Den politiske kandestøber* is set in the city of Hamburg. Two members of the city council decide to play a trick on a local artisan, Herman von Bremen, who spends most of his time discussing politics. They convince him that he has been elected mayor of Hamburg and put before him some difficult cases to solve, which increasingly confuse him and finally cure him of all political ambitions. Though the morality is clear—"Every man a little beyond himself is a fool"—the comedy within the comedy shows Herman to be a more sympathetic person than the councillors, and probably not only in the eyes of modern democratic readers, since his opinions in many cases show wisdom and moderation of the kind often praised by Holberg. In *Erasmus Montanus,* such contradictions are more palpable. A farm boy, Rasmus Berg, has studied at the University of Copenhagen and returns home with a Latin name and an unstoppable urge to engage the local people in learned disputes, whereby he alienates such friendly, if naive, local citizens as the deacon, the overseer, and, particularly, his future father-in-law, Jeronimus. Once again a trick is played on the hero: he is trapped by a lieutenant into joining the army and thereafter beaten up by a brutal corporal until he implores his captors to free him and promises to change his ways and his wrongheaded ideas. Even though Erasmus is both ridiculous and unsympathetic, however, so are his antagonists, and besides, Erasmus is intelligent, and most important, he is right even if in the end he has to renounce his proposition that the earth is round rather than flat. Thus, in all this comedy there is, deep down, a touch of something like tragedy, the faint contours of a Galileo forced to accept the rules of a corrupt society. Søren Kierkegaard, the Danish philosopher, writes: "I grieve when I see or read *Erasmus Montanus*; he is right, and is subject to the *masses*" (*The Journals of Søren Kierkegaard* [London, 1938], p. 37). Most readers—rightly—do not see Erasmus in quite that light.

In his preface to the first edition of the comedies, Holberg relates how *Jeppe paa bierget* was played rather poorly the first time, "because of a confusion among the actors," and this confusion is in a sense symbolic: of Holberg's plays it is the one most often played, and its popularity is partly due to Jeppe's complex character, which, over the years, has been the cause of many different and often contradictory interpretations. Jeppe is an alcoholic farmer, hounded by the local squire and cheated and maltreated by his wife, Nille. When Nille sends him to town to buy soap, Jeppe spends all the money on drink and falls asleep on a dungheap, where he is found by Baron Nilus and his company. To entertain his master, one of the servants proposes that a comedy be played, whereby Jeppe is taken to the palace and placed in the baron's bed, where he later wakes up, believing at first he has arrived in heaven. Soon, however, the soft-spoken Jeppe, aided by quantities of liquor, changes into a tyrant and finally falls into a drunken stupor. He is placed once more on the dungheap, and, when he awakes, brought to court and sentenced to death by poisoning. He is then drugged, hung up in the gallows (the rope under his arms), and found by his wife, who first cries to see him dead but, when he awakens and asks for a drink, proceeds to whip him until he is rescued by his former judges. Jeppe is finally told about the tricks played on him and leaves the scene ashamed, whereupon Baron Nilus proceeds to address the spectators with a poem showing the danger of elevating farmers and artisans above their proper state. The play, then, depends for its success on a series of grotesquely incongruent situations, but it is also cruel. The Danish poet Adam Oehlenschläger found the baron's epilogue quite revolting, as do many modern readers, for the same reason that henpecked Jeppe, with his warm heart, his humor, and intelligence, moves the audience. Indeed, there are distant overtones of Holberg's admired philosopher Socrates here, not only in the pairing with a shrewish wife or the poison scene, but in the way the two men answer their judges. It has been claimed that such a reading—psychologizing and sentimentalizing—is unhistorical. But readers should also be warned against the so-called intentional fallacy. The truth is that, for a modern audience (and whether Holberg intended it or not), the text of the play is curiously at odds with the morality of the epilogue, showing once more how Holberg's humor is of a complex kind, full of an irony that points forward to such later masters of tragicomedy as Henrik Ibsen.

Holberg's poetic rapture came to a close as suddenly as it began. Exhausted, he applied for a leave of absence and spent the winter of 1725 in Paris, where he tried in vain to get some of his work (in his own translation) performed. At home in Copenhagen, Montaigu's group faced financial difficulties and finally gave a last performance on February 25, 1727, for which Holberg wrote a dramatic prologue, *Den danske comoedies liigbegjængelse* (Funeral of the Danish Theater). The work that ends Holberg's poetic rapture, however, is not a play but a strangely uninspired long poem entitled *Metamorphosis* (1726), by Holberg's own admission in the preface "without doubt my last poetic work, since I am getting very serious as well as lazy, leaving to young people an art I can no longer master." Among classical works, Ovid's *Metamorphoses* was a particular favorite of Holberg's, which is not surprising considering his special interest in characters of confusing psychology. Examples are the singer Tigellius, subject of his second satirical poem, and Miss Leonora, heroine of the *Den vægelsindede,* or historical persons such as Queen Christina of Sweden and Marie Grubbe, formerly married to the viceroy of Norway and later, when Holberg met her, married to a brutal ferryman serving a prison sentence yet happier with him than with her former husbands. Holberg's own life was complex, not only in his volatile temperament—he was an irascible and sometimes paranoiac man who admired the Stoics—but in his life's story of a fatherless high school student who became his country's most famous playwright. This metamorphosis Holberg set out to explore in the first section of his Latin autobiography, published on the last day of the year 1727. In the great Copenhagen fire of 1728 he lost not only all his personal belongings, but his apartment, where he had produced all the works from his decade of "poetic rapture"—the fire underlining once more the end of the most important stage of his life.

In 1730 Holberg finally became professor of a subject he both loved and was qualified to teach: history. His scholarly production during the 1730s is characterized by his many books on historical subjects, though he served as university president from 1735 to 1736 and even gave up his professorship in 1737 to become bursar of the university. His *Dannemarks og Norges beskrivelse* (Description of Denmark and Norway) appeared in 1729. It was a book for which he had collected materials as far back as his Oxford days, and it resembles the 1713 *Anhang* in being cultural history rather than topography. Between the years 1732 and 1735 Holberg's major historical work appeared, *Dannemarks riges historie* (History of the State of Denmark), which examines causes and effects and emphasizes cultural as much as it does political history, showing Holberg to be a pioneer of modern historiography. Considering the strict censorship of his times, Holberg was also a man of some courage, though in no way a revolutionary. He was a staunch defender of the absolutist state (against such critics as Molesworth and Montesquieu), feeling that its championship of the burgher class created new opportunities and more equality. Holberg's next book, a description of Bergen (*Bergens beskrivelse*, 1737), was based on the manuscript of one Edvard Edvardsen (1630–95), who was assistant principal at Bergen High School when Holberg first studied there. Holberg organized the unwieldy material and added interesting and amusing comments of his own, making the book one of his most charming. He remembers his mother's next-door neighbor, the great poet Dorothe Engelbretsdatter (1634–1716), though mainly because of her old-fashioned Bergen costume, and he tells with pride of his own great-grandfather, Ludvig Munthe, whose forebears, everyone in Bergen agreed, were of nobility.

Two other historical works belong to this stage in Holberg's production: a general church history (*Almindelig kirkehistorie*, 1739)—derivative but unbiased—and a history of the Jews (*Den jødiske historie*, 1742). A certain anti-Catholic sentiment is noticeable in some of Holberg's writings, and he is also critical of all aggressive atheism, but otherwise he shares the deism and the religious tolerance of the Enlightenment, being equally against the authoritarian attitude of conventional orthodoxy and the private and emotional nature of contemporary pietism. Some of the great theological problems of the day, such as the presence of evil in the world, Holberg often discussed but did not try to solve. Instead, he emphasized the social aspect of religion as a school for practical morality, claiming that children must be taught to be human before they can become Christians.

Historical, or rather psychohistorical, are also Holberg's history of great men (*Helte-historier*, 1739) and history of great women (*Heltinde-historier*, 1745), in which, as in Plutarch's similar accounts, several pairs of historical characters—Socrates and Epaminondas, Zenobia and Catherine the Great, and so on—are introduced, compared, and contrasted. Although Holberg often criticized military leaders for wasting human lives, he—the son of a colonel—also admired some of the famous field marshals of his day. As a historian, he came to emphasize more and more the importance of the great individual in historical development, as well as, in terms of a country's population, the importance of what he called "enthusiasm," his term for modern nationalism. Many of the introductions and comparisons belong to Holberg's most interesting essays, which are concerned with ethical evaluation rather than pure description and analysis. Hence they form a natural introduction to the last, moralistic stage in Holberg's writing career, consisting of a volume of science fiction, *Niels Klim* (1741), and seven volumes of essays (*Moralske tanker,* 1–2, 1744; and *Epistler,* 1–5, 1748–54).

Niels Klim (Eng. tr. *Journey to the World Underground,* 1742) was written in Latin and later translated into several modern languages, making it Holberg's most popular book. It pretends to be the memoir of a real person, one Niels Klim (1620–90), whom Holberg knew from his Bergen childhood. Niels Klim, who was interested in exploring caves in the vicinity of Bergen, fell through a hole into the interior of the hollow earth, landing eventually on the planet Nazar with its empire of Potu. Potu (Utop[ia] backward) gives Holberg the opportunity to outline his ideal society—a reflection of his own temperament, with its curious mixture of conservative and progressive elements. The form of government is hereditary monarchy, the senate is composed of none but large-landowners, and the Potuans, who are slow-thinking (but right-thinking) trees, do not suffer reformists gladly. There is religious freedom, however, and academies are coeducational institutions ("two young virgins learned navigation") that teach no theology, emphasize science, and have no room for the sophistic disputations so common at the University of Copenhagen. Women, though they are also good mothers, hold high positions in society, as seen by the case of Palmka, who was president of the senate in her hometown (Niels Kilm: "Bless me! thought I . . . What if the daughter of Counsellor Sørensen [of Bergen], that all-accomplished young lady, were to plead at the bar instead of her stupid father?"). Colonel Holberg's son also appears to be something of a pacifist, telling of the Potuans that "in time of war the conquerors, returning from the field, instead of that joy and triumph with which we celebrate victories and sing Te Deum, pass some days in deep silence, as if they were ashamed of having been obliged to shed blood."

The greater part of *Niels Klim* is inspired by an interest in the purely fantastic, like some of Holberg's models, such as Jonathan Swift's *Gulliver's Travels,* Daniel Defoe's *Robinson Crusoe,* and Montesquieu's *Lettres persanes.* Niels travels around the planet Nazar, visiting some two dozen lands, including Mascattia, the land of philosophers; Jochtane, the land of many religions; Quamboia, where people grow more voluptuous with age; and

Cocklecu, where women do what men do on Earth: rule the land and rape their partners (while men are kitchen boys or prostitutes). Holberg's fascination with metamorphoses of whatever kind is still active, as is his interest in warfare: when Niels proposes a law preventing women from holding public office, he is banished to the firmament. He later returns to establish his own empire, conducts military campaigns to subject his neighboring countries, becomes overambitious, and finally, fleeing from a lost battle, tumbles back to Earth through the same cavernous passage he had entered several years earlier. Niels Klim's memoir is completed by one Master Abeline (also an authentic Bergen name), who tells of how the old Niels Klim, at certain times of the year, would visit the famous cavern, from which he always returned "with his eyes swollen and his face all bathed in tears," a story symbolic of Professor Holberg's own situation as he said an ultimate goodbye to the remnants of his "poetic rapture." Even so, though *Niels Klim* is rich in progressive ideas and colorful invention (and in modern times the subject of a comic strip as well as of a much-acclaimed theatrical performance), it still pales in comparison with the pulsating life of Holberg's best comedies.

In 1737 Holberg had published a volume of Latin epigrams, and he used some of them as introductions to his "moral thoughts" (*Moralske tanker,* 1744), sixty-three essays written in the style of Montaigne. The subjects are varied, but though Holberg as always uses humor to teach his moral lessons, the essays are generally of a serious nature: on fearing God, on hypochondria, on studies beneficial and detrimental, on the deprived taste in modern plays, and so on. *Moralske tanker* is a more ambitious and more elegantly written book than the five volumes of "epistles" (*Epistler*) that followed, which are generally more humorous and more telling of Holberg's almost omnivorous intellectual appetite. The epistles in many cases are addressed to an imaginary friend or colleague, and subjects include "The Advantage of Cats over Dogs," "Apologia for the Devil," "What It Takes to be a Good Teacher," "Defense of Masquerades," and some essays concerning, among other things, Holberg's health, his frugality, his refusal to attend Italian operas, and his preference of women's company over that of men. All in all, they provide a lively portrait of the author, a person at the same time bigoted and tolerant, obstinate yet changeable, humorous, entertaining, and as a stylist immensely readable. Of Holberg's 539 epistles, one (no. 447) gives details of the last ten years of his life and is usually added to his three published Latin autobiographies (1728, 1737, 1743), thus completing Ludvig Holberg's interesting memoirs. When they appeared in English in the year 1827, the translator had left out "a few coarse pleasantries by which the fastidiousness of some readers might have been offended."

Holberg had placed most of his money in several estates near Copenhagen, which he willed to the old (1584) Sorø Academy for Young Noblemen; in return, he received from King Frederik V the title of baron (1747). To his annoyance, some of his colleagues smiled at this, remembering only too well how Holberg had ridiculed office seekers in such comedies as *Den honnette ambition* (1731; The Honorable Ambition). After 1746, when the pietistic King Christian IV was succeeded on the throne of Denmark by his lighthearted son, Frederik V, theatrical activities were gradually revived, and for the Royal Theater, newly established in 1748, Holberg wrote an additional six comedies, none of which, however, belongs to his commonly produced plays.

Ludvig Holberg was an intensely active person. He had no wife, children, or close colleagues, and all his energies went into writing and into private or public (university) business activities. Throughout his life he particularly appreciated his musical evenings with a few friends and in his old age is said to have attended and enjoyed parties at the court of King Frederik V. Strangely, though he seemed so entirely a city person, Holberg was happiest in the country. Though the modern romantic love of nature is the product of later generations, Holberg was basically a constructive personality who, beyond being a mercantilist and a physiocrat, found aesthetic pleasure in "seeing the growth of the soil, the planting and harvesting, and seeing cows and sheep walking as if in a procession to their gathering places morning and evening" (*Epistler* 1, no. 29). Typically, he made his ideal citizens of Potu trees. While checking the university's forest lands in August 1753, he caught a severe cold; he died in January 1754, at the age of sixty-nine. Shortly before, he had written a friend: "It is enough that throughout my life I have tried to be useful to my country; hence I want to die now that my strength is leaving me."

The people of Denmark and Norway have always agreed that Holberg is the father of Danish and Norwegian literature and theater, though they have sometimes emphasized different aspects of his life and works. The Danes naturally have seen Holberg's years in Copenhagen after his return from England as important for his development. They have looked on him as a person of tolerance and moderation, and among his literary works they have emphasized his comedies. In Norway, Holberg's Bergen childhood and his two years in England have been seen as particularly formative, Holberg has often been viewed as politically radical, and in addition to his plays, his historical and essayistic production has been much enjoyed, both in itself and as a boost to Norwegian nationalism during the union with Denmark. The Danish critic Georg Brandes identified with Holberg as the good European who single-handedly brought international Enlightenment to provincial Denmark-Norway. No Norwegian learned more from Holberg than Henrik Ibsen. Not only did he savor Holberg's sense of the absurd (Stockmann, umbrella in hand, chasing his former allies around the table in *An Enemy of the People*), but he carried on Holberg's educational program, including the fight for women's rights. Most important, Ibsen explored Holberg's type of irony in realistic plays that made him the father of modern tragicomedy.

FROM HOLBERG TO TULLIN

During the second half of the eighteenth century we find, in Scandinavia as elsewhere in Europe, a change in human sensibility: reason gives way to sentiment, and dignity to grace, as can be seen in the changing style in music between, say, Handel and Mozart, or in contemporary portraits, where gravity is replaced by a smiling charm. The city is less central and the park landscape correspondingly prominent as a theme for writers, who begin using poetry as much as prose to present their ideas about humankind's place in the universe.

Political life in Denmark-Norway did not change radically. The kings were singularly ineffectual. Frederik V (1746–66), though friendly and popular, was a philandering alcoholic, and his son and successor Christian VII (1766–1808), mentally instable. With the exception of a two-year rule by the enlightened despot Johann Friedrich Struensee (Christian VII's private doctor) in 1770–72, however, the twin countries were run by experienced and conscientious statesmen. There was considerable dissatisfaction among the farmers of West and South Norway, but there were no revolutions, and the Dano-Norwegian union continued largely undisturbed until its dissolution in 1814.

Through his gift to Sorø Academy, Holberg had wished to promote a new kind of educational establishment, where members of the Danish nobility and burgher classes would be trained to be well-informed and sophisticated young men of the world. On several occasions he had also praised science academies, like the Royal Society in London, for their free inquiry into the laws of nature and the universe. Six years after Holberg's death Trondheim became the home of Norway's first science academy, founded in 1760 by the scientist and theologian Johan Gunnerus (1718–73) and the historians Peder Suhm (1728–98) and Gerhard Schøning (1722–80).

Schøning's major project, which he continued even after he had become a professor at Sorø Academy in Denmark, was his history of Norway (*Norges riges historie*, 1–3, 1771–73), in which, following the French writers Montesquieu and Paul Henri Mallet, he claimed that the Germanic peoples had originated in Scandinavia, from where they brought the concept of freedom to Continental Europe. Instead of "Scandinavia," Schøning at all times used the word "Norway," making his country the cradle of freedom. Schøning was also in charge of a magnificent edition (1777–80) of Snorri Sturluson's (1179–1241) *Heimskringla* (ca. 1230; first Eng. tr. *History of the Norse Kings*, 1844), which, with his own historical works, became a powerful inspiration for Norwegian nationalism during the second half of the eighteenth century. Further inspired by the new teachings of Rousseau, Norwegian writers following Schøning found a favorite motif in "the free Norwegian farmer," free in contrast to his Danish colleague, who was enslaved by the landed gentry and, between the years 1733 and 1788, was not allowed to move from the place of his birth. In 1771 Selskabet til de skiønne og nyttige Videnskabers Forfremmelse (Society for the Advancement of the Beautiful and Useful Sciences)—founded in 1759 and popularly referred to as Det Smagende Selskab (The Society of Taste)—gave its annual prize to Hans Bull (1739–83) for his poem "Om landmandens lyksalighed" (About the Happy Farmer), with lines like the following:

> Life, action, every place. Here seeding new-plowed field
> There sawing useful boards, or tap the mountain's yield.
> While spineless slaves endure a life without attraction,
> A free Norwegian finds his strength increased by action
> And pride in ownership; his unrestricted right
> Makes all his troubles sweet and all his burdens light.

The preference for sentiment over reason in literature is particularly evident in the drama of the times. Holberg in one of his epistles complained about the new taste in plays with their emphasis on the visually attractive rather than on idea content. But the growing burgher class did not want to see its members ridiculed in Holberg's (as they felt) rather coarse comedies and favored instead the sentimental plays newly imported from France (Philippe Néricault Destouches, Denis Diderot), England (Samuel Richardson's *Pamela*, dramatized by Voltaire), and Germany (Gotthold Lessing). Soon sentimental plays were produced locally, by Dorothea Biehl in Copenhagen and Enevold Falsen in Christiania, and such Norwegian writers as Bredal, Nordahl Brun, and Claus Fasting attempted to produce operas and tragedies after Italian and French patterns for the Danish stage.

In poetry French influence gave way to English, exemplified by the work of Alexander Pope, whose "Essay on Man" inspired much of the didactic poetry of the North, while his nature poems (mainly "Windsor Forest") served as models for a whole tradition of Scandinavian landscape poetry. Links with the German poetic tradition became more important after the middle of the century, partly through the ascendancy of the German-inspired pietism during the reign of Christian VI, partly through the presence in Copenhagen in 1759–71 of the German poet Friedrich Gottlieb Klopstock (1724–1803), whose influence, however, was much greater among Danes than among Norwegians.

The great English prose writers of the day, such as Henry Fielding and Laurence Sterne, did not have important followers in Denmark-Norway, even though their works were early translated into Danish. English popular weeklies, however, such as *The Tatler* and, particularly, *The Spectator,* were soon imitated in Scandinavia, first by the Swedes (Olof von Dalin's *Den svenska Argus*, 1732–34; The Swedish Argus), then by the Danes, as in Jens Schielderup Sneedorff's *Den patriotiske tilskuer* (1761–63; The Patriotic Spectator), and finally by the Norwegian Claus Fasting in his *Provinzialblade* (Provincial Papers). By that time Norway's first newspaper, *Norske intelligenssedler* (Norwegian Intelligence Papers), had already been founded in Christiania (1763). It ran articles on a variety of subjects, from moral matters to recent advances in agriculture, and some poetry, though it was mostly advertisements. A publication of great importance for the intellectual life in Denmark-Norway was the monthly journal *Minerva,* edited jointly by Christen Pram and Knud Lyhne Rahbek from 1785 to 1789 and by Rahbek alone until 1797. Most people of some prominence in the twin kingdoms contributed to its discussion of such issues as educational and agricultural reform and the freedom of writers and journalists. Much of this new interest in the cultivation of Danish prose was inspired by the epistolary literature of Ludvig Holberg, who, in turn, had learned some of his manner from the early English *Spectator* literature.

Throughout the Age of Enlightenment there was in Scandinavia a strong undercurrent of pietism and, later, sentimentalism. Pietism had its roots among German Protestants reacting against the Lutheran orthodoxy, which had developed into a cold and inflexible bureaucracy. The pietists returned feeling and fantasy to church life, renewed the sense of mysticism by emphasizing individual devotion and an intensified experience of God, and turned their religion into a practical Christianity of the heart. They shared with men and women of the Enlightenment a deep concern with tolerance in religious matters. Among the pietists, Count Zinzendorf's Moravian

Brethren stand out for their interest in music and poetry. The spiritual verse of the pietists has brilliant description of nature and a deeply felt religious enthusiasm, though it often appears as edifying literature with long-winded and saccharine extravaganzas, showing a transition to sentimentalism. Sentimentalism as a movement grew during the second part of the eighteenth century. It continued and secularized pietism's religious experience of nature, resulting in a modish and sometimes excessive emotionalism, with daydreaming and a tearful demeanor.

In Norway pietism did not produce native verse of lasting importance. Foreign hymns, however, were circulated throughout the countryside and helped prepare the ground for the strong fundamentalist movement of the following century known as Haugeanism. In 1734 a Norwegian woman of noble background, Birgitte Christine Kaas (1682–1761), published some translations of hymns from the German, and in 1740 a hymnbook was published and circulated in Norway which contained several hymns by the great Danish pietist poet Hans Adolph Brorson (1694–1764), Holberg's contemporary. Many of Brorson's hymns, set to Norwegian folk tunes, have become the most beloved songs in Norway, partly because of their childlike simplicity, as in the Christmas song "Her kommer dine arme smaa" (Here Come Your Little Poor Ones), or because of the "Norwegian" mountain imagery, as in "Den store hvide flok vi se / som tusind bjerge fuld af sne" (The Vast, Unnumbered Throngs that Show / Like Thousand Mountains Full of Snow). This last hymn, from Brorson's later collection, *Svane-sang* (1765; Swan Song), was set to a Norwegian folk tune and, in Grieg's famous arrangement, gradually became known all over Norway and Norwegian America.

A sentimentalist rather than a pietist, Christian Braunmann Tullin (1728–65) for some time enjoyed an undeserved reputation as the most prominent poet in Denmark-Norway after Holberg, undeserved because some of the then-unknown Danish poets of the time were clearly more gifted. Son of a Norwegian farmer turned businessman, Tullin studied theology in Copenhagen and then returned to Norway, where he operated a factory, at the same time holding the office of mayor of Christiania (Oslo). His life shows some parallels with that of Holberg: he was a man of weak constitution, a gifted musician and linguist, with friends among people of influence. But he lacked Holberg's iron will and concern for his personal health and, feted and idolized by members of Christiania high society, he died at the young age of thirty-six. At the university Tullin had come under the influence of the pietist professor J. F. Reuss, and though, like Holberg, Tullin later changed his religion in the direction of conventional deism, he never lost his understanding of the value of emotions in poetry. What he particularly shared with Holberg was a deep concern with improved education and greater freedom for women. Tullin was an eager reader of the moralistic journals, English and Danish, of his day, and in his collected works in three volumes from 1771, the greater part consists of prose essays, somewhat in the style of Holberg's epistles. The first volume is devoted to poetry, epitaphs, occasional verse, and two large poems for which, in 1760 and 1763, he won the prize established by the newly founded Smagende Selskab. The first poem, "Søefarten, dens oprindelse og virkninger" (Navigation: Its Origins and Effects), was written in elegant alexandrines (six-footed iambs) and described the golden age of seafaring, then (inspired by Rousseau) its decline under the influence of human greed and violence, and finally its restitution through God's direct intervention. Tullin's second prize-winning poem, "Skabningens ypperlighed i henseende til de skabte tings orden og sammenhæng" (The Excellency of Creation, with Respect to the Order and Coherence of All Things Created), is written in the spirit of a happy deism. Nature is described as infinite, purposeful, and attractive down to its smallest detail, with some of the spirit, if not the enthusiasm, of Henrik Wergeland's cosmologies of two generations later.

Tullin was best known as a writer of pastoral poetry, a genre cultivated since early classical times (by poets such as Theocritus) and particularly popular in Europe during the mid-eighteenth century. The poem "Thyrsis til Melikrona" (Thyrsis to Melicrona) (with the shepherd's name taken from Theocritus) has a provocative amphibrachic ($x—x$) rhythm and was probably written to an existing melody. Tullin today is remembered first and foremost for his poem "Maidagen" (The May Day), a description of the scenery around the estate of Bogstad in Sørkedalen outside Christiania and written on the occasion of Morten Leuch's marriage to Mathia Collett in 1758. It is *the* classical Dano-Norwegian nature poem, surviving in anthologies and textbooks, like Thomas Gray's more rightly famous "Elegy," for more than two hundred years. Tullin describes the lines, colors, and sounds of the landscape in twenty-nine eight-lined stanzas, somewhat too topographic, detailed, and artificial for modern taste and yet charming as an example of a literary rococo painting. It has been translated into Swedish, Icelandic, German, Dutch, English, and French and was praised by no lesser person than the German writer Gotthold Lessing. Holberg had learned his poetry from the French and his ways of thinking from the English. Tullin learned his poetry from the English. His second prize poem ("Skabningens ypperlighed") has much in common with Pope's "Essay on Man," and his more lyrical nature poems show the influence of Young's *Night Thoughts*.

During the second half of the eighteenth century Norwegian writers belonged to one of two schools, the French classical line from Holberg or the somewhat more sentimental and English-oriented line from Tullin.

Norwegian poetry at the middle of the eighteenth century was also briefly influenced by German verse, which in turn had connections with the emotional language of the pietists. Klopstock's unrhymed poetry, which later influenced the great Danish poet Johannes Ewald (1743–81), had no appeal for Tullin, but it did inspire his countryman Peter Christopher Stenersen (1723–76). Stenersen, from Gudbrandsdal in East Norway, spent most of his life as a clergyman in Denmark. He had already written a dissertation on unrhymed poetry when, in 1754, he wrote his famous "Choriambic Ode" on the occasion of a local wedding. The poem, of twenty-four so-called asclepiadean stanzas, is a relatively successful attempt to apply a strictly syllabic meter in an accented language like Danish and the first example of unrhymed poetry by a Norwegian. Other poems by Stenersen—for instance, a well-known drinking song, "Ode til selskabsbrødrene" (Ode to the Bon Vivants), in sapphic meter (as in the *Odes* of Horace)—have regular rhymes, and unrhymed verse was not used thereafter in Norwegian poetry until the time of Henrik Wergeland.

DET NORSKE SELSKAB

Until World War II the majority of Norwegians still had a rural background, and in an urban or foreign milieu they tended to seek each other out and stick together, whether as immigrants from the country in nineteenth-century Christiania, as emigrants in America, or, one hundred years earlier, as students in Copenhagen. In the early 1770s these Norwegian students in Copenhagen found a leader in Niels Krog Bredal (1732–78), a friendly bachelor who had written the first Danish opera, *Gram og Signe* (1754; Gram and Signe), was mayor of his hometown of Trondheim from 1757 to 1770, and served thereafter as director of the Royal Theater in Copenhagen. When his most recent, and by no means memorable, opera, *Tronfølgen i Sidon* (1771; The Succession to the Throne of Sidon), was criticized by a young Dane, Peter Rosenstand-Goiske, in his dramatic journal, Bredal wrote and produced a farce similarly entitled *Den dramatiske journal*. The farce was booed by the Copenhagen students (an incident later celebrated in Johannes Ewald's tragicomedy, *De brutale klappere* [The Brutal Booers]), and Bredal in the spring of 1772 had to leave his directorship after only one year. The Norwegians in Copenhagen, however, recovered from their wounded patriotism when another countryman, Johan Nordahl Brun

(1745–1816), won a prize for the best Danish tragedy with his *Zarine* (1771), a rather unremarkable attempt to imitate classical French drama. More important, as it later turned out, was Brun's drinking song "For Norge kiempers fødeland" (1772; To Norway, Home of Giants), which, with revolutionary lines such as "and yet one day we'll wake again / And break our bondage and our chain," became a Norwegian "Marseillaise." Because it was unprintable in the strictly censored Twin Nations, the song may have led indirectly to the establishment (on April 30, 1772) of the well-known Norske Selskab (Norwegian Society) in Copenhagen as a place where students could freely celebrate their patriotism and private longing for the old country. Members would meet over a glass of punch in Madame Juel's Tavern. They had a secretary, Ole Gjerløv Meyer, who, as a glowing patriot and poet manqué, was representative: over the years more than twenty of the two hundred members tried their hand at poetry, which the society published in three collections (1775, 1783, 1793). Though the society may have been given too much emphasis in past histories of Danish and Norwegian literature, its members produced some singable verse of lasting value, and above all, they created and consolidated a Norwegian national consciousness, which did not appear in its full flowering until after the dissolution of the Danish-Norwegian union in 1814.

Unlike his Norwegian "Marseillaise," Johan Nordahl Brun was not revolutionary, though he was definitely a nationalist: he had worked as a secretary for Bishop Gunnerus and was much inspired by Schøning's history of Norway. He wrote Norway's first national play, *Einar Tamberskielve* (1772), about an eleventh-century athlete and hero from Brun's home district of Trøndelag. In his poetry (1791) he celebrated such new themes as Norway's mountain scenery ("Bor jeg paa de høje fjeld" [When I Live in the Mountains High]) and Norway's winter sports ("Min norske vinter er saa vakker" [My Norwegian Winter Is So Beautiful]), both of them subjects unthinkable to Holberg, who, however, would have approved of Brun's description of Norwegian business enterprise in the festive national song for the city of Bergen, written to a melody by Jean-Baptiste Lully and still popular. Also lasting have been some of Brun's hymns (1786) for Easter and Pentecost ("Jesus lever," "Aand over aander" [Jesus Liveth, Spirit Above Spirits]), inspired by a robust orthodoxy and free from the rationalism and emotionalism of his age.

Brun's membership in Det Norske Selskab was of short duration. He returned to Norway in 1772 and ended his career forty-five years later as bishop of Bergen. A brilliant public speaker, he has often been compared to the nineteenth-century poet and playwright Bjørnstjerne Bjørnson, whom he does *not* resemble in his politics, being a royalist and a staunch conservative to the end of his days. In the Norwegian Society, however, Brun had been surrounded by many people of opposite character—perpetual students, womanizers, drunks—such as the short-lived Johan Vibe (1748–82), author of a couple of popular drinking songs, and Johan Herman Wessel (1746–85), an ingenious versifier and the greatest poet in Det Norske Selskab. At times Wessel gave private instruction in foreign languages, but he lived otherwise, as well as he could, from his literary production, including a weekly paper, *Votre Serviteur Otiosis* (1784–85; At Your Service, Members of the Leisure Class). In this sense he is Norway's first professional writer, a Norwegian Bellman—of lesser scope, and unmusical, but with a remarkable gift for meter and a true sense of what is genuine in literature. He turned his satirical gifts against all forms of pretense, and since he looked on most things as sham, his serious poetry is almost nonexistent ("Ode til søvnen" [1775; Ode to Sleep] is a noteworthy exception). In literary matters members of Det Norske Selskab wished to uphold the old classical ideals, as can be seen from the motto inscribed on their membership ring: *vos exemplaria graeca* ["let the things of Greece be an example to you"]. Wessel shared their conservative attitude, admired French theater, and had little understanding of the new trends in literature, whether English-inspired nature poetry or the overly emotional verse of the Danish followers of Klopstock.

Wessel was also a man of taste who saw that the Norwegian imitations of French tragedy were ridiculous rather than sublime. In his five-act "tragedy," *Kierlighed uden strømper* (1772; Love without Stockings), he created a popular parody, in which he observed Boileau's strict unities and other rules of classical French drama. The comic effect is based on the incongruity of high style and low reality: the hero lacks the right kind of stockings for his wedding and steals them from his rival, with dire results: in the last scene the hero, the heroine, the rival, and their servants all stab themselves to death. *Kierlighed uden strømper* is enjoyable reading—Wessel's alexandrines are among the best in all Danish and Norwegian literature—and as a singspiel, with music by the normally serious composer Paolo Scalabrini, it is still popular on the stage in Denmark and Norway. Wessel is otherwise known for his comic tales in verse, of which several belong to the classics of Danish and Norwegian literature. In "Smeden og bageren" (printed 1784; The Smith and the Baker), ridiculing Dano-Norwegian court procedure, a peaceful baker is executed instead of a murderous smith, because the village has only one smith but two bakers. As a master of light verse, Wessel has no equal in Norwegian literature and has remained a model for later poets, including Herman Wildenvey.

Less gifted than Wessel but also less doctrinaire in his literary taste was the third leading member of Det Norske Selskab, Claus Fasting (1746–91), whose journalism is more important than his creative writing (his play *Hermione* [1772] was one of the tragedies justly parodied by Wessel in *Kierlighed uden strømper*). Fasting was well read and liberal in his views, he admired French drama but also the Klopstock-inspired Ewald, and he had an early understanding of the new trends in English literature, from Richardson to Ossian. Fasting was a collaborator in two Danish journals, *Kritisk journal* and *Kritisk tilskuer* (Critical Journal; Critical Spectator), before he returned to his birthplace, Bergen, where he founded and edited a weekly paper called *Provinzialblade* (1779–81; Provincial Papers), a forerunner of Aasmund Vinje's more famous journal *Dølen*. Unlike Wessel, Fasting thought highly of the contemporary English nature poems and praised the Norwegian attempts in this new genre. In September 1774 Det Smagende Selskab announced a "prize for the best attempt in painterly poetry, whereby Pope's 'Windsor Forest' could serve as example. One would have to choose some place in the Danish states, which are remarkable either for their graceful or for their frightening scenery, as in the first case the Sound or one of the Royal Castles, and in the second case the Maelstrom or the waterfall Sarpen in Norway."

The result was a new tradition of Norwegian nature poetry. Edvard Colbjørnsen (1751–92) wrote about spring in a way that made Fasting exclaim enthusiastically in *Kritisk tilskuer*, "What a poem, what imagery! Oh, fatherland! Oh, Norway!" (The poem had appeared in the first collection [1775] published by Det Norske Selskab.) Det Smagende Selskab gave its prize to Thomas de Rosing Stockfleth (1748–1808) for his poem about Sarpen, and to Peter Harboe Frimann (1752–1839) for his poem about St. Sunniva's Monastery at Selje (1774, printed 1777), a description of an idyllic spot in West Norway, while his poem about the montain Hornelen is an example of the "frightening" scenery recommended by Det Smagende Selskab. Frimann was a poet of good taste and with a sense of modern literature: he wrote verses full of rococo grace ("Ode til søvnen" [1775; Ode to Sleep]) and one of the first ballad imitations in Dano-Norwegian literature ("Axel Thorson"; 1775), while in his poem about Hornelen (1777), he abandons the alexandrine and introduces, as one of the first Norwegian poets, an ottavelike stanza. Despite his taste and refinement, Peter Frimann did not win the reputation of his older brother, Claus Frimann (1746–1829), whose own poem about Hornelen won (we now think unjustly) Det Smagende Selskab's prize. But Claus Frimann, a minister in the Norwegian countryside, later published some folk songs in simple meters about everyday life among farmers and fishermen. Many of the songs in his two collections, *Almuens sange* (1790; Songs of the People) and *Den syngende sømand* (1793; The Singing Sailor), have a poetic simplicity rarely heard in the period between Brorson and the great romantic poets of the following century. They were also popular, and many of them were set to music.

Thomas de Rosing Stockfleth was briefly a member of Det Norske Selskab and, in addition to his prize poem on Sarpen, earned a reputation for an earlier poem called "Heimatkomsten" (1771, printed 1798; The Homecoming). In 1729 a Bergen poetaster, Ole Camstrup, had written a poem in dialect about a farmer at a wedding party, and five years later (1734) Michael Heiberg (1705–57) composed a similar poem, also written in dialect and called "Bonden i brudlaupsgarden" (The Farmer at the Wedding). This poem of twenty-one stanzas, written in the same meter as Petter Dass's *Nordlands trompet,* gradually became well known and marks the beginning of Norwegian literature written in nynorsk. In "Heimatkomsten," Stockfleth continues the tradition of dialect poetry and describes in forty-four stanzas the feelings and experiences of a soldier in the royal guards returning to his home parish in Gudbrandsdalen after eight years in Copenhagen. The meter—nine-line stanzas of six, four, or three trochees—is based on an old folk melody and was taken up by another and more important specialist in dialect poetry, Edvard Storm (1749–94). Storm left his home district of Gudbrandsdalen at the age of twenty and spent the rest of his life as a poet and pedagogue in Copenhagen. His friends there appear to have been Danes rather than his countrymen in Det Norske Selskab—he apparently resented their criticism of the Danish poet Ewald—but even so he is the most truly nationalistic of all Norwegian poets in Copenhagen, ever inspired by memories of his childhood in Gudbrandsdal. Storm, according to his student, the great Danish poet Adam Oehlenschläger, spoke a dialect-colored Norwegian and collected dialect words from many parts of Norway. He is best known for his lively dialect songs from Gudbrandsdal celebrating spring, such as "Markja grønast" (printed 1802; Eng. tr. "Fields and Woods Are Crowned with Verdure," 1881), or the homecoming from the mountain chalet, "Oss har gjort kva gjerast skulle" (printed 1802; Eng. tr. "We Have Done Our Bounden Duty," 1881), and for his ballad (in Danish; printed 1782) about the defeat in 1658 of the Scottish army under Colonel Sinclair at Kringen in Gudbrandsdal.

The last years of Det Norske Selskab saw the continuation of the anacreontic tradition of drinking songs in poetry by Jens Zetlitz (1761–1821), a gifted and versatile troubadour whose poetry filled the third of the society's poetry collections (1793). Zetlitz continued the tradition begun by Hans

Bull by writing about the free Norwegian farmer, an inspiration also for Jonas Rein (1760–1821), whose melancholy temper inspired poetry that earned him a reputation as a master of elegiac verse. Though conventional in form—he was a favorite of Wessel's—Rein, even more than Fasting, oriented himself toward new political and poetic ideas. He was inspired by the slogans of the French Revolution, as well as by the poetry of Friedrich von Schiller and the philosophy of Immanuel Kant. Like Nordahl Brun, he attended the Constitutional Assembly of 1814 at Eidsvoll, where his anti-Swedish position later cost him the appointment of bishop of Bergen after Brun.

Other people from the last years of Det Norske Selskab who represented the new nationalistic ideas were Christen Pram, Nicolai Wergeland, and Niels Treschow. Christen Pram (1756–1821), editor of the periodical *Minerva*, first tried himself at nature poetry with "Emilias kilde" (1782; Emilia's Spring) and then published an epic poem in fifteen songs, *Stærkodder* (1785; about the ancient hero Starkad), for which he won local fame and was admired even in Sweden. Pram is also important as a pioneer in the development of Dano-Norwegian fiction, being the only Norwegian short-story writer from the eighteenth century. His stories—inspired partly by Voltaire, partly by Oliver Goldsmith—were popular in their time, and some of them, such as "Hans Kruuskop" and "Jørgen"—both from the year 1786—still make enjoyable reading. Pram should be remembered furthermore for his ten-volume historical report, written after an official journey through Norway in the years 1804–6, and for his prize-winning thesis on a separate Norwegian university (1795). Pram's idea that a Norwegian university should be established in Norway was strongly supported by Nicolai Wergeland (1780–1848), whose dissertation on this topic, *Mnemosyne* (1811), fired Norwegian patriotism, though it offended most Danes, who felt that their university had served the Norwegians well. An exception was the Dane Enevold Falsen (1755–1808). As a young man he had come from Copenhagen to Christiania, where he was highly thought of, both as a judge and as a keen supporter of the local theater. Falsen was active on the stage and as a translator and writer of plays—his musical, *Dragedukken* (1797; The Leprechaun), was popular in Danish and Norwegian theaters for several generations—but he is remembered among his new countrymen mainly for his gallant defense (1793) of a separate university for Norway. The old dream became a reality in 1811, and Niels Treschow (1751–1833), one of the most prominent philosophers in Denmark-Norway, moved back to his home country to become its first university professor.

Norwegian Literature
1800–1860

Harald Naess

4

It has been said that the intellectual movement now known as the Enlightenment was born among the English, displayed its finest flowering in France, and ended in Germany, where Immanuel Kant's *Critique of Pure Reason* (1781; *Kritik der reinen Vernunft*) gave rise to a new subjectivism in philosophy, literature, and the arts. The new movement, known as romanticism, spread to England, France, and the rest of Europe, including such Scandinavian countries as Denmark and Sweden. Norway was late in accepting the new ideas of romanticism, but it was a Norwegian-born philosopher, Henrich Steffens (1773–1845), who first introduced these ideas in Denmark-Norway. Steffens had studied geology in Denmark and in Germany, where he came under the influence of the German philosopher Friedrich Schelling and his views of the unity of nature and history. Steffens visited Jena, the stronghold of the romantic movement in Germany; stayed with Johann Goethe at Weimar; met Friedrich von Schiller; and gradually befriended many of the central names in German romanticism, the brothers Schlegel as well as Ludwig Tieck and Novalis. In 1801 he published his *Beitrag zur inneren Naturgeschichte der Erde* (Contributions to the Inner Science of the Earth), in which he outlined a teleological evolutionary system that made him famous among his contemporaries. In 1802 he returned to Denmark-Norway, where his lectures and conversations influenced such leading men in Danish romanticism as the poets Adam Oehlenschläger, Adolph Wilhelm Schack von Staffeldt, and N. F. S. Grundtvig. Though Steffens had hoped for an academic position in Denmark or Norway, he spent the rest of his life as a professor in Germany, and his many works, including a ten-volume autobiography, were written in German. He always remembered Norway, the "romantic" country of his birth, which he visited three times, though his influence there was felt less and less. In 1830 Norway's first great romantic work, the cosmological poem *Skabelsen, mennesket, og Messias* (Creation, Man, and Messiah), was dedicated by its author, Henrik Wergeland, to, among several people, "Henrik Steffens, you Norway's blown-away laurel leaf."

The period 1800–1830, a golden age in the literature of Denmark and Sweden, produced no poetic works of lasting importance in Norway, and it has been said defensively that the country's artistic resources all went into the making of its liberal constitution, signed at Eidsvoll on May 17, 1814. In fact, many of the ideas of romanticism—national pride, love of home and countryside—had already been developed in the previous century among members of Det Norske Selskab (The Norwegian Society) in Copenhagen and were strongly felt by farmers and civil servants. What was lacking was the great poet who could bring those ideas to life. The result was a literary period of mostly occasional poetry, songs inspired by the 17th of May Constitution, with texts by such minor poets as Simon Olaus Wolf (1796–1859) and Conrad Nicolai Schwach (1793–1860), and by Hans Hanson (1777–1837), who is remembered for being one of the first Norwegians of the nineteenth century to use dialect in his poetry. "Astri, mi Astri" (1797; printed 1816; Eng. tr. "Astri! My Astri!" 1881), his adaptation of a text by Horace, has become widely known as a popular "folk song." A somewhat more ambitious poet was Henrik Anker Bjerregaard (1792–1842), known not only for his prize-winning national anthem "Sønner af Norge" (1820; Eng. tr. "Minstrel Awaken," 1881), but for a popular musical, *Fjeldeventyret* (1824; The Mountain Adventure), for which Norway's first composer, Waldemar Thrane, provided the melodies, including the charming dialect song "Aagots fjeldsang" (Eng. tr. "Aagot's Mountain Song," 1872). The most important literary artist of the period was the novelist and short-story writer Mauritz Hansen (see "Beginnings of the Norwegian Novel," below).

THE CULTURAL DEBATE OF THE 1830S

A central literary topic throughout the pre-romantic and romantic periods was the free Norwegian farmer, Holberg's "nobleman in miniature," a theme that also inspired the civil servants in the Eidsvoll Constitutional Assembly when they decreed that two-thirds of the members of the Norwegian Storting, or parliament, should come from the rural areas. They soon had second thoughts, realizing that the Storting could be dominated by farmers, which is what happened for the first time in the year 1833. The next thirty years were characterized by a struggle between the civil servants and the farmers, with the latter finally winning when, in 1869, they united with schoolteachers and lawyers to form the liberal party later known as Venstre.

If we overlook the insignificant literary contributions of the Eidsvoll generation, Norwegian literature in the nineteenth century can be said to have begun around 1830 with a cultural debate between the poets Johan Welhaven and Henrik Wergeland, between a defender of traditional bourgeois values (Welhaven) and a purveyor of new liberal ideas (Wergeland) that were rooted in the optimism and religious tolerance of the previous century and reached their full flowering during the golden age of Norwegian literature in the 1880s.

The Danish critic Johan Ludvig Heiberg, writing about Det Norske Selskab in Copenhagen and its opposition to the Danish poet Johannes Ewald, claimed that the society, with its neoclassical ideals, ought rather to be called "Danish," since it emphasized "Danish" aesthetic ideals, namely, simple, clear, correct, and elegant expression, while the society's antagonists, including the poet Ewald, were less "Danish" and less national because of their love of pathos and their reliance on German, rather than French, models. Late in life Heiberg's relative and admirer in Norway, Johan Welhaven, wrote a book entitled *Ewald og de norske digtere* (1863; Ewald and the Norwegian Poets), in which he praised the Norwegian stand against the emotional style of Ewald and by doing so justified his own youthful attack on Ewald's great admirer in Norway, Henrik Wergeland, an attack that had led to years of cultural debate in the 1830s. Ostensibly, it was an attack on Wergeland's total neglect of what Welhaven, like Heiberg, considered basic in poetry—simple, clear, correct, and elegant expression—but the attacks and counterattacks were also inspired by a difference in temperament between the conservative, introverted Welhaven and the outgoing, enthusiastic Wergeland. Wergeland, with his highly personal style, his promethean spirit, and his mystical experience of nature, could more rightly be called a typical poet of the romantic era, but at the same time he praised the progressive spirit of the Enlightenment. Welhaven, in contrast, had strong links with the neoclassical ideals of the previous century and was a romantic more in the general sense of a nostalgic votary of the past. During the first decades of the newborn nation the patriotism of both antagonists was discussed and it was generally felt that Wergeland was the more Norwegian. A correct view would be to see the two writers, each in his own way, as both national and international.

Wergeland's international orientation was above all political. Unlike the conservative Welhaven, he was inspired by the European fight for freedom and wrote songs for the oppressed people of Spain and Russia, for the blacks of America, and, particularly, for the admission of Jews to the kingdom of Norway. His heroes in poetry were such freedom fighters as Lord Byron and Claude Joseph Rouget de l'Isle, and he refused to recognize the greatness of the Danish poet Oehlenschläger, since, Wergeland claimed, Oehlenschläger had done nothing to alleviate the political and social oppression in Denmark.

Although Wergeland wrote poetry describing the beauty of the Norwegian landscape, his nationalism was primarily directed toward the Norwegian people, their way of life, their folk music, and their speech. He was the first to speak out, theoretically and systematically, for the reformation of the Norwegian language; he was also concerned about raising the educational level among farmers and workers and edited some edifying periodicals. Above all, he worked to increase the national sentiment among the lower classes—as in the celebration of the Norwegian 17th of May Constitution—which made him, along with his violinist friend, Ole Bull, the great hero of early nineteenth-century Norwegian nationalism.

Welhaven, in contrast, deploring the dilettantism of early nineteenth-century Norwegian poetry, felt that Norway could not create a new literature out of nothing and therefore depended on the inspiration and influence of foreign literatures, for which reason he was referred to as a Danomaniac. He and his gifted friends in the Intelligence party—Jonas Collett, P. A. Munch, and A. M. Schweigaard—were also tied to Germany, and indeed to the liberal forces there known as Jung Deutschland (Young Germany). Their sense of the practical, of everyday detail, as they found it in the humorous verse of the Swedish poet Carl Michael Bellman, helped prepare the way for international realism in Norway.

But Welhaven, as a typical representative of the Norwegian civil-servant class, was also aware of his national responsibilities. When, many years later, he looked back on his youthful attack on Wergeland, he felt no need to apologize, since he had served his country in taking a stand against the exaggerated pathos that threatened to destroy the first literary attempts of the new nation. With his love of simplicity Welhaven was naturally inspired by the medieval folk ballads, as well as by the whole idea of Norwegian folk literature, and among the artists of the so-called National Breakthrough who tried to present the young nation ideally in music, painting, and verse, Welhaven was the preeminent poet. Typically, many of the songs that describe the romantic Norwegian landscape, songs cherished by middle-class city dwellers down to the present day, have words written by Welhaven.

Johan Sebastian Cammermeyer Welhaven (1807–73) grew up in Bergen. His father, pastor at the Bergen hospital, was a lovable man; his mother, clear-thinking and sharp-tongued, was related to the famous Danish critic Johan Ludvig Heiberg. As a child, Welhaven was much impressed by the magnificent landscape of West Norway with its striking harmony of cold mountain glaciers and idyllic fjord havens. Most of Welhaven's poetry deals with similar contrasts in his own personality and with his unfulfilled dreams of harmony.

With his good looks, his sharp tongue, and his sense of poetry, Welhaven soon made himself known among members of the Christiania Student Association. In August 1830 he opened his attack on Henrik Wergeland with a poem in *Morgenbladet* (Morning Paper), and during the next four years he gathered around himself a group of gifted students, the so-called Intelligence party, whose enemies were members of the "Norwegian party," also referred to as "Screamers" and "Patriots." Welhaven's friends gradually left the student association and formed their own organization, with a paper, *Vidar*, in whose pages Welhaven continued his attacks on Wergeland and the "Patriots." In Old Norse mythology Vidar is the young god who kills the Midgard Serpent, and, from J. L. Heiberg, Welhaven had borrowed the concept of the literary critic as a knight at arms, fighting literary dilettantism in particular and provincialism in general. His cycle of sonnets, *Norges dæmring* (1834; Norway's Dawn), which attacked the cultural self-sufficiency of the young nation, was much criticized for its unconstructive tone and further isolated Welhaven from his people. In the summer of 1836 he visited France, where he was impressed by the architecture and art of Paris. A certain appreciation of new ideas in international art and politics appears to have been no more than a passing mood, however: Welhaven's sense of the contemporary was tied completely to his local fight for aesthetic principles, and once the anti-Wergeland movement had died down by the late 1830s, Welhaven's creative writings became more and more the product of an essentially elegiac and backward-looking temperament. His first collection of poetry, *Digte* 1839 (Poems), does contain memories of his fight with Wergeland, poorly disguised as poems from biblical and classical mythology ("Goliath," "Sisyphos"), but more central is his tasteful and metrically pleasing nature poetry ("Bergens stift" [The Bergen See], "Byens kirkegaard" [The City Cemetery]). The collection also contained a group of poems from his visit to France, including the oft-quoted "Republikanerne"

(The Republicans), which, with its ironic treatment of young revolutionaries, shows Welhaven's general conservatism.

In the midst of Welhaven's battle with Henrik Wergeland, a strange and gradually tempestuous romance developed between Camilla Wergeland, who had always admired her brother's adversary, and Welhaven, who was both attracted to and afraid of Henrik's sister. Some of the poems in the 1839 collection contain veiled references to Camilla or discussions of opinions that she shared with her lover, particularly her contempt for the male ideal of a physically and socially desirable, but essentially soulless, bride. Some of these narrative poems—"Den første kærlighed" (The First Love), "Efter soiréen" (After the Soirée)—contain Welhaven's most radical thinking, but the ideas were first fully realized by Camilla Wergeland Collett in her novel *Amtmandens døttre*. Welhaven's relationship to Camilla Collett came to an end in the late 1830s, when he was engaged to Ida Kjerulf—secretly, since her family was against her marriage to a person without a permanent position. Ida contracted tuberculosis and died in 1840, one month after Welhaven received a temporary lectureship in philosophy at the university. He was tenured in 1843 and married one Josephine Bidoulac, though with the understanding that Ida would continue to be his only true love. This sentiment colors several of the poems in his collection *Nyere digte* (1845; Recent Poems), such as "Det omvendte bæger" (The Upturned Beaker), about a knight who rejects the potion of forgetfulness offered him by the elves, because he wishes to "preserve his sorrow." The collection also contains an apologia for his own sarcastic temperament ("Det tornede træ" [The Thorny Tree]), a philosophic poem on the nature of poetry ("Digtets aand" [The Spirit of the Poem]), and a colorful national ballad, "Aasgaardsrejen" (The Riders in the Sky), of which Welhaven was especially proud. His next collection, *Halvthundrede digte* (Fifty Poems) from 1848, contains further examples of his national ballads and lyric nature poetry, as well as his poem about Ida Kjerulf called "Den salige" (The Blessed One), Norwegian literature's most beautiful in memoriam. As a poet Welhaven was unable to renew himself. He published two more collections of poetry (1851, 1860), less important than his work from the 1840s, though with a fine song of resignation ("En sangers bøn" [A Minstrel's Prayer]) and melancholy nature poems of great beauty (such as "Lokkende toner" [Alluring Melodies]).

Welhaven was remembered by his contemporaries as a literary critic of note and a gifted writer of nature poetry. It is in this latter capacity that he has gained a name for himself in the consciousness of later generations. In that outburst of creative energy referred to as the National Breakthrough, which culminated in the 1840s but had a long-lasting effect among people of conservative taste, Welhaven was the preeminent poet, as Halfdan Kjerulf was the composer and Hans Gude and Adolf Tidemand the painters. His poetry, in musical settings by Kjerulf, has been preserved in the repertoire of the Oslo Student Chorus (founded by Kjerulf) and received added significance as the verbal expression of Norway's romantic landscape painting. Welhaven's personal longing for harmony gradually took on a religious note, which may even color the wistful refrain of "Lokkende toner": "Tirilill tove / langt, langt bort i skove" (Til-til torest, far away in the forest). To most readers today, however, this poetic birdcall—Norwegian literature's "blaue Blume"—simply symbolizes the general longing of Norwegian city dwellers, whose nature-loving hearts Welhaven touched like no other poet.

HENRIK ARNOLD WERGELAND

Nicolai Wergeland, the father of Henrik Wergeland (1808–45), grew up in Bergen, where he was first apprenticed to a goldsmith but later, with the help of friends, sent to grammar school. After studying theology in Copenhagen, he was appointed lecturer at the cathedral school in Kristiansand, where he met and married Alette Thaulow, of a respected and artistically gifted family. Nicolai Wergeland, though a fine teacher and a learned man, could be as arrogant and pedantic as his wife was charming and generous, but in the upbringing of his children he was unusually understanding and forgiving. Inspired by Rousseau's *Emile,* he devised for his oldest child, Henrik, a private "Henrikopaedia," forty-three rules of benevolent pedagogy, and outside the home "classroom," where he was the strict schoolmaster, he gave his sons and daughters free rein. His book *Mnemosyne* (1811), which proposed a separate university for Norway, was well accepted by patriotic Norwegians but less so by Danes, who felt that his remarks on Denmark's exploitation of Norway during the union period were tactless and unjustified. Wergeland, however, continued his anti-Danish line both as a member of the constitutional assembly at Eidsvoll in 1814 and more particularly in a book about Denmark's "political crimes" against the kingdom of Norway (1816), a hateful and poorly researched attack that was much criticized and contributed to making the family's last years in Kristiansand difficult. Even so, after leaving Kristiansand in 1817 for a position as minister to Eidsvoll, Nicolai Wergeland looked back on the Kristiansand years as the happiest in his life. Henrik, who was nine years old when they moved, always carried with him a touch of the Kristiansand dialect, though he later considered scenic and historic Eidsvoll to have been his true home.

During the 1820s Henrik Wergeland attended Oslo Cathedral School and Oslo University, where he received a divinity degree in 1829. His tolerant views on the subject of hell destroyed his chances of top grades in theology, but otherwise he did well at school, though it is generally agreed that his student life was wilder than most. His first story had appeared in print when he was thirteen, and his first play when he was nineteen, a farce published under the pseudonym Siful Sifadda, "half brother of my better self," a name Wergeland later attached to most of his lighter work. At the same time, and under the influence of a series of love affairs in which the beloved assumed the role of a lodestar—his "Stella"—he rejected his sinful desires and devised his own Platonic philosophy. According to it, humans' earthbound and spiritual instincts are driven forward and upward by mutual longing, whereby they slowly develop into more perfect forms. The ideas are present in *Digte. Første ring* (1829; Poems: First Cycle), Wergeland's first and remarkable collection of poetry, and are further developed in the gigantic cosmological poem *Skabelsen, mennesket og Messias* (1830; Creation, Man, and Messias), which, one month after its appearance, provoked Welhaven's anonymous attack in the Christiania (Oslo) paper *Morgenbladet*:

How long will you indulge in senseless raving
Or crazy brandishing of Quixote's spear?
. . . .
Your place assured a thousand votes will fix,
The place the Muse reserves for—lunatics.

Welhaven's poem was the introduction to young Norway's first cultural debate, in which the participants were chiefly the two poets, though other critics were also involved. In 1832 Welhaven provided a more complete investigation of Wergeland's poetry (*Henrik Wergelands digtekunst* [Henrik Wergeland's Poetry]), which called forth a defense by Wergeland's father, who emphasized his son's genius as opposed to the poetic craftsmanship of Welhaven, but which also moved Wergeland to write henceforth in a simpler vein.

After his theological exam Wergeland stayed for the most part at home in Eidsvoll, trying there to practice his plans for improving the lot of the lower classes. In 1830 he accompanied his father to Sweden, where he established contact with such Swedish liberals as Gustav Hierta and C. F. Ridderstad. He next visited England and France, and in 1832 he accompanied his English friend Philip Pope on a tour of West Norway, travels that later left their mark on his poetry. Nicolai and Henrik Wergeland both had a good relationship with the king of Sweden and Norway, but in his personal conduct Wergeland was often his own worst enemy. On May 17, 1829, he had been an instigator of Norway's independence festivities, which displeased the king, who wished to see them replaced by a celebration of his own November 4 constitution. Wergeland had also been involved in some court cases, and in 1833 he had published two books of poetry (*Spaniolen* [The Spaniard] and *Caesaris*) in which he attacked the political tyranny of Ferdinand VII of Spain and Nicholas I of Russia, whose friendship was important to Sweden. Though he had passed his theological practicum with good grades, Wergeland realized that, with his past record of rebellion, he could not expect to receive a living, and in 1834 he therefore began studying medicine, which he gave up after two years in order to accept a temporary appointment as university librarian. In 1838 one of his plays, *Campbellerne* (The Campbells), received a prize and was performed at the Christiania theater. "My proudest moment" is Wergeland's description of a "theater battle" in which the spectators and the police combined forces to throw out booers from Welhaven's Intelligence party. The incident marks the end of the Welhaven/Wergeland "cultural" debate.

With his earnings from the performance of *Campbellerne*, Wergeland was able to buy a home. At this time he also met his future wife, Amalie Bekkevold, and it was his hope that he might obtain a living and settle down to married life. When the king visited Christiania in December 1838, Wergeland wrote his beautiful poem "Kongens ankomst" (The King's Arrival), which was published in *Morgenbladet* and later translated into French for the king to read. Wergeland's father also met with Karl Johan on several occasions and found the king to be well-disposed. In February, however, Wergeland, with some German acquaintances, visited a friend at the Royal Guard. They had a party and were surprised by a former enemy of Wergeland, now head officer of the watch, who had the irregularities reported to the king. Wergeland's friend was sentenced, and Wergeland himself lost his chance to obtain a living. The incident inspired a moving sunset poem to Amalie, "Smukke skyer" (1839; Beautiful Clouds), in which the poet describes how his living was changed to a beautiful red cloud. But Karl Johan generously offered Wergeland a yearly stipend from private funds, money Wergeland accepted on condition that it be regarded as payment for his efforts to improve public education. His paper *For arbeidsklassen* (1840–45; For the Working Class), a nonprofit project, was sent out in several thousand copies and consolidated Wergeland's popularity with the common people.

In November 1840 Wergeland was appointed national archivist, at the same time that his old enemy, Welhaven, received a temporary appointment as lecturer in philosophy. Neither candidate was particularly qualified, and in Wergeland's case, the old accusation that the poet had sold himself to the king was brought up again, this time by Wergeland's former friend L. K. Daa, who attacked him anonymously in the press. Wergeland replied, first in a humorous vein, later with bitter invective, for which he was sued and fined. No incident in Wergeland's life affected him more deeply than his breach with Daa. During the years 1840–41 Wergeland produced much of his finest lyric poetry, including poems written to his wife in gratitude for her support during this difficult period in his life. In the spring of 1840 they moved into a new home, "The Grotto," where Wergeland was able to cultivate his interest in gardening and where, after 1842, he spent some happy years. Wergeland had suggested that the Norwegian Constitution be amended to permit Jews to enter Norway, and on each occasion when the bill was discussed by the Norwegian parliament (in 1842 and again in 1844), he published a collection of poetry: *Jøden* (1842; The Jew) and *Jødinden* (1844; The Jewess). By that time he had already developed the disease that was to end his life within a year, though it was a year full of activity for the poet. His poem *Den engelske lods* (1844; The English Pilot), a melodrama set in a framework of beautiful nature poetry, turned out to be particularly popular. He revised his *Skabelsen* and began writing his memoirs. In April, because of mounting debt, he was forced to sell the Grotto and move to a smaller house. Here he completed his memoirs, called *Hasselnødder* (Hazelnuts), began work on a play against emigration to America (*Fjeldstuen* [The Mountain Cabin]), and wrote some of his best poems. His sickbed, ending with his death on July 12, 1845, was remarkable also in other ways: many of his estranged friends came back to visit him, and the news of his courage and activity even spread abroad, where Mëir Goldschmidt, Danish poet and feared editor of a satirical weekly, described in a newspaper how Wergeland was lying on his deathbed, how he knew his situation yet wrote poems about his own death, without whimpering, without sentimentality, singing triumphal songs and looking smiling into the face of death. And he added, in a personal letter to Wergeland (July 7, 1845), "Thinking of you thus makes me proud to be a human being."

While Welhaven's writings are contained in four octavo-sized books, Wergeland's collected works fill twenty-five large volumes. What is still being read, however, does not include his *Norges konstitutions historie* (1841–43, Eng. tr. History of the Constitution), though it is valuable for its interviews with members of the constitutional assembly, nor his dramatic production, most of it marred by hyperbole and poor psychology. It also does not include much of his prose, except for his lively autobiography *Hasselnødder,* and even much of his poetry, some of which, such as the gigantic *Skabelsen, mennesket og messias,* can be enjoyed only in parts. What remains, then, are single poems of extraordinary feeling and beauty, enough to make Wergeland, in the curious wording of his Danish biographer Aage Kabell, "Norway's, or Scandinavia's, greatest poet" (*Wergeland* [Oslo, 1956], 1:9).

Wergeland was a theologian and the son of a theologian, and in his work religion has a central place. He showed little understanding of the fundamentalism (Haugeanism) that was then gaining ground in Norwegian society, and the deism of the eighteenth century did not satisfy him. Nevertheless, he admired the religious tolerance and progressive spirit of the Enlightenment, as can be seen in his poem "Eivindvig" (1833), in which he celebrates the good works of the rationalist minister Nils Dahl in his parish of Eivindvig. Wergeland's religion is evolutionary and pantheistic, men are "germs in the slime left by spirits," and "Higher and higher, through spirals, / Rises the army of spirits / Up to God" ("Napoleon" [1829; Eng. tr. 1960]). He saw God's presence in animals ("Min lille kanin" [1829; Eng. tr. "My Little Rabbit," 1960]) and flowers, as in this stanza from "Med en Buket" (1838; Eng. tr. "With a Bouquet," 1960):

He has no soul, who does not count
Nature an open book, nor knowst
That the gray lichen on the mount
Can speak a language, like the rose.

Many of his nature poems also describe a mystical transition between biological forms. In what is perhaps his finest single collection of poems, *Jan van Huysums blomsterstykke* (1840; Eng. tr. *Jan van Huysum's Flower Piece,* 1960), a Dutch family, massacred by Spanish soldiers, is reincarnated as flowers, first in nature and later on the canvas of the great Dutch master. A similar mystical experience of God and nature, but more charmingly fairytale-like, is found in Wergeland's last poem, "Den smukke familie" (1845; Eng. tr. "The Beautiful Family," 1960), in which the buds of the poet's potted rose tree are revealed as servants of his dead mother, who has sent them to prepare the clothing in which his soul shall pass away.

Wergeland was a person of great enthusiasm and warm human relationships, and his poems to women, admired men, and children are among his most memorable. His love poems range from the ethereal odes to Stella to the more earthly *Digte* from 1838, most of them addressed to his future wife, Amalie Bekkevold, with titles such as "Den første omfavnelse" (Eng. tr. "The First Embrace," 1960) and "Den elsktes slummer" (Eng. tr. "The

Loved One's Slumber," 1960). His poems of praise are remarkable for the immediacy and intensity of the emotions expressed, as in his poems to various Norwegian nationalists or to their sometime enemy, King Karl Johan. His songs for children, many of them written for his paper *For arbeidsklassen,* are patriotic, moralistic, and humorous and have remained popular to the present day. Wergeland's poems to the children of nature—trees, insects, animals—are more serious, often being disguises for statements about the persecuted artist, as in the case of the stately "Til en gran" (1833; Eng. tr. "To a Pine Tree," 1960) or the charming "Den første sommerfugl" (1837; Eng. tr. "The First Butterfly," 1960), in which Wergeland feels that "like Saint Stephen, all alone, must thou stand and face the stone." Wergeland's poems about himself in 1844–45—his sickness ("Paa sygelejet" [Eng. tr. "On the Sickbed," 1960]), his having to sell the Grotto ("Auction over Grotten" [Eng. tr. "The Grotto at Auction," 1960]), his waking nights at the hospital ("Paa hospitalet, om natten" [Eng. tr. "By Night in the Hospital," 1960] and "Anden nat paa hospitalet" [Eng. tr. "First/Second Night in the Hospital," 1960]), his final desperate plea to be spared an early death, and his resignation ("Til foraaret" [Eng. tr. "To Spring"] and "Til min gyldenlak" [Eng. tr. "To My Wallflower," 1960])—were published in the daily press and contributed to making his courageous stand known at home and abroad. The poem that best describes Wergeland's temperament, however, is "Mig selv" (Eng. tr. "Myself," 1960) from 1841, showing his sentimentality ("Into my dog's eyes I lower my sorrows as in a deep well"), his irascibility ("I love not blue sky everlasting, as I do hate stupid staring eyes"), and his resilience ("Like the insect's sting in the mussel, insults breed pearls only in my heart").

Henrik Wergeland was above all a poet concerned with the political, social, and environmental problems of his day. Unlike most of his colleagues from the romantic era, he did not consider the past to be a primary inspiration for poets. His poem "Til en ung digter" (Eng. tr. "To a Young Poet," 1960) from 1833 begins with the following exhortation:

Bard! Look thou not behind thee,
Not toward the rune-covered stones,
Not toward the grave-mound, barbaric days hiding!
Those shields, let them lie! Let them molder those bones!

From the same year are his two collections *Caesaris* and *Spaniolen* about political freedom for the people of Poland and Spain. In 1843, when his famous violinist friend left for the United States, Wergeland wrote the poem "Norge til Amerika ved Ole Bulls didrejse" (Norway to America, on the Occasion of Ole Bull's Journey Thither), in three of whose five stanzas he speaks of Carolina's blacks, whose chains of slavery Ole Bull should try to break with his magic bow. Though Wergeland's efforts to help the Jews in Norway did not immediately result in a repeal of the "Jew Paragraph" in the constitution, the poet continued to the end to fight with words. These words he called in an 1842 poem his "Army of Truth," in which his concession, "Oh how frail your power seemeth, / To be fighting / For the truth mankind is slighting," is followed by his battle cry, "Forward, then, with fearless faces, / Truth's firm line!"

Nothing is more typical of the autobiographical Wergeland poem than its changing mood, from pride and despair to trust and humility. One of his greatest single poems, "Følg kaldet!" (Eng. tr. "Follow the Call!" 1960) from *Jødinden* 1844), deplores

All the wretched poet's woe,
Of a little nation born,
In a spot remote, forlorn,
With a speech
Which can never further reach
Than the uttered breath may go.

It then describes the earth in striking pictures, its pristine past and its future of endless possibilities, concluding,

There is nothing, great or small,
Nothing fruitless, no decay,
There is purpose in its fall,
Howso vaguely cast away.

This happy evolutionary tale is framed by a discussion of the poet's mission in the world. Wergeland finds that, like the shaman surrounded by a few Lapps, "He will crave no longer now / Thronging millions ranged below, / Just a little band of friends."

William Wordsworth's statement in the preface to *Lyrical Ballads* (1800) that "poetry takes its origin from emotion recollected in tranquillity" fits Welhaven's poems, but not Wergeland's, which so often bear the stamp of immediacy, though later revisions show how the poet tried to avoid crudities and repetitions. Wergeland's imagery is always striking and far-ranging, as are his themes. Generally, his prosody seems less interesting than that of Welhaven with its many different stanzaic forms. Of Wergeland's early poems (*Digte. Første ring*, 1829)—many of them celebrating Stella, his version of the eternal feminine—most are unrhymed or else unstrophic, often with refrains and dialogue and suggesting a connection with the emotional poetry of the preromantic era, such as that of Johannes Ewald. Later collections show his attempt—possibly under the influence of Welhaven—to observe the accepted conventions of his day, and there are poems of great formal beauty, such as "Anden nat paa hospitalet," in which the so-called Heine stanza (four lines of three iambs/anapests) is used with great sophistication. Generally, however, Wergeland continued to favor unrhymed and unstanzaic verse, which makes him a precursor of modern poetry, somewhat in the style of Walt Whitman, whose "Song of Myself" resembles Wergeland's similarly named poem in form as well as content. It is interesting to note that also in this respect, Wergeland, with his strong roots in the progressive spirit of the eighteenth century, heralds ideas of the twentieth century.

THE NATIONAL BREAKTHROUGH

Wergeland, we must assume, would have supported the revolutions of 1848 —the rise of liberal forces in Paris, Vienna, Berlin, and Rome—and the first Norwegian Labor Association, established by Marcus Thrane as a result of these international events. The mood in Norway during the 1840s and 1850s, however, turned national rather than international. Young Norwegian painters, frightened by the unrest in Germany, left the art school in Düsseldorf and came home, where they began exploring the imposing scenery of interior Norway. In Christiania they formed their own artists' association, where poets and musicians were also active and where, on March 28–30, 1849, they put on an entertainment program that has since come to be viewed as the epitome of a movement known in Norwegian intellectual history as national romanticism. The central event was a piece of gesamtkunst called "Brudefærden i Hardanger" (The Bridal Procession in Hardanger). It consisted of a large painting by Hans Gude (the fjord landscape) and Adolf Tidemand (the rowing boats with colorful passengers) and a corresponding poem by Andreas Munch, set to music by Halfdan Kjerulf and sung by the Oslo Student Chorus. The audience was made up of intellectual city dwellers whose eyes had been opened to the natural and cultural beauties of the countryside—its scenery, folk literature, folk music, folk art, folk language. Though they were nationalists of a kind very different from Wergeland's revolutionary freedom fighters, these conservative civil servants nevertheless staged an intellectual revolution of lasting importance for the development of Norwegian culture.

The first painters to discover the Norwegian mountain landscape were probably Johan Flintoe and Peder Balke, as well as the more famous Johan

Christian Dahl (1788–1857), who also appreciated the value of the rustic arts and architecture of Norway. Though he spent most of his life as a professor (and colleague of Caspar David Friedrich) at the academy in Dresden, Dahl undertook several tours of Norway, from which he brought back some two hundred sketches of Norwegian mountain scenery. Dahl's landscapes were a great inspirational force for Norwegian painters and poets alike. His success in organizing a Norwegian Society for the Preservation of Ancient Monuments (1844) led to many similar efforts and helped rescue the medieval Norwegian stave churches from senseless destruction. Tidemand, though from a different (Düsseldorf) school of painting, visited Dahl in Dresden two years earlier (1842) and was greatly inspired by the older painter's patriotism and enthusiasm. In turn, his own national romantic genre paintings were a major inspiration for Bjørnson's "rustic tales."

With the exception of Welhaven, the poets of the national romantic movement did not produce much memorable verse. Andreas Munch (1811–84), formerly a respected writer of elegiac and religious poetry, is now remembered mainly as the author of the text in Kjerulf's song "Brudefærden i Hardanger." Jørgen Moe (1813–82) was the quintessential national romantic poet, with poems based on pictures by Gude and Tidemand or, as in the case of the famous "Fanitullen" (1849; The Devil's Reel), on folk music and local legend. Moe is the preeminent landscape poet of eastern Norway and the author of attractive prose and poetry for children, particularly his *I brønden og i kjærnet* (1851; In the Well and in the Pond), later included in elementary school readers. He is better known, however, as the collector, with Peter Christen Asbjørnsen (1812–85), of the folktales of Norway. Asbjørnsen and Moe first met when they were preparing for the university entrance examination in the late 1820s. They were interested in tales, found Andreas Faye's Norwegian collection from 1833 unsatisfactory, and decided to make their own. They followed the example of the brothers Grimm, except in language, which they wanted to bring closer to the original folk tradition. Of the two, Asbjørnsen had the greater sense of rough realism; Moe, the more refined style and theoretical background. The first issue of the tales (Norske folkeeventyr [Norwegian Folktales] appeared in December 1841 and was followed by three more in the years 1842–44. A second edition appeared in 1851 with a scholarly introduction by Moe. Asbjørnsen in the meantime (1845–48) had published two volumes of Norwegian legends (*Norske huldreeventyr og folkesagn* [Norwegian Folk Legends]), which show him as the first true recorder of Norwegian folk language and folk life. He was an eager outdoorsman, and his legends often appear within a frame story describing a fishing or hunting tour, as in his

"Kvernsagn" (Eng. tr. "Legends of the Mill," 1859): "When the world goes against me, and it is very seldom it forgets to do so whenever there is an opportunity, I have always felt a relief in taking walks in the open air as an alleviation of my portion of troubles and anxieties." These opening lines are followed by the account of his meeting with storytelling woodsmen.

Particularly important for the development of nineteenth-century Norwegian prose was Asbjørnsen and Moe's decision to try to preserve the storyteller's own idiom with its native words and simplified sentence structure. Camilla and Jonas Collett criticized the "rough" language used in the tales and, after befriending the two collectors, helped compose some of the descriptive introductions to Asbjørnsen's legends. On the whole, however, Asbjørnsen and Moe remained true to their original intent of keeping the language close to everyday speech. Another friend, Bernhard Herre (1812–49), also contributed some tales and wrote *En jægers erindringer* (1849; A Sportsman's Memoirs), remarkable for both its poetic rendering of landscape moods and its modern language, and an early precursor of Knut Hamsun's more famous novel *Pan* (1894).

Moe later devoted himself to his duties in the Norwegian state church as minister and bishop, and Asbjørnsen to his career in forestry and zoology, though he continued his folkloristic studies by expanding and revising the old collections. Asbjørnsen was also interested in art. He had joined the Christiania Art Association during its brief existence in 1848–50, where he met and befriended Gude and Tidemand. More than thirty years later, however, when the time came to find illustrators for the tales, Asbjørnsen wisely chose such younger artists as Erik Werenskiold and Theodore Kittelsen. Asbjørnsen and Moe's folktales were the single most important product of Norwegian national romanticism, and the illustrated edition (now numbering 150 tales, including Asbjørnsen's legends) has remained a classic since its first appearance in 1879. George Webbe Dasent, the first English translator of the tales (1859), wrote: "The language and tone are perhaps rather lower than in some other collections, but it must be remembered that these are the tales of 'hempen homespuns,' of Norse yeomen, of *Norske Bønder,* who call a spade a spade, and who burn tallow, not wax; and yet in no collection of tales is the general tone so chaste, are the great principles of morality better worked out, and right and wrong kept so steadily in sight."

These farmers were also presented in a popular student comedy *Til sæters* (1850; Meeting at the Mountain Pasture) by Claus Pavels Riis (1826–86) and, more seriously, in a rustic tale, *En fjeldbygd* (1851; A Mountain Village), by Nikolai Ramm Østgaard (1812–73), whose sense of realism and genuine country language stand out among prose writers of the National Breakthrough.

To explain the sudden burst of creativity in nineteenth-century Norway, it has been common to point to some extraordinary national enthusiasm as the driving force. To Wergeland's pride in the 17th of May Constitution was added a corresponding pride in Norway's distant past, created in part through the publication in 1851–63 of Peter A. Munch's six-volume *Det norske folks historie* (History of the Norwegian People). Like most men of Norway's national romanticism, Peter Andreas Munch (1810–63) belonged to the circle around Welhaven. He was personally pro-Danish, though not like Welhaven a Scandinavianist. Rather, he wished to give to Norway a history as glorious as that of Denmark and Sweden; indeed, he set out to show how the people of Sweden and Denmark had originally come from northern Norway! With his great learning and his use of new source materials, Munch impressed and inspired contemporary historians. He was also a brilliant philologist, responsible for the publication during the years 1845–50 of many medieval codices, including *Den eldre Edda* (Eng. tr. *The Poetic Edda*, 1926), *Speculum Regale* (Eng. tr. *The King's Mirror*, 1917), and *Norges gamle love* 1–3 (The Old Laws of Norway). More popular, and important for the strengthening of a national romantic sentiment in Norway, were his *Nordens gamle gude- og heltesagn* (1840; 10th ed., 1971; Eng. tr. *Norse Mythology*, 1926) and especially his translation of Snorri Sturluson's *Norges kongesagaer,* also known as *Heimskringla* (1859; Eng. tr. 1894 and others). Munch, who had praised the language of Asbjørnsen and Moe's folktales, tried in his translation of Snorri to bring the narration closer to Norwegian parlance by using special words not found in Danish. In later translations, and with illustrations furnished by Werenskiold and others, the *Heimskringla* has gradually become a people's classic, much like the folktales. And, again like the folktales, it was a powerful influence on the new generation of Norwegian writers, for example, on Bjørnson in his rustic tales and on Ibsen in his historical dramas.

In the cities Norwegian folk music was looked down on as primitive and ugly and was first appreciated only by professional musicians. The greatest fiddler in the folk music tradition, Torgeir Augundsson, was discovered by Ole Bull as early as 1831, and in January 1849 the two artists gave a concert in Christiania which inspired Welhaven's poem about the artist from the "snow-covered mountains, where our art, in tones as well as speech, can forever find refreshing inspiration." Though most members of the audience were less impressed than Welhaven, folk music was slowly accepted. In 1852–53 the minister and hymn writer Magnus Brostrup Landstad (1803–89) published the first major collection of Norwegian medieval folk ballads, for which the organist Ludvig Lindeman (1812–87) provided 114 melodies. Lindeman had made his first transcriptions in 1840, and during the next forty years he collected some fifteen hundred folk tunes, many of them used (and harmonically improved) by Edvard Grieg, from his *Norske folkeviser og danse* (1869; Twenty-five Norwegian Folk Songs and Dances) to his last composition, *Fire Salmer* (Four Psalms) from 1906. Where the Norwegian folk tunes had texts, they were printed either in Danish (old hymns) or in Norwegian dialect, and the dialect texts were important for the development of Norway's second language, nynorsk. Typically, Grieg, with his deep understanding of folk music, was the first Norwegian composer to use nynorsk extensively in art songs.

AASEN AND VINJE AND THE DEVELOPMENT OF NYNORSK

Wergeland had prophesied that Norway would have its own Norwegian language by the end of the nineteenth century. The method was one of gradually mixing more and more specifically Norwegian words into the generally accepted Danish standard until the resulting Dano-Norwegian was finally "purely" Norwegian. Wergeland's line was taken up by the language reformer Knud Knudsen (1812–95), many of whose suggested spelling and lexical changes have since been incorporated into the Dano-Norwegian now known as *bokmål* (formerly *riksmål*), the larger of Norway's two official languages. P. A. Munch, a staunch defender of the accepted Danish standard, attacked both Wergeland and (twenty years later) Knudsen, claiming that their "language reforms" would result in nothing more than a superficially Norwegianized Danish. According to Munch, a truly Norwegian standard could be created only by "bringing one of our purest dialects into a proper form and using Old Norse as a guide" ("Om norsk sprogreformation" [1832; On Norwegian Language Reformation], article in the student paper *Vidar*). Few had expected that this idea would actually be carried out, as it was, twenty years later, by a self-taught linguist and poet, Ivar Aasen (1813–96).

Having collected dialect material on his travels around the Norwegian countryside, Ivar Aasen in 1848 published a grammar of "the Norwegian Folk Language" and two years later a dictionary of the same language. In his very positive reviews of Aasen's works, P. A. Munch expressed his wish to see the new language in actual usage and was not disappointed: in 1853 Aasen published *Prøver af landsmaalet i Norge* (Samples of the Norwegian Country Language), in which he showed how his standard could be used in a variety of situations, from everyday dialogue to poetry (he included his own translations of passages from Shakespeare, Schiller, Esaias Tegnér, and others). Though Aasen remained personally a modest man throughout his life, a sign of a certain confidence in the future of nynorsk (formerly *landsmål*) is his use of the word "Norwegian" rather than "Norwegian Folk Language" when his grammar and dictionary appeared in their second editions: *Norsk grammatik* (1864) and *Norsk ordbog* (1873). By that time Aasen had also gained a certain reputation as a dramatist and poet through his musical one-act play *Ervingen* (1855; The Heir) and his collection of poetry called *Symra* (1863; Anemone). *Ervingen,* often seen on the Norwegian amateur stages of the past, is not a great play, though it is interesting for its timely theme: an emigrant returns from America to claim his allodial rights in Norway. The songs in the play have become particularly popular: Aasen is a better poet than dramatist, as is also seen in *Symra,* a collection of songs that are, in Aasen's own words, "cheering rather than scoffing / songs that suit our way of life and show our way of thinking." The songs are national, elegiac, moralistic, and suggest a connection with the classical tradition of Claus Frimann. Aasen is more varied in his prosody, however, with meters ranging from Old Norse verse forms ("Gamle Norig" [Old Norway] and "Haraldshaugen" [Harald's Mound]) to ottava rima ("Sumarkvelden" [Summer Evening]). Above all, the poems are simple and singable, several of which (for instance "Millom bakkar og berg utmed havet" [Eng. tr. "'Mong the Rocks of the North Sea's Blue Water"]) are among the most popular songs of Norway, appreciated even by those who otherwise look down on nynorsk.

Aasmund Vinje (1818–70), another pioneer in the history of nynorsk, was a more remarkable poet than Aasen and also a gifted journalist and interesting as a transitional figure between romanticism and early realism. The son of a tenant farmer, Vinje had the same humble background as Aasen, though he was more ambitious, attaining a law degree at the advanced age of thirty-eight. He was a man of shifting and often contradictory loyalties, critical of the civil-servant class as well as of farmers, and he antagonized many of his colleagues, such as Ibsen (who wrote in *Kjærlighedens komedie,* "Not everyone who loves to rake the muck, / is therefore Aasmund Vinje's equal"). As a journalist he was the table-talker rather than the debater, offering curious and humorous associations and allusions, which made him popular as a speaker among farmers at cattle shows, though—with the pioneering sociologist Ejlert Sundt (1817–75)—he was critical of the lack of hygiene found in the rural areas of the country. He was a city person also in his enthusiasm for the university and for such technical innovations as the railroad, as well as in his love of nature walks: Vinje was one of Norway's first mountain tourists. Between 1858 and 1870 he owned and edited a weekly journal, *Dølen* (Man from the Valley), a publication somewhat in the style of Addison and Steele's *Spectator*, in which he printed many of his poems and stories. In June 1860 his subscribers had to wait six months for the next issue and received by way of compensation an account of Vinje's journey from Christiania via Sweden and the East Norwegian mountains to Trondheim, where he attended the coronation of King Charles XV. *Ferdaminni fraa sumaren* 1860 (1861; Travel Account from the Summer of 1860) became his most popular work, full of irony and interesting observations and also some poetry, including his most famous poem, "Ved Rondarne" (Eng. tr. "Homecoming at Rondane," 1948 and others). In developing his Dano-Norwegian, Knud Knudsen had tried to replace words of foreign origin with Norwegian expressions. Vinje did the same for nynorsk, often adding the replaced word in parentheses after a suggested neologism. More important was his effort to simplify his syntax, bringing it closer to the short-sentence structure of everyday speech. While his younger colleagues, Bjørnson and Ibsen, visited Germany and Italy, Vinje, like other liberal romantics—Erik Gustav Geijer, N. F. S. Grundtvig, Henrik Wergeland—was drawn to England. But after a visit to that country in 1862–63, Vinje published *A Norseman's View of Britain and the British* (1863; Norw. tr. *Bretland og britarne*, 1873), which is critical of the materialism and class differences found among the English.

In Vinje's poetry a common theme is that of creativity and ennoblement through suffering, as in the poem "Den særde" (Eng. tr. "The Wounded Heart," 1908), which is somewhat reminiscent of Wergeland's poetry of self. An elegiac mood also colors the poem "Vaaren" (Eng. tr. "Springtide," 1908), written in hexameters with end rhyme, internal rhyme, and alliteration, and made popular, like other poems by Vinje, through Grieg's musical setting (See *Fifty Songs for High Voice*, 1908).

One of Vinje's last pieces in *Dølen* was a characterization of the recently deceased economist A. M. Schweigaard, whom Vinje criticizes for his political and cultural conservatism, especially his stand against the farming class and its struggle for a Norwegian Norway. One year earlier (1869) the political party Venstre (Left) had been founded, and fifteen years later (1884) its dynamic leader Johan Sverdrup was able to form Norway's first parliamentarian government. The new party gave Aasen's and Vinje's fledgling nynorsk movement its much-needed political support. After 1885 nynorsk texts were introduced in elementary school readers, and in 1892 municipalities were given the power to choose which of the two norms—

bokmål or nynorsk—would be used in each of the country's school districts. By that time nynorsk was recognized as Norway's second official language, with a weekly newspaper and internationally known writers such as Arne Garborg.

BEGINNINGS OF THE NORWEGIAN NOVEL: HANSEN AND COLLETT

The modern European novel was developed in the hundred years between Holberg's *Niels Klim* (1741) and Asbjørnsen and Moe's *Norske folkeeventyr* (1841). In England, Richardson was active, and Fielding, Goldsmith, Austen, Scott, Dickens; in Germany, Wieland, Goethe, Jean Paul, Tieck, Novalis, Fouqué, E. T. A. Hoffmann, Chamisso; in France, Voltaire, Rousseau, de Stael, Dumas (*père*), Stendhal, Balzac; in America, Cooper. Many of them were read and appreciated in Norway, in addition to such Swedish writers as Carl Jonas Love Almquist and, particularly, Fredrika Bremer, and such Danes as Steen Steensen Blicher, Bernhard Severin Ingemann, Carsten Hauch, Thomasine Gyllembourg, and Hans Christian Andersen. Norway, in contrast—and despite the achievements of Christen Pram in the previous century—lacked a prose tradition of vigor and originality. Women of the upper middle classes would read works in the original and, in the kitchen or the weaving parlor, retell their contents to their servants, who, in turn, delighted the children of the house with their store of folktales and legends. Contemporary diarists, however, complained that there was still no "entertainment literature" available from the hand of Norwegian writers—with the exception of the work of Mauritz Hansen.

Mauritz Hansen

Mauritz Hansen (1794–1842) was related to some of Denmark's most important literary figures, and his family had great hopes for his future as a writer. Unfortunately, during his short life he had to augment his meager income as a teacher by writing for periodical publications, with the result that very little of his extensive literary production is fully developed. In his life, as in his many textbooks for schools, Hansen was a man of liberal outlook. He was an evolutionist before the time of Darwin, he tried to give his daughter a high school education (forty years before the first Norwegian woman passed the university entrance examination), and he worked actively for the language-reform program later adopted by Knud Knudsen. In his novels and short stories, the many foreign quotations (from Latin, Italian, French, English, and German) seem to indicate an educated audience, and yet in most cases the action caters to the melodramatic taste of the lower classes: they are stories of misalliances, adultery, illegitimate children, murder, fortune telling, robbery, women disguised as men, and so on, often in the style of an opera libretto, with involved and incredible plot lines. That is also the case in his best-known novel, *Keadan* (1825), about one Wilhelm Brandt, accused of having murdered his friend and rival suitor. Letters and documents are quoted frequently, and where the narrator is present, he acts as a guide, addressing the reader and explaining his narrative scheme. The fact that Hansen sometimes gets the names of his characters mixed up shows how he was often obliged to work under pressure. He is more successful in the short story, where his in medias res introductions are sometimes brief and effective: "The murder of Hans Kopperud, who during the bridal night was stabbed to death by the bride, was written up in the *Berling Times*; I remember it very well, though I was young at the time" ("Den myrdede brudgom," 1828; The Murdered Bridegroom). In an earlier story, "Luren" (1817; The Alpenhorn), the plot is more typically introduced with a piece of largely unrelated nature description, but the narrative itself touches on a social problem of some importance: a proud farmer's unwillingness to accept his daughter's sweetheart because the young man is a person without property. In the 1850s the theme was taken up by Bjørnson in his rustic tales, which is why "Luren" has sometimes been termed Norway's first example of this popular genre.

Hansen's stories—eight volumes, or more than thirty-five hundred pages—were published in 1855–58 by his friend Conrad Nicolai Schwach but were soon forgotten when Bjørnson's rustic tales began to appear on the Norwegian book market. Hansen himself is remembered mainly for being the only notable name in the generation of writers immediately before Wergeland. In his day, however, he was a person much admired by such later masters of prose as Jørgen Moe and Camilla Collett, even by the young Henrik Ibsen, who used some of Hansen's melodrama in his plays (e.g., the shipwreck scenes in *Keadan* and *Peer Gynt*'s final act). As a problem writer, though, Ibsen is more indebted to Camilla Collett, the true founder of the Norwegian novel.

Camilla Collett

Camilla Collett (1813–95) was Henrik Wergeland's sister and grew up with him and two other brothers and a sister at Eidsvoll, where she enjoyed a fairly unrestricted childhood. During her teens she spent one unhappy year at school in Christiania and two more at the Moravian Institute at Christiansfeld, Germany, from which she returned home in 1829, full of resentment over women's underprivileged position in society, only to see her older sister married off to a person she did not love. Camilla had inherited her father's difficult temperament. She was, like him, a very private person, and her isolation within the family grew when she fell in love with Welhaven, Henrik and Nicolai Wergeland's enemy. Her diaries from the 1830s tell of her sense of hopelessness when Welhaven, though much attracted to her beauty and intelligence, told her they were not suited to each other. Still, like her brother Henrik, she was able to turn her disappointment into art: the diary entries became exercises in literary style and, twenty years later, an important source book for her first and only novel.

In 1841 Camilla married Jonas Collett, another member of the Intelligence party. She told him she still loved Welhaven, but Collett was an understanding and endlessly tolerant husband, a faithful supporter of his wife's literary activities as well as the father of her four children. After her husband's death in 1851, Camilla Collett spent some time in Copenhagen, where 12 *breve* (1851; Twelve Letters) by twenty-one-year-old Mathilde Fibiger had recently given rise to a public discussion of women's emancipation. Camilla Collett was inspired to realize her old dream of publishing a contemporary novel, showing the ill effects of ancient prejudice against women. *Amtmandens døttre* (Eng. tr. *The District Governor's Daughters*, 1992) appeared in two parts in 1854–55. It was followed in 1860 by a collection of short stories and in 1862 by a volume of memoirs, *I de lange nætter* (During the Long Nights), with interesting and moving pictures of Henrik Wergeland and herself as children and adults. Camilla Collett's later production consists almost entirely of polemical writings supporting women's rights—all of them inspired by her indignation and most of them well written. Her *Sidste blade* (Last Papers) appeared in three installments in 1868–73. A book with the striking title *Fra de stummes lejr* (1877; From the Encampment of Mutes) discusses women in literature, while the title of her two last collections, *Mod strømmen* (1879, 1885; Against the Current), refers to a well-known Norwegian fairy tale about an obstreperous wife whose body drifted upstream after she drowned in a river. Though Camilla Collett's feminist essays are still highly readable, she is remembered mainly for *Amtmandens døttre*, Norwegian literature's first novel.

The governor and his wife have four daughters: one is dead after an unhappy marriage, another is unhappily married, a third is in love with a penniless vicar, and the youngest, Sophie, though different from the others— more beautiful, gifted, reflective—falls in love with her tutor, the handsome, serious-looking Kold, who also loves her. Their emotions are secret, however, and only a sudden danger can break the "natural modesty of her gender," so that she confesses her love to an overjoyed Kold. But that same evening, he, in order to hide this joyful experience from an interfering friend, vehemently denies his love. Sophie, listening at the door, overhears the conversation and, believing she has been exposed to typical male exploitation, refuses further contact with Kold. Some time later she is wooed by a prosperous widower of great charm and dignity, to whose little daughter she is particularly attracted, and she finally consents to marry him after the usual pressure from her mother. On the day before the wedding she meets Kold and learns the truth about his love. She feels that she still loves him, yet she decides not to upset her family's plans for her wedding.

Though an improvement on *Keadan*, *Amtmandens døttre* shares many of the formal inadequacies of the earlier novel, such as the use of letters and diary excerpts, improbable action and an intrusive narrator. But it is in many ways a poetic book, with beautiful passages and effective use of symbols and quoted poetry: Collett was a well-read author and there are reminiscences of (and references to) other writers throughout her text. Heinrich Heine's ironic lines from *Buch der Lieder* (1827) "Du hast Diamanten und Perlen / Hast alles was Menschenbegehr / Und hast die schönsten Augen / Mein Liebchen was willst du mehr?" (You have diamonds and pearls / Have everything one could desire / You have the most beautiful eyes / What more could you want?) had been expanded in several poems by Welhaven, in which he attacked the contemporary ideal of the smiling and superficial doll-woman. Collett used ideas from Welhaven's poems in her novel, exchanging his irony for her own open anger and accusation. Her novel is, in Ibsen's words (letter to Ludwig Passarge, June 16, 1880), the story of "something actually lived through," and this sense of realism sets it apart from most early Norwegian fiction. The plot is interesting as both social and literary history: its rendering of local topography, architecture, and garden culture, and its frequent references to the Wergeland/Welhaven controversy. As a psychological novel it contains some well-made portraits: the alcoholic Brandt (modeled on George Frederik von Krogh), the governor and his wife, Kold (with features taken from Welhaven), and Sophie, a tomboy slowly and not without protest learning to accept the resignation of womanhood. Its ending is open, and while a conventional reading sees Sophie's fate as tragic, more recent interpretations have emphasized the challenge of (step)motherhood as a positive solution to Sophie's problem.

Amtmandens døttre is a novel of commitment, fired by the author's continuous indignation over the subjugation of women, whose education aims to polish off every trace of individuality and smother every spark of independence and whose goal in life is to be not happy but married. "Do you know what a Norwegian housewife is?" asks the narrator, and answers: "I don't know a single woman who, through her charm or her intellect, inspires a wide circle of people, and yet I know many who both could and should be such an inspiration."

Camilla Collett differed from her brother Henrik in lacking understanding of the lower classes, their dialect, their rights, and their artistic and intellectual gifts. There was a genteel arrogance about her, which explains why she preferred the company of the Danophiles in the Intelligence party and criticized the rough country language of Asbjørnsen and Moe's folktales. Nevertheless, she shared the strong emotions of her brother: what in him was enthusiasm and optimism, was in her a never-ending indignation; what he did for the oppressed political and social classes, she did for women. Many found her company trying; the English critic Edmund Gosse described her as "singularly unpleasing," and Bjørnson, a possible competitor for the epithet "founder of the Norwegian novel," warned her first biographer: "Beware of Mrs. Collett! Everlastingly dissatisfied and endlessly overvalued" (letter to Clara Bergsøe, June 7, 1896). But *Amtmandens døttre* inspired both Ibsen's *Kjærlighedens komedie* and Jonas Lie's *Familjen paa Gilje*, and Alexander Kielland wrote the author three days after her seventieth birthday: "I don't believe I have ever brought up the problem of women's rights without asking myself: what would Mrs. Collett have said about it? For any writer in our country, taking up the woman issue means running into Camilla Collett, and during his work that writer will straighten his back, like a soldier feeling the general is looking at him."

Norwegian Literature 1860–1910

by James McFarlane

5

A PROFILE OF THE AGE 1860–1910

The Cultural and Intellectual Climate

The half-century leading up to the outbreak of the First World War is a period characterized by unprecedented and—by any standards—extraordinary change in Western society and culture.

In the course of these years the world's economy expanded at a rate never before seen or equaled since. It was an age that witnessed an explosive growth in urban living, in the development of the metropolitan city, and in industrialization. The achievements of science and of scientific method—in electromagnetism, in thermodynamics, in spectroscopy and cosmology and many other fields of inquiry—not only yielded startlingly new insights into the nature of the physical universe but also made impressive contributions to the material well-being of the individual and of society. Communications were changed out of all recognition by the spread of the railways and the development of the internal combustion engine. New sources of power, such as electricity and oil, were exploited. The chemical industry launched new synthetic materials.

Perhaps even more significant than these material and outwardly visible changes were the shifts of perception and sensibility which accompanied these more overt manifestations of change: the radical revaluation of all values (to use Nietzsche's phrase); the transformation of patterns of faith, belief, and understanding; the new insights into the nature both of the physical universe and of the ways of the conscious and unconscious mind.

Institutions that at one time must have seemed unassailable were subjected in these years to a rigorous and critical scrutiny that questioned their essential validity; truths that down the ages had been accepted as absolutes were assigned to a new relativism; established moral codes and standards were, under challenge, found to be less than wholly immutable; many of the accepted certainties of conventional thinking were invaded by doubt and skepticism; much of what, to earlier generations, had seemed solid, four-square, and fixed began to look disturbingly fluid and unpredictable.

In matters of art and literature, it is widely held that the changes effected in this age were of a kind and a magnitude different from any of the earlier divisions in Western history; scholars speak of a "great divide," a "chasm" greater than that which divided antiquity from the Dark Ages, or the Dark Ages from the Middle Ages. Compared to this division, it has been argued, all earlier historical movements or epochs in the history of Western litera-ture—the medieval, for example, or the baroque, or neoclassicism or ro-manticism—are merely subclassifications. The totality of change wrought in these few crucial decades is, it is claimed, of such profundity and immen-sity that even today it is still difficult for us to comprehend.

In addition to sharing in this global process of civilizational change, Scandinavia—and within it Norway—underwent related changes deriving more directly from the native social, economic, and cultural conditions per-taining at the time. Geographically remote regions and isolated commu-nities were made more easily accessible by the improvement in communica-tions, and with this access came a disproportionately severe impact on local conditions and lifestyle. The domestic economy of the *bygd*—the parish or village or rural community that had traditionally served as the natural social or administrative unit—was exposed to increasing influence from outside. The spread of industry gave a strong impetus to the development of towns and helped to stimulate the emergence of a new, urban-based working class. Social conflict became variously and progressively polarized: the peasant (*bonde*) versus the professional (*embetsmann*), the rural versus the urban, the liberal-minded versus the conservative-minded, the political left versus the political right. This last confrontation culminated in Norway in the crisis of 1884 with the formation of the country's first left-wing government.

Turning to the literature of the period, we see that Scandinavia played a remarkable role. From the status of a minor literary force at mid-nineteenth century, little known and perhaps even less regarded on the international scene, it emerged from virtual obscurity to become within a few brief de-cades one of the leaders of the literary world. For Scandinavia, it was an age of extraordinary creativity in the field of literature; and its major figures—Kierkegaard, Ibsen, and Strindberg conspicuous among them—were in the very vanguard of change and justifiably took their rank among the most in-fluential writers of the age in the Western world.

When it comes to Norwegian literature, the shape of the period (defined rather arbitrarily at the head of this chapter as 1860 to 1910) was rough-hewn by two separate and symbolic acts of repudiation separated from each other by a quarter of a century: the first by Henrik Ibsen in the mid-1860s, the second by Knut Hamsun in the early 1890s. Each highlights a crucial moment of transition from one literary credo to another; each inaugurates a period of literary endeavor within a particular style or idiom or system of values which proved to be both innovative and remarkably productive. With their aid we can view more clearly the essential structural pattern of the age.

The Repudiation of National Romanticism

In its origins, Ibsen's *Brand* (1866; Eng. tr. 1891 and others) was above all an act of repudiation and disavowal, a breakaway from what the author had come to see as a whole world of false values and spurious ideals. In the opening stanzas of the earliest version of this work—the so-called Epic Brand— Ibsen exhorted his countrymen (his "fellows in guilt," as he called them) to break free from their current obsessions with the past. The past, he insisted, was dead; the ancient grandeur of the heroic age was but a rouged and embalmed corpse, pestilential; there could be no resuscitation; decay and disintegration had to fulfill their natural life-sustaining role:

> What is dead no lie will bring to life.
> What is dead must go down into the dark.
> Dead things have only one purpose: that
> of yielding nourishment for the new-sown seed.

He declared his intention of turning away from the deceitful sentimentalities of his own earlier work, away from ineffectual dreams of the future based on this "lying pretense" in order to face instead the realities of the present-day world:

> See, this is why I have turned my sight and mind
> away from the soul-dead tales of our past,
> away from our lying dreams of a bright future,
> and go into the misty world of the present.

With this forthright repudiation of the values of national romanticism came also a radical revision on Ibsen's part of the role of the poet in society. No longer did he see his task as that of some latter-day skald, extolling past heroism, idealizing events, building public morale, and nourishing national pride; rather, he was the solitary detached observer, the dispassionate recorder, setting out the truth with honesty and courage, however unpalatable that truth might be.

The decision was, of course, not taken in an intellectual vacuum; many of the anti-idealistic, anti-metaphysical, and anti-theological doctrines that came to prominence in these years obviously contributed to the cultural climate that prompted it. In Norway's case, three bodies of belief from wider Europe may be readily identified: positivism, associated with the name of Auguste Comte (1798–1857) and defined by him in his *Catéchisme positiviste* (1852; Eng. tr. *The Catechism of Positive Religion*, 1855), a doctrine that advocated the application of the scientific method of "positive spirit" to all aspects of human activity, claiming that all true knowledge derived from the examination, description, and classification of observable phenomena; utilitarianism, particularly as interpreted by John Stuart Mill in *On Liberty* (1859), *Utilitarianism* (1863), and—somewhat later but most influentially—*The Subjection of Women* (1869); and the theory of evolution as expounded by Charles Darwin in *On the Origin of Species* (1859) and *The Descent of Man* (1871).

This declaration on Ibsen's part cannot really be thought of as a manifesto, for the text of the "Epic Brand" was not discovered and made public until the turn of the century. But it can nevertheless be seen as heralding a period of some twenty-five years in which Norwegian literature came to speak with a distinctive voice: to concern itself with life as lived in the present day instead of with the heroic past; to address itself to contemporary "problems" rather than sentimentalized edification; to see things "realistically" or "naturalistically," attaching first priority to the recording of perceived "truth" rather than the pursuit of idealized "beauty"; to reflect the immediacy of experience through the practice of precise and detailed observation; to speak out boldly, with honesty and courage, even though this might shock or offend; and to increase public awareness of the pressure of deterministic forces—social, economic, environmental, political—on the life of the individual.

The emergent trend toward a realistic, problem-oriented literature in Scandinavia was, in circumstances of quite spectacular publicity, given both direction and definition by Georg Brandes in Denmark in 1871. In a series of widely reported public lectures begun that year in Copenhagen—lectures that were eventually combined with others and published under the title of *Hovedstrømninger i det nittende Aarhundredes Litteratur* (1872–90; Eng. tr. *Main Currents in Nineteenth-Century Literature,* 1901 and others)— Brandes laid down what he held to be the crucial test for contemporary literature: "What shows a literature to be living in our day is the fact of its subjecting problems to debate." It was also Brandes who came to provide the distinctive term for this particular literary phenomenon in Scandinavia: the Modern Breakthrough.

The Repudiation of Realism and Naturalism

Inevitably, in the fullness of time the orthodoxy of "problem literature" and the dominance of the realistic or naturalistc mode themselves came under attack. As though in substantiation of what Ibsen's Dr. Stockmann had said in 1881—that "the life of a normally constituted truth is generally, say, about seventeen or eighteen years, at most twenty"—this challenge came at the beginning of the nineties. It was mounted by Knut Hamsun, whose repudiation of the prevailing naturalistic style in literature as well as of its widely esteemed practitioners was as vehement and as forthright as Ibsen's had been of national romanticism a quarter of a century earlier.

The transition from the one style to the other was, of course, not as abrupt or as unconditional as this (necessarily brief) account may seem to imply. Individual authors responded to the changing cultural climate in their own personal and often idiosyncratic ways. The traditions of realism and naturalism were not abandoned overnight but often persisted, perhaps in modified form, for many years in the case of some writers. The newer postnaturalistic or "modernist" mode manifested itself in a variety of ways and enriched the vocabulary of critical taxonomy with a range of terms of greater or lesser precision: impressionism, neoromanticism, symbolism, decadence, and others.

The break found its most conspicuous expression in a series of three lectures—"Norsk literatur" (Norwegian Literature), "Psykologisk literatur" (Psychological Literature), and "Mode literatur" (Fashionable Literature)—that Hamsun delivered in 1891 at various venues around the country, including Christiania (Oslo). These deliberately "pugnacious" and "destructive" lectures (as he himself called them) were directed in the main against the then "big four" of Norwegian literature: Ibsen, Bjørnson, Kielland, and Lie. In particular, he attacked their predisposition to write about "types" instead of fully rounded characters, the emphasis they gave to the description of commonplace quotidian events, their obsession with simple and undifferentiated emotions, and their conception of the individual as a predictable product of social, economic, and other environmental forces. Against these, Hamsun set out the merits of "psychological" literature, which addresses itself to the complexities of the modern mind, to the irrationalities of contemporary living. This approach implies not a denial but an extension of "scientific" observation away from the external world of material detail, of visible objects, and of conscious decision-making to embrace the more ambiguous and random reactions of the senses and of the unconscious mind. He argued that it is the author's duty to respond to the faintest vibrations of the soul, to bring all his innate sensitivity to bear on these phenomena, to capture them and record them in his work: "I shall pin down even the vaguest flicker [in the mind], and hold it under my magnifying glass."

These lectures echo ideas that had been forming in his mind over the previous year or two and to which he had given expression in two recently published articles: "Kristofer Janson" (1888), and—more important—"Fra det ubevidste Sjæleliv" (From the Unconscious Life of the Mind), published in the periodical *Samtiden* (Our Times) in 1890. In the former, Hamsun draws what was for him a fundamental distinction between literature as "popular education" and literature as "art." To write with the object of improving the people is to debase the real nature of literature, which can only be to produce in the reader the authentic thrill: "The writer must always, on all occasions, find the vibrant word . . . that which by its trenchancy can so wound my soul that it whimpers. . . . One must know and recognize not merely the outward meaning but also the secret power [of words]. . . . There are overtones and undertones in words and there are lateral tones." The debating of problems for largely didactic purposes or the simple chronicling of familiar everyday events he sees therefore as inimical to the true aims of the "modern" writers.

It is, however, in "Fra det ubevidste Sjæleliv" that Hamsun defines with great authority the essential nature of the new writing he was advocating. He takes as his starting point—as indeed Strindberg had done earlier in his "Preface to *Miss Julie*"—the distinctive psychological makeup of "modern" man, his split and disharmonic mind. He draws attention to the strange and inexplicable moods and thoughts that invade this mind, things often too elusive to be seized and held fast. If only writers concerned themselves with these phenomena, these inexplicable, unpredictable, anguished states of mind, instead of forever chronicling the commonplace events of daily living—betrothals and evening balls and excursions and similar domestic encounters—how very much greater would be our understanding of life in the modern age:

> We would learn something about the secret stirrings that go on unnoticed in the remote corners of the mind, the incalculable chaos of impressions, the delicate life of the imagination seen under the magnifying glass; the wanderings of these thoughts and feelings out into the

blue; untrodden, trackless journeyings by brain and heart, strange workings of the nerves, the whisper of the blood, the entreaty of the bone, all the unconscious life of the mind.

This essay, of which the novel *Sult* (1890; Eng. tr. *Hunger,* 1899 and others) is the creative counterpart, is important not only in marking the transition within Norwegian literature from the "problematic" to the "psychological" but also because it anticipates—even in its phraseology—much of the discussion in the wider world of literature outside Scandinavia a quarter of a century later about the "stream of consciousness" novel. In those much-quoted phrases that tell of "tracing the atoms as they fall on the mind," of the "disconnected and incoherent patterns scored on the unconscious," of the "reveries between brackets of reality," of the "tangles of mental association" there is clearly an echo of Hamsun's words of 1890.

HENRIK IBSEN

Henrik Ibsen is widely acclaimed as the father of modern drama. His bold decision, after completing *Peer Gynt* in 1867, to abandon verse as the medium of dramatic composition in order to write prose plays about contemporary problems is now seen as an event of the most far-reaching significance. His subsequent emergence in the 1880s and 1890s from comparative Scandinavian obscurity to the status of a writer of European and international renown was unprecedented. His skill in making drama an instrument for the formation of public opinion was consummate. These were the years when the publication of a new Ibsen play, its prompt translation into a range of other languages, and its swift performance over a wide spread of the theatrical capitals of Europe were events of prime social and cultural significance.

But although to the world of his contemporaries it was the provocative and the innovative elements in his work which made the chief impact, posterity has come to value qualities there of a much more enduring kind. There is the recognition that, central to his achievement of creating the modern realistic prose drama, his work of exploring and exploiting the resources of prose dialogue in ways never before imagined, let alone attempted, resulted in the creation of a "poésie du théâtre" of immense power and subtlety. Add to this his supreme mastery of the dramatic medium in all its aspects, the penetration and profundity of his insights, and the formidable shaping power of his imagination, and the reasons for the continuing appeal of his work are immediately evident.

Ibsen's creative career slots neatly into the second half of the nineteenth century, spanning the period from 1850—the year of publication of his first drama, *Catilina* (Eng. tr. *Catiline,* 1922 and others)—to the December days of 1899, which witnessed the appearance of his last work, *Når vi døde vågner* (Eng. tr. *When We Dead Awaken,* 1900 and others). But although conceived and written exclusively within the nineteenth century, Ibsen's work is arguably even more significant as an all-pervasive influence on world drama in the present century. The tradition in drama which, for Bertolt Brecht, was made up of those "great attempts to give the problems of the age a theatrical structure" (*Brecht on Theatre* [1957], p. 130), and which might well be thought to include the names of Maxim Gorky, Gerhart Hauptmann, Frank Wedekind, George Bernard Shaw, Georg Kaiser, Eugene O'Neill, and Arthur Miller, clearly draws nourishment from Ibsen's earlier achievements in the field of the realistic problem play. That other group of writers—among them one might number Maurice Maeterlinck, Hugo von Hofmannsthal, Anton Chekhov, William Butler Yeats, and Federico García Lorca—for whom the practice of drama meant above all the struggle with words and symbols in the context of theater in an effort to communicate life's more elusive truths, found their inspiration not so much in Ibsen's more obviously polemical works but rather in the subtle techniques of those dramas that convey their meaning by more oblique means. There have been few areas of world drama in the twentieth century left untouched, directly or indirectly, by the force of his continuing presence.

Henrik Johan Ibsen was born on March 20, 1828, the second child of a prosperous businessman, in Skien, a small timber port about one hundred miles down the coast from Norway's capital city of Christiania (now Oslo). His memories of childhood, recollected in later life, were somber: he recalled particularly the pillory, the jail, the madhouse—"only buildings, nothing green"—and how the many sawmills filled the air with a sound like that of moaning women. When he was eight years old, his father went bankrupt; the lifestyle of the family deteriorated abruptly, and the associated sense of shame and social isolation left an enduring mark on Ibsen's personality. He had ambitions to study as an artist, but at the age of fifteen he was apprenticed to an apothecary in Grimstad, a little farther down the coast. Here he stayed for six years. When no more than eighteen, he fathered an illegitimate child by one of the servant girls in the house; he supported his son and the mother for the next fourteen years, but the incident remained one of the darker secrets of his life.

In what few leisure hours he had, he painted, wrote verse, and studied for the university entrance examination. Out of his reading of the set Latin texts—especially Sallust and Cicero, which Ibsen (to use his own phrase) "lapped up"—there grew his first substantial composition: the tragedy of *Catilina,* a work in which echoes of the revolutionary year 1848 are also distinctly audible. Published in 1850 under the pseudonym Brynjolf Bjarme, it attracted disappointingly little attention. Its basic theme nevertheless set a pattern for much of Ibsen's later drama—a theme that the author (on the occasion of the publication of a second revised edition in 1875) defined as "the clash of ability and aspiration, of will and possibility, at once the tragedy and the comedy of mankind and the individual."

In the spring of 1850 Ibsen quit Grimstad for Christiania, where he hoped to gain admission to the university as a student. In the big city there was not only the theater to enjoy, but also journalistic enterprises to join, such as the periodical *Andhrimner* (named after the Norse gods' cook), which he helped to edit. He also completed a second play, very much in the national romantic mode, which was accepted for production by the theater in Christiania: *Kjæmpehøjen* (Eng. tr. *The Warrior's Barrow* [also *The Burial Mound*], 1922 and others) was performed there on September 26, 1850, the first performance ever of an Ibsen play. It was not a success with the public and was not published in book form until 1902.

In 1851 opportunity knocked for Ibsen: he was appointed "dramatic author" to the recently established Norwegian theater in Bergen. The experience he gained there over the next six years was of fundamental importance for the course of his future career. Not merely encouraged to write for the theater, he was in fact required by the terms of his appointment to do so. There were enviable opportunities for having his own work staged. Moreover, he was expected to contribute to the day-to-day practical running of the theater and in consequence acquired valuable experience in all aspects of dramatic production and a profound insight into the peculiarities and potentialities of the medium. He was given leave in 1852 to undertake a study tour of theaters in Denmark and Germany, and over the following years he was able to build up an unrivaled knowledge of those plays that formed the popular European repertoire of the day.

Five of his own plays, written in these years, were produced in Bergen annually on the anniversary on January 2 of the theater's founding: 1853, *Sancthansnatten* (Eng. tr. *St. John's Night,* 1957 and 1970), a rather inept "fairy-tale comedy" that Ibsen in later life was inclined to disown; 1854, a revised version of *Kjæmpehøjen*; 1855, *Fru Inger til Østeraad* (rev. ed. *Fru Inger til Østråt,* 1874; Eng. tr. *Lady Inger of Østråt,* 1890 and others), a historical drama of Scribean-style intrigue; 1856, *Gildet paa Solhoug* (Eng. tr. *The Feast at Solhoug,* 1908 and others), a lyrical piece that took inspiration from the author's study of Landstad's collection of Norwegian folk ballads and which was the first real theatrical success Ibsen enjoyed, its performance being appreciatively received by the Bergen audience; and 1857, *Olaf Liljekrans* (Eng. tr. 1921 and 1970), a play based on a fragment he had begun in 1850 and that he now (vainly) sought to bring to life by piling intrigue on improbable intrigue. In sum, they met with only mixed success from the critics and the public. It was while he was in Bergen that he met his future wife, Suzannah (née Thoresen), though it was some years before they could afford to marry. Their son and only child, Sigurd, was born on December 23, 1859.

In the summer of 1857 Ibsen asked to be released from his contract with Bergen in order to take up an appointment with the Norwegian Theater in Christiania. The years that followed, until his departure in the spring of 1864 to live in Italy, saw his fortunes—at least in the personal and economic sense—at their nadir. The theater he had joined was in a parlous financial position; he himself fell victim to depression and was several times near suicide. His work was repeatedly rejected by the more established theaters; even when his plays did reach the boards, they were discouragingly received. His debts mounted; he was under regular public attack on account of his policies for the theater; his marriage also seems to have been under strain. Eventually, in 1862, the theater went bankrupt, and Ibsen found himself living from hand to mouth.

Nevertheless, in the course of these years he was able to complete three dramas of a quality much higher than anything he had written earlier. *Hærmændene paa Helgeland* (Eng. tr. *The Vikings at Helgeland,* 1890 and others) was published as a supplement to the weekly *Illustreret Nyhedsblad* (Illustrated Newspaper) in April 1858: a "saga drama," it marked a crucial step in Ibsen's growing recognition of the genuinely poetic potential of prose dialogue, though to today's reader it smacks somewhat of pastiche. *Kjærlighedens komedie* (Eng. tr. *Love's Comedy,* 1890 and others), printed as a Christmas supplement to the same periodical in December 1862, reverted to verse as its medium—but this time it was a verse of style and elegance which served as a splendid vehicle for the pointed wit of its comments on love and marriage. It provoked a storm of protest from the public, which objected to the views expressed. Finally, in this period the historical tragedy *Kongsemnerne* (1863; Eng. tr. *The Pretenders,* 1890 and others) again adopted prose as its linguistic medium. But there was a difference. Instead of being, as in *Hærmændene,* an archaic speech deliberately designed to be reminiscent of the language of the past, it was cast in a less time-bound idiom, closer to modern speech. Although the work must be classed among

Ibsen's historico-nationalistic plays—his last, as time was to show—its main concern was psychological rather than chauvinistic. It addressed itself to the problem of *inner* qualification or disqualification as evident in the historical figures of Haakon and Skule; contemporaries were quick to see in it also a comparative commentary on the different poetic talents of Bjørnson and Ibsen himself. It was played (in a series of fifteen performances) in January 1864 at the Christiania Theater, in a production by the author himself, and was enthusiastically received by the public.

To these years there also belong some significant works in the field of lyric and narrative poetry. Ever since his Grimstad days, Ibsen had continued to write poetry—shorter lyrics, occasional verse for weddings and other events, prologues, and other pieces; and some of them, such as "Bergmanden" (1851 and 1861; Eng. tr. "The Miner," 1902 and others), and "Lysræd" (1855; Eng. tr. "Afraid of Light," 1902 and others), contribute significantly to our understanding of his outlook on life. During his Christiania period he also published the longer reflective poem "Paa Vidderne" (1959; Eng. tr. "On the Heights," 1910 and others) and the poem cycle "I billedgalleriet" (1859; Eng. tr. "In the Picture Gallery," 1986), which consists of twenty-three separate but related poems, most of them sonnets. In 1862 there appeared "Terje Vigen" (Eng. tr. 1917 and others), a longer narrative poem that holds strong subjective elements within its account of a sailor's hard struggle against adversity and despair and his final victory over circumstances as well as over himself.

In an effort to ease his desperate financial situation, Ibsen made several applications to the government for travel grants and was awarded two modest sums in 1862 and 1863 to enable him to collect folk songs and folktales in rural Norway. In the autumn of 1863 he was given a further grant to allow him a year's study abroad "to study art, art history, and literature." In April 1864 he left Norway for Italy. He lived abroad for the next twenty-seven years, chiefly in Rome, Dresden and Munich, returning to Norway only for short visits in 1874 and 1885.

The changes wrought in Ibsen by this break were profound: changes in belief, in attitude, in values, in lifestyle, and above all in the nature and thrust of his work. Recent public events, especially what he felt had been Norway's contemptible behavior vis-à-vis Denmark in the Dano-Prussian war earlier that same year, left his feelings in turmoil: a mixture of shame, anger, distaste, and guilt. In distancing himself from home, he was better able to see his own earlier career and works in perspective, and he was not pleased with what he saw. He was moved to a passionate denial of many of the things he had once uncritically accepted and to a repudiation of what he now viewed as a whole world of false values and spurious standards.

Strangely compounded with these largely negative feelings was an equally new and powerful experience: the encounter with Mediterranean Europe, its gentle landscape, its wide skies, its serene art. In a speech given in Copenhagen in 1898, he recalled it as "a feeling of being released from darkness into light, escaping through a tunnel from mists into sunshine." The cultural shock made him look long and hard at those assumptions that had served him hitherto and to take stock anew of life. He felt revulsion at the way he had allowed his pen to serve what he now judged to be the false ideals of national romanticism. He was moved to a fundamental reappraisal of things he had himself witnessed and indeed suffered under: the public hypocrisies, the blinkered vision, the self-deception, the wishful thinking, the cultural chauvinism that had been his lot for what he realized was half a lifetime.

He began work on *Brand* (1866; Eng. prose tr. 1891, verse tr. 1894 and others) and saw in the very act of composition an opportunity for the cathartic discharge of venom: "I had standing on my desk [he wrote in a letter to Peter Hansen, October 28, 1870] an empty beer glass with a scorpion in it. From time to time the creature became sickly; then I used to throw a piece of soft fruit to it, which it would then furiously attack and empty its poison into; then it grew well again. Is there not something similar to that about us poets?"

As originally conceived, *Brand* was to be a long epic poem; and Ibsen worked at it in this form for well over a year, completing more than two hundred eight-line stanzas. Although the manuscript of this work went astray and was not published until 1907 under the title of *Den episke Brand* (Eng. prose tr. *The Epic Brand*, 1972), it can now be seen as a document of prime significance for plotting the way Ibsen's mind was working during these very crucial months. Then one day, probably in July 1865, Ibsen found himself in the Church of St. Peter in Rome. He described the experience in a letter to Bjørnson on September 12, 1865:

> Suddenly the form for what I had to say came to me, forcefully and clearly. Now I have thrown overboard the thing that has been tormenting me for a whole year without my having got anywhere; and in the middle of July I began on something new which progressed as nothing has ever progressed for me before. It is new in the sense that the writing of it began then; but the content and drift of it have been hanging over me like a nightmare since those many unhappy events

back home made me look within myself and look at our way of life there, and think about things that previously went drifting by me and that in any case I never gave serious thought to. It is a dramatic poem, with a contemporary theme, serious minded in content, five acts in rhyming verse.

In the work that the world now knows as *Brand*, Ibsen set out to castigate his countrymen for their spinelessness, their duplicity, their evasiveness, their readiness to seek an easy compromise; and it set up, by way of contrast, a central character whose strength of will is the supreme factor, whose motto is "All or nothing," and who is ready to sacrifice all to the imperatives of his chosen mission.

Brand was an immediate artistic and commercial success. It won for its author official financial support from the Norwegian Storting, and it assured Ibsen once and for all a firm material basis for his future career. Thereafter, Ibsen astonished his friends in Rome by the new elegance of his dress, the new cut of his beard, the new dignity of his manner, and even the new firmness of his handwriting.

After *Brand,* as Ibsen was himself later to affirm, *Peer Gynt* (1867; Eng. tr. 1892 and others) followed, as it were, of its own accord. The essential complementarity of these two "dramatic poems" has often been commented on: from Arne Garborg, who in his 1876 article "Peer Gynt" described the poem as the "correlating caricature" of *Brand,* to W. H. Auden, in this century (*The Dyer's Hand,* 1968), who saw the two eponymous heroes respectively as the apotheosis of "apostle and genius." Ibsen himself (in a letter to Edmund Gosse, April 30, 1872) declared bluntly that *Brand* was *Peer Gynt's* "modsætning," that is, variously its antithesis, its opposite, its counterpart, its contrary. After the stern, unbending self-discipline of Brand, the later play follows the career of an unprincipled, unstable, evasive daydreamer who is happy to adopt as his motto "To thine own self—be enough." Yet Ibsen himself was also ready to acknowledge that both characters were in their own distinctive ways self-portraits: "Brand is myself in my best moments," he wrote later in a letter to Peter Hansen (October 28, 1870); and he went on to admit that many of Peer Gynt's characteristics were there as a result of a process of "self-dissection." At the same time, *Peer Gynt* is a richly inventive work, the product of a highly fertile imagination, and peopled with mystic and symbolic figures like the Buttonmoulder, the Strange Passenger, the Thin Man, the Boyg, and the family of trolls which have shown themselves to possess a timeless validity.

The impact of these two works on the Scandinavian reading public was immense. *Brand* went through four editions in its first year of publication and by the end of the century had reached fourteen editions. *Peer Gynt* was sold out even before publication day, and a second and larger printing was rushed out within fourteen days of the first; by the end of the century it had reached its eleventh edition. In the theater, by contrast, *Brand* had to wait nearly twenty years for its first performance (in Stockholm in Swedish translation) and was not performed in full in Norway until 1904; *Peer Gynt* had its theatrical premiere in Christiania in 1876. Together they established Ibsen's reputation as Scandinavia's best-known and most widely discussed author of the age.

Between the completion of *Peer Gynt* in 1867 (when its author was in his fortieth year) and the publication ten years later of the first of what the world came to think of as the characteristically "Ibsenist" dramas—*Samfundets støtter* (1877; Eng. tr. *Pillars of Society,* 1888 and others)—there lay a distinctly Germanic middle age, a decade of very mixed endeavor and achievement. In 1868 Ibsen left Italy to take up residence in Dresden; here he remained until moving to Munich in 1875 and eventually back to Italy in 1880. In these ten years he wrote only two plays: *De unges forbund* (1869; Eng. tr. *The League of Youth,* 1890 and others) and the monumental "double drama" *Kejser og Galilæer* (1873; Eng. tr. *Emperor and Galilean,* 1876 and others, the first Ibsen play to be translated into English). Ibsen felt that both these plays were clearly German in their general style and inspiration. The former play—"reminiscent of 'Knackwurst' and beer," as Ibsen put it in the aforementioned letter to Peter Hansen—was composed in a mood of anger and exasperation following some of the criticism that had been directed at *Peer Gynt* in Scandinavia; in it he aimed a biting satire against some of his contemporaries "up North," including (though Ibsen was later to deny it) Bjørnstjerne Bjørnson (letter to Bjørnson, December 9, 1867). For his medium, he adopted a prose dialogue in a contemporary idiom, a sharp contrast to the verse rhythms of *Brand* and *Peer Gynt* but anticipating in some measure the prose of his later works.

Kejser og Galilæer was also, in Ibsen's mind, "a completely and wholly realistic piece of writing" (letter to Ludvig Daae, February 23, 1873), written from a growing conviction of the incomparable power of prose as a medium for drama. In a letter to Edmund Gosse (January 15, 1874), who had the temerity to suggest to him that the play might have been better in verse, Ibsen gave an altogether peremptory reply: "You think that my play should have been in verse and that it would have gained thereby. On that point I must contradict you, for the play is—as you will have noted—cast in a form as realistic as possible. . . . If I had used verse, I would have run counter to my own intentions and to the task I had set myself." Although therefore these two plays—in their shared Germanic origins and in their realistic intent—have much in common, in practically every other respect they are greatly dissimilar: one is a highly contrived comedy, locally allusive, rather Holbergian in its construction and manner; and the other is cosmic in its significance, monumentally proportioned, and intent on communicating a deeply pondered *Weltanschauung*. The ten acts of *Kejser og Galilæer* follow the career of Julian the Apostate: his rise to imperial power and his attempts to reintroduce the old paganism into the Christianized Roman Empire of the fourth century A.D.; it advances the concept of "the third realm" by which conflicting values of the two bodies of belief may be reconciled and synthesized and a new age inaugurated. But despite giving the drama a specific historical setting, Ibsen was always quick to insist on the essential relevance of the events to the modern world and to stress the timeless nature of the underlying conflict.

It was in this decade too that Ibsen felt the compulsion to make a final reckoning of his work in the field of lyric poetry. He addressed himself to the task of selecting from the considerable body of lyric, narrative, and occasional poetry that he had written in his earlier years those items he judged to be worthy of publication in more permanent form; some of them he also subjected to quite major revision. This selection, his one published volume of poems, appeared in 1871 with the title of *Digte* (Poems; Eng. tr. in selections, 1902 and 1912; in full, 1986), and a second and somewhat augmented edition was published in 1875. Alongside some of Ibsen's longer and already well-known poems, such as "Terje Vigen" (1862) and "Paa Vidderne" (1859), it included some poems that (in their origins at least) date back to Ibsen's earliest years in Christiania in the 1850s (such as "Spillemænd" ["Fiddlers"], "En svane" ["A Swan"], "Fugl og fuglefænger" ["Bird and Birdcatcher"], and "Bergmanden" ["Miner"]), several of the love poems and other pieces he wrote in his twenties during his time in Bergen (such as "Byggeplaner" ["Blue-Print"], "Markblomster og potteplanter" ["The Wild Flowers and the Pot-Plants"], and "En fuglevise" ["A Birdsong"]), certain poems he had written in the mid-1860s following the stress of the Dano-Prussian war (such as "En broder i nød" ["A Brother in Peril"], "Troens grund" ["Grounds for Confidence"], "Mindets magt" ["The Power of Memory"] and "Abraham Lincolns mord" ["Abraham Lincoln's Murder"]), along with other pieces of more recent composition (e.g., "Ballonbrev til en svensk dame" ["Balloon-Letter to a Swedish Lady"] and "Rimbrev til fru Heiberg" ["Rhyme-Letter to Mrs. Heiberg"]). The effort he put into this undertaking (which he described to Georg Brandes as "a confounded labor") was tantamount to a declaration on his part—quite as eloquent as anything he had to say elsewhere on the question of the role of verse in drama—that he felt he needed at this point in his career to draw a line under his accomplishments as a lyric poet; after the 1870s he wrote virtually no more poetry.

The year 1871 was fraught with significance for Ibsen in yet one further respect. His *Digte,* the fruit of many months of anguished self-examination and self-discovery, appeared in May. The following month he finally began the task of writing his vast new historical drama, the research for which had occupied him intermittently over the previous seven years. He was convinced it would be his masterpiece and was in a mood of heightened tension. Shortly afterward, in July, he was visited in Dresden by Georg Brandes, a young scholar and critic who was beginning to earn recognition in his native Denmark but who as yet lacked the wider European reputation he was later destined to achieve. For three days they animatedly exchanged news and views, and each found enormous stimulation in the encounter. Brandes returned home to Copenhagen, vibrant with excitement, impatient for action. In November of that year he delivered the first of a series of lectures which that winter took intellectual Copenhagen by storm and which, when they were published in 1872, were a most potent influence in the creation of the new "problem" literature that came to dominate the literary scene in Scandinavia for the greater part of the next two decades. Their most memorable assertion—"What shows a literature in our day to be a living one is the fact of its subjecting problems to debate"—set the keynote for the new way of literary endeavor. Ibsen, with great percipience, at once recognized the full and, in the literal sense, epoch-making significance of these lectures, claiming that they bore witness to "a mortal combat between two epochs" and adding: "No more dangerous book could fall into the hands of a pregnant writer. It is one of those works that place a yawning gulf between yesterday and today" (letter to Brandes, April 4, 1872).

Ibsen was not the first of Norway's writers to respond to the new call for a literature that would take as its prime purpose the debating of social and other problems; notably Bjørnson's two dramas of 1875, *En fallit* and *Redaktøren,* take clear chronological precedence. But with *Samfundets støtter* (1877), Ibsen was quick to join the ranks of those who felt a crusading zeal in identifying and indicting the ills and evils, the immoral and corrupt practices of contemporary society. In this instance it is the hypocrisies of the business world, the criminal irresponsibility of running the so-called coffin ships, and the choking illiberalism of a small provincial society (in contrast to the openness and freedom in the New World) that serve to feed the dramatic debate. The play marked the start of a quite extraordinary and sustained period of creativity in Ibsen's life, one that lasted until the end of the century and created for him first a European and then an international reputation of the highest distinction.

Two years after *Samfundets støtter,* he published *Et dukkehjem* (1879; Eng. tr. *A Doll's House,* 1880 and others), which, by its tendentious treatment of the theme of woman's role in marriage and in society, dominated public debate in Scandinavia. In his own preliminary notes for what he called his "modern-day tragedy," Ibsen set out the ideological basis of his play: "There are two kinds of moral law, two kinds of conscience, one in man and a completely different one in woman. They do not understand each other; but in matters of practical living the woman is judged by man's law, as if she were not a woman but a man. . . . A woman cannot be herself in contemporary society; it is an exclusively male society with laws drafted by men, and with counsel and judges who judge feminine conduct from the male point of view" (*Oxford Ibsen,* 5:436). Within three months of its publication it had been played in the major theaters of all the Scandinavian capitals. It was quickly translated into German and English; and—as an index of the spread of the world's familiarity with this Norwegian dramatist—it had by the end of the century been translated into French, Italian, Spanish, Portuguese, Dutch, Russian, Polish, Serbo-Croat, and Hungarian. In Germany its history of performance was complicated by the fact that Ibsen, under pressure and protest, had provided an alternative ending to the play, by which Nora at the end renounces her decision to abandon her family and finds reconciliation with her husband in the final moments. This was the version adopted for its German premiere in Flensburg and subsequently seen in Berlin and Hamburg and several other cities; not until March 3, 1880, was the authentic version seen—in Munich, in the presence of the author. The first English performance was (most unexpectedly) in Milwaukee; London had to wait until 1889 for its first substantial production, an occasion that was hailed as "the most dramatic event of the decade." The year 1889 also witnessed performances of the play in Belgrade, Turin, and Brussels; it was Paris's turn in 1894. Although clearly a product of its own age and the social and sexual values of that age, *Et dukkehjem* at its deeper levels nevertheless addresses problems that are timeless, as the play's continuing appeal to modern audiences the world over testifies.

Gengangere (1881; Eng. tr. *Ghosts,* 1885 and others) appeared after a further interval of two years. Strictly disciplined in its dramatic form, it largely obeys the rules of classical drama as they relate to the "unities." The "ghosts" of the title are those dead ideas of the past which continue to haunt the life of the living, with dire consequences. Once again it is a woman who is the center of the action: Mrs. Alving, who seeks to fight herself free from the stifling and life-defeating forces from the past which envelop her life. Ibsen's preliminary notes for the play again make explicit reference to the status of women in contemporary society: "These women of the modern age, mistreated as daughters, as sisters, as wives, not educated in accordance with their talents, debarred from following their mission, deprived of their inheritance, embittered in mind—these are the ones who serve as mothers of the new generation. What will be the result?" Even more audacious than *Et dukkehjem* in its choice of themes, it admitted into its world such matters as venereal disease, incest, and euthanasia; and it set the individual's pursuit of happiness above the more conventional calls of duty and social responsibility. This time the resulting public agitation, amounting in some quarters to total moral outrage, seriously affected the play's ability to communicate with its audience. It was so vehemently attacked in the Scandinavian press that the book sales were decimated. For years the major theaters of Scandinavia were afraid to touch it. In Germany public performances of it were banned by the police. The first fully public performance in England, licensed by the Lord Chamberlain, was not until 1914. Its world premiere, performed in the original Norwegian, was not even in Europe: it took place at the Aurora Turner Hall in Chicago in 1882. The real breakthrough in the theater came when, in the years 1889 to 1891, the new wave of "independent theaters"—the Freie Bühne of Berlin, the Théâtre Libre of Paris, and the Independent Theatre of London—chose *Gengangere* as the work that they felt best matched their theatrical policies and aspirations. Only then was the explosive power of the play felt by the wider public, perhaps augmented by its delayed-action effect.

These three "problem plays" from the years 1877 to 1881 formed in Ibsen's mind a kind of miniseries, within which the separate works quickly took color from one another; in particular, he thought that *Et dukkehjem* acted as a kind of introduction to or preparation for the more extreme *Gengangere*. Together these plays set out to identify and condemn those aspects of contemporary society which in Ibsen's view inhibited the free self-realization of the individual: the hypocrisies of the world of business, the outworn conventions of social behavior, the insincerities of organized religion, the bigoted attitudes toward sex and marriage. Central to all three dramas is an attempt to define in dramatic terms the real nature of freedom as something that is essentially a matter of individual decision and individual responsibility, something personal that has to be striven for with courage and determination. All three plays document a process of emancipation by ordeal;

and all three principals—Bernick, Nora, and Mrs. Alving—progress from some initial and rudimentary stage of personal integrity to a more refined one.

En folkefiende (1881; Eng. tr. *An Enemy of the People,* 1888 and others) was clearly written in anger at the hostile reception of the Scandinavian critics and public to *Gengangere.* In a play that traces the incredulous exasperation of one who, for publishing unpalatable truths about the polluted sources of a community's economy, is subjected to abuse and even physical violence from his fellow citizens, Ibsen gave his own spirited answer to the attacks that had been made on him. But the hurt and distress he felt on that occasion was not to be assuaged simply by writing this one play: the disturbance inflicted on his views on life and meaning and truth was much more profound that that, and Georg Brandes was surely right to see *Vildanden* (1884; Eng. tr. *The Wild Duck,* 1890 and others) and *Rosmersholm* (1886; Eng. tr. 1891 and others) as also traceable to this common point of origin. The former looks at the possibly tragic consequences of telling the truth without due regard to the circumstances; the latter follows the destiny of one whose dementia similarly was the pursuit of truth, one who also had improving designs on his fellow creatures but whose ultimate achievement is equally unavailing.

Taken together, however, these plays mark a period of transition in Ibsen's more mature work. *En folkefiende* has a continuing appeal as an accessible, not too highly wrought work: "Written in half the time Ibsen usually devoted to a play," wrote William Archer in *Play-Making* (1912, p. 79), "it is an outburst of humorous indignation . . . a straightforward spirited melody." By contrast, the general assessment of *Vildanden* and *Rosmersholm* is that they belong among the more elusive, more subtle, and more complex of the works: Sigurd Bødtker, for instance, designated *Vildanden* "the master's masterpiece" (*Verdens Gang,* no. 81 [1904]), while on behalf of *Rosmersholm* it is frequently claimed that never were Ibsen's constructional and evocative skills more confidently exploited. Ibsen himself, writing to his publisher in 1884, was moved to admit that he thought of *Vildanden* as something rather special in his oeuvre, and he added that here his methods were new and that some of the country's younger dramatists might be encouraged by his example to launch out along new paths. Thus *En folkefiende* could be taken as marking the close of one stage of Ibsen's more mature development: the completion of a period when the dramatist's objective was the more specifically Brandesian one of subjecting problems to debate. *Vildanden*—transitional, intractable—came at a time when its author's dramatic powers were addressing new and challenging problems of a less socially deterministic kind, and *Rosmersholm* might be seen as inaugurating a newer, more psychologically oriented mode which, with variations and modifications, served him for his final series of six plays: *Fruen fra havet* (1888; Eng. tr. *The Lady from the Sea*, 1890 and others), *Hedda Gabler* (1890; Eng. tr. 1891 and others), *Bygmester Solness* (1892; Eng. tr. *The Master Builder,* 1893 and others), *Lille Eyolf* (1894; Eng. tr. *Little Eyolf,* 1895 and others), *John Gabriel Borkman* (1896; Eng. tr. 1897 and others), and *Når vi døde vågner* (1899; Eng. tr. *When We Dead Awaken,* 1900 and others).

As the sweep of Ibsen's authorship over these years took the dramatist from the social to the psychological, from the polemical to the visionary, from the naturalistic to the symbolic, from the demonstrative to the evocative, he found himself engrossed in the problems of dramatic language and what it could be made to "say." Ever since his renunciation of verse as an acceptable medium for drama, he had been fascinated by what he had called "the far more difficult art of prose"; his conviction that, below the surface of what might seem to be nothing more than the commonplaces of everyday speech, one might communicate unsuspected subtleties and profundities impressed him as an insight that opened up new and important possibilities for drama. It was Ibsen's success in this matter that later drew admiring phrases from those who were themselves preeminently sensitive practitioners of language—most immediately, Hofmannsthal, Henry James, Chekhov, and Maeterlinck in the nineties, and later James Joyce, Rainer Maria Rilke, and Luigi Pirandello.

Vildanden, Ibsen insisted, had to be interpreted as "tragicomedy." Gregers Werle, with his relentless "idealistic demands," wreaks havoc in a humble household that in essence seeks little more than to live at ease within its own comfortable illusions; but the tragedy of Hedvig's death is sharpened by comic elements that add an extra resonance to the play. There is little comic relief of this kind in the somber *Rosmersholm,* which traces the tragic consequences of the interaction between a naturally conservative-minded man and a naturally radically minded woman when they try to make their life together: he, diffident, contemplative, with his roots deep in a landed tradition; she, passionate, strong-willed, and of dubious origins. Rosmer is also persuaded to feel that, not unlike Gregers Werle, he has an improving mission in life, an interventionist role: to go out into the wider world and work for the creation of a new generation of "free, happy, and noble-minded people." But there is a fatal mismatch between the confident strength required for this course of action and his own sensitive, self-questioning, and (in the end) guilt-ridden soul.

In an age that showed a growing fascination with the nature of the unconscious mind, with the phenomena of hypnotism, magnetism, and mental suggestion, *Fruen fra havet* gives evidence of Ibsen's own ever-increasing preoccupation with the mysterious ways of the mind. He found himself drawn to the technical problem of how most effectively in drama to communicate something of the irrational ways of the human psyche, how to externalize those warring forces that do battle for control of the mind, the neuroses, the mysterious logic by which the deeper layers of the human personality are ordered. Ellida Wangel acknowledges the power exerted over her by what she calls "det dragende," a compulsive force akin to the sea's undertow, an amalgam of all those ambivalent drives and urges and impulses that can often hold the individual helpless in their grip. Ibsen's adopted method was to try to create, in a play otherwise conventionally naturalistic in its structure, an extra dimension of meaning by the use of images. Wangel himself comes in the course of the play to the belated realization that his wife actually *thinks* in images, in large measure lives out her life in images. Only in the light of this understanding does her conduct acquire meaning and intelligibility, and perhaps it is only by an analogous process that a valid reading of the play as a whole is to be achieved.

His next play, *Hedda Gabler,* was unenthusiastically received on its publication. It was met with bewilderment by critics in all parts of Europe, who complained at the sheer difficulty of finding any general meaning in it, at the unreality of the main character, at the many obscurities and inconsistencies. On its opening night in Copenhagen the audience laughed in all the wrong places; after the Christiania production the following night, the critic of the journal *Samtiden* dismissed the play in two terse lines: "*Hedda Gabler,* a play in four acts by Henrik Ibsen. An unrewarding play, which hardly any of the cast will remember with any real satisfaction." Even Ibsen's most ardent admirers in the English-speaking world—such as Edmund Gosse, William Archer, and Henry James—were mystified and disappointed by it; in James's phrase, they felt "snubbed." As for the declared anti-Ibsenists of the day, their published abuse knew no bounds. Later generations have decisively reversed this assessment of the play; it is now among the more frequently performed works in the oeuvre and a great favorite of audiences the world over.

Among the quite extensive notes and jottings that Ibsen made while at work on the play, two entries seem to offer a key to its meaning. One relates to the eponymous heroine: "The demonic thing about Hedda is that she wants to exert an influence over another person." The other describes the flawed character of Løvborg: "The despairing thing about him is that he wants to control the world but cannot control himself." The world of *Hedda Gabler* is thus an arena where minds do battle, where the desire to dominate and manipulate and control is the compulsive motive, but where in this succession of encounters and conflicts some fatal inadequacy brings ultimate defeat.

In 1891, after the completion of *Hedda Gabler,* Ibsen returned to Norway and settled down in Christiania, where he lived for the rest of his life. It was in the autumn of that same year that he attended lectures by Knut Hamsun in which his own dramatic practice was vehemently attacked by the younger man. In 1892 Ibsen's son Sigurd married Bjørnson's daughter Bergliot. There was much about his next drama, *Bygmester Solness,* to prompt his contemporaries into asking the question, How far could Solness be thought of as representing a self-portrait of the artist? And how nearly did the play's dramatic conflict mirror the inner doubts and questionings of its creator? Some were quick to relate the undoubted erotic elements there to Ibsen's own encounters of these years, notably with Emilie Bardach and Helene Raff. There was speculation about how far the Solness ménage took color from Ibsen's own marital relations. The conflict (of which Solness is so aware) between the practice of one's art and the pursuit of happiness, together with the sacrifices seemingly demanded thereby on all sides, was seen as something Ibsen had experienced on his own nerves. And in the recurrent theme in the play of youth's threat to the older generation some claimed to hear echoes of the real-life, Hamsun-inspired hostility. Central to the play is the theme of potency—artistic as well as sexual—and the menace that lurks in a situation marked by declining powers; it carries a message that creativity seems to be something that inevitably feeds on the lives and happiness of others, leaving a trail of victims.

Duty, obligation, remorse, and the overriding need for expiation—these are the elements that make up the Solness marriage. Aline, the wife, lives a chill, withdrawn, and self-punishingly dutiful life—the word *plikt* (duty) seemingly forever on her lips. Into this guilt-ridden household the young, assertive, amoral Hilde erupts with a kind of Nietzschean force and reveals herself as an extraordinarily Ibsenist creation. In the haunting exchanges between Hilde and Solness which make up so much of the play, the sexual overtones are unmistakable; they speak of the delights of giving free rein to a "robust conscience," of the thrill of seduction and abduction, of the pleasures of following the ways of untamed creatures, of trolls and raiding vikings and birds of prey. In the end, however, the man is the one possessed: "*My—my* master builder," Hilde cries ecstatically at the final curtain as Solness falls to his death.

Ibsen's next play, *Lille Eyolf* (1894), is an extraordinary tour de force, though it was not immediately recognized as such by contemporary readers and audiences. Indeed, it was long dismissed as one of his weaker plays: "strangely and painfully meager," Henry James put it in a letter to Elizabeth Robbins (see her *Theatre and Friendship*, 1932). Later generations of critics, however, have come to see it as a work of highly intricate orchestration, in which Ibsen set himself challenges in the way of dramatic communication which are daunting in their complexity.

It is clear from the earlier drafts of the play that Ibsen radically changed his purpose in the course of writing it. The result was a complex weave of nuance and suggestiveness overlaid with the profoundest irony, an artistic and technical achievement unsurpassed among Ibsen's dramas. Like all the plays of his last years, its world is the creation of a mind haunted by problems of personal relations in conditions of stress and by the way these problems bear down on individual happiness and faith. Basic to the situation in the play are the fraught sexual and marital relations between Alfred Allmers, the husband, and his wife, Rita. Superimposed on these are the obligations and aspirations of parenthood, elements to which the title of the play as well as its dramatic structure give special prominence: the rights and duties of fatherhood, the demands and frustrations of motherhood. And as a further overlay are those relationships, which even at first encounter are oblique and which as the play progresses become ever more insubstantial and uncertain, attaching to the putative half-sister/half-sister-in-law/half-aunt Asta, who eventually turns out to be none of these things. The action of the play then follows the consequences of the impact of domestic disaster—young Eyolf's death by drowning—on the individuals concerned and on their continuing relationships.

The emotional geometry of *John Gabriel Borkman* (1896) shows an overall similarity with that of *Lille Eyolf*: at the heart of the new play there is a triangular pattern of husband, wife, and wife's twin sister, a lattice of sexual and kinship relationships, with the destiny of the son as one of the spoils to be fought over. The son, Erhart, is positioned at the climax of the drama at the intersection of no fewer than five different forces seeking to determine his fate: those exerted by Gunhild, his dominating and hate-filled mother; by John Gabriel, his assertive and paranoid father; by Ella Rentheim, his mortally sick aunt, who seeks to stake her claim on his loyalty; by Mrs. Wilton, a seductive divorcee; and by the natural sexual drives of his own youthful manhood. Once again one of the chief motivating springs of the drama is a woman's humiliatingly unfulfilled sexuality: Ella wrings from Borkman the monstrous admission that, as part of a squalid business deal, he had traded her love for a bank directorship in pursuit of what he grandly thinks of as a glorious mission in life: the creation of material wealth. Within this arena of interlocking personal relationships, the play explores the dynamics of obsession and self-delusion. Borkman constructs for himself a comprehensive personal myth, in which he plays the central role of Nietzschean Superman, a Napoleon of industrial development. But this is mere self-delusion: a natural consequence of this deceptive and deceitful world in which, as he and the minor bank clerk Foldal in a deeply moving scene come to realize, even friendship is merely a form of mutual self-deception.

When Ibsen subtitled his next play, *Når vi døde vågner* (1899), a "dramatic epilogue," it was not with the immediate intention of announcing to the world the end of his career as a writer. All the term implied, he said, was that here was the culmination of that series of dramas which had begun with *Et dukkehjem* in 1879, and that if he were to write anything else, it would be "with new weapons and in new armor" (letter to Moritz Prozor, March 6, 1900). Not long afterward, he changed his mind somewhat and saw his play rather as rounding off a more tightly drawn series that had begun with *Bygmester Solness* in 1892. Then, on March 15, 1900, only a few days after making this pronouncement, Ibsen suffered his first stroke, which left him incapable of any further literary activity.

In the light of these events, therefore, *Når vi døde vågner* inevitably acquired an extra significance as the final dramatic comment to an entire creative career that had spanned half a century. The central figure of Rubek— the artist-sculptor and (in Irene's dismissively contemptuous term) "poet"—carries with it an invitation to see the play as one last and merciless piece of self-analysis, as a final pitiless assessment of the sacrifices that art demands of life and of the conflict between an individual's calling and the pursuit of happiness.

Ibsen died on May 23, 1906.

BJØRNSTJERNE BJØRNSON

In a speech at the unveiling of a statue of Bjørnstjerne Bjørnson in Molde some years ago, the distinguished speaker, then professor of Scandinavian literature at Oslo University, asked rhetorically, "Who was the greatest Norwegian?" Rejecting from his short list the names of some other possible contenders, ranging chronologically from St. Olav all the way down to Fridtjof Nansen, he finally settled firmly on Bjørnson. Although of course, the special pieties of the occasion had some bearing on the final choice, what is nevertheless significant is the precise nature of the question that resulted in this answer: the greatest Norwegian, not the greatest Norwegian writer. For held within it is a pointer to the peculiar essence of the greatness of Bjørnson.

He was manifold. In 1858, at the start of what was to be a long and crowded career, he catalogued some of the things he had recently been doing, quite apart from what he was actually being paid to do, namely, running the Bergen theater. He had, he said, been writing polemic pieces in the press, giving talks in various merchants' and workingmen's clubs, writing poems for patriotic occasions, arguing politics, and a host of other things. He accepted that all this had seriously interfered with his writing, delaying the completion of the story he was currently engaged on: *Arne*. He called it, wryly, "dissipation of effort." Yet behind the words one senses that he reveled in it. Certainly he succeeded in elevating it into a triumphant way of life.

In addition to a lifetime of prolific authorship—as poet, dramatist, novelist, and polemicist—Bjørnson was also at various times theater director, editor, political activist, public speaker, journalist, and a score of other things. In all these roles he somehow managed to appear somewhat greater than life-size. An imposing physical presence, a powerful voice, and a natural eloquence made him a notable orator. He was a man of hugely generous impulses, impatient of all that was petty, and he was not slow to make his impatience known. He was a natural leader—indeed, his contemporaries referred to him on occasion as "the uncrowned king of Norway." He left the stamp of his personality on many aspects of Norwegian life over more than half a century.

But there was a reciprocity here as well. If the people (or at least those who were not implacably opposed to him) seemed to have need of him, accepting him as a spokesman, as one who could articulate their deeper aspirations, the reverse was also true: he needed a public, *his* public, before he could achieve complete fulfillment. Without that essential element, he seemed to lack a whole and vital dimension. He was, in all senses, a very public man.

Bjørnstjerne Martinius Bjørnson was born on December 8, 1832. Throughout his life he carried happy memories of his childhood days in Romsdal (where his father was a minister of the church) and of his school days in Molde. In 1850 he went to Christiania to prepare for university studies, and there he found himself in the company of Ibsen (four years his elder) and of Vinje. But even at this early stage the "dissipation of effort" syndrome was already active. His reading went more into his own personal choice of authors—such as Wergeland, but also Goethe and Alphonse Lamartine—instead of the pensum; he gave time to his own efforts at writing, determined as he was even at this stage that he would be a writer; he got himself implicated in Marcus Thrane's workers' movement; and he gave freely of his time and energy to the campaign for a Norwegian theater in Christiania.

In 1854 he broke off his studies and wrote drama criticism and book reviews for the Christiania newspaper *Morgenbladet*. When he eventually addressed himself seriously to his own writing, however, the results were immediate. He wrote his one-act "saga drama" *Mellem slagene* (1857; Between the Battles; Eng. tr. *Between the Acts,* 1941) in the astonishingly brief period of fourteen days, stimulated—as he himself recorded—by the experience of a student outing to Uppsala in 1856, where his sense of Scandinavian past glory was aroused. Displacing to the twelfth century the plot of a modern play he had been planning, he found himself the author of instant drama of no mean technical quality. His other work of this year, a short narrative piece of the genre that was to become known as the *bondefortelling* (peasant tale), with the title *Synnøve Solbakken* (Eng. tr. under various titles, 1858 and others), was a much more significant achievement and betokened a genuine breakthrough for the young writer. It not only introduced the public to a new narrative style, fresher, crisper, more direct than the kind that readers had become accustomed to; it also inaugurated what was virtually a national campaign, a program in national pride.

The mid-nineteenth century was witnessing a powerful and still-growing national consciousness, something that had been gathering strength ever since Napoleonic times: a conviction that the destiny of Norway—"a new country but an ancient kingdom"—was intimately yet subtly related to its great and heroic past, and that its present state of culture and its standing in the modern community of nations had an inherent distinctiveness that it was necessary to foster. The key figure in this national self-awareness, the custodian of those traditional values—spiritual, moral, existential—was the Norwegian peasant, the *bonde*. He was seen as the living embodiment of an exemplary way of life upon which a glorious future could be built. Much later in life, in a speech marking the fiftieth anniversary of this seminal work, Bjørnson confessed what his didactic intent had been: "Many people regarded *Synnøve* as being simply a novel, mere belles lettres. With *Synnøve* I intended something more than that. I was not writing merely to put together a book. What I wrote was a plea on behalf of the peasant. . . . We had come to understand that the language of the sagas lived on in our peasants, and their way of life was close to that of the sagas. The life of our nation was to be built on our history; and now the peasants were to provide the foundations."

The "tale," this not-easily-definable shorter narrative form, was a natural choice for Bjørnson to select as one of the main vehicles for his cultural campaign; in its economy of form he found an excellent match for the terseness of his didactic intent. He was, of course, by no means the only writer in Europe in this age writing within the tradition of the "village story." Inside Scandinavia itself, two or three decades earlier, there had been the earthily regional tales of Steen Steensen Blicher, firmly rooted in his native Jutland; Bertold Auerbach had given a picture of Black Forest peasant life in his *Dorfgeschichten* (Village Tales); and Jeremias Gotthelf had had didactic designs (not wholly dissimilar from Bjørnson's) in writing his Novellen of Swiss peasant life. Within Scandinavia, and doubtless contributing significantly to the formation of Bjørnson's own narrative style, were two other different but complementary literary influences: the collection of Norwegian folktales by Asbjørnsen and Moe which reconstructed with startling liveliness and freshness of vision tales that had lived on only in oral tradition; and the often seemingly ingenuous but essentially highly sophisticated tales of Denmark's Hans Christian Andersen. The continuing link between past and present, between ancient Norway and the modern peasant was something to be emphasized with pride; to do this was to make a defiant defense of peasant culture against the often supercilious hostility of the townspeople with their "Danophile" ways and also to mount a program of popular education for the peasants themselves, who were in large measure either heedless or indeed unaware of their heritage.

In the earlier stage of this phase of his authorship the most important peasant tales, after *Synnøve Solbakken,* were *Arne* (1859; Eng. tr. 1866 and others) and *En glad gut* (1860; Eng. tr. *A Happy Boy* and other titles, 1870 and others). *Fiskerjenten* (1868; Eng. tr. *The Fisher Girl* and other titles, 1869 and others) further added to this group of works; and finally, *Brudeslåtten* (1872; Eng. tr. *The Wedding March* and other titles, 1882 and others) might be thought to complete the narrative component of the "rotation of crops." The emphasis in these works on what the nationally romantic mind of the day considered characteristic viking virtues—powerful but undemonstrative feeling, strength of will and purpose, stern self-discipline, loyalty to kinsman and friend, ruthlessness in a just cause if necessary—together with the attempt to catch something of the laconic but doom-laden directness of saga language was all very much part of Bjørnson's strategy. In their more immediate objective these tales were in large measure successful; by the sheer popularity of their appeal they undoubtedly had a great social impact and affected the lives and attitudes of people in a very real way.

Complementing these prose works, and forming the other powerful thrust in his two-pronged cultural campaign, were his saga dramas of these years. Three dramas followed *Mellem slagene* at brief intervals: *Halte-Hulda* (1858), a blank-verse piece written in Bergen, where Bjørnson had only recently taken over from Ibsen at the theater as producer; *Kong Sverre* (1861; King Sverre), also in blank verse, but written in Rome during Bjørnson's residence there between 1860 and 1862; and *Sigurd Slembe* (1862; Eng. tr. 1888), a dramatic trilogy, part in blank verse, part in prose. *Halte-Hulda*, set in the time of transition in Norway's history between the decline of heathen beliefs and the rise of Christianity, inevitably invites comparison with Ibsen's *Hærmændene på Helgeland*, which not only has virtually the same chronological setting but was also published in the same year as Bjørnson's play. Bjørnson used his play as the occasion for writing a major article, published in *Bergensposten* (The Bergen Post), on modern drama as he conceived it should be, which is greatly revealing about his own practice and aspirations. But it is *Sigurd Slembe* that marks the high point of his dramatic composition of these years. His two years in Bergen had been strenuous in the extreme. His work in the theater was intensely demanding: it is reported that in one winter alone he was responsible for putting on twenty-five plays. He married and assumed all the new responsibilities that came with setting up a household. He took over the editorship of *Bergensposten* and made it a fiercely campaigning newspaper. He found himself in the thick of political in-fighting. He felt he must find respite; and that respite he would seek in Italy.

In Rome he was able to collect his strength, gather his ideas, extend his reading (especially of Schiller and Shakespeare), discover the art of the Mediterranean, fall in love with the Italian landscape, and review his personal position. It is not inappropriate to see *Sigurd Slembe* as part of this review. It is a powerfully structured piece. Taking its material largely from Snorri Sturluson's *Heimskringla*, it follows the career and ultimate downfall of a gifted man, well endowed by nature, blood, and position to exercise great influence for good but who because of inner flaws of character suffers eventual defeat. What he lacks is self-control and self-discipline; and these qualities, the play insists, are the essentials of greatness, just as balance and equilibrium are the necessary concomitants of great art. In contrast to Sigurd, Bjørnson created in the figure of Harald Jarl a character of subtle modernity, a man who, though humiliated and banished by his half-brother, finds any thought of revenge or of the reacquisition of power distasteful, who wins a brief happiness from life through his friendship with a young boy and is merely sickened by the plots of those who seek his reinstatement. Once again, as with *Halte-Hulda*, there is an invitation to make an Ibsenist connection—for only two years later came *Kongsemnerne,* Ibsen's own dramatic variant on the theme of the nature of leadership and the essential qualifications and disqualifications that attach to it. *Sigurd Slembe* established beyond all doubt Bjørnson's reputation as Norway's leading writer of the day, and on his return to Norway from the South in 1863 the warmth of his welcome was heartening.

Four other substantial or otherwise significant works, of a quite different order from the tales and the saga dramas, complete the tally of works finished by 1872: two dramas, one epic poem cycle, and a collected edition of poems. The first of these plays, *Maria Stuart i Skotland* (1864; Eng. tr. *Mary, Queen of Scots,* 1897), was prompted partly by his admiration for Friedrich von Schiller and partly by his disagreement with the interpretation Schiller puts on the queen's character in his own drama, *Maria Stuart.* In any event, Bjørnson's Mary is a less interesting figure than his weak and vacillating Darnley, based on the fascinating idea that the reason for his weakness is "because there is something deep within him to which he is loyal, a longing, a memory, a love," and he knows himself that this is so.

Bjørnson's other play of these years is more important for what it presages than for what it actually is. From his earliest days as a writer, Bjørnson had shown an interest in the potential for *borgerlig* drama, what was variously known in other parts of Europe as *bürgerliches Drama, proverbes dramatiques,* "domestic drama," or "drama of middle-class life." His first saga drama, *Mellem slagene,* was apparently a "historicized" domestic drama of modern times. Now it was perhaps time for that original plan to be resuscitated. *De nygifte* (1865; The Newly Married Couple; Eng. tr. *A Lesson in Marriage,* 1911) is a play modest in its dimensions but firm in its touch. Using only five characters, it took a timeless problem—a husband's break with his rich parents-in-law and his fight to retain his wife's affection—and examined it in a modern setting. What is not yet there is the element of argumentative debate that informs the later problem dramas, and it is no surprise to find that Georg Brandes dismissed it as a play about pale young lovers feeding on milk and water. But it points forward to the profounder shift in the nature of Bjørnson's drama from 1875 onward.

Possibly the most unexpected thing about the epic poem cycle *Arnljot Gelline* (1870; Eng. tr. 1917) is that it is dedicated to "Scandinavia's folk high schools." This dedication betrays the presence of Grundtvigian problematics behind the historical setting. Although medieval in its subject matter and placed in the time of Olav Haraldsson, it had clear modern connotations. Some of the individual poems in the cycle are among Bjørnson's finest works. In the same year, he collected and published the best of his lyric po-

etry in a volume entitled *Digte og sange* (1870; Eng. tr. *Poems and Songs*, 1915).
Bjørnson is probably more highly esteemed by Norwegians for his poems
than for any other part of his literary achievement, despite the fact that their
first publication in book form took place relatively late in his career, when he
was thirty-eight, and also that he published no further volumes of poetry
during his lifetime (though he did bring out, in 1880 and 1900, revised and
augmented editions). Even so, there are a modest 140 items in the final edition; and in the thirteen volumes of his collected works they fill only two
hundred pages. Nevertheless, they have entered the national consciousness
and have won the general affection of the people in a unique way. They are
full of associations for a Norwegian, overtones that foreign readers probably could never share. One grows up with them in Norway, hears them first
perhaps in the childhood home, meets them in school; one of them, "Ja, vi
elsker dette landet" (Yes, We Love This Country), is the national anthem;
they have stimulated many composers to set them to music, and as sung
works they have earned extra popularity.

The poems in *Digte* range over a great variety of styles: love poems; nature descriptions; verses in honor of loved ones, great contemporaries, or
figures of past history; occasional poems for anniversaries or other special
occasions. Sometimes they can be didactic: one describes the role of the
poet as that of "weekday preacher." Some are highly personal statements,
full of genuine pathos and immediacy of feeling; others consciously try to
speak for the nation. At their best, they have a simplicity and directness of
language, a concreteness of image, and a beauty of sound that gives them a
unique splendor in Norwegian literature.

After their publication Bjørnson was, for the second time in his life,
moved to seek refuge and respite in Rome. By the year 1873 he had become
deeply implicated in political arguments at several levels; matters reached a
head when he managed to give grave public offense to many by urging the
Danes to seek reconciliation with their German neighbors over the Schles-
wig problem. The phrase he used—that they should "change their signals"—gave the name to the subsequent bitter exchanges: the "Signal
Feud," whose furor finally drove him abroad. He remained resident in
Rome until 1875, and once again he found there spiritual renewal and revi-
talization.

The year 1875, with the publication and subsequent stage performances
(in Stockholm) of his two plays *En fallit* (1875; Eng. tr. *The Bankrupt*, 1914)
and *Redaktøren* (1875; Eng. tr. *The Editor*, 1914), marks the ultimate transition in his work from the historical to the modern, from a residual romanticism to a hard-hitting realism, from themes of peasant life and traditional

heroism to the strident world of the urban and commercial affairs of the contemporary age. These two plays, together with *Det ny system* (1879; Eng. tr. *The New System*, 1913) four years later, inaugurated the new age of the problem play in Norway. Of the three, *En fallit* attracted most public attention, becoming a great box-office success in many parts of Europe. And once again there was the now almost predictable Ibsenist cross-reference—this time to *Samfundets støtter* (1877), which explored the same arena of business ethics and personal probity and in time became an even greater success with the wider European public.

In these plays one finds a gallery of representative figures whose destinies document their author's optimistic faith in the power of common goodness and decency. The bankrupt, the editor, and the director general of "the new system" all fight a rearguard action, showing much resourcefulness but little integrity when their positions of power and authority are threatened. But their defeat by a largely unarticulated community good is theatrical rather than dramatic.

Kongen (1877; Eng. tr. *The King*, 1914) mounts an attack on selected (and, as Bjørnson believed, ossified) social institutions: in this instance, the monarchy. A king who comes to realize that by his position and his authority he has been acting a lie, who then attempts to bring the established institutions of state and church into line with his own ideals, is the dramatic correlative of the ideas that Bjørnson put to Christiania students later that same year in a speech entitled "Om at være i sandhed" (On Being in Truth). The king's offense, in contrast to the editor's and the bankrupt's, is thus sublime, and that in itself gives dramatic force to the work.

Kaptejn Mansana (1875; Eng. tr. *Captain Mansana*, 1883 and others), written soon after Bjørnson's return to Norway, is in compass little more than a sketch (its original title was "A Sketch from Italy") and gives a short rehearsal to a theme that was to inform much of his later work: the unwholesome effect of a sick society on one of its members. *Magnhild* (1877; Eng. tr. 1883 and others), which followed two years later, is not quite a fully rounded novel (it is defined as "*En fortælling*," a "tale," on its title page), its comparative brevity being less of disciplined economy than lack of amplitude. It takes as its opening situation one that was to become familiar in contemporary problem literature—the young, innocent girl who finds herself married to an older and more experienced man—and works through the consequences for her and for the young composer whom she loves. In its incidental attacks on the institution of marriage the way society seemed to have made it, it shows a brisker realism and a sharper vision than before as well as a lack of sentimentality new in Bjørnson's work. It also betrays a fundamental transformation in his attitude toward peasant life and culture, a sharp criticism instead of a romantic appreciation.

Indeed, not only in his view of peasant culture but in many other respects his ideas and beliefs were in ferment at this time. He lost faith in Christianity the way it was presented by the Church and lost patience with the Grundt-vigians; his reading of these years included much that was critical of ortho-dox belief. His address "On Being in Truth" to the Student Association in Christiania in October 1877, the very day after the publication of *Magnhild*, was his immediate attempt to define his new position.

From this point on, the pattern of Bjørnson's authorship seems to stabi-lize: its fluctuations become less extreme, and it even becomes more set in its ways. It has been suggested that all the works that follow this period of intel-lectual crisis fall conveniently under two headings: first, those that deal with private and largely individual problems such as home and marriage, sexual relations, parents and children, the education of the young, and the rights of women; and second, those that treat the individual's relations with some su-praprersonal authority in, for example, the affairs of community and church, of party and country, of politics and religion. To the former category one might assign the dramas *Leonarda* (1879; Eng. tr. 1911 and others), *En hanske* (1883; Eng. tr. *A Gauntlet,* 1886 and others), *Geografi og kærlighed* (1885; Eng. tr. *Love and Geography,* 1914), *Laboremus* (1901; Eng. tr. 1914), *Daglannet* (1904; Land of Dag), and *Når den ny vin blomstrer* (1909; Eng. tr. *When the New Wine Blooms,* 1911), together with the narrative works *Støv* (1882; Eng. tr. *Dust,* 1884 and others) and *Det flager i byen og på havnen* (1884; Flags Are Hoisted in Town and Harbor; Eng. tr. *The Heritage of the Kurts,* 1892). In the second category one might include the dramas *Over ævne I* (1883; Eng. tr. *Pastor Sang* and other titles, 1893 and others), *Over ævne II* (1895; Eng. tr. *Beyond Human Might,* 1914 and others), *Paul Lange og Tora Parsberg* (1898; Eng. tr. *Paul Lange and Tora Parsberg,* 1899), and the novel *På guds veje* (1889; Eng. tr. *In God's Ways,* 1889 and others).

Prominent among the matters treated in these later works is the degraded position of women in the contemporary community, their subjection by so-ciety's existing institutions and conventions. The iniquities of the double standard of morality as applied to men and women, the tyrannies exercised by one partner over the other within marriage, the traditional lack of candor and honesty between husband and wife (especially as it related to *his* past), the perpetuation of women's ignorance of sexual matters before marriage and their restricted educational opportunities generally—all these themes make their appearance. In his passionate rejection of these social evils, Bjørnson is often inclined to deal in stark contrasts of black and white, good and evil. Seen with today's eyes, this rigidity tends to diminish the artistic integrity of the work, inhibiting subtlety.

Leonarda addresses the problem of women and divorce. The divorced Leonarda establishes herself as the most "moral" character of all, not excluding the bishop. That is not too difficult, since the men are all drunkards, lechers, slanderers, or bigots. As a piece of drama, (as distinct from dramatized pleading) it tends to lose its way in a maze of emotional entanglements, and perhaps sacrifices too much to the one supremely theatrical moment when Leonarda triumphantly reveals that the alleged secret lover is none other than her divorced husband. In *En hanske,* the heroine, Svava Riis, discovers that her father is an old libertine, and her fiancé no better. She demands the same standards of morality for both men and women, both before and within marriage, and literally throws down the gauntlet to her fiancé by striking him in the face. The play aroused enormous controversy, and for yet another time in his life Bjørnson found himself at the center of a storm of protest. But not all was stridency in these plays: in *Geografi og kjærlighed,* marriage is examined through the medium of comedy, with the wife taking revenge on her egotistical scholar husband by leaving home for a period. *Daglannet* allows a similar wifely victory over an overbearing husband, and in *Når den ny vin blomstrer,* written when Bjørnson was in his late seventies, he invests the wife with what had traditionally been the husband's authority and sends her out into the great world of commerce as a career woman.

Det flager i byen og på havnen was Bjørnson's first attempt at a full-scale novel. At its ideological center is the question of the proper education of girls which, it suggests, must strive to be a real preparation for life, including adequate biological instruction. But the narrative is prolix and the long didactic passages wearisome. It is in the second group of works, however, of which *Over ævne I* is unquestionably the most brilliant, that Bjørnson seems most at ease with his material. This intensely moving drama reflects Bjørnson's newly won conviction that innate decency and morality count for more than any officially promulgated Christian faith and that belief in the miraculous is not sustainable. Humankind should recognize and accept its natural limitations. But the work is more than just a vehicle for ideas. It grew organically through five years of gestation: first planned as a comedy, then nearly rewritten as a novel in 1880, it was three more years before it found its final shape. What might have been yet another stage-mounted denunciation (like *En hanske*) ended as a poised, laconic piece in two acts, taut, concentrated, and yet resonant with meaning. Its complementary Second Part of twelve years later examined the same area of fanatic idealism but in the context of revolutionary politics rather than religion. It lacks the controlled power of the First Part, however.

På guds veje also puts the proposition familar from *Over ævne*: that there is no great overlap between orthodox Christianity and true morality. The personal relationships in the novel, which is constructed on a lattice of the loyalties and attractions of two married couples, are made subordinate to the clash of beliefs represented by the two men, one a parson and the other a doctor.

Paul Lange og Tora Parsberg shows no diminution in Bjørnson's creative powers. It carries an indictment of the ways of politics that ruthlessly and unscrupulously hound to death an opponent for the sake of party gain, its pleas made explicit in the heroine's final words: "Oh why must it be that the good men so often become martyrs? Will we never reach the stage where they can become leaders?"

REALISM AND NATURALISM

Jonas Lie

Jonas Lie (1833–1908) enjoys a deserved reputation as the founder of the Norwegian novel and his country's first great practitioner in the field of fiction. Apart from an early volume of verse (*Digte* [1867, later augmented 1889; Poems]), a dramatic poem (*Faustina Strozzi* 1875), an unsuccessful tragicomedy (*Grabows Kat* [1880; Grabow's Cat]), and one or two other undistinguished attempts at drama in the 1890s, Lie found the narrative form—both novel and short story—the most congenial for his prolific talents. As the author of more than thirty books, during his lifetime he was hailed as a writer in whose novels ordinary people could recognize themselves and their like. He did for the seagoing communities what Bjørnson had done for peasants: treated them as subjects for serious literary consideration. He led the way in many different fields: he was the first for nearly two centuries to write with intimate familiarity of Nordland and its mysterious ways; he wrote the first novels of the sea, the first novels of the world of business and commerce, and even the first novels of love and marriage of modern Norway.

Improbably, bankruptcy was the spur that, in 1868, transformed the thirty-five-year-old lawyer and dilettante poetaster into a novelist of stature. He had always intended to make writing his vocation, and his choice of a legal training and a lawyer's profession had been meant to provide the material conditions on which he could base a literary career. But a series of ill-judged speculations left him with heavy debts; motivated by a fierce resolve to pay off his creditors, he turned to writing both as a means of personal ful-fillment and as a source of income.

With encouragement from his friend Bjørnson and the active help of his wife, Thomasine, he addressed himself to what was to be his first novel: *Den fremsynte eller Billeder fra Nordland* (1870; Eng. tr. *The Visionary, or Pictures from Nordland,* 1894). The fact that he was a late starter left its mark on his style: detachment, precision, careful attention to significant detail—virtues that one associates with the legal mind—together with a sense of assurance and balance gave his work poise and maturity. To this was added, at a deeper level, a sense of fantasy that Lie himself attributed to the presence of gypsy blood in his veins but which must surely also have been fed by his experience of mystery-ridden Nordland in his most impressionable years. Structurally, the novel is doubtless too elaborate for its touchingly simple theme of the love of a mentally unstable boy, gifted with second sight, for his childhood sweetheart. It manages to incorporate a fictional narrator (who nevertheless soon disappears), two sets of posthumous papers, some flashback reminis-cence, and some interpolated folktales. But the novel's genuine vitality and freshness of vision are at once evident; there is magic in the book, but it lies in the creation of atmosphere, in the counterpoint of romantic mood and re-alistic detail, rather than in the organization of its parts.

Lie was quick to remedy this weakness in his next novels: *Tremasteren "Fremtiden"* (1872; Eng. tr. *The Barque "Future,"* 1879) and *Lodsen og hans hustru* (1874; Eng. tr. *The Pilot and His Wife,* 1876). Their architecture is much more disciplined; the narrative is made to flow more smoothly; the detail is more concerned with daily living in a defined community. In the former novel, commercial practices and business ethics come in for special scrutiny; in the latter, it was seafaring life that provided the narrative with its mise-en-scène. Always, however—here as elsewhere in his novels of this pe-riod—the realistic detail was "poetically mirrored," as Lie himself was anx-ious to insist. This feel for the highly charged significance of otherwise pos-sibly trivial detail, a quality that has led some to call his realism "impressionistic," continued to inform his novels of the next few years. It is to be found in the admittedly rather second-rank novels *Thomas Ross* (1878) and *Adam Schrader* (1879), and, rather more effectively, in *Rutland* (1880), in which the themes of the sea and married love are deftly fused. As always when Lie is at his best, the inner landscape of the mind and the external land-scape (or seascape) of the setting symbolically and mutually sustain and re-inforce each other: "The reader must be brought to understand the particu-lar mental state of the hero," Lie insisted; "it is this that the various images serve" (letter to his publisher, F. V. Hegel, November 15, 1870).

Lie, who had earlier acquired a taste for foreign living from a three-year sojourn in Italy in the early 1870s, left Norway in 1878 and remained abroad for the next twenty-eight years: first in Germany and Austria (Stuttgart, Dresden, Berchtesgaden) and from 1882 until 1906 in Paris. Here he found it easier to broaden his horizons and to respond with enthusiasm to some of the exciting ideas of the age; his correspondence of these years bears eloquent witness to the new impulses, the "bubbling fermentation," he felt within him. Having deliberately held himself aloof in those earlier years of his authorship from the tempestuous social debates of the age, taking pride in being of his contemporaries one of the least programmatical, he now found a new zest in commitment: to "problems," to social reform, to popular enlightenment. Ibsen's *Gengangere,* when it appeared in 1881, made an enormous impression on him; he won much greater insight into the significance of Georg Brandes's activist endeavors in literature and criticism; he began to revise his earlier ideas about the role of the artist in society and the wider responsibilities of the writer.

Yet his commitment was tempered by a controlled detachment, characteristic of Lie's general style. The encoded strictures in his next novel, *Gaa paa!* (1882; Go Ahead!), on the theme of stagnation and renewal in Norwegian society, on the conflict between youth and age and the resistance of conservatism to reform, are for some so oblique as to require a quite sophisticated exegesis. *Livsslaven* (1883; Eng. tr. *One of Life's Slaves,* 1895) is, by contrast, much more direct in its strategies, much more Zola-like in its depiction of working-class life, much more outspoken about the class struggle, and much more explicit about what Lie defined as the "explosive material" in society.

The same year saw the publication of what is generally regarded as Lie's masterpiece: *Familjen paa Gilje* (1883; Eng. tr. *The Family at Gilje,* 1920). Ostensibly a descriptive period piece—it carries the subtitle "Et Interieur fra Firtiaarene" (An Interior from the Forties)—it has a powerful undercurrent of contemporary social criticism within its precisely observed and coolly recorded details of life in a small mountain community earlier in the century. The position of women in marriage and society, the ways of established authority, and the dead hand of convention are all examined in a fashion that is deliberately low-key and typical of Lie's detached commitment. Too low-key, indeed, for many of his contemporaries, who (like Kielland) failed to understand why the author had not been more outspokenly condemnatory, had not "exposed the gluttonous, guzzling officials as the fathers of the present-day ones" (see Georg Brandes, *Brevveksling,* 4:354).

Before the decade was out, Lie had published a further four novels, bringing his tally for the eighties to eight. They all contributed significantly, by their narrative style as well as by their thematic preoccupations, to the concept of an "eighties literature" in Norway: a concern for social issues, an honesty of vision, an attention to precise detail, a tendency to didacticism, a quickness to point up the moral values inherent in quotidian event and circumstance, particularly as they bore on the relationship between men and women. In *En malstrøm* (1884; A Maelstrom)—for which Lie at one time proposed the title "Children of Drunkenness"—the central problem is alcoholism and its consequences for a one-time prosperous family. Similarly, the very title of *Kommandørens døtre* (1886; Eng. tr. *The Commodore's Daughters,* 1892), making as it does an undisguised reference to Camilla Collett's classic feminist novel *Amtmandens døttre* of earlier years, immediately declares its allegiance to a liberal and progressive philosophy of life and announces its concern with what Lie on this occasion called "the finest and healthiest struggle we have: women's rights." There is a further possible literary allusion, and with it an index of its didactic purposes, in the title of Lie's next novel, *Et samliv* (1887; A Life Together); it echoes Nora's reverberant curtain line in *Et dukkehjem,* as she slams the door on what to her has proved to be a hollow relationship: "so that our life together would become a real marriage." The tensions that beset a loveless marriage, the jealousies and incompatibilities, the possessiveness, and the problems of communication between the partners are explored here with understanding and sensitivity. *Maisa Jons* (1889) is an attempt to address the problems facing a young working-class woman in the big city, who by virtue of her occupation of seamstress swings between her own life of domestic poverty and the high living of those in whose houses she plies her trade. Lie recognized the challenge of this book and faced it squarely: the need to enter into the life, the attitudes and feelings, and the very language of a working woman to present it from within honestly and unsentimentally. He himself was not displeased with the results.

With the publication of *Onde magter* (1890; Evil Powers), a distinct change is evident in Lie's authorship. One detects a new cynicism, a greater pessimism, a readier awareness of the darker forces at work in the individual—forces not always for good. He wrote to a friend: "I began to *see* people for what they are, . . . previously I had taken them for what they gave themselves out to be. I well knew that there was envy in the world, and meanness and such like, but they were evil and remote things; then I discovered they are quite close at hand. I saw envy cross my own threshold, and realized that it was to be found in the best of people—in me, in you, in everyone." *Onde magter,* in part a reproach to Bjørnson, with whom he had recently quarreled, was the first and most direct manifestation of this new realization: a study of the ways in which envy, suspicion, and the compulsions of ambition can invade and destroy friendship. These insights then opened his eyes to a new dimension of meaning to the traditional troll of folklore, that creation of Norwegian folktale and legend, in which Lie found a useful correlative for the darker forces that inhabit the mind and the soul. The introduction to his two-volume collection of shorter pieces, entitled *Trold* (1891–92; Trolls; Eng. tr. *Weird Tales from Northern Seas,* 1893), points up this extended significance: "There are trolls in people," Lie insisted there, and not only of the more traditional and primitive kind—like superstition, fear of the supernatural, and dread—but also of a more sophisticated nature which reside in the psyche: drives and urges and impulses and compulsions that are only too obviously part of modern, "civilized" living. *Trold,* therefore, while using the mold of the folktale, nevertheless intentionally functions at two levels: the one, primitive magic and nature mysticism, and the other, psychological and symbolic complexity.

Four more of Lie's novels appeared before the turn of the century and continued his exploration of the various facets of this view of life. *Niobe* (1893; Eng. tr. 1897) looks at the stresses in contemporary life between parents and children, between a long-suffering older generation and the age's dilettante youth, in a demonstration of how it can end in death, in imprisonment, and in multiple self-destruction of a startlingly violent kind. *Naar sol gaar ned* (1895; When the Sun Goes Down) again, as the title intimates, takes the perspective of an older man in assessing contemporary living and finds unholy consequences in the irresponsible adoption of "modern" standards and values. *Dyre Rein,* the most assured of the novels of this group, added a further and very effective narrative dimension: the fact of the protagonist's self-consciousness and self-knowledge within the events as they occur. By tracing the hero's own awareness of the darker psychic forces within himself and recording the onset of personal tragedy that follows from this very awareness, this novel took Lie's narrative art an important step further. Finally, *Faste Forland* (1899) is a slighter work, in part a rather ironic self-portrait, about the perils of financial speculation and the demoralizing effect it can have on individual integrity.

It was left to one of Lie's last and most powerful novels, *Naar jerntæppet falder* (1901; When the Iron Curtain Falls), to emphasize the cathartic and therapeutic value of withstanding the stress of these dark inner forces and winning. A group of passengers on an Atlantic steamer suddenly hears in midocean that an infernal machine planted on the ship will blow them up within the hour; in such circumstances, a kind of shorthand definition for any serious crisis with which life might confront the individual, each person is made to show his self-control or lack of it. When it is later discovered that the whole thing has been a false alarm, each individual passenger sees himself and his fellows in a much clearer light.

It is probable that Lie learned much in matters of narrative technique from Gustave Flaubert; he was also impressed by Emile Zola. Lie's name is often coupled with that of Charles Dickens, but it is perhaps with the Austrian Adalbert Stifter that the affinities are closest. They have much in common, both in the "poetic realism" of their art as well as in their attitude to life. It is their shared belief that passionate and intemperate behavior, the loss of self-control, pose an unrelenting threat to human happiness. Stifter stated, "We all have tigerlike proclivities." And Lie wrote in a letter to Hegel (April 15, 1880), "Passion, this wild beast within man, breaks out the moment he least expects it. To win the moral struggle, to emerge from the fires of passion cleansed and purged, is to achieve life's greatest victory."

Kristian Elster, père

A lesser talent, but one that made its own distinctive contribution to the annals of the day, was that of Kristian Elster, *père* (1841–81). Elster died when only forty; his literary production during his lifetime was of modest compass, though already he was being recognized as a man of genuine promise. The posthumous publication of his novel *Farlige folk* (1881; Dangerous People) shortly after his death from pneumonia on April 11, 1881, aroused immediate attention in his native Norway, and it was translated into Swedish three years later by no less a person than Gustaf af Geijerstam.

Elster brought a touch of internationalism into what was perhaps in danger of becoming a rather inbred literary scene. He spent some years in Germany while seeking to qualify himself in forestry, and his enthusiasm for certain features of German regional writing prompted him later to translate Berthold Auerbach and Fritz Reuter. His greatest enthusiasm was reserved for Ivan Turgenev, however, whom he also translated.

As a nineteen-year-old, Elster first tried his hand at literary composition with a saga drama, which was accepted by the Christiania Theater only to be withdrawn by its author, one of many acts of irresolution that occurred at key moments in his life in consequence of his crippling lack of self-confidence. A second saga drama, *Eystein Meyla* (1863), was also accepted for production and this time even performed, but it was not well received. Nevertheless, Elster succeeded in catching the approving eye of Bjørnson, who was convinced that the young man had a future as a writer.

When, after some time abroad, Elster returned to Christiania, it was essentially as a literary critic, book reviewer, journalist and commentator; and it is among the fugitive pieces written in these roles that the clearest impression can be obtained of the qualities he expected of the literature of the day: good writing had to give priority to truth and honesty and precision rather than lend itself to the elegant generalizations of the older school. Here too one finds his comments on some of the leading topics of the current debate: the character of pietism, the merits of peasant culture as compared with city values, the language question, and the folk high school movement. There are rich pickings here for anyone today seeking an entry into the intellectual climate of the age.

Two novellas, "En korsgang" (1871; Penitential Journey) and the more substantial *Solskyer* (1877; Sun Clouds), the former a peasant tale set in western Norway and the latter a moving but structurally implausible piece, first reached the public through the medium of periodical publication. *Solskyer* adopts a rather inappropriate epistolary form, purporting to be "letters from a country doctor to his friend," presumably so that Elster can sustain a kind of first-person confessional idiom; but the writer's capacity for total recall and his ability to reproduce long conversations verbatim (even on occasions when he was not present!) strains credulity. Elster's supple descriptive prose is, however, a delight to read.

His novel *Tora Trondal* (1879), his only work to appear in book form in his lifetime, is a composition of three carefully juxtaposed characters: the eponymous heroine, a disappointed dreamer, set—it is often suggested, in the manner of Turgenev—between two very different types of men, one a weary, moody, overcultivated aesthete and the other a man of action with a social conscience. It was the quality of the debate among the participants, who are skillfully prevented from seeming to be mere mouthpieces for a line of argument, which gave the work a large part of its contemporary appeal. The figure of the ironic aesthete appears once again in the shorter and well-resolved narrative piece *En fremmed fugl* (1881; A Strange Bird), in which an argument in favor of a more responsible commitment to life is deftly presented.

Elster's major work is without doubt *Farlige folk*. The mix of characters was clearly selected with meticulous care, ranging from the patrician and merchant classes, professionals, and officials down to the peasants, fishermen, and workers. The hero, the doctor Knut Holt, brings a breath of the great world outside when he returns (not unlike Lona Hessel in Ibsen's *Samfundets støtter*) to his native village after a long period abroad. He arrives with a new outlook on life and a new vocabulary (which includes terms such as "proletariat" and "capitalist") and is impatient with those who seek cautious liberal solutions to life's problems. The "dangerous people" of the title are those of the left who pose a threat to the entrenched privileges of those in possession of wealth or authority and who support the striking workers and sow dissension with their radical talk of class warfare. Once again, however, for Elster, the problems of narrative structure, of how to organize a plot, to direct an action, gave him greatest difficulty; and the highly melodramatic climax—with the implausible intervention of an old flame (the "Pampas Woman") from South America—seriously detracts from the artistic worth of the novel. Nevertheless, it was a work of burning actuality in its day which still, more than a century later, is impressive for the sincerity of its author's social conscience.

Alexander Kielland

It is hard to think of Alexander Kielland (1849–1906) other than as a kind of eighties concentrate. Most obviously, in the straight chronological sense: his first major work appeared in 1880, his last in 1891. Into this relatively brief span he managed to pack nine novels, three plays, and a clutch of short stories, after which, at the age of forty-two, he virtually abandoned imaginative writing; he died at the age of 57. Second, and equally obviously, in a thematic sense: his works brought the major preoccupations of the decade—the sense of social concern, the moral outrage prompted by so many contemporary institutions and practices, the struggle for individual integrity—into sharp focus. And third, though possibly more elusively, in a stylistic sense: the elegant irony, the mordant satire, the brilliant wit, the controlled form.

Born on February 18, 1849, into a wealthy Stavanger family, Kielland began by taking a law degree, marrying at the age of twenty-three, and seeming to settle down and manage a brickworks. He then became ruefully aware that all he was fit for was "to tell jokes, play the flute, and fish for salmon." In 1878 he cut free and left for Paris, where he remained resident for some months. It was here that he met Bjørnson and here that his first short stories were written. For most of his life he lived in Stavanger, except for two longer periods abroad in Copenhagen (1881–83) and in Paris (1886–88), and in 1892 he became mayor of the town. In 1902 he moved to Molde, where he held the position of district governor. He died in Bergen on April 6, 1906.

Although Kielland's final reputation is that of a novelist, his first published work was a play, *Paa hjemveien* (1878; On the Way Home), which appeared in the periodical *Nyt norsk tidsskrift* (New Norwegian Periodical). It was followed the next year, through the good offices of Bjørnson, by his first independently published book: a collection of short stories, for the most part written in Paris, with the title *Novelletter* (1879; Short Stories: Eng. tr. *Tales of Two Countries*, 1891). With their quiet wit and their elegance of style, they made an immediate impact; and Kielland, who clearly at this stage found the short-story form congenial, quickly followed them up with a second collection entitled *Nye novelletter* (1880; New Short Stories; Eng. tr. *Tales of Two Countries*, 1891).

His first novel, *Garman & Worse* (1880; Eng. tr. 1885), was begun at the encouragement of Georg Brandes, who had urged him to try the longer narrative form. It was an immediate public success, and posterity tends to accept it as Kielland's masterpiece. Located in his native Stavanger, the eponymous firm of merchants which serves as the focus of the narrative is a sort of thinly disguised "Kielland & Son" (as he put it in a letter to Edvard Brandes), with many of the characters modeled on members of his own family. The detailing in the book was thus the result of intimate familiarity and incorporated much personal recollection. But the most distinctive thing about the novel in its own day was the sharpness of its social comment, its account of the struggle of sensitive minds for survival in a ruthless commercial world, and the bitterness of the conflicts between youth and age, rich and poor, integrity and authority. It is a novel that clearly betrays Kielland's contempt for the kind of narrative realism that prided itself on dispassionate and objective description, that kept itself in check, that held back from taking sides: "I light a bonfire in the middle, as it were, in which I want to burn some social evil or other; and round this are grouped a flock of characters upon whom the gleams of the fire fall more or less strongly, but always only with illumination from the fire" (letter to Georg Brandes, November 6, 1884).

With his next novel, *Arbeidsfolk* (1881; Workers), Kielland sought to intensify the polemic but only succeeded in making it cruder. His assault on the corrupt ways of bureaucracy, the arrogance of the jack-in-office, and the social evils that follow is carried by a plot in which implausibility vies with sentimentality for control. To call it Dickensian, as some who were impressed by the wealth of minor characterization have done, is to flatter it rather than define it; Brandes said that it reminded him of William Makepeace Thackeray and urged its author to address himself rather to Flaubert as a model, to concentrate on fewer characters and show them in greater depth.

Indignation continued to fuel a succession of works—indignation at the deceits of public life, at the hypocrisies of institutionalized religion, at the reactionary ruthlessness of those in authority, at the duplicities of capitalism. *Else* (1881; Eng. tr. *Elsie: a Christmas Story*, 1894), a slighter, more disciplined, and more effective work than its immediate predecessor, took as its target the smug self-satisfaction of the well-to-do; *Skipper Worse* (1882; Eng. tr. 1885), which explored the earlier history of the firm of Garman & Worse, returned to the attack on the world of officialdom against the background of the religious movement known as Haugeanism; and *To novelletter fra Danmark* (1882; Two Short Stories from Denmark; Eng. tr. in *Norse Tales and Sketches,* 1896) takes issue with "the crime they call wealth."

His next two novels form a pair: *Gift* (1883; Poison) and *Fortuna* (1884; Eng. tr. of both in *Professor Lovdahl,* 1904). They follow the fortunes of Abraham Løvdahl, whom the author described as his own "unhappy doppelgänger," from childhood up through the iniquities of the contemporary grammar school system and on to his later business career and the dubious morality of the marketplace. But although the two qualities one had now come to expect from a Kielland novel—the sharp social criticism and the careful realistic description of the Stavanger milieu—were still conspicuously present, there was now a newer element: a firm and assured psychological treatment of the hero as he suffers under the constant inner conflict of his two inherited natures, one from his father and the other from his mother.

The two novels that followed similarly have much in common: *Sne* (1886; Eng. tr. *Snow,* 1887) and *Sankt Hans fest* (1887; Midsummer Festival). They both addressed themselves to various aspects of religious bigotry and hypocrisy: the former to the ambiguous role played by the established church in the political struggles of 1884 between the monarchical right and the parties of the left; the latter, at a rather more parochial level, to the presumption of those low-church clerics who "think they have God in their pockets."

These were also the years in which Kielland once again tried his hand at drama, something he had not attempted since publishing his three so-called dramatic *proverbes* under the title *For scenen* (1880; For the Stage). Although claiming to despise the drama form, he nevertheless wrote in successive years *Tre par* (1886; Eng. tr. *Three Couples,* 1917), *Bettys formynder* (1887; Betty's Guardian), and *Professoren* (1888; The Professor). They are all distinctly lightweight, poking fun at various aspects of contemporary life, though the last of the three succeeded in giving much offense in some quarters by its crude caricature of the Hegelian scholar M. J. Monrad.

In 1889 Kielland took over the editorship of the local Stavanger newspaper, using it as a vehicle for his left-wing political views. *Jacob* (1891) was destined to be his last novel. It must have impressed his readers—and indeed, himself—as all too predictable: the story of a country lad who comes to the big city and, beginning with petty thieving, works his way up to wealth, power, and authority by shady practices. It can only have reinforced his feeling that he had now written himself out. He wrote no more novels, though he continued a wide-ranging correspondence into which he put the best of his compositional skills and stylistic abilities. A last book, *Omkring Napoleon* (1905; Eng. tr. *Napoleon's Men and Methods*, 1907), was a modest monument to his historical interests in later life.

Kielland rightly ranks as a great stylist. His is a preeminently "literary" style, a sophisticated blending of many disparate elements culled from his wide reading in European literature and thought, of which only those who consult his letters—in themselves a major component of his total authorship and admirably readable—can have a full sense. Undertaken partly under the tutelage of Georg Brandes (himself surely the most systematically voracious book reader of the century), Kielland's eager reading of English, French, German, and Russian writers as well as those of his native Scandinavia nourished and shaped his own narrative artistry. France beckoned when he first seriously began to contemplate a writer's career; and when Brandes criticized one of his earlier works as being "too English," Kielland replied that he "would ten times rather bear French arms"; an early enthusiasm for Flaubert and the brothers Goncourt led ultimately to a profound (though qualified) admiration for Zola. He gave close study to Darwin, found much to stimulate him in Herbert Spenser, devoured the works of Mill—"You must read the *whole* of Stuart Mill," he counseled his sister in 1880—and read Dickens avidly. He discovered a close sense of affinity with Heine's irony and later admitted in a letter to Georg Brandes (August 11, 1891): "I admire him in a way and to a degree I have never confessed to anyone—I think from a kind of envy." He found much to respond to in Turgenev. But pride of place among these many literary influences must surely go to Søren Kierkegaard—"the author I have loved most," as he once said in a letter to George Brandes (January 2, 1880)—to whom Kielland turned time and time again for inspiration and whose uncompromising hostility to hypocrisy in all its forms served as a model.

His radicalism was the unusual product of a highly developed social conscience combined with a deep sense of guilt at the material well-being that had been his by the accident of birth. "The force that drives me and puts heat into my words," he wrote to his brother (January 31, 1982), "is a bad conscience, and the knowledge that I am personally so well off." It is here that one finds the reason why his novels, even at those moments when they seek to impress as being determinedly and objectively realistic, are profoundly subjective, and why much of the overt social criticism is nevertheless oblique self-criticism. In the last analysis, however, it might be argued (with corroboration from Kielland himself) that the real key to his authorship lies in his profound admiration for John Stuart Mill, something that he had in common with Georg Brandes; it was, he said in a letter to Edvard Brandes (April 8, 1881), a matter of great pride to him to have been an honest adherent of utilitarianism in his writing, and "you come down to this in the end if you want to write anything about me."

Amalie Skram

From the very beginning of her authorship, Amalie Skram (1846–1905) was confident of the essential difference between realism and naturalism. Reviewing Alexander Kielland's *Garman & Worse* in 1880, she designated Kielland a "realist" because (she claimed) he concerned himself simply with the *revealed* phenomena of existence: those aspects of life which were immediately and directly accessible to our sense perceptions, things that "stand in the light," whereas the naturalist writer was concerned with "subterranean anatomy," the identification of sources, the nature and extent of those factors that actually determine the course of events, the mechanics of cause and effect. Her phrases stand almost as a manifesto, defining an approach to literary composition which sustained her own writing throughout her creative career and which in consequence helped to determine the course of Norwegian literature for a whole generation.

To date, her achievement as a novelist has been evaluated at less than its true worth. But with the steady growth of interest over the last decades of the twentieth century in women's literature, Amalie Skram is now emerging in the general consciousness as a writer who made an important and unique contribution in this field. As a woman writing about women and their problems, bringing all her feminine insight to bear, and having experienced herself the particular constraints society imposed on women in this age, she and her work are rightly attracting renewed attention and a revised and much more appreciative assessment.

Before her first appearance in print in 1877, destiny had furnished Amalie Skram with a wealth of experience of life. Born into a lower middle-class family in Bergen on August 22, 1846, she was exposed at an early age to the stresses that accompany the aspirations of a family eager—doubtless, in this instance, excessively so—to improve its social status. Her father's bankruptcy in pursuit of these ambitions, followed by his abrupt departure for America in 1864, pressured her into marriage at the early age of eighteen to a ship's captain, a personable man some nine years her senior. For more than ten years she accompanied her husband on his voyages to distant parts of the world, including North and Latin America and Australia, giving her an enviably wide experience of the world and its ways. But despite their separate efforts, it became evident in time that their marriage was not destined to survive. Courageously (in that day and age), she determined to break free, a decision that brought her to the brink of a nervous breakdown. The marriage was eventually dissolved in 1882.

She had already enjoyed the company of a circle of radical artists and writers at her home in Bergen. She had also made her first tentative beginnings as an author, initially with a sensitive appreciation of J. P. Jacobsen's *Marie Grubbe*, followed in time by other critical pieces in the periodical press on contemporary authors: Ibsen, Bjørnson, Garborg, and others. Her first modest excursion into imaginative writing came with the publication in 1882 of a short story, "Madam Høiers lejefolk" (1882; Madame Høier's Renters).

A second marriage in 1884 to the Danish author Erik Skram brought her economic security and the opportunity to address herself more single-mindedly than before to her chosen vocation of writing. For the greater part of her later life she remained resident in Copenhagen or elsewhere in Denmark. (Her estrangement from her native Norway—the consequence of what she felt was a wounding lack of interest on the part of the country of her birth in her more mature authorship—was such that she subsequently disclaimed her Norwegian affiliations, requesting that her gravestone identify her as "A Danish citizen, a Danish subject, and a Danish author.")

Her first major work, a novel, was an immediate succès de scandale. *Constance Ring* (1885; Eng. tr. 1988), which the respected publishing house of Gyldendal felt compelled to reject because of its explicitly frank treatment of sexual matters (exacerbated by the fact that the author was a woman), in consequence had to find a private publisher. It appeared on the scene only shortly before the Christiania Boheme uproar (see "Hans Jæger and the Christiania Boheme," below) and greatly fueled public debate about the state of contemporary morals. It succeeded in polarizing even more sharply the current political arguments: the radicals, most vocal among them Arne Garborg, awarded it high praise, while it was received with cries of outrage by the conservatives, who characterized it as immoral. Addressing itself to the wider problems of love and marriage, to the tradition that kept women in ignorance of the realities of sex in advance of marriage, to the double standard of conduct in sexual matters for men and women, and to the deception on the part of men in the marital context which constituted a constant affront to the female partner, it represented a bold and courageous statement, made with all the authority of one who had had experience of such matters at close quarters. Garborg's description of it (*Nyt tidsskrift*, 1885)—"the profoundly sad story of a woman who, like all women and all human beings, is created to love but cannot"—has become standard. The work stands to-day as an uncompromising exposure of sexual mores in Norway in the eighties as seen from the woman's point of view.

In the same year her second excursion into short story form, "Karens jul" (1885; Eng. tr. "Karen's Christmas" in *Slaves of Love,* 1982), appeared in the Christmas pages of the Danish newspaper *Politiken* (Politics).

Skram then began a period of great productivity, maintaining over the next decade or so—in parallel, as it were—two distinct narrative objectives. On the one side she continued with a succession of erotic works, examining the social and psychological tensions, especially in a marital context, that she felt she needed to bring to the attention of the public. There is no doubt that in these works, particularly, she stood in strong empathetic relationship to her characters—"I weep my way through all my books," she once claimed in a letter to Bjørnson (1894)—and that writing, for her, involved a deeply se-rious commitment. Three novels and a play between 1888 and 1893 constitute a recognizable group: *Lucie* (1888) examines the incom-patibilities in a marriage between a one-time prostitute and a lawyer, and probes the man's class-ridden prejudices, which make him incapable of ap-preciating the fundamentally sterling qualities of his wife; *Fru Inès* (1981; Mrs. Inès), in which a deeply sensual Spanish woman is trapped in a loveless marriage that brings her no fulfillment, but when she seeks happiness with a young Englishman, she nevertheless finds that her hot-blooded nature only acts as a tragic barrier between them; *Forraadt* (1892; Eng. tr. *Betrayed,* 1987), which takes as its theme the marriage between a young innocent girl and an older experienced man; and, last in this group, the drama *Agnete* (1893), which in its (admittedly rather wooden) treatment of the man-woman relationship invites, but does not really merit, comparison with Ibsen's *Et dukkehjem.*

Of this group, *Forraadt* stands out as a work of genuine power and sub-tlety. The autobiographical cross-references are, of course, obvious: the girl is not yet eighteen, and the man is a sea captain of thirty. Her protracted ini-tiation into the hitherto unknown world of male sexuality, a world that she finds shocking and odious but which at the same time piques her curiosity, is described with an insight clearly deriving from firsthand experience. These novels offer an anatomy of marriage as she sees it. For women, she declared later in a letter to her husband, marriage is "in most cases a hell which they enter." Suffering is the inevitable accompaniment; and disaster, for one or both parties, the nearly inevitable culmination.

Throughout these years and until 1898 Skram was also at work on the se-ries of four novels that posterity tends to recognize as her greatest achievement and that collectively have been given the name *Hellemyrsfolket* (1887–98; The People of Hellemyr). This series is a comprehensive work with a broad epic sweep, tracing the history of a west coast family from the time of the 1820s and on through four generations. The account of the family's destiny begins with *Sjur Gabriel* (1887), the story of the miserably hard struggle for existence in a small fishing village just north of Bergen, where the land is poor, the fishing meager, and cheap brandy an ever-present temptation. The sequel, *To venner* (1887; Two Friends), came out the same year. It takes up the family history again in the 1850s and first follows the destinies of the children of the original couple as they seek and find work in Bergen, but then concentrates on one of the grandchildren, Sivert, and his early seafaring experiences. The third volume, *S. G. Myre* (1890), continues the history of Sivert as he tries to break free of his working-class origins and establish himself in a social milieu that is nevertheless determined to preserve its privileges. Finally, the fourth volume, *Afkom* (1898; Offspring), which appeared after a break of eight years, brings the family history up to the eighties. A fifth volume, to be called "Offspring of Offspring," never materialized. In sum, *Hellemyrsfolket* documents with a wealth of authentic detail the social history of these years and life as it was lived in certain contexts: at the level of extreme poverty, where misery is endured almost as though it were an inherited evil, and among the entrepreneurial class, with its often duplicitous ways. Everywhere there is an overriding sense of the vulnerability of individuals, so many of whom are defenseless against the economic and social forces ranged against them from without and the psychological compulsions from within.

The catalog of Skram's authorship must also make reference to three other publications of the nineties: a slim volume entitled *Børnefortællinger* (1890; Children's Stories), short pieces that (as one must always be careful to point out) are more *about* children, uniquely defenseless as they are in society, than *for* them; and two novels with a hospital setting: *Professor Hieronimus* (1895) and *Paa St. Jørgen* (1895; Eng. tr. *Under Observation,* 1992, contains both works), based largely on her own experiences of her stay in a mental hospital after a breakdown in 1894. These two works have tended to stand in the shadow of what was felt to be the "major" series, but the importance of their place in her oeuvre should not be overlooked: they are highly personal and indeed passionate statements about the nature of authority and the way it can sometimes (for example, in a mental hospital) be exercised. *Julehelg* (1900; Christmas Season) bears witness to her readiness in later years to turn to religion, after having broken emphatically with Christianity in earlier life; but as a novel it lacks the strength and rigor of her earlier work.

Toward the end of her life Skram returned, at one point in her correspondence, to the same basic conviction about life and writing that she had singled out (in her Kielland review) at the very outset of her career: the need to look at causes and not simply at effects. Evil, for her, she said, was a consequence of circumstance, an almost predictable result stemming from identifiable conditions. The compulsion to explore those causes—and the causes of those causes—is in fact her own dementia, her own magnificent obsession. She continued her letter: "If there was anything I wanted to achieve by what I have written, it was to get people to understand, to look, and to judge mildly."

Her naturalism was of the kind that sought to make its impact by the innate eloquence of what was recorded and not by the superimposition of authorial comment. Her work shows an extraordinarily sharp eye for detail. Her novels take us through a world of rich particulars: on land and on sea, in cottage and in mansion, in kitchen and parlor and byre, on festival days and at funerals. In the pages of her novels we find a fascinating inventory: of utensils and implements, of clothing and food and furniture and possessions. When she sends her characters to sea, the details are authentic as only they can be from extensive firsthand experience: the beauties and perils of the elements, the precise shipboard routines, the duties of officer and man, the excitements and the longueurs. Unvarnished objective chronicling is the technique that gives her work its power. Occasionally, her unrelenting adherence to the naturalistic tenets as they relate to heredity and environment strikes the reader as overassertive. But her stature in the history of Norwegian literature and especially her contribution to women's literature are now beyond dispute.

Arne Garborg

It is perhaps revealing that the three most powerful influences on Arne Garborg (1851–1924) in his formative years were dark: a repressed and unhappy childhood, a distaste for his own native district, and a deep sense of guilt at seeming to run away from his family responsibilities.

He was born on January 25, 1851, in the district of Jæren in South West Norway, a strangely flat, treeless landscape of sandbanks, shallow bays, and moorland bog from which Garborg as a young man escaped with a sense of release. In *Knudaheibrev* (1901); Knudahei Letters, chap. 1) he wrote, "Uglier and uglier it appeared to me the older I became. And without the least sigh I left it." In contrast to most other regional writers of the day, who derived much inspiration and strength from their sense of loyalty to their native parts, Garborg for long years felt bereft of any firm territorial allegiance—something that must surely have contributed to the sense of restlessness and rootlessness that accompanied him through life.

An initially happy childhood was all too soon invaded by gloom and oppressiveness when his father fell prey to religious mania and imposed a stern, even tyrannical, pietist regime on the household. Books, apart from the Bible, were forbidden; childhood games were discouraged; and even schooling was denied the boy for a period. His relationship with his father grew ever more complex and tormenting and ended only with the father's suicide when Garborg was nineteen.

His overwhelming desire to escape from these home circumstances was, however, in conflict with his duties and responsibilites as *odelsgut* (oldest son and heir to a farm) to remain and work the family smallholding. When he did eventually break free and leave for the city, it was with profound feelings of guilt, which never quite left him.

His life became a restless search for a system of beliefs and values which would give meaning to existence and serve as the basis for his own conduct. He went through many differing stages, passed through more than one personal crisis, embraced numerous causes, and contributed by his writings to many of the major controversies of the day, so much so that his work progressively and revealingly reflects the great number of ideological preoccupations and shifts in the public mind.

Coming to Christiania in 1873, he sustained himself through his studies by casual journalism, mainly of a polemical nature. His first novel, *Ein fritenkjar* (1878; A Freethinker), began to appear as a serial in 1878 and was eventually published in book form in 1881. In 1883 he published *Bondestudentar* (1883; Peasant Students), "that profound and serious book about Norway's poverty," as Georg Brandes called it. Written in landsmål (nynorsk), it addressed itself to the growing tension between the culture of the city and the ways of the valleys as experienced by that new phenomenon heralded by the title of the book: the peasant student at the university. The novel is remarkable not only for the finely observed naturalistic descriptions of life in Christiania in the 1870s but also for its assured handling of the psychological aspects of the hero's problems as he seeks to reconcile his countryman's values with the urban scene.

Garborg became ever more radical in his thinking, and he expressed himself forthrightly both in his published writing and in his private correspondence on the burning topics of the day: the religious controversies that centered on the clash of positivism, pietism, and Grundtvigianism; the so-called morality debates, especially those associated with the publication of Hans Jæger's *Fra Kristiania-bohêmen* (1885; From Christiania's Boheme); the place of women in society; and the threat to rural life and values from the spread of modern urban living.

Bondestudentar seemed to provide him with a congenial idiom with which to continue his novel writing; and both his next novels—*Mannfolk* (1886; Menfolk) and its feminine counterpart, *Hjaa ho Mor* (1890; Living with Mother)—take his naturalistic style to new extremes. Both novels were in their own way contributions to the great morality debate of the eighties, the former in its treatment of the sexual problems of young men in the face of poverty and social repression, and the latter in its examination of how modern conditions of living bear on a young girl seeking to preserve her respectability. Contrary perhaps to popular expectation, *Mannfolk* was not banned by the authorities as Christian Krohg's *Albertine* had been, but it was equally audacious and explicit in its treatment of sexual relations and equally condemnatory of the oppressive social conditions and conventions that made free and natural relationships impossible. *Hjaa ho Mor* shows Garborg's naturalistic technique at its most extended, and although the novel aroused relatively little attention in its native Norway, it enjoyed resounding success in Germany, where it was the third of Garborg's novels to be translated into German.

These were the years in which Garborg also had profound personal problems. He lost his job as state auditor in 1887; he suffered financial difficulties, and he also seemed unable to find any firm and lasting basis for a philosophy of life. He sought enlightenment from many different sources at this time: anarchism, Buddhism, Nietzscheanism, spiritualism. A happier interlude in this period is represented by his *Kolbotnbrev* (1890; Kolbotn Letters), written originally as contributions to a periodical from the cottage in the mountains where for eighteen months he lived with his newly wedded wife. In these letters he describes with ironic humor the small details of daily living, his reflections on life, and the varying moods of nature as he observed them.

Trætte mænd (1891; Weary Men), his next novel and probably his greatest popular success, marked a profound inner crisis of conscience. It was written in a spirit of Idealistic Reaction—Garborg's own term for what he felt was happening to him and to many of his contemporaries. Prompted in part by his reading of Nietzsche, in whom he recognized an implacable opponent of the modish "decadence," it served as a denunciation of those who pursued their libertine ways under the hypocritical guise of "free love," and it spoke out against an atheism and a materialism bereft of any spiritual value. Writing on this occasion in riksmål (bokmål), Garborg opted for a diary form of narrative; it traces the break-up of personality in one rendered progressively incapable of genuine emotion by his own unauthentic lifestyle and brought near destruction until finally he is able to find some measure of salvation in Christianity. The adoption of the diary form was inevitably interpreted as an invitation to read the work as the author's personal confession, as an announcement of his own conversion à la Joris Karl Huysmans, though Garborg denied this. In effect, however, this novel was a way of writing himself free of many of the beliefs and values to which he had himself earlier given allegiance.

With *Fred* (1892; Eng. tr. *Peace,* 1929), Garborg returned "home" in more than one sense: he moved back to Jæren to live; he gave his novel a specifically Jæren setting, and he incorporated into it much of the darkly remembered realities of his childhood home. The central character, Enok Hove, is clearly and admittedly modeled on Garborg's own father: a rough but fundamentally sincere peasant, loyal to the land and to the family tradition, in the grip of a religious fanaticism so totally at odds with these inherited values that he is destroyed by it. The almost inhuman compulsions of strict pietism, the inner torment felt by one who strives to obey but is haunted by inadequacy, means that only in the grave does he find the "peace" proclaimed by the title. The novel is written with deep sensitivity and with great insight into the manic mind of the central character. Some of the nature descriptions—of seascape and landscape—are passages of great virtuosity, carefully composed to reinforce and counterpoint the events that pass across the inner landscape of the mind.

Garborg was by temperament a natural intellectual. He was probably the most well read of Norwegian writers at this time and took some pains to try to keep himself abreast of the day's ideas. His contemporaries recognized in him a cosmopolitan spirit; one critic in 1894 called him the most "European" of the country's authors. He was one of the founders of the periodical *Syn og segn* (Seen and Heard), and to it he contributed a long article on Nietzsche in its first year of publication, in which he anticipated much of what only later came to be accepted truths. The same year he wrote a self-revealing article for *Samtiden,* "Troen på livet" (1895; Faith in Life), in which he points to the overriding need to affirm life, finding in this central belief the basis of "the *thinking* religion."

The more explicit treatment of religious themes begun by *Fred* remained predominant in Garborg's writing over the next two decades. In particular, three works that continue the chronicle of the Hove family pivot about the problem of the nature of true religion: the drama *Læraren* (1896; The

Teacher); *Den burtkomne faderen* (1899; Eng. tr. *The Lost Father,* 1920), a lyrical novel in diary form; and *Heimkomin son* (1908; The Son Returned), containing a collection of unconventional sermons on biblical texts. They were joined by other more philosophical works, such as *Jesus Messias* (1906), an outline of his own liberal theology, and *Den burtkomne Messias* (1907; The Lost Messiah), a rejoinder to those who criticized the former work. They all belong in essence to Garborg's continual striving to define what he felt the message of Christianity really was: an appeal to brotherhood and love.

Standing distinctively among these later works is the splendidly lyrical *Haugtussa* (1895; The Mound Elf), a poem cycle of some seventy pieces, in which Garborg set out to create a vision of an earlier unspoilt Jæren, of an age still untainted by pietism and capitalism and other modern evils. Taking its inspiration from folktale and folk song, it tells of Haugtussa, a simple maiden who nevertheless has visionary powers, and of her struggle with the trolls, that is, the darker, more elemental forces in life, and her ultimate victory, brought about by her simple goodness and virtue. Here the Jæren landscape is presented with an affection that testifies how triumphantly Garborg had by now overcome his earlier distaste. The limpid lyricism of the pieces, their sheer singability, has attracted the attention of more than one composer; and the well-known Grieg setting—an eight-song cycle known as "The Mountain Maid"—is one of the best-loved items in the repertoire. A modernized sequel entitled *I helheim* (1901; In Hell), in which Haugtussa visits the realm of the dead, has more overt contemporary allusiveness but is much inferior to its predecessor.

Garborg was a writer of unusual versatility: a novelist of power, an occasional dramatist, a lyric poet of haunting quality in the exquisite *Haugtussa,* a pamphleteer and polemicist, an able letter writer, a translator of Shakespeare and of Goethe's *Faust* and of the *Odyssey.* But essentially, it was Garborg's genius for becoming implicated in things and ideas which lends his work significance, and anyone who seeks to understand the controversies and cross-currents of this complex age will find much enlightenment in his work.

Other Writers of the Period

One figure prominent in the literary life of Norway and of Scandinavia at this time—though her renown derives perhaps more from the power of her personality and the rich eclecticism of her connections, both literary and otherwise, than from any high distinction in her work—was the writer Magdalena Thoresen (1819–1903). Born in Denmark, she came to Norway at the age of twenty-three after a somewhat tempestuous youth and early womanhood. Here she married a clergyman and settled in Bergen. Ibsen, recently appointed dramatic author to Ole Bull's theater there, was a not-infrequent visitor to her house and in time married her stepdaughter, Suzannah. (Much later in life, at a moment of marital tension, Ibsen in a letter to Suzannah described his mother-in-law as "that damned old sinner of a stepmother of yours.") When Bjørnson succeeded to Ibsen's job in the theater, Thoresen, now a widow, found herself passionately attracted to him. A year or two later she moved to Denmark, where she counted Georg Brandes among her friends. She is thought to have served as the model for several characters in the works of others: notably, for Ibsen's Rebecca West and Ellida Wangel and for Bjørnson's Maria Stuart and Leonarda.

Thoresen's own work is mostly written in a kind of Norwegian-flavored Danish, though the settings are generally Norwegian. It includes lyric poetry—*Digte af en dame* (1860; Poems by a Lady)—along with several volumes of peasant tales in the manner of Bjørnson—*Fortællinger* (1863; Tales), *Signes historie* (1864; The Story of Signe), *Solen i Siljedalen* (1868; The Sun in Siljedal), and *Nyere fortællinger* (1877; New Tales)—and two dramas—*Inden døre* (1877; Behind Doors) and *Kristofer Valkendorf og Hanseaterne* (1879; Kristofer Valkendorf and the Hanseatics). Her most engaging works are, however, those narratives in which she blends the factually descriptive with the imaginative: *Billeder fra vestkysten af Norge* (1872; Pictures from the West Coast of Norway) and *Billeder fra Midnatsolens land* (2 vols., 1884 and 1886; Pictures from the Land of the Midnight Sun). Her published letters are eminently readable.

It is the fate of Kristofer Janson (1841–1917) to be remembered today more readily for oblique reasons rather than for his more positive contributions to Norwegian letters. He is recognized as having been the model for Pastor Sang in Bjørnson's *Over ævne, I*, as well as for Ibsen's Hjalmar Ekdal, and he also served as the subject matter of an important article in 1888 by Knut Hamsun which was influential in launching a whole new literary movement.

Nevertheless it should not be forgotten that he was also a poet and novelist in his own right. In particular, his historical novels *Fraa dansketidi* (1875; From Our Time under Denmark)—written, like most of Janson's early work, in nynorsk—and *Vore bedsteforældre* (1882; Our Grandparents) were highly popular reading in their day, and in 1876 Janson, like only Bjørnson, Ibsen, and Lie before him, received a Norwegian state salary. But it was his unique contribution, at a most formative period, to the development of Norwegian-American cultural relations during his lifetime which most deserves acknowledgment. In 1879–80 he toured the midwestern states as a lecturer and described his experiences in *Amerikanske forholde* (1881; American Conditions). During a second visit to America he was accepted into the ministry of the American Unitarian Association, and for eleven years (1882 –93) he worked as a pastor to the Norwegian immigrant communities in and around Minneapolis. Knut Hamsun was resident for some months in his house in the spring and summer of 1884 and acted as a kind of secretary and assistant to him. During these years Janson was also active as a writer as well as a clergyman; a play (or what he called a "dramatized sermon"), *Helvedes børn* (1884), was translated into English and published in Chicago in 1885 as *Children of Hell*; he also wrote several novels, including *Præriens saga* (1885; The Saga of the Prairie), *Et arbeidsdyr* (1889; A Work Animal), and *Bag gardinet* (1889; Behind the Curtain), important works in the field of Norwegian-American literature. His memoirs, written some time after his return to Norway, *Hva jeg har oplevet* (1913; What I Have Experienced), are very revealing, both about himself and about the age in which he lived.

FROM THE EIGHTIES TO THE NEW CENTURY

Hans Jæger and the Christiania Boheme

In the one major work by which he became known to his contemporaries in the 1880s, the two-volume novel *Fra Kristiania-bohêmen* (1885; From Christiania's Boheme), Hans Jæger (1854–1910) offers an indirect description of himself as "a child of the future, prematurely born." It was a phrase at once both arrogant and defensive: on the one hand, a defiant declaration that he knew how "advanced" his views were, how very much ahead of their time; on the other, a sad acknowledgment that he felt misunderstood on all sides in his efforts to tell the unpalatable truth about the society he lived in.

In any event, it was the overreaction of a nervous Ministry of Justice which, by impounding his book and imprisoning its author, contrived for him the particular notoriety that has assured him a lasting place in the literary annals of the age. Shock and outrage were the ingredients from which his reputation was initially formed. But times *did* change, and social and moral attitudes with them. The growing permissiveness of the new century gave to his phrases a prescience of which he could hardly have been aware when he uttered them; modern sensibilities register only mild shock at his once-so-outrageous book, and it stands revealed as an earnest and prolix work of small literary value. By contrast, the novel trilogy he wrote in later life between the years 1893 and 1903 has won a measure of belated recognition.

Originally, Hans Jæger had planned a seagoing career for himself; he went to sea at the early age of fourteen, and four years later had already taken his master's ticket. But in 1875 he abandoned these plans, moved to Christiania, matriculated as a student, and at the same time took employment as a parliamentary clerk. He read avidly: in philosophy, especially Kant, Fichte, and Hegel; and in literature, where Zola became one of his main passions.

These were the years when the temperature of public debate rose dramatically in Norway, and works of literature on their appearance were judged as much by the nature of their contribution to the ideological discussion as they were for any literary excellence. Few areas of contention were exempt from literary scrutiny in these years: religion, the nature of Christianity, the role of the Church, the rights of women, class conflict, sexual morality, property and the law, politics, economic exploitation, and poverty. Bjørnson's *Redaktøren* and *En fallit* fired the opening shots in 1875 (the same year Jæger took up residence in Christiania) with their assault on the ethics of capitalism, the hypocrisies of politics, and the disadvantaged position of women in society. The year 1877 continued the cannonade: Bjørnson's drama *Kongen* and his novel *Magnhild* provoked a furious reaction from the public; and Ibsen entered the fray with *Samfundets støtter*, which tore down the facade of society's smug and self-satisfied respectability to reveal the dishonesties and pretensions on which that society rested. In 1879 women's rights were placed at the head of the literary agenda, with Ibsen's *Et dukkehjem*, Bjørnson's *Leonarda*, and the publication of a revised and augmented edition of Camilla Collett's *Amtmandens døttre*. As the seventies gave way to the eighties, the public debate became increasingly and explicitly sexual and showed a readiness to address problems in this area which had earlier been passed over with averted eyes. A peak was reached in 1881 with Ibsen's *Gengangere,* which generated perhaps the strongest shock waves ever registered by a work of literature in Norwegian society: in addition to the (by this time) predictable attacks on organized religion, the hollowness of bourgeois respectability, and the evils of the institution of marriage, Ibsen's play also embraced such themes as prostitution, cohabitation, extramarital sex, incest, and venereal disease.

Jæger's first major intervention in this heated atmosphere of debate came in the same year as *Gengangere*: in the autumn of 1881 he participated in a public meeting in the Workers' Association called to consider the growing problem of prostitution in the capital city. (Most of his speech was later imported verbatim into his novel *Fra Kristiania-bohêmen*.) His provocative remarks were widely reported and condemned as puerile, immature, ignorant, and cynical, and created much outrage in certain circles, particularly his assertion that monogamous marriage, by limiting a man to one intimate relationship when he had the capacity within him for twenty, cheated him of nineteen-twentieths of the content of his life. It was in the institution of marriage as currently in force that he found one of the root causes of the evil of prostitution: a social convention, reinforced by the law, which prevented "free love," the open and unfettered association of men and women in the pursuit of happiness. The other main cause was to be found in the shameful economic exploitation of women, which drove them to the streets simply to survive. Other public appearances added to his notoriety. In furtherance of his ideas, he also wrote two ineffectual dramas—*Olga* (1883) and *En intellektuell forførelse* (1884; An Intellectual Seduction)—works that rightly convinced him that drama was not his medium.

Fra Kristiania-bohêmen came the following year. He acknowledged in his preface that the book was "a monstrosity" in a double sense: as literature, because he knew he lacked any original literary talent; and as social comment, because he could not achieve what he wanted to achieve without writing "naturalistically" and thus inevitably giving offense: "Naturalism is—to define it briefly—deterministic literature. And determinism is based on the conviction that human beings, given the de facto conditions prevailing, cannot act otherwise than as they do. . . . Determinism insists that one can never with any moral justification hold an individual responsible for his actions."

In its intent, the novel is a work of conspicuous earnestness, a protracted indictment of contemporary society and its values and institutions. Its thesis is that the prevailing moral codes and behavioral patterns were such that they inevitably—"deterministically"—destroyed individual freedom and happiness, robbed people of their rightful inheritance, drained their natural energy, crippled their initiative, and corrupted their ideals. Jæger attempts to demonstrate this view by tracing the careers of the (largely autobiographical) Herman Eek and his friend Jarmann, both of whom are finally defeated by life. The novel became a repository for much material from the author's own life: recollections of incidents when he was a sailor, endless descriptions of sexual encounters with women of various kinds in various places, and the verbatim text of lectures he had once delivered, along with quotations from the press comment they had drawn. The whole was interspersed with passages of programmatic (and, it was alleged, occasionally blasphemous) argumentation about religion, philosophy, Darwinism, and other ideas of the day.

There is no gainsaying the sincerity with which these views were held, no doubting the passionate intensity of his beliefs, no disguising the contempt he felt for those who in his opinion were living furtive lives in a squalid world of untruth. The book was a deliberate exercise in social subversion. Redemption could come only with the adoption of a Bohemian lifestyle:

There is in our society a small group of people—most of them the sons of fine, upstanding parents—for whom modern society is a barren, dreary desert, where they can find no place to settle so that they merely wander, thirsting for life. This little group are the prematurely born children of the future, its first seed . . . with needs that can only be satisfied under some freer, richer, and finer form of society which it is the prerogative of the future to create—these are the exiled, homeless Bohemians.

One thing was certain, he declared: the numbers of the Boheme were growing; and could they but be brought to a clear understanding of the real situation in society, "they would all rise up as one man to fight a hard, sustained, and well-planned battle to undermine the three gigantic granite blocks holding up the old culture and the old society and all their poverty of spirit: Christianity, the moral code, and the old conception of the law." Alas, the fervor with which these views were held failed to be transmuted into any genuine literary passion. The pace of the book is slow, and its obsessively sexual preoccupations (once the original capacity to shock is diminished) become wearisome. Nevertheless, it retains a measure of historical significance as a work that marks a breakthrough in the frank and uninhibited treatment of sexual matters in literature.

Continuing trouble with the authorities in the years 1886 to 1888, with further fines and imprisonment, began to take its toll on Jæger, both physically and psychologically. Even more devastating, however, was the anguish of an unhappy love affair, in which he and the painter Christian Krohg were in competition for the same Bohemian woman—a triangle of sexual tension which lasted six weeks but which took Jæger most of the rest of his life to write himself free from. This he did in his trilogy of novels written between 1893 and 1903—*Syk kjærlihet* (1893; Sick Love), *Bekjendelser* (1902; Confessions), and *Fængsel og fortvilelse* (1903; Prison and Despair)—works that were virtually unknown to his contemporaries but which have now won a measure of belated recognition. Printed abroad in Paris, they were in their day banned throughout Scandinavia and in consequence sold not much more than a handful of copies; they had to wait for their reprinting in Norway in 1969 and 1970 to gain a wider circulation. Written in the first person, they are as much documentary autobiography as they are novels; the central character bears Jæger's own name, and there is no effort to disguise the real identity of the other two main characters. Letters, diary entries, and other items of "actuality" are incorporated, though the whole is nevertheless thoroughly *composed*. By their almost painfully honest and brutally frank descriptions of sex, its practices and perversions, these confessional revelations of a highly complex emotional life must have struck his contemporaries as being more suited to a work of clinical and psychological pathology than to what was generally thought of as literature; today's reader—the "future" for whom Jæger was perhaps deliberately writing—brings different criteria to bear and finds in these works a *document humain* of deep fascination. These novels directly engage the modern sensibility, and thus contribute to Jæger's literary status, in the kind of way the hitherto better-known *Fra Kristiania-bohêmen* no longer does.

The punitive actions of the authorities in banning *Fra Kristiania-bohêmen* and imprisoning its author provoked many at the time to vehement protest against what was seen as a denial of freedom of expression, a view that was reinforced when the novel *Albertine* (1886) by the painter Christian Krohg (1852–1925), Jæger's friend and fellow Bohemian, was similarly banned. Krohg was primarily a painter but also exercised a considerable influence on the literature of his day by his pen. Between 1886 and 1890 he edited a journal with the significant title of *Impressionisten* (The Impressionist), which appeared at irregular intervals, with Jæger as its most loyal, and most iconoclastic, contributor. The "Albertine" motif—the arrest by the authorities of an innocent girl who had been driven to prostitution—was one that Krohg had treated on canvas on several occasions. In its narrative treatment, Krohg gives a psychologically sensitive portrayal of the young girl, which drew the warm critical approval of Georg Brandes and other influential voices at the time. It was his one literary work with any claim to survival.

Much more a product of the Boheme than one of its shaping forces, Gabriel Finne (1866–99) might best be described as one of naturalism's epigones, with all the derivativeness of a second-generation adherent. He was (considering his early death at the age of thirty-three) a comparatively productive writer. His debut came in 1889 with a feebly constructed novel of Bohemian life entitled *Filosofen* (The Philosopher), which did little for his reputation. Everything else that he wrote belongs in time to the nineties but in spirit to the eighties: one collection of short stories, *Unge syndere* (1890; Young Sinners), which attracted attention more by its provocativeness than by its literary merit; seven novels, of which *Doktor Wangs børn* (1890; Dr. Wang's Children), *To damer* (1891; Two Ladies), *Rachel* (1895), and *I af-*

grunden (1898; In the Abyss) are probably the best; and four plays, of which perhaps only the one-act *Uglen* (1893; The Owl) is worth a second glance.

His view of naturalism, in both the phrases he used to define it and the way it took shape in his works, was strictly orthodox, if not to say crudely simple; the deterministic forces of heredity and environment, the helplessness of the individual—male contrasting with female—in the grip of inner drives and outer imperatives recur again and again as themes. Only perhaps in *Doktor Wangs børn*, which was given the accolade of a reissue in 1971, are there elements of genuine insight which lift this novel above the rest of Finne's work.

It was the novelist Peter Egge, writing in his memoirs apropos his one-time friend and colleague Arne Dybfest (1869–92), who remarked that the nineties were not propitious years for those young people who had become "spiritually aware." The eighties, he admitted, "had been crude and wild; yet they were confident and full of the joy of battle. The world was soon to be set to rights. Science was all-powerful. The disappointments that followed were great. This affected the young, who bore no blame for the bankruptcy. They grew weary and bored. Terms like 'decadent' and 'fin de siècle' were on everyone's lips. I heard them so often . . . they made me feel sick" (*Minner*, 1: 248).

Dybfest, whose life had been "blighted" (the term is Egge's) from birth, fell victim to the compulsions of decadence at an early age. As a very young man, he had—like his more famous contemporary, Knut Hamsun, before him—first tried and then rejected the life of the American Midwest. As a declared anarchist he wrote for some journals during his time there. He also visited Albert Parson (of the famous Haymarket Square riot) in prison in Chicago, an incident that figured in his first published book, which bore the defiant title of *Blandt anarkister* (1890; Among Anarchists), written after his return to Norway. In it, he proclaimed his political beliefs in terms of almost religious fervor.

For his next book, a novel, he turned rather to Nietzsche for his ideological framework and to decadent sex for his theme; *Ira* (1891) has as its eponymous heroine a one-eyed woman obsessed by her own sex drives; the variousness of her domination over the effete, introverted, and perverted Harry Mohr is dwelt on to the point of (almost literal) nausea. And yet, as Egge has rightly insisted, "the style has fire, music, beauty. The book . . . did have something unique to itself" (*Minner*, 1:206).

Dybfest's preoccupations show little change in his next—and last—book: *To noveller* (1892; Two Short Stories), published posthumously. One of these stories, "En ensom" (A Lonely Person), tells of a man who finds himself strangely attracted to an ugly and lonely middle-aged spinster, whose aroused passions find consummation in a climax in which death and sexuality are combined in an almost parodistically decadent fashion.

Dybfest himself died at the early age of twenty-three by drowning, whether by a sailing accident or by suicidal design can never be certain. His talent was clearly limited and his authorship flawed, but as one of the few Norwegian examples of European decadence he is perhaps not unworthy of some measure of attention.

Gunnar Heiberg

Toward the end of his life Gunnar Heiberg (1857–1929) published what he might well have suspected would be his last book. It was a selection of some of his essays, *Salt og sukker* (1924; Salt and Sugar), a title that could stand as the author's own wry assessment of the blend of qualities he felt his life's work presented. Acerbic, bitingly satirical, wickedly sarcastic when his indignation took command, he was at the same time possessed of a vision of love and passion and a faith in the potential for good in the individual which inform all that he wrote.

Although it is as a dramatist that Heiberg mainly features in the history of Norwegian literature, his contribution to the literature of his day was highly personal: he made his debut as a lyric poet, and a good third of his total authorship consisted of collections of essays, articles, and other studies. With hindsight, therefore, it is not surprising to note that when his dramatic style moved away from an early preoccupation with surface realism, it matured into a vehicle in which lyricism and the crisp, spare precision of the essayist are subtly compounded.

He was twenty-one and still a student when he first appeared in print with two poems: "Menneskets genesis" (1878; The Genesis of Mankind) in the pages of *Nyt norsk tidsskrift* and "En soirée dansante" (1878; An Evening Party with Dance) in an anonymous publication, the only other item in which was (improbably) a piece by Hans Jæger on Kant's philosophy. The former poem in particular was an astonishing personal declaration of faith, which nevertheless succeeded in giving great offense in conservative circles and to the university authorities. In urging a reinterpretation of the myth of the Creation and the Fall, whereby Cain is hailed as the personification of the free human spirit, Heiberg was declaring his loyalty to the radical beliefs of the Modern Breakthrough and (obliquely) giving expression to his admiration for Georg Brandes.

His first major work was, however, in dramatic form, and drama remained the main vehicle for his ideas on life and love over the next thirty years, in the course of which he wrote more than a dozen full-length works. Despite the forthrightness of its message, *Tante Ulrikke* (1884; Aunt Ulrikke) was the product of cautious endeavor and some uncertainty; Heiberg worked on it for three to four years, refining and revising, before he deemed it complete. It was then rejected by a fearful Christiania Theater; and although it was accepted for production by the theater in Bergen, Heiberg subsequently withdrew it. It takes as its central figure one of Norway's great women activists of these years, Aasta Hansteen (who had also served as a model for Lona Hessel in Ibsen's *Samfundets støtter*), and debates passionately and vehemently the current problems of social justice and the legitimate rights of the individual.

The same year as *Tante Ulrikke* was published, Heiberg was appointed artistic director of the National Theater in Bergen; he remained there from 1884 to 1888. His experience in this post was invaluable for his understanding of the practical and the more theatrical dimensions of drama, but the demands of the job were such as to preclude any thoughts of further dramatic composition for the time being.

The nineties represent the most productive period of Heiberg's career, and the dramas he wrote then trace an inner development away from the realistic problem play to a greater preoccupation with the psychologically oriented concerns of the new decade. Between 1890 and 1899 Heiberg wrote eight plays, ranging from satirical lampoons to impressionistic comedy, from the exploration of human sexuality to the exposure of political chicanery.

Kong Midas (1890; King Midas) is (it is often claimed) the most Heibergian of Heiberg's plays: not the most accomplished, but the one in which his natural talents were given their freest play. Essentially, it was an assault on those figures, public and private alike, who combine unshakable confidence in the rectitude of their beliefs with a sense of God-given compulsion to impose them on their fellows. The inspiration was in part literary—from the figure of Gregers Werle in Ibsen's *Vildanden*—but in the main drawn from the actuality of contemporary debate. Bjørnstjerne Bjørnson was unmistakably built into the main character—Ramseth, an editor—and so savagely lampooned that the Christiania Theater did not dare to accept the work for performance. Despite the threatened ire of Bjørnson, however, Copenhagen's Royal Theater performed the work, where it attracted great attention.

In these years Heiberg was hammering out his own distinctive style of dramatic dialogue. The earlier ponderousness is gone, and the tone often approaches banter; the communication of mood and feeling takes priority over the furtherance of action; events follow one another not in accordance with some rigid dramatic logic but loosely, associatively. This style is employed with great assurance in the next two plays, *Kunstnere* (1893; Artists) and *Gerts have* (1894; Gert's Garden); yet beyond the often seemingly throw-away dialogue, behind the lighthearted facade, one is made aware of a lurking serious reality.

Heiberg's next play, *Balkonen* (1894; Eng. tr. *The Balcony*, 1922), continues his exploration of the nature of love and passion but in a much more intense and deliberate manner than in the previous dramas. It offers homage to ecstasy; it sees passion and sexual fulfillment as the great imperatives of life, to be acknowledged and obeyed and given precedence over all social convention. In its formal structure, the play is highly stylized. Julie, a deeply passionate woman (reminiscent in many respects of Rita in Ibsen's *Lille Eyolf*), is seen in her successive relationships to three men: the first a calculating materialist, the second an ineffectual idealist, and the third a figure of primitive sexuality. The materialist is without understanding of the life of the senses and is repudiated by his wife; the man of culture and refinement can see passion only as a force hostile to what he considers civilized living: "it belongs to the dark, it steals from the intelligence, from the character, from the will." To allow the things that conventional society esteems—possessions, social and professional advancement, respectability—to prevail is "to civilize love out of your body," as she puts it. These values are irreconcilable with the deeper, darker instincts that drive her; she lives out her belief that fulfillment is achieved only by total surrender to the sovereign claims of Eros.

The complement to *Balkonen* came some ten years later with *Kjærlighedens tragedie* (1904; Eng. tr. *The Tragedy of Love*, 1921), probably Heiberg's most resolved play. In it he explores further the convoluted nature of erotic love in a domestic world of conflicting social and psychological forces. This time the mood is less exalted than in the earlier play, the dramatic conventions more realistic, the emotional fluctuations less extreme. Between the earlier and the later play came Heiberg's sensitive critical analysis of Ibsen's *Når vi døde vågner*, a study that sheds much light on Heiberg's intentions in writing *Kjærlighedens tragedie*. Central to the action once again is the tension between the all-demanding desires of a sensual woman and the more subdued, more temperate, more distracted love of her husband, whose conduct is dictated by mundane considerations. Unable to compromise, the wife takes her own life. This act prompts the comment from a somewhat Obstfelder-like observer of these events in the play: "Is it not more beautiful that love should kill rather than die?"

Heiberg's other plays of these years have a more time-bound message than these two distinctive plays of eroticism; they also tend to revert to a more realistic dramatic idiom and to a more direct concern with contemporary social and political problems, though the legitimate stance of the individual in the problematic situation is always clearly in focus. *Det store lod* (1895; The Big Lottery Prize) addresses the question of how the acquisition of sudden wealth can undermine and contaminate one's principles, in this case a workers' leader. *Folkeraadet* (1897; The People's Council) is a political satire, so heavily loaded with contemporary allusion that it is difficult for a latter-day reader to respond fully to it. *Harald Svans mor* (1899; Harald Svan's Mother) examines the problems of the daily press and the threats to the integrity of the individual journalist which are ever-present in the situation. Finally, *Kjærlighet til næsten* (1902; Love of One's Neighbor) is a comedy on the theme of unauthentic altruism, the way in which declarations of philanthropic intent and protestations of selfless dedication to truth and goodness can serve as merely a disguise for self-seeking and self-love. Heiberg continued in a political vein in his drama about the events of 1905, the dissolution of the union between Norway and Sweden, in *Jeg vil værge mit land* (1912; I Shall Defend My Country); it is instructive to read his volume of essays, entitled *1905* (1923), in connection with the play. Less well dramatically resolved is his last play, *Paradesengen* (1913; Bed of State), a somewhat impudent piece about the problems faced by the children of the great in living up to public expectations and prompted by the death of Bjørnson three years earlier.

His volumes of essays bear witness to a genuinely European mind. He spent a fair amount of his life abroad, in Copenhagen and other European cities and above all Paris. His *Pariserbreve* (1900; Letters from Paris) is a selection of his journalist reports to *Verdens Gang* (Way of the World) from the French capital about the Dreyfus affair; and *Franske visitter* (1919; French Visits) gives further evidence of his attachment to France. When he writes about the theater—in, for example, *Ibsen og Bjørnson på scenen* (1918; Ibsen and Bjørnson on the Stage) and *Norsk teater* (1920; Norwegian Theater)—he speaks with the authority of one who was directly and personally engaged.

Heiberg was virtually destined to be an epigone: after the great achievements of Ibsen and Bjørnson in the field of drama, it was inevitable that in the next generation there should be some falling away and that a great deal of what was written would be derivative. Heiberg was always ready to acknowledge Ibsen's greatness—in his speech on the occasion of Ibsen's seventieth birthday he thanked the great man for having taught Norwegians both how to respect and how to disrespect—and among his own generation he had no real rivals in the field of drama. But posterity has proved to be severely selective in picking those few of his works considered to be of lasting significance.

Sigbjørn Obstfelder and the Lyric Poetry of the Age

The reputation of Sigbjørn Obstfelder (1866–1900) for many years after his death suffered from what might be termed stereotypification. As perhaps no other, it was said, he incarnated the spirit of the fin de siècle. His life seemed an enactment of all that was characteristic of the age: a tormented search for meaning in existence at times brought him close to losing the balance of his mind and ultimately brought him to an untimely death from tuberculosis at the age of thirty-three at the very turn of the century. It was as though his soul, so closely attuned to the spirit of the age, could not endure the passing of the decade. Several writers, including Rilke, are suspected of having later used him as a model on which to base some fictional character representative of the age.

In chronological terms, his oeuvre, modest in size, exquisite in tone, belonged wholly to the decade of the nineties. His first volume of poems appeared in 1893; his last and incomplete piece of work was published posthumously in 1900. To the years between belong some plays and dramatic fragments, a novel and several shorter prose works, a group of compositions he called "poems in prose," and a large number of fugitive pieces, sketches, reminiscences, and articles.

More recent assessments of his achievement nevertheless see much more to admire than this obvious quality of typicality. He is recognized as having a uniquely fine though limited distinction. Despite his indebtedness in many ways to some of his near-contemporaries both inside and outside Scandinavia—to Maeterlinck, to Charles Baudelaire, to Walt Whitman—his originality of purpose and achievement is evident. His growing recognition as a modernist innovator, with his sensitive exploration of the potentialities of poetic form and the creatively experimental use of language in his endeavor to "say the unsayable," has awarded him a significance in the development of Norwegian and European modernism which had previously attracted less than its due attention.

Born in Stavanger on November 21, 1866, the seventh of sixteen children, Obstfelder gave early evidence of imaginative talent and a precocious skill with words. He entered the university as a student of philology but left himself free also to pursue his interests in music, literature, and philosophy. He was particularly strongly drawn to Kierkegaard.

Then, in 1888, there came one of those highly personal, perhaps even eccentric, decisions that arose from the clash within him of two powerful motivations: a feeling on the one hand that life required of him some effort to make a practical and material contribution to society; and on the other hand an intuitive sense that art—supremely in its most impractical form of music—was the vocation that lay closest to his own talents. In what must at the time have seemed like an act of stern self-discipline, he abandoned his arts course at the university, took up the study of civil engineering, and with his newly won technical qualifications emigrated to America to join his younger brother in 1890. But life in America—in Milwaukee at first, later in Washington Heights and Chicago—became a matter of disappointment and frustration. It swung the pendulum of his mind away from engineering and back to artistic ambition. He determined to return to Norway to devote himself to musical composition. But this inner conflict had left him weary and dispirited, and he suffered mental collapse.

This self-same inner conflict—between the practical and the imaginatively creative, between the imperatives of social betterment and the claims of individual fulfillment—remained with him throughout his life and found expression in many distinctive and idiosyncratic ways in his writing. After his breakdown he decided with quiet deliberation on a literary career, publishing his first poems in periodical form in 1892. But in the years that followed he also wrote many articles on the controversial questions of the day: on temperance, on problems of architecture, on the aesthetics of painting, on sexual morality, and—most especially—on the role and the rights of women in society.

After his literary debut in the pages of *Samtiden,* his verse collection *Digte* (1893; Poems) appeared the following year. It contains some thirty pieces, some of which had been written in America as early as 1890. It was to be his one and only published volume of verse.

Digte is filled with the brooding sense of one who feels isolated, alienated, and estranged from life, who is bewildered and sometimes fearful yet often overwhelmed by feelings of awe and joy. One (much-quoted) individual poem has established itself as the purest distillation of Obstfelder's attitude to life: "Jeg ser" (I See), with its images of empty facades, masklike faces, and threatening nature:

. . . .
So this is the earth.
So this is the home of mankind.
. . . .
I see, I see . . .

I must surely have come to some wrong planet!
It is so strange here . . .

These poems broke with traditional practice in several respects, nowhere more conspicuously than in their use of language. Rhyme in them is given a much lower priority than in traditional Norwegian poetry up to that time, and they favor loose rhythmical patterns at the expense of regular meter. This technique resulted in an audaciously reductive style. Extreme simplicity of phrase was clearly intended to startle the reader into attention, but there is no doubt that on occasion it approached perilously close to banality, which led some contemporary critics to dismiss his work as arrant nonsense, offering little more than "the fantasies of delirium."

In the earlier poems in this volume, words are clearly things that lend themselves to delighted manipulation: Obstfelder exults in their tonal qualities (e.g., "Regn" [Rain]), is excited by their rhythmical patterns (e.g., "Orkan" [Tempest]), delights in the shock of unusual word compounds and juxtapositions (e.g., "Vår" [Spring]), the counterpointing of the technological and the mystical. With time this exuberance in the use of words yielded to a profounder sense of their innate inadequacy. In anticipation of T. S. Eliot, he found himself regretting the inability of words to say anything other than what he was no longer concerned to say. His continuing efforts to find ways of nevertheless saying "det usigelige" (the unsayable) became one of his major obsessions.

The later poems in this volume begin to show a greater confidence of technique and possibly reflected a growing familiarity with French symbolist poetry. The themes become more somber, and death and decay become things of absorbing fascination (e.g., "Han sår" [He Sows], "Billet doux"). Woman in all her manifest roles—virgin, mother, comforter, goddess, whore, vampire—also is a recurring enigmatical factor in the poet's search for a faith, a set of values to live by, a philosophy of life.

Evident too is the shift of emphasis from a predominantly musical idiom to one that has more direct affinity with visual art, especially with painting. Many of these poems are verbalized landscape paintings (e.g., "Kval" [Torment], "Navnøs" [Nameless]), interiors (e.g., "Genre"), portraits. In an essay (1896) on Edvard Munch, Obstfelder considers the nature of Munch's genius in terms that reflect back revealingly on his own poems of this time. Permeating all these poems is a sense of the instability of the modern world, the lack of fixed points of reference, the loss of absolutes, the disconcerting speed of all things.

It was, however, probably in the form of the European modish prose poem that Obstfelder felt most completely at ease. What Baudelaire called the suppleness and flexibility of poetic prose, its power to accommodate the ebb and flow of waking and dreaming thought, allusive and associative, exerted a powerful appeal on Obstfelder. Again, his output in this genre was modest in size—only twenty-five pieces found their way into the *Samlede skrifter* (1917; Collected Works). They were never collected separately in book form, nor have they yet found an English translator. Nevertheless, among their number they include some pieces—for example, "Bugen" (The Belly) and "Byen" (The Town)—that are, in their nightmarish way, among the most haunting works Obstfelder ever wrote.

Such is the nature of Obstfelder's natural prose style that it would not be out of order to think of his other excursions into prose narrative, in the form of short story or novella, as being essentially extended prose poems. *To novelletter* (1895; Two Short Stories) and *Korset* (1896; The Cross) share the same quality of supple allusive prose that one finds in the best of his prose poems. The two stories in the former publication—"Liv" and "Sletten" (Eng. tr. "The Plain," 1982)—both explore the shifting moods and the inner anguish of haunted lovers. Here, perhaps for the first time in Obstfelder's authorship, the theme of erotic love is given close narrative analysis. *Korset*, the longest but arguably the least artistically resolved of Obstfelder's narrative works, continues without advancing this preoccupation.

Of Obstfelder's three dramas, it is charitable to suggest that they work best as book drama rather than on the stage. *De røde draaber* (1897; The Red Drops) and the two one-act plays "Om vaaren" (In Spring; written 1895–96, performed 1902) and "Esther" (written 1892, published 1899) can be taken as adding to the Maeterlinckean tradition of symbolist drama without making any original or lasting contribution.

The work that more than any other will ensure Obstfelder's position in the annals of European and world literature is one that his untimely death left unfinished: the novel in diary form *En præsts dagbog* (1900; Eng. tr. *A Priest's Diary*, 1987). Rilke described it as "the story of a soul who, in his despairing attempts to approach God, actually becomes more estranged from Him, a prey to an intellectual fever that brings him to despair" (Maurice Betz, *Rilke Vivant*, Paris 1937, 118). The priestly diarist is a man sustained by a conviction that within the chaotic and often menacing immediacy of life there lies some ordering explanation. His quest for meaning in existence drives him on compulsively to interrogate every experience and every sense impression, even though he knows he will emerge wounded from the ordeal. It stands today as a work of extreme honesty, full of the immediacy of experience, and remarkable as much for the delicacy of its recognitions as for the resonance of its courage.

At the age of sixty-eight, Nils Collett Vogt (1864–1937) looked back—in his autobiographical *Fra gutt til mann* (1932; From Boy to Man)—at his first published collection of poems, *Digte* (1887; Poems), and confessed that, were he ever to contemplate putting together a fully representative anthology of his poetry, only one of those early works would survive his critical scrutiny: "Var jeg blot en gran i skogen" (Were I but a Fir Tree in the Forest). In any event, this poem has become what is probably his best-known work. It is widely anthologized, learned by rote by generations of schoolchildren, and the object of much popular affection.

It can also now be seen as heralding much of what his later poetry was concerned to say, as well as typifying his personal mode of saying it. *Digte* was unusual in its day in at least two respects. The first and most obvious was that, in a decade in which drama and the novel were the genres that writers seemed to turn to most readily as those best suited to their socially oriented purposes, here was an author who chose to make his debut as a lyric poet; and in so doing he can now be seen as anticipating in some measure the changing sensibilities of the nineties. The second was the unexpected compounding it represented: on the one hand it was in intent as well as in content a radically socialist statement, an attempt on the part of the author to define his progressive aspirations as they had taken shape under the conservative pressures of his childhood and domestic upbringing; and on the other it was in format entirely traditional, employing a carefully metered, rhymed, and structured style that echoed the poet's personal enthusiasms—for Wergeland and Bjørnson, for Heinrich Heine, Lord Byron, and Percy Bysshe Shelley. This somewhat uneasy combination of form and content possibly bears some correlation to his anguished uncertainties. What, he repeatedly wonders, did the times intend for him? How, as "a child of one's age," does one resolve the conflicting pressures of the times into which one was born? These were questions to which "Var jeg blot en gran i skogen" was one of the tentative answers he essayed in this book; the questions persisted throughout his life and work to the very end.

The lyric continued to be the literary genre in which Vogt felt most at ease. In middle life, it is true, he turned briefly to the novel form and wrote two novels that took as their theme the conflict between the younger and older generations: *Familiens sorg* (1899; The Family's Sorrow) and *Harriet Blich* (1903). And in later life he also wrote a series of dramas, beginning with two pieces published under the joint title of *Spændte sind* (1910; Tense Minds); one of them, originally called *Ingrid*, was published later in a new version with the title *De skadeskudte* (1916; The Wounded Ones). He continued with *Moren* (1913; The Mother), *Therese* (1914), *Karneval* (1920; Carnival), and *Forbi er forbi* (1929; Past Is Past). But it is essentially as a lyric poet that Vogt achieved and still maintains his modest position in literary history. In the course of his career he published nine separate collections of poems, which fall in terms of chronology as well as by virtue of their overall style into two obvious groups. To the earlier belong (following the *Digte* of 1887) five publications: *Fra vaar til høst* (1894; From Spring to Autumn), *Musik og vaar* (1896; Music and Spring), *Det dyre brød* (1900; Dear Bread), *Fra Kristiania* (1904; From Christiania), and *Septemberbrand* (1907; September Fire). To the later group belong *Hjemkomst* (1917; Homecoming), *Ned fra bjerget* (1924; Down from the Mountain), and *Vind og bølge* (1927; Wind and Wave).

They show him to be above all a contemplative poet, pondering the uncertainty of being, the search for identity, the quest for life's purpose. And he affirms, as is evident even in many of the titles of his books, that it is in the first instance to natural phenomena that we turn when we seek answers to life's profounder mysteries: to wind and wave and mountain and sea and bird and forest as we perceive them in their seasonal progression. He is a poet of mood, of quiet feeling, of "stillness," a word that recurs again and again in his poems. He writes with special reverence of the quietude of autumn, though always with an acknowledgment—tacit or direct—that storm and gale present a constant threat, in the natural landscape as also in the landscape of the mind. As a contemplative poet, he shows a deep sense of place and writes with particular affection of streets and squares and other topographical features that have at some time meant much to him. He also, especially in *Det dyre brød* and *Septemberbrand*, reveals a rare talent for literary portraiture; and some of his poems about other writers of his own generation and earlier—on Vinje, Ibsen, Kielland, Amalie Skram, and others— may be counted among his finest pieces. Also deserving of special mention is the Cantata he wrote for the centenary celebrations in 1914 of the Constitution, and which was included in *Hjemkomst*. Two volumes of reminiscences, written in his late sixties, *Fra gutt til mann* and *Oplevelser* (1934; Experiences), give an insight into the nature of the man and the age in which he lived.

While still only nineteen years old and before even a word of his work had appeared in print, Vilhelm Krag (1871–1933) won instant public acclaim with his poem "Fandango" and was hailed as the prophet of a new movement in Norwegian literature. On October 25, 1890, his poem, presented to the Students' Association in Christiania in a public reading, was received with rapturous applause as the harbinger of a new literary epoch. The chord that it struck—and the musical imagery here is particularly appropriate—found an immediate response in the hearts of a public satiated with naturalism and its endlessly drab inventories of common life and its concern for "problems." The colorfulness of the poem's exotic Persian theme, the musicality of its language, the sensuous vibrancy of its imagery, its air of gentle melancholy and sweet sorrow made it a distinctly and almost polemically antinaturalist statement. It was only later that the reader of the poem on that occasion, the art historian Jens Thiis, proposed the term "neoromantic" to characterize it.

The immoderate expectations created by this startling debut were, however, less than triumphantly fulfilled. The volume of poems that Krag published the following year, *Digte* (1891; Poems), which included "Fandango," went some way toward confirming him as a poet of genuine sensitivity to the musical qualities of language; but the book can now be seen as containing much that was merely derivatively romantic. Little is there to sustain the notion that here was an innovative lyric genius speaking with a new authority.

Krag nevertheless persevered for some time in the same idiom with *Nat. Digte i prosa* (1892, Night. Poems in Prose) and *Sange fra Syden* (1893; Songs from the South): these works told of a world of dreams and visions, of weariness and longing, of the mystic and the exotic. But it perhaps betrays something of the direction in which Krag was moving that he was driven in the latter book to the admission: "I am so weary of these Pascha verses . . . of the vague melody of this sorrowfulness." It now reads almost like a confession on the author's part that his neoromantic vein was already exhausted even while he was still in his early twenties.

Krag's subsequent career was, in a quantitative sense, impressively productive. As early as 1893 he had turned to dramatic composition and by 1907 had published eight plays, of which nevertheless perhaps only one, *Baldevins bryllup* (1900; Baldevin's Wedding), has any lasting, though even then limited, value. He also soon turned to the novel form, and between 1895 and 1920 he published close to a score of novels, among them the somewhat sentimental *Lille Bodil* (1902; Little Bodil) and the comic *Major von Knarren og hans venner* (1906; Major von Knarren and His Friends). He also continued with great facility to write lyric poetry, and his later publications include *Nye digte* (1897; New Poems), *Vestlandsviser* (1898; Songs from the West Country), and *Viser og vers* (1919; Songs and Verses). In his later years he wrote four volumes of his reminiscences.

But these many publications progressively created for their author a very different reputation from that which "Fandango" had seemed to presage. Krag eventually found fulfillment in a quiet withdrawal into regionalism. He described with deep affection and quiet humor the life and people of that part of Norway where he was born and to which he gave his undying allegiance, and for which he personally created the term "Sørlandet"—the South Country. Its gentle landscape, its charming seascapes, its islands and its skerries, its wildlife, and above all its "characters" and their speech find— in admittedly somewhat idealized form—their deeply sympathetic chronicler in Vilhelm Krag.

Long classed as a mere camp follower of the Bohemian culture of the nineties, renowned as a femme fatale of legendary beauty, and notorious for her alleged promiscuity within the company of writers and artists to which she belonged, Dagny Juel (1867–1901) has nevertheless in recent years won from posterity a measure of recognition as a writer whose work, though modest in size, nevertheless spoke with a distinctive voice.

Born into comfortable circumstances, sensitive by nature, and well educated, she went at the age of twenty-six to Berlin to study music. There she fell in with the group of writers, artists, and intellectuals who used the tavern "Zum schwarzen Ferkel" as their meeting place. It was a cosmopolitan group that at various times included the Scandinavians August Strindberg, Edvard Munch, Bengt Lidforss, and Holger Drachmann, the German poet Richard Dehmel, and the tempestuous Pole Stanislav Przybyszewski (whom Juel soon married). Within this company she held erotic sway in her own inimitable fashion, and her transmuted presence is detectable still in the works of those who knew and enjoyed her and responded to her dynamic personality.

Juel also had literary ambitions on her own account. As early as 1893 she wrote a short story, "Rediviva" (published posthumously in 1977), a slight first-person tale of illicit love, of "psychic murder" (to use Strindberg's phrase), and of the spiritual torment it brings in its train for the woman concerned. But in its focus on the themes of erotic love and death, of inner torment and the vain search for happiness, it set a pattern for much of her later work.

Thereafter Dagny Juel turned away from prose narrative to try her hand at drama, lyric poetry, and prose poetry, though the chronological sequence of these works is uncertain. What is known is that she (unsuccessfully) submitted her drama *Den sterkere* (The Stronger) to the Christiania Theater in 1895, then had it accepted for publication in the periodical *Samtiden* in 1896. To invite (as by its choice of title it seems to do) comparison with Strindberg is merely grotesque, though there are derivative echoes of the master in the way in which it fastens on the nature of sexual attraction and its potential as an agent of domination in the relations between man and woman, in the battle between mind and mind. This work, together with the other plays she is known to have written in the course of the next year or two—*Ravnegård* (Ravenwood), *Synden* (The Sin), and *Når solen går ned* (When the Sun Goes Down)—are all explorations in a kind of Maeterlinckean idiom of woman's inner anguish within a triangular erotic situation. The last three works first saw print in Polish translation around the turn of the century, but they had to wait until 1978 for their Norwegian publication.

As a lyric poet she has flatteringly been called "the Camilla Collett of the Norwegian lyric," doubtless in acknowledgment of the specifically feminist quality of her work; others have seen an affinity rather with Obstfelder, one of whose short stories she translated into German and published in the German periodical *Pan*. Her *Digte* (Poems), written probably in the years 1896 and 1897, remained unpublished and virtually unknown until 1975, when it was printed in *Samtiden*. In these poems she reveals herself as the tormented victim of existential and sexual angst, a solitary and divided soul endlessly seeking the consummation that is forever denied her, the peace of mind that forever eludes her.

Like Obstfelder, she was also drawn to attempt the medium of the prose poem, perhaps the genre most congenial to her modest talents. The title of her one published work in this form—"Sing mir das Lied vom Leben und vom Tode" (Sing to Me the Song of Life and of Death; published in *Samtiden*, 1900)—suggests, however, that the more immediate inspiration in this instance was Richard Dehmel. Once again the dominant themes are those of death and sex, love and anguish, and the pity of living. Here, as in her other works, she speaks with the mannerisms but also with the authentic tones of the period, and the imaginative and tormented mind behind the poem is painfully evident.

Deserted in her last years by friends, assailed by ill health and depression, wearied by her husband's alcoholism and frequent marital infidelities, Juel met her own violent death by pistol shot in distant Tiflis in what may have been a suicide pact.

Other Writers of the Period

Many and various were the constituent elements compounded in the life and work of Per Sivle (1857–1904): the regional, the religious, the radical, the political, the patriotic, and others. Some of these elements sustained him through difficult periods of ill health and nervous depression until he capitulated in a final surrender to suicide at the age of forty-seven. Others he found strength in fighting himself free from: as when he shook off the oppressive pietism of his youth—which had prompted his earliest works, the epic poem *En digters drøm* (1878, under the pseudonym of Simon de Vita; A Poet's Dream) and his first *Digte* (1879; Poems)—and gave his new allegiance to radical left-wing politics.

Sivle represented in part a strange throwback to the ideals of the earlier national romanticism. Throughout his life he was fired with admiration and pride by the events of Norway's glorious past, and in some of his later poems he showed much ingenuity and skill in relating contemporary political issues to historical and legendary events of the past. In the same way, his patriotism—which had its roots deep in his love of his native Hordaland: its landscape, its people, its language, and its peasant culture—was at the more national level tempered by this continuing romantic overlay.

His authorship was modest in its proportions and uneven in quality. Much of it was deliberately addressed to a localized or regional readership and often deftly exploited the resources of dialect speech. His *Vossa-Stubba* (1887; Voss Fragments), a collection of short tales and other pieces put in the mouth of the local yarnspinner Kolbein Hausa, draws on his memories of a rural childhood and incorporates a sense of robust peasant humor; his later *Nye Vossa-stubbar* (1894; New Voss Fragments) and *Sivle-stubbar* (1895; Sivle Fragments) continue his delight in the tradition of the oral narrative. *Sogor* (1887; Tales) is more self-consciously wrought but is nevertheless revealing of the author's caring personality.

Sivle's one larger-scale work—the working-class novel *Streik* (1891; Strike)—shows him to be unequal to the structural demands of the longer narrative form; it lacks the disciplined cohesion that properly belongs to the novel and is best read as a loose concatenation of shorter stories and episodes. But the intensity of feeling that informs the novel, his passionate sympathy for the struggle of the workers against injustice and repression, is eloquent on every page; and it marks the start of a new tradition of working-class literature in Norway, placing its emphasis on social and political values rather than psychological insights.

Thereafter Sivle tended to turn more to the lyric as the literary form he found most congenial, and in the next few years he published five collections of verse: *Noreg* (1894; Norway), *Bersøglis- og andre viser* (1895; Bare Truth Songs and Other Songs), *Skaldemål* (1896; Skaldic Speech), *En fyrstikke og andre viser* (1898; A Match and Other Songs), and *Olavs-Kvæde* (1901; Olav Songs). Here again the quality of the individual poems is unequal: sentimental at times, florid even, nevertheless they can on occasion move the reader by the genuineness of their recognitions and the courage of their humane convictions.

"Scrupulousness" is the word that best describes the dominant quality of the work of Tryggve Andersen (1866–1920). He was the declared enemy of anything in literature—in his own work as in that of others—which he felt was in any way *løgnagtig*, that is, spurious or dishonest, whether in language, mood, historical detail, or any other element. He became one of the most accomplished short-story writers of his generation in Norway, though he was too meticulous a stylist and too self-critical an artist ever to achieve more than a quantitatively modest output.

As a young man he had aspirations for an academic career, and at the university he energetically pursued studies in Egyptology, a choice in tune with his own cast of mind. But he fell afoul of the authorities because of his involvement in a scandal and was rusticated for two years, after which he never returned to his studies. He made his literary debut in 1895 with a short story, "Den døde mand" (The Dead Man), a low-key study in the macabre; but it was his next piece that made his reputation with the public and has remained his best-known work: *I cancelliraadens dage* (1897; In the Days of the Chancery Councillor), set in the Napoleonic age and centered on village life as it was then in eastern Norway. In structure it was, however, more a cycle of short stories than the novel it proclaimed itself to be. In it he exhibited a severely disciplined style, unsentimental, with nothing "merely" confessional or self-revelatory.

A volume of poems the following year, *Digte* (1898; Poems), did little but demonstrate that metrical form was not really his métier, which may well explain why his next prose work, the novel *Mot kvæld* (1900; Toward Evening), was a deeply personal statement, as subjective as his earlier novel had been objective. Lacking facility in the lyric, he perhaps needed some manner of expression for what lay closest to his heart, and found it in this particular form; which may also explain why he himself called the work his best—and best-loved—book.

Thereafter he made the short story his preferred form. Four published collections constitute his main subsequent achievement: *Gamle folk* (1904; Old Folk; see "Den gylne hevn" ["Gilded Revenge"] in *Slaves of Love*, 1982); *Bispesønnen* (1907; The Bishop's Son); *Hjemfærd* (1913; Homeward Bound), and *Fabler og hændelser* (1915; Fables and Occurrences). His *Dagbok fra en sjøreise* (written 1902–3, published posthumously in 1923; Diary from a Voyage at Sea) is essentially a set of notes for a novel about the sea which never came to fruition. Throughout his life he remained a characteristically nineties figure, a neoromantic who would himself have welcomed the comparison with some of the larger figures of German romanticism, especially Novalis and E. T. A. Hoffmann.

The obituary for Nils Kjær (1870–1924) called him "the foremost writer in our language, the golden pen." The phrase would have delighted him. As an essayist—he himself came to prefer the Holbergian "epistle" to describe the literary genre within which he mainly operated—he clearly took immense pride in his ability to construct a well-turned phrase, to achieve a style both elegant and witty. And his supreme skill in this area has been widely acknowledged by both critics and the public. Yet behind the many self-deprecating phrases he used, one detects an unmistakable intellectual arrogance. Looking back over his career at the end of his life, he wrote: "I have been what the English in olden days called an 'Idler.' I have dashed off some little pieces about happy summers and happy islands, but my modest literary output was never designed to do more than provide me with my daily bread. I have therefore been able to lead a completely carefree life. I gave up the idea once and for all that I might 'go to the ant, and be wise.'"

He could, on this and many other occasions, be obsessively defensive; yet his words betray an eagerness to imply the existence of hidden reserves that he was simply too sluggardly, too indolent, to deploy. His own excursions into more imaginative writing, however, into the fields of the short story and of drama, called his bluff and exposed—to himself perhaps as well as to others—a hollowness, a creative vacuum at the center.

The high polish of his first selections of essays—*Essays. Fremmede forfattere* (1895; Essays: Foreign Authors), which gave evidence of his wide if eclectic reading, and *Bøger og billeder* (1898; Books and Pictures), the fruits of a period of residence in Italy—was evident. It was in these books that he laid the foundations for the graceful, allusive, and eminently readable prose style that he was to make so much his own.

His later volumes of essays—*I forbigaaende* (1903; In Passing), *Smaa epistler* (1908; Small Epistles), *Nye epistler* (1912; New Epistles), *Svundne somre* (1920; Vanished Summers), and *Siste epistler* (1924; Last Epistles)— became increasingly opinionated. Thus alongside pleasantly entertaining but essentially innocuous descriptive items of life and its ways in that part of the country he knew and loved (Sørlandet), there began to obtrude pieces of a more polemical kind, offering comment on the social and political and cultural problems of the day. These revealed Kjær as a great traditionalist, a highly conservative if not reactionary thinker, who in his later years was prepared to espouse anti-Semitism and Mussolini's fascism in phrases that make quite startling reading today.

Kjær also tried his skill as a short-story writer, in the collection entitled

Det evige savn (1907; The Eternal Loss), and as a dramatist. Of his four plays—*Regnskabets dag* (1902; Day of Reckoning), *Mimosas hjemkomst* (1907, Mimosa's Homecoming), *Det lykkelige valg* (1913; The Happy Choice/Election), and *For træet er der haab* (1917; For the Tree There Is Hope)—only *Det lykkelige valg* has retained its power to entertain a modern audience, even though some of the targets of its political satire—the temperance movement, the language conflict, and the women's rights movement—have with the passage of time shifted their ground somewhat.

The life story of Ragnhild Jølsen (1875–1908) in some ways resembles that of Dagny Juel: like her, Jølsen came from a comfortable middle-class home and was in her younger years very close to her father, whom she later disappointed by her unconventional lifestyle and her pursuit of sexual freedom. As also in the case of Juel, a woman's inner anguish is the subject of much of her writing, and she ended her life at the early age of thirty-three with an overdose of drugs. Nevertheless, Ragnhild Jølsen differed from Dagny Juel in gradually leaving behind her the ideas and manners of neo-romanticism and instead adopting the more objective mode of the new century. The region, the family tradition, and its financial failure all figured conspicuously in her writing. The language of her last works is as local and as everyday as that of Duun and Undset and marks an interesting transition to the new realism of the 1907 generation.

Jølsen was born and raised at Ekeberg at Enebak, an estate that had been in the family possession for centuries and where her father had more recently established a match factory. After her father's bankruptcy, the family moved to nearby Christiania, where she attended Nissen School for girls. Her teenage years were somewhat wayward even for this emancipated age, and she went through some quite tempestuous love affairs, being also for a time engaged to the writer Thomas Krag. At the age of twenty-one she returned with her parents to Enebak, and here she spent the rest of her short life, except for brief stays in Denmark, Germany, and Italy. Jølsen's first three novels, *Ves mor* (1903; Ve's Mother), *Rikka Gan* (1904), and *Fernanda Mona* (1905), are explorations of female psychology, modern in their emphasis on a powerful and unusual eroticism though showing something of the mannered and stilted style of the apprentice writer. Very different is the language of her two last novels, in which she draws on local folkloric material that she had collected at Enebak over many years. *Hollases krønike* (1906; Hollas's Chronicle), like Tryggve Andersen's *I Cancelliraadens dage*, is a collection of country tales set in times long past. The central figure, Hollas, brings to mind the evil character of Sintram in Selma Lagerlöf's *Gösta Berlings saga* (1890), while the use of dialect in the text shows a connection with the Norwegian *heimstaddikting* (regional literature), so popular at the turn of the century (as in the work of Jens Tvedt, Vetle Vislie, and others). Dialect is used even more extensively in Jølsen's last book, *Brukshistorier* (1907; Stories from the Factory), whose humor and contemporary idiom has made it the most popular of her works. In an article from 1964, the Norwegian writer Jens Bjørneboe claimed that after her visit to Italy "her language changed completely and for the first time she wrote pure Norwegian, without any trace of Danish chancelry style. And what she writes is not romantically 'felt from inside,' but the result of clear and incisive observation, sharp, ruthless, and full of humor. *Brukshistorier* is not Ragnhild Jølsen's most important book, but it is the best, the best written" (*Bøker og mennesker* [1979], p. 199). The title of one story, "Felelåten i engen" (The Fiddle Tune in the Meadow), recalls "Felen i vilde skogen" (The Fiddle in the Wild Forest) by Norway's greatest master of the short story, Hans E. Kinck (see below), whose art was clearly a great influence on Ragnhild Jølsen.

KNUT HAMSUN

For a novelist and writer recognized as supremely gifted in the art of precise observation, whose work is characterized by the most meticulous detailing of the minute and fleeting phenomena of the life of the mind and the ways of the individual, and whose ironic scrutiny of society and its ways is both sustained and penetrating, Knut Hamsun could on occasion be oddly slapdash when it came to recording the events of his own career. When, at the age of twenty-five, he recalled for the benefit of friends what he could remember of the outlines of his earlier life, he got quite a few things wrong. Nevertheless, what his hasty autobiographical note—indirectly and obliquely—manages to reveal of the nature of its author makes it a document of genuine significance. He began by getting the year of his birth wrong:

> Born 4 August 1860 [actually 1859] at Lom—or perhaps Vaage—in Gudbrandsdal at Garmostræet (smallholding). Father from Vaage, mother from Lom. Peder Pedersen and Thora Olsdatter. The middle one of 7 brothers and sisters. In '62 [actually 1863] my parents moved to Hammerø in Nordland, bought [actually rented] the farm at Hamsund. 5 brothers and two sisters [one of whom did not survive to adulthood]. Was in Nordland until 1873; went to Lom, confirmed there '74. Moved back home. Wrote some nonsense [a novel, *Den gaadefulde: En kjærlighedshistorie fra Nordland* (The Enigmatic Man). Af Kn. Pedersen, 1877] which was published in Tromsø. . . . In a shop

in Hammerø for one year. . . . Went to Vesteraal (cannot remember the year [1877]); was given a post as a deputy teacher in one of the fjords. Wrote some nonsense [a novel, *Bjørger. Fortælling af Knud Ped-ersen Hamsund*, 1878] which was published in Bodø. Next year a job as a clerk with the sheriff, serving as assistant sheriff. One year in this. Went '79 to Hardanger, wrote some nonsense [?] which was not pub-lished; went to Copenhagen with some different nonsense [the novel *Frida*, which was never published and the manuscript of which is pre-sumed lost] which Hegel [of the Gyldendal publishing house] wouldn't take, even though it was much better nonsense than my ear-lier work. Arrived impoverished in Christiania [in January 1880] with perhaps a hundred books and a couple of shirts. Remained in Chris-tiania some months, *had* to leave. . . . got work on the roads at Gjøvik. Was there a long time, God knows how long—I believe a couple of years.

These years were the time of rising "America fever" in Norway, and the young writer was not immune. His elder brother Peter had already settled in the Midwest, and as the emigration figures began to reach their peak in 1882, Hamsun saw a promising future for himself in the New World. Partly by borrowing, partly by cajolery, he organized a passage for himself and arrived in Wisconsin in February 1882. His autobiographical note continues in a way that is both summary and dismissive:

Was helped to get a ticket to America, went to America, worked on farms for some months, in shops a couple of years, on the prairie for a year, from there [in January 1884] to Minneapolis and to [Kristofer] Janson for a year [acting as his secretary], fell ill, got help to return home [in September 1884] to die, came to Valdres. Remained there two years, did not die, came to Christiania, wrote a little for the news-papers, starved horribly at times, was again helped to get a ticket to America, and once again I had to go over to America [arriving in Sep-tember 1886]. Again. I hated the country. Tram conductor for nine months in Chicago, traveled West, worked on the prairie another year, kept myself in Minneapolis by lectures at 10 cents a ticket.

Hamsun's hopes and aspirations during his second stay in America differed from what they had been on his first visit. Now the objective was to make what money he could, pay off his accumulated debts, and then establish himself back in Norway and pursue a regular literary career. The clipped phrases of his autobiographical note pay less than full credit to the active literary and cultural life he led in America during his second stay: he continued to write short fiction, and he was an assiduous free-lance journalist. He also put much effort into an ambitious series of public lectures in Minneapolis in the winter of 1887–88 on modern European literature, beginning his review with Balzac, Flaubert, and Zola, then assessing the achievements of the leading contemporary Scandinavian writers (including Bjørnson, Ibsen, Lie, and Strindberg), and rounding the series off with three general lectures on the prevailing literary scene. His return to Scandinavia brought no immediate breakthrough, however; and he had to work doggedly and wait impatiently before his reputation began eventually to acquire shape and substance. His autobiographical note becomes at this point even more laconic:

> With the help of some kind people came back home [from America], sailed on past Christiania, did not even come ashore there, but hid myself on board a day and a half and continued on to Copenhagen. Without money, pawned my raincoat, got a room in St. Hansgade for the 6 kroner I got for the raincoat. Was helped by Edvard Brandes, wrote an article for a few kroner in *Politiken*, wrote the first published chapter of *Hunger* [in the Danish periodical *Ny Jord*, 1888]. Then things got better.

Things did not "get better," however, without the exercise of enormous determination on his part to succeed as a writer, in the course of which he suffered considerable privation. Partly through the good offices of Edvard Brandes in Copenhagen, he gained entrée into the literary circles associated with the new periodical *Ny Jord* (Virgin Soil). It was here in 1888 that he published those items that first drew the attention of the public to this writer of perhaps more than usual talent. First came an article about his one-time colleague and associate in Minneapolis, Kristofer Janson; then, and much more important, a short but arresting piece of fiction entitled "Sult" (Hunger). This fragment was eventually incorporated two years later into his first major and startlingly innovative novel, *Sult* (1890; Eng. tr. *Hunger*, 1899 and others)

Hamsun's past experience and considerable talents as a public lecturer also helped to establish him as a challenging and distinctive personality, as well as furthering his career as an author. Invited in December 1888 to deliver two public lectures to the Danish Students Association on the subject of his experiences in America, he went on to develop and expand his provocative views into a small book published a few months later: *Fra det moderne Amerikas aandsliv* (1889; Eng. tr. *The Cultural Life of Modern America*, 1969). Hamsun admitted that the book was biased but that he remained unconcerned so long as it brought his name to the attention of the reading public: "Unlike other books about America [it] asserts *my* biased view of that philistine land and is violently *contra*. Here at home I will simply be abused in all the papers for it. . . . But if I am successful in driving it into people's brains that I do have literary powers, despite my biased views, I shall be content" (*Selected Letters*, p. 99). In this he achieved a fair measure of success at a moment that was crucial to his career; Georg Brandes was prompted in his review of the book to comment: "Here is a new and outstanding Norwegian prose writer, an author who thinks independently, who has something to say, is able to say it, has already made something of himself and will do more" (*Verdens Gang*, May 9, 1889). For the remainder of 1889 and the early part of 1890 Hamsun was sustained by this single objective, though often necessarily driven by sheer poverty into writing fugitive items of sometimes hack journalism; one series of articles that he contributed to *Dagbladet* (The Daily Paper) about a contemporary religious figure, however, did subsequently achieve the greater permanence of book form: *Lars Oftedal* (1889). Nevertheless, his overriding intent was to complete his partly finished novel for publication. As he explained to a correspondent at this time, "Hunger" was only one section of a work with three other sections that he was writing on the same theme: "the nuances of hunger, the shifting mental states of a starving person." In the late spring of the following year he completed the novel, and it was published in June 1890.

This persistence and dedication, allied to an almost visionary sense of the direction in which the "new" literature was heading, ultimately achieved the breakthrough he had been working for; and it has been rightly said that the ten years of intense literary activity between 1888 and 1898, beginning with his return from America and ending with his departure for a visit to Russia, constitute the most important decade in his career as an author. A second novel, *Mysterier* (Eng. tr. *Mysteries,* 1927 and others), appeared in 1892. Two further novels, *Redaktør Lynge* (Editor Lynge) and *Ny Jord* (Eng. tr. *Shallow Soil,* 1914), were published in April and November of 1893, respectively. The haunting novel *Pan* (Eng. tr. *Pan,* 1920 and others) was published only twelve months later, in December 1894. Two excursions into the field of drama followed next: *Ved rikets port* (1895; At the Gate of the Kingdom) and *Livets spil* (1896; The Game of Life); a volume of short stories, *Siesta* (1897), appeared the following year; and, completing this decade of endeavor, there came first another play, *Aftenrøde* (1898; Evening Red), in June, and finally the novel *Victoria* (1898) in October.

The central theme of *Sult* is that of privation at several levels—physical, psychological, erotic, social—and of the fight of a sensitive and vulnerable individual to build up inner defenses in the interest of sheer survival. Hamsun himself acknowledged that much of the real strength of the novel came from the limitation he imposed on its range of references: "The book deliberately plays on a single string," he wrote to a correspondent, "but attempts to draw from that one string hundreds of tones." Written in a highly individualistic style, it created no little sensation among the more discerning Scandinavian readers of the day; and time has confirmed that it was a key document in inaugurating a new mode of literature, not merely domestically within Scandinavia but in the wider world of European and international literature.

After the publication of *Sult* Hamsun plunged into a new frenzy of work. In the summer of 1890 he formed a plan for a major new novel, whose distinguishing feature was to be a manifesto-like preface in which he would spell out his new, iconoclastic, and revolutionary credo. In the end the notion of a preface was abandoned, and instead he decided on two separate and different ways of making his ideas known (and perhaps at the same time winning a more immediate financial return): he would publish a programmatic article in the newly launched Norwegian journal *Samtiden*, and he would undertake an extended lecture tour of major towns and cities of Norway to promulgate his combative views in a more personal and direct way.

His article "Fra det ubevidste sjæleliv" (From the Unconscious Life of the Mind) accordingly appeared in the autumn of 1890 (see "The Repudiation of Realism and Naturalism," earlier in this chapter)). In it he urged the new generation of writers to address themselves to the subtleties and complexities of the inner mental and emotional life of the individual, to the strange and inexplicable moods and thoughts that invade the mind and that are challengingly elusive: "They last a second, a minute, they come and go like a moving, winking light; but they have left their mark, deposited some kind of sensation, before they vanished." It is uncannily as though he were rehearsing some of the catch phrases of the modernism of two or three decades later—those that tell of tracing the atoms as they fall on the mind, of the disconnected and incoherent patterns scored on the unconscious, of the reveries between brackets of reality, of the tangles of mental association. Only by giving attention to these phenomena, he insisted, would literature liberate itself from the ennui of the merely general and typical; and in so doing, it would find a genuine rapport with the spirit of the modern world.

For his lecture tour he prepared a series of three lectures to be given successively at each venue, entitled "Norwegian Literature," "Psychological Literature," and "Fashionable Literature." He set out to demolish the literary values and practices of the older generation of writers (being especially severe on Bjørnson, Kielland, Ibsen, and Lie), to decry what he felt was their crippling obsession with typified characters and predictable quotidian events, and to advocate instead a literature of greater psychological refinement and sensitivity. Much of the spring and autumn of 1891 was taken up with these lectures, including appearances in Christiania, Bergen, Trondheim, Stavanger, Kristiansand, and other major Norwegian towns.

The novel to which these more programmatic and histrionic activities served as a complement was *Mysterier,* which appeared in 1892. From the start the novel was planned as something psychological in temper and elitist in its values, a combination perhaps best defined by the term Georg Brandes had recently applied to the work of Friedrich Nietzsche: "aristocratic radicalism." As Hamsun confessed in a letter to his German translator:

It is to be a big psychological novel. . . . Actually I work very slowly. I am completely incapable of writing for the masses: novels about betrothals and evening balls and childbearing, with stress on external event, I regard as too cheap and they do not interest me. With what little I do produce, I address myself to a culturally sophisticated and select group of people, and it is recognition by this select public that I value. (*Selected Letters,* p. 132)

The novel traced the bizarre sequence of events one summer after the unheralded appearance in a little Norwegian coastal town of "a stranger, a certain Nagel, a remarkable and peculiar charlatan, who did a lot of extraordinary things and who disappeared again just as suddenly as he had come." His approach to life was essentially what Eduard von Hartmann, in his *Die Philosophie des Unbewussten* (1869; Eng. tr. *Philosophy of the Unconscious,* 1884), had earlier defined as the "mystical" mind, a reliance on thoughts and feelings and judgments that are independent of any ponderously rational or logical processes and are determined by the greater immediacy of the workings of the unconscious mind. Nagel emerges as a highly modernist figure, a "fractional" character of the sort that Strindberg had recently identified as typically "modern" in his Preface to *Miss Julie* (1888), not to be added up in whole numbers and "inconsistent" only if one attempted to measure him by a commonsense logic too coarse-meshed to catch the altogether more elusive "subjective logic of the blood," as Nagel himself puts it. More important, to adopt such criteria would be entirely contrary to Hamsun's view of the nature of psychological literature. To Hamsun's keen disappointment, *Mysterier* created less public attention when it appeared than *Sult* had done; but posterity has come to regard it as one of Hamsun's most seminal works, one that established him as being firmly in the vanguard of the emergent modernist novel in Europe.

After completing *Mysterier* Hamsun moved to Denmark and spent the better part of a year there, first in Copenhagen and then on the island of Samsø. His next two novels in strict chronological sequence—*Redaktør Lynge,* a literary caricature of Olav Thommessen and an indictment of his editorship of the newspaper *Verdens Gang,* and *Ny Jord,* a rather conventional satire of artists' life in Christiania—show him reverting for a brief period to a more traditional style of narrative; although not without literary merit, they are not considered as belonging among the more accomplished of Hamsun's works. A substantial part of the next three years, 1893–95, he spent in Paris, where he hoped to broaden his horizons and at the same time gain some knowledge of French. It was during his time in France that he finally met his admired Strindberg; he also made the acquaintance here of the German playwright Frank Wedekind and the Danish novelist Herman Bang.

It was in Paris, in the autumn of 1893, that he began his next and deeply fascinating novel *Pan,* which he finally completed during the late summer of 1894 in Kristiansand on an extended visit back to Norway. It purports to be the recollections, in quasi-diary form, of Thomas Glahn, a young retired lieutenant, of the events during a stay in North Norway two years earlier. The narrative is in itself a stylistic tour de force, strangely born of the defiance with which Hamsun vowed to confront his many detractors, who dismissed him as a mere charlatan, "an apostle of humbug." Each chapter, he claimed, was as carefully composed as a poem; each line was gone over with meticulous attention. It focused, he said, on the mysterious life of Nordland, the regions of the Lapps, and the superstitions that ruled the land of the midnight sun; it had been his endeavor to capture in the book something of the spirit of Rousseau, the sensibilities and sensitivities of the nature-worshiping soul. At the same time, the psychological complexities—centering on the relationship between Glahn and the heroine, Edvarda—are formidable; love, after its first passionate and reciprocal declaration, becomes a desperate and inexorable drama of alternating doubt and reassurance, attraction and repulsion in a recognizably existentialist mode.

One can only speculate as to why, after *Pan,* Hamsun turned away from prose fiction to try his hand at drama. Possibly, it was a kind of arrogance that spurred him to challenge Ibsen—then Norway's greatest living writer—on his own ground; possibly, it was in part to try to augment his own uncertain income by seeking theatrical royalties. The three plays *Ved rikets port, Livets spil,* and *Aftenrøde* do in fact form a trilogy, whose continuing hero, Ivar Kareno, begins his career as a philosopher of Nietzschean convictions, suffers defeat both in his academic and in his domestic life, and is eventually reduced to an ineffectual opportunist in his later years. Hamsun was himself convinced that these dramas were works of considerable power; of *Livets spil* he once wrote to Bjørnson: "It is the most profound book I have ever written; and I have put into it all my bitter brooding reflections." All three plays were given performances at the Christiania Theater but have failed to win from posterity the kind of acclaim their creator had obviously hoped for. Nor, indeed, did any of Hamsun's later dramatic or quasi-dramatic works do much to revise this assessment: *Munken Vendt* (1902; Friar Vendt), a highly inventive dramatic poem reminiscent in some respects of *Peer Gynt,* is nevertheless structurally weak, and *Dronning Tamara* (1903; Queen Tamara) and the later *Livet i vold* (1910; Eng. tr. *In the Grip of Life,* 1924) do little to redress the balance.

In 1898 he published *Victoria,* widely held to be one of the most moving love stories in Norwegian literature. A simple synopsis suggests sentimentality, even banality: the story of the love of a poor boy, Johannes, for Victoria, a rich man's daughter, who betrays him for the wealthier Otto to save her father from bankruptcy but who dies at a relatively early age from tuberculosis. All this action is held suspended in a lattice of other complex emotional relationships. What gives *Victoria* its fascination and distinction, however, is the way it explores the inner life—the dreams and visions and mental imagery—of Johannes, a writer and poet and obvious Hamsun look-alike, in his search for love and for life's meaning: "Love is . . . the origin of the world, the ruler of the world; but all its ways are filled with blossoms and blood, blossoms and blood."

The years between the completion of *Victoria* in 1898 and the start of his "Wanderer" sequence of novels six years later mark a somewhat unsettled period in Hamsun's career. In 1898 he married Bergljot Bech, a young divorcee; unfortunately, the marriage did not bring the stability and happiness Hamsun (now in his fortieth year) had been longing for, and it was dissolved in 1906. (His second marriage—to Marie Andersen, an actress—was in 1909.) In 1898, with his new bride, he traveled to Finland, where he lived for a year before embarking on a journey to Russia, Caucasia, and Turkey. His impressions from this trip he incorporated in a book, *I æventyrland* (1903; In a Wondrous Land). A volume of short stories, *Kratskog* (1903; Brushwood), complemented his earlier exploration of this genre in *Siesta* (1897) and encouraged him to complete a further collection two years later, *Stridende liv* (1905; Struggling Life).

The one really distinctive product of these exploratory years, however, was a volume of poems, *Det vilde kor* (1904; The Wild Chorus), Hamsun's sole excursion into the genre of lyric poetry—the only form of literature, he averred, which is not both pretentious and meaningless, but simply meaningless. In this collection he reveals himself as a poet who took delight in breaking with tradition, who was ready to admit an audaciously new range of linguistic reference and metrical patterning into his work—things that proved to have considerable appeal to the succeeding generation of lyric poets, especially Herman Wildenvey and Olaf Bull.

Enjoying a powerful measure of shared identity are the six novels that belong to the years between 1906 and 1912: the three so-called Wanderer novels—*Under høststjernen* (1906; Eng. tr. *Under the Autumn Star,* 1922 and others), *En vandrer spiller med sordin* (1909; Eng. tr. *On Muted Strings,* 1922 and others), and *Den siste glæde* (1912; Eng. tr. *Look Back on Happiness,* 1940)—and the three others that completed the output for these years—*Sværmere* (Eng. tr. *Dreamers,* 1921, and *Mothwise,* 1922), *Benoni* (1908; Eng. tr. 1925), and *Rosa* (1908; Eng. tr. 1925). Together they embody a distinct shift of style and narrative technique from those of the novels of the nineties: although in these later works there is still some measure of self-identification with the heroes—indeed, the first-person narrator of the "Wanderer" books bears the name of Knut Pedersen, Hamsun's original name—the mood is one of increasingly ironic detachment and resignation. The role the novelist adopts is that of detached observer rather than active participant. The perspective is now middle-aged, even elderly; life's genuine values are seen as residing in the greater quietude and simplicity of rural life; and the reader is made aware of the author's growing impatience and indeed irascibility with many of the more modern sophistications of the new century: tourism, women's emancipation, the popular press, commercialized sport.

When, in 1911, Hamsun bought and subsequently ran a farm at Hamarøy in North Norway, he was in his early fifties; yet, in quantitative terms at least, he still had a large part of his creative career ahead of him, including ten major novels. His adopted pattern of life close to the soil, both in Nordland and later (from 1918 onward) at Nørholm near Grimstad in South Norway, was the outward correlative of his changed sense of values. He was acutely conscious of the inroads made by an urbanized "civilization" into what he held to be the simpler, sterner virtues of the more traditional way of Norwegian life. The beliefs and attitudes and values sustaining the later novels are no longer exuberantly inserted into the text and debated as they were earlier, but more obliquely and pervasively implied. These works assume a settled and largely pastoral (even at times feudal) scheme of values and carry a strong anti-intellectual and antidemocratic message. They exhort by implication to a life of honest labor and a distrust of clever cerebration.

The twin novels from the time around the beginning of the First World War—*Børn av tiden* (1913; Eng. tr. *Children of the Age*, 1924) and its sequel, *Segelfoss by* (1915; Eng. tr. *Segelfoss Town*, 1925)—explore the social and economic changes in a small community consequent on the spread of the new commercialism and the insidious encroachment of industrialization. The crude entrepreneurial ways of capitalism undermine the traditional patriarchal pattern of life, and the one ineffectual outsider figure can only look on impotently.

The novel that followed, *Markens grøde* (1917; Eng. tr. *Growth of the Soil*, 1920), was Hamsun's one attempt to provide in fiction a positive example of those values he set store by, and for once he held back from the satire and the irony that make their positive point negatively. In this story of the career of Isak, "a lumbering barge of a man," he paid homage to the simple life of honest toil on the land, to its tribulations and its rewards, and to its essential role in preserving the continuity of life: "Generation to generation, breeding ever anew; and when you die, the new stock goes on. That's the meaning of eternal life." The result was, despite the presence of many separate elements typical of Hamsun at his sovereign best—his irrepressible inventiveness, his dry humor, and the fluency of his style—possibly the least characteristic novel he wrote. It won for its author the Nobel Prize in 1920 and brought him international fame.

Konerne ved vandposten (1920; Eng. tr. *The Women at the Pump*, 1928 and others) reverts to a more typical Hamsun idiom and style; it mounts a bitter satirical attack on many of the things that drew his disapproval at the time, such as organized labor, book learning and modern education, democracy, and the English nation. The central character, Oliver, is an emasculated cripple—a transparent enough symbol for the degenerate life of the modern day. This novel was followed by another somber work in which the symbolism spoke with simple directness: the action of *Siste kapitel* (1923; Eng. tr. *Chapter the Last*, 1929) is located in a mountain sanatorium, and its dominant themes are sickness, depression, and death.

The four-year gap between *Siste kapitel* and his next book, *Landstrykere* (1927; Eng. tr. *Vagabonds*, 1930, and *Wayfarers*, 1980), was the longest interval in Hamsun's career up to this point; and when the new novel did appear, it proved to be the longest book he ever wrote. Moreover, over the following seven years it developed into a trilogy with the addition of *August* (1930; Eng. tr. 1931) and *Men livet lever* (1933; Eng. tr. *The Road Leads On*, 1934). In these three novels, Hamsun develops in depth one of his most memorable characters: August, the irrepressible schemer and small-time entrepreneur, the extravagant poseur and inveterate liar, and the embodiment of all that restlessness and rootlessness which for Hamsun seemed to epitomize the unauthentic spirit of the contemporary age. These books trace the events of August's career in his dealings with Edevart and other friends and associates at three carefully selected and spaced points in time: when the hero is aged twenty-seven, forty-seven, and sixty-seven, respectively. The canvas that Hamsun worked on was broad, and he took the opportunity to create a gallery of more than sixty supporting figures and gave himself freedom to pass much overt social comment, including his profound distaste for the once-prevalent emigration fever and for the ideological pollution that he felt came from the New World.

Hamsun's last novel, *Ringen sluttet* (1936; Eng. tr. *The Ring Is Closed,* 1937), does indeed stand as a kind of epilogue to his life and career, even though he was unable to realize his plan for writing a sequel and was thus moved to call the book "a torso." The ground it moved over was familiar; in essence, it offered a variation on those themes that had served him in his fiction for most of the interwar years.

His last years, sadly, found him the subject of political rather than literary judgment; so that when Thomas Mann spoke of him in 1951, the syntactical ordering of the sentence was only too typical—referring to him as "a man broken by politics, though still the quondam creator of highly discriminate narrative works." In 1940, at the age of eighty-one, and only a few days after the German invasion of Norway, Hamsun threw his great influence on the side of the Nazis, publishing the first of a series of wartime articles in which he acted as an eloquent apologist for Hitler. It was a decision compounded possibly of three elements: his lifelong approval of authoritarian forms of government, his contempt for what he held were the ineffectualities of democracy, and an intense and long-standing antipathy toward the English. After the war he was arraigned and, at the end of a protracted investigation, officially declared to be suffering from "permanently enfeebled mental powers." Whereupon at the age of eighty-nine, as though to give the lie to uncomprehending officialdom, Hamsun wrote and published his astonishing apologia, *Paa gjengrodde stier* (1949; Eng. tr. *On Overgrown Paths,* 1967), a brilliant evocation of a man living in bewildered ignorance, a work with passages of unimpaired vigor and full of the authentic magic of his style.

He died on February 19, 1952, at the age of ninety-two.

HANS KINCK

Hans Ernst Kinck (1865–1926) was extraordinarily productive. From the time of his debut as a writer in 1892 until his death (and even later, for some of his publications appeared posthumously) he brought out a seemingly inexhaustible stream of books: novels (including one in three volumes); collections of short stories, dramas, and dramatic poetry; volumes of historical, literary, and cultural essays; biographical studies and much more: in all, more than two score publications. But quantity was in no sense at the expense of quality, for he also demonstrated himself to be one of the most startlingly original authors writing in Norwegian in the last hundred years. Sadly, his work has not attracted the attention of translators to the extent that its quality merits. The consequence is that—in the English-speaking world, at least—he is relatively little known.

Fundamental to his work is a sense of society's essential duality, of a continuing great divide, whereby some clash or confrontation of cultures provides the base pattern against which life is lived. This duality is something to which his mind returns in fascination time and time again, finding an almost endless variety of manifestations, in the past as well as the present, in other civilizations as well as that closest to home. Even as a child he was aware—almost in the blood, as it were—of this pattern at the level of family: his father, a doctor, was a member of the professional class, while his mother was the daughter of a peasant family. He found himself responding to similar dualities in other arenas of life: social, psychological, and even topographical, as in the sense of contraries he felt when the family moved from Setesdal's "ballad valley" to the "sea-salt rationalism" of the Hardanger coast. As a young man he could hardly fail to become aware of the endless public debate about Norway's "two cultures": the *embetsmannskultur* and the *bondekultur*, terms so semantically complex that they only begin to yield their fuller meaning within the broadest context of Norwegian social history: one the lifestyle and values of a professional or official class, still trailing clouds of immigrant Dano-German glory from its past; and the other those of the yeoman farmer, clinging to the myth of his one-time heroic origins and zealous for—or jealous of—his rights. Such was the fascination of these concepts for Kinck that it is not too fanciful to see the greater part of his authorship as a kind of protracted attempt to give definition to them through the medium of literature.

This interest was soon to manifest itself in his writing. His formal education was largely in the classics and philology: Latin, Greek, and Old Norse. But he also read widely in philosophy, especially German philosophy of the eighteenth and nineteenth centuries. For a time he entertained the idea of following an academic career, and he wrote a short dissertation on the relation between medieval ballad poetry and the heroic poetry of northern antiquity; but he soon abandoned the idea. His literary debut was *Huldren* (1892; The Half Wit), the story of an illegitimate but imaginative child who is set apart from the rest of the rural community. Kinck followed this work with *Ungt Folk* (1893; Eng. tr. *A Young People,* 1929), set like its predecessor in Hardanger, in which the clash of the two cultures is given a more conspicuous and central motivating place. Common to both works is a deep sensitivity to the psychological shifts and tensions behind outer events.

His next book was written in Paris: *Flaggermus-vinger* (1896; Bat's Wings), a collection of short stories. The book has the subtitle "Eventyr vestfra" (Stories from the West [of Norway]), intimating the importance of the setting, a background of nature and natural forces against which the individual makes his—or very often her—way. In, for example, "Hvidsymre i utslaatten" (Eng. tr. "White Anemones," in *Slaves of Love,* 1982), the sense of harmony between external nature and inner feeling is intense: "She turned off up the valley and into the mountains. . . . She did not rest, did not stop to recover her breath. Steadily she continued across the wet bogland, across the mountain knolls and up the steep hillsides. She wasn't aware of walking. It was as if a strongly running stream of silent tears swept her up each hillside." The mood of these stories is characterized by a skillful blending of the realistic and the mystical, and with this collection Kinck created a distinctive poetic prose style of great suppleness and suggestiveness.

Flaggermus-vinger was the first result of Kinck's preoccupation with the form of the short story, a fascination that led him to publish eleven volumes of short stories in the course of his career. In chronological terms, they group themselves mainly into two periods: 1896–1908 and 1917–26. Thematically, they defy any rigid classification, though certain rough groupings may serve as an approximate guide. Some collections take themes of love and the nature of erotic behavior: they include, from the earlier period, *Vaarnætter* (1901; Spring Nights), *Naar kærlighed dør* (1903; When Love Dies), and *Livsaanderne* (1906; The Spirits of Life), and, from the later period, *Kirken brænder* (1917; The Church Is Burning). Other collections are in a more pastoral mood, many of them in the tradition of the village story or the German *Dorfgeschichte,* among which might be included *Fra hav til hei* (1897; From Sea to Mountain), *Masker og mennesker* (1908; Masks and People), and, from his later career, *Fra Fonneland til Svabergssveen* (1922; From Fonneland to Svabergssveen). Two other allegorical collections from his later period show a certain affinity: *Guldalder* (1920; Golden Age) and *Foraaret i Mikropolis* (1926; Spring in Micropolis), both of which turn to classical antiquity, while the distinctive *Trækfugle og andre* (1899; Migratory Birds and Others) offers a kind of comparative cultural study, through the medium of narrative, of the impact of Mediterranean life and landscape and art on the northern temperament. Finally, *Torvet i Cirta* (1929; The Market in Cirta), which also looks to the ancient world, was published posthumously.

Generalization about these genial and greatly varied works tends to detract from what is their essential strength: their highly individual character. Nevertheless, it may be said that they evince a complex authorial personality with a penetratingly analytical mind: one that has profound sympathy for the more vulnerable members of society, for those who lack the hard outer skin that might protect them; one that knows the way society's impersonal and intolerant forces can wound and hurt; that penetrates deep not only into the individual psyche, its moods, reactions, irrationalities, but also into the collective psyche, the group loyalties, the tribal mores, the ingrained attitudes and conventions that often pass unscrutinized and unchallenged from generation to generation. By their quality they constitute a quite extraordinary achievement and establish Kinck's position as probably Norway's supreme short-story writer of all time.

After the tautness and brevity of the pieces in *Flaggermus-vinger,* Kinck moved to the other end of the formal spectrum: to a broad epic narrative that was eventually to fill two volumes. *Sus* (1896; Soughing) was followed after an interval of two years by *Hugormen* (1898; The Adder); they relate the career of Herman Ek (the name was taken from *Fra Kristiania–bohêmen*) in his attempts to come to terms with the two cultures. Kinck later reworked the two novels as one, and in 1923 it was published under the title *Herman Ek*. In some ways immediately reminiscent of Kinck himself, Ek is the son of a man of refined disposition and a woman of practical resource. He spends his childhood in a valley in southern Norway, which is clearly Kinck's familiar Setesdal; he then goes on to the university, where he follows the public debate about the two cultures. He feels ambivalently placed between these two warring classes, bound to both by his inherited loyalties, but at the same time deeply aware of their separate faults. He sees around him officials who are quick to declare their concern for the well-being of the peasant but who cherish a secret contempt for him; and he sees peasants who conceal their hatred for those who have moved in and taken over "their" country and who will cheerfully play them false given half a chance. This external, social divide is counterpointed in the novel by the inner psychological split of the central character as he tries to find his role in life, in Ek's case as a reforming entrepreneur in a peasant environment. Finally, losing all patience, he decides to inflict "development" on the valley and its people, to despoil its rivers with his industries, and to turn proud and independent craftsmen into units of paid labor. But war—this peculiarly Norwegian variant of the orthodox class war of the textbooks—is joined, and the local people take fitting vengeance. Variations on this basic theme of the two cultures are found also in Kinck's next four novels: *Fru Anny Porse* (1900), *Doktor Gabriel Jahr* (1902), *Emigranter* (1904; Emigrants), and *Præsten* (1907; The Clergyman).

For the next ten years or so, Kinck's creative energies were channeled into drama or dramatic poetry. *Driftekaren* (1908; The Drover), his foremost achievement, is a great, powerful, sprawling, five-part dramatic statement held together not by any cohesive action but by the power of the central figure. Vraal, larger than life, horsedealer and poet in one, dominates the play almost in the manner of a Brand or a Peer Gynt in his anguished, multifaceted search for wholeness, before finally finding salvation in the love of a good woman. *Driftekaren* is a massively impressive work, but it is not easily accessible; not only is the action highly and indeed perhaps even wantonly episodic, making it difficult to follow, but it is also couched in a language of formidable density.

Forming a special group in themselves are Kinck's Italian plays. In 1906 he had written a play based on a character from Boccaccio's *Decamerone: Agilulf den vise* (1906; Agilulf the Wise), a work in which Kinck found his way to a highly personal solution to the problems of dramatic verse, creating a language of fluid, rhythmical power. There followed, at irregular intervals, *Den sidste gjæst* (1910; The Last Guest), *Bryllupet i Genua* (1911; The Wedding in Genoa), *Mot karneval* (1915; Toward Carnival), and finally *Lisabetta's brødre* (1921; Lisabetta's Brothers). Kinck's skill in psychological portrayal is very evident in these plays; especially memorable is his unorthodox but persuasive reading of the character of Machiavelli in *Mot karneval*. This work, written in prose, is—despite its historical displacement—as modern in its analysis of realpolitik as any contemporary study.

Undoubtedly, the major work of these years is, however, the three-volume novel *Sneskavlen brast* (1918–19; The Avalanche Broke). In it Kinck returns, as though in obedience to some obsessive compulsion, to the theme of social conflict in an age of transition. As it follows the changing fortunes of a small rural community in western Norway in the late 1870s, riven by conflicting loyalties and ambitions, the novel weaves into its broad tapestry many of the themes Kinck had explored earlier in *Ungt folk*, *Fru Anny Porse*, and *Emigranter*. A spread of characters from both sides of the class divide play out their individual destinies against a somber background of political change, shifting ideologies, and spiritual degeneration. Conflict is endemic: between the sexes, between the generations, but above all between the classes. *Storfolk* and *bonde*, upper class and peasant class, the rich and the poor are ranged against each other, each with its own kind of passionate intensity and each in its own distinctive way essentially flawed. The "important people," enjoying positions of privilege and authority, have become effete, corrupt, and degenerate; they fight defensively to preserve what they have. The peasants, generally driven more by greed and envy than by idealism, are out for change and a share of life's spoils; but the clear implication is that, should they succeed, they will fall victim to the same spiritual degeneracy of those they have supplanted—they will themselves (as one of the characters comments) become the new bureaucracy. It is a world in which there is room for some characters of compassion and genuine humanity (of which the young girl Sophie is the most moving example), but they are few and vulnerable. In its general message of the futility of the struggle, *Sneskavlen brast* could well be reflecting the mood of the years in which it was written: the end of the First World War.

The inventory of Kinck's authorship is by no means exhausted by a listing of his narrative, dramatic, and poetic works. He was also an enthusiastic essayist, whose interests ranged over many fields, including art, literature, cultural history, and politics. Whenever in this capacity he turned his attention to his beloved Italy—as he did in the essay collections *Italienere* (1904; Italians), *Gammel jord* (1907; Ancient Soil), and *Stammens røst* (1919; The Voice of the Race)—he was invariably extremely well informed and offered a wealth of original ideas. The biographical *Renæssancemennesker* (1916; Renaissance Figures) complements his Machiavellian drama *Mot karneval*. His essays on art and literature, in which he ranged widely from the medieval and the Renaissance to the modern, are collected under the title *Mange slags kunst* (1921; Many Kinds of Art); and there was a further, posthumous collection two years after his death: *Kunst og kunstnere* (1928; Art and Artists). Occupying a somewhat special place in his essayistic work is *Rormanden overbord* (1920; Helmsman Overboard), made up of pieces he wrote during and after the war, pieces roughly coterminous in time with *Sneskavlen brast*, on which they are an oblique commentary. They reflect his concern about the social and cultural dangers inherent in the postwar situation, and they outline his views about how to maintain the integrity of the individual and of the "folk" in the face of such threats. Though modest in compass, these essays nevertheless reveal much of Kinck's philosophy of life in these years.

Norwegian Literature
1910–1950

by William Mishler

6

THE HISTORICAL AND SOCIAL CONTEXT

After five hundred years of political union with (and under) Denmark and later Sweden, Norway in 1905 became a sovereign nation, a monarchy like its two sister countries. Haakon VII, elected king in 1905, lived until 1957, and Norwegian history during the fifty years of his rule can be seen as a drama in five acts: the first promising years of the new nation, followed, during the neutrality of World War I, by years of anxiety and greed, then by the gradual prosperity and complacency of the postwar years, which ended in catastrophe when, on April 9, 1940, Norway was attacked by Germany. After two months of fighting, Norwegian soldiers surrendered to the German occupation forces, which stayed in the country for five years. The king and his government did not surrender, however, but fled to England, from where Norway, thanks to its large merchant marine, was able to support its allies in their struggle against Hitler's Germany. The last act of the historical drama is made up of the reconstruction years, when, after the war, Norway welcomed its king and government home from exile and, four years later, in 1949, gave up its traditional neutrality to join the North Atlantic Treaty Organization (NATO).

The optimism of the post-1905 years can be seen, for example, in the building of the Rjukan power station in 1907, which marks the beginnings of Norway's important hydroelectric industry, and in the opening of the Oslo-Bergen railway in 1909. Industrialization meant emigration from the countryside to new and old urban areas. In 1905 only 28 percent of Norway's population lived in cities; in 1930 the percentage was 30, and in 1946, 50 (in 1985 it was higher than 80). Also in the early years of the new nation civil rights were extended to individuals who had earlier not been able to participate in politics: by the year 1898 all men could vote and by the year 1913, all women. By that time, too, a woman for the first time had been admitted as a student to the university (1882), received a Ph.D. degree (1906), and won a seat in the Norwegian parliament (1911). After an early attempt at organization and the subsequent crackdown by the government in the 1850s, Norwegian labor leaders were finally able to form a permanent political party in 1887. In the new century, particularly during the 1920s, there was a radicalization of the Labor party, which gradually established strong links with Moscow. Of special importance for writers and other intellectuals of a radical bent was a student movement, led by a returned emigrant from America, Erling Falk, and named Mot Dag (Toward Day) after the title of its periodical. The Labor party won the election in 1928 and formed its first government but was forced out after two weeks. The country was not ready for socialism, and moreover during a brief period in the early 1930s experienced a conservative backlash when the agrarian party (1931–33) came to power: there were clashes between workers and the military, a group of nationalist Norwegians occupied part of Danish Greenland, and the head of the Department of Defense was the later notorious Vidkunn Quisling. The first lasting Labor government was formed in 1935, and the party was continuously in power until 1963.

During World War II Quisling—by now leader of his own party, called Nasjonal samling (National Unification)—had been installed by the German occupiers as "president of the ministry." There was a strong Norwegian Resistance movement, some of whose members were caught and executed, while others—ministers of the church, teachers, students, and intellectuals generally—were sent to concentration camps. A large number of collaborators—idealists and opportunists, including fifteen writers—after the war received punishment ranging from small fines to the reintroduced death sentence. The events of the war years as well as the postwar prosecutions formed a powerful inspiration for Norwegian writers and painters.

The opposition between civil servants and farmers, which had characterized the nineteenth-century Norwegian countryside, was gradually replaced by new patterns. Norway's population doubled between the years 1800 and 1900, and since there was not enough farmland to go around, several hundred thousand farmers left for America, and others emigrated to the nearest town to find work in a factory. When the civil servants, many of them by now the sons of farmers, moved into the government offices in developing urban areas, they were joined by the new class of industrial workers, who were also the sons of farmers or farmworkers. The new social division, then, was between city dwellers and those who chose to remain country people.

Life in the countryside was dominated by the strong position of religion, in the established state church as well as in the fundamentalist, and sometimes nonconformist, "prayer houses." When theology instruction at the university, under the influence of international scholarship, became too liberal for the fundamentalist forces, they established in 1908 their own seminary, which influenced religious life in Norway throughout the century. More open-minded and, particularly, more national were followers of the nineteenth-century Danish religious leader N. F. S. Grundtvig. The stronghold of this brand of Christianity was the folk high schools, which, with their interest in national history, folk language, and folk art, had an impact on the many Norwegian writers who set out to find and describe the "soul of the people." Some of these writers, in turn, were influenced in this enterprise by a form of neoromantic Christian esotericism called anthroposophy, which had been brought to Norway in the first decade of the century by the movement's founder, the Austrian seer Rudolf Steiner (1865–1925).

For the farmers who moved to the cities, the speed of the urbanization process varied with place and people. Some farmers, who were proud of their rustic heritage, formed *bygdelag*, or provincial societies, in which the dialect, folk music, and folk dance of the province in question were cultivated, and their activities were supported by the liberal government, whose members were often farmers' sons and speakers of Norway's second language, *nynorsk*. In 1912 a special nynorsk theater was established, Det Norske Teatret (The Norwegian Theater), which gradually became one of the most distinguished theaters in the country. In the early years it played folk comedies, set in Oslo's working-class areas and often using dialect speech, which—together with the *bygdelag*, teetotaler, and young workers' movements—helped ease the city/country conflict.

Life among city intellectuals was characterized by an international rather than national outlook. Among members of the political left, the cool rationality of such system builders as Freud and Marx was particularly appealing, albeit, especially with regard to Freud, in simplified and superficial versions. Freud was (mis)read as promoting a view of childhood as a lost paradise and as fostering a back-to-nature mysticism, an interpretation that, however, never reached the same proportions in Norway as in, say, Sweden. The main proponent of Freudianism in Norway was Freud's aberrant student, Wilhelm Reich. He stayed in Norway from 1934 until he was expelled in 1939, and had many followers, from psychology professor Harald Schjelderup to novelist Sigurd Hoel. One of the notable characteristics of both forms of radicalism, the Marxism of the Mot Dag group and the cultural radicalism of the Freudians (there was a certain overlap between the two), was that neither inspired much sympathy among the socialists or the workers. Both tended to view these leftist intellectuals as impractical theorists with little understanding of everyday politics.

In the twenties and thirties, however, the radicals caused a great stir in the newspapers and other forums of public debate, and a group of powerful conservatives arose to combat them. The conservatives were upset over the attack on established religion and the new openness in the discussion of sexuality. Some of them joined with the rural fundamentalists and had the 1933 National Theater production of Marc Connelly's *Green Pastures* (in which God appeared on stage) banned; others were later to embrace an upper-class and urban type of Christianity, referred to as the Oxford Movement and introduced to Norway by its American founder, Frank Buchman, in 1934.

In urban graphic arts, the subjective and often tragic manner of the 1890s gradually gave way to an optimistic monumental art, depicting general themes such as "Mother Earth" or "History of the Labor Movement" and spanning a whole generation of artistic activity, from Edvard Munch's Aula decorations (1916) and Gustav Vigeland's sculpture park (1924–43) to the murals of Oslo City Hall (ca. 1950). While the size and scope of these art works correspond to the great epic novels of a rural genius like Uppdal or Duun, the typical Norwegian city writer of the mid-1900s tended more often to be preoccupied with his or her own personal psyche.

PROSE WRITERS OF THE EARLY TWENTIETH CENTURY

Many of the writers who became prominent in Norway between 1905 and 1914 grew up during the 1870s and 1880s, the period known as the Modern Breakthrough when the literary movements of realism and naturalism made their tardy but triumphant appearance in Scandinavia. In Norway it was then that a generation of gifted writers—Henrik Ibsen, Bjørnstjerne Bjørnson, Jonas Lie, Alexander Kielland, and Arne Garborg—answered the call of the prominent Danish critic, Georg Brandes, for a literature that would turn away from outmoded romantic ways of thinking and feeling and, instead, "bring up problems for debate." For approximately twenty years these writers and their colleagues responded with works that drew attention to problematical areas in which society either was undergoing rapid change or was under pressure to do so, such as women's rights, education, sexual morals, class relations, urbanization, and industrialization.

During the nineties and fin de siècle, Norway, like other European and

Scandinavian countries, experienced a neoromantic revival. Symbolism, mysticism, world-weary pessimism, a fascination for the uncanny all figured prominently both in literature and in the other arts. Ibsen's later plays—for example, *Fruen fra havet*, *Bygmester Solness*, *Når vi døde vågner*—manifest a predilection for dark allegory and a tantalizing mystical bent. Knut Hamsun's brilliant early novels—*Sult*, *Pan*—turn their energies, somewhat in the manner of Dostoevski, toward an exploration of various abnormal aspects of the psyche. The brooding, death-obsessed paintings of Edvard Munch and the haunted expressionistic poetry of Sigbjørn Obstfelder clearly belong to this same climate of feeling.

To designate such works as neoromantic is not to suggest that they represent a philosophical break with earlier realism or naturalism. Rather, despite their marked difference in tonality, they bring these movements to their logical conclusion. Realism and naturalism had at first been adopted by writers like Ibsen as modes of thinking and writing which promised to clear away the fog of religious thinking and to present in the aesthetic domain an order of truth analogous to that obtained by positivistic science. This promise, however, along with its initial robust optimism, gradually gave way to pessimism as artists increasingly came to grapple with the intractability of biological and social conditioning.

Then, as the new century dawned, political and social developments again brought about a shift in mood. As the question of Norway's relationship with Sweden became acute, its writers shifted their focus away from the ultimate and inward concerns favored by the neoromantic movement back toward more immediate ones. Once independence from Sweden had been achieved, many of Norway's writers became interested in stitching together the fabric of their national identity. That is, they turned to the past—either the distant Middle Ages or more recent history—to discover the deep continuities in the Norwegian national psyche and to assess the gains and losses involved in Norway's move into the twentieth century.

Like their great predecessors from the Modern Breakthrough, they wrote in the realistic mode, but unlike the men and women of the Modern Breakthrough, the new realists were for the most part not interested in stressing the newness of Norway's situation. While often critical in their assessment of present developments, they were not rebels or iconoclasts. Rather, it is as if Norway's recent independence had placed a burden of responsibility on its writers which increased their sense of *pietas* (reverence). Where Ibsen and his contemporaries had been willing to criticize and in some cases tear down, their twentieth-century progeny clearly understood their mission to be one of assessment, understanding, and, in the final analysis, endorsement. Witnesses to rapid but orderly cultural change, they wrote to present an accounting. Thus many of them cultivated the historical or multigenerational family novel, building complex spans between present and past on which eras and phases of culture might be displayed.

The literary critic Daniel Haakonsen has coined the term "ethical realism" to describe the spirit of the entire interwar period. The term refers primarily to the novel, in which straightforward storytelling was the order of the day and the primary symbolic operations were those of mediation and balance between present and past, individual and group. Of course, the same terms figured in the works of the writers of the Modern Breakthrough, but there they tended to meet in irreconcilable opposition. When they reappeared two or three generations later, it was generally to undergo a complex set of permutations which ends in synthesis. In other words, the important modification in Norway's literary agenda in the early twentieth century is that, while remaining realistic or naturalistic in technique, it becomes, in Claude Levi-Strauss's sense of the term, "mythical." Its principal task is to achieve harmony among multiple stories fundamentally at odds. In contrast to the atheistic or agnostic ethos of the Modern Breakthrough, many neorealistic writers invoke religion (i.e., Christianity) or a mystical sense of Norway's history and destiny as synthesizing agents.

Another way to make the same point is to note that *twentieth*-century modernism (except in the case of several poets, whose work was not primarily received in that sense) makes no appearance in Norwegian literature until after the Second World War. European modernism is predicated on the "death of God," on the collapse of "common sense," on the feeling that the parts no longer cohere. But Norway's experience, despite the First World War, in which it did not participate, was hardly one of incoherence. Rapid change, certainly, but not chaos: Norwegians were industrializing and modernizing their country in a rational, supervised, and potentially profitable way. They were tapping their waterfalls for energy and arranging themselves into labor unions that would elect the socialist governments that transformed twentieth-century Norway in one of history's most successful feats of social engineering. The literature of the period reflects the transformation as it is occurring with a sense of stoical nostalgia and, in the best instances, a complex grasp of the enormity of the conflicts involved.

Three Chroniclers:
Peter Egge, Johan Bojer, Gabriel Scott
Prolific writers, Egge, Bojer, and Scott produced only one or two novels apiece for which they are primarily remembered today. All are works that

present a strong and positive view of peasant culture. Many of the novels by Peter Egge (1869–1959) are valued for their accurate depiction of the culture of Trøndelag, with its intractable conflict between the families of the peasants who had lived in the area for several centuries and the families of the more recently arrived government officials. Related to this conflict is the more general one between traditional and modern culture, which Egge also portrays in several of his novels. In his best works Egge can be seen as a kind of Norwegian Thomas Hardy, a regional novelist who finds in the alteration and demise of peasant culture a theme of great magnitude. Unlike Hardy, however, Egge draws no metaphysical conclusions from the mournful fates of his protagonists. He is more intent on exhibiting their psychological strength than on drawing philosophical implications from their defeat. It is a mark of the strength of certain of Egge's novels that also artistically they merit comparison to Hardy's works.

Egge published his first novel in 1891, *Almue* (Common People), which deals with the resistance of small-town people to art, and from then on published a book a year until 1917; only a few have retained their interest for readers today. His enduring reputation rests on *Inde i fjordene* (1920; In the Inner Fjords), *Jægtvig og hans Gud* (1923; Jægtvig and His God), and *Hansine Solstad* (1925; Eng. tr. 1939), the last generally considered to be Egge's masterpiece. Here the milieu from the Trondheim of the latter years of the nineteenth century is rendered with the care of a cultural historian. The character Hansine Solstad is an outwardly unremarkable woman from the working class who remains undefeated despite long years of poverty and unwarranted suspicion. Her portrait is affecting because it is drawn realistically and unsentimentally.

After *Hansine Solstad* Egge continued to publish novels, but none as memorable as the well-crafted, realistic, low-key novels of the twenties. His four volumes of memoirs, published in 1948–55, when Egge was in his eighties, contain vivid accounts of writers from Ibsen to Undset.

In his autobiography, *Læregutt* (1942; Apprentice), Johan Bojer (1872–1959) writes about a case that deeply affected him when he was a boy in his native Trondheim. A bricklayer named Lyngvær Hagerup, a radical leftist who had made his way in local politics and been elected to parliament, publicly admitted that once in his youth he had spent a few days in jail for a petty crime. His career was ruined. This incident prompted Bojer to write his first important novel, *Et folketog* (1896; A Procession). In Bojer's view, politics promotes false values and blurs the boundary between truth and falsehood in public life. The notion is further explored in several subsequent novels, of which the most successful and, at the time, popular was *Troens magt* (1903;

The Power of Faith; Eng. tr. *The Power of a Lie*, 1908 and others). The novel enjoyed considerable success in France, where it was read in the context of the Dreyfus affair.

After the war the tenor of Bojer's work changed. Where once he had focused his criticism on the psychological mechanisms engendered by modern life, he now proposed a message of idealism and altruism. The best of these works is *Den store hunger* (1916; Eng. tr. *The Great Hunger*, 1918 and others), in which altruism is seen as the remedy to the ills of modern life. The novels of Bojer that continue to be read today, however, are the ones he wrote in the twenties, which are free of explicit ideological analysis. They are *Den siste viking* (1921; Eng. tr. *Last of the Vikings*, 1923 and others), *Vor egen stamme* (1924; Our Own Stock; Eng. tr. *Emigrants*, 1925), and *Folk ved sjøen* (1929; Eng. tr. *Folk by the Sea*, 1931). The first of them is considered by critics to be the best novel written about sailors and the sea in Norwegian literature. In it Bojer looks back to his youth and in a series of variegated episodes describes the adventures of fishermen-peasants from Trøndelag as they sail to the fishing banks of Lofoten. It was a way of life already in its final days because of the advent of steamships, so there is a note of restrained pathos to Bojer's tale. In this work and the other two novels, the second about Norwegian emigrants in North America and the last again about fishermen from Trøndelag, Bojer has no message to preach. In portraying the lives of ordinary people simply and artistically, he was making the best case for the national and human values in which he most believed.

Gabriel Scott (1874–1958) lived and wrote in southern Norway, an area he loved and frequently described in his works. Questions about good and evil concerned Scott throughout his career. In the 1940s he wrote his autobiography in the form of a novel trilogy—*En drøm om en drøm* (1940–47; A Dream of a Dream)—in which the main character, Finn Eggen, is preoccupied with discovering how a good God can permit evil to exist in the world and ultimately concludes that the source of existence is unqualified goodness. Scott dealt with the struggle between good and evil in historical terms in his first major work, *Jernbyrden* (1915; Eng. tr. *The Burden of Iron*, 1935). Set in the 1800s, the novel identifies the moral corruption and greed of the upper classes as the origin of evil. Scott's sympathies, like most of the writers of this period who chronicled the demise of their traditional way of life, are with the peasants.

A peasant fisherman named Markus is the central character in Scott's next work, generally considered to be his masterpiece, the novel *Kilden* (1918; The Spring; Eng. tr. *Markus the Fisherman*, 1931). In telling Markus's life story, Scott merges his narrative voice with his character's wise and simple one, stringing everyday incidents realistically narrated and philosophical reflections into a seamless prose poem. This work draws its inspiration from three equally important sources: Scott's love of nature, particularly Norway's southern seacoast; his respect for the values of peasant culture; and his admiration for the philosophy of Spinoza.

Scott continued to address himself to moral and religious questions in his subsequent works, in the form of legends and folktales as well as in novels of peasant life, among them the humorous and poetic *Det gyldne evangelium* (1921; Eng. tr. *The Golden Gospel*, 1928). The work that Scott considered his best is *Helgenen* (1935; The Saint), a story about a peasant boy who is miraculously cured by a holy picture.

Scott began his career as an author of children's books, several of which have become classics: *Hollænder-Jonas eller gutten sin egen* (1908; Dutchman Jonas or His Own Boy), *Sølvfaks* (1912; The Cat Silver), and *Kari Kveldsmat* (1913; Kari Supper; Eng. tr. *Kari*, 1931).

Three Analysts of a Changing Age:
Nini Roll Anker, Kristian Elster, Sven Elvestad
The rapidity with which power changed hands in Norway at the end of the nineteenth and the beginning of the twentieth century induced some writers to focus on the culture itself and attempt to lay bare some prominent mechanisms driving it. Such is the case with Nini Roll Anker, Kristian Elster, and Sven Elvestad. Briefly put, their undertaking is more sociological than aesthetic; character matters less for them than cultural context.

Nini Roll Anker (1873–1942) grew up in a family of civil servants during the late nineteenth century when her class was in decline. When she married, it was into a wealthy merchant family. During her long career she wrote about the condition of women in both classes, as well as the lot of poor working women. In her novels she analyzed the forces in each of these settings which crippled women emotionally and erotically and thereby prevented them from realizing their potential. She wrote not so much to obtain equal treatment for women as to communicate a sense that women understood better than men the sacredness of life. Politics was not the issue for her, but rather the great personal and social damage caused by the sexual repression of women. In many of her works she communicates a message concerning the necessity of avoiding or undoing repression so that both men and women might be saved from the mechanization inherent in modern life and the threat of annihilation by war. In a lecture held in 1918 she said: "Many people speak of and wait for a 'new type of woman.' Instead we women ought to place our hope in a new and better type of man—in men who would be wise enough to bow their heads in reverence for the army of working women who still, all over the world, feel themselves to be the chosen ones because they know that in their willingness to serve life rests the fate of humanity, also men's."

Anker generally wrote in the tendentious spirit of the radicals of the Modern Breakthrough. She placed her characters in well-defined social environments and set them to debating about politics and ideology. Despite this polemical thrust, however, she did not make caricatures even of the reactionaries and puritans, who for her are the villains. She had a compassionate understanding of the insuperable financial and social forces that bend and twist human lives.

Anker began her writing career in 1906 with a volume of short stories, *Lill-Anna og andre* (1906; Little Anna and Others), which focused on the conditions of working women. She achieved wide public attention and recognition with her next two novels, *Benedicte Stendal* (1909) and *Det svake kjøn* (1915; The Weaker Sex), both about the disastrous effects of women's traditional education. In the trilogy that some critics consider her best work, *Huset i Søgaten* (1923; The House on Lake Street), *I Amtmandsgaarden* (1925; On the District Governor's Estate), *Under skraataket* (1927; Beneath the Slanting Roof), Anker depicts life in a Norwegian civil-service family during three generations, from 1840 to the First World War. From the standpoint of cultural history, the trilogy is also valuable for its faithful portrait of lower-middle-class life in Trondheim.

Anker's fervent devotion to life as an absolute value inspired her to write several powerful antiwar works. One was a play, *Kirken* (1921; The Church), and another was her last novel, *Kvinnen og den svarte fuglen* (1945; The Woman and the Black Bird), which was written in 1942 but because of its strong pacifist message could not be published until after the war.

Kristian Elster (1881–1947) presents his fictions against a backdrop of rapid political and social change, but he is far less polemical and engaged than Anker. Politics in his novels is not considered with a view to its inherent dynamics. Instead, it is seen as an arena in which men undergo psychological and ethical testing. Thematically, there is a kinship between Anker and Elster in that one of his central concerns was the fate of the civil-service class.

Elster, son of the novelist Kristian Elster, came, like Nini Roll Anker, from a family of government officials and experienced the rapid diminution of his class's power as he grew up. One of his most widely read books, *Av skyggernes slegt* (1919; From a Race of Shadows), depicts a government official's family encountering the modern period, while *Bonde Veirskjæg* (1930;

Farmer Weatherbeard) treats a comparable process for a peasant and his family.

An important earlier work by Elster is the trilogy *I lære* (1911; Apprenticeship), *Landeveien* (1912; The Road), *Mester* (1913; Master). Clearly autobiographical, these books depict a young man's development against the background of politics. In 1919 Elster published his reminiscences of the war period in a novel called *Min Bror Harris* (My Brother Harris). Here he was particularly critical of the individualism characteristic of Christiania's literary and artistic milieu from the turn of the century.

Elster was a prolific writer. In addition to his many novels, he wrote a popular history of Norwegian literature (2 vols., 1923–24, republished in 6 vols., 1934–35), some literary studies (on Ibsen's poetry, Goethe, and Kierkegaard), and several volumes of his collected book and theater reviews.

Sven Elvestad (1884–1934) was a journalist and, under the pseudonym Stein Riverton, author of detective novels—indeed, the creator of this genre in Norwegian literature. In novels such as *Angsten* (1910; Fear) and *De fortaptes hus* (1911; The House of the Lost), he confirmed the tradition of Tryggve Andersen and produced intriguing portraits of people suffering from alienation and guilt. His book of sketches, *Aar og dag. Stemninger og skildringer* (1913; Years and Days: Moods and Portraits), contains a suggestive essay called "Løpet mot døden" (The Race toward Death), in which, thirteen years before Sigmund Freud's *Das Unbehagan in der Kultur (Civilization and Its Discontents)*, he proposes that civilization carries the seeds of its own destruction. He continued this line of thought in *Professor Umbrosus* (1922).

Elvestad also produced a fine collection of short stories, *Himmel og hav* (1922; Heaven and Sea), and a book of interviews, *13 mennesker* (1932; Thirteen People), which became his most popular work.

THE EPIC NOVELISTS: UNDSET, DUUN, UPPDAL, FALKBERGET

Epic scope and accomplishment characterize the work of a surprising number of modern Norwegian novelists, of whom the most important are Sigrid Undset, Olav Duun, Kristofer Uppdal, and Johan Falkberget. Together their writings represent perhaps the most significant body of imaginative literature to have been produced in twentieth-century Norway. While these writers do not form a school or group—indeed, they differ widely both in religious and philosophical outlook and in political ideology—they can with the benefit of hindsight be seen to have taken on a common task: that of placing their contemporary moment within the framework of national history in such a way as to give to its current contradictions inspiring and instructive precedents.

Modernism in literature and the other arts became prominent in countries such as France, England, and Germany, which had experienced the First World War directly. In the aftermath of that upheaval the modernism of Ezra Pound, James Joyce, T. S. Eliot, and others marked a sea change in consciousness, an obligatory repudiation of the very premises by which history previously had been understood. The task facing Norwegian artists, spared a direct experience of the abyss of the war, was different from that of their European contemporaries. While Norwegians too had to grapple with the twentieth century and the disappearance of many components of their traditional culture, modernity presented a different face to them. Rather than chaos, their national experience was one of wide-ranging rationalization, secularization, and social reorganization, all of which were occurring at a rapid pace. In a sense, it was Norway's very success along these lines, that is, in exploiting its resources and organizing itself politically and socially, that threatened to alienate it from its past and the values and standards enshrined there. Each of its epic novelists took on the important mission of framing the ethical debate implicit in Norway's new circumstances in narrative terms that offered a sense of historical continuity. And as is so often the case in modern Norwegian literature, Ibsen, in this regard as well, turns out to have been a forerunner. With his history plays such as *Kejser og Galilæer* and *Kongsemnerne*, he had given important lessons in how modern psychological and philosophical conflicts could be convincingly incarnated in characters from antiquity or the Middle Ages.

Sigrid Undset

Of the aforementioned epic novelists, Sigrid Undset (1882–1949) is probably the most important. A writer of international reputation, she was awarded the Nobel Prize for her novel *Kristin Lavransdatter* in 1928.

Her father, Ingvald Undset, was a well-known archaeologist who communicated his fondness for historical research to his daughter, with whom he had a close relationship. He died when she was eleven years old, and the family's finances declined. After high school Sigrid Undset, who had hoped to become a painter, went to business school and in 1898 at the age of sixteen began working as an office clerk. She continued in this occupation for the next ten years, storing in her memory the frequently disheartening experiences of modern working women which she was later to use in her novels of contemporary life. In her free time she read widely in history and literature and began to write fiction. The first manuscript she attempted to publish was a novel set in the Middle Ages. It was rejected. The editor, with advice that would come to haunt him, told her to forget about writing historical novels, for which in his view she had no talent, and to try her hand at one set in the present. Apparently following his advice, she wrote a novel with a contemporary setting, *Fru Martha Oulie,* published in 1907, and her writing career was launched. In 1912 she married a painter, Anders Svarstad, who had three children from a previous marriage. She had three children with him, then separated from him in 1919 and moved to Lillehammer, where in the following years she wrote the historical novels on which her renown mainly rests. In 1924 she became a Roman Catholic.

Undset's conversion marked the end of at least one phase of a quest for religious certainty which can be followed in the works she wrote between 1907 and 1918, novels such as the aforementioned *Fru Martha Oulie,* and *Jenny* (1911; Eng. tr. 1920 and others), *Vaaren* (1914; Spring), *Splinten av troldspeilet* (1917; Eng. tr. *Images in a Mirror,* 1938), and the short-story collections *Den lykkelige alder* (1908; The Happy Age), *Fattige skjæbner* (1913; Poor Existences), and *De kloge jomfruer* (1918; The Wise Virgins)—the last two partly translated as *Four Stories* (1959). With the exception of the novel *Fortællingen om Viga-Ljot og Vigdis* (1910; The Tale of Viga-Ljot and Vigdis), they are set in the present and narrated, as are all Undset's novels, in a realistic manner and with a quality of writing that is comparable to, for example, Theodore Dreiser's, that is, sturdy and often powerful.

Fru Martha Oulie is a novel about a woman trying to find her way between the ethical demands of marriage and the personal fulfillment offered by illicit love. Its opening sentence, "I have been unfaithful to my husband," sounds a motif that would echo throughout Undset's entire body of work. On their own and with no system of belief in which to set their experiences, the heroines of her early novels find little fulfillment either in the traditional roles of wife and mother or in that of the modern emancipated woman. Mrs. Oulie declares: "In the old days I used to get angry when I read in books that a woman could be happy only if she merged herself with another person. But now I agree and say Amen to it, just as I do to all the other threadbare and down-at-the-heel truths that I opposed in my youth." In *Vaaren,* it is children who supply the heroine with her raison d'être: "As long as I have my children," she declares, "I know that I can go on living—gladly, no matter what else life might have in store for me."

But resignation, duty, and the demands of motherhood could not in themselves truly quiet the fundamental uneasiness at the heart of Undset's characters. The women in all her novels experience their condition as built on an insoluble dilemma. As women, usually as daughters who have been loved in their childhood, they are motivated by a need to offer and receive love, but this need, for the various reasons that the novels explore, cannot be met. Motherhood satisfies the need to love, at least in part, and while it is the solution adopted by several heroines, Undset is a sufficiently shrewd psychologist to suggest, even while seeming to approve of her characters' maternal altruism, that it may also be a mask for a displaced narcissism.

In other words, while Undset frames her fictions from a distinctly female standpoint, she then works them out in ways that suggest that gender ultimately is a distraction. Human love contains no solution to the dilemma it itself proposes. Implicitly, then, Undset's viewpoint was religious well before she converted to Catholicism, which is not to say that as an artist she drew on her adopted religion for answers. Rather, she found in it a transcendent position from which she could recognize the problems inherent in human relations as insoluble. If anything, Catholicism enhanced her instinctive realism.

Perhaps Undset's strongest formulation of the dilemma posed by love, among the novels set in the modern period, occurs in *Jenny*, the work considered to be her first artistic success. Twenty-eight-year-old Jenny Winge, an aspiring painter, meets the somewhat younger Helge Gram in Rome and for the first time falls in love. The two are happy in Rome, but their relationship falls apart when they go back to Norway. There Jenny becomes the lover of Helge's father, a man who had also wanted to be a painter. She breaks up with him when she gets pregnant. Back in Rome, she again meets Helge, who compels her to have sex with him. Depressed, Jenny commits suicide.

It is not the drastic plot that gives this novel its interest but the double perspective Undset brings to bear on it. On the one hand, she shows that from a psychological or sociological standpoint Jenny has ample justification for what she does; on the other hand, she tries to convince the reader that Jenny has made all the wrong choices. Given her needs and circumstances, Jenny was prone to fall victim; and yet her status as victim does not, in the narrator's eyes, excuse her. Certainly she is not responsible for the way in which her need to be loved was engendered in her, yet ethically she must bear its consequences.

How much is the modern period to blame? While *Jenny* and Undset's other modern novels pose the question of the extent to which people are condemned to the kind of narcissism that prevents them from making responsible and ethically correct decisions, what motive does modern life offer for not considering one's own needs as primary? The general response given in these novels is simply the somber one of the hindsight view of the damages incurred.

But has it always been so? Are narcissism, self-centeredness, and egoism particularly modern phenomena? It was apparently to pose the question in its starkest terms that Undset chose to set it in the context of the Middle Ages. Of course, she had always had a keen historical interest in the period, but beyond the intrinsic fascination she felt for it, she made clear on several occasions that writing historical fiction was her way of posing present-day problems in a heightened and clarified form. In 1910, for example, after publishing *Viga-Ljot og Vigdis,* she wrote:

> I felt sure that I understood the early Middle Ages, a time when what was pure and unchangeably human in people stood undisguised. Social forms were so simple that the individual was able to grow and develop freely. . . . If one peels off the layer of notions and ideas peculiar to one's own time, one can step directly into the medieval period and see life from its standpoint—one discovers that it coincides with one's own. Then one can write as a contemporary. For of course one can only write novels about one's own contemporary period.

This statement expresses in clear terms that for all its accuracy of historical detail, the fourteenth century in which *Kristin Lavransdatter* is set is conceived of as a timeless realm in which what Undset calls "the human heart" might reveal itself. The present is projected into the past so that the inessentials of the present may fall away and human relations stand forth in all their purity.

In volume 1, *Kransen* (1920; Eng. tr. *The Bridal Wreath,* 1930), we follow Kristin from the time she is a young girl, the apple of her father's eye, to the time of her marriage. In these years Kristin turns away from the fiancé her father has chosen for her, a good but unexciting man, and falls in love with a dashing knight named Erlend. He is drawn as a very "modern" character—restless, divided, passionate, bored. In his need to satisfy his desire for Kristin he presents a male, and more culpable, version of the narcissistic character of which Kristin, of course, presents the female counterpart. Her condition is less culpable and more intractable since it has been implanted in her by her father's love, against which the child has no defense.

Volume 2, *Husfrue* (1921; Eng. tr. *The Mistress of Husaby,* 1930), shows us Kristin as Erlend's wife. This volume describes her daily life in all its aspects as she repeatedly gives birth and contends with her husband's difficult and dangerous character. He becomes involved in a plot against the king, which eventually requires her to travel to meet the king and plead for her husband's pardon.

Volume 3, *Korset* (1922; Eng. tr. *The Cross*, 1930), gives us the final years of Kristin and Erlend's marriage, following the course of their passion as it continues to endure and flare beneath its load of accumulated bitterness. At last Erlend is killed in an armed scuffle. Kristin's life is ended by the Black Death. In her final days, in an act of ultimate altruism, she cares for plague victims and then is stricken down.

This plot outline is a mere sketch of the rich network of human relations Undset draws in this extraordinary work. There are murders and political intrigues, branching subplots involving Kristin's parents, her sister, her former fiancé, her spiritual advisers, Erlend's former mistresses, and others. For all its length there is a huge steadiness to Undset's composition, a patient elaboration of detail contrasting with quick, saga-inspired narrative sweeps. Throughout the whole, the reader is kept informed of odors, tastes, textures, moods, visible nature in its shifting variety. And though we know that in the Middle Ages the relative importance of food and sex was the inverse of what it is in modern times, the book carries conviction: readers are led to believe that this is how people actually lived in the Middle Ages.

The abstractness Undset aimed at by placing her tale in the fourteenth century she achieved. She highlighted the dilemma of egoism by removing it from the present, where it is ubiquitous and thus irresolvable, and placing it in a feudal period where by definition it could not be the norm. The human bond in the feudal period was governed by a code of fealty within a hierarchical structure. Kristin's and Erlend's versions of self-centeredness are glaring exceptions in a world where everyone else who is not breaking the law is bound by fidelity to one's word. Whether medieval people actually succeeded in living up to their ethical code is not Undset's point. She does not idealize the Middle Ages. But at least then people knew that ethical code. Underlying the muddle of human emotion was a clear spiritual geometry.

Undset's next novel, *Olav Audunssøn i Hestviken* (1925; Olav Audunssøn of Hestviken; Eng. tr. *The Axe* and *The Snake Pit*, 1928–29), and its sequel, *Olav Audunssøn og hans børn* (1927; Olav Audunssøn and His Children; Eng. tr. *In the Wilderness* and *The Son Avenger*, 1929–30), are set in the latter half of the thirteenth century. In these novels, the psychology is more narrowly Catholic. It concerns Olav's need to confess a murder he committed in his youth and his inability to do so. The language of Olav's inner monologues is also more weighted with technical theological notions than in

Kristin Lavransdatter, of which the tetralogy is in several ways a harsher rendition.

The relationship between Olav and Ingunn is one that like Kristin's and Erlend's has been tainted from the start, but it unfolds in its later phase without the incitement of sexual attraction. Olav's inability to go to confession or to disengage himself from the heroic code of honor, based on renown, is a more blatant and less excusable form of Kristin's self-preoccupation. But there is great psychological power in these books, particularly in the accounts of Olav's relationship with his unacknowledged son, and a grimness in the marshaling of consequences which gives them their own kind of grandeur.

After these novels Undset wrote four novels set in the present and offering a fairly straightforward critique of its values: *Gymnadenia* (1929; Eng. tr. *The Wild Orchid,* 1931), *Den brændende busk* (1930; Eng. tr. *The Burning Bush,* 1932), *Ida Elisabeth* (1932; Eng. tr. 1933), and *Den trofaste hustru* (1936; Eng. tr. *The Faithful Wife,* 1937). She also wrote essays, hagiographical works, and memoirs, all exemplifying her direct sort of realism and high standard of craftsmanship.

Olav Duun

In her funeral eulogy for Olav Duun (1876–1939), Sigrid Undset called him Norway's greatest writer. They were novelists of a comparable ambition and magnitude, creators of serial novels of epic proportions which attempted to capture essential aspects of their nation's culture in the very years when it was undergoing significant changes. Their art is informed by a profound understanding of human character both in its timeless workings and as it is shaped by social and historical contingencies. Alike in the scope and quality of their art, in practice they form a kind of naturally contrasting pair.

Undset wrote in conservative bokmål, tinged, in her historical novels, with archaic turns of phrase and vocabulary. To give these books a flavor of the sagas, she kept her sentences fairly simple in structure, though she did not hesitate on occasion to use complex sentences or a wide-ranging vocabulary, particularly when describing natural scenery or the inner workings of a character's psychology. Duun, by contrast, wrote in nynorsk (or, more correctly, in the dialect of his home district of Namdal), with a degree of understatement, verbal restraint, and stylistic simplicity that approaches pure laconism. Reading Undset, one is aware of listening to the voice of high or learned culture; reading Duun—though he was an educated man and a teacher—one has the impression of listening to the voice of peasant culture at its pithiest and most pungent.

In their views of history the two authors also form an interesting contrast. Undset's focus is on the couple and the nuclear family. Clearly, she sees them as the enduring units at the heart of culture, relatively impervious to historical change. Indeed, as mentioned above, she shifts her focus from present to past to eliminate from her analysis of character those distracting aspects specific to it from the twentieth century. In essence, she views the human being as drawn by two opposing forces: love and egoism. Whether set in the fourteenth or the twentieth century, her novels examine the various factors that cause people to erect and maintain their defenses or to try, when drawn by love, to open them.

Duun's perspective, in contrast, is focused on the individual as he or she was formed by cultural and family history and is presently affected by the surrounding group. For Duun, history is a living process. Rather than looking through it or beneath it to timeless essences, he is concerned in his art with following its waxings and wanings as they manifest themselves in culture. He studies in particular how these changes are reflected in the shifting balance that exists between the individual and the group. Indeed, if we reduce his work to a formula, we can say that it is concerned with the integrity of the individual and the forces that threaten or sustain it. Chief among the hostile forces are the ones that emanate from the group in the forms of small-mindedness, jealousy, vindictiveness, and greed. Beyond these, Duun is a master at suggesting the workings of some mysterious fatality in things themselves. Conversely, the sustaining forces spring mainly from some primordial source of vitality on which certain individuals, in ways that he studies in novel after novel, can draw.

The primary access to this source of strength is the *ætt*, the clan, generations of the extended family as it unfolds in time and produces new versions of its founders. Here Duun's vision bears some similarity to those of the great realists and naturalists of the nineteenth century, such as Honoré de Balzac and Emile Zola, though without their scientific underpinnings and consequent positivistic pessimism. In Duun's world, heredity is not a fatality but a mysterious resource. His masterpiece, the six-volume family saga called *Juvikfolke* (1918–23; Eng. tr. *The People of Juvik*, 1930–35), traces its workings through six generations. At the very bottom of the past—as Odin Setran, one of the saga's main characters, proclaims—is an openness, a wellspring of possibility from which the present can draw strength in inexplicable ways.

Duun came from Namdal in northern Trøndelag, the area that served as the setting for all his writings. The small village where he grew up was important to him both for its old traditions and for its apparently large number of eccentric and highly individualistic characters. He lived at his family home until he was twenty-five, then left for the teachers' college in Levanger. In 1908 he married and moved to Botne near Holmestrand, where he worked as a teacher until he was fifty-one. He published a book a year for twenty years.

Duun's first novels, *Marjane* (1908), *På tvert,* (1909; Wayward), *Nøkksjølia* (1910), *Hilderøya* (1912), and *På Lyngsøya* (1917; On Lyngsøya), are studies of human beings who have been either defeated by stronger rivals or at least forced into permanent attitudes of resistance. The novels are psychologically acute accounts of the workings of power as it breaks certain characters and arouses others to fierce resistance. Individual psychology is set within a historical and sociological framework: the specifics of peasant life in one particular northern Norwegian village. Duun went on to write two novels, *Tre venner* (1914; Three Friends) and *Harald* (1915), concerning the other side of the coin. In them he told the story of men who were not losers in life but winners, men who enjoyed general esteem, who were *lykkemenn* (i.e., inherently fortunate individuals). But good luck does not necessarily make good people. The protagonist of the first novel is a psychologically and morally empty individual, and the protagonist of the latter can find no object or project that engages him. In Duun's next novel, *Det gode samvitet* (1916; Eng. tr. *Good Conscience,* 1928), he traces the rise of the modern sensibility over three generations, the gradual diminishing of group awareness and the corresponding increase in individualism.

In retrospect, all these novels look like a preparation for *Juvik-folke,* Duun's greatest work. In these six novels, Duun traces the history of a family over six generations, from 1814 to 1914. Though the work is as local and specific in its setting and details as all Duun's other writings, in fact it is a psychological portrait of Norway from the time of the vikings to the present. Here is the program of the whole as stated by Odin Setran, the hero of the latter half of the saga:

> I want to show you a people who stumbled their way to the present out of the old time and the darkness, surrounded by nothing but the dark forces. I want to show the man who wrestled with Satan, and won, for he is the greatest of them. Yes, won so that they dared to breathe and laugh as they pleased; it was a great day, it lasted perhaps for centuries. Oh I see them, the whole crowd of them moving, stripping off the darkness and the powers and rushing blindly forward into the light and then standing there, gazing around and seeing practically nothing. I feel I am right in the midst of them, that I have made the

journey with them, the whole way in darkness! I want to show you the time when they all were aware of each other. And then the time when one or the other of them became aware of himself. And at last when they will see the battle, the great battle, when it will be all against one and one against all. And he who shall lose everything but still win.

The first three novels, *Juvikingar* (1918; Eng. tr. *The Trough*, 1930), *I blinda* (1919; Eng. tr. *The Blind Man*, 1931), and *Storbrylloppe* (1920; Eng. tr. *The Big Wedding*, 1932), show us the last of the old-style Juvikings, Per-Anders, a viking and a heathen who lives his life with great unreflective vitality. None of his sons has his same superb balance. They are either a little crazier than he or a little more weighted with conscience. The third of these novels is set in the 1870s, and in it we note the arrival of modern culture with its shift from a barter to a money economy.

The last three novels, *I eventyre* (1921; In Fairyland; Eng. tr. *Odin*, 1933), *I ungdommen* (1921; In Youth; Eng. tr. *Odin Grows Up*, 1934), and *I stormen* (1922; Eng. tr. *The Storm*, 1935), trace the life of Odin Setran, who embodies many of the strengths of the old Juvikings along with a conscience and modern shrewdness. His ambition is to bring prosperity and happiness to his village. He succeeds in becoming mayor and director of a fish-oil factory. Throughout his life he has had a rival, a diabolic character, Lauris, who lacks Odin's mystically unbroken contact with his ancestors. In the final pages of the novel, when both men are at risk of drowning, Odin overcomes his rival by refusing to kill him. He allows Lauris to live at the expense of his own life. Odin becomes a sacrificial hero out of compassion and self-respect, in this way fusing the two distinct codes of the Christian and pagan cultures that comprise him.

Duun's next major work was a trilogy that openly addresses the conflict between good and evil: *Medmenneske* (1929; Fellow Man), *Ragnhild* (1931), *Siste leveåre* (1933; Last Year). In the first novel, an evil man is killed by his daughter-in-law, a good person who perceives the harm the man is doing to other people, including his son, and who finds the instinctive courage to act. In the subsequent volumes, which are not as powerful as the first, we watch the aftereffects of her deed.

In Duun's final works, *Samtid* (1936, Contemporaries) and *Menneske og maktene* (1938; Mankind and the Powers; Eng. tr. *The Floodtide of Fate*, 1961), he moves away from his earlier notion of inherited or inherent cultural strength as a remedy to the evils of modern times. Written in the shadow of the approach of World War II, these novels explore the catastrophic workings of mass psychology under extreme pressure without proposing any remedies other than the mysterious presence of goodness in certain people. Duun uses symbolism and compression to enhance the tension and sense of doom in these works. In *Menneske og maktene*, he gathers a group of characters on an island that according to a prophecy is doomed to be destroyed by a flood. The first six chapters of the novel present us with the stories of the various characters and show their different strategies for meeting the incipient catastrophe. The final chapter presents the storm. Without attempting to explain why certain human beings, when put to the test, are able to perform in noble and altruistic ways, Duun ends his writing career by showing that this nevertheless is the case.

Kristofer Uppdal

Kristofer Uppdal (1878–1961), novelist, poet, and essayist, was another writer with epic intentions. Where Duun wrote about peasants and village culture and Undset about people of the lower, middle, and upper classes, Uppdal wrote about the new working class that had recently been created in Norway by the advent of industrialism. Neither the deep continuities nor the unchanging aspects of history interested Uppdal, but rather the way in which it was being radically transformed by the proletarian worker. These were the people who had recently left their villages by the thousands and gone to work in factories, in mines, or as itinerant laborers, building roads and laying railroad track. For Uppdal, the proletarian worker was not only a new sociological and historical phenomenon, he carried philosophical and even religious significance as well.

In addition to being a novelist, Uppdal was an important poet who produced some of Norway's first modernist verse. Particularly his erotic poetry in the volumes *Elskhug* (1919; Love) and *Altarelden* (1920; Altar Fire) is innovative in spirit and technique, written in a free-verse style similar to Walt Whitman's and that of the Finno-Swedish modernists. In his later years Uppdal devoted his energies primarily to poetry of a difficult philosophical sort.

A striking aspect of Norway's industrialization is the rapidity with which the workers in the factories and on the railroads were organized into unions. Outlawed in the 1880s, unions continued to be formed in secret. By the turn of the century they were legal, and from 1905 to 1908 membership in the Arbeidsmannsforbundet (Norwegian Labor Union) quintupled. With large numbers came great possibilities, the heady prospect of radical change both in the present and in the distant future. In a series of ten novels with the collective title *Dansen gjenom skuggeheimen* (1911–24; The Dance through

the World of Shadows), Uppdal focused on several aspects of the prole-
tarian/union process.

In the first half of the series, he tells the stories of several young men as
they grow up and step into this new mode of life, this new network of relationships. In the latter half of the series, particularly volumes 7 and 10, he
considers the complex relationships between the worker and the labor
union, the body that both empowers and potentially restricts him.

Uppdal was born on a farm in northern Trøndelag. In his youth he
worked as a farm laborer and shepherd and in his father's livery stable. After
spending some time in a folk high school, he worked for twelve years as a
miner and itinerant laborer, traveling the length and breadth of Norway. He
joined the union in 1899 and subsequently served in several elected positions.

Uppdal wrote in nynorsk. His first novel, *Ved Akerselva* (1910; By the
Aker River), which was republished in 1923 as part of the *Dansen* series, describes social unrest in a farming village and then follows the life of a man
who becomes an itinerant worker and eventually a hobo. He goes through a
social and psychological degeneration but is finally able, through the effects
of solitude, to reach a more genuine sense of himself. It is unlikely that Uppdal had conceived his plan for a series of interrelated novels when he wrote
this novel, but the curve it describes indicates the tendency in all his subsequent writings. Ultimately, he is interested in the worker as a type of new
man, a kind of modern hero, the man who takes charge and remakes himself.

His next novel is the one that gives the series its name, *Dansen gjenom
skuggeheimen* (1911; The Dance through the World of Shadows). Aesthetically, it is one of the best of the group. The plot concerns an artistically
gifted boy who leaves his northern village at age sixteen and, while leading
the life of an itinerant laborer, has numerous erotic affairs. Eventually, he returns to his native village as a construction worker. Here he falls in love with
the daughter of the richest farmer in the village and marries her, in this way
reestablishing his connection with his past. Uppdal's language in this novel
is powerful and evocative, amounting to prose poetry in its sensuous descriptions. Both in his novels and even more in his poetry, Uppdal honors
Eros as a cosmic force, the agency through which human beings are able to
surpass their limits and establish contact with the cosmos.

Another important novel in the series is *Stigeren* (The Mining Foreman),
from 1914. Set in a mining town in the period from the 1880s to the end of
World War I, it portrays the public and private life of a labor-union official,
his relationship with the workers and engineers on the one hand and with

his wife on the other. Uppdal shows the tensions inside the labor movement, as one branch of it becomes increasingly radical and the other tends in the direction of democratic socialism. The main character is unable to handle these conflicting pressures and in the end flees to the mountains.

Three of the novels in the second half of the series reflect Uppdal's own contemporary experience in the labor union. They do not have the energy and color, the sense of freedom and sensuous immediacy of the earlier volumes. But *Domkyrkjebyggjaren* (The Cathedral Builder), from 1921, is a powerful study of an idealist who unsuccessfully tries to communicate to his colleagues his sense of the labor movement as a religious undertaking.

Herdsla (The Test), the last novel of the series, contains a poem called "Songen om rallaren" (Song of the Itinerant Worker), part of which extols the worker in the following terms:

On his way through the country, he sows factories. Shakes
    them out of his sleeve.
Factories to spin and weave clothes. To warm people. And to
    make them fair to the eye.
At the end of his workday, the laborer ambles away, pleased
    with his work. Half-naked. Maybe a little chilled,
    having sweated through a tough shift. And frighteningly
    dirty, after hard labor.
But like a bountiful king he walks away from it all.
What value have the things he has made for the one who makes
    everything?
Himself, his value is the same. More.
Things have value only for those who can make nothing.

Dansen gjenom skuggeheimen, then, culminates in a vision of the worker as the new, free, powerful human being. Though Uppdal recognizes that the labor movement is full of problems, that it contains self-serving and even corrupt individuals—having worked as a union official himself, he was not naive in that regard—he nevertheless looks to labor's future with a visionary's glance.

After completing his epic cycle of novels in 1924, Uppdal worked on a large-scale poetic project that was published in three volumes in 1947, under the collective title *Kulten*. Kulten is the name of a prophet like Nietzsche's Zarathustra, who alternates between relating the events of the last three years of his life (he dies in the final volume) and preaching his new religion. The religion is a dark compendium of the teachings of Zarathustra, Buddha, Jesus, and pessimistic modern philosophers such as Schopenhauer and Nietzsche. The work is difficult to read for several reasons. Twelve hundred pages long, it is written in a version of Uppdal's Trøndelag dialect which, according to commentator Philip Houm, he worked to make as archaic as possible. The style is sometimes cryptic to the point of the mysterious, sometimes verbose. And the message is gloomy. Kulten is an impoverished wanderer who on several occasions mentions that he has earlier been confined against his will in a madhouse. He feels himself to be an unrecognized genius. Now he is full of contempt for the average unenlightened human being who fails to grasp that it is through suffering that the meaning of life can best be understood and its purposes served. Apparently, Uppdal intended the figure to be seen both as a specific human being living in a specific part of Norway and as representative of all humanity—and, of course, as his own spokesman.

Johan Falkberget

Norway's other great proletarian novelist, Johan Falkberget (1879–1967), wrote epic novels set in the coal-mining area of Røros. A Christian and a socialist, Falkberget, unlike his fellow novelist Uppdal, did not celebrate the newness of the present in the figure of the proletarian worker, but summoned up visions of the worker's lot in the past to serve as inspirations for the present. He thus created a kind of visionary fusion of eras. In his greatest novels, those written in the second half of his career—*Den fjerde nattevakt* (1923; Eng. tr. *The Fourth Night Watch*, 1968), *Christianus Sextus* (3 vols., 1927–35), and *Nattens brød* (4 vols., The Bread of Night, 1940–59)—Falkberget mirrored present problems in those of the past in ways suggesting, first, that the human condition is essentially unchanging, and second, that in an earlier time, before the advent of capitalism, people had more psychological and religious resources on which to draw. With his great learning and considerable art, Falkberget worked to give Norwegians a more useful past, so to speak, than the one they actually had—a heartening vision with which to confront the grim present. These works are usually called historical novels, as indeed in a conventional sense they are. Falkberget was an autodidact who researched the local history around Røros in southern Trøndelag, his native area, with a thoroughness that won him two honorary doctorates and high professional praise. The local color, folklore, customs, language, all the minutiae of daily life are rendered with loving accuracy. But the lookout point from which the action is seen is religious, and the underlying paradigm of the plots is mythical. These are stories of death and renewal, of purification through suffering. In this they are in some ways akin to Sigrid Undset's great medieval novels, though Falkberget's socialistic

Lutheran humanism is perhaps warmer and more relenting than Undset's stern Catholicism.

The Røros area of southern Trøndelag has been a mining district since the middle of the seventeenth century and has attracted large numbers of workers from Sweden and Germany. Judging from Falkberget's novels, there was a remarkable mix of languages, customs, and cultures in the place: ancient superstitions connected to the underground and the working of metals, many strata of religious beliefs, modern scientific and technological understanding, and military lore from a variety of armies and campaigns.

Falkberget grew up steeped in this mixture. He was fond of calling himself a "mountain man," of pointing out that his family had lived in Røros for three-hundred years and that he looked at the world and wrote his novels "in the light of his miner's lamp." His father had worked in the mines as an ore assessor. A literate man, he read Zola's *Germinal* aloud to his son when the latter was a boy. Johan began working in the mines when he was eleven and continued until he was twenty-five, when he quit in order to write.

His first works were sketches of miners and life in the mountains. Then he wrote some novels about working people, the most important of which are *Svarte fjelde* (1907; Black Mountains), *Ved den evige sne* (1908; By the Eternal Snow), and *Urtidsnat* (1909; Primordial Night), which depict different groups of workers—itinerant railroad laborers, farmers, miners—and show the great differences and conflicts among their various ways of life. In these works Falkberget developed his particular strengths as a storyteller: a characterization that is almost Dickensian in its quirkiness and a sensuously expressionistic manner of describing nature.

Though the conditions in Falkberget's novels of working life are often grim, there is little indignation motivating their description. Life as viewed by Falkberget is moved by powerful, timeless forces, one of the greatest of which is Eros. Falkberget next wrote several historical novels in which lovers are parted by war (*Eli Sjursdatter*, [1913]), by class difference (*Av jarleætt* [1915; Of Noble Family]), and by unresolved guilt (*Lisbet paa Jarnfjeld* [1915; Eng. tr. *Lisbeth of Jarnfjeld*, 1930]). In 1923 he wrote his first historical novel of epic scope, *Den fjerde nattevakt* (1923; Eng. tr. *The Fourth Night Watch*, 1968). Before doing so, however, he wrote a novel set in the present about a family of uprooted workers which is generally considered to be the most significant of his early works: *Brændoffer* (1918; The Burnt Offering). The book is divided into two parts, the first of which concerns a family of indentured servants who move from the country to the city and who, in the second part, perish in their new surroundings. Falkberget's presentation of cause and effect is grimly naturalistic. Social conditions and heredity grind the family down, destroying their possibilities for love and happiness. The Danish novelist Hans Kirk, a Marxist, wrote of the novel: "There has scarcely been written an imaginative work in world literature which more pitilessly depicts brutal capitalism before the working class had built its defenses, the unions. It is a masterpiece, and if there is one book in Scandinavia which fulfills Gorky's criterion for socialist realism—that people be portrayed as products of the labor process—this is the one" (*Falkberget nå* [Oslo, 1980], p. 13).

Though capitalism is clearly shown to be a major factor in the tragedy of this family, the message of the novel is not one of resistance. Capitalism is viewed as a fatality and as a moral failing—a manifestation of greed, not a particular social system for exchanging goods and services. In 1920 Falkberget renewed his charge against capitalism in a lighter mode with a popular book of comic sketches about a capitalist war profiteer, *Bør Børson jr.*

Den fjerde nattevakt is set in the early years of the nineteenth century. It is the story of an illicit love affair between an arrogant Lutheran minister and a peasant woman, and the devastating consequences in both their lives. Ultimately, the minister is humbled through his fall into sin, and through his suffering he acquires wisdom. The power of the work is in Falkberget's wonderfully individualized portraits and his manner of juxtaposing them. It is clear that he draws his characters with great love and sympathy, seeing in them a potential for greatness which adversity only enhances.

After four years of research Falkberget published the first volume of *Christianus Sextus*. The title refers to the copper mine, named for the Danish-Norwegian King Christian VI (1730–46), where the action is located in the early years of the eighteenth century. Falkberget chose this troubled period of Scandinavian history, after the end of the Great Nordic War (1701–20), for its resonance with the situation of modern Norway in the years following the First World War. Both were periods of great unemployment, food shortages, displacement of populations, and accompanying social unrest. In this way the troubles of the two periods are in a sense relativized and shown to be superficially different versions of perpetually recurring human woes. *Christianus Sextus* can properly be called a collective novel. It has little in the way of plot. Each volume is built up of series of episodes that show how people react to adversity, how they are driven by their passions, and how they are purified through suffering. It is an enormous book of portraits, the faces and bodies of largely unremarkable people caught at significant junctures for varying periods of time in the narrator's glance.

Falkberget's next and final novel, a work in four volumes, *Nattens brød*

(1940–59; The Bread of Night), is considered his masterpiece. Set in the latter half of the seventeenth century, it is characterized by the same richness of detail and episode, historical accuracy, and profusion of bizarre and interesting characters as his earlier historical novels, at the same time as it is held together by a powerful central narrative. It concerns a young woman named An-Magritt, whose name forms the title of the first volume, a figure conceived along ideal lines whose failings nevertheless keep her within the limits of credibility. Chief among them is her pride, her unwillingness to humble herself. In creating An-Magritt, Falkberget said that he was seeing the dawn of modern Norway, of 1814 and 1905, the dates of Norway's independence. With this remark Falkberget reveals his intention of stepping back into the past in order to revise it, to imagine an ideal mix of capitalism and socialism. An-Magritt is a strong, intelligent, loving, but unsentimental peasant who through her work, her business schemes, her inventions, her mercantilist principles, brings profit and well-being to Røros. She is helped by the Swedish bailiff Hedström, a character who incarnates the principles of socialistic Christianity and who lends her money for her enterprises.

IN SEARCH OF NORWAY'S SOUL

With the exception of Kristofer Uppdal, Norway's great epic novelists helped to suture the gap in Norwegian history created by centuries of Danish rule. Uppdal's work, though, was akin to theirs in its attempt to portray the historical emergence of the new proletarian class in Norway and to suggest its potentially revolutionary significance. It was to history, in other words, that all these writers turned in their attempt to render in their art the very new and very old phenomenon that was twentieth-century Norway. Although it is not possible to draw hard and fast lines of demarcation in literary history, we might identify another important group of writers as those who chose to approach Norway more from an anthropological than a historical standpoint. Broadly speaking, they were artists with organicist notions of culture similar to those of the great romantic thinkers of the nineteenth century, Johann Gottfried von Herder and N. F. S. Grundtvig. For them, both the moderns and their nineteenth-century forebears, a nation is to be conceived of as a living being with its own specific individuality, or "folk soul."

A prime characteristic of this soul is that it is not to be found in cities, prey as they are to the desiccating forces of rationalism and mechanism. All the writers we are about to consider fix their attention on local, rural cultures, either on the specific places and people themselves or, just as often, on their significance, their mystical import. Many of these writers were fired by the ambition to preserve the specificity of Norway, its multirootedness in the local, so to speak, against the homogenizing effects of modern international industrial culture. In Scandinavia, rootedness in the local had been endorsed and promoted by the great Danish poet, theologian, and educator N. F. S. Grundtvig (1783–1872) at the beginning of the nineteenth century. The folk high school movement he founded had produced several schools in Norway which continued to radiate an intense and frequently mystically tinged patriotism.

In the twentieth century two thinkers who were particularly significant in breathing new life into Norway's quest for her folk soul were the Norwegian author Hans E. Kinck (1865–1926) and the Austrian thinker Rudolf Steiner (1861–1925). Different in many ways, especially in their metaphysics, both were nevertheless neoromantic thinkers who, thanks to the persistence with which they were able to communicate their inspirational views of Norway, exerted considerable influence on its twentieth-century literature.

In his novels, plays, and essays, Kinck carried out a kind of "psychohistory" of the country, probing into the layers of the national unconscious for the residues of the unresolved conflicts of history. He showed them to be layered in strata, from pagan to Christian, according to group and locality. Though profoundly patriotic, Kinck was not interested in delivering a conventionally idealistic or sentimental picture of Norway. Indeed, what he saw as particularly Norwegian was the bizarre, the idiosyncratic, the tough and gnarled viking root that neither Christianity nor modern times had succeeded in extirpating.

Rudolf Steiner, in contrast, was a Christian mystic, though a very idiosyncratic one. He named his system of thought "anthroposophy," distinguishing it from Theosophy, with which he was for a time affiliated. Anthroposophy combines elements of Goethean science, esoteric Christianity, theosophy, German *Geistesgeschicte* (intellectual history), and various strands of occultism such as alchemy and astrology into an extraordinarily complex system that nevertheless is based on a few simple ideas. One of them is that behind the visible world is another world of spiritual forces. To understand the logic of the workings of these forces is to grasp the secrets of the cosmos and of human history, for both, according to Steiner, unfold according to a grand set of interlocking analogies.

In 1910 Steiner gave a series of lectures in Christiania entitled *Die Mission einzelner Volksseelen im Zusammenhange mit der germanisch-nordischen Mythologie* (The Mission of Particular Folk Souls in Connection with Germanic-Nordic Mythology), which announced the transcendent significance of the role that Norway, to the extent that she was able to maintain contact with her dual heritage, pagan and Christian, was to play in world culture. It was an inspiring message to which several Norwegian artists were ready to listen.

Tore Ørjasæter

Tore Ørjasæter (1886–1968) came from Skjåk in Gudbrandsdal, the heartland of Norway. His village was next to Lom, where his friend, the poet Olav Aukrust, lived. Of the two, Aukrust was the visionary and Ørjasæter the mystic. Aukrust was profoundly influenced by Rudolf Steiner's anthroposophy, whereas, if Ørjasæter was, it was probably by way of Aukrust. Aukrust gathers himself in his poetry for ecstatic leaps and apocalyptic visions; Ørjasæter speaks with a quieter, homelier, less bardic voice, often about his dividedness and longing for wholeness. Both are national poets, writing of Norway as a land with a holy past and a sacred destiny. For Aukrust, that meant turning his glance to the past and to the local; for Ørjasæter, it implied an attempt to achieve a synthesis of the present and the past and a sense of psychological wholeness.

As a teacher's son and an intellectual Ørjasæter grew up with a certain emotional gap between himself and his native village. In his first book of poems (1908) he writes of his desire to be free and travel, but in the title poem, "Ættararv" (Family Inheritance), he also says:

To live on the farm
son after his father
this is the best
fate for a man.

In 1913 Ørjasæter published the first volume of the trilogy *Gudbrand Langleite,* an epic poem cycle for which, along with a cycle of poems called *Elvesong* (1932; Riversong), he is chiefly known. In 1920 came volume 2, entitled *Bru-millom* (The Bridge Between), and in 1927, *Skuggen* (The Shadow). In 1941 Ørjasæter published the whole in a new, reworked edition. The trilogy depicts the inner development of the artist while measuring the change in the times in which he is living. It follows the poet from his youth in the village through his travels and eventual return. In accomplishing this cycle, he has achieved the inner freedom necessary to begin to write poetry, but he suffers from a feeling that with this vocation he has been given a task beyond his powers to accomplish. He is impeded by forces of

"fate," in particular the suffering inherent in erotic love, and also by a mysterious dark aspect of his vocation which he names "the shadow."

One of Ørjasæter's most famous erotic poems is "Elgen" (The Moose),
from the first volume of *Gudbrand Langleite*. It shows a powerful, lonely
bull moose meeting a cow in the forest. At the first exchange of glances between them, the moose is shot and dies. An equally sorrowful treatment of
Eros occurs in the collection from 1915, *Mannskvæde* (Man's Song):

Man bears woman on his way of the cross
over a brambly moor
on his broad shoulders he bears
the heavy burden of his own blood.

This treatment, which sees erotic suffering in terms of Christian mysticism,
allows Ørjasæter to invoke Christ as a mediating agent.

The "shadow" from which Gudbrand struggles to free himself in the final
volume of the trilogy manifests itself in the figure of Elland Falkjom, a devil-
may-care fiddle player, who threatens to lead Gudbrand astray through his
recklessness. Interestingly enough, the figure appears to be modeled on
Ørjasæter's friend, Olav Aukrust. In terms of the poem, however,
Gudbrand becomes free of the shadow when he recognizes it as a part of
himself, perhaps the demonic aspect of his own ambition.

Elvesong, Ørjasæter's most popular book, recasts his persistent conflict
between will and fate in terms that allow them to be resolved. It is a cycle of
poems that follows a frozen drop of water as it melts, falls into a river, and
eventually finds its way to the sea. These poems are suffused with an almost
Buddhist understanding of the limitations inherent in the personal ego and
in a correspondingly joyous sense of freedom when it dissolves. The over-
arching metaphor of the river journey permits Ørjasæter to clothe his allegory in quiet, specific descriptions of landscape, stream, and ocean. *Livet
skal vinne* (1939; Life Will Win) contains poems about his fear of the coming war and his impressions of Nazi Germany. Ørjasæter affirms his belief
that "life will win / even if the earth should perish." This volume also contains Ørjasæter's strongest statement concerning Christ as a cosmic force of
unity.

After the war, in addition to several more volumes of poetry, Ørjasæter
published two powerfully expressionistic plays, *Christophoros* (1948) and
Den lange bryllaupsreisa (1949; The Long Honeymoon). The latter is tech-
nically innovative in the manner of August Strindberg's *Dream Play*, part of
the action occurring in an after-death state. It deals with modern fears and
forms of guilt—war, for example, and the atom bomb.

His last volume, *Klårhaust* (1963; Clear Autumn), contains some wonderfully calm and steady poems of farewell and insight: "Your lack of weapons was itself your shield."

Olav Aukrust

Olav Aukrust (1883–1929) came from the village of Lom in Gudbrandsdal. Or, more precisely, from the neighboring narrow Bøver valley, which, surrounded by high mountains, remains untouched by sunshine for several months of the year. The images in Aukrust's poetry were furnished by this landscape, particularly by the dramatic tension in the struggle between light and dark. He grew up in a severely pietistic household. As a boy he was keenly interested in religious and philosophical questions, reading writers such as Søren Kierkegaard, William James, and Henri Bergson. In literature he was fond of Thomas Carlyle and Ralph Waldo Emerson, and among Norwegians, Bjørnstjerne Bjørnson and Sigbjørn Obstfelder. His favorite poet was the national poet of Norway, Henrik Wergeland, whom he tried to emulate in his own poetry and to whom he is often favorably compared.

As an adult he worked as a teacher and, from 1914 to 1917, as a principal in a folk high school in the mountain district of Dovre. Crucial to his development were the years he spent in teacher training, 1907–8, when he lived at the house of the poet and preacher Ivar Mortensson Egnund. It was Mortensson who introduced Aukrust to the ideas of Rudolf Steiner and who with his own translation of the medieval *Edda* poems gave an example of a poet putting himself in the service of Norway's national spirit. For Mortensson, the folk soul of Norway was to be found in its folklore, folk poetry, dialects, pagan mythology, and medieval Christian piety. He saw the role of the poet as a religious one: to steep himself in his cultural heritage and then rearticulate it for the present. All this aroused an enthusiastic response in Aukrust.

Much of Aukrust's adult life was marked by serious illness. He was unable to continue his school work after 1917. In 1915 he published his first poems in newspapers and journals. On the basis of these works alone the poet and novelist Arne Garborg proclaimed Aukrust to be Norway's greatest living poet. In the same year, in the spring, an ecstatic religious experience made a decisive impact on him. Although he frequently referred to this experience in later years, he said it could not be put into words—only, he explained to friends, that it was as if he had gazed directly into the hidden connectedness in everything. In the following year he published his first book of poems, *Himmelvarden* (The Cairn of Heaven), a volume of 330 pages.

Himmelvarden is a book of lyrics which describes and in a sense enacts the struggle of the poet to become a religious initiate and seer. Aukrust uses the mountain as a metaphor for his steep and difficult climb. Many of the poems describe his inner sufferings and torments, sometimes in elaborate metaphors and allegories, sometimes with direct, almost naked diction, as in the following literal translation:

When the mind is desolate
when there is no more joy
and memory sits within
by empty, forgotten nests
when sorrow weeps bereft
pleading, sinking to its knees
when hope is met by fear
which draws all things down
in a dark deepened by tears and horror
and sunders the last trembling bridge:
then be with me, then be with me
then pray for me, then pray for me
for faith, faith, faith!

Most of Aukrust's poems defy translation. They are written in powerful nynorsk, each word as if hewn from the local rock. Employing complicated patterns of stressed and unstressed syllables, dissonance, assonance, and always heavy end rhymes, they are locked as securely in their Norwegian bodies as Gerard Manley Hopkins's are in his English ones—to which, in their complicated music and religious fervor, they bear a resemblance.

After eleven years marked by sickness and the struggle to write, Aukrust published *Hamar i Hellom* (1926); the title, he said, was the name of an old parish prophet. Concerned with Norway at the level of the village, it was the first volume of a projected trilogy. The next was to deal with Norway as a nation, and finally, the third volume was to place Norway in a universal context. These last two volumes were never finished, but the poems that had been completed were published posthumously in *Solrenning* (1930; Sunrise). In *Hamar i Hellom*, Aukrust wrote poems describing the customs and lore of the Norwegian mountain village, hoping to give vital instances of old Norwegian culture which could be marshaled against Norway's present cultural decline.

Unquestionably, Aukrust was a major poet; future critics and historians must try to determine the extent to which his passionate nationalism restricted or enhanced his literary gifts.

Inge Krokann

Inge Krokann (1893–1962) was a nationalistic novelist in the spirit of Olav Aukrust, who indeed was Krokann's great inspiration. Krokann also studied to be a folk high school teacher and imbibed during his training the same romantic theories of language and culture as inspired Aukrust. Also like Aukrust, Krokann was incapacitated during much of his adult life by tuberculosis. Notions of suffering and purgation figured significantly in the writings of both men. Wisdom they considered a kind of crystallized pain, and insight something to be gained by moving through life as if it were a way of the cross. The patron saint of Norway, the martyred Christian King Olav, stood for both men as a holy national prototype.

Krokann's novels exemplify his theories. His first one, *I Dovre-sno* (1929; In Dovre Cold), published in the year Aukrust died, is set in Oppdal in the fifteenth century, a time of national decline for Norway. The Danish and Swedish kings were fighting for control of the country, the Church was corrupt, the local chiefs were weak. A group of peasants appeal to a man named Roald, proprietor of a large farm named Lo, to lead them. Roald is a natural chief, possessed of great virtues and coming from a strong family, but his youth has been spent in service to the Catholic Church and in this way he has divided himself from his pagan roots. The split in his consciousness is of course a metaphor for Norway's split, just as his eventual defeat and tragic death is a metonymy for Norway during its years of subjugation. The influence of Undset and Duun can also be noted here and in other of Krokann's novels. Like the people of Juvik, Krokann's characters are in mystical contact with their dead ancestors. Krokann intended *I Dovre-sno* to be a single novel, but on completing it, he decided to write a series of novels about the family at Lo. They are *Gjenom fonna* (1931; Through the Snowdrift), *På Linfeksing* (1934; On Linfeksing [the name of the hero's horse]), and *Under himmelteiknet* (1941; Under the Sign of Heaven).

Krokann is a somewhat schematic novelist, committed to demonstrating a thesis. Like Duun, Undset, and Falkberget, he was enormously learned in the history and folklore of his area, but in terms of verbal artistry and psychological insight he is not their peer. His books make difficult reading, and part of their weight derives from the fact that Krokann, like Uppdal, writes in dense local dialect.

In 1939, before finishing the Dovre series of novels, Krokann published a powerful novel about lynch justice in a small pietistic village in the west of Norway: *Blodrøter* (Blood Roots). Set at the end of the nineteenth century and based on an actual case, it is a grim study of small-mindedness and mass suggestion which has little of the national romantic about it, other than that once again suffering brings insight to the falsely accused protagonist.

Olav Nygard

Like Tore Ørjasæter and Olav Aukrust, Olav Nygard (1884–1924), a friend of Ørjasæter, was a visionary nynorsk poet who succumbed to tuberculosis. Of the three, he is the one who suffered most from material poverty. After completing a few years of folk high school, he spent the rest of his short life struggling to eke out a living while attempting to write and withstand the complications of his disease. His letters frequently make sad reading. Nygard published his first book of poems in 1913, *Flodmaal* (High Water Mark), then spent the next seven years trying to earn money at odd jobs: "I was living in Bergen doing menial labor. There was a time when I survived for more than a month on roughly forty cents a day. That's when I got sick for the first time, as perhaps you remember," he wrote to Hulda Garborg, to explain his silence and his final resentful unwillingness to publish.

Because of its formal perfection, Nygard's poetry is often seen as influenced by Olaf Bull's. By his own account, the poets who meant most to him were Shakespeare (some of whose sonnets he translated), John Keats, Percy Bysshe Shelley, Robert Burns (whom he also translated), and the Norwegian Henrik Wergeland. The major theme of much of his poetry, as one might expect, is death:

I love my affliction which broke new paths
to the lovely castle of my feelings.
I have found my soul and found my refuge
In the blood which from my lungs has sprung.

Or:

Earth receive
the gift you gave me;
a stone I shake
my body from me;
light of foot, I
tread my gravepath.

As this last example suggests, though Nygard's poetry is often melancholy, it is also often bright with courage. In addition to *Flodmaal,* he published three more small volumes: *Runemaal* (1914; Rune Language), *Kvæde* (1915; Poems), and *Ved vebande* (1923; On the Border of Holy Place). All three collections have a high percentage of accomplished and moving poems, but in the last Nygard rises to great heights. He approaches death as sacred ground, unsentimentally and clearly, and with a compression and unflinching seriousness reminiscent at times of Emily Dickinson. His ambition to be on a level with his fate, to meet it worthily and even with gratitude, also recalls Wergeland's mystical serenity on his deathbed.

Though he had a hard lot in life, Nygard died confident that the body of his work would survive: "In this faith I have lived, in the faith I die, that my time will come, though it may take fifty years after my burial."

Alf Larsen

Poet, essayist, literary critic, journal editor, and polemicist, Alf Larsen (1885–1967) is the writer in Norway who most explicitly and militantly attached himself to Rudolf Steiner's anthroposophy, though it did not have the effect on him, as it did on Aukrust, of turning him toward local culture. Larsen vigorously eschewed the provincial. While paying Aukrust the homage of imitating him in his own poetry, it was Aukrust the religious quester, rather than the nationalist, that Larsen admired. The poles of Larsen's poetry are the cosmos, whose workings he interpreted through Steiner, and the natural world, particularly the sea and the shore and the woods surrounding his house.

His first books of poems were gloomy: *Vinterlandet* (1912; Winter Land), *Indgangen* (1915; Entry; a Norwegian reworking of the first volume, originally in Danish), *Billeder fra den gamle stue* (1916; Pictures from the Old Parlor), and *Digte* (1919; Poems). Pessimistic in tone, many of these poems describe the sea, especially in its gray, forbidding moods. Then, with *Vindens sus* (1927; The Rush of the Wind), nature takes on a transparency. By this time Larsen had read Steiner's *Occult Science*, which changed his understanding of the physical world. No longer feeling himself estranged from nature, he can contemplate its working with a wider range of sympathy.

As long as Larsen fixes his eyes on the specifics of the natural world around him or remains aware of himself as a fallible human being, he is an engaging artist. After *Vindens sus* he published *Jordens drøm* (1930; Earth's Dream), *I jordens lys* (1946; In the Light of the Earth), *Stemninger ved Okeanos' bredder* (1949; Moods on Oceanus's Shore), *Høsthav* (1958; Autumn Sea), *En tangkrans* (1959; A Crown of Seaweed), *Den jordiske vandringsmann* (1968; The Earthly Pilgrim), and *Siste strofer* (1969; Last Stanzas).

Larsen also published two superb collections of literary criticism, *Den kongelige kunst* (1948; The Royal Art) and *I kunstens tjeneste* (1964; In the Service of Art). His essays on Melville, Conrad, Dostoevski are tactful, empathic, and full of insight. Also to be noted is a collection of aphorisms, *Nattetanker* (1951; Night Thoughts), which contains many interesting and moving reflections.

Ingeborg Refling Hagen

Ingeborg Refling Hagen (1895–1989), short-story writer, novelist, poet, and educator, was an avowed follower of Hans Kinck, who praised her first work, *Naar elv skifter leie* (When the Stream Shifts Direction), when it appeared in 1920. It is a collection of tales that, like all her work, depict village life in her native Hedmark. Like Kinck, Hagen portrays what one might call the split in Norway's folk soul, the opposition between the dark pagan past and the light forces of the modern Christian period. Unlike Kinck, however, she writes from the standpoint of a Christian socialist. The focus of her work is primarily on women, especially as they are involved with the forces of Eros and death.

Ingeborg Refling Hagen grew up in a poor peasant household, where her mother, despite overwork, did everything she could to instill a love of traditional literature in her children. Whether they were folktales, fairy tales, or Bible stories, she made certain she had stories to tell her children every day. Hagen gives a vivid account of these moments in the first volume—*Vi må greie oss selv* (1948; We Must Manage Alone)—of her four-volume autobiography, whose collective title is *Livsfrisen* (Life Frieze).

In her novels such as *Loke saar havre* (1922; Loki Sows Oats), *Ugild* (1923; The Uncompensated), and *Fostersverdet* (1928; The Family Sword), she unrolls nightmare visions of Hedmark between the late Middle Ages and the nineteenth century. Often using folk narrators, Hagen weaves narratives in which the boundaries between realism, vision, and nightmare are erased. In a rhythmic prose that accords with the often horrific material, Hagen tells tales of extreme poverty: the selling of indentured servants, killings, abortions, witchcraft, cruelty, doomed love, and so on. In story after story, dreamy young women, wandering through a world of horrors, are enmeshed in the coils of Eros and drawn down to disaster.

Hagen's work became more moderate and balanced in tone during the thirties. Then she wrote what, from an aesthetic standpoint, is her most successful work, the novel trilogy *Tre døgn på storskogen* (Three Days and Nights in the Deep Woods), which consists of *Kjørekaren* (1937; The Teamster), *Sognebudet* (1938; The Sick Visit), and *Den nye læreren* (1939; The New Teacher). It was also during the thirties that Hagen produced her most popular book: a collection of prose poems and free verse with the title *Jeg vil hem att* (1932; I Want to Go Home Again). These poems are spoken by emigrants to America who remember the old country with sadness and nostalgia.

Ole Edevart Rölvaag

The theme of Norwegian emigration to America was primarily useful to writers like Ingeborg Refling Hagen and Johan Bojer as a means of commenting on forces at work in the Norway of their day, but to O. E. Rölvaag (1876–1931), who was actually living the life of an emigrant, the theme had a different and greater immediacy. Only a writer who had lived on the prairies, as Rölvaag had, could understand the intractability of America. Insisting on being taken on its own terms, America welcomed foreign people while excluding their cultures. Though Rölvaag wrote *Giants in the Earth* in Norwegian and for a Norwegian audience, the novel is no allegory through which Norway might perceive itself. Instead, it has become a classic of American midwestern fiction, assigned to successive generations of high school students as a means of giving them some sense of the hidden cost imposed by the melting pot.

Born in Helgeland in northern Norway to a family of fishermen, Rölvaag yielded to his curiosity to travel abroad when his uncle offered to pay his way to South Dakota. Impelled by a strong desire to learn and eventually to write, Rölvaag left his uncle's farm after three years of hard work to attend Augustana Academy, a small, church-affiliated college in South Dakota. After graduating, Rölvaag went on to get his bachelor's degree from St. Olaf College in Northfield, Minnesota. He left for a year of graduate studies at the University of Oslo, and then, after working at various teaching positions, he returned in 1906 to St. Olaf's, where he became chairman of its Norwegian Department, a position he held for the rest of his life, dividing his energies between teaching and writing.

In 1912, under the pseudonym Paal Mørck, he wrote his first book, *Amerikabreve* (America Letters; Eng. tr. *The Third Life of Per Smevik*, 1971), an epistolary novel based on his experiences in South Dakota. A second novel, *Paa glemte veie* (1914; On Forgotten Roads), was followed by two more, *To tullinger* (1920; Two Fools; Eng. tr. *Pure Gold*, 1930) and *Længselens baat* (1921; Eng. tr. *The Boat of Longing*, 1933), both published under his own name. In a book of essays, *Omkring fædrearven* (1922; Concerning Our Heritage), Rölvaag strongly encouraged the Norwegian-American community to preserve its language and culture.

When he read in a newspaper that the novelist Johan Bojer intended to visit the United States and write a novel about Norwegian emigrant life, Rölvaag took a leave of absence from his teaching and in the course of a year produced the first volume of his major work, *I de dage* (1924; In Those Days). He finished the second volume, *Riket grundlegges* (1925; The Founding of the Kingdom), and two years later (1927) published an English translation of both books: *Giants in the Earth: A Saga of the Prairie*. It is a novel that works on two levels. On one it gives a vividly circumstantial account of the life of typical Norwegian settlers in the American Midwest, while on the other, in the two main characters, Per Hansa and his wife Beret, Rölvaag created striking embodiments of the opposing forces he felt at work in himself and his fellow emigrants. Per Hansa stands for the spirit of adventure and conquest, while Beret exemplifies the fear of the unknown and nostalgia for the culture that has been left behind. Beret sees her husband's enterprise as an act of arrogance, and his attempt to establish himself on the godforsaken and endless prairie seems to her a challenge tossed in the face of God. Her reason threatens to give way as she watches him struggle, while he feels he has no choice but to redouble his efforts. For all its careful ethnology and occasional charm, *Giants in the Earth* is a bleakly modern book.

Rölvaag wrote two more volumes in the series, *Peder Seier* (1928; Eng. tr. *Peder Victorious*, 1929) and *Den signede dag* (1931; The Blessed Day; Eng. tr. *Their Father's God*, 1931), which continue the account of Beret and her children and chronicle her doomed attempt to maintain some semblance of Norwegian culture in America. Her children grow up desiring only to become Americans. Rölvaag intended to write another volume in which he would have shown the continuing assimilation of Peder Seier but died before he could realize his intention.

TWO MODERN MASTERS: VESAAS AND SANDEL

The modernist writer is one for whom meaning has become problematic: the premises for simple, straightforward meaning—a coherent interior self and a public world of stable truths and values—have vanished, and in their place the artist senses the increasing fragility of the inner self and the widening gap between language and reality. Attempting to shake off his or her acute sense of alienation and unreality, the writer, paradoxically, invokes the very threat of incoherence and meaninglessness in terms compelling enough to overcome it. Tarjei Vesaas and Cora Sandel, while not modernists in the radical mode of Joyce or Eliot, are nevertheless recognizably part of the international modernist tradition in the sense that they are both writers for whom the old novel of empiricism and realism is no longer valid. An intense, subtly layered inwardness characterizes Sandel's work, and rich formal inventiveness typifies that of Vesaas.

In prose of great formal beauty, Sandel repeatedly brings her protagonists—most often women—to a point of breakdown in human relations where a frightening gap of unmediated reality opens before them. A chasm of cosmic indifference or basic malevolence (often it is hard to say which) threatens to engulf them. Countering this threat, Sandel is brave enough to posit only the art with which it is rendered. For her, the aesthetic is perhaps the sole area of freedom and value. Vesaas, in contrast, uses a wide range of formal means in his novels and short stories, from subtly psychological realism to symbol and allegory, to impart an almost mystical sense of the inarticulable substratum in things. Art for him is not a thing of finished perfection but a means of probing further and further into the mystery of silence.

Tarjei Vesaas

"The force that sustains life," wrote Tarjei Vesaas (1897–1970) in his essay "Poesi og tronge tider" (1939; Poetry and Difficult Times), "streams from an eternal sun, and the great events in life proceed in accord with it: birth, love, death, new birth. As before. This is the force that sustains poetry, that stirs desire for the intangible, the fragile and frightening and inexpressible. And then poetry and secret dreams *must* grow."

Vesaas is a major writer who, particularly in the latter and more experimental half of his career, explored the tenuous and difficult area between the great solar order and the dark, lunatic, sabotaging forces. For him, both language and dreams are allied with the latter, leading into the dark. As his career went on, he pursued these forces to greater and greater lengths. Words seem to arise in Vesaas's most compelling texts in the mysterious way that water fills up the footprint of an explorer in new, possibly dangerous terrain.

One of Norway's modern writers who can be read in an international context, Vesaas came from Vinje in Telemark and wrote in nynorsk. He grew up on a farm, Vesaas, and spent his adult years living and writing (married to the poet Halldis Moren Vesaas) on another farm, Midtbø, not far from the first one. Vesaas had published nine novels and a play by the time of his first major artistic success, *Det store spelet* (The Great Game; Eng. tr. *The Great Cycle*, 1967) in 1934. This novel tells the story of a boy who grows up on a farm, feeling trapped by the prospect of having to take it over from his father. His father's atavistic love of the earth repels him. At one point, when his father embraces him and tells him that he, the son, will never leave, the boy feels nauseous. These feelings, Vesaas has written, were similar to ones he experienced in his youth, when, as the oldest son—the *odelsgut*—he stood first in line to inherit the family farm. Though he felt a strong connection to the land, he felt an even stronger desire to become a writer. Transmuting his real-life refusal into fictional acceptance, Vesaas has the boy in *Det store spelet* overcome his feelings of repulsion as his father gets older. Called on one day to kill a horse that has become too old to work, the young man has a sudden insight into the eternal play of life and death which enables him to accept his place and to assume the role of the one who balances life and death, as his father had done before him. In 1935 Vesaas published a sequel, *Kvinnor ropar heim* (Women Call Home), an elegiac description of farm life whose mood was inspired by his own happy marriage.

By 1940, when Vesaas published his novel *Kimen* (Eng. tr. *The Seed*, 1964), he had written thirteen novels and two collections of short stories. Stylistically, he had become a master at exploiting the tendencies inherent in nynorsk toward simple sentence structure, understatement, and concise and predominantly concrete vocabulary to the point where his language seemed to hum and vibrate with the force of the unspoken. His artful plainness calls attention to itself, taking on a sphinxlike quality. He had learned to heighten realism with allegory in a way that endowed everyday events with secret and dreamlike significance. *Kimen* tells the story of a peaceful island that is visited by a mentally unbalanced man. He becomes deranged when he sees some riled pigs devouring their young. In a subsequent fit of madness, he kills a young girl. The village people pursue him and kill him. That night, in a huge barn, the people assemble to assess what they have done. The father of the slain girl says that violence cannot be tolerated, and his rejection of the logic of the day's events promises a healing of them. His word, the seed referred to in the title, reinstitutes the ethical, humane order. In retrospect, *Kimen* appears to epitomize and exorcise the Second World War, in which Norway had become embroiled the year the novel was published.

Huset i mørkret (1945; Eng. tr. *The House in the Dark*, 1976) was written during the occupation of Norway. Here Vesaas has further simplified his narrative means to pure allegory. No names or events from the real world are mentioned. Everything is abstract and menacing: the dark house is Norway, the occupying forces are called "the arrow people." Because there is no ambiguity as to what is being described, Vesaas can trim the allegory to a minimum of plot and concentrate on evoking an atmosphere of suspicion and dread. In this way, the novel takes on a universality that allows it to be applied correlatively to all modern situations of dictatorial oppression.

Such allegories can be less effective, however, when their referent is not clear. In some of the novels Vesaas wrote after the war, the ineffable occasionally presses so hard on the narrative that the effect is strained and claustrophobic. Such criticism can be directed in particular to *Tårnet* (1948; The Tower), *Signalet* (1950; The Signal), and *Brannen* (1961; The Fire). The general sense of Vesaas's endeavors nevertheless is clear in these works. Proceeding in the manner of earlier Scandinavian expressionists, like Pär Lagerkvist and August Strindberg, Vesaas attempts to present direct, concentrated images for the repressed nightmare beneath modern reality.

Both more accessible and aesthetically successful is the novel *Fuglane* (1957; Eng. tr. *The Birds*, 1968), Vesaas's masterpiece. Allegory, symbol, abstraction, and understatement are effectively combined to tell the touching story of a simpleminded man, Mattis, and of the events that lead to his death. Mattis lives with his sister, Hege, and spends most of his time thinking his simple private thoughts and paying attention to the mute messages of the natural world. Vesaas renders the flight of birds, the look of trees, the invitingness of flat stones with the kind of presence and power they presumably have for a mind freed of practical and utilitarian concerns. Mattis is a character who belongs in the company of Benjy from William Faulkner's *Sound and the Fury,* or even Prince Myshkin from Dostoevski's *Idiot.* When a hard-working, practical lumberjack moves in with Hege, intruding on Mattis's idyll, Mattis retreats. Vesaas renders his inevitable destruction with great power and tact.

Vesaas received the Nordic Prize in literature for his novel *Is-slottet* (1963; Eng. tr. *The Ice Palace*, 1966), an intriguing mixture of symbolism and depth psychology which has also been made into a movie. In this work, Vesaas presents us with two girls, Siss and Unn, who are bound together in a way that leaves ambiguous whether they are two halves of the same being or independent characters tied by some strange psychic connection. At the climax of the novel, one of the girls wanders into the ice castle of the title, a frozen waterfall, and dies there. The other girl, who also feels a strong pull toward death, manages to save herself. It is an eerie work, written with great poetic compression and open to a puzzling variety of interpretations. Vesaas's final novels, *Bruene* (1966; Eng. tr. *The Bridges,* 1969) and *Båten om kvelden* (1968; Eng. tr. *The Boat in the Evening,* 1971), are perhaps best seen as prose poems, the latter with many references to Vesaas's youth.

Vesaas also published several volumes of poetry and short stories. The short-story collections *Vindane* (1952; The Winds), which won first prize in a European competition, and *Ein vakker dag* (1959; A Beautiful Day) contain examples of the full range of his art: psychologically apt portrayals of childhood and first love, lyrical descriptions of animals and farm life, and powerfully condensed symbolist tales reminiscent of Kafka or Lagerkvist. Vesaas published his first volume of poetry in his fifties, *Kjeldene* (1946; The

Springs). The language and form were fairly conventional, but in subsequent volumes, *Leiken og lynet* (1947; Games and Lightning), *Lykka for ferdesmenn* (1949; Happiness for Travelers), *Løynde eldars land* (1953; Eng. tr. *Land of Hidden Fires*, 1973), and *Ver ny, vår draum* (1956; Be New, Our Dream), he developed into a powerful modernistic poet.

Cora Sandel

While Tarjei Vesaas was a master of the modernistic symbolical and/or expressionist tale, Cora Sandel (pseudonym of Sara Fabricius) (1880–1974) deployed her considerable art in novels and tales of self-conscious psychological realism. That is, she tells her stories by narrating the effects of the world on her subtly tuned and bravely feminine sensibility. A deep sense of pathos and irony infuses all Sandel's fiction. Her children and adolescent girls are amazed and fearful at the loss of vitality and intelligence that they see occurring among their domesticated, browbeaten, or—in the case of the defiant—outcast older sisters. And from this recognition Sandel's art bestows compassion and sympathy on all the various creatures, men and animals included, that are subject to mistreatment and oppression.

Sandel's major work is a trilogy of novels about her fictional alter ego, Alberte, of which she published the first volume when she was forty-six: *Alberte og Jakob* (1926; Eng. tr. *Alberta and Jacob*, 1962). The novel tells the story of Alberte's childhood in her northern city above the polar circle. Jakob is Alberte's brother, her confidant and ally until he makes his escape by going to sea. In careful, telling detail, Sandel lets the reader feel the cold and darkness of the place, the family's straitened means, the awful respectability of the middle-class ladies in the town with their "oilcloth sofas and porcelain dogs." As Alberte looks around her, her only prospect seems to become one of these ladies, buying security with a conventional marriage. The only women she notices living outside this frame are a crazy old lady and a prostitute. The volume ends with a half-hearted suicide attempt on Alberte's part, followed by a new resolve to live.

Volume 2, *Alberte og friheten* (1931; Eng. tr. *Alberta and Freedom*, 1963), tells the story of Alberte in Paris. She works as a model, keenly aware of her poverty, spending her days wandering, she says, "through the back streets of life." "There was another life she should have been living, something else than this. Somewhere there is a path she is not finding." Lonely, almost morbidly sensitive, but with a toughness that ultimately saves her, she experiences a love affair with one man and then marriage to another, a painter as self-preoccupied as she though brutally insensitive. She helps a friend go through an abortion. Unhappy in her marriage and stuck in her career, Alberte begins to write notes on small scraps of paper that she keeps in the bottom of her trunk.

The final volume, *Bare Alberte* (1939; Eng. tr. *Alberta Alone*, 1965), chronicles Alberte's painful steps in becoming an artist. Among the most difficult is the handing over of her son, whom she had had against her husband's wishes, into his custody. With no money and with a gathering awareness that she is first and foremost an artist, she returns to Norway and finally writes a novel very much like the one we have just read.

Sandel's other books include the novels *Kranes konditori* (1945; Eng. tr. *Krane's Café*, 1968) and *Kjøp ikke Dondi* (1958; Don't Buy Dondi; Eng. tr. *The Leech*, 1960) and the following collections of short stories: *En blå sofa* (1927; A Blue Sofa), *Carmen og Maja* (1932; Carmen and Maja), *Mange takk, doktor* (1935; Many Thanks, Doctor), *Dyr jeg har kjent* (1945; Animals I Have Known), *Figurer på mørk bunn* (1949; Figures Against a Dark Background), and *Vårt vanskelige liv* (1960; Our Difficult Life). In these works Sandel turns her attention to struggles similar to those in the Alberte books, that is, to portraits of children, dreamers, trapped housewives, passionate and inept people who struggle to maintain themselves against the forces of small-mindedness, bigotry, and bottom-line common sense. Occasionally, Sandel narrates these struggles with the cold but angry objectivity of the outsider, as in the remarkable and chilling short story "Kunsten å myrde" (The Art of Murder) from *Mange takk, doktor*, in which a peasant woman who has twice gotten pregnant without being married is inexorably pushed by her family toward suicide. Sometimes Sandel enters into the feelings and thoughts of her imperiled protagonists with tactfully controlled anger and insight. An example of this kind of story is "Barnet som elsket veier" (The Child Who Loved Roads) from the volume with that title (1973).

THREE PUBLIC POETS: WILDENVEY, BULL, ØVERLAND

Though very different in tone and subject matter, Herman Wildenvey, Olaf Bull, and Arnulf Øverland were alike in their great popularity, both during their careers and afterward. In his way, each is a kind of national poet, canonized in the general culture through anthologies, literary histories, and textbooks. All three wrote rhetorical verse, that is, verse that signals its intention to speak to a large audience through its choice of standard themes, its clarity of diction, its public persona, and such standard poetic devices as rhyme and regular stanza forms. As far as the function of this sort of poetry is concerned, one perhaps may see it, like the Norwegian epic novel, as a self-conscious alternative to the modernism that was flourishing in Europe and beginning to stir in parts of Scandinavia.

Herman Wildenvey

If "national poet" is too heavy a term for such a lighthearted poet, Herman Wildenvey (1886–1959) qualifies by way of his enormous popularity. He is Norway's acknowledged master of light verse, elegant and charming. He published his first book of poetry, *Campanula* (under his original name of Herman Portaas), at age sixteen and then left Norway for America, where he lived for three years. On his return to Norway, he worked as a porter and tour guide at a tourist hotel, where he wrote his first collection of poems to be published under the euphonious pseudonym Herman Wildenvey, *Nyinger* (1907; Bonfires). The first edition sold out in four days. He had found exactly the tone that would make him, and keep him, a best seller, one that was both ironic and coquettish, modest and flippant. A master of rhyme and meter, he was able to make his poetry seem both graceful and effortless. Combining realism and romanticism, pathos and irony, he continually catches the reader off guard and in a position to be charmed.

After bringing this new note into Norwegian poetry, Wildenvey went on to publish more than twenty books of verse and several collected editions. *Owls to Athens* (1935) contains a selection of his poetry in English translation.

Singing out mellifluously in praise of pleasure and a carpe diem approach to life, Wildenvey remained afloat for many decades in Norway's literary waters by insisting on his superficiality, his lack of seriousness. To the extent that he had a philosophy, it was a comfortable pantheism, an aesthete's unshakable conviction that the beauty of the part implies that the whole must also be beautiful. More than by his philosophy, however, he held his readers by his insouciance, his disdain for the Protestant work ethic, his unconcern with the moral and ethical questions that, particularly in the difficult thirties, were preoccupying so many of his literary colleagues. He could also be something of a philistine when it came to passing judgment on modernistic literature—James Joyce, for example, whom he mocked at length in several poems. But again, it was not to hear his critical opinions that his large audience turned to him, but rather to see him play the faun. And of course, to be offered advice like the following:

Let the bird in your hand fly away in a rush
Then open your heart and stretch out your hand—
For those better birds, the two in the bush.

Wildenvey also wrote a novel, two collections of stories, a play, and four volumes of autobiography.

Olaf Bull

A much more serious poet than Herman Wildenvey, Olaf Bull (1883–1933), is an equally "pure" poet in the sense that, with the exception of a little journalism, he worked at nothing but poetry. Born in Christiania (Oslo) and educated there, he studied science as well as literature at the university. Thereafter, he lived the life of an urban aesthete, intellectual and Bohemian. He traveled widely, living for extended periods of time in Denmark, France, and Italy. He was particularly devoted to France and French culture and drew extensively on the thought of Henri Bergson in his poetry.

Bull's production includes *Digte* (1909; Poems), *Nye digte* (1913; New Poems), *Digte og noveller* (1916; Poems and Short Stories), *Samlede digte 1909–1919* (1919; Collected Poems), *Stjernerne* (1924; The Stars), *Metope* (1927), *De hundrede aar* (1928; The Hundred Years), *Kjærlighet* (1929; Love), *Oinos og Eros* (1930; Oinos and Eros), *Oslo-hus* (1931; Oslo House [a prologue]), and *Ignis Ardens* (1932).

His poetry has a Victorian formality, finish, and seriousness to it. Crafted with intense care with regard to rhyme and meter, it is marked by moods of frank eroticism, idealistic gratitude for beauty, and wistful melancholy. Matthew Arnold suggested himself as perhaps a kindred spirit in English poetry, though Bull is more intensely physical, more passionately appreciative of nature, particularly the season of spring with flowering beauty and abundant vitality, as in his poem "Vaarbrytning" (The Break of Spring). Widely read, Bull did not hesitate in his poetry to draw on his knowledge of history, literature, philosophy, and science, as in his monumental poem "De hundrede aar" (1927; The Hundred Years), in which he unrolls a panorama of Norwegian cultural history from Wergeland to Bjørnson in powerfully declamatory lines. He was especially interested in modern physics, puzzling in several major poems over the implications of Einstein's theory of relativity. This learning, however, particularly in his early works, does not get in the way of his powerful feelings nor does it protect him from deep metaphysical anxiety.

"Stenen" (The Stone), from his first volume of poems, gives a striking picture of this anxiety. The poet imagines that he is in outer space, "beyond outermost eternity," when he sees a demon approaching him. The demon shows him a stone he is about to drop. In the next instant it will disappear "and never cease falling." The thought of this stone, says the demon, will plant an uneasiness in the poet's mind that will never die. Terrified, the poet awakes:

> But the dream remained in the night of my heart;
> from youth to mature age
> my mind sought in vain to grasp
> the stone that is always falling.

The thought of the stone, that is, of matter, of all life, as subject to insuperable gravity led the poet to seek refuge in poems celebrating wine, art, love, learning, and culture. An early example is "Ved et glas vin en vaarnat" (1909; A Glass of Wine on a Spring Night):

> Soul, draw your curtain aside
> the night is cold and fine, and the moon
> herself serves herself in your wine
> . . . .
> But innumerable stars like islands lie
> in the heavens' etheric sea
> which is why, my friends, we must die.

Many of Bull's poems concern the women to whom he has turned for relief from his lonely despair. These poems, though marvelously wrought, may perhaps strike today's reader as somewhat patronizing. Woman is assigned the role of the naive experiencer of life, the medium through which the poet can absorb the world freed of its burden of thought. The following lines are from a poem entitled "Foraar" (1909; Spring):

> Look, the swallows rise in a dance, in a dance sink down
> and my thoughts turn again to the time
> when *she* was with me to call the swallows swallows,
> to be more than happy to call the blue air blue.

In this way woman becomes vital to Bull as the primary object of passion to be recalled in tranquility. From "Ars Longa" (1924):

> I *have to* act in this way, my dear
> wherever I may love or happen to be!
> I have to radically change and
> consume all that is dear to me.

Bull's masterpiece along these lines is the poem "Metope" from the volume of the same name (1927). It begins:

> *You* will I tenderly in iron rhythms master

you will I deeply and lastingly conserve
in poetry's eternally youthful alabaster.

It is a Keatsian attempt to transmute a poignant moment of love into a poem
that will not only save the lovers by memorializing them, but also save them
by merging them with their archetypal originaries, Pan and Psyche. In its
desperate effort to salvage something from the moment to set against the
working of time, it also resembles Arnold's "Dover Beach," except that with
Bull both the lovers are seen, for all their feeling, as utterly separate. Indeed,
the pathos of the poem springs from the unreachable and unassuageable
anxiety that the poet can sense in his lover.

At times one can sense a certain paradox in Bull's poetry, which is that his
very success as an artist removes him from the objects under contemplation,
turning them into hermetically sealed art works. For help in overcoming
this painful dichotomy, Bull appealed to Bergson's notion of reality as an
unsegmentable continuum that, though not apprehensible by the rational,
logical mind, could nevertheless be experienced through intuition. Toward
the end of his career he wrote some long philosophical poems that he described as "Bergson set to verse." "Ignis Ardens," a lengthy cantata written
for a university doctoral ceremony, is an example. It traces the evolution of
the cosmos and of life on earth in great stately rhythms, finding in this
movement a record of the forward movement of spirit. "Nature is an abyss,"
it concludes; "but," replies the chorus, "God is the Ground."

Here at last was a force to set against the poet's gift and demiurge, celebrated in a poem entitled "Fantasi" (Imagination) from his first volume:

Like love is the desire to gather together
and turn earth's desert into an Eden
Again like love's must that force be
that fuses separate thoughts by its festive glow.

Only in imagination's bridal chamber
do flower and woman blessedly unite
and smile-dimples turn into lilies
and mouths into roses, miracle flamed.

But all things that in scattered confusion
lie aspiring darkly toward each other
must die a death, and then merely as souls
assemble behind a solitary forehead's heaven

Then the thinker becomes a god, life glowing
behind the hand pressing in upon his eyes—
And his heavy head inclines, as if weighted
down by the violence of those countless encounters.

Valuable for the serious student of Olaf Bull are two volumes of his letters
(1989) and a collection of his aphorisms, *Ekko og regnbue* (1987; Echo and
Rainbow).

Arnulf Øverland

Clarity and decisiveness characterize all the writings—whether poems, stories, or essays—of Arnulf Øverland (1889–1968). It is as if his words have
been scrubbed of ambiguity and placed on the page with entire conviction.
A great polemicist, Øverland attacked first and foremost conventional
Christianity. His first book, *Den ensomme fest* (1911; The Lonely Feast), includes a poem about the death of a young girl entitled "Et år er gått" (A Year
Has Passed), in which we find these mordant lines:

You wanted to live.
But darkness embraced your soul.
God went walking over the earth,
and quite by accident happened
to tread on your soul with his heel.

In another poem, "Ved krusifikset" (By the Crucifix), Øverland angrily
waves Jesus away, questioning what his suffering has to do with the poet's
own. It seems particularly bitter to him that death, which strikes all people,
provides no link between them. Following from this perception, many of
the poems in Øverland's first collections are chiseled statements of loneliness, bitterness, fear, anxiety, and a sense of life's pointlessness. For all their
bleakness, however, they maintain a brave attitude and a refusal to accept
false comfort.

It is in the last poem of the collection from 1915, entitled *Advent,* that
Øverland finds the agency that will free him from self-enclosure: Norway itself. While war rages elsewhere in Europe, Norway, with its valiant history
and rugged geography, presents itself to the poet's eye as the source of solidarity for which he has been searching. With this poem Øverland took a giant step into the role of national poet, which for the rest of his career he was
to maintain as successfully as anyone since Bjørnson. In his next collection,
Brød og vin (1919; Bread and Wine), we find the poem "Rettergang" (Trial),

which declares the poet's belief and traces his future course of action. God, in the figure of a stern judge, tells the poet,

One [presumably Jesus] is not enough for me.
Many are born to suffer.
You shall join the common flock
and struggle in the ranks of the nameless.

You could have chosen the way
of peace, if you had had a choice
You could have bought happiness for yourself
if only your soul had been for sale.

Implied here is that the poet is on his way to socialism. Like his friends the novelist Sigurd Hoel and the playwright Helge Krog, Øverland became involved with the Marxist thinker Erling Falk (1887–1940), who through his organization Mot Dag exerted considerable influence on Norway's left-wing intellectuals in the period between the wars. Øverland began to write for Falk's journal *Mot dag* in 1922 and remained a faithful socialist until after the Second World War, when the news of the suppression of intellectuals within Russia caused him to speak out in sharp abjuration.

His next collection, *Berget det blå* (1927; The Mountain in the Blue), opens with another long, strident, programmatic poem, "Riket er ditt!" (The Kingdom Is Yours!), in which Øverland angrily reacts to the special regard in which Jesus is held at the expense of the common man:

A child is born in Bethlehem,
and children are born in every home

and many of them have found peace
at a place of execution.

Further along in the poem, he cries out:

I say again to serving maid and slave
Save yourselves!
. . . .
Oh, brothers in humiliation and sisters in shame,
still, we are like him!

As this passage suggests, however, Øverland's anti-Christian polemics contain more than a grain of ambiguity and sympathy. In an attempt to speak more immediately to readers who, whatever their adult beliefs, had been formed by a Christian culture, Øverland increasingly adopted biblical tones in his poetry. This effort reached its apogee in the volume *Ord i alvor til det norske folk* (1940; Words Spoken Seriously to the Norwegian People), in which he proposed generic nonreligious verses, which still had the *sound* of religious verses, to be used in ceremonies such as baptisms and burials.

As an essayist and cultural figure Øverland aroused considerable public debate at various times in his career by fighting in three causes: against organized Christianity; for the conservative form of Norwegian (Dano-Norwegian or riksmål); and against modernism in the arts, especially poetry—as can be seen in his notorious "Tungetale fra Parnasset" (1953; Speaking in Tongues from Parnassus) in the collection *I beundring og forargelse* (1954; In Admiration and Indignation). As this essay makes clear, part of Øverland's strength derived from a certain degree of narrow-mindedness. For example, though he had been educated as a painter and for many years functioned as an art critic in the newspapers, he never sought to disguise that he knew very little and cared even less about modern art.

Øverland was clear-sighted early on and brave in the actual event as far as Hitler and the danger of nazism was concerned. In 1935 he published a clear analysis of the imminent danger of Hitler in "Da kom Hitler" (Then Came Hitler) in the essay collection *Det frie ord* (The Free Word) and repeated his warning in the famous poem "Du må ikke sove" (You Must Not Sleep) from the collection *Den røde front* (1937; The Red Front). Øverland's outspokenness caused him to be arrested by the Germans in 1941, and he spent the remaining war years in captivity. From jail he smuggled out some of his most beloved patriotic poems, such as "Til kongen" (To the King) and "Vi overlever alt!" (We Shall Survive Everything!). These poems were published in 1945 in a volume bearing the title of the second of them.

Not limited to polemical and national topics, Øverland also wrote many personal poems. The volume in which he most successfully fused his public and private persona was *Hustavler* (1929; Almanac), in which, in addition to poems about Norway, he handled such personal topics as love and death and friendship, writing with warmth, his usual admirable directness, and even a certain vulnerability.

NORDAHL GRIEG AND OTHER SOCIALIST WRITERS

Among leftist writers in Norway in the first half of the twentieth century, we can distinguish those of middle-class background who came by their views through an intellectual process, usually instigated by contact with Erling Falk and his Mot Dag movement, from those who grew up in working-class homes and were drawn to the left by feelings of solidarity and/or revolutionary hope. Prominent members of the former group are Arnulf Øverland, Sigurd Hoel, and Helge Krog; and of the latter, Oskar Braaten and Rudolf Nilsen. Nordahl Grieg is a more complicated case: from the middle-class and well educated (brother of the powerful publisher Harald Grieg), he acquired his sympathy for workers and revolutionaries more slowly—the result of his experiences as a sailor in the Norwegian merchant marine and, particularly, a two-year stay in Russia in the early 1930s.

Oskar Braaten (1881–1939) was Norway's first author to write about Oslo's proletarian East End, where he was born and where, among its narrow streets and dismal apartment houses, he grew up. In his plays, short stories, and novels, he portrayed individuals and types from this milieu, always remaining close to his direct experience. Despite his subject matter, however, Braaten is not generally seen as a proletarian writer in the manner, say, of Johan Falkberget or Kristofer Uppdal, because his view of working people was not ideological. Having grown up in presocialist Norway, Braaten was not indignant on the worker's behalf, nor did he have a vision of their historical mission. The characters who figure in his works usually aspire to nothing grander than to take a step into the lower middle class. Braaten treats their modest ambitions with sympathy and understanding, sometimes with grotesque humor, employing a tone and narrative devices reminiscent of the folktale.

Braaten's first book of short stories, *Kring fabrikken* (Around the Factory), appeared in 1910. It consists of sketches from the outskirts of Christiania, showing the lives of working girls and street children and realistically revealing the cramped and squalid conditions of the large apartment houses in which they lived. Braaten continued to write short stories on these themes, gathering and publishing his *Oslo-fortellinger* (Oslo Tales) in 1935.

His plays *Ungen* (1911; The Child) and *Den store barnedåpen* (1925; The Great Baptism) continue to be popular, thanks to their humor and warmth. Both give positive portraits of working-class mothers, showing them as strong, primitive, and generous. In the first play, Braaten suggests that it is in motherhood that a woman finds true fulfillment, and in the latter, he directs criticism at the Norwegian state church for its reluctance to baptize children who have been born out of wedlock. In addition to writing plays for Det Norske Teatret (Oslo's nynorsk theater), Braaten was involved with it in other ways from the time of its founding in 1912, working there in a variety of capacities and eventually as its director.

Braaten's novels *Kammerset* (1917; The Boudoir), *Ulvehiet* (1919; The Wolf Den), and *Matilde* (1920) are studies in the emotional costs exacted by flight from a proletarian environment. In the thirties, feeling that he had exhausted his material, Braaten turned to the theory of psychoanalysis and recast his theme of social ambivalence in psychological terms in two novels, *Prinsesse Terese* (1931; Princess Terese) and *Masken* (1933; The Mask). His last work, the novel *Fugleburet* (1937; The Bird Cage), is a character study focusing on the phenomenon of religious hysteria.

Rudolf Nilsen (1901–29) also came from Oslo's proletarian East End, but unlike Oskar Braaten, he was intensely committed to the working class and the cause of socialism. Friendship, solidarity, and revolution are the dominant themes in his poetry, which his technical skill and sense of irony generally preserved from becoming merely hortatory. Nilsen looked to the Russian Revolution as a beacon of hope for working people and—frequently with optimism, often with indignation, and sometimes with sober pessimism—wrote of the forces that fostered or opposed the implementation of its ideals.

His three collections are *På stengrunn* (1925; On Stony Ground), *På gjensyn* (1926; Au Revoir), and *Hverdagen* (1929; The Ordinary Day). His best-known poem is "Nr. 13" (Number 13), about the apartment house where he grew up, "where the poor people live" dreaming about "Atlantis, Utopia—about a better fate and portion / than this life in which others own you, heart and soul."

Intense and contradictory, Nordahl Grieg (1902–1943) was an engaged political writer of the left. He used his poems, novels, plays, and journalism as occasions for debate and advocacy, placing aesthetic and purely philosophical concerns in second place. His poetry is strongly rhetorical in the positive sense, seeking to move its listener by an irresistible force of feeling, and his novels and plays make their polemical points with an immediacy that solicits a direct response.

Born in Bergen, Grieg went to sea as soon as he had completed high school. At the age of twenty he published his first book of poems, *Rundt Kap det gode Haab* (Around the Cape of Good Hope). It is strongly patriotic and full of feelings of solidarity and indignation on behalf of the workers:

The engine keeps on pounding
As it did all yesterday
And now it's quitting time.
Today. Or is it yesterday?

Experiences from this voyage form the background for his first novel, *Skibet gaar videre* (1924; Eng. tr. *The Ship Sails On*, 1927), which aroused indignation because of its frank account of prostitution and venereal disease in port towns. While the novel was instrumental in getting the Red Cross to direct its efforts toward improving such conditions, it also angered some of Grieg's fellow sailors.

An indication of Grieg's strange ambivalence vis-à-vis totalitarianism can be found in the novel's portrait of the ship's captain, a lonely leader "who must rule over everything and everyone." Though a socialist, Grieg, like many of his fellow intellectuals between the wars, had a tendency to look to strong men for leadership. This reverence for the heroic was strengthened by the year he spent studying at Oxford, during which he wrote a thesis on Rudyard Kipling and the British Empire. During the same year, he wrote most of the poems in *Stene i strømmen* (1925; Stones in the Stream), a collection that conjures up the cool rippling streams of Norway with wonderful effect.

Having seen revolution and militancy at close hand, Grieg wrote some plays concerning ends and means in politics, of which one of the most interesting is the experimental *Barrabas* (1927). It raises the question of whether pacifism or armed struggle is best suited to achieve world peace, a matter of both political and deep personal concern to Grieg, touching as it does on the theme of the hero. His most satisfying treatment of this theme, however—indeed, it is one of his major works—is the volume of essays and translations he wrote in honor of the English romantic and young war poets: *De unge døde* (1932; The Young Dead).

Like several of his Norwegian colleagues, Grieg looked to Russia as the bulwark against fascism. After spending two years in the Soviet Republic, which confirmed his faith in Russia as a social experiment and in Marxism as a philosophy, he wrote two plays that aimed to portray the class struggle in Norway in the strongest terms: *Vår ære og vår makt* (1935; Eng. tr. *Our Honor and Our Glory,* 1971) and *Men imorgen* (1936; But Tomorrow). In the first, shipowners are set against sailors and attacked for their profiteering during the First World War. Abandoning verisimilitude and using cinematic techniques, caricatural types, and shock effects, Grieg seeks to arouse indignation in his audience and win them to his views.

A play that uses similar techniques, though with greater artistic control, is *Nederlaget* (1937; The Defeat). Considered by many critics to be Grieg's masterpiece, it is based on the events of the Communard Uprising in Paris but alludes to the contemporary Spanish Civil War. Again Grieg poses the question of pacificism versus armed struggle, this time provocatively defending the use of force in terms that clearly refer to the notorious show trials in Moscow. One of the characters in the play says, "The good can win only through violence. This is the bitter lesson we have learned." Grieg stood alone among Norwegian writers and intellectuals in defending the Soviet Republic for its use of violence against its people.

In defense of his position regarding Russia, Grieg wrote *Ung må verden ennu være* (1938; Young as Yet the World Must Be [a line from Wergeland's poem "Follow the Call"]), a large journalistic novel set in a variety of locations—Moscow, Oslo, England, Spain—and arguing the case for an active and committed approach to political problems. He exemplified his theory during World War II by participating as directly as he could on the side of the Allies. He was part of the team that moved Norway's gold from its treasury to England, and after the German occupation of Norway, he served as an officer in England, broadcasting talks and poems of encouragement back to Norway. In them he spoke repeatedly about his hopes for peace and in defense of humane values. Seeking ever closer contact with the war, he flew as a correspondent on English bombing raids to Germany, and on the night of December 2, 1943, he was shot down. For his Norwegian readers, at least, the manner of his death cannot help but cast a retroactive glow on his writings.

THE RADICAL FREUDIANS: HOEL AND KROG

Though Sigmund Freud's theories had been introduced into Norway as early as 1907 by Ragnar Vogt, one of the country's leading psychiatrists, in his textbook of psychology, it was not until the late twenties that they were presented to the public at large. In 1929 Kristian Schjelderup published his translation of Freud's *Vorlesungen zur Einführung in die Psychoanalyse* (1916 –17; Introductory Lectures on Psychoanalysis), two years after his brother, Harald Schjelderup, professor of psychology at the University of Oslo, had given a major discussion of Freud in his textbook of psychology. The air in Norway was charged with expectancy regarding Freud, one might say, since in the rest of Europe and in America his theories had been the subject of discussion and debate for at least a decade. In the popular mind, Freud tended to be thought of as a racy and, for many, dangerous thinker, and it was decidedly in this light that he came to be viewed by a vocal contingent of conservative Norwegians, once they began to detect his influence on their national literature.

The specific cause of the alarm was a novel published by Sigurd Hoel in 1931, *En dag i oktober* (Eng. tr. *One Day in October,* 1932)—or rather, the fact that this novel, which many viewed as a typically decadent and nihilistic example of literary Freudianism, had been awarded second prize in a literary contest sponsored by the publisher Gyldendal. No less a figure than conservative leader C. J. Hambro attacked Hoel in print, accusing him of being a cynical proponent of both Freudianism and Soviet materialism. The attack on Hoel and "dirty" literature (*smusslitteraturen*) was carried further in a notorious editorial in the right-wing newspaper *Morgenbladet* (The Morning Paper), bearing the title "A Dirty Stream Is Inundating the Country." In other words, as the thirties got under way in Norway, public opinion was sharply polarized concerning Freud and his impact on culture.

Sigurd Hoel

Sigurd Hoel (1890–1960) was an important cultural figure in Norway for four decades, both for his novels and short stories, which were very popular, and for the considerable influence he wielded in the fields of journalism and literary criticism.

He was born in Odalen and spent his youth on a farm. He studied in Oslo, received his *artium* degree in 1909, and then went on to study mathematics. He was a teacher for some years, secretary in the Academy of Science, and coeditor of Erling Falk's journal *Mot dag* from 1921 to 1924. He served as literary critic for several socialist or liberal newspapers, first *Social-Demokraten* (The Social Democrat), then *Arbeiderbladet* (The Worker's Paper) (1918–31) and *Dagbladet* (The Daily Paper) (1932–36). Other important positions he held were literary consultant to the Gyldendal publishing house and editor of its *Den gule serien* (Yellow Series, so named for the cover of the book jackets), for which he supervised the translation of many central works of foreign literature. After the war, like his friend Arnulf Øverland, he worked for the cause of riksmål and served as the chairman of the Riksmålsforbundet (Riksmål Alliance).

The editorship of *Mot dag* was an important early step for Hoel, at the time a mere twenty-one-year-old student not long removed from the provinces. Erling Falk was a charismatic leader who had gathered an impressive circle of intellectuals around himself, and to shine in such a circle might have seemed an intimidating task. Despite his youth, Hoel wrote his editorials in *Mot dag* in a clear and elegant style, with cutting irony and abundant self-confidence. From this point on, Hoel remained an important trend setter and arbiter of taste, praising and castigating with equal vigor. His essays have been collected in the following volumes: *Tanker i mørketid* (1945; Thoughts in a Dark Time), *Tanker fra mange tider* (1948; Thoughts from Many Times), *Tanker mellom barken og veden* (1952; Thoughts between a Rock and a Hard Place), and *Tanker om norsk diktning* (1955; Thoughts about Norwegian Literature).

Unlike Øverland, Hoel did not adopt Marxism as his creed, maintaining his independence vis-à-vis Falk even when serving as his coeditor. Rather than class struggle, Hoel viewed society's taboo on sexuality as the primary cause of the human unhappiness he detected around him. Hoel became keenly interested in Freud's theories in his youth and later in his life underwent analysis with Wilhelm Reich during the several years the latter spent in Norway after fleeing Nazi Germany. The impact of psychoanalysis is apparent everywhere in Hoel's novels, beginning with the one for which he first became widely known, *Syndere i sommersol* (1927; Eng. tr. *Sinners in Summertime*, 1930), a lighthearted portrayal of a group of young people who go on summer vacation together in southern Norway. It has remained one of Hoel's most popular books, though now it is read chiefly for its humor and as an engaging portrait of the wild twenties. (After the war Hoel wrote an amusing and melancholy sequel, *Jeg er blitt glad i en annen* [1951; I Have Fallen in Love with Someone Else], which takes up the stories of the young "sinners" thirty years later.) The young people are consciously modern, struggling to evince enlightened attitudes toward sex and love, but in the end pairing off in conventional couples. One of the characters, the liberated Evelyn, makes a remark that will reverberate further in Hoel's work: "Yes, I think we're heading for disaster. I think that many women in our generation are also heading for disaster—hopelessly, miserably, lamentably. That's what I think." In other words, the prognosis for enlightened women, even those living among enlightened men, was not good.

Hoel's next novel, *En dag i oktober*, was the one that unleashed the aforementioned debate about psychoanalysis and dirty literature. Not shocking for its portrayal of sex, the novel clearly upset its critics by its attack on middle-class marriage and perhaps by a certain clinical coldness on the part of the narrator. The plot concerns the crisis and suicide of a character named Tordis Ravn, the wife of the protagonist, a decent, enlightened woman who does not speak in the course of the twenty-four hours portrayed. Employing the technique of the collective novel, Hoel shifts the focus of the narrative from one couple to another living in the building, both of which are suffering from their awful marriages. These relationships are portrayed with a certain amount of farce, but the central problem, Dr. Ravn's relationship to his wife, is handled seriously. Dr. Ravn is a scientist whose singleminded devotion to his work has led him to exclude his wife from his life. Carefully and plausibly depicting Dr. Ravn's resentment of his wife's love, Hoel reveals the sexual anxiety inhibiting the character's unconscious.

Hoel carried this sort of investigation further in his next novel, which is one of his most accomplished: *Veien til verdens ende* (1933; The Road to the End of the World). Drawing on his own memories of his rural upbringing,

Hoel recounts the life of a boy named Anders from age three to the advent of puberty. The reader is shown the world as Anders experiences it: his mother, father, the hired help, the animals, the weather, all with their numinous or menacing glow. Here Hoel tries not to articulate the causes of anxiety but directly to convey the feelings that are colored by it. This novel has some of the same power as the early portions of James Joyce's *Portrait of the Artist as a Young Man*. Hoel continued to use this autobiographical material in a fine collection of short stories, *Prinsessen på glassberget* (1939; The Princess on the Glass Mountain).

The effects of a strict pietistic background form the point of focus in *Fjorten dager før frostnettene* (1934; Fourteen Days before the Frost Nights). It is another story of a professional man, this time a doctor, who, though outwardly successful, has made an emotional mess of his life by his inability to receive or extend love. Aesthetically, the novel is weakened by a certain schematism and the willed quality of its resolution. In the intervals when he was not writing novels delving into psychological matters, Hoel produced two novels that were broad, satirical reviews of contemporary society: *Sesam, Sesam* (1938) and *Ved foten av Babels tårn* (1956; At the Foot of Babel's Tower).

After the war he returned to his psychological investigation of character in one of his most important works, *Møte ved milepelen* (1947; Eng. tr. *Meeting at the Milestone,* 1951). Here Hoel, like many other Norwegian novelists, took up the disturbing question of why a large number of Norwegians became Nazi sympathizers and collaborators during the war. True to his insight into male sexual anxiety, Hoel drew a character who in his youth ran away from his sweetheart when she told him she was pregnant. She has a son, who grows up affected by his father's absence and as a result becomes a Nazi. Around this central plot, which unfolds like an intriguing puzzle, Hoel has produced an exciting picture of the war years, full of drama and tension.

In *Stevnemøte med glemte år* (1954; Rendezvous with Forgotten Years), Hoel looks back to the war years with a certain nostalgia. For many who threw themselves into the Resistance movement and worked in the underground, it was a time of heroism, of solidarity, lighted by the assurance that comes from fighting in a good cause. In the figure of Sven Arneberg, Hoel draws a glowing portrait of the good soldier. In contrast to him, the narrator is another one of Hoel's self-analyzing intellectuals. And as background to these two, Hoel presents a large portrait gallery of human types, both heroes and villains.

Hoel returned to the question of guilt in his last book, *Trollringen* (1958;

Eng. tr. *The Troll Circle,* 1991), a sequel to a historical novel he wrote in 1941, *Arvestålet* (The Heirloom Dagger). Set in a Norwegian village in the first half of the nineteenth century, it presents a powerful picture of the forces of superstition, small-mindedness, and aggression. Here is Hoel's greatest attempt to get at the neurotic link that binds human beings together so tragically. At the end the hero, who has been unjustly condemned to death, reflects on his situation: "Everything cohered in a single strange weave with some kind of pattern in it that he could glimpse, but not see entire. He felt that if he could see the whole pattern, he would be able to turn his fate around." A similar attempt to perceive underlying patterns and understand them formed the driving motive of Sigurd Hoel's writing.

Helge Krog
Helge Krog (1889–1962), dramatist and essayist, was a good friend of Arnulf Øverland and Sigurd Hoel. These three formed what became known as the "radical triumvirate" in Norwegian literature during the 1930s. As in the case of his friends, Krog's encounter with the Marxist thinker Erling Falk was of crucial importance. Marxism helped Krog see relationships among phenomena that until that point had seemed random or contradictory to him. From this he drew the conclusion that the struggle was hopeless unless conducted on all fronts simultaneously.

For Krog the playwright, this meant, at first, writing plays that centered on the inequities in society in a direct and explicit manner and then, in his more successful works, plays that dealt with the relationship between people's erotic lives and their social and political behavior. *Det store vi* (1917; The Big We) is a play about unfair wages and the economic power of the press, and *Jarlshus* (1923; Earl's House) concerns the relationship between striking workers and their employer. Neither of these rather earnest plays is among Krog's popular successes.

Far more interesting and enjoyable is the series Krog wrote in which women, somewhat in the manner of Nora in Ibsen's *Et dukkehjem,* and later Julie and Karen in Heiberg's *Balkonen* and *Kjærlighedens tragedie,* respectively, break the rules of conventional middle-class marriage. Like Heiberg's, Krog's plays are light in tone. The dialogue is witty and epigrammatic in the manner of George Bernard Shaw or the Swedish author Hjalmar Söderberg, a great favorite of Krog's. Indeed, Sonja, from Krog's first erotic comedy *Konkylien* (1929; Eng. tr. *The Sounding Shell*), bears a close resemblance to Söderberg's Gertrud, from the novel of the same name. Both women move from male partner to male partner, driven not by a taste for promiscuity but by fidelity to the ideal of love, which they do not wish to see degraded by male egotism or the tedium of the everyday. Cecilie Darre, in Krog's next play, *Underveis* (1931; Eng. tr. *On the Way*, 1939), is a female Communist doctor who is going to have a child but refuses to marry. Her refusal leads to a break with her family, the family of her child's father, and finally her radical friends (among whom is a fictionalized version of Erling Falk). At the end of the play, again like Nora or Gertrud, she stands in proud, undefeated isolation. This play caused a storm of discussion when it was first produced in 1931.

Krog's third erotic play is *Opbrudd* (1936; Eng. tr. *Break-Up*, 1939). In a spirit similar to Øverland's statement or program poems from the same period, it is a work with a clear message directed against bourgeois, individualistic attitudes and toward purportedly more rational and honest ones. In this play, the central character, Vibeke, is positioned between two men, her husband and her lover, both of whom are selfish individualists. In the course of the afternoon portrayed by the play, Vibeke gains insight into the falseness of her relationship to these two and her need to liberate herself: "I believe I have to learn how to think and feel in a new way . . . how to *be* in a new way. I want to go to the living, I want to go to people and offer myself to them, then we'll see."

Krog was also a superb essayist—logical, clear, intelligent, uncompromising. His essays are gathered in the following collections, whose titles suggest his movement away from purely literary topics toward more broadly cultural-political ones: *Meninger om bøker og forfattere* (1929; Opinions about Books and Authors), *Meninger om mange ting* (1933; Opinions about Many Things), *Meninger. Litteratur, kristendom, politikk* (1947; (Opinions: Literature, Christianity, Politics), *Rent ut sagt* (1954; Frankly Speaking), *Sant å si* (1956; To Tell the Truth). In *6te kolonne—?* (1946; Sixth Column—?), he raised the question of the role of big business in occupied Norway.

Although Helge Krog was perhaps not the most original literary talent among the writers of the twenties and thirties, he is still greatly respected for the moral qualities he displayed in his writing and in his life, honesty in particular.

CHRISTIAN PSYCHOLOGICAL NOVELISTS: FANGEN AND CHRISTIANSEN

Ronald Fangen

Ronald Fangen (1895–1945) and Sigurd Hoel bore a certain mirror resemblance to each other. Both were intellectuals who pursued in their works the reciprocal relationship between private and societal psychology. Both were international in their intellectual orientation, clearly influenced in their writing by wide reading in modern European and American literature. And where Hoel was a follower of Freud and Reich, Fangen turned to Otto Weininger and Alfred Adler. Both writers were preoccupied by questions of guilt and atonement.

Both wrote several novels in which the protagonists live outwardly successful lives that, in a moment of existential crisis, they perceive to be hollow. Delving into the emptiness, they find guilt. Delving into the guilt, they find the moment in which they refused love or had it withheld from them. For Hoel, the moment brings the relief of insight; for Fangen, it permits insight into what in religious terms is often called "hardness of heart." About midway through his career Fangen became a Christian, converted by the American evangelist Frank Buchman, who brought his Oxford Movement to Oslo in 1934. Of the two, Hoel is the greater stylist, the more polished man of letters.

One feels that Hoel's assurance, like Øverland's, derived at least in part from his resolute atheism. Fangen, in contrast, spent the years of his early adulthood in tense metaphysical uncertainty. A book of his essays published after the First World War, *Streiftog i digtning og tænkning* (1919; Forays in Literature and Thought), shows him split in his allegiance between a religious thinker such as Dostoevski and rationalists such as H. G. Wells and Romain Rolland.

Fangen used this dichotomy in his first literary success, the play *Syndefald* (1920; The Fall), in which two Protestant ministers both love the same woman, causing one of them to weaken under the strain of jealousy and renounce his faith. Fangen's next two plays, *Fienden* (1922; The Enemy) and *Den forjættede dag* (1926; The Promised Day), articulate similar moral and existential dilemmas. Despite Fangen's beliefs, his plays do not present pat answers. In *Den forjættede dag*, for example, a woman in a comfortable, middle-class household who has devoted her life to her husband and children is finally compensated for her years of service by the confession of her dying husband that he has always been in love with another woman, hardly a case of virtue rewarded.

Fangen's early novels portray representative figures—the idealist, the nihilist, the superficial success, and so on—poised against the background of the hectic twenties: *Nogen unge mennesker* (1929; Some Young People); its sequel, *Erik* (1931); *Duel* (1932; Eng. tr. *Duel*, 1934); and *Allerede nu* (1932; Already Now), in which the Erik from the novel by that name instills meaning into his life by converting to Christianity. Christian conversion also provides the solution in Fangen's next two novels, which, from an artistic standpoint, are among his strongest: *En kvinnes vei* (1933; A Woman's Way) and *Mannen som elsket rettferdigheten* (1934; The Man Who Loved Justice). They are both psychologically penetrating analyses of characters who have closed themselves off from love, Esther in the first novel because she was not given love as a child, and Gottfried Stein in the second because he is inordinately preoccupied with the ideal of justice and demanding his due. Esther flees her unhappiness by becoming a perfectionist in her work; Stein pushes his demand for justice to the point of killing the judge who had unjustly condemned him to jail. When both these characters arrive at the end of their tethers, they adopt a religious solution to their dilemmas in a psychologically convincing way.

Another artistic success for Fangen was the novel *Kvernen som maler langsomt* (1939; The Mill That Grinds Slowly). In this novel, he pits a group of established and wealthy businessmen from Bergen against a group of proletarian settlers from the town's suburb. Again the story concerns people seeking what they consider to be their rightful due in an aggressive, legalistic way, and again the solution is provided by religious insight, this time delivered by the sons and daughters of the contestants. After the war Fangen, like Hoel, took up the question of Norwegian defection to nazism. In his novel from 1945, *En lysets engel* (The Angel of Light; Eng. tr. *Both Are My Cousins,* 1948), Fangen poses two idealists against each other, one who dies in a concentration camp and one who fights for the Nazi cause. Not Fangen's strongest work from an artistic standpoint, it nevertheless poses the interesting question of the degree to which idealism itself may give rise to evil.

Sigurd Christiansen

Sigurd Christiansen (1891–1947) had certain marked affinities with Ronald Fangen, in the sense that both were influenced by modern psychological theories and both took a Christian approach to questions. Christiansen, however, did not write explicitly as a Christian apologist nor, however well read he may have been in Freud, did he carry out his investigation of character and motive in a modern spirit. As a character in one of his novels says, "If a person has found himself and become better through spiritual anguish, no one should take his feeling of guilt away. For it is helpful to the one who bears it."

Christiansen's central works are two trilogies, one from the twenties and one from the thirties. The first—*Inngangen* (1925; The Entrance), *Sverdene* (1927; The Swords), *Riket* (1929; The Kingdom)—is a family novel that perhaps owes something of its scope and seriousness to works like Undset's *Kristin Lavransdatter* or Duun's *Juvik-folke*. It tells the story of a father and his sons, each of whom chooses a different path in life. The father is a modest industrial arts teacher whose decency and goodness place a challenge before his sons to be as inwardly successful as he has been in his own quiet way. One becomes an artist, two become religious converts, and another is able to come to terms with himself after living through a marital crisis. A particularly interesting aspect of the work is its depiction of various forms of low-church Protestantism (pietistic, evangelical) and the impact they have on the family.

Christiansen's first great success with a large public came with the novel *To levende og en død* (1931; Eng. tr. *Two Living and One Dead*, 1932), which won first prize in a pan-Scandinavian competition for the year's best novel. It is a short work, written quickly, expressly for the competition, so it is tighter and more straightforward than much of Christiansen's other fiction. It concerns a post-office worker who offered no resistance when a robbery was committed in his post office and as a result was branded a coward by his colleagues. Christiansen studies the effects of shame on the man and on his relationship with his wife. A similar theme is treated in *Agner i stormen* (1931; Eng. tr. *Chaff Before the Wind*, 1934).

Christiansen's second great trilogy—*Drømmen og livet* (1935; Dream and Life), *Det ensomme hjerte* (1938; The Solitary Heart), *Menneskenes lodd* (1945; Man's Lot)—tells the life story of a novelist. Though obviously drawing its materials from Christiansen's own life, it is not an autobiography in a narrow sense. It is uniquely focused on the idea—the *ideal*—and the process of becoming a literary artist, a vocation that for Jørgen Wendt and his creator is equivalent to a sacred priesthood. In the first volume, we experience Jørgen's early childhood and discover the world through his remarkably sensitive eyes. In volume 2, he discovers that he is "one of those whom God's finger has pointed to." In volume 3, at the cost of much loneliness, suffering, and hard work, Jørgen Wendt becomes a novelist. One of the great works in modern Norwegian literature depicting the artist's artistic vocation, the trilogy has been compared to Cora Sandel's books about Alberte.

CITY AND WILDERNESS

Soon the night will be done. Rat gray
the joyless dawn oozes into being.
An average day. With clouds. And a sky

like an old slice of dirty white bread.
Everything seems strange. Too familiar
unreal. While you, who are new, were
like one I'd loved for thousands of years.

These lines, written by Gunnar Larsen (1900–1958) when he was a nine-teen-year-old student, indicate the tension in him between the modernist and the romantic. Despite the promise shown by his poetry, Larsen soon abandoned it for prose, pursuing the dichotomy inherent in his sensibility in five novels. He also worked as a journalist, wrote a biography of the ex-plorer Henry Stanley, and translated Ernest Hemingway's *The Sun Also Rises*.

Son of a shipowner, Larsen was born and lived in Oslo. With the excep-tion of those in his second novel, his characters tend to be businessmen or professionals, upper-class urban people who react intensely to nature when-ever they have occasion to step outside the city. His first novel, *I sommer* (1932; This Summer), tells the story of a love affair between a young man and an unhappily married woman. What gives the book its considerable charm is the vaguely ironic, slightly distanced tone of the narrator as he re-cords his adventures through small, sharply observed details.

Larsen's next book, *To mistenkelige personer* (1933; Two Suspicious Char-acters), is based on a real event and portrays the adventures of two men who are fleeing the law after murdering a sheriff. A kind of "documentary novel" before the term was coined, it tells its story by noting in specific and con-vincing detail the features of the landscapes through which the characters move.

Weekend i evigheten (1932; Weekend in Eternity), Larsen's next novel, consists almost entirely of an inner monologue delivered by an Oslo lawyer during a weekend camping trip. The external world makes its presence felt only by way of brief italicized remarks or bits of conversation. Otherwise, the reader is carried backward along the current of the protagonist's remi-niscences to a point in time when a seemingly insignificant event, a chance meeting with a woman, had what turned out to be a determining effect on his life. It is an eerie, dreamy, and romantic work in which symbol and sug-gestion weave a web of implicit meaning.

In their relationship with women, Larsen's male characters tend to be passive, choosing inactivity as a means of preserving an ideal of woman formed during their adolescence. In *Bull* (1938), his fourth novel, Larsen tells the story of two such romantic idealists, a man and a woman who would have been the realization of each other's dream, but unfortunately, they never meet.

Larsen's final novel, *Sneen som falt ifjor* (1948; The Snows of Yesteryear), consists of the reflections of a man who chose not to act the part of a hero during the war. He is a kind of antihero, a melancholy intellectual who, like all Larsen's protagonists, has his most meaningful relationship with nonhuman nature.

Mikkjel Fønhus (1894–1973), a more robust romantic, ensured himself a place in Norwegian literature by writing about aspects of his country which are presumably known and loved by every Norwegian: its landscape and animals. In a prose that is both sensitive and accurate, poetic and sharply descriptive, Fønhus wrote more than forty novels and volumes of stories, in about half of which wild animals are the protagonists. And in the others, in which human beings are given a more significant role, the point of focus is still the natural world.

After completing his secondary education in Oslo, Fønhus abandoned his plans to study law. He returned to his family farm in Sør-Aurdal in Valdres and devoted himself to a life of hunting, hiking, and fishing, and then of writing wildlife stories based on his experiences. He achieved a popular success with his second book, *Der vildmarken suser* (1919; The Wind in the Wilderness), in which he described the ways of the creatures in the forests, ponds, and mountain plateaus of his native Valdres. In telling the adventures of bear and elk and other animals in this and other books, Fønhus succeeds in locating himself at the animal's point of view in a way that is convincing, exciting, and unsentimental.

Many of Fønhus's novels are devoted to one specific animal: the elk, the fox, the beaver. Some of his most popular ones are *Troll-elgen* (1921; Eng. tr. *The Trail of the Elk*, 1923), *Under polarlyset* (1922; Eng. tr. *Northern Lights*, 1925), and *Skogenes eventyrer* (1920; The Adventurer of the Forests; Eng. tr. *Jaampa, the Silver Fox*, 1931). Fønhus also traveled abroad in quest of adventure, to Canada, for example, for a novel about lumberjacks, and to Africa for another about big-game hunters. All his books display his great love of animals. Though he was an eager hunter, especially in his youth, he also worked for animal rights, particularly on behalf of bears.

CONFRONTING THE BEAST WITHIN: AKSEL SANDEMOSE

Aksel Sandemose (1899–1965) was and remains a great force of renewal in modern Norwegian prose literature. A rule breaker in his private life as well as in his art, Sandemose wrote novels that contain elements of the essay, the short story, the autobiography, and the tall tale, as well as philosophical and moralistic reflection. He took the Norwegian novel away from its well-beaten tracks (epic naturalism, psychological analysis) and made it more flexible and disturbing than it had been for a long time. Two factors in particular contribute to this disturbing quality. First, he did not hesitate to compose his works in what sounds like his own speaking voice—passionate, sharp, or melancholy. Like H. C. Andersen or Strindberg before him, Sandemose altered his chosen genre by eliminating distance. Frequently, he seems to be telling the drastic truth, or at least to be just on the point of telling it. And since, as he wrote in *Det svunde er en drøm* (1946; The Past Is a Dream), "murder and love are the only topics worth writing about," it can happen that his readers stay up late, turning the pages with strangely ambiguous motives. Of course, like his contemporary Henry Miller, whom he in some ways resembles, he can also try his reader's patience. Miller and Sandemose are both proletarian autodidacts who worked in their youths at a variety of jobs, traveled widely, read enormously—particularly in Freud or anyone else who attempted to throw light on the conjunction of love and death and the classic perversions of masochism and sadism. Both lash out against the strictures of lower- and middle-class morality, seeing them as the weapons of a hated slave mentality. Further, both see organized groups, from the pecking order of the small group to the vast hierarchies of the modern state, as inevitably stupid and cruel. But while Miller is Rabelaisian, comic, mainly viewing human affairs as farce, Sandemose tends toward a pessimistic final assessment. As strong as Eros may be, Sandemose seems ultimately to see it working in the cause of death.

Aksel Sandemose was born in Nykøbing, in Jutland, Denmark. His mother was Norwegian. He grew up in difficult circumstances because the family had little money, and he left school at age fifteen to become a sailor. After wide travels and many jobs he published a book of short stories, *Fortællinger fra Labrador* (1923; Tales from Labrador), written in Danish and based on his experiences as a lumberjack in Canada. He published five subsequent books in Danish, none of which today is counted among his important works, other perhaps than *Klabavtermanden* (1927; The Klabauterman), a tale about life at sea, which owes something to Conrad and which Sandemose rewrote and published in Norwegian later in his career (*Klabautermannen*, 1932).

In 1929 he moved to Norway and in short order wrote two major novels. *En sjømann går iland* (1931; A Sailor Disembarks) tells about Espen Arnakke's life as a lumberjack in Newfoundland, in a place ominously named Misery Harbor, and gives a vivid portrayal of the rivalries and jealousies that flourish in the closed society of a logging crew. They eventually lead Espen to murder a man named John Wakefield. Wakefield had taken Espen's girlfriend from him, but Espen's motivation is more complex than simple anger or revenge. As in all Sandemose's novels, old patterns and forces such as sibling rivalry, homoeroticism, and masochism are at work.

These buried roots of forces are next illuminated in Sandemose's second novel about Espen Arnakke, considered by many to be his best: *En flyktning krysser sitt spor* (1933; Eng. tr. *A Fugitive Crosses His Tracks,* 1936), with the subtitle "Tale of a Murderer's Childhood." Like Sigurd Hoel's *Veien til verdens ende,* which was published in the same year, it has attained a prominent place among the many classic depictions of childhood in rural Scandinavia. Of the two books, Sandemose's is by far the darker. As in the films of Ingmar Bergman, childhood is seen as one unending process of humiliation. The name of the town in which Espen grows up is Jante, and Sandemose's formulation of "The Jante Law"—the first of which is, "Thou shalt not believe thou art something"—has become part of contemporary Scandinavian consciousness, something everyone knows even if unaware of its provenance. Following the thread of Espen Arnakke's anxious memories, Sandemose's novel shows how the small town can close around the individual, humiliating him, stifling him, infecting him with anger and guilt and a dangerous need for punishment.

Sandemose returned to the closed male group in *Vi pynter oss med horn* (1936; Eng. tr. *Horns for Our Adornment,* 1938), a novel set in the period before the First World War and following a group of sailors on a half-year voyage from Norway to Iceland and across the Atlantic to Newfoundland, where the protagonist dies. Sandemose considered it to be the final and best formulation of the Espen Arnakke problem, but, perhaps because of its more freewheeling and experimental form, it lacks the intensity of the earlier works.

In 1941 Sandemose fled occupied Norway and moved to Sweden, where he wrote *Det svundne er en drøm,* a novel concerned with his classic themes of rivalry, betrayal, jealousy, and murder, now richly complicated by his memories of the war and the Nazi invasion of Norway. In *Varulven* (1958; Eng. tr. *The Werewolf,* 1965), Sandemose again looked back to the war years. *Varulven* tells the story of three people bound in an erotic triangle and examines the passions and tensions of their relationship as a means of casting light on the general violence of the times. It is one of Sandemose's most mature and disturbing works. Again he portrays the destructive potential of the small-town environment, with its violent repression of adolescent sexuality, and convincingly shows it to form the nucleus of the guilt and disorder manifested in the later lives of his characters. In probing into the causes of violence, however, Sandemose does not pretend to have understood it completely. As an artist he senses a darkness in human beings which ultimately defies analysis. As his narrator states, "The Werewolf is a murderer of children. He sniffs his way to the foetus in its mother's womb and rips it out. He forever sniffs his way to the sources of life. He is the thing that at all times human beings have tried not to see, to place outside of themselves. And in this way it has become more real than the humans themselves."

After the war Sandemose lived in southern Norway and for four years (1951–55) published a journal of which he was the editor and sole contributor: *Årstidene* (The Seasons). Throwing off the restraints of genre, he could now carry on a direct and uninhibited monologue with his readers. The autobiographical segments from these interesting and often charming essays are collected in the volume *Rejsen til Kjørkelvik* (1954; The Journey to Kjørkelvik).

OTHER POETS WITH ROOTS IN THE NATIONAL

The following poets all wrote in nynorsk and continued, more or less, in the line of Aukrust. Hans Henrik Holm (1896–1980) lived the life of an independent scholar and poet. Born and raised in Oslo, he became passionately involved in the study of rural village culture in Norway, especially that of Setesdal and Telemark. He collected samples of the folklore, dialects, and customs of these areas and in the course of his investigations became interested in tracing the evolution of and interaction among particular strands of these cultures. The way in which he chose to display his erudition was in the form of enormous epic poems.

The first volume of the first of these poems was published in 1933: *Jonsoknatt* (St. John's Eve), a folio volume of 279 pages. Here Holm gathers a group of peasants around a midsummer night's fire and has them sing folk songs and tell fairy tales, folktales, legends, and myths. Though written in verse, the language does not function as poetry, chiefly because Holm sought to render it in a form of nynorsk as quaint and archaic as possible. From 1966 to 1972 he published five subsequent volumes in his epic work and a sixth volume in prose giving his analysis of the whole. He produced a second cycle of poems called *Bygdir i solrøyk* (1949–51; Villages in Sun Haze), as well as seven other independent volumes of verse.

Einar Skjæraasen (1900–1966) began as a writer in standard Norwegian in the manner of Olaf Bull and Arnulf Øverland but wrote his most successful verse in the form of folk songs in the dialect of his native Trysil. Best known among his collections are *Skritt forbi min dør* (1938; Steps Past My Door), *Så stiger sevjene* (1945; Then the Saps Rise), and *Danse mi vise Gråte min sang* (1949; Dance My Tune, Weep My Song).

Also from Trysil, Halldis Moren Vesaas (1907–), wife of novelist and poet Tarjei Vesaas, has published seven books of poetry: *Harpe og dolk* (1929; Harp and Dagger), *Morgonen* (1930; The Morning), *Strender* (1933; Shores), *Lykkelege hender* (1936; Happy Hands), *Tung tids tale* (1945; Speech from a Heavy Time), *Treet* (1947; The Tree), and *I ein annan skog* (1955; In Another Forest). Making her literary debut in the thirties, at a time when not many women poets were being published in Norway, she wrote with a sense of herself as speaking for women in general. In her own words, her poems were intended to express

a woman's feelings, a woman's viewpoint, a woman's life. . . . Program or not, my poems in the years that followed [the debut in the thirties] naturally became an expression of all the most typical feelings and experiences of women in general, since it was in these years I married, got a home, became a mother. "My circle is small and the ring of my thoughts goes around my finger." It couldn't have been otherwise in that period of my life. Later, I think the ring got wider. Beyond the tree in the front yard is another forest. Women's issues were no longer predominant, neither as inspiration nor as theme. (Quoted in the poetry collection *Ord over grind* [Words across the Gate], 1971, p. 2)

Indeed, Halldis Moren Vesaas has written poems inspired by her gratitude for love, pregnancy, and motherhood which, despite the risk of sentimentality, are strong and vivid. Other poems express uneasiness over the precarious abundance of life, its exposure to harm and death. During the war this tone darkened to grief and outrage. While the level of technical craftsmanship in her poems varies widely, their emotional quality is consistently strong. Vesaas is known also for her translations into nynorsk and for her two volumes of memoirs, *I Midtbøs bakkar* (1974; In the Hills of Midtbø) and *Båten om dagen* (1976; The Boat in the Day).

Aslaug Vaa (1889–1965) was from Kviteseid in Telemark, the same region with which Hans Henrik Holm was concerned in his poetry. She too had her roots in local language and lore, writing in a dialect-tinged nynorsk but not in an antiquarian way. Her references are international as well as national, reflecting the many years she lived in France and Germany with her husband, the psychoanalyst and student of Wilhelm Reich, Ola Raknes. After her debut (at age forty-five, after raising five children) with a book of poems chiefly concerned with local Telemark lore, *Nord i leite* (1934; In the North), her poetry became both wider in scope and more inward.

Nevertheless, she did not lose touch with older folkloric poetic forms. Both from Olav Aukrust, an important early influence, and later from William Blake, she learned how to express complex, modern content in simple diction and balladic forms. In Blake, she recognized what she called an "important secret weapon against spiritual death" in the quality of "innocence"—something "absolutely primordial and inward" (see Leif Mæhle's afterword in Vaa's *Dikt i utvalg* [Selected Poems], 1954).

In her second book of poems, *Skuggen og strendan* (1935; The Shadow and the Shore), she writes in the title poem:

From shadow to shore
from shore to shadow
I'll run till my heart
shall beat no more.

The shadow stands for her solitude, and the shore represents the place where other people gather to greet visitors from foreign lands. In these poems she is often aware of the evil and the pain in the world:

If one is beaten
it is because one is blind
one is tired
one is frightened.

In her third book of poems, *Villarkonn* (1936; Sinister Magic), several important pieces show her turning against an exclusively intellectual, that is, psychoanalytical, view of life:

You cut me into pieces
and dismember me
thinking that thus
you can discover me.
Thinking that thus
you can find the human root
and the law of all her being.

In this same collection are also some gentle and innocent poems in praise of village life.

Vaa's later collections—*På vegakanten* (1939; On the Side of the Road), *Fotefar* (1947; Footsteps), *Skjenkarsveinens visur* (1954; The Barman's

Songs), and *Bustader* (1963; Dwellings)—continue to combine poems of innocence with poems that move toward holistic awareness:

A dove and a water drop
each is a thing
that encircles the globe
in one living ring.

Water and dove
within me are telling
each place on earth
for me is a dwelling.

In these poems she also draws closer to nature in an attempt to discover her real identity and to look at death squarely.

Vaa also wrote poetic pieces for the stage, some drawing on local Telemark lore, such as, *Tjugendagen* (1947; The Twentieth Day of Christmas), and some dealing with the meeting of African and European culture, for example, *Honningfuglen og leoparden* (1965; The Honey Bird and the Leopard).

Jakob Sande (1906–67) wrote folk songs characterized by macabre humor, nautical lore, and radical politics. His songs became particularly popular during the radical sixties in Norway. Two of his folk-song collections are *Skreddarsveinen* (1958; The Tailor's Apprentice) and *Hestevrinsk og fløytelåt* (1964; Horse Whinnies and Flute Music).

Åsmund Sveen (1910–63) published four books of poetry in which the dominant feeling is erotic anxiety: *Andletet* (1932; The Face), *Jordelden* (1933; Earth Fire), *Eros syng* (1935; Eros Sings), and *Såmannen* (1940; The Sower). In 1943 he published a book of folk songs, *Bygdeviser* (Village Songs), in which he sings about the seasons and traditional farming life. Two posthumous publications—*Brunnen* (1963; The Well) and *Tonemesteren* (1966; Tone Master)—contain poems that introduce mythical themes and continue to depict erotic love in a tragic light.

FOUR MODERNIST POETS:
REISS-ANDERSEN, BOYSON, GILL, JACOBSEN

Gunnar Reiss-Andersen
In his poetry, Gunnar Reiss-Andersen (1896–1964) frequently presented himself as forever standing between two realities: summer and spring, future and past, land and ocean, this world and some other one. A mystic and a

kind of Platonist, he wrote poems characterized by nostalgia, longing, and a sense of mystery and regret. As he drew ever closer to the split in himself, his work took on a recognizably modernist air. Indeed, the span of his long career can be seen as a kind of bridge extending from the modern poets of early twentieth-century Norway to the modernists of the postwar years.

In one of his early poems ("Sjøfarersangen" [1921; Song of the Seafarer]), Reiss-Andersen's persona is lost in time, adrift between vast epochs:

A thousand years I have traveled
yes, for more than a thousand years.
The night is the shadow of nights
and the day the reflection of days.

Later in the same poem, he writes: "I am the limitless world's / forever homeless son." This theme is also expressed in seasonal terms, as in the poem "Rovfuglen" (1923, Bird of Prey):

Windy summer will come
to us, too, my friend.
But right when spring is over
we want it back again.

This feeling of homelessness, of being neither here nor there, leads Reiss-Andersen to a use of double negatives, which became one of his most characteristic trademarks. His most anthologized poem, "Til hjertene" (1926; To Hearts), begins:

Never forget her
whom you never met
who perhaps will meet you
after death.

In poem after poem, Reiss-Andersen sang the praises of this unattainable Anima figure, a sort of gnostic Sophia, who refused to allow the poet to betray her with a real woman in the actual world.

In Reiss-Andersen's symbolism, spring stands for a state that has passed, the time of a nearly forgotten but crucial initiation, and summer for a state that nearly coincides with itself, that is full of the feel of present things. In the poem "Sensommerdagene" (Late Summer Days) from 1940, the present impinges threateningly: "The thunder roars: The bull out there in the dark has huge lungs. / The fall moon rises: / Look, the bull has bloody horns." At first one thinks that the reference is to the current war, as it may well be, but the stanza concludes on a note of cosmic optimism: "But to each kernel / hidden in each blade of wheat / travels a beam of life from every single star!"

During the war Reiss-Andersen, like many of his fellow poets, wrote patriotic poems, which often have the feel of having been pressed on him by the situation. Indeed, throughout his career he wrote a great deal of occasional poetry. But in the years following the war he returned to his central theme and produced his greatest work by rearticulating his nearly gnostic sense of having drifted far from home. In "Prinsen av Isola" (1949; The Prince of Isola) from the book by that title, he addresses his own soul as the only living being in a world of dead simulacra. It is a wonderfully sustained visionary poem that ends with a cry of dichotomous longing: "Oh, beloved, forever beloved in a sea of stone / Oh, body of light against the summer sea! / Oh, I recall you, blue future memories."

In his last book, *År på en strand* (1962; Years on a Beach), Reiss-Andersen published some of his strongest work. "Huset på den andre siden" (The House on the Other Side) is a kind of Kubla Khan vision in which the poet's actual house faces the dwelling place of the imagination on the other shore. The final stanza begins by assigning some names to the forces that have been drawing the poet:

> Bent over my Bible, I can
> whisper: Light and lead me, Christ.
> Over on the other shore
> Whisper Faustus and Mephisto.

In other words, he completes the circle, ending where he began with the tension of the in-between. For as the poem "Crepusculum" from the same volume indicates, there is nothing in the actual, contemporary world to induce him to settle into it. On the contrary: "In a land abandoned by spirit, the gray termites come marching in / lords of emptiness with an unending desire in their jaws."

Emil Boyson

Emil Boyson (1897–1979) may be the most French of Norwegian poets. His poems are musical, subtle, and difficult in a manner reminiscent of Stéphane Mallarmé, whom Boyson both studied and translated. In meticulously ordered verse and with words of sober abstraction, Boyson clears a space of emptiness in his poetry in which his objects can gently rearise. But when they do, they insist on their reality. Boyson's, in other words, is not a poetry in which objects flash and vanish in the shattering brilliance of an empty transcendence. Boyson fixes his glance on them with patient calm, frequently apprehending them in the twilight, which for him is a time not of colorless absence but of half-hidden mystery, as in "Vei i natten" (1939; The Road in the Night):

Alone on the desolate plain
the moon, solace of wanderers,
followed me; while my heart bent
its silence toward ash-pale autumn.

Death's mild emptiness loomed
where I drank of the moon's welling—
mutely I wandered, drawn by the allure
of a goal beyond all the mountains.

Boyson was a student of Edmund Husserl's phenomenology and in his later years translated Roman Ingarden's introduction to Husserl's *Phenomenology* into Norwegian. Boyson seems to have been drawn to phenomenology as a means of assuring himself of the actuality of the world, its veridical presence. It appears to have helped him overcome his nagging suspicion that the world around him was no more than a play of shadows on an unreal ground. After a conversion to Roman Catholicism in his early adulthood, it was natural for Boyson, given his involvement with French culture, to move from phenomenology to a study of French existentialism, particularly that of Gabriel Marcel.

These philosophical and religious concerns of Boyson's are mentioned not because knowledge of them is required for an appreciation of his poetry, but to give an indication of the direction of his thinking. Ultimately, Boyson can rely on the reality and goodness he senses in the world around him, because both are founded on love. Speaking to his wife, he writes in the final two stanzas of "Til vokteren" (1939; The Guardian):

When you are gone, I shall see
of the world's endless abundance
only death's sore on the Cross's tree
and enclosed in bread, a mystery.

Yet while your beauty is still near me
before a stronger one commands—
see to everything that grows, and be
the silence of my heart before I speak.

Boyson has not had a particularly large following in Norway, perhaps because he is something of an anomaly, but among poets and critics he is held in high esteem. His collections are *Varsler og møter* (1934; Warnings and Encounters), *Tegn og tydning* (1935; Signs and Interpretation), *Gjemt i mørket* (1939; Hidden in the Dark), *Sjelen og udyret* (1946; The Soul and the Monster), and *Gjenkjennelse* (1957; Recognition). Of Boyson's prose work, *Yngre herre på besøk* (1936; Young Gentleman Pays a Visit) and *Vandring mot havet* (1937; Wandering toward the Sea) are of some interest as early examples of a Norwegian experimental novel. Boyson was also a master translator of modern poetry from a variety of languages: English, French, German, and Spanish.

Claes Gill

Claes Gill (1910–73) produced only two slim volumes of verse, *Fragment av et magisk liv* (1939; Fragments of a Magical Life) and *Ord i jærn* (1942; Words in Iron), thirty-four poems in all. When the books first appeared, they were considered puzzling and mysterious. Initially, Arnulf Øverland, acting as a publisher's consultant, had rejected the first of them as too bizarre. Now, roughly a half-century later, though still mysterious, both have acquired landmark status as modernist texts in Norwegian literature.

Promises of other volumes of poetry went unfulfilled during the remaining thirty-one years of Gill's life, during which he earned his living as a successful theater actor. Partly because of his actor's aura and partly because he frequently gave interviews that contained subtly discordant accounts of his past—and of course, because he forever delayed publication of further poems—Gill acquired nearly mythical status during his lifetime. In the following poem, "Den gudommelige orden" (1939; Divine Order), we see him assuming the dramatic persona of the modern poet:

Anima mundi in all things: coal, paper and ocean,
the steamers' dark moan of pleasures in foreign ports,
a foreign grave.

Years of fanatical effort have given me a magic wand;
I kiss the whiteness of my woman in noble paper;
with noble letters.

The esoteric reference to "anima mundi," the unmediated discord by which the poem is organized, the shift from a "dark" sensuality to a "noble," courtly attitude toward woman, all make us feel at once that we have left the common sense of the compact majority far behind and entered a world where Yeats and Mallarmé are important presences. As in Mallarmé's work, the poem traces a typically modernist trajectory from spirit to matter to sensuality to death—to end with a sudden movement of awareness of itself as a poem. In the last two lines we discover that we are observing the poet in the act of writing. The loop has completed itself, and the poem has become reflexive. Enclosed within his poem, the poet "fanatically" struggles to bring forth the autonomous word that both conjures its object into presence and celebrates its absence.

Despite Gill's attitude of self-assurance, one frequently senses in his poems a fear that language may not really be able to stand up to the force of transient phenomena. Often Gill seems to aspire to reach beneath the phenomenal surface of things toward an esoteric substratum, only to be blocked by the feeling that the mystery may have been generated by an impossibility inherent in his own act of apprehension: "I will arise / and go to that lost land / where all is revealed as writing on water." Perhaps language does not fix things in a lasting structure but flows away like the things themselves. But if this is the case, and if language is no match for death, poetry may paradoxically achieve a kind of permanence for itself by drawing death's portrait, as in one of Gill's final poems, the laconic "Flyktende ungdom" (1942; Fleeing Youth):

Fleeing youth!
A hind
hunted by a pack
of belling hounds

The great Hunter
at his post
scrutinizes—coldly,
calmly—his hands.

Rolf Jacobsen

Rolf Jacobsen (1907–) is one of the few Norwegian poets with an international reputation, thanks in part to recognition and translations by the American poet Robert Bly (*Twenty Poems,* 1977) and more recently by Roger Greenwald (*The Silence Afterwards,* 1982).

He is a different sort of modernist than Gill or Boyson, without the Yeatsian mannerisms and plangency of the one nor the tense philosophically charged awareness of the other. A newspaper editor by profession, Jacobsen fills his poems with everything the news excludes: a geological sense of history; a naive intimacy with forest, ocean, and landscape; a wry and divided taste for the city; a fierce detestation for ecological damage; and a tactful, utterly nondogmatic sense of the holiness of life, particularly as it manifests itself in unprotected beings like trees and old people.

From his first book of poems, *Jord og jern* (1933; Earth and Iron), Jacobsen wrote free verse distinguished by compelling rhythms and startling images:

Speckling the country, the yellow bogs
are like blotches of plague.

Pale gray in the rain and hooded with fog, they send their
sadness like endless seas among thin forests.

We are far from any conventional view of nature here, far even from being able to say what the poet's attitude is to the—objectively speaking—innocent bogs. Clearly, they carry a whiff of death and corruption, releasing their essence at the end of the poem into the poet's mind like a kind of narcotic:

And all of them have this haunting breath
this bitter smell of sweet wine. Many miles
away in the forest I can feel it
numbing my thought like a drug.

It was this peculiar rapport with things, conveyed in striking images and in a free verse that convincingly mimed the movements of the poet's feeling, which distinguished Jacobsen's poetry from the start, making it hard to categorize. Because he wrote poems about trains, electrical turbines, office windows, racing automobiles, airplanes, and so on, he was often taken as a kind of futurist, like Emilio Marinetti, as if modern civilization had found in him another troubadour. But even his first book contained clear signs that Jacobsen was not really on the side of the machine:

Have you heard the air hammers' drum-fire against the rivet on rail,
    building, the high iron sides of ships?
—Then you have seen the flag of war snapping in the wind!
—Then you have heard the machine guns
spewing their steel into the enemy's heart.

Two years later, in *Vrimmel* (1935; Tumult), a stronger undertone of sadness and compassion entered Jacobsen's poetry. Age, decay, and rust began to evoke a gentle sympathy from him. War, business, and industry seemed driven by an energy as indifferent and unstoppable as Vesuvius's. One senses Jacobsen's underlying dismay at the destructiveness inherent in modern civilization, but as an artist he refuses to react conventionally and simplistically to it. His poetry fixes the permanent natural world and the speeded-up world of the modern city in a kind of metaphorical mirror relationship to each other, each commenting on the other, each striving to overcome the other. Jacobsen's sympathies are perhaps on the side of nature, but his intuition and wisdom seem to suggest that even the gasoline-driven cities may simply be nature moving at another tempo, one ultimately indifferent to the fate of humans.

Jacobsen is a master poet, so it is difficult to say which are his best books. *Fjerntog* (1951; Express Train) and *Hemmelig liv* (1954; Secret Life) are perhaps the collections that display his gifts most abundantly. Many of these poems seem to spring from some passionate sixth sense that allows Jacobsen to look to the edge of the thing he is considering and render its aura more powerfully than the thing itself. "Tistlenes sommer" (1951; Thistle Summer), "Butikk-kvartalet" (1954; Shops), "Vinden og fontenen" (1954; The Wind and the Fountain), "Den omvendte sommeren" (1954; Inverted Summer), "Tømmer" (1954; Timber), and "Stavkirker" (1954; Stave Churches) are some prime examples of his hauntingly intuitive art. And there are many more, both in these two collections and in such later ones as *Sommeren i gresset* (1956; Summer in the Grass), *Stillheten efterpå* (1965; The Silence Afterwards), *Headlines* (1969), *Pass for dørene—dørene lukkes* (1972; Watch the Doors—The Doors Are Closing), *Pusteøvelse* (1975; Breathing Exercise), *Tenk på noe annet* (1979; Think about Something Else), and *Nattåpent* (1985; Open 24 Hours).

Generally speaking, what one notices in Jacobsen's later poetry is that he becomes less modernistic as time goes on. He becomes more of an explicit and public poet—not in a pompous way, but from a need to speak clearly and directly about ecological matters, taking the word in its widest and deepest sense.

Norwegian Literature since 1950

Jan I. Sjåvik

7

In 1950 Norway was still in the process of recovering both materially and spiritually from World War II and the German occupation of the country. The material rebuilding process was led by the majority Labor government, which embarked on an ambitious program of industrial reconstruction and economic development. The people also hungered for books, however, for few new titles had been published during the war because of Nazi censorship and the self-imposed silence of most writers. Established and new authors now sought to satisfy this pent-up demand.

Many writers continued to focus on time-honored themes and genres, the so-called ocean-death-love motifs of lyric poetry or, in fiction, the psychological novel. There was also the enduring emphasis on ethical considerations, as in Johan Borgen's *Lillelord* trilogy and in some of Jens Bjørneboe's works, in which these concerns are fused with a need to understand the tragedy of nazism. There were still others, particularly Sigurd Hoel and Aksel Sandemose, who through their novels searched for the roots of the war, both in the social conditions of the community in question and in the psychological makeup of its individuals.

The war had also led to a distrust of ideologies and to a recognition of the need for open and pluralistic discussion, but the public debate was carried on, in true Norwegian fashion, with more vigor than wisdom. Among journals holding on to their standards was *Vinduet* (The Window), founded in 1947. It provided a view of world writing while giving space to the new literature at home. Although the editor tried to avoid appearing too obviously partisan, the journal's position in the debate was often thought of as radical. The journal *Spektrum* (1946–54; Spectrum) provided a conservative and anthroposophic counterbalance, while specific socialist ideas were debated in *Kontakt* (1947–54; Contact). A left-leaning publication of a different sort was the illustrated weekly periodical *Arbeidermagasinet* (1927–70; The Worker's Magazine), later renamed *Magasinet for alle* (The Magazine for All). Edited by Nils Johan Rud for almost fifty years, it continued to offer publishing opportunities and helpful guidance to many budding literary talents.

PROSE FICTION 1950–1965

The fiction of the early 1950s reflects many of the burning issues of the day, such as the fear of nuclear war, Norway's decision to join NATO (1949), and the mutual distrust of the superpowers. By the mid-fifties increased international stability as well as generally better living conditions at home had led to a feeling of permanence that tended to change the scope of what was written. Short novels and collections of short stories gave way to longer novels and series of novels. As in the novel of the 1930s, the focus was often on the psychology of the individual, who was typically portrayed in Freudian terms, though the ideas of Carl Gustav Jung began to have some impact as well. The literary existentialism of Jean-Paul Sartre and Albert Camus also became known in Norway. It is nevertheless true that many of the new prose writers of the 1950s were not particularly inventive: such older authors as Aksel Sandemose and Tarjei Vesaas were, susprisingly, among the more "modern" novelists during the early postwar years.

Johan Borgen
When Johan Borgen (1902–79) died, an obituary in a national newspaper referred to his "golden pen." As a journalist, critic, novelist, short-story writer, and playwright, Borgen had been a veritable institution in Norwegian cultural life. Born into a bourgeois family from Christiania's fashionable west side, he was known to be a member of the radical left. But he was not politically active and spent his life investigating the intricacies of human nature. His debut took place as early as 1925, but neither this first book, a collection of short stories entitled *Mot mørket* (Toward Darkness), nor several volumes that followed have the significance of his later work.

Borgen's breakthrough as a writer came after the war with a series of short-story collections, *Hvetebrødsdager* (1948; Honeymoon), *Noveller om kjærlighet* (1952; Short Stories about Love), and *Natt og dag* (1954; Night

and Day). The best of the stories are among the finest in Norwegian literature and have as their key concern the struggle for a fullness of love and the
search for, and experience of, a personal identity. The striving for identity is
also an important aspect of Borgen's largest and most significant work, the
trilogy *Lillelord* (1955; Eng. tr. 1982), *De mørke kilder* (1956; The Dark
Fountains), and *Vi har ham nå* (1957; We've Got Him Now). *Lillelord*, the
most highly accomplished of the three books, tells the story of a young man,
Wilfred Sagen, who grows up in an upper-middle-class environment in
Kristiania (Oslo) before World War I, and offers a penetrating analysis of
both Wilfred Sagen's cultural milieu and the development of his personality
as he sets out to find himself. The second volume tells about his success in
business, but failure in art, during the First World War, while the final part
of the trilogy shows him leading a double life during World War II, when he
both served the occupants as a guard along the Swedish border and worked
to bring Jewish refugees to safety in Sweden. The antidote to the sterility of
Wilfred's existence is embodied by a young Jewish woman, Miriam, who
touches his life at several critical junctures and with whom he at one time has
a love relationship. In the end, however, not even she is able to save him
from suicide.

Borgen's next novel, *Jeg* (1959; I), departs from the realistic conventions
employed in the *Lillelord* trilogy. The protagonist is split into two personalities, one of whom engages in experience while the other is purely the observer. At issue is both the definition of identity and the question of whether
a unified personality is possible. Because the author has chosen to split the
protagonist's consciousness, the character is given the opportunity to
choose between the possibilities present in his divided self. Borgen's emphasis in *Jeg* is on the importance of choice and responsibility in human life.
His next novel, *Blåtind* (1964; Blue Mountain), is thematically connected
with the *Lillelord* books through the character of another Jewish woman
who, like Miriam, represents wholeness and human solidarity, in opposition to men whose personalities have been divided through their concern
for power and status. Later novels such as *Den røde tåken* (1967; The Red
Mist), *Min arm, min tarm* (1972; My Arm, My Intestine), and *Eksempler*
(1974; Examples) all focus on the personality question.

Sigurd Evensmo
Sigurd Evensmo (1912–78), who like Borgen was also a journalist and a
critic, is known primarily for his World War II novel *Englandsfarere* (1945;
Eng. tr. *Boat for England*, 1947) about the attempted escape and subsequent
arrest and execution of a group of Norwegian patriots. Its theme, the ques-

tion of what qualities are required of a person who wants to live in full solidarity with others, also recurs in Evensmo's most important work, the Karl Martin trilogy. Its three volumes, *Grenseland* (1947; Border Country), *Flaggermusene* (1949; The Bats), and *Hjemover* (1951; Homeward), recount the life of the young Karl Martin as he grows up on the border between city and country as well as the one between proletariat and lower middle class, and then go on to describe his young manhood as a journalist of the left in the 1930s and finally some of his mature years during the war. The trilogy combines a general interest in social conditions with a special concern for the protagonist's human development. More particularly, the final volume focuses on the ethics of Karl Martin's choices: is his political involvement motivated by a concern for his fellow citizens or is it, rather, a manifestation of his desire to flee from more personal, and therefore more demanding, responsibilities? Evensmo's authorship as a whole has centered on the question of how to mediate between political necessity and individual morality, a problem that also informs his later books, such as the short-story collection *Glassveggen* (1954; The Glass Wall) and two futuristic novels entitled *Gåten fra år null* (1957; The Riddle from Year Zero) and *Miraklet på Blindern* (1966; The Miracle at Blindern). *Femten døgn med Gordona* (1963; Fifteen Days with Gordona) is a political thriller, while *Inn i din tid* (1976; Into Your Time) and *Ut i kulda* (1978; Out into the Cold) are volumes of memoirs.

Kåre Holt

The main theme in the novels of Kåre Holt (1917–) is the corrupting effect of power on those who hold it and the suffering endured by those who are nothing but pawns in the games of the rulers. Holt had written several books before the war and throughout the 1940s, but his real breakthrough came with the novel *Det store veiskillet* (1949; The Great Crossroads). An existentialist work inspired by Sartre, it tells the story of a young man forced to choose among several options available to him at the beginning of the war. In a manner reminiscent of Johan Borgen's technique ten years later in *Jeg*, the novel casts its protagonist in three different roles: a black marketeer, a Nazi torturer and informer, and a leader in the Resistance. In each of the three versions of the story, the protagonist has to deal with himself as he appears in the two other roles, which makes for a highly complex and engaging narrative.

Holt's concern with the question of choice and responsibility is evident also in his next three books, *Brødre* (1951; Brothers), *Hevnen hører meg til* (1953; Vengeance Is Mine), and *Mennesker ved en grense* (1954; People along a Border). In the subsequent series of three novels, *Det stolte nederlag* (1956; The Proud Defeat), *Storm under morgenstjerne* (1958; Storm beneath a Morning Star), and *Opprørere ved havet* (1960; Rebels by the Ocean), Holt took his material from the history of Norwegian organized labor, covering the time from the earliest attempts at unionization under Marcus Thrane in the 1850s, through the establishment and development of the Labor party shortly before the turn of the century, and concluding with a dramatic incident in the town of Hammerfest in 1921.

Holt's major work is the trilogy *Kongen* (The King), composed of the volumes *Mannen fra utskjæret* (1965; The Man from the Outer Skerry), *Fredløs mann* (1967; Outlaw), and *Hersker og trell* (1969; Ruler and Slave) and dealing with the life and times of King Sverre, a twelfth-century pretender to the throne of Norway. Focusing not on Sverre's political ideas but rather on the effect of power on the individual who becomes a slave both to his ambitions and to circumstances, the author shows how the cost of political and military achievement has to be borne by the masses of common men and women, whose labor and suffering made possible the greatness of their leader. Holt's interest in the more distant history of Norway also manifests itself in a play, *Kristina av Tunsberg* (1971; Christina of Tunsberg), and the novel *Farvel til en kvinne* (1972; Farewell to a Woman), in which the themes of power and violence are explored in the imagined lives of those who buried the Oseberg viking ship. In *Oppstandelsen* (1971; The Resurrection), the author expresses the view that even leaders of democracies will withhold information from the people if it serves their personal interests, while in the novel *Folket ved Svansjøen* (1973; The People of Swan Lake), in which the fate of a small Sami community is chronicled, the focus is once more on the victims of power.

The explorer and national hero Roald Amundsen is the subject of Holt's most hotly debated book, the semidocumentary novel *Kappløpet* (1974; The Race; Eng. tr. *The Race: A Novel of Polar Exploration*, 1976). Holt attempts to demythologize Amundsen by presenting him as a vain and ruthless man ridden by ambition, but since it is difficult to distinguish between passages in which the author relies strictly on his sources and those in which he uses them creatively, many readers have found this handling of documentary material objectionable. A novel in a similar vein is *Sjøhelten* (1975; The Naval Hero), in which Holt takes on Admiral Peter Wessel Tordenskiold (1690–1720), another Norwegian much admired by his countrymen. *Sønn av himmel og jord* (1978; Son of Heaven and Earth), in which Holt draws on the life of Hans Egede, an early Protestant missionary to Greenland, is a third example of the author's use of biographical material. His novel *De lange mil*

til paradiset (1977; The Long Miles to Paradise), in contrast, is autobiographical in nature. Holt's most substantial works from the 1980s are
Gjester fra det ukjente (1980; Guests from the Unknown), a narrative drawing on stories and legends that have been handed down in his own family,
and his two-volume autobiography, *Sannferdig beretning om mitt liv som
løgner* (1982; A Truthful Narrative about My Life as a Liar) and *Veien videre.
Ny sannferdig beretning om mitt liv som løgner* (1983; The Road Leads on: A
New Truthful Narrative about My Life as a Liar). Of lesser importance are
Mørke smil (1981; Dark Smiles), a spoof on spy stories and other kinds of
thrillers, and the brief narrative *Vandringen* (1986; The Journey), which is
heavily dependent on the writings of the explorers Fridtjof Nansen and
Hjalmar Johansen.

Paal Brekke

Paal Brekke (1923–) is known chiefly as a lyric poet, but he has also written
three novels of some significance. *På flukt* (1946; Fleeing) takes place
among Norwegian refugees in Stockholm during the war, while *Aldrende
Orfeus* (1951; Aging Orpheus) deals with the difference between two generations of artists. In Norwegian literature this book, written somewhat in the
style of James Joyce, has a composition and a narrative technique well in advance of its time. *Og hekken vokste kjempehøy* (1953; And the Hedge Grew
Enormous), by contrast, is a murder mystery of sorts, investigating the relationship of passivity, lack of emotional involvement, and violence.

Jens Bjørneboe

Jens Bjørneboe (1920–76) is one of the most European of Norwegian
writers. He was profoundly influenced by the ideas of Rudolf Steiner, founder of the anthroposophic movement, and by the political and dramatic
ideas of Bertolt Brecht. Though his major contribution to literature has
been in the fields of the novel, drama, and debate, his debut was a volume of
poetry, *Dikt* (1951; Poems), followed by two other collections, *Ariadne*
(1953) and *Den store by* (1958; The Great City). All Bjørneboe's poetry dis-
plays a tension between introverted metaphysics and a need to bring about
social and intellectual change. Like many members of his generation,
Bjørneboe was deeply moved by the war experience. His first novel, *Før
hanen galer* (1952; Before the Cock Crow), was a study of the experiments
performed by Nazi doctors on concentration-camp inmates during the war.
It portrays a physician whose shockingly split mind harbors both a scien-
tifically objective inhumanity and the feelings of a sensitive and caring private person. The book attracted much attention, but Bjørneboe's next

novel, *Jonas* (1955; Eng. tr. *The Last of These,* 1959), created an even greater stir, since it attacked teachers, administrators, and pedagogical ideas in the Norwegian school system. The main character, a dyslexic eight-year-old boy, is labeled "developmentally disabled" by his teachers and saved from destruction only because he meets a caring adult who espouses ideas similar to those of the author. In *Under en hårdere himmel* (1957; Under a Harder Sky), Bjørneboe takes on—for the first of many times—Norwegian judicial authorities. The novel criticizes the treatment of Norwegian war criminals after the war while defending certain collaborators who, in Bjørneboe's opinion, acted in good faith. *Blåmann* (1959) portrays the development of an artist, and *Den onde hyrde* (1960; The Evil Shepherd)—written while the author was carrying on a running feud with the Norwegian state prosecutor—attacks the way young criminals are treated by the courts and in the prisons. *Drømmen og hjulet* (1964; The Dream and the Wheel) connects with *Blåmann* in being a portrait of an artist, in this case the writer Ragnhild Jølsen.

Bjørneboe's fascination with the problem of evil led to what is generally regarded as his finest novel, *Frihetens øyeblikk* (1966; Eng. tr. *Moment of Freedom,* 1975), the first volume of a trilogy commonly referred to as the "History of Bestiality." The narrator is a Servant of Justice in a small European country who has set himself the task of chronicling the evils and injustices of Western civilization, and readers are spared none of the gruesome details in his seemingly endless catalog of atrocities. The substance of the matter is, however, that though existence appears to be meaningless, writing—that is, the production of texts—is a mechanism through which humans may endure life in an otherwise empty world. The trilogy's remaining volumes, *Kruttårnet* (1969; The Gunpowder Tower) and *Stillheten* (1973; The Silence), contain variations on the same theme.

Bjørneboe's last work of fiction was *Haiene* (1974; The Sharks), a novel of the sea in the tradition of Herman Melville. Telling the story of a ship's final voyage, it has its share of violence and brutality, though in the end there is a hope that the battling members of the crew will find their way to unity and reconciliation.

Alfred Hauge
Like Bjørneboe, Alfred Hauge (1915–87) displayed a clear concern with spiritual values in his writing, and with psychology in general, in which area his thinking was strongly influenced by the views of Jung. Unlike Bjørneboe, however, Hauge was a committed Christian whose artistic struggle took place on two fronts: he had to overcome prejudice against

high culture in the low church environment to which he belonged, and he needed to clear away the doubt, on the part of many members of the Norwegian cultural elite, that there could be true artistic value in literature that openly expressed a Christian view of life. This double challenge is part of the reason why Hauge remained a productive writer to the end of his life and a major innovator, both thematically and formally.

Hauge's first book, *Septemberfrost* (1941; The Frost of September), about the difficult years of national isolation before 1814, had a strong patriotic appeal. A second novel, *Tuntreet blør* (1942; The Yard Tree Is Bleeding), describes a rural crisis in the 1920s, while *Ropet* (1946; The Call) tells the story of a writer torn between his calling and the condemnation of art found in his fundamentalist environment, thus thematizing the author's own predicament.

Hauge's breakthrough came with a broadly conceived social/family/psychological novel in two volumes, *Året har ingen vår* (1948; The Year Has No Spring) and *Fossen og bålet* (1949; The Waterfall and the Bonfire), set in the author's home district and treating a family's striving for salvation. In *Ingen kjenner dagen* (1955; Nobody Knows the Day), the protagonist is a minister who has sacrificed his artistic talents for his religion and who is now taking stock of his life and finding it wanting. In *Kvinner på Galgebakken* (1958; Women on Gallows Hill), in contrast, a middle-aged man is looking back on his life and discovering that he has sacrificed the needs of others to satisfy his own vain ambitions.

Hauge had been attracted to the story of the pioneer immigrant Cleng Peerson, who, like the author, hailed from southwestern Norway. For twenty years he collected materials relating to this father of organized Norwegian emigration to America before presenting it in fictionalized form as a trilogy.

The first part, *Hundevakt* (1961; Midwatch), deals with the background of the emigration; the second volume, *Landkjenning* (1964; Landfall), portrays the journey itself, and the final volume, *Ankerfeste* (1965; Anchorage), tells about life in the new country. Hauge's Cleng Peerson trilogy is a fine example of both the historical novel in general and its subgenre, the emigration novel, but Hauge is also concerned with the psychological, religious, and ethical dimensions of his subject matter. The book was later published in a two-volume English edition (*Cleng Peerson*, 1975) as part of the sesquicentennial celebration of the Norwegian emigration to America.

Hauge's most ambitious work is his Utstein Monastery cycle, named after a historical landmark in his part of the country and consisting of five novels and two collections of poetry. The cycle was launched through the experimental novel *Mysterium* (1967; Mystery) and attempts to analyze the role played in human life by such qualities as empathy, tenderness, and the ability to help others cope with suffering of various kinds. A Jungian *Bildungsroman* with a Christian slant, it was followed by *Legenden om Svein og Maria* (1968; The Legend of Svein and Mary), a reworking of Hauge's earlier novel *Veien til det døde paradiset* (1951; The Road to the Dead Paradise), and two collections of poetry titled *Det evige sekund* (1970; The Eternal Second) and *I Rindbrads land* (1983; In Rindbrad's Country). The second half of the cycle consists of a trilogy that Hauge named "Århundre" (Century), composed of the volumes *Perlemorstrand* (1974; Mother-of-Pearl Shore), *Leviathan* (1979), and *Serafen* (1984; The Seraph). Set in southwestern Norway, the trilogy is a study of the twentieth century, which Hauge regards as a time of both spiritual and environmental crisis, and attempts to demonstrate how the present age is ruled by the twin emotions of greed and fear. Hauge also contributed to other literary genres, notably with two volumes of autobiography, *Barndom* (1975; Childhood) and *Ungdom* (1977; Youth).

Terje Stigen
Like Alfred Hauge, Terje Stigen (1922–), who comes from Finnmark, is strongly tied to the particular part of the country where he grew up. Primarily a teller of tales, who at times sacrifices other considerations for the sake of the story, Stigen is the most prolific writer of his generation.

Stigen's first novel, *To døgn* (1950; Two Days), shows, like most of the novels written at the time, the effects of World War II in Norway. Three more books followed before his breakthrough with *Vindstille underveis* (1956; Eng. tr. *An Interrupted Passage,* 1974), a short-story cycle with a frame establishing the necessary connection between the individual tales and with the all-consuming power of love as a general theme. Several more novels from the 1950s and early 1960s are, primarily, examples of the well-told tale. The short-story collection *Glasskulen* (1963; Eng. tr. *The Crystal Ball,* 1971) is set in northern Norway, as is the novel *Til det ytterste skjær* (1964; To the Outermost Skerry). *Krystallstjernen* (1965; The Crystal Star) narrates the happy adolescence of its protagonist, while *Timer i grenseland* (1966; Hours in a Borderland) has the German occupation as its setting. In yet another novel, *Det flyktige hjerte* (1967; The Wavering Heart), which takes place around the year 1800, the protagonist, Richard Blæsius, is an unhappy minister unable to escape his misery except through his art. But art has its price: what could have led to a fullness of emotional experience has to be used as raw material for art, and so his life is impoverished.

De tente lys (1968; The Lighted Candles) is also a historical novel. It takes place shortly after the death of St. Olav (1030) and shows the conflict between those who simply want to live in peace and those who look at their fellow humans as pawns in a power game. *Det siste paradiset* (1969; The Last Paradise) deals with the industrialization of a small town in northern Norway, and *Kains merke* (1971; The Mark of Cain) treats the lasting effect of a person's wartime experiences. *Besettelse* (1970; Obsession) is a psychological novel about a male teacher and one of his female students; *Min Marion* (1972; My Marion) argues for the right of the handicapped to experience a normal conjugal love relationship; *Skumsøylen* (1973; The Foam Pillar) is yet another story of love, this time between a strong woman and a weak man; and *Peter Johannes Lookhas* (1974), about a writer in an authoritarian state, is a plea for freedom of expression. *Avikfjord* (1977), *Huset og byen* (1978; The House and the City), *Rekviem over en sommer* (1979; Requiem for a Summer), and *Øgler i Avikfjord* (1980; Lizards in Avikfjord) constitute a series of novels that take place before and during World War II. Searching the past to find our true selves is the theme of *Bak våre masker* (1983; Behind Our Masks); *Baldershavn* (1984), in which Richard Blæsius returns as the first-person narrator, is a study in evil, jealousy, and revenge; and *Ved foten av kunnskapens tre* (1986; At the Foot of the Tree of Knowledge) is a tale of power and violence culminating in sabotage and reprisals on a small island in northern Norway during World War II. *Katedralen* (1987; The Cathedral) is a first-person narrative about deprivation and survival in Germany at the close of the war, while *Monolitten* (1988; The Monolith), which has the same setting but takes place before and during the war, explores once more the problem of evil. *Treskjæreren Johannes* (1990; The Woodcutter Johannes) is Stigen's most recent novel.

Stigen has also written essays and radio plays, some of them available in a volume titled *Den røde sommerfugl* (1974; The Red Butterfly).

Åsta Holth

Though not as productive as Terje Stigen, Åsta Holth (1904–) shares with her colleague a talent for storytelling. Holth started out writing short stories, but her real contributions are her two novel series. A trilogy consisting of *Kornet og freden* (1955; The Grain and the Peace), *Steinen blømer* (1963; The Stone Blossoms), and *Kapellet* (1967; The Chapel) tells the saga of seventeenth-century Finnish immigrants in the region along the Swedish-Norwegian border. A second trilogy with titles *Gullsmeden* (1958; The Goldsmith), *Presten* (1971; The Minister), and *Johannes* (1975) deals with the same material. Holth uses some of her own ancestors as characters in her books, but her purpose is to portray their environment rather than their personalities. Generally, in Holth's books women are her strongest figures.

Ragnhild Magerøy

Ragnhild Magerøy (1920–) shares Holth's interest in strong women characters. In her trilogy *Gunhild* (1957), *Forbannet kvinne* (1958; Cursed Woman), and *Kjærleiken spør ikke* (1960; Love Asks No Questions), she portrays the lives of three women from the same family who are married to weak men. *Lengsel, men ingen vinge* (1962; Longing, But No Wing) takes place during World War II and tells the story of a young girl who can find love and tenderness only among the German occupants. *Dronning uten rike* (1966; Queen without Empire), in contrast, is set in the Middle Ages, as is a whole series of later novels: *Mens nornene spinner* (1969; While the Norns Are Spinning), *Himmelen er gul* (1970; The Sky Is Yellow), *Nikolas* (1972), *Kvassere enn sverdet* (1974; Sharper Than the Sword), *Baglerbispen* (1976; The Bagler Bishop), *De som dro sudr* (1979; Those Who Went South), and *Den lange vandringen* (1980; The Long Journey), the last two about a group of pilgrims. *Miriams kilde* (1985; Miriam's Spring) is a volume of short stories, many with Jewish themes. Magerøy's strengths are her insight into the feminine psyche and her ability to portray accurately the settings of her stories.

Vera Henriksen

Like Magerøy, Vera Henriksen (1927–) writes about women in a distant past. A trilogy consisting of *Sølvhammeren* (1961; The Silver Hammer), *Jærtegn* (1962; A Sign from God), and *Helgenkongen* (1963; The Saint King) takes place during the eleventh century and has a woman protagonist of exceptional strength of personality. In contrast, *Glassberget* (1966; The Glass Mountain) is a novel of modern marriage. Henriksen's most ambitious work is a series of novels about life at the time of the Reformation: *Trollsteinen* (1970; The Magic Stone), *Pilgrimsferd* (1971; Pilgrimage), *Blåbreen* (1973; The Blue Glacier), *Staupet* (1975; The Goblet), and *Skjærsild* (1977; Purgatory). Though all these books can be read as contributions to a contemporary debate about sex roles, their greatest strength is Henriksen's narrative skill. Drawing heavily on medieval documents, Henriksen focused her attention once more on the time around the year A.D. 1000. Some of the titles are *Dronningsagaen* (1979; The Saga of the Queen), which is set in southern Sweden; *Bodvars saga* (The Saga of Bodvar) consisting of the volumes *Odins ravner* (1983; The Ravens of Odin) and *Spydet* (1984; The Spear), in which the action takes place in and around Iceland;

and *Runekorset* (1986; The Runic Cross), which is set in Greenland and America. In addition to being literary works in their own right, several of these titles offer interesting reinterpretations of the Icelandic sagas, which are a major inspiration for Henriksen's medieval novels. Henriksen's most recent novel, *Silhuetter mot hvitt lys* (1990; Silhouettes on White Light), is set during and after World War II.

Finn Carling

Finn Carling (1925–) differs from most other Norwegian writers of his generation in that his focus is not on the everyday realities of life, whether explored in the historical or the contemporary novel, but on the relationship between reality and fantasy. *Broen* (1949; The Bridge), *Stemmene og nuet* (1950; The Voices and the Moment), *Arenaen* (1951; The Arena), *Piken og fuglen* (1951; The Girl and the Bird), *Skyggen* (1954; The Shadow), *Fangen i det blå tårn* (1954; The Prisoner in the Blue Tower), and *Desertøren* (1956; The Deserter) are prose works with stylized characters, extensive use of symbols, and playful narrative patterns. In the last of these novels, *Desertøren*, Carling also touched on his own situation as a handicapped person, and his next book, the autobiography *Kilden og muren* (1958; Eng. tr. *And Yet We Are Human*, 1962), is a personal discussion of what it means to suffer from cerebral palsy.

The autobiography initiated a change in Carling's authorship. He now wanted to explore the life situations of other social minorities and published *Blind verden* (1962; Blind World), *De homofile* (1965; Homosexuals), and *Skapende sinn* (1970; Creative Minds), the last volume containing interviews with writers. *Resten er taushet* (1973; The Rest Is Silence) examines the process of dying, *Skapt i vårt bilde* (1975; Created in Our Image) is a contribution to the contemporary debate of how to treat persons differing from the accepted social norm, and *Hvite skygger på svart bunn* (1976; White Shadows against Black) discusses African problems. Like these semidocumentary accounts, two works of fiction from the same period also show a need to depart from the dreamlike qualities of Carling's first books: *Sensommerdøgn* (1960; Days of Late Summer) is a realistic and psychological exploration of why some men are unable to establish a complete erotic relationship with one woman, while *Kometene* (1964; The Comets) describes the psychological damage inflicted on some characters by their hypocritical surroundings.

Most of Carling's fictional works from the 1970s, however, emphasize fantasy and dream, which makes them seem similar to his early books. *Gjesten* (1970; The Guest), a study in puberty, objects to the tendency of some political theoreticians to forget they are dealing with living human be-ings; *Fiendene* (1974; The Enemies) is an unsettling discussion, in the form of a novel, of the violence and brutality of the modern world; *Marginalene* (1977; The Marginalds), considered by many to be Carling's best book, is a cycle of short stories about people who are different in one way or another; and *Tårnseileren* (1979; The Swift), with its composite portrait of an uncon-ventional person, shows that human identity is an elusive thing, highly de-pendent on the perceptions of one's associates.

In the 1980s Carling became increasingly pessimistic. *Visirene* (1981; The Visors) is a revelation of universal selfishness, *Museumstekster* (1982; Mu-seum Texts) imagines that a nuclear war has taken place before the period in which the book is set, and in *Fabel X* (1984) Carling makes use of techniques drawn from science fiction to construct his frightening picture of the world. *Lille Orlando* (1986; Little Orlando) is a novel of education and at the same time a portrait of the cruelty and cynicism of Western culture. The author's most recent novel is *Gjensyn med en fremtid* (1988; Meeting a Future Again), in which he makes extensive use of autobiographical material.

Carling has also made contributions in other genres, such as drama and poetry. *Gitrene* (1966; The Bars) is an experimental drama based on the bib-lical story of Abraham's sacrifice of Isaac. The plays *Slangen* (1970; The Snake) and *Skudd* (1971; Shot) both have protagonists who must suffer for the actions of others. Carling's most recent publication is a book of poetry, *Det innerste rommet* (1990; The Innermost Room).

Arne Skouen

The situation of the handicapped is also central to the authorship of Arne Skouen (1913–). Best known as a film maker and as a columnist in the Oslo daily *Dagbladet* (The Daily Paper), Skouen in addition has written novels and plays. *Fest i Port des Galets* (1947; Eng. tr. *Stoker's Mess*, 1948) tells about a group of Norwegian sailors and focuses on the process of maturation as experienced by the protagonist, which is also a theme in the next novel, *Gategutter* (1948; Street Urchins). *Pappa tar gull* (1962; Daddy Takes Gold) and *Pappas dans* (1964; Daddy's Dance) are primarily satirical novels without much purpose beyond entertainment, but the final Daddy novel, *Pappa blir voksen* (1966; Daddy Grows Up), represents a return to the ques-tion of maturation.

Torborg Nedreaas

Torborg Nedreaas (1906–87) began writing popular fiction for the weekly press, and some of these early stories have been collected in *Før det ringer tredje gang* (1945; Before the Third Bell). *Bak skapet står øksen* (1945; The Ax Is behind the Cupboard), a collection of short stories about young girls who befriend the German occupants during the war, was her first attempt at serious literature. A novel, *Av måneskinn gror det ingenting* (1947; Eng. tr. *Nothing Grows by Moonlight,* 1987), further explores men's emotional and sexual exploitation of women.

Nedreaas's greatest achievements are several narratives focused on the development and growth of a young girl called Herdis. *Trylleglasset* (1950; The Magic Prism), a cycle of short stories, portrays Herdis, her parents, and their environment, a socially mixed Bergen neighborhood, during the First World War. Nedreaas tells her tale from a socialist and feminist perspective and continues the account in two of the stories in the collection *Stoppested* (1953; Bus Stop) and in the novel *Musikk fra en blå brønn* (1960; Eng. tr. *Music from a Blue Well,* 1988). *Ved neste nymåne* (1971; By the Next New Moon), another novel, tells about Herdis's teenage years. As in the earlier books, attention is concentrated on her emotional and intellectual life, but the author is now more aggressive in her portrayal of the materialism of the Bergen plutocracy.

Nedreaas's political radicalism is expressed in the novel *De varme hendene* (1952; The Warm Hands), a powerful attack on Norway's membership in NATO. *Den siste polka* (1965; The Last Polka) is a short-story collection with emphasis on women and children. Nedreaas also wrote radio plays and essays.

Agnar Mykle

Like Nedreaas, Agnar Mykle (1915–) comes from a petty-bourgeois background; unlike her, however, he voices his opposition to his origins not in political terms, but in the expressed need for personal, particularly sexual, liberation. *Taustigen* (1948; The Rope Ladder) is a collection of short stories by an excellent stylist concentrating his attention on the conflict between expectations and everyday reality. The novel *Tyven, tyven skal du hete* (1951; The Thief, the Thief You Will Be Called [Norwegian nursery rhyme]; Eng. tr. *The Hotel Room,* 1963) is a defense of the right to sexual freedom, though at the same time it points to a connection between sexual exploitation and physical brutality. A similar concern appears in *Jeg er like glad, sa gutten* (1952; I Couldn't Care Less, Said the Boy), a collection of short stories.

Mykle's fame rests on two novels, *Lasso rundt fru Luna* (1954; Eng. tr. *Lasso Round the Moon,* 1960) and *Sangen om den røde rubin* (1956; Eng. tr. *The Song of the Red Ruby,* 1961). They tell the story of the youth and young manhood of the composer Ask Burlefot, who, like Mykle, has grown up in a narrow-minded bourgeois environment. The novels are largely about his search for liberation and personal development, particularly in the erotic sphere. To this end he takes advantage of several women for whom he does not really care, while his upbringing keeps him at a distance from the one he does love. It is possible to view Burlefot's story not only as a novel of male development, but as a more general portrait of male subjugation of women.

Because of the sexually explicit scenes in *Sangen om den røde rubin,* some reviewers claimed Mykle had violated the Norwegian obscenity statute. A decision to prosecute was made, and Oslo City Court found the book to be in violation of the law, although both the author and the publisher were cleared of criminal charges. The High Court subsequently overturned the verdict regarding the book. The case gave both the author and his novel unrestrained publicity and had the effect of liberalizing the standard of obscenity in Norway, paving the way for the frank depiction of sexuality which became common in the 1970s and 1980s.

The novel *Rubicon* (1965; Eng. tr. 1966) constitutes a follow-up of sorts to the two Burlefot novels, but it is far weaker artistically. A better book, *Largo* (1967), contains two short stories, one of which has *crimen bestialis* as its theme. Mykle has not remained active as a writer.

Kjell Askildsen

Mykle has not been as prolific as some of his colleagues, and neither has Kjell Askildsen (1929–), but unlike Mykle, Askildsen has been appreciated by critics and fellow writers more than by the public at large. His earliest books, the short-story collection *Heretter følger jeg deg helt hjem* (1953; Hereafter I Will Go with You All the Way Home) and the novels *Herr Leonard Leonard* (1955; Mr. Leonard Leonard) and *Davids bror* (1957; David's Brother), deal with people who rebel against a stifling milieu and repressive authority figures. Formally interesting is the short-story collection *Kulisser* (1966; Stage Decorations), which contains examples of advanced use of stream-of-consciousness and point-of-view techniques. A brief novel, *Omgivelser* (1969; Surroundings), is a study in everyday role playing, while *Kjære, kjære Oluf* (1974; Dear, Dear Oluf), another short novel, shows how conflicts in marriage are a consequence of the subjection of women. After the novel *Hverdag* (1976; Every Day) Askildsen during the 1980s published two more volumes of short stories. *Ingenting for ingenting* (1982; Nothing for Nothing) focuses on the male psyche, including men's inability to communicate, their jealousy, and their need to control women. *Thomas F's siste nedtegnelser til almenheten* (1983; Thomas F's Last Notes for the General

Public), which contains two stories, has as its main themes alienation and the question of identity. *En plutselig frigjørende tanke* (1987; A Suddenly Liberating Idea) is, with the exception of the title story, a collection of material from Askildsen's earlier volumes of stories. Askildsen's most recent book is a collection of short stories entitled *Et stort øde landskap* (1991; A Large Deserted Landscape).

Axel Jensen

Axel Jensen (1932–) differs from most of his contemporaries both in his subject matter and in his way of dealing with it. After a rather insignificant first novel, *Dyretemmerens kors* (1955; The Cross of the Animal Tamer), he published the autobiographical first-person novel *Ikaros* (1957; Eng. tr. *Icarus, a Young Man in the Sahara*, 1959). It is an intense and emotional report of a geographical and spiritual journey and, for the author, a means of voicing his distaste for contemporary ideologies and his anger at a world created by his elders. The protagonist in Jensen's next book, *Line* (1959; Eng. tr. *A Girl I Knew*, 1962), is a budding writer and "angry young man" of the 1950s who has difficulty adjusting to his social milieu in contemporary Oslo. The novel *Joachim* (1961), which takes place in Greece, is of lesser artistic significance, while the science-fiction story *Epp* (1965; Eng. tr. 1965) is regarded as one of the most important Norwegian pieces of social and cultural criticism from the 1960s. Its setting is a society of the future which has been made so efficient that human qualities of life have all but disappeared. The book's protagonist and diarist, Epp, accepts the status quo and reveals his lack of emotional and intellectual acuity through his style, causing readers to compare their own situation with the conditions portrayed in the book. After a nine-year break Jensen published two books on India, the travelogue *Mor India* (1974; Mother India) and the poetry collection *Onalila. En liten østvestpoesi* (1974; Onalila: A Little East-West Poem). He has also published two autobiographical books, *Junior eller Drømmen om pølsefabrikken som bibliotek* (1978; Junior, or the Dream of the Sausage Factory as Library) and *Senior* (1979).

Finn Alnæs

Finn Alnæs (1932–91) was one of the most ambitious writers in postwar Norwegian literature. His novels are long; they treat philosophical, particularly ethical, questions of the greatest significance; and their protagonists are often larger-than-life, heroic individuals. Alnæs's first novel, *Koloss* (1963; Colossus), established the author as one of his country's foremost prose writers. Brage Bragesson, the protagonist, is superhuman both physically and mentally; he performs a series of notable feats and probes his psyche for his true motives. The importance of ethical action is brought into particularly sharp focus at the end of the book when, during a blizzard, Bragesson saves the life of his bitterest enemy. *Gemini* (1968) thematizes the conflict between two approaches to the writer's vocation. Of two writers, who are also twin brothers, one produces the kind of cynical literature Alnæs wished to combat, while the other one—the author's alter ego—speaks in favor of placing the human spirit in opposition to political and cultural degeneration. Alnæs comes across as a radical individualist with a cosmic perspective.

In his next novel, *Festningen Faller* (1971; The Fortress of Faller), in which the stylized action takes place in the future in some Western industrial society, Alnæs forces his readers to face the question of individual responsibility in a mass community where technology reigns.

Alnæs's most ambitious project is a cycle of novels called *Ildfesten* (Festival of Fire), which, according to his plan, was to include eight volumes and have as its central theme the joy of life in its various forms. The first volume of the octet is *Musica* (1978), in which, in addition to music, environmentalism is a major concern. This emphasis is continued in the second volume, *Dynamis* (1982), in which the author also attempted to thematize the infinite. His protagonist and spokesman is Fartein Glitra, an astrophysicist who has abandoned the Einsteinian view of the universe. To Glitra there is no such thing as a defined space, only spaces between smaller and larger aggregates of matter, and he maintains that humans will be able to survive on this planet only if they adopt a world view based on the infinitude of the universe. Alnæs published a collection of essays, *På frihetens pinebenk* (1972; On the Rack of Freedom); *Naturkatedral* (1976; Nature Cathedral), written in praise of the beauties of the Norwegian landscape; and *Svart snø* (1976; Black Snow), which documents an environmentalist "direct action" at Mardøla in 1970.

Ebba Haslund

The authorship of Ebba Haslund (1917–) is focused on the lives of women in Oslo's middle class. Haslund's first book was a volume of short stories, *Også vi*— (1945; We, Too), which was followed by some novels: *Siste halvår* (1946; The Last Half Year), *Det hendte ingenting* (1948; Eng. tr. *Nothing Happened*, 1987), *Middag hos Molla* (1951; Dinner with Molla), *Krise i august* (1954; Crisis in August), *Drømmen om Nadja* (1956; The Dream of Nadja), *Hvor går du, Vanda?* (1960; Where Are You Going, Vanda?), *Det trange hjerte* (1965; The Narrow Heart), *Syndebukkens krets* (1968; Tropic

of the Scapegoat), *Bare et lite sammenbrudd* (1975; Only a Small Breakdown), and *Behag og bedrag* (1978; Pleasure and Deception). One of Haslund's strengths is her ability to portray women convincingly: her psychological insight is considerable. The protagonist is usually in the middle of a
marriage crisis or adjustment crisis of some sort, and a recurring motif concerns the many mechanisms by which women are subjected to men's norms,
making them into something different from what they could have been if
granted the opportunity to choose for themselves. *Døgnfluens lengsel* (1984;
The Longing of the Mayfly), though it takes place in a middle-class environment similar to that of Haslund's earlier books, has the additional theme of
religious conversion.

Haslund has also written radio plays, children's books, and essays, as well
as two volumes of autobiography, *Som plommen i egget* (1987; Like the Yolk
in the Egg) and *Med vingehest i manesjen* (1989; With a Winged Horse in the
Arena).

Bergljot Hobæk Haff

Like many of Haslund's books, *Raset* (1956; Landslide) by Bergljot Hobæk
Haff (1925–) tells the story of a marriage in distress. An erotically gifted
woman is married to an inhibited and unimaginative physician who, because he feels inferior to his wife, wishes to control her. The novel ends in
death and insanity, but despite its theme it is not a one-sided book, because
its point of view belongs to the male first-person narrator. *Raset* was followed by *Liv* (1958), a less successful novel, and *Du finner ham aldri* (1960;
You Will Never Find Him), in which Haff returns to the question of women
who are destroyed by a patriarchal society. *Bålet* (1962; The Bonfire) portrays a woman who has to choose between two men, of which one represents goodness and service while the other is the typically evil and domineering autocrat. For Haff, this novel marks the beginning of a trend away from
psychological realism and in the direction of symbol and allegory: the protagonist in *Bålet* represents all humanity having to choose between good
and evil.

Also concerned with the question of good and evil is the large and heavy
whore who serves as first-person narrator in *Skjøgens bok* (1965; The Book of
the Harlot); she is a woman endowed with a rare ability to comprehend the
underlying motives of human actions. *Den sorte kappe* (1969; The Black
Cloak), which takes place in a city on the Mediterranean, portrays a Norwegian shipowner who has difficulties distinguishing between nuns and
prostitutes. The moral of the story: male society, which has put women on a
pedestal not to honor them but rather to marginalize and trivialize them,

will have to reap its just reward. *Sønnen* (1971; The Son) begins as the story of a young man controlled by his mother and ends as an allegory of the impossibility of Christian charity. *Heksen* (1974; The Witch), set during the time of the witch hunts, is a general meditation on suffering, particularly with reference to the artist, whose responsibility it is to take over the inarticulate cry of anguish and transform it into song so that it may be heard and understood. *Gudsmoren* (1977; The Mother of God) is an original and highly experimental story in which the biblical Christmas narrative is transposed into contemporary Norwegian reality, and *Jeg, Bakunin* (1983; I, Bakunin) is a fictitious first-person account from the hand of the great Russian revolutionary. Though a "historical novel" based on fictitious letters and other documents, it leads the reader to engage in moral and ethical reflection on contemporary problems. So does Haff's most recent and most political novel, *Den gudommelige tragedie* (1989; The Divine Tragedy), in which God, expelled from Heaven by the white archangel Gabriel, settles among the black miners of Soweto.

LYRIC POETRY 1950–1965

Lyric poetry was a strong genre in the 1930s. Wildenvey and Øverland were the dominant names, though there were many others, and most of them employed traditional means of expression, modernist tendencies being largely unknown (for exceptions, see the discussions of Reiss-Andersen, Boyson, Gill, and Jacobsen in Chapter 6). During World War II and the German occupation, when it became necessary to enlist the poets in the war effort, poems were even more traditional in form and content since they had to express the concerns of average men and women. Other conservative factors were the lack of stimulation from the outside and the deliberate slowdown in the publishing of native works during the war years when the country's literary life simply ground to a halt.

After the liberation in the spring of 1945 there was a flood of printed materials, but most of the published poetry had been written earlier or was in line with prewar sentiments. This situation changed with the return of Norwegian poets who had spent part of the war years in Sweden, where they had become acquainted with such *fyrtiotalister* (poets of the forties) as Erik Lindegren and Karl Vennberg, whose work was a local manifestation of European modernism. Because their central themes of anxiety, isolation, and critical pessimism, as well as their obscure style, were poetic values directly opposed to those called for by the people of an occupied country, considerable time had to pass before the new ideas took root: the change during the first few postwar years was gradual and extremely tentative, more in the direction of a late symbolism than modernism in its strictest sense. One source of inspiration was T. S. Eliot's *Waste Land* (1924), a translation of which was provided by Paal Brekke in 1949, and motivation for change was also provided by the work of certain Danish poets associated with the periodical *Heretica* (1948–53). When modernism began to manifest itself in the work of such poets as Brekke and Erling Christie, who maintained that the twentieth-century fragmentation of reality must be accompanied by a fragmentation of poetic form, it was met by a strong rearguard action led by the poet Arnulf Øverland. Øverland's essay "Tungetale fra Parnasset" (1953; Glossolalia [Speaking in Tongues] from Parnassus) has since given the controversy its name of *Tungetale-debatten* (The Glossolalia Debate).

Paal Brekke

Paal Brekke (1923–) was the standard-bearer of modernism in Norway during the 1950s. Having fled to Sweden as a seventeen-year-old schoolboy at the beginning of the war, he had come into contact with the work of Edith Södergran, Gunnar Ekelöf, Karl Vennberg, and Erik Lindegren, which he introduced in Norway after his return home. His first volume of poetry, however, was rather traditional (*Jeg gikk så lange veier* [1945; I Walked Such Long Roads]). Far more significant was the modernistic *Skyggefektning* (1949; Shadow Fencing), which was inspired by Eliot's *Waste Land* and received a quite negative reception. After writing three novels, Brekke returned to poetry with his *Løft min krone, vind fra intet* (1957; Lift My Crown, Wind from Nothingness), in which the modernistic vocabulary and fragmented world view still dominate, but kernels of goodness and beauty are nevertheless to be found, particularly in the poet's treatment of love. In *Roerne fra Itaka* (1960; The Oarsmen of Ithaca), Brekke inveighs against the consumerist ideology of the modern welfare state, and his use of the classical motif lends an especially strong ironic tone to the volume.

A journey to India in 1960 (described in *En mundfull av Ganges* [1962; A Mouthful of Ganges]) nudged Brekke in the direction of closer involvement in political and social life. His next volume of poetry, *Det skjeve smil i rosa* (1965; The Wry Smile in Pink), is a satirical treatment of the whole of Western life, but again particularly its consumerist aspects, and the documentary poetry and prose of *Granatmannen kommer* (1968; The Grenade Man Is Coming) likewise is an indictment of contemporary reality. The poems contained in *Aftenen er stille* (1972; The Evening Is Quiet) give an ironical portrait of the kind of life offered to old people in the welfare state. *Flimmer. Og strek* (1980; Shimmering. And Lines) is the title of Brekke's most recent volume of poetry. Brekke has also worked as a translator and reviewer. *Til sin tid* (1970; At Its Time) is a collection of literary articles spanning the years 1945–70. A similar volume is *Farvel'ets rester* (1981, The Remnants of the Farewell).

Erling Christie

Another modernistic point man in the 1950s, Erling Christie (1928–) was, like Brekke, also a critic. *Tendenser og profiler* (1955; Trends and Profiles) contains articles that he wrote in the early part of the decade and in which he introduced such names as T. S. Eliot, Rainer Maria Rilke, and W. H. Auden to the Norwegian public. His own poetry was first published in *Drøm om havet* (1954; Dream of the Ocean) and *Serenade for blå gitar* (1956; Serenade for a Blue Guitar), in which, despite his modernist technique, the choice of words is often traditional. The satirical poetry of *Minus* (1959), in contrast, is highly economical, and the poetry of *Tegnene slukner* (1960; The Signs Are Extinguished) is more concrete than that of the earlier volumes, showing that Christie had managed to liberate himself from his teachers. Christie's promising career was cut short by an accident in 1960.

André Bjerke

André Bjerke (1918–85) was one of the cultural leaders siding with Øverland in the debate over modernism. Formerly a radical who admired classical verse for its adherence to strict prosodic rules, Bjerke was forced by the occupation to write conventional poetry. *Syngende jord* (1940; Singing Earth) and *Fakkeltog* (1942; Torchlight Parade) are collections of such material, while *Regnbuen* (1946; The Rainbow) and *Eskapader* (1948; Escapades) show the influence of Rudolf Steiner's anthroposophy. *Den hemmelige sommer* (1951; The Secret Summer) established an image of Bjerke that has remained with the public since then, unaltered by his many later collections. Childhood, love, art, and play are some of the central themes in this poetry, and they are expressed in the elegant language of his formally perfect verse. Bjerke also produced high-quality translations of drama and poetry from world literature. In addition, he wrote some of Norway's finest mystery novels (under the pseudonym of Bernhard Borge) and was a prolific contributor to Norwegian public debate, particularly the issue of language reform, where—again with Øverland—he favored a conservative line.

Inger Hagerup

Whereas love was one of Bjerke's several central themes, it was a constant preoccupation with Inger Hagerup (1905–85), who wrote about the relationship between man and woman in all its aspects. *Jeg gikk meg vill i skogene* (1939; I Lost My Way in the Woods), her first volume of poetry, also contained social and political poems, but *Flukten til Amerika* (1942; The Flight to America) consisted mostly of love poems. Hagerup is particularly well known for her Resistance poetry, however, a famous example of which is "Aust-Vågøy," written in 1941 and included in *Videre* (1944; Further), a collection of war poems published in Sweden. Hagerup returned to her central theme of love in *Den syvende natt* (1947; The Seventh Night) and *Sånn vil du ha meg* (1949; Thus You Want Me), as well as in volumes from the 1950s, *Drømmeboken* (1954; The Dream Book) and *Strofe med vinden* (1958;Stanza in the Wind). In addition to love, childhood and death are important themes in *Fra hjertets krater* (1964; From the Crater of the Heart). Hagerup also wrote children's verse, radio plays, and a three-volume autobiography.

Astrid Hjertenæs Andersen

A strong vitalism is present also in the poetry of Astrid Hjertenæs Andersen (1915–85). Her first two collections, *De ville traner* (1945; The Wild Cranes) and *De unge søylene* (1948; The Young Pillars), are rather ordinary, but her later poetry, inspired by modernism, is the work of a refined artist fully able to create expressive and concrete nature images, as in *Skilpaddehagen* (1950; The Turtle Garden) and *Strandens kvinner* (1955; The Women of the Shore). In *Vandrersken* (1957; The Wandering Woman), the erotic becomes a significant motif; and in *Pastoraler* (1960; Pastorals), *Frokost i det grønne* (1964; Breakfast in the Green), and *Rosenbusken* (1972; The Rosebush), Andersen departs from her earlier, somewhat complicated style. Her precise images and carefully chosen words give the better poems in these volumes an almost classical simplicity. Andersen also published volumes of poetic prose, such as *Doktor Gnomen* (1967; Doctor Gnomen), *Hyrdefløyten* (1968; The Shepherd's Flute), and *Svaner og nåtid* (1973; Swans and the Present).

Marie Takvam

Love in its various aspects is a main theme also in the poetry of Marie Takvam (1926–), who voices her concern about the role of women in society as well. *Dåp under sju stjerner* (1952; Baptism under Seven Stars) and *Syngjande kjelder* (1954; Singing Springs) contain genuine expressions of zest for life and love, while in *Signal* (1959; Signals), the poet is more critical of contemporary society. This attitude intensified in volumes such as *Merke etter liv* (1962; Marks of Life), *Mosaikk i lys* (1965; Mosaic in Light), *Brød og tran* (1969; Bread and Cod Liver Oil), and *Auge, hender* (1975; Eyes,

Hands). Takvam, who writes in nynorsk, has also published a novel, *Dansaren* (1975; The Dancer), about a woman's love of a bisexual man.

Tor Jonsson

The poetry of Tor Jonsson (1916–51) exhibits a strong ideological motivation. Rooted in the Norwegian countryside (Hamsun's and Aukrust's birthplace, Lom), Jonsson uses nature images to illustrate what he perceives to be a fundamental conflict in our lives, the tension between striving for security and concern for others. Though he had appeared in print as early as 1932 (in *Arbeidermagasinet*), Jonsson did not have his first book published until almost a decade later. *Mogning i mørket* (1942; Maturation in Darkness) was followed by *Berg ved blått vatn* (1946; Mountains by a Blue Lake) and *Jarnnetter* (1948; Iron Nights), both of which contain sharp attacks on poverty and other forms of social injustice.

Jonsson was also a journalist, writing in nynorsk and with a leftish slant. Some of his articles were collected in a volume titled *Nesler* (1950; Nettles), and a second collection called *Nesler* was published in 1952, after Jonsson's suicide, as was an unfinished collection of poetry, *Ei dagbok for mitt hjarte* (1951; A Diary for My Heart). Jonsson's collected prose and poetry has since become available in a two-volume edition (1956–60) containing unpublished poetry and prose; a one-act play, *Siste stikk* (1950; The Last Trick); and an essay by the poet Tore Ørjasæter. Ørjasæter describes Jonsson's verse as masculine and compressed, with striking use of rhythm and alliteration, but otherwise simple in its use of effects—a poetry of powerful imagery and great clarity and with a message that stands out firm and vivid. As a nynorsk poet, journalist, and satirist, this lonely and promising writer was in many ways a twentieth-century Aasmund Vinje.

Hans Børli

Hans Børli (1918–89), like Tor Jonsson, had his origins in a rural environment. A logger by trade, he began his writing career by publishing several volumes of undistinguished poetry: *Tyrielden* (1945; The Pitch Fire), *Villfugl* (1947; Wild Bird), *Men støtt kom nye vårer* (1949; But Constantly New Springs Came), and *Likevel må du leve* (1952; You Still Must Live). Many of the early poems are humorous, and others are sharply critical of contemporary society; later collections, in which free verse is often used, contain poetry of a much more personal kind. Some of these volumes are *Ser jeg en blomme i skogen* (1954; If I See a Flower in the Forest), *Dagene* (1958; The Days), *Jeg vil fange en fugl* (1960; I Want to Catch a Bird), *Ved bålet* (1962; By the Fire), *Hver liten ting* (1964; Each Little Thing), *Som rop ved elver*

(1969; Like Cries by Rivers), *Isfulgen* (1970; The Ice Bird), *Vindharpe* (1974; Wind Harp), *Vinden ser aldri på veiviserne* (1976; The Wind Never Looks at the Road Signs), *Dagen er et brev* (1981; The Day Is a Letter), and *Frosne tranebær* (1984; Frozen Cranberries). Børli also wrote prose narratives whose setting is his forest world.

Alf Prøysen

The life of common people in the countryside also forms the backdrop in the poetry of Alf Prøysen (1914–70), probably the most widely known of the Norwegian writers of the 1950s and 1960s. His first book was a collection of short stories, *Dørstokken heme* (1945; The Threshhold at Home), but it was his ballads that caused his popularity to soar. Written in dialect and with melodies sometimes borrowed from others though usually composed by the author himself, they were performed by Prøysen on Norwegian radio and heard and loved by listeners all over the country. Prøysen gradually published several collections of these ballads, many of them full of satire and social criticism, though the poet is first and foremost a humorist. Titles include *Drengstuviser* (1948; Ballads from the Room of the Hired Men), *Skøyerviser* (1952; Joking Ballads), *Tolv viser på villstrå* (1964; Twelve Ballads Gone Astray), and *Så seile vi på Mjøsa* (1969; Then We'll be Sailing on Mjøsa).

Prøysen was equally well known and loved for his children's songs, published in such collections as *Musevisa* (1949; The Ballad of the Mice), *Lillebrors vise* (1949; Little Brother's Ballad), and *Teddybjørnen og andre viser* (1950; The Teddy Bear and Other Ballads). One of Prøysen's numerous successes was *Trost i taklampa* (1950; A Robin in the Ceiling Lamp), a satirical and humorous novel whose background is the migration from the countryside to the cities after World War II.

Harald Sverdrup

During World War II Harald Sverdrup (1923–) served as an airman in England and, after the invasion of France in 1943, on the Continent. His war experiences recur in his poetry as sources of imagery whenever he needs to describe something ugly and life-denying. Sverdrup's poetic celebration of the life force is passionate and unqualified, and his earliest collections of poetry, *Drøm og drift* (1948; Dream and Desire) and *Evig byggende Babel* (1949; Eternally Building Babel), contain poems full of powerfully conceived but unpolished erotic imagery. Later collections, however, such as *Han finner sin elskede* (1953; He Finds His Beloved), *Syngende natt* (1955; Singing Night), and *Sankt Elms ild* (1958; St. Elmo's Fire), show that Sverdrup has matured artistically. This progress is further demonstrated by *Isbjørnfantasi*

(1961; Polar Bear Fantasy) and *Sang til solen* (1964; Song to the Sun), in which his vitalism is expressed in highly refined imagery. *Farlig vind* (1969; Dangerous Wind), *Fredløse ord* (1971; Outlawed Words), and *Grønn kalender* (1974; Green Calendar) contain satirical poems, showing a degree of social engagement, especially in *Grønn kalender,* in which the poet speaks out strongly on behalf of environmental concerns. Other volumes of poetry are *Gamle Louis og andre dikt* (1976; Old Louis [Armstrong] and Other Poems), *Fugleskremsel* (1980; Scarecrow), and *Gokstadskipet* (1980; The Gokstad Ship). *Vårt trygge liv* (1982; Our Safe Life) consists of poems about the war experiences of Sverdrup and others, while *Lysets øyeblikk* (1985; Moments of Light) contains many of Sverdrup's finest erotic poems. His most recent collection is *Tranene danser* (1989; The Cranes Are Dancing).

Sverdrup has also written radio plays, travelogues, and a novel, *Paradisets barn* (1968; Children of Paradise), as well as a volume of childhood memoirs entitled *Slips i tretoppen* (1989; Necktie in the Treetop).

Olav H. Hauge

Like Tor Jonsson and Hans Børli, Olav H. Hauge (1908–) is firmly rooted in his native soil. In his case that soil has nourished him by means of an apple orchard that he has tended over the years on his father's smallholding in Hardanger and that has both furnished imagery for his poetry and afforded him sufficient leisure to write. Hauge was close to forty at the time of his debut, and in his first book of verse, *Glør i oska* (1946; Embers in the Ashes), he was considerably indebted to earlier poets such as Olav Aukrust and Olav Nygard, who, like Hauge, wrote in nynorsk and had strong ties to the land. His second volume of poetry, *Under bergfallet* (1951; Beneath the Crag), however, proved that Hauge was already in the process of finding his own voice as a poet: he abandoned the abstractions and the romanticism of his predecessors and turned to everyday physical nature for his inspiration. *Seint rodnar skog i djuvet* (1956; Slowly the Woods Redden in the Gorge) and *På Ørnetuva* (1961; On Eagle Mound) show years of laborious striving for a clarity of vision and a style even more simplified with increasingly powerful images, while *Dropar i austavind* (1966; Drops in the East Wind) and *Spør vinden* (1971; Ask the Wind) represent a further turning toward concrete, everyday subjects.

Hauge stands as one of the foremost modernists in postwar Norwegian poetry and indeed as one of the great poets of Norway. He is well informed about both the literature of his native land and world letters, having been active as a translator (self-taught) from several foreign languages. Like earlier poets in the nynorsk tradition—Ivar Aasen, Aasmund Vinje, and Arne Garborg—and like his contemporary Tarjei Vesaas, Hauge has remained within a fixed native sphere and at the same time has transcended it through his wide-ranging intellect: he is one of Norway's most outward-directed writers. Hauge has continued writing poetry into advanced age, and even the most recent edition of his works, *Dikt i samling* (1985; Collected Poems), contains fourteen new poems. Selections of Hauge's poetry have appeared in English under the titles *Don't Give Me the Whole Truth* (1985) and *Trusting Your Life to Water and Eternity* (1987).

Ernst Orvil

Among the poets of the 1960s and 1970s, Ernst Orvil (1898–1985) belonged to the older generation; indeed, he could have been the grandfather of some of his colleagues. He is probably still best known as a dramatist, since during the 1950s several of his plays were performed with considerable success at the National Theater and other theaters in Norway. Orvil was a hedonist and a utilitarian who encouraged what he called "ethical pleasure" in his readers or viewers, that is, a sense of qualitative discrimination between pleasurable experiences, of which erotic love is deemed paramount. With his elegant plays Orvil continued a line in Norwegian drama from Heiberg to Krog, by showing individuals who deny the natural pleasure-seeking instinct within them, especially women who are weighed down by their fears or inhibitions.

Orvil had already published half a dozen novels when his first collection of poetry appeared in 1940, and he continued to cultivate the prose genres throughout his life. In his half-century of active writing he produced nearly fifty books, differing in genre but not in style. Typical of Orvil's prose is its artistry, a playful choice of words, syntax, dialogue, and story line which did not fit the realistic framework of most Norwegian postwar writing, though his admirers found his style amusing and liberating. It is suited to verse writing rather than to conventional prose, and Orvil is therefore preeminently a poet—indeed, a poet who continued to develop his talent throughout a long career. Resignation and a new concern with the little things of life color his verse of the late 1950s (e.g., the collection *Lisbet* from 1957), while in the 1970s—for example, in the collections *Brekasjer* (1970; Breakages) and *Nok sagt* (1972; Enough Said)—he discusses such psychological and social problems as personal identity and conservation of the environment. This poetry is characterized by a new tone of humor and good-natured banter, somewhat in the style of Orvil's much younger colleague Jan Erik Vold, a major champion of Orvil's poetry. Vold edited the posthumous collection

Siste dikt (1988; Last Poems) and the first volume of Orvil's collected poems, *Samlede dikt. 1940–1955* (1990).

Stein Mehren

A fundamental conflict in the early poetry of Stein Mehren (1935–) is the opposition of experience and expression, as seen in his first book, *Gjennom stillheten en natt* (1960; Through Stillness One Night), in which striking metaphors and intimate experience of nature are contrasted with alienation and a sense of the unreal. *Hildring i speil* (1961; Mirage in a Mirror) is a further exploration of this relationship between language and the world. In *Alene med en himmel* (1962; Alone with a Heaven) and *Mot en verden av lys* (1963; Toward a World of Light), the poet accepts the fact that we can apprehend the world only through language, at the same time as he strives, successfully at times, to apprehend the world in its immediacy. Moments of such transcendence Mehren finds in the meeting of man and woman, humans and nature, and in adult consciousness and intimately relived childhood.

In *Gobelin Europa* (1965), *Tids alder* (1966; Time's Age), and *Vind runer* (1967; Wind Runes), the treatment of these same themes is clearer and more concentrated than before, but there are also poems in which Mehren satirizes modern technological society. At the same time, he turned to new means of expression, publishing volumes containing aphorisms and essays as well as poetry. In *Aurora, det niende mørke* (1969; Aurora, the Ninth Darkness) and *Kongespillet* (1971; The King Play), books in which the journey is used as a symbol of humans' attempt to achieve insight, Mehren, the philosopher, shows how our civilization needs to liberate itself from technological systems and find its way back to a mode of existence that can restore immediacy to human life. *Maskinen og menneskekroppen* (1970; The Machine and the Human Body) is a collection of essays dealing with the same problem and containing attacks on technified sexuality, and *De utydelige* (1972; The Indistinct Ones) and *Titanene* (1974; The Titans) are semi-essayistic novels in which Mehren criticizes the ideological commitment of many of his contemporaries, mostly of the radical left. *Den store frigjøringen* (1973; The Great Liberation), *Kunstens vilkår og den nye puritanismen* (1974; The Condition of Art and the New Puritanism), and *En rytter til fots* (1975; An Equestrian on Foot) contain polemical, satirical, and parodical essays on literature and culture. Other collections of essays include *Her har du mitt liv* (1984; Here You Have My Life) and *Vår tids bilde som entropi og visjon* (1987; A Picture of Our Times as Entropy and Vision). *Dikt for enhver som våger* (1973; Poems for Each Who Dares), *Menneske bær ditt bilde frem* (1975;

Man, Carry Your Image Forth), *Trettende stjernebilde* (1977; Thirteenth Constellation), *Vintersolhverv* (1979; Winter Solstice), and *Den usynlige regnbuen* (1981; The Invisible Rainbow) are further expressions of Mehren's view that language constitutes reality.

With the passage of time his poetry has become increasingly philosophical. In *Timenes time* (1983; The Hour of Hours), Mehren tries to show how poetic power can arise when the past and the present are brought together in a higher unity, and in *Corona—formørkelsen og dens lys* (1986; Corona—The Eclipse and Its Light), how two poles in a pair of opposites retain traces of each other so that there is no presence without traces of absence and no absence without traces of presence. *Fortapt i verden. Syngende* (1988; Lost in the World: Singing) deals with longing and love, while *Det andre lyset* (1989; The Other Light) takes up the light-and-darkness motif of *Corona*. *Skjul og forandring* (1990; Concealment and Change) is the title of Mehren's most recent collection.

Arnljot Eggen

Like many poets of his generation, Arnljot Eggen (1923–) has his roots in a rural environment and writes in nynorsk. His first volumes, *Eld og is* (1951; Fire and Ice) and *Jegeren* (1955; The Hunter), are those of a poet highly dependent on his predecessors in the nynorsk poetic tradition. In *Sendebod* (1959; The Messenger), however, he leaves that tradition and places himself squarely within modernism. But his next collections, *Eit hovud i havet* (1965; A Head in the Ocean) and *Roller og røynd* (1967; Roles and Reality), represent a departure from the individualism associated with modernism. Eggen had become critical of contemporary consumer society and spoke out in favor of collectivist values: *Sprekken i muren* (1969; The Crack in the Wall), *Baksideviser* (1970; Seamy Side Ballads), *Knaben-balladen og andre tekster* (1974; The Knaben Ballads and Other Texts), and *Skulder ved skulder* (1977; Shoulder to Shoulder) are all marked by the poet's engagement in the issues of the day. *Det flyktige varige* (1988; The Changing Enduring) is a collection of poems and aphorisms.

Eggen has also worked as a translator. He has written children's books and radio plays and has participated in group theater projects, such as the writing and staging of the radical play *Pendlerne* (1973; The Commuters).

Arnold Eidslott

Arnold Eidslott (1926–) shares with his contemporaries both a modernist form and a contempt for the new consumer society. *Vinden taler til den døve* (1953; The Wind Speaks to the Deaf) expresses a mythical, anthroposophical, and Christian view of life, as well as a dislike of materialism. In *Manes* (1965) and *Memento* (1967), the poems are more tightly composed than in the first collection, with imagery both compressed and powerful. The two volumes *Ved midnatt da havet sank* (1971; At Midnight When the Ocean Receded) and *Rekviem for Lasarus* (1973) promulgate a brand of Christianity close to that of Søren Kierkegaard. Since then Eidslott has published a large number of collections, most recently *Adam imago Dei* (1984), *Advarsel i kode* (1987; Warning in Code), and *De navnløses kor* (1989; Choir of the Nameless). Like everything Eidslott has written, they deal with our relationship to God.

Georg Johannesen
Several of the aforementioned poets gradually assumed a stance of social and political engagement. Georg Johannesen (1931–), in contrast, began his career by writing a political novel, *Høst i mars* (1957; Autumn in March). The books tells the story of two seventeen-year-olds whose pure love, resulting in the conception of a child, is destroyed by the society of their elders. That society is seen to be sick and its illness is transferred to the two young parents when an abortion is performed to make them socially reintegrated; as a result, the girl becomes neurotic and the boy a terrorist. *Høst i mars* is a powerful indictment of contemporary social reality and of the language of the older generation. The acerbic tone of *Dikt 1959* (1959; Poems 1959) points to a poet of the disillusioned postwar generation, while Johannesen's next collection, *Ars moriendi eller de syv dødsmåter* (1965; Ars moriendi, or the Seven Ways of Death) offers a modern interpretation of the seven deadly sins. Each of the forty-nine poems, one for each day of seven weeks, consists of three three-line stanzas in a sparse style with compressed, often surreal imagery; the collection is a powerful protest against the barrenness of modern life. Similarly, *Nye dikt* (1966; New Poems) attempts to tear the reader away from conventional ways of thinking. *Om den norske tenkemåten* (1975; About the Norwegian Way of Thinking) is a collection of articles and contributions to the public debate, while *Om den norske skrivemåten* (1981; About the Norwegian Way of Writing) contains essays mostly on literature.

Three recent books by Johannesen are difficult to classify. *Tredje kongebok* (1978; The Third Book of Kings) and *Johannes' bok* (1978; The Book of John) are prose pastiches modeled on biblical literature, while *Simons bok* (1980; The Book of Simon) imitates classical military narrative. Johannesen's purpose, however, is to comment—critically, as always—on conditions in contemporary society. His most recent book, *Romanen om Mong-*

stad (1989; The Novel about Mongstad), is a political satire by "Guri Johns, with an afterword by Georg Johannesen."

THE *PROFIL* REBELS AND THEIR CONTEMPORARIES

There are several reasons why the intellectual and cultural climate in Norway was ready for a change around the middle of the 1960s. The ambitious development efforts of the postwar Labor government had been successful and allowed virtually all Norwegians a measure of material well-being. With their physical needs satisfied and a strong sense that poverty and want were things of the past, people began contemplating the cost of their present standard of living. Even in the 1950s and early 1960s some of the poets had been critical of the new consumer society, and there was an increasing understanding of the true price to be paid for progress, such as centralization, urbanization, pollution of the environment, and depletion of natural resources.

The concern for conditions at home went hand in hand with attention to developments abroad, as more and more people began to see how the industrialized nations were taking gross advantage of human beings in the third world. The issues were brought into focus by the war in Vietnam, which was regarded as just another manifestation of how greedy capitalism uses any means at its disposal to protect its privileges and its ability to exploit. Having had their fill of the fruits of capitalism, many intellectuals turned to the extreme left for guidance, finding it in the writings of the young Karl Marx or the ideas of Mao Zedong. With the fervor of true believers, they went to work attempting to create a socialist millennium through revolution and the dictatorship of the proletariat. The ultimate goal was still somewhat at a distance, but these latter-day leftists received an infusion of enthusiasm when Norway, by its referendum of September 25, 1972, narrowly rejected membership in the European Economic Community (EEC). This decision, and the struggle that preceded it, left its marks on the authorship of such writers as Espen Haavardsholm and Dag Solstad.

Another factor that helped bring about a change in the intellectual climate had to do with the material conditions under which Norwegian writers worked. Every year since 1964 the Storting (parliament) has empowered the Norwegian Cultural Council to buy and distribute to libraries one thousand copies of each belletristic volume published in Norway by a Norwegian writer. This policy has made it far more attractive than before for younger talents to embark seriously on a writing career, at the same time making experimental work more feasible. A negative side effect of the new policy was the publication of much substandard writing, since the financial risk to the publishing houses was reduced.

The *Profil* rebellion of 1966 has become a standard reference point in Norwegian literary history. Originally a minor journal for students of language and literature at the University of Oslo, *Profil* (1959–), by its February 1966 issue, had become the rallying point for one of the most closely knit groups in Norwegian letters of the twentieth century. The success of the rebellion depended on several circumstances, not least the fact that literary institutions in Norway were greatly in need of renewal. The *Profil* group counted among its members several gifted new writers, particularly in the area of prose, and since newspapers were happy to receive the stimulation provided by younger reviewers, the rebels were welcomed with open arms in the daily press.

Those associated with *Profil* wanted to guide Norwegian letters in the direction of modernism and a specifically Norwegian literary tradition. Tor Obrestad referred to the medieval visionary poem "Draumkvede" in his explanation of what he considered to be proper modernistic literature. Dag Solstad departed from the middle-class realistic and psychological novel, as it had been practiced in Norway, and wanted to create a more broadly based literature through the use of folktale, myth, and dreams, a genre clearly inspired by Jung. Solstad never turned his ideas into reality, however, possibly because the genre had been preempted by the old-fashioned writer Alfred Hauge, who gave his *Mysterium* (1967) a structure closely based on dreams and the following year brought folktale and myth into *Legenden om Svein og Maria*.

In the early 1970s many of the young *Profil* writers turned toward the Maoist form of Marxism-Leninism and adopted a new literary program in which everyday reality, presented in documentary fashion, would take the place of myth and in which a concern with politics became more important than folktales. Purely literary questions were no longer of much interest, and the journal, now associated with a Marxist-Leninist youth organization, placed a premium on serving the people by preparing the country for the coming revolution. Nevertheless, as a crucible of new ideas, *Profil* affected Norwegian letters in two ways: the concept of "literature" was greatly expanded, even to include such pedestrian documents as a plan for Norwegian road building, and the traditional distinctions between genres were in large measure abandoned.

Dag Solstad

Dag Solstad (1941–) is generally considered the most talented of the *Profil* writers. His debut took place a year before the rebellion, when he published *Spiraler* (1965; Spirals), a Kafka-inspired volume of short stories dealing with loneliness and isolation. It was followed by another collection of short prose, *Svingstol* (1967; A Turning Chair), written in a terse style reminiscent of Tarjei Vesaas. Solstad's first novel, *Irr! Grønt!* (1969; Patina! Green!), has as its protagonist a student from the country who is searching for liberation by consciously playing a variety of roles, an idea Solstad got from the Polish writer Witold Gombrowicz, whom he had recently introduced to Norwegian readers (in a 1969 article in *Vinduet* [The Window]). Solstad, however, claimed that such liberation cannot be achieved, since everybody is subject to the roles imposed on them by late capitalism. His second novel, *Arild Asnes, 1970* (1971), describes an attempt at a more radical break with conventional society. Asnes, a writer, is a socialist intellectual who, paradoxically, is given freedom to write so that he may confirm the bases for existence under capitalism but who instead converts to Marxist—Leninism. An important aspect of the novel is the story of how Asnes overcomes his distaste for the simple and direct language of the Marxists and, in the end, learns to make it his own manner of expression.

Arild Asnes created a big stir, and even more so Solstad's next novel, *25. septemberplassen* (1974; The 25th of September Square), a chronicle of the postwar era in Norway. In it Solstad wants to show how the working class was betrayed by its Labor party leaders, who abandoned true socialism and collaborated with American capitalist interests. The play *Kamerat Stalin eller familien Nordby* (1975; Comrade Stalin, or the Nordby Family) is little more than an interlude, followed by a novel trilogy consisting of *Svik. Førkrigsår* (1977; Betrayal: Prewar Years), *Krig. 1940* (1978; War: 1940), and *Brød og våpen* (1980; Bread and Weapons). Here Solstad gives his Marxist-inspired version of events before and during World War II, attempting, among other things, to show that the Norwegian Nazis, the German occupants, and the Norwegian bourgeoisie had common interests. The trilogy is at the same time a realistically told story about members of the working class in trying times.

By the end of the 1970s the fact could no longer be ignored that the existing Norwegian working class had no desire for a Marxist-Leninist revolution and that no such desire could be generated despite the best efforts of the committed revolutionary writers. In addition, the hope earlier found in Mao's China had all but disappeared, and some committed writers found a need to pause and review their earlier activities and the ideology behind them. Solstad's attempt at such an examination of his past came under the unwieldy title of *Gymnaslærer Pedersens beretning om den store politiske vek-*

sen som har hjemsøkt vårt land (1982; High School Teacher Pedersen's Account of the Great Political Revival Which Has Visited Our Country). Primarily a first-person novel about the position of the radical intellectual in modern society and the relationship between literature and politics, it is also an intertextual tour de force in which the author projects a both ironic and nostalgic attitude toward the immediate past. In Solstad's next novel, *Forsøk på å beskrive det ugjennomtrengelige* (1984; An Attempt to Describe the Impenetrable), in contrast, attention is focused on the immediately contemporary society, where, Solstad seems to say, it is extremely difficult for decent human beings to exist.

Solstad's *Roman 1987* (1987; Novel 1987) earned him the 1988 Nordic Literary Prize. It is another reckoning with the Marxist-Leninist movement, and also, like *Gymnaslærer Pedersens beretning*, is told in the first person, this time by a historian who abandons a promising career in teaching and research to become one with the working class. Though his attempt fails, he insists that the experience was worth the effort. Similarly, Solstad seems not to regret his own past. His most recent book, *Medaljens forside* (1990; The Seamless Side), is a "novel" about one of Norway's major industrial enterprises, commissioned by the Aker Group for its sesquicentennial.

Tor Obrestad

While Solstad has so far confined himself to prose, Tor Obrestad (1938–) has also written poetry. The oldest member of the *Profil* group and often regarded as one of its central figures, Obrestad, who writes in nynorsk, first appeared on the literary scene with a collection of poetry, *Kollisjon* (1966; Collision), and a volume of short stories, *Vind* (1966; Wind). Both books are rather traditional; Obrestsad had learned from Arne Garborg, Tarjei Vesaas, and Franz Kafka, and deals with individual rather than social problems. That changed in his next works, the poetry collections *Vårt daglige brød* (1968; Our Daily Bread) and *Den norske løve* (1970; The Norwegian Lion) and the novel *Marionettar* (1969; Marionettes), in which the author comes across as a full-blown revolutionary. Obrestad's best-known book, however, is *Sauda! Streik!* (1972; Sauda! Strike!), a documentary novel about an illegal strike at a large industrial plant in western Norway. The novel celebrates the victory of the workers and is a major literary document from the 1970s. Two more collections of poetry from the first half of the decade also glorify the proletariat and the revolution: *Sauda og Shanghai* (1973; Sauda and Shanghai) and *Stå saman* (1974; Stand Together). *Tolken* (1975; The Interpreter) is a collection of short stories, while *Stå på!* (1976;

Hang In!) is another novel based on a labor conflict. *Vinterdikt* (1979; Winter Poems) is a volume of poetry in the style of Obrestad's early verse.

Obrestad's voice became less strident in the early 1980s. The novel *Ein gong må du seie adjø* (1981; Someday You Must Say Good-Bye), though still a piece of political literature, does not exhibit the propaganda and the faith in easy solutions which characterize most of his work, and *Sjå Jæren, gamle Jæren* (1982; Look at Jæren, Old Jæren), a collection of short stories and other prose texts about this West Norwegian district, is free of the author's didacticism and contains some of his finest pieces. *Misteltein* (1988; Mistletoe) is a volume of poetry in which Obrestad reaches back to Old Norse myths for inspiration, thus returning to the original program of the *Profil* group.

Espen Haavardsholm

Espen Haavardsholm (1945–), like Solstad and Obrestad, began his writing career with a focus on the problems of the individual. Alienation and absurdity are central motifs in the short-story collection *Tidevann* (1966; Tidewater), and the author—faithful to the early aesthetic ideas of the *Profil* group—relies on the language of myth and dream. In the novel *Munnene* (1968; The Mouths), however, Haavardsholm departs from his earlier preoccupation with the single individual to portray four young people in an interpersonal situation. *Den avskyelige snømannen* (1970; The Abominable Snowman) contains short stories written in a rather minimalist style in which the author eschews complicated imagery and seeks to allow everyday reality to speak for itself. In another collection of short prose, the semidocumentary *Zink* (1971; Zinc), with its focus on the power structures in Norwegian society, Haavardsholm advocates the Marxist-Leninist revolution by addressing the reader directly. *Grip dagen* (1973; Seize the Day) is a political diary recording the events surrounding the EEC referendum in 1972. It has a strong ideological basis, as does *Historiens kraftlinjer* (1975; The Lines of Force in History), in which Haavardsholm tells the story of a young worker's visit to Albania, praising that country's version of Communism without asking whether or not Albania's poverty and backwardness may be ideologically determined.

The 1980s brought a change to Haavardsholm's authorship. The novel *Drift* (1980; Drive) is not as politically dogmatic as his earlier books and actually warns against making ideology a substitute for religion. Since Haavardsholm has created a protagonist who is a traditional Norwegian Communist rather than a Marxist-Leninist Maoist, however, the book should perhaps not be read directly as a commentary on the author's own experiences during the 1970s.

Svarte fugler over kornåkeren (1981; Black Birds over the Grain Field) is a rather uninteresting collection of short stories, but Haavardsholm's next book, a novel titled *Store fri* (1983; Big Break), attracted a great deal of attention. In this political love story, which thematizes the conflict between surface radicalism and latent puritanism in the liberated cultural elite, the author examines in particular the educational ideas of this group, whose children were raised in a spirit of freedom. The novel *Roger, gult* (1986; Roger, Yellow), which uses Aksel Sandemose's psychoanalytical novels as intertext, tells about a group of boys growing up in Oslo in the 1960s.

Haavardsholm has also contributed to the genres of literary biography and criticism. *Kartskisser* (1969; Sketched Maps) is a collection of literary essays which antedates the onset of Marxism-Leninism, while *Poesi, maktspråk* (1976; Poetry, Language of Power) is a collection of criticism, interviews, and polemical prose with a strong ideological slant. Haavardsholm's most recent publication (1989) is a well-written biography of the novelist Aksel Sandemose.

Edvard Hoem

Edvard Hoem (1949–), also a Marxist-Leninist, made his debut with a collection of poetry, *Som grøne musikantar* (1969; Like Green Musicians), which was followed first by a lyrical novel, *Landet av honning og aske* (1970; The Land of Honey and Ashes), and then by a book that gave Hoem his breakthrough as a writer and set the tone for much of his authorship: the novel *Anna Lena* (1971). A retrospective portrayal of life in a peripheral community on Norway's west coast, *Anna Lena* shows how the forces of capital dictate where people may or may not live and work. Centralization of population and the means of production was part of the price paid for the Labor government's economic miracle in the 1950s, and Hoem, like his colleague Solstad, wished to point out that the true idea of socialism had been compromised. Along similar lines, *Kjærleikens ferjereiser* (1974; Eng. tr. *The Ferry Crossing*, 1989) aims to show how people are victims of social forces they do not understand. In terms of composition and narrative technique, the novel is highly original, but there is a certain triteness to its political message: like Solstad's *Arild Asnes*, it ends as one of the characters walks around selling the Marxist-Leninist newspaper *Klassekampen* (The Class Struggle).

In 1978 Hoem announced plans for a trilogy with the common title *Gi meg de brennende hjerter* (Give Me the Burning Hearts), a line taken from Rudolf Nilsen's classical poem "Revolusjonens røst" (1926; The Voice of the Revolution). Two parts have been completed—*Melding frå Petrograd* (1978; Message from Petrograd) and *Fjerne Berlin* (1980; Distant Berlin)— but volume 3 has not appeared, perhaps because the project suffers from insurmountable internal contradictions. Hoem has, however, produced a volume of poetry, *Du er blitt glad i dette landet* (1982; You Have Become Fond of This Country), and three more novels. *Prøvetid* (1984; Rehearsal) is about a middle-aged divorced actor and his various love affairs while he is rehearsing Strindberg's *Miss Julie*. *Heimlandet barndom* (1985; The Homeland Childhood) tells with great sensitivity of the childhood and youth of a boy growing up in a rural and fundamentalist environment, while in *Ave Eva* (1987), the old myth of Paradise Lost (including Eve's blame) is given a contemporary West Norwegian setting. Hoem's most recent publication (1989) is a biography of Nordahl Grieg. Hoem writes in nynorsk.

Jon Michelet

Jon Michelet (1944–) is primarily a journalist who has had a great deal of success as a writer of thrillers. Clearly anticapitalist and anti-imperialist, most of his books are centered on his antihero, the middle-aged detective Vilhelm Thygesen. They include *Den drukner ei som henges skal* (1975; He That Is Born to be Hanged Shall Never Be Drowned), *Mellom barken og veden* (1975; Between a Rock and a Hard Place), *Jernkorset* (1976; The Iron Cross), *Hvit som snø* (1980; White as Snow), *Den gule djevelens by* (1981; The City of the Yellow Devil), and *Panamaskipet* (1984; The Panama Ship). Most notable among them is *Jernkorset,* which explores residual nazism in Norway. Michelet has also written two thrillers critical of the Norwegian government for giving in to Soviet demands regarding Spitzbergen: *Orions belte* (1977; Eng. tr. *Orion's Belt,* 1986), which was later filmed, and *Angrepet på Longyearbyen* (1978; The Attack on Longyearbyen). *Terra Roxa* (1982) is considered Michelet's most significant venture into the writing of more serious literature, while *Jerv (jervere jervest?)* [1983; Wolverine (More Wolverine, Most Wolverine?)] has been rather unsuccessful. *Le Coconut* (1989), a valiant attempt to transcend the genre of the thriller, is hardly better. Michelet's strength is his ability to tell a fast-paced story in which character portrayal is secondary to action. His hard-boiled style is oral and easy to follow, though some readers find that his realism depends too much on excessive use of vulgar language.

Tor Edvin Dahl

Tor Edvin Dahl (1943–) shares Michelet's gift as a storyteller, which has made him a good writer of mysteries and, more significantly, has enabled him to write about young people's problems in a captivating manner, as can be seen even in his first book, the short-story collection *En sommer full av regn* (1968; A Summer Full of Rain). *Ikke om håp, men heller ikke om håpløshet* (1969; Not about Hope, but Neither about Despair) and *Syv noveller om nødvendige mord* (1971; Seven Short Stories about Necessary Murders) contain short stories in which Dahl shows how dreams and myths about love often lead people astray. The idea of Christianity as a cure for existential despair is already present at this point in Dahl's authorship, as it is in the novels *Den andre* (1972; The Other One), *Hege og Lind* (1974; Hege and Lind), and *Romanen om Eva* (1975; The Novel about Eva). Dahl received much acclaim for *Guds tjener* (1973; The Servant of God), a religious *Bildungsroman* set in a pentecostal environment, which the author clearly knows from the inside. Particularly impressive in Dahl's analysis of the protagonist's development is the sophisticated use of time and point-of-view techniques. *Abrahams barn* (1982; The Children of Abraham), a serious mystery novel set in a similar environment, has the same formal qualities and gives an effective presentation of Dahl's ideas about the role of love, faith, and their opposites in human relationships. The novel *Josef kommer hjem* (1986; Joseph Comes Home) deals with similar themes but without the mystery-story aspect.

Øystein Lønn
Satire and black humor are trademarks of Øystein Lønn (1936–), who made his debut with a volume of short stories, *Prosesjonen* (1966; The Procession). The novel *Kontinentene* (1967; The Continents) takes place in the future, after a nuclear war. *Arkeologene* (1971; The Archaeologists) is a novel dealing with doomed attempts to reconstruct the past, while the short-story collection *Historie* (1973; History) treats the history of Europe in the twentieth century. The novel *Hirtshals Hirtshals* (1975), an open work in Umberto Eco's sense of the term, offers a many-faceted portrait of the present age and places heavy demands on the reader. *Lu. Fortelling* (1977; Lu: A Story) tends toward the mystery story; *Veien til Cordoba* (1981; The Road to Cordoba), a novel, tells about a journey made by the protagonist to recover the past and understand the present; while *Bjanders reise* (1984; Bjander's Journey), also a novel, is again a mystery story. Though it deals with the smuggling and distribution of heroin, it is at the same time a political novel, showing how the use of drugs is only one of many symptoms of a fundamentally sick society. *Tom Rebers siste retrett* (1988; Tom Reber's Last Retreat) is Lønn's most recent novel, in which the theme is again modern, inauthentic living.

Kjell Hallbing

Some of the writers discussed in this chapter have also written in less serious genres. Examples are Tor Edvin Dahl and Kjartan Fløgstad, who have both published detective fiction. It is worthy of note that the most prolific writer in all Norwegian literature is Kjell Hallbing (1934–), whose books about U.S. Marshal Morgan Kane—written under the pseudonym Louis Masterson—are widely read in Norway, where for quite some time there has been a large and durable market for translated westerns. Hallbing has been able to exploit this market and develop a devoted following. His Morgan Kane novels, which take place mostly in the western U.S. during the closing years of the nineteenth century, are relatively short and can consequently be read in one sitting. The conflicts are clearly drawn, the characterization is superficial, the story is heavily loaded with sex and gratuitous violence, and the actions of the protagonist are such as to confirm masculine myths deeply embedded in Norwegian culture. Although Hallbing is said to be well informed about U.S. history, he has not attempted to transcend the popular conception of life in the American West.

Bjørg Vik

Bjørg Vik (1935–) is one of several woman writers who made their debut before the *Profil* rebellion but who have published most of their significant works in the 1970s and 1980s. Helped along in the beginning by Nils Johan Rud, the editor of *Magasinet,* Vik started out writing rather traditional short stories, which show the influence of Cora Sandel and are, for the most part, variations on the theme of women in love. Such stories make up her early collections—*Søndag ettermiddag* (1963; Sunday Afternoon), *Nødrop fra en myk sofa* (1966; Cries of Distress from a Soft Sofa), and *Det grådige hjerte* (1968; The Greedy Heart)—about erotic encounters and the attending conflicts, or about moments of marital infidelity that, perhaps paradoxically, revitalize stale relationships. The novel *Gråt elskede mann* (1970; Cry, Beloved Man) deals with similar themes at the same time as it attempts to achieve a deeper understanding of gender roles. In the short-story volumes *Kvinneakvariet* (1972; Eng. tr. *An Aquarium of Women,* 1987) and *Fortellinger om frihet* (1975; Stories of Freedom), Vik has clearly benefited from her active feminist involvement: she portrays contemporary women in various social positions, all of them women who need to deal with conflicts stemming from the structures of a patriarchal society.

   En håndfull lengsel (1979; A Handful of Longing; Eng. tr. *Out of Season and Other Stories,* 1983), one of Vik's finest volumes of stories, gives evidence of continued artistic growth. The protagonists are women in their middle years who, like many earlier Vik characters, have to make decisions regarding their love lives. *Snart er det høst* (1982; Soon It Will Be Fall) and *En gjenglemt petunia* (1985; A Forgotten Petunia) show how Vik has continued to enlarge her thematic sphere; she now writes about women *and* men, young and old, with sympathy and understanding. Vik refers to *Små nøkler, store rom* (1988; Small Keys, Large Rooms) as a novel, though it may be read as a collection of short stories connected by common characters and environment. The protagonist is a young Oslo girl, Elsi, whose childhood and youth during World War II and the following years is portrayed with great sensitivity, a treatment somewhat reminiscent of that of Torborg Nedreaas in her trilogy about Herdis. The story in *Små nøkler* is continued in *Poplene på St. Hanshaugen* (1991; The Poplars of St. Hanshaugen).

Liv Køltzov

A member of the circle around *Profil* in the mid-1960s, Liv Køltzov (1945–) first published a volume of short stories, *Øyet i treet* (1969; The Eye in the Tree), and then two novels, *Hvem bestemmer over Bjørg og Unni?* (1972; Who Decides about Bjørg and Unni?) and *Historien om Eli* (1975; The Story of Eli). Køltzov's main theme is the position of women in contemporary Norway, the social dimension of their lives as well as their attempts at liberation from gender stereotypes at home. The two friends Bjørg and Unni, for example, are galvanized into social action by the need to oppose a highway project, and this political involvement affects their attitude toward the men in their lives. The novel *Løp, mann* (1980; Run, Man) is the story of a slowly disintegrating marriage, while the two short stories contained in *April/November* (1983) portray women who are grappling with a sense of meaninglessness. Køltzov's most recent novel, *Hvem har ditt ansikt?* (1987; Who Has Your Face?), explores the question of how a woman's identity is formed by the roles played in her association with parents, siblings, friends, and mate. The novel differs from Køltzov's earlier feminist books by being a love story, and one in which love is portrayed as a positive force in the relationship between man and woman.

Gerd Brantenberg

While many Norwegian women authors—like Bjørg Vik—are influenced by a moderate feminism, Gerd Brantenberg (1941–) stands as Norway's foremost representative of feminist lesbian literature. Her first novel, *Opp alle jordens homofile* (1973; Rise up, All Homosexuals of the Earth; Eng. tr. *What Comes Naturally*, 1986), is a first-person narrative about coming out of the closet in Norway during the early 1970s. It has a quick and engaging style and offers an evenhanded treatment of the way life is experienced by lesbian women. Brantenberg's next book, *Egalias døtre* (1977; Eng. tr. *Egalia's Daughters: A Satire of the Sexes*, 1985), describes the country of Egalia, where women rule and make social and even linguistic structures support their interests, and where an unsuccessful rebellion is staged by young men who would like to do some of the things that are done only by women. *Ja, vi slutter* (1978; Yes, We Are Quitting) is a diary about the agony of giving up smoking.

The novel *Sangen om St. Croix* (1979; The Ballad of St. Croix) is a more ambitious undertaking and tells the story of a generation of schoolgirls in Fredrikstad, the author's hometown. An expert storyteller, Brantenberg is also a social historian who offers a genuine account of girls growing up in Norway in the early 1950s. The joys and pains of their lives are portrayed with humor and warmth in a second volume, *Ved fergestedet* (1985; At the Ferry), which covers the second half of the decade, when the girls have become teenagers in high school. A third volume set in the same environment is titled *For alle vinder* (1989; Spread by the Winds) and focuses on the character Inger Holm, who also appears in the previous two books. Her coming to terms with her lesbian identity constitutes a major theme. A novel with the title *Favntak* (1983; Embraces), which deals with a similar topic, is less successful. It discusses the situation of lesbian women trying to break out of their marriages; but the story is told in an esoteric manner that makes it difficult for most readers to identify with the characters.

Knut Faldbakken

The conventional realistic-psychological novel—with a strong admixture of sensationalism—has been continued in the authorship of Knut Faldbakken (1941–), who is not, however, without social concerns: in his works the individual always exists against the background of others. Sexuality is Faldbakken's main theme, and in his novels he has explored its many aspects and variations. *Den grå regnbuen* (1967; The Gray Rainbow) is a study of three young people who learn that sex alone does not satisfy, *Sin mors hus* (1969; His Mother's House) treats the mother/son incest motif from a Freudian point of view, and *Maude danser* (1971; Maude Dances; Eng. tr. *The Sleeping Prince*, 1988) portrays the twisted sexuality of a middle-aged woman. Rather less interesting are the three short stories that make up *Eventyr* (1970; Tales). Faldbakken's definitive breakthrough came with *Insektsommer* (1972; Eng. tr. *Insectsummer*, 1991), a sensitive account of a young boy's encounter with the erotic, seen as a force both liberating and dangerous.

With the novel *Uår. Aftenlandet* (1974; Famine: The Occident) and its sequel *Uår. Sweetwater* (1976; Famine: Sweetwater), Faldbakken's work took a turn toward greater social engagement. The author describes a technologically advanced society that has begun to self-destruct, and his protagonists are persons who have decided to move to a large landfill, there to live as scavengers. A complicated mythical pattern underlies the fast-paced and action-filled narrative. In *Adams dagbok* (1978; Eng. tr. *Adam's Diary*, 1988), Faldbakken returns to questions of sexuality and gender roles. The novel explores three versions of the modern male and was followed in 1980 by *E 18* (Highway 18)—a novel about youth, sex, and drugs—and *Bryllupsreisen* (1982; Eng. tr. *The Honeymoon*, 1987), which set off a heated debate in the Norwegian media. Its male protagonist finally attempts to solve the personal and sexual problems of an uneasy relationship with his wife by striking her, and since the cure appears to work, Faldbakken was accused of advancing a simplistic and morally unacceptable Nietzschean solution to marital difficulties (he denied the charge).

Faldbakken has published three other novels. In *Glahn* (1985)—a rewriting of Knut Hamsun's famous novel *Pan* (1894)—and *Bad boy* (1988) he takes as his theme male sexual identity and male identity in general. Both novels present men engaging in some of the sexual acts for which Faldbakken's protagonists are famous, from voyeurism to transvestism. The novel *Til verdens ende* (1991; To the End of the World), written in anticipation of the quincentennial of Christopher Columbus's first voyage to America, argues in favor of the view that Columbus hailed from Western Norway. In addition to being a prolific novelist, Faldbakken is a respected critic and for a time served as the editor of the literary journal *Vinduet*. He has also written for the stage on themes similar to those in his novels. Two of his best-known plays are *Tyren og jomfruen* (1976; The Bull and the Virgin) and *Livet med Marilyn* (1987; Life with Marilyn). The second, like the novel *Bryllupsreisen*, deals with a decomposing marriage and ends with a faint, inverted echo of Ibsen's *Et dukkehjem* as the husband leaves his wife and son to recover his identity.

Einar Økland

Although he made his debut before the *Profil* revolt, Einar Økland (1940–) belongs to the group in terms of both age and affiliation. *Ein gul dag* (1963; A Yellow Day), his first book, is a rather conventional collection of private poetry; the poems contained in *Mandragora* (1966) are more concretely tied to the poet's West Norwegian reality. It was a volume of short stories, however, that established Økland's reputation in contemporary literature.

Svart i det grøne (1967; Black in the Green) contains sensitive stories dealing with childhood and youth—one of Økland's strengths—and antirealistic, even bizarre, tales such as "Black and Decker." It is the story of a would-be handyman who borrows a power drill, falls in love with it, and then uses it to murder its owner and dispose of his body: technology, to Økland, can be a threat both physically and spiritually.

In the short-story collection *Vandreduene* (1968; The Passenger Pigeons), Økland, like some other *Profil* members at the time, attempted to undermine the use of metaphoric language. *Amatør-album* (1969; Amateur Album), an autobiographical work containing both poetry and prose and illustrated with snapshots from the author's childhood and youth, is also valuable as a social and historical document. The title of the novel *Galskap* (1971; Craziness) is both an echo from its intertext, Shakespeare's *Hamlet,* and a reference to the fact that the protagonist loses his ability to vary the amplitude of his emotional responses. Økland's next book, *Gull-alder* (1972; Golden Age), in whose best sections the author looks back to his childhood, is a combination of narrative, poetry, and drama, while *Stille stunder* (1974; Quiet Moments) is a carefully crafted short-story cycle. Like Økland's other works from the early 1970s, the poetry collection *Bronsehesten* (1975; The Bronze Horse) is colored by the author's typical self-irony rather than by the enthusiasm for political and social criticism so common among his colleagues. In *Romantikk. Folkeminne* (1979; Romanticism: Folklore), Økland continues the autobiographical tradition from *Gull-alder,* while *Blå roser. Folkeminne* (1983; Blue Roses: Folklore) is a pessimistic exploration of contemporary society. Økland, who writes in nynorsk, has also published criticism and children's books.

Jan Erik Vold
Much like Økland, Jan Erik Vold (1939–) pays continual attention to his own origins: born and reared in Oslo, he has expressed his love for this city with more force and clarity than any other modern poet. Vold is also an internationalist, however, who has received impulses from American poetry, from William Carlos Williams to Bob Dylan. Narcissism is the theme of *Mellom speil og speil* (1965; Between Mirror and Mirror), while *Blikket* (1966; The Glance) represents an extreme inward turn: the same five words are arranged in a maximum of different ways. HEKT (1966; GRAB) is another variation on the theme of narcissism, but at the same time, the use of everyday situations shows the poet turning outward toward other human beings. HEKT also tends toward use of the absurd, and this trait, along with a strong sense of humor, characterizes Vold's next book, a volume of prose texts

titled *fra rom til rom* SAD & CRAZY (1967; From Room to Room SAD & CRAZY). The success of Vold's search for contact is seen in *Mor Godhjertas glade versjon. Ja* (1968; Mother Goodheart's Happy Version. Yes), in which the individual poems are focused on objects of the everyday world. This Norwegian response to "the new simplicity" wave of other Scandinavian countries contains easily accessible poetry and became an immediate success with critics and the public at large. Vold's distrust of metaphoric language is accentuated in such other books as *kykelipi* (1969; Cock-a-Diddle-Dee) and *spor, snø* (1970; Tracks, Snow), which emphasize visual images, devoid of commentary. In his next volumes, *Bok 8: Liv* (1973; Book 8: Liv), *Buster brenner* (1976; Buster Burns), and *S.* (1978), Vold has continued in the tradition of concretism and simple forms, inspired by haiku poetry and Zen Buddhism. *Sirkel, sirkel* (1979; Circle, Circle) contains similar poems, written after a trip around the world. Eight years later came *Sorgen. Sangen. Veien* (1987; The Sorrow. The Song. The Road), followed by *En som het Abel Ek* (1988; One Named Abel Ek) and *Elg* (1989; Moose). Vold's poetry has remained concrete and simple, focusing on fundamental aspects of our existence: love, sorrow, and the details of everyday life.

Throughout his career Vold has been one of the most visible cultural personalities of Norway, prominent as editor, translator, critic, and cultural journalist. *Entusiastiske essays* (1976; Enthusiastic Essays) and *Det norske syndromet* (1980; The Norwegian Syndrome) are collections of his newspaper articles and other criticism.

Paal-Helge Haugen

Like Vold, Paal-Helge Haugen (1945–) shows a strong affinity for contemporary American poetry, some of which he has translated into Norwegian. He has also absorbed impressions from Japanese and Chinese poetry, and the haiku tradition has clearly influenced his verse. Haugen first received a measure of fame for his novel *Anne* (1968), which introduced documentarism into Norwegian literature and earned a Norwegian literary prize. It is the story of the life and death of a young girl suffering from tuberculosis, told partly through Anne's own lyrical perceptions of the world around her and partly through excerpts from religious, educational, and medical literature. *Anne* is an open work, inviting the reader to participate in the production of meaning.

Haugen's first volumes of poetry were *På botnen av ein mørk sommar* (1967; At the Bottom of a Dark Summer) and *Sangbok* (1969; Songbook). These early works are characterized by the absence of complex metaphoric language and by simple and striking images drawn from everyday life. In his next volumes, *Det synlege menneske* (1975; The Visible Figure) and *Fram i lyset, tydeleg* (1978; Outlined in the Light), these trends are continued, though with an increased concern for contemporary cultural and political problems.

Haugen writes in nynorsk, and the rural background (in his case, Setesdal) is strong in his poetry. The poems in *Steingjerde* (1979; Eng. tr. *Stone Fences,* 1986) cover a child's sensuous discovery of its surroundings, the beginning social awareness of a young boy, and the preadolescent's first experience of internal conflicts. The book gives a picture not only of a developing human being, but of a whole community in transition. With Erling Kittelsen, Haugen has also published a literary experiment titled *I dette hus* (1984; In This House), in which every second poem (poetic prose) is by Haugen and the themes are creation, history, and the relationship between nature and culture. *Det overvintra lyset* (1985; Hibernated Light) is a volume of poetry about love and war, and *Inga anna tid, ingen annan stad* (1986; No Other Time, No Other Place) is a musical drama written in collaboration with the composers Gunnar Germeten, Jr., and Rolf Inge Godøy and treating a woman's struggle for identity and liberation from a domineering man. Haugen has also written a fine book for children, *Herr Tidemann reiser* (1980; Mr. Tidemann Goes Traveling).

Arild Nyquist

The first book published by Arild Nyquist (1937–), *Ringer i et sommervann* (1963; Ripples in a Summer Lake), is considered a fine but traditional novel about childhood. Seven years later came the volume *Dexter og Dodater* (1970; Dexts and Dotes [Texts and Notes])—a mixture of prose, prose poetry, and what could almost be referred to as verse—which is a daring experiment with style, composition, and typography, and which, as it has turned out, is quite characteristic of the author. *Frakken tegner og forteller* (1971; The Overcoat Draws and Narrates) is also a highly unconventional book, telling about a visit to the king by the novelist and his old coat, and *Nå er det jul igjen! og andre dikt* (1972; Now It Is Christmas Again! and Other Poems) is its equivalent in verse (not all readers realized it was intended as a volume of nonsense poetry and it created quite a controversy).

Nyquist has been a very prolific writer whose work is characterized by humor and warmth and by irony and satire. Among his books in the 1970s and 1980s are *Abel XIV* (1973), a fantastic narrative of the life and death of Abel; *Eplehøst* (1974; Apple Harvest), a volume of poetic prose starting out with a spoof on Sigbjørn Obstfelder's poem "Jeg ser"; *Barndom* (1976; Childhood), the story of a boy growing up in the 1950s; and *R; fortellinger for nordmenn* (1977; R: Stories for Norwegians), a volume of five typical Nyquist stories. *Kollvikabrev* (1978; Letters from Kollvika) tells about the author's life in Stamsund in northern Norway. *Skalden Odvar og andre svingslag* (1980; The Poet Oddvar and Other Swinging Hits) is a collection of satirical prose, while *Abborfiske i Norge* (1981; Perch Fishing in Norway) is a fantastic and satirical novel in which the author takes on such forces in Norwegian society as business, industry, the press, the agricultural establishment, the government, the Conservative party, the Labor party, and the feminist movement. *På Geilo, sa Tom* (1982; At Geilo, Said Tom) is a volume of internally connected stories about life, love, and fishing, and about death and uncontrollable fear. *Mr. Balubers trompet* (1984; Mr. Baluber's Trumpet) contains almost one hundred prose and verse texts. *Havet. Et dikt om livet og døden* (1985; The Ocean: A Poem about Life and Death)—Nyquist's greatest poetic achievement—presents history and reality as a dance of death, while *Løp, Johan—vent! (Brannen)* [1986; Run, John—Wait! (The Fire)] is a metanovel focusing on murder and suicide. Nyquist's most recent book is *Giacomettis forunderlige reise* (1988; Giacometti's Marvelous Journey), a bitingly satirical novel consisting of six stories and a frame.

Nyquist has written seven books for children, the most recent of which is *Slemme Lars* (1987; Mean Lars). He is also a rock-'n'-roll lyricist and performer.

Jon Bing and Tor Åge Bringsværd

With the exception of Axel Jensen's *Epp* and two novels by Sigurd Evensmo, the collaborative authorship of Jon Bing (1944–) and Tor Åge Bringsværd (1939–) constitutes the most serious venture into science fiction in postwar Norwegian literature. Bing and Bringsværd made their double debut with a collection of short stories, *Rundt solen i ring* (1967; Around the Sun in a Circle), which is full of humor and satire, as is their play *Å miste et romskip* (1969; Losing a Spaceship). When writing on his own, Bing emphasizes the effects of a technological society on individuals, as in his book *Komplex* (1969; Complex), a mixture of novel and short-story collection, and *Det myke landskapet* (1970; The Soft Landscape). The short stories in *Knuteskrift* (1974; Knot Writing) explore elements of science fiction in contemporary life. The novel *Dobbeltgjengere* (1983; Doppelgangers), with its meditation on the nature of human and artificial intelligence, is a contribution to the contemporary debate about people and computers.

Bringsværd is more satirically inclined than Bing and focuses his attention on society rather than on individuals. His short-story collection *Probok* (1969; Pro-Book), for example, portrays a Norwegian millennial society of the future in which fundamentalist worshipers inhabit the cities while non-believers and other sinners have been expelled to the countryside. The novel *Bazar* (1970; Bazaar) tells about apartments that have moved out of their buildings and garages that are driving around hunting for people. Bringsværd's burlesque humor is displayed in a large number of books from the 1970s, such as *Den som har begge beina på jorda står stille* (1974; He Who Has Both Feet on the Ground Stands Still), *Syvsoverskens dystre frokost* (1976; The Somber Breakfast of the Sleepyhead)—both of which take place in an international milieu—and *Pinocchio-papirene* (1978; The Pinocchio Papers). In the 1980s Bringsværd departed from his earlier use of science fiction. *Gobi—Barndommens måne* (1985; Eng. tr. *Gobi, Childhood's Moon*, 1991), a novel set during the time of the medieval children's crusades, is both a book about the horrors of war and an allegory of the dangers of uncritical reliance on religious faith and ideologies. Its protagonist returns in *Gobi—Djengis Khan* (1987; Gobi—Genghis Khan), in which the theme of war is continued, with the conclusion that each person carries with him his own enemy in his heart and mind. The third volume in the series, *Gobi—Djevelens skinn og ben* (1989; Gobi—The Devil's Skin and Bones), is an exploration of individual identity and the problem of evil.

Bing's authorship also includes significant contributions in the fields of law and information science, while Brengsværd has published many books for young people.

Kjell Heggelund

Kjell Heggelund (1932–) is a literary historian whose three volumes of poetry from the 1960s established him as a poet of note. He belongs to a generation of poets characterized by their attempt to liberate themselves from modernism and symbolism, and Heggelund, to reach this goal, took the route of a cool and distancing irony. In *Reisekretser* (1966; Circles of Travel), he creates distance to his material through a special use of time, while in *I min tid* (1967; In My Time), in which the poet addresses another, and present, human being, distance is created by a mixture of humor and seriousness, as well as by several levels of style, from high poetry to everyday language. *Punkt. 8* (1968; Point. 8) is a verse cycle in which the language of advertising and the weekly press is tested for its poetic qualities.

Kjell Erik Vindtorn

Like his colleague Jan Erik Vold, Kjell Erik Vindtorn (1942–) has had considerable success as a reader of his own poetry, often to musical accompaniment. Since his debut with *Sentrifuge* (1970; Centrifuge), he has published a large number of books, including *Det nedbrente luftslott* (1988; The Burned-Down Castle in the Air) and, most recently, *Til deg som søv bort dine draumar* (1990; To You Who Sleep Away Your Dreams). Vindtorn writes surrealistic poetry and attempts to recall the spirit of a 1960s-style "happening" in his works and performances. His poetic world includes all manner of objects and ideas and represents an effort to recreate the cosmos as it may have been before the advent of language. Vindtorn's strength lies in the originality and force of his poetic images.

Herbjørg Wassmo
Though Herbjørg Wassmo (1942–) first published two collections of poetry, *Vingeslag* (1976; Beating Wings) and *Flotid* (1977; High Tide), her reputation as one of Norway's foremost writers of the 1980s is based largely on her novel trilogy about Tora, one of many books in the postwar years which treats the stigma of women and children who were lovers or offspring of members of the German occupation forces in Norway during World War II. Tora is the daughter of a German soldier and his Norwegian girlfriend. In *Huset med den blinde glassveranda* (1981; Eng. tr. *The House with the Blind Glass Windows*, 1987), she lives in a small island community in northern Norway with her mother and a stepfather who abuses her sexually, and she is able to survive emotionally only because of her extraordinary imagination and the safety afforded her by a childless aunt and uncle, who provide some joy in her otherwise dreary existence. In the second volume, *Det stumme rommet* (1983; The Mute Room), Tora has left home to attend secondary school but finds herself pregnant by her stepfather. At the end of the book, she secretly gives birth to and buries a stillborn child. The third volume, *Hudløs himmel* (1986; Sensitive Sky), which garnered Wassmo the Nordic Literary Prize for 1987, shows the gradual disintegration of Tora's personality after the death of her aunt. Her escapes into the secret life of her imagination take on the characteristics of mental illness, and in the end psychic health and living no longer seem possible. The strength of the trilogy, in addition to its outstanding character portrayal, lies in its poetic language and its realistic descriptions of social life in northern Norway in the 1950s. A direct opposite of Tora is the protagonist of *Dinas bok* (1989; Dina's Book), a novel set in the 1840s and 1850s. It tells the story of a woman of almost superhuman strength who rules among men in the harsh and competitive world that was the northern Norway of a century and a half ago.

Veien å gå (1984; The Road To Go) is a documentary novel from World War II which describes a North Norwegian family and its flight to Sweden during the winter of 1944. Wassmo has also written two radio plays, *Juni-*

vinter (1983; Winter in June) and *Mellomlanding* (1985; Stopover), the latter about an encounter, after sixteen years and marriages on both sides, between a woman and a man who had had a son together.

Erling Gjelsvik

Erling Gjelsvik (1949–) has so far written three novels. The first-person narrator of *Dødt løp* (1978; Dead Run) has read too much Hemingway, is visiting Spain, and goes from one adventure to another. A woman he encounters in France, however, teaches him to limit his display of macho vitality. The theme of the book is the conflict between male and female values as well as the need to distinguish between real and narrated life. In *Den som lever ved sverd* (1981; He Who Lives by the Sword), a young couple, Jørn and Siren, travels the Americas in the late 1960s. Once more the plot is made up of a series of adventures, which end when Jørn is unceremoniously murdered by two young rednecks next to the Dallas-Fort Worth airport. The theme of young vitality is continued in *Stormsvalene* (1986; The Stormy Petrels), which describes, sometimes in monotonous detail, the generation of Norwegian high school seniors that helped radicalize Norwegian political life in 1968. Gjelsvik has yet to demonstrate that he is able to transcend the motifs of substance abuse, violence, and gratuitous sex in his work.

Lars Saabye Christensen

Lars Saabye Christensen (1953–) made his debut with a collection of poetry and short prose, *Historien om Gly* (1976; The Story of Gly), and has since published four more volumes of poetry, though he is better known as a writer of fiction. *Jokeren* (1981; Eng. tr. *The Joker,* 1990) is a mystery story, told in the first person by a former bank robber who, after finding his own obituary in the newspaper, turns detective. *Sneglene* (1987; The Snails), also a mystery story, is valuable for its poetic qualities. Christensen's breakthrough came with the novel *Beatles* (1984), which tells about the growing-up years of four teenage boys from Oslo during the 1960s. It is both a fine portrait of youth and a significant memorial to an important decade. Christensen's most recent novel, *Herman* (1988; Eng. tr. 1990), another portrait of childhood and youth in Oslo during the 1960s, stands out for its elegant use of language and deep insight into the mind of an unusual boy. Christensen has also written plays and filmscripts.

NORWEGIAN DRAMA IN THE SIXTIES, SEVENTIES, AND EIGHTIES

The main problem for Norwegian drama in the twentieth century has been to liberate itself from the influence of the type of drama created by Henrik Ibsen, which has since come to be regarded both as the perfect drama of a certain kind and as dramatic perfection per se. Ibsen's legacy has been felt also in his definition of the role of the dramatist: first and foremost a *dikter* (poet, writer) and only secondarily a theater professional.

Norway has been slow to give up the Ibsen tradition. In the 1920s and 1930s the influence of film and early epic theater could be seen in the work of a dramatist like Nordahl Grieg, but in a small country, with few and financially weak theaters, there is little opportunity for experiment. After the war, which brought theater development to a standstill, there was nobody of Ibsen's stature who consistently attempted to write for the theater, and though several major writers occasionally wrote plays during the 1950s, there was not enough activity for a new theater tradition to get under way. Radio (and later television), however, provided some chances for experimental work, and several well-known novelists wrote radio plays, among them Johan Borgen and Tarjei Vesaas.

A revival of drama began taking place in the mid-1960s, as some of the established theaters added small auxiliary stages where lesser-known plays could be performed without great financial commitment. Another trend furthering experimentation was the establishment of regional theaters around the country in the early 1970s. Also, in addition to the normal state-supported institutions, some player collectives worked independently, so that, all in all, enough institutional developments existed to create a more open critical forum. At the same time, playwrights became more closely involved with the theater companies, a case in point being Edvard Hoem, who started out as an artist-in-residence at the regional theater in Molde.

Jens Bjørneboe

The most durable influence on postwar Norwegian drama came from Bertolt Brecht, whose epic theater strongly affected Jens Bjørneboe. His first play was *Til lykke med dagen* (1965; Many Happy Returns), a provocative satire on the Norwegian prison system (which he had earlier exposed in his novel *Den onde hyrde*). *Fugleelskerne* (1966; The Bird Lovers), Bjørneboe's best play, is set in an Italian village, where a bird refuge is about to be established by a company of German bird lovers, whose leaders are former war criminals. They are recognized by some of the locals, who want revenge for their suffering during the war, but in the end the Germans have their way because they have money. The lesson to be learned is that capital equals power. Bjørneboe's next play, *Semmelweis* (1968), is a more general exploration of the concept of authority. Semmelweis is the Hungarian phy-

sician who first discovered the cause of childbirth fever; in the play he suc-
cumbs to the pressures of his medical colleagues who refuse to believe in the
virtues of washing one's hands. *Amputasjon* (1971; Amputation) is a parody,
showing how authoritarian society trims up its members so that they will fit
into the accepted molds, while *Dongery* (1975; Dungarees) is a satire on the
mentality of modern business.

Sverre Udnæs

Sverre Udnæs (1939–82) was one of the most highly gifted theater professionals in postwar Norway. His oeuvre consists of twenty separate works
written for television, radio, film, and stage. During his lifetime Udnæs
published eight of these pieces in a total of four volumes: *Tre TV-spill* (1976;
Three TV Plays), *I dette hvite lyset og to andre spill* (1977; In This White Light
and Two Other Plays), *Kollisjonen* (1978; The Collision), and *Løvfall* (1979;
Falling Leaves). The remaining twelve pieces have been collected in *Dra-
matikk 1964–1982* (1988; Drama 1964–1982), edited by Jan Erik Vold.
    Known particularly for his artful dialogues, Udnæs wrote brilliantly
probing psychological plays, often placed in the setting of the nuclear family, in which he investigated hatred, destructiveness, and the longing for
love. Enormously productive as a writer and a director, he has earned a
steadily growing reputation.

Edvard Hoem

Also known as a novelist, Edvard Hoem has worked extensively in theater.
His first play was the Brecht-inspired *Kvinnene langs fjorden* (1973; The
Women by the Fjord), about the powerlessness of women workers and
small factories having to struggle for survival. *Musikken gjennom Gleng*
(1977; The Music through Gleng) and *Tusen fjordar, tusen fjell* (1977; A
Thousand Fjords, a Thousand Mountains) are thematically connected with
some of Hoem's novels in that they show the necessity of maintaining vital
communities in the less central parts of the country. *Der storbåra bryt* (1979;
Where the Big Wave Breaks) depicts the lives of common people at the end
of the Napoleonic Wars, including their reception of the new idea of liberty.
God natt, Europa (1983; Eng. tr., *Good Night, Europe,* 1989), Hoem's most
successful drama to date, portrays an old politician and war hero attempting
to come to terms with his past and in the process discovering that he is no
great hero after all. *Lenins madam* (1983; Lenin's Woman), about an
aborted revolution in a small Norwegian town of the 1920s, mirrors the failure of Hoem's own Marxist-Leninist generation. Hoem's most recent play
is *Sankt Olavs skrin* (1989; St. Olav's Casket).

Peder W. Cappelen

Unlike Bjørneboe and Hoem, Peder W. Cappelen (1931–92) largely eschewed politics and ideology in his plays. Although a dramatist from the beginning of his writing career, Cappelen first gained the attention of critics for his epistolary nature descriptions, in which he reflected on the function of ritual, dream, and imagination in national culture and individual development. Two of his works in this genre are *Vidda på ny* (1974; New Look at the Highlands) and *Fugl i en vår* (1979; Birds in a Spring). In his dramatic practice, Cappelen was also very much of a loner, though he learned from Shakespeare, Strindberg, and the medieval mystery play.

Cappelen's plays fall into the categories of historical drama and plays based on folk literature and folk belief. His historical plays, often written in a mixture of prose and blank verse, draw on early Norwegian history and medieval literature. In *Kark* (1974), Cappelen used a tenth-century episode recorded in Snorri Sturluson's *Heimskringla* to make a statement about the relationship between imagination and reason and between women and men. It is also a political play in that it shows graphically the unjust treatment of women in medieval Christianity. *Sverre—Berget og ordet* (1977; Sverre—The Mountain and the Word) is similarly based on early (twelfth-century) Norwegian history. Cappelen's most ambitious work in this genre is a trilogy consisting of *Lucie, jomfru til Austråt* (1980; Lucie, Maid of Austråt), *Dyveke, duen på Akershus* (1982; Dyveke, Dove of Akershus), and *Knut Alvsson* (1984), all of which are set in the early sixteenth century during Norway's union with Denmark.

Cappelen's first folklore play was *Tornerose, den sovende skjønnhet* (1968; Briar Rose, the Sleeping Beauty). Others in this genre are *Trollspill* (1975; Troll Play) and, the most significant, *Hvittenland* (1981; Eng. tr., *Whittenland*, 1989). Cappelen used an array of figures from Scandinavian mythology and Norwegian folklore to stage a conflict between opposing forces and ideals, such as summer and winter, nature and technology, emotions and intellect, and stewardship and domination. In the end, good triumphs over evil.

Other recent works by Cappelen are *Eufemianatten* (1986; Euphemia Night), in which Håkon V and other historical characters act against a mythological-folkloristic background, and *Kolbrennaren* (1988; The Charcoal Burner), a mixture of comedy, folk drama, and farce. Cappelen also wrote books for children.

Bjørg Vik

Although primarily a short-story writer, Bjørg Vik has had a significant effect on Norwegian drama by bringing feminist concerns to the stage. Her first play, *To akter for fem kvinner* (1974; Two Acts for Five Women), in which she takes a strong feminist position, consists of a discussion among five women who represent different attitudes and reactions to the place of woman in society. *Hurra, det ble en pike!* (1974; Hurrah, It's a Girl!), a series of skits for young amateur actors, advocates feminist and environmentalist views. *Sorgenfri* (1978; Sans Souci) tells about love relationships in three settings and three generations.

Det trassige håp (1981; The Defiant Hope) consists of five radio plays: *Ferie* (Vacation), *Magma, Døtre* (Eng. tr., *Daughters,* 1989), *Forværelset* (The Anteroom), and *Myrtel. Døtre,* a study in isolation and generation gaps between women, is the most accomplished of these plays and has also been adapted for the stage. *En øy av galskap* (1984; An Island of Craziness) is another radio play, while *Fribillett til Soria Moria* (1984; A Free Ticket to Soria Moria) was written as a television drama.

Cecilie Løveid

Cecilie Løveid (1951–) is one of the most unconventional and most interesting writers of her generation. *Most* (1972; Juice) is a love story told in poetry and prose. Similar texts are *Tenk om isen skulle komme* (1974; What if the Ice Were to Come) and *Sug* (1979; Eng. tr. *Sea Swell,* 1986), the most important of these books. A novel made from bits of prose, prose poems, and formal poetry, *Sug* tells the story of an unwed mother and her search for love. The book is notable for the poetic qualities of its language, for its daring formal experiments, and for the fact that Løveid makes her female protagonist a hunter rather than prey in the love relationships portrayed. Other collections of poetry are *Mørkets muligheter* (1976; The Possibilities of Darkness) and *Fanget villrose* (1977; Captured Wild Rose).

During the 1980s Løveid worked primarily with drama for radio, television, and stage. *Du, bli her!* (1983; Listen: Stay Here!) was performed on radio in 1980, and *Måkespisere* (1983; Eng. tr. *Seagull Eaters,* 1989), the more successful of the two plays, on radio in 1982. *Måkespisere* is set in Løveid's native city of Bergen before and during World War II and tells about a young working-class girl who wants to become an actress but whose hopes are crushed by a cruel world: her landlord seduces her with food, she gets pregnant and gives birth, her baby is taken away to be raised for the Führer, and in the end she is "rinsed and hung up to dry." The play has a strong intertextual dimension, with quotes from an old manual on homemaking, Ibsen's *Gengangere,* and Chekhov's *Chaika* (1896; Seagull) hovering in the background. *Vift* (1985; Great Fun) is a radio play in which a young girl is initiated into the world of adults.

Løveid has worked directly with a major theater in Bergen on several of her plays, such as *Vinteren revner* (1983; The Winter Cracks) and *Balansedame* (1986; Tightrope Walker), a meditation on the significance of birth, which, for Løveid, is both a return to the boundaries of individuality and an experience holding the possibility of ecstasy. *Fornuftige dyr* (1986; Rational Animals) has as its theme the animality of man and the irrationality of love. Its male protagonist fathers a child by one woman, leaves her for another, returns to his first lover, and, years later, falls for his own daughter, now in her teens: actions that he is able to rationalize in the name of freedom. In *Dobbel nytelse* (1988; Double Delight), which takes its title from a line in *Fornuftige dyr,* Løveid continues her exploration of the forces of desire.

THE 1980S: TOWARD POSTMODERNISM

Like its predecessors, "romanticism" and "modernism," "postmodernism" is a slippery concept and difficult to define. It is sometimes thought of as synonymous with "self-reflexivity" as it appears in metafiction, but that is only partially true. Postmodernism is paradoxical in a more general sense, in that, freed from dreams of dialectic harmony, it celebrates the contradictions of existence. It portrays the dominant culture from inside, attempting to show that this culture carries within it the seeds of its own demise. It has an intensely parodic attitude toward a world in which it nevertheless attempts to root itself. Its paradoxes reveal and contest prevailing norms by incarnating both the norm and its undoing in the text. Some of the characteristics of postmodern literature include explicit dramatization of both narrator and reader; extreme intertextuality, often through parody of other texts; a breakdown of the temporal and spatial organization of the narrative; subversion of conventions, norms, and codes; and a dehumanization of literary figures, often achieved through the use of odd names. Postmodernist literature attempts to break down expectations and even the concept of causality.

Postmodernist tendencies may be observed in several of the Norwegian writers discussed above. Alfred Hauge's *Århundre* trilogy accentuates its own fictional status in the extreme. Arild Nyquist's *Abborfiske i Norge,* whose title is a takeoff on Richard Brautigan's *Trout Fishing in America* (1967; Norw. tr. *Ørretfiske i Amerika*), names a major character Abborfiske and presents a text full of discontinuities. Edvard Hoem appears as a minor character in his own novel *Kjærleikens ferjereiser,* and so on. Several writers—Ole Robert Sunde, Jon

Fosse, Lisbeth Hiide, Ingvar Ambjørnsen, Mari Osmundsen, and others—have touched on various aspects of postmodernism in their books. This presentation discusses only two writers who may be regarded as postmodernist point men in the Norwegian literature of the 1980s.

Kjartan Fløgstad

Kjartan Fløgstad (1944–) first published two volumes of modernist poetry, *Valfart* (1968; Pilgrimage) and *Seremoniar* (1969; Ceremonies). Unlike most of his contemporaries, he displayed no overt political engagement but offered a deeply felt experience of both nature and city environments. His next book, a mixture of narrative and essayistic prose entitled *Den hemmelege jubel* (1970; The Secret Jubilation), showed that he was a widely read, incisive, and engaging man of letters. The short-story collection *Fangliner* (1972; Painters) and the novel *Rasmus* (1974) draw on Fløgstad's own experience as a sailor in the merchant marine and as a worker in industry. Rather than, say, Dag Solstad, who admits that his novels about workers from the same time period were written for members of the intelligentsia rather than for the workers themselves, Fløgstad offers genuine portraits of daily life in the factory and on board the merchant ship and writes in a manner accessible to the common person. Two mystery novels, written in the mid-1970s, can also be regarded as literature for the people.

The foundation of Fløgstad's literary reputation, and his first foray into postmodernism, is the novel *Dalen Portland* (1977; Eng. tr. *Dollar Road*, 1989), for which he received the Nordic Literary Prize. A Bakhtinian account of changes brought about in a small community in western Norway when the area was industrialized, the book blends the realistic and the fantastic throughout. The lives of several members of one family are chronicled, and the characters are taken by their author to a large number of places at home and abroad. The text contains elements of the picaresque as well as other popular literary forms, and its self-reflexivity is shown in an otherwise realistic scene, in which one of the characters encounters a figure who states that his name is Kjartan Fløgstad and that he is knocking on a boiler in the factory to see if he can hear the hollow ringing sounds of the language. In his next novel, *Fyr og flamme* (1980; Fire and Flame), the author went further along the postmodernist road. Subtitled "Av handling" (Dis Sertation), the book is, in one sense, both a traditional story and a discussion of its subject and, in another sense, neither of the two. A hybrid text, difficult to categorize, *Fyr og flamme* encompasses many different discourses, and like the text, its central character, Hertingen, is larger than life.

Fløgstad's next book reads more like a traditional novel. *U 3* (1983) takes its title from the U2 episode in the middle of the Cold War and is more overtly political in the traditional sense than either of its predecessors. The protagonist, Alf Hellot, is an officer in the Norwegian Air Force, and he becomes the reader's guide to the history of Norwegian defense policy during the postwar era. The story culminates with the news of the downing of the U2 spy plane, after which Hellot, ever loyal to his people, terminates his life while on a mission to warn of what is happening to Norway as a result of its NATO collaboration with the United States. The postmodern aspects of the novel are found primarily in the relationship between its characters and the narrator, who has at his disposal such aids as the fictional retrospectroscope, by means of which he is able to gather the information needed to tell the story.

Fløgstad's most hotly debated book is *Det 7. klima* (1986; The Seventh Climate), the fictional biography of one Salim Mahmood, an Asian immigrant to Norway who becomes a writer and data linguist. The novel offers the author's view of what is happening to Norwegian cultural and intellectual life, but his views are presented in a difficult manner so that, when the book first appeared, most of the critics reacted with a great deal of frustration and only limited understanding. Fløgstad's contributions to the debate about the book have been collected in *Tyrannosaurus text* (1988), which, like two other volumes of essays, *Loven vest for Pecos* (1981; The Law West of Pecos) and *Ordlyden* (1983; The Sound/Community of Words), serves as a good introduction to Fløgstad the intellectual. Fløgstad writes in nynorsk.

Jan Kjærstad

The place of Jan Kjærstad (1953–) in Norwegian postmodernism is partly a function of his art, partly a result of his position in the literary institution. As editor of *Vinduet* he was accused of favoring writers who agreed with his particular view of literature; his answer to this charge was that he simply wanted to allow another generation of critics to develop. Kjærstad's first book was a collection of short stories, *Kloden dreier stille rundt* (1980; The Planet Quietly Rotates), in which many of his characteristics as a writer are already evident: his love of Oslo, his engagement with the issues of the day, his humor, and his concern for the social and ethical dimensions of art. The final story in the book exemplifies several of these traits, in that a writer named J. is charged at the final judgment with having written immoral literature and sent to Hell by a God who speaks nynorsk! The novel *Speil. Leseserie fra det 20. århundre* (1982; Mirrors: A Series of Readings from the Twentieth Century) was also well received. Relatively traditional in composition, it deals with the timely topic of the arms race and with violence in general. Kjærstad's definitive breakthrough came with his novel *Homo Falsus eller: Det perfekte mord* (1984; Homo Falsus; or, The Perfect Murder), which has many postmodernist traits. It is a novel about modern men and women, who are seduced by the language of their society, who are themselves seducers, and who hide behind masks and roles. The protagonist is a young woman who has taken on both the role of the person Greta Garbo and some of Garbo's movie roles, and who carries out a game of seduction in which several male representatives of power are made mysteriously to disappear at the climax of the sexual act. The narrator of the story, who represents himself to the reader as identical with the book's author, offers a running commentary on the action and the writing process until it becomes clear that he, too, is only a character, that he is Greta's next victim, that she is the real author of the book, and that she uses rather conventional means to get rid of her victims. *Homo Falsus* thus thematizes some problematic aspects of contemporary life and art.

Kjærstad's most recent novel is *Det store eventyret* (1987; The Great Adventure), in which Norway has become an island located in the Indian Ocean, where the protagonist is carrying out a monumental search for love among remnants of a culture based on writing. Like Fløgstad's *Det 7. klima, Det store eventyret* becomes a defense of intellectual culture at a time when the reality of the natural world and the reality of writing are both being replaced by the unreality of the media industry's transitory images.

LITERARY CRITICISM AND SCHOLARSHIP

In 1950 the historical-biographical method was still dominant in Norwegian criticism. Associated with the name of Francis Bull (1887–1974), professor of Scandinavian literary history at the University of Oslo, this approach to literary study resulted in much valuable work, from Kjølv Egeland's *Nordahl Grieg* (1953) to Gudrun Hovde Gvåle's *O. E. Rølvaag* (1962). Bull's method was, however, strongly opposed by what was referred to as the aesthetic-philosophical school, consisting primarily of students of Peter Rokseth (1891–1945), a scholar in the field of French literature. The foremost representative of this school was Daniel Haakonsen (1917–89), whose early work includes *Skabelsen i Henrik Wergelands diktning* (1951; The Creation in Henrik Wergeland's Work) and *Henrik Ibsens realisme* (1957; Henrik Ibsen's Realism). Else Høst, another Roksethian, wrote monographs on two Ibsen plays, *Hedda Gabler* (1958) and *Vildanden* (1967; The Wild Duck).

Rokseth's followers paved the way for the ideas of the Anglo-American New Criticism, which gradually penetrated Norwegian literary studies, though it never achieved a position in Norway comparable to its dominance in America. According to the New Critics, the literary work constituted a unified whole and the job of the critic was to demonstrate how all the work's parts contributed to that whole. In many cases, Norwegian critics combined the neocritical focus on the individual work with the older historical-biographical approach; examples are Ellisiv Steen's study of *Kristin Lavransdatter* (1959) and Kjølv Egeland's *Skyld og skjebne* (1960; Guilt and Fate), a study of four novels by Sigurd Hoel. Some of the most typical examples of Norwegian New Criticism are to be found in the literature on Knut Hamsun, such as Rolf Vige's *Pan* (1963) and Rolf Nyboe Nettum's *Konflikt og visjon* (1970; Conflict and Vision). In Norway, as elsewhere, the close reading of the New Criticism is normally applied to individual works, though it has occasionally been used in studies devoted to whole authorships, such as Ingard Hauge's *Tanker og tro i Welhavens poesi* (1955; Ideas and Faith in Welhaven's Poetry), Johannes A. Dale's *Olav Nygard* (1957), and Bjarte Birkeland's *Per Sivle* (1961). An example of value-centered criticism applied to a complete oeuvre rather than to individual works is Aasmund Brynildsen's book of four Hamsun essays, *Svermeren og hans demon* (1973; The Dreamer and His Demon). Brynildsen also wrote other essays, anchored in a culturally conservative humanism, on a large number of topics.

Myth criticism has not been widely practiced among Norwegian critics, an exception being Asbjørn Aarseth, whose *Dyret i mennesket* (1975; The Animal in Man) offers a controversial interpretation of Ibsen's *Peer Gynt*. Structuralism has also had little impact on traditional literary scholarship, though it may be seen as an influence on Irene Engelstad's *Fortellingens mønstre. En strukturell analyse av norske folkeeventyr* (1976; The Patterns of the Story: A Structural Analysis of Norwegian Folktales). Neo-Marxist ideological criticism, in contrast, was early a significant force, manifesting itself in such books as Nils Magne Knutsen's *Makt, avmakt. En studie av Hamsuns* Benoni *og* Rosa (1975; Power, Powerlessness: A Study of Hamsun's *Benoni* and *Rosa*) and in studies of Arne Garborg by Harald Bache-Wiig, Gunnar Foss, and Åsfrid Svensen. Marxist criticism went hand in hand with the revolutionary literature of the *Profil* group and appears to have declined in the 1980s. As the postmodernist movement manifested itself in the literature of this decade, poststructuralism received a great deal of attention from the critics. The central figure in this trend is Atle Kittang.

His book *Litteraturkritiske problem* (1975; Problems in Literary Criticism) contained a discussion of the hermeneutics of suspicion, and he has since introduced both deconstruction and French neo-Freudianism to Norway. Among his major works are *Luft, vind, ingenting. Hamsuns desillusjonsromanar frå Sult til Ringen sluttet* (1984; Air, Wind, Nothing: Hamsun's Novels of Disillusionment from *Hunger* to *The Ring Is Closed*) and *Møtestader* (1988; Meeting Places), a collection of articles and essays.

Contemporary criticism in Norway is characterized by openness toward a variety of methods and philosophical underpinnings. Book-length studies are published by both the Norwegian University Press and the more traditional publishing houses, and outlets for articles are such literary journals as *Edda* and *Norsk litterær årbok* (Norwegian Literary Yearbook) as well as more general periodicals. It is also becoming increasingly common for several scholar-critics to work together on state-supported projects. One such group project was "Litteraturhistorieskrivningens teori og praksis" (The Theory and Practice of Literary Historiography), which, supported by the Norwegian Research Council for General Scholarship, was carried out by the departments of comparative literature at the universities of Bergen and Oslo. A spin-off from this project is Asbjørn Aarseth's *Realismen som myte* (1981; Realism as Myth).

Norwegian Children's Literature

Margaret Hayford O'Leary

8

EARLY HISTORY

Norwegian children's literature did not come of age until the late nineteenth century. Books for children were produced in Norway before that time, but numbers were small compared to those of other European countries. During the eighteenth century Lutheran fundamentalism was strong in Norway and little need was felt for reading material other than the Lord's Prayer and the Creed. Nevertheless, the spirit of the European Enlightenment, with its belief that knowledge creates good people, gradually gained a foothold in the country, and by the 1770s creation of a literature for children had become part of the struggle for independence and for a Norwegian language. Even after the dissolution of the union with Denmark in 1814, however, Danish language and Danish culture continued to be dominant.

In the early 1800s literature written for children was of the Christian/moralistic kind, its characters were models of perfect behavior rather than realistically portrayed, and neither the language nor the reality depicted had much relation to Norwegian society, since most of the material was translated into Danish from German or English. The first book written by a Norwegian author for Norwegian children was a reader by Simon Kildal (1761–1822) with the cumbersome title *Øvelse-bog til bogstav-kjendskab, rigtig staven og retlæsning, bestemt til vejledelse for forældre og ungdomslærere, som ville komme deres vigtige kald ihu: at anføre børn paa en fornuftig maade til at læse, tænke og frygte Gud. Til brug for drængebørn* (2d ed. 1804; Exercise Book for Familiarity with the Alphabet, Correct Spelling and Reading, Intended for the Guidance of Parents and Teachers Who Wish to Keep in Mind Their Call: To Lead Children in a Sensible Way to Read, Think, and Fear God. For Use with Boy Children). Although this book is an example of the religious/moralistic type of Norwegian children's literature, there was a parallel worldly/moralistic tradition, originally inspired by the rationalism of the Enlightenment but gradually heavily influenced by the ideas of European romanticism. In the eighteenth century it had been generally held that young people, as future adults, needed to be educated and guided, but with romanticism came a new view of children as God's angels and the flowers of the field, and for the first time books were written not only to teach but to entertain them. Works by such authors as Mauritz Hansen (1794–1842), Henrik Wergeland (1808–45), and Jørgen Moe (1813–82) exemplify the worldly, romantic type of children's literature, though Wergeland spanned both traditions. Although none of them was primarily a children's author, they laid the foundation of a national children's literature of literary quality. They believed that Norway's future lay in educating its children, and they also worked toward the creation of a Norwegian language so that children could learn to read in a language closer to the language they spoke, rather than in Danish.

Mauritz Hansen's work is all but forgotten today, except for his children's book, *Lille Alvilde og bjørnen* (1829; Little Alvilde and the Bear), a romantic depiction of nature, people, and religion, which shows the power of innocence. Although not intended for children, it became popular among them and has been called the first literary tale in Norwegian children's literature. Hansen was a pioneer in the creation of the Norwegian children's magazine with his *Billed-magazin for børn* (1838–39; Picture Magazine for Children): though elsewhere in Europe children's magazines had existed since the eighteenth century, *Billed-magazin* represented something new for Norway. Hansen also published two collections of fables for children, *Halvhundrede fabler med billeder for børn* (1838; Fifty Fables with Pictures for Children) and *Fem og tyve fabler med billeder for børn* (1842; Twenty-Five Fables with Pictures for Children), both of them free retellings of German fables.

Although Henrik Wergeland wrote only one book explicitly for children, *Vinterblommer i barnekammeret; original og fri oversatt samling for børn* (1840; Winter Flowers in the Nursery: Original and Freely Translated Collection for Children), during the last years of his life he published separately several children's poems, songs, and tales. Thus, with his national reputation as a personal friend of children, he has an important position in the history of Norwegian children's literature. Living in the age of romanticism and being himself in many ways a romantic, Wergeland was at the same time a man of the Enlightenment and shared its belief in human perfectibility through education.

Jørgen Moe, who is best known for his folktale collaboration with Peter

Christen Asbjørnsen, published his only children's book in 1851: *I brønden og i kjærnet: Smaahistorier for børn* (In the Well and in the Pond: Little Stories for Children). For the first time in Norwegian children's literature, children are portrayed with psychological insight and without open moralizing. Furthermore, Moe tried to make the language style more Norwegian and oral: though his spelling and grammar are largely Danish, he attempted to use Norwegian vocabulary. The book has rightly been considered the first original Norwegian children's book, though it had little influence on the writing of the next several decades.

The latter half of the nineteenth century saw a change in the view of children and childhood and a decline in the authority of religion. In Norway, as elsewhere in Europe, children were allowed to read books for amusement rather than solely for education and moral example, and though children's literature on the whole tended to remain religious and moralistic, there was a gradual movement away from the dark, pietistic religiosity of previous decades, as can be seen in the work of Marie Wexelsen (1832–1911). Her poems and stories, with their more fully developed characters, are clearly inspired by the "happy" Christianity of the Danish poet and religious leader N. F. S. Grundtvig. Wexelsen is now known mainly for her Christmas song "Jeg er så glad hver julekveld" (1860; Eng. tr. "I Am So Glad Each Christmas Eve").

The decline in the authority of religion was noticeable also in the Norwegians schools: from having been largely institutions of religious instruction they became schools of general education for all people, including working-class and rural children—and girls as well as boys. There is a connection between this increased availability of education for girls and the appearance of women as writers of children's books. Nearly all women authors of this period were from the civil-servant class—schoolteachers or the wives or daughters of pastors—writing under initials or pseudonyms at first and only much later under their own names. These women tended to continue the religious tradition and to focus their attention on the everyday lives of girls, while men branched out into adventure stories for boys. Examples of well-known women writers include Gustava Kielland (1800–1889) and Hanna Winsnes (1789–1872). In her memoirs, which she dictated when she was past eighty, Kielland provided a lively picture of a Norwegian childhood during the hard times before 1814 and the first years of union with Sweden. She is best known for her lively Christmas song "O, jul med din glede og barnlige lyst" (Eng. tr. "Oh, Christmas with Joy and Childlike Delight"). Winsnes, great-grandmother of the writer Barbra Ring, is best known for her cookbook from 1845 (which went through thirteen impressions by 1921), but she also wrote a religious textbook for children in which she retold parts of the Bible in verse (1846) and a story, *Aftnerne paa Egelund* (1852; Evenings at Egelund), which became quite popular, being reprinted as late as 1923. Winsnes represents the end of the tradition of religious moralism.

Among male authors, Oluf Vilhelm Falck Ytter (1832–1914) was a central figure in Norwegian children's literature from the 1860s to the beginning of the 1900s. He wrote adventure stories (inspired by Robinson Crusoe), translated American and English classics for young people, edited youth and children's magazines, and promoted the athletics movement. His most popular Robinson Crusoe imitation, *Haakon Haakonson* (1869), was reprinted as late as 1990.

THE GOLDEN AGE (1890–1914)

Though religion continued to play an important role in nineteenth-century Norwegian schools, stern fundamentalist theories of child rearing gradually gave way to the gentler view of Grundtvigianism. Toward the end of the century the stark social vision of naturalism also challenged the earlier romantic image of ennoblement through poverty, so that children were increasingly viewed as individuals in their own right. As more and more children learned to read, there was an increasing demand for books to teach reading as well as books for children to read in their leisure time. One of the most important figures in the new Norwegian schools was the author Nordahl Rolfsen (1848–1928), an idealist inspired by the work of Henrik Wergeland and Bjørnstjerne Bjørnson. Rolfsen believed that education was the key to erasing the distinction between social classes, and because he recognized the importance of literature for child development, he made it his life's work to help create a national children's literature through the production of children's magazines, books for leisure reading, and school readers. His magazine *Illustreret tidende for børn* (1885–92; Illustrated Newspaper for Children) was considered outstanding in Scandinavia, and many of Norway's best-known children's authors of the time published their stories in the magazine before they appeared in book form. The magazine led directly to Rolfsen's major work, his five-volume *Læsebog for folkeskolen* (Reader for the Elementary School), beginning in 1891 and including by 1894 a nynorsk edition. The readers contained contemporary children's literature and served to familiarize children and their parents with works by such authors as Jørgen Moe, Henrik Wergeland, and Bjørnstjerne Bjørnson, among others. Rolfsen's greatest contribution to children's literature, however, was his work for the establishment and supervision of centrally administered school libraries, of which by the year 1903 there were eighteen hundred. He headed the central steering committee for schoolbook collections from its inception in 1896 until 1914, and his committee recommended titles to be included in school libraries and even published children's books.

While children's literature on the whole paralleled the development in literature generally, it tended to be more conservative and less critical of society. It recorded the daily lives of children, but now children from all classes of society: particularly in the nynorsk literature, children from rural areas were depicted for their own sake, not merely as colorful stereotypes or background figures. Some of the best nynorsk writers include Per Sivle (1857–1904), Kristen Stalleland (1861–1949), Hallvard Ellestad Bergh (1850–1922), and Rasmus Løland (1861–1907). Most of them wrote for both children and adults, and many of their so-called children's books were not originally intended for children: the distinction between children's literature and literature for adults was not as sharp as it is today.

Among the most important bokmål writers of the Golden Age are Bernt Lie (1868–1916), Dikken Zwilgmeyer (1853–1913), and Barbra Ring (1870–1955), all of whom write about life in the small towns; and Lars Kjølstad (1861–1932), Hans Aanrud (1863–1953), and Gabriel Scott (1874–1958), whose books are set in rural eastern Norway. Dikken Zwilgmeyer was one of the outstanding children's authors of the 1890s. She is best known for her series of thirteen Inger Johanne books, which are still popular (Eng. tr. *What Ever Happened to Inger Johanne, As Told by Herself*, 1919, and *Inger Johanne's Lively Doings*, 1926). Writing directly for children, she understood the psychology of young people and avoided direct moralizing: moral lessons are brought out only as a natural consequence of the story. The character of Inger Johanne also represented something new in Norwegian children's literature: a girl who, fresh and unafraid to do anything the boys could do, departed from the rigid sex roles of the times. Zwilgmeyer, whose books have been translated into many languages, was included in *The Junior Book of Authors* (1934).

Like Zwilgmeyer, Barbra Ring came from a family of civil servants and landowners, and the background and temperament of her female characters resemble those of Zwilgmeyer: they reject the traditional female role, preferring outdoor activity to housework. Ring is a great humorist. She creates amusing situations by placing a child in an unaccustomed milieu or by contrasting a child's naive way of thinking with the adult's more rigid behavior and thought patterns. Her books have been translated into several foreign languages as well as into nynorsk. Best known are *Tertit* (1905), *Peik* (1909;

Eng. tr. 1932), and *Fjeldmus og Bymus* (1909; Mountain Mouse and Town Mouse [nicknames for Petra and her cousin]), which, with some other titles, were later (1917–18) collected into the seven-volume *Peik og Fjeldmus* books. (In 1927 *Fjeldmus* was published in America and England as, respectively, *The Tomboy Cousin* and *Tales of a Country Mouse*). Barbra Ring is also known as the originator of the Norwegian *ungpikebøker* (young girl books) about love and infatuation, such as *Babbens dagbok* (Babben's Diary), with which the thirty-four-year-old author made her debut in 1904.

In contrast to Zwilgmeyer and Ring, Hans Aanrud wrote about the farming communities of eastern Norway. He is remembered for stories such as *Sidsel Sidsærk* (1903; Eng. tr. *Sidsel Longskirt, a Girl of Norway*, 1935) and *Sølve Solfeng* (1910; Eng. tr. *Solve Suntrap*, 1935), set in the idyllic, stable, and orderly world of Norway one hundred years ago. Aanrud's books have been translated into several foreign languages. Like Aanrud, Gabriel Scott wrote about rural Norway, particularly the southern coast. Of his many books for children, the humorous *Tripp. Trapp. Træsko. Fortælling om tre smaa venner paa landet* (1902; Trip. Trap. Wooden Shoe. Tale about Three Little Friends in the Country) represents a new trend in the Norwegian children's literature after the turn of the century, with its lighter and more amusing tone.

The last decades of the nineteenth century are important also for children's poetry, mainly in the form of collections of songs, nursery rhymes, lullabies, and so on that had long been part of a strong Norwegian oral tradition. A collection by Elling Holst (1849–1937), *Norsk billedbog for børn* (1888; Norwegian Picture Book for Children) contains some songs that are still familiar, including "Ro, ro til fiskeskjær" (Row, Row to the Fishing Ground) and "Ride, ride ranke" (Ride, Ride Upright). Another important collection of children's songs was made by Margrethe Munthe (1860–1931): *Kom skal vi synge* (1905, 1907, 1918; Come, Let's Sing), which has continued to be published.

The Golden Age of children's literature came to an end during the first decades of the twentieth century, when all its central writers either died or stopped writing for children. The new generation of authors was less active in the field of children's literature, now generally limited to standardized realistic stories with little experimentation, though there was an increased emphasis on the individual and individual problems. Nynorsk literature often showed the hero or heroine overcoming a difficult social background— what has been called "children's book realism," in which bold and brave moral boys and girls defy the established society and succeed where adults have failed.

Though there were rapid changes in Norwegian society after the secession of 1905—industrialization, problems in labor relations, migration to the cities, and so on—little evidence of such social turmoil is apparent in children's literature. Nevertheless, we find a freer attitude toward religion and child rearing and, during the 1930s, greater political awareness (but still no treatment of the lives of industrial workers). There were also formal changes, in that the earlier collections of short, episodic stories were replaced by longer, more connected texts. The output of children's literature increased between the wars, but little of lasting value was produced: the growing number of children who could read and the rise of the entertainment industry may have contributed to the proliferation of poor-quality books. Flight from reality is common, usually in the form of stories of wild adventure or the pursuit of criminals. Especially popular were such translated series as *Frøken detektiv* (Nancy Drew books) and *Hardy Boys* books. There was a clear distinction between books for boys and books for girls, books were designated for specific age groups, and for the first time, children's literature was considered a separate—and inferior—category of the national literature. Many of the books produced after World War I were set at a time before the turn of the century, being written by older authors reminiscing about their childhood. During the German occupation of Norway in 1940–45 virtually nothing of worth was published, since there was a complete authors' strike. Even so, though it was not until after World War II that a large number of good writers were dedicated to children's literature, a few authors from the period between the wars are worth mentioning, mainly authors of literature for adults who also wrote children's books. Regine Normann (1867–1939), Kristian Elster (1881–1947), and Marie Hamsun (1881–1969) are still read today, while Sven Moren (1871–1938), Olav Duun (1876–1939), Halvor Floden (1884–1956), Sigrunn Okkenhaug (1889–1939), Ragnvald Vaage (1889–1966), and Halldis Moren Vesaas (1907–) are prominent among those writing in nynorsk.

Regine Normann was especially important as a writer of fairy tales, which, with their blend of art tale and genuine folktale, have been compared favorably to those of Asbjørnsen and Moe and the brothers Grimm. Her *Eventyr* (1925; Fairy Tales) and *Nye eventyr* (1926; New Fairy Tales) were republished in 1967 as *Ringelihorn og andre eventyr* (Ringelihorn and Other Fairy Tales), illustrated by the artist Kaare Espolin Johnson and supported by the Norwegian Cultural Fund. Another of her titles to be reissued is her first children's book, *Den graa kat og den sorte* (1916, 1969; The Gray Cat and the Black One).

Somewhat surprising is the interest shown by the novelist (and misogynist) Knut Hamsun in the writings of his wife Marie: he encouraged her to publish the little anecdotes she used to tell in letters to him, and the result was the four-volume series *Bygdebarn* (1924–32; Eng. tr. *A Norwegian Farm*, 1933, and *A Norwegian Family*, 1934), which have since become classics in Norway and abroad. As late as 1955 Marie Hamsun published a story, *Tina Toppen*, which was a runner-up for the international Hans Christian Andersen prize.

In 1950 Halvor Floden became the only children's author ever to receive the Norwegian state artist's salary. Writing in nynorsk, he worked during his long career for the right of children to use their own language at school. Many of his stories have been included in modern school readers, even in bokmål versions; some of his books have been dramatized; and one—*Frik med fela* (1917; Frick with the Fiddle)—is available in German and English translations (*Frick, Story for Children*, 1926). Floden wrote about the problems of handicapped and orphaned children, gypsies, and the German occupation of Norway during World War II.

In children's books by Halldis Moren Vesaas, the milieu has been compared to that of Hans Aanrud and Halvor Floden, though Vesaas's style is more leisurely. Titles include *Du får gjera det, du* (1935; You Had Better Do It), *Den grøne hatten* (1938; The Green Hat), and *Tidleg på våren* (1949; Early in the Spring), which have been well received by critics and translated into several other Scandinavian languages and German. Vesaas also contributed to Norwegian children's literature through her modernization of books by Per Sivle and Rasmus Løland and her collaboration with Torbjørn Egner on his readers for elementary schools.

AFTER WORLD WAR II

The postwar period was one of tremendous economic growth and rebuilding, with full employment. For the first time, the state showed an interest in children's literature, first by awarding a prize each year, beginning in 1948, for the best children's book and later by supporting authors through the Norwegian Cultural Council. Little of literary value was written about the war years, though there was a major debate about how the occupation should be dealt with in children's books. The general tendency, which would continue until the 1970s, was to protect children from its harsh reality. Authors, in the words of Sonja Hagemann, "projected their own dreams and longings for goodness and friendliness into their books" (Hagemann, 3:137). The period from the late 1940s to the 1960s has been characterized as a new golden age of Norwegian literature for small children, a situation due in large part to the influence of radio. The radio show *Barnetime for de minste* (Children's Hour for the Little Ones) served a function similar to that of the children's magazines from the 1800s by providing a place for new authors to try out their work and hone their style. Some of the most important children's authors received their start on this program, including Alf Prøysen (1914–70), Thorbjørn Egner (1912–90), and Anne-Cath. (Catharina) Vestly (1920–).

Alf Prøysen is best remembered for his many songs and for his stories about Teskjekjerringa (Mrs. Pepperpot; lit.: "The Old Teaspoon Woman"), beginning with *Kjerringa som ble så lita som ei teskje* (1957; The Old Woman Who Became as Little as a Teaspoon; Eng. tr. *Little Old Mrs. Pepperpot*, 1959 and others). Prøysen's work has been translated into many languages, including Japanese. In 1970 he was awarded the Norwegian Cultural Council's Special Award and, after his death, the Special Award of the Ministry of Church and Education for his contribution to children's literature.

Thorbjørn Egner was an extremely versatile author who wrote stories, poems, and songs, and who always illustrated his own books. He also translated and retold A. A. Milne's *Winnie the Pooh* (1926; Norw. tr. *Ole Brum*, 1947) and created a Norwegian radio version of Hugh Lofting's *Doctor Doolittle* (1954; Norw. tr. *Doktor Dyregod*, 1954). Egner's most original work is *Folk og røvere i Kardemomme by* (1955; Eng. tr. *The Singing Town*, 1959; People and Robbers in Cardemom Town*, 1968), in which, partly under the influence of English writing, he broke with the powerful realistic tradition in Norwegian children's literature. His optimistic, friendly view of humanity permeates his books, where even the little creatures who cause tooth decay are presented as lovable (*Karius og Baktus*, 1949; Eng. tr. *Karius and Baktus*, 1962 and others). Though books by Egner have appeared in more than twenty different languages, perhaps his most far-reaching work has been his sixteen-volume series of readers for Norwegian schools (1950–72). In addition to collecting classical children's stories and poems, he was able to get such well-known authors as Arnuld Øverland, Tarjei Vesaas, Inger Hagerup, and Halldis Moren Vesaas to write directly for the series.

Though Anne-Cath. Vestly may not measure up to either Prøysen or Egner in literary quality, her books have been translated into many languages and her importance for children's literature is undeniable. She is popular among Norwegian children both as a writer and as a radio and television performer. Beginning with the series *Ole Alexander Fili-bom-bom-bom* (1953), she was the first Norwegian author to write about children growing up in apartment buildings in the city. In the *Aurora* books (1966–; Eng. tr. *Hallo, Aurora,* 1973 and others), she writes about the reversal of gender roles, and in the series beginning with *Lillebror og Knerten* (1962; Little Brother and Peanut), about the problem of latch-key children. Although Vestly does take up social problems, she still manages to create an idyll, in which the adults are all patient, kind, loving, and sensible—able to solve both their own and their children's problems. Vestly has also edited *Barnas store sangbok* (1952; The Children's Big Songbook).

Despite the postwar increase in literature for the very young, the majority of children's books continued to be written for older children, and though these books represent no radical change from what had existed before, the 1940s and 1950s were a time of renewal. There was a reaction against the poor-quality series of the 1930s, with higher standards for style and composition, and there was experimentation of the kind found in literature for adults, with collective and reportage novels, use of symbols, and nonsense literature. There was little or no political propaganda in children's books, but social concerns were more central than before, categories for boys' books and girls' books began to disappear, and books had both male and female protagonists, with the girl sometimes more aggressively bold than the boy. Especially during the 1950s and 1960s such authors as Jo Tenfjord (1918–) and Aimée Sommerfelt (1892–1975) responded to the Cold War by writing books promoting international understanding. Indeed, there was general agreement among authors that children's books should further the ideals of peace, tolerance, hope, and understanding beyond national boundaries, as well as respect for the individual.

Aimée Sommerfelt began writing in the 1930s, but she did not make her real breakthrough until 1950 with her book *Miriam* (Eng. tr., 1963), in which she takes a stand against the anti-Semitism that had sprung up in Norway during the war. *Veien til Agra* (1959; Eng. tr. *The Road to Agra,* 1961) became an international success: it was translated into more than twenty languages and won several international prizes, including the Jane Addams Prize in 1962. Sommerfelt believed that the only way to make children understand such world problems as hunger, poverty, and homelessness was to relate the issues directly to the personal lives of young readers. *Veien til Agra* has been used in schools to teach children to think globally.

Zinken Hopp (1905–87) is Norway's only internationally known nonsense writer. She was influenced by Lewis Carroll's *Alice's Adventures in Wonderland* and *Through the Looking Glass,* both of which she translated into

Norwegian. Hopp's *Trollkrittet* (1948; Eng. tr. *The Magic Chalk,* 1959) has been translated into a dozen languages and published in eastern Europe, Japan, and the United States. In 1958 Hopp won the French Oscar Prize.

The documentary novel was introduced into Norwegian children's literature by Leif Hamre (1914–90), a member of the Norwegian Air Force during and after World War II who made his literary debut with *Otter Tre To kaller* (1957; Eng. tr. *Leap into Danger,* 1959, and *Otter Three Two Calling,* 1961). With this and his subsequent books about air pilots, he created a new kind of hero who, in doing his utmost on the job, conquers his own fear. Hamre, whose books are available in seventeen languages, has been awarded many national and international prizes.

Other notable authors from the 1950s and 1960s include Finn Havrevold (1905–88), who received the Damm Prize in 1952 for *Sommereventyret* (1952; Eng. tr. *Summer Adventure,* 1962) and again in 1955 for *Den ensomme kriger* (1955; The Lonely Warrior); Ebba Haslund (1917–), who has written four books for children with the common theme of rebellion against gender-role expectations; and Babbis Friis-Baastad (1921–70), who was also awarded the Damm Prize for her first book, *Æresord* (1959; Word of Honor), and who wrote about our need for listening more often to our own consciences and about tolerance and understanding of those who are different. Baastad's *Kjersti* (1962; Eng. tr. *Kristy's Courage,* 1965), about a handicapped girl, has been translated into a dozen languages. It won the Damm Prize and received honorable mention in the international Hans Christian Andersen competition. Philip Newt (1939–) wrote the first mass-produced picture book for the blind, *Rulle på eventyr* (1977; Eng. tr. *Roly Goes Exploring: A Book for Blind and Sighted Children,* 1977), which has cardboard cutouts of different shapes and a text written in both extra-large letters and Braille.

THE 1970S AND 1980S

Nineteen sixty-eight, the year of the youth revolution, marked a turning point in Norwegian literature, including literature for children. By the 1970s the distinction between boys' books and girls' books had been dropped by most Scandinavian publishers. Children's authors were influenced by neo-Marxist theory and were criticial of all forms of authority—whether society, school, church, or parents—and for the first time we find political propaganda, of both the right and the left, served openly in children's books. Popular genres included science fiction, magical realism, and political fables, as well as the social realism found in books for adults. Many of the important issues were global—pollution, fear of nuclear war, the relationship between the strong and the weak, the rich and the poor—but such problems as divorce and the collapse of the nuclear family were also taken up. The old theme of death, taboo in the immediate postwar period, was revived again in the 1970s, and by the end of the decade it had become a common element.

Although their techniques are different, Thormod Haugen (1945–) and Per Knutsen (1951–) both write about difficult family situations, Haugen with a psychological/mystical perspective and Knutsen with a more realistic approach. Haugen's books can all be seen as variations of one central theme, the oppressed and frightened child, as in *Nattfuglene* (1975; Eng. tr. *The Night Birds*, 1982), and have been translated into more than a dozen languages. Examples of Knutsen's books are *Du må plante flere blomster, Line-Liv* (1977; You Have to Plant More Flowers, Line-Liv), about family problems, and *Jeg vil ikke* (1978; I Don't Want To), about a rebelling star athlete.

Two of the most important writers of science fiction for both children and adults are Tor Åge Bringsværd (1939–) and Jon Bing (1944–). While Bing and Bringsværd are known for their jointly written books for adults, their children's books are produced separately, Bing concentrating on science-fiction novels for children and Bringsværd on utopian picture books. Bing has written three novels about space-traveling librarians, *Azur—kapteinenes planet* (1975; Azure—Planet of the Captains) and its sequels *Zalt—dampherrenes planet* (1976; Zalt—Planet of the Steam Lords) and *Mitz—gjenferdenes planet* (1982; Mitz—Planet of the Ghosts). Bringsværd's work includes *T-banetrollet Knerten Gundersen* (1969; The Subway Troll, Knerten Gundersen), *Ruffen—sjøormen* (1973; Ruffen—the Sea Serpent), and *Det blå folket og karamellfabrikken* (1974; The Blue People and the Caramels Factory). More surrealistic is *Alice lengter tilbake* (1983; Alice Longs to Go Back), in which two Norwegian children meet Alice in Wonderland in her old age and retrace her steps, finding the old rabbit hole, and so on. Thore Hansen (1942–), who has illustrated books by Bing and Bringsværd, also writes his own children's books, such as *De flygende hvalers land* (1976; Land of the Flying Whales), which introduces Bobadilla and Neseblomsten, a rhinoceros who wants a flower on his nose instead of a horn.

Among writers of children's poetry of the 1970s, the most important are Inger Hagerup (1905–85), with *Den sommeren* (1971; That Summer), illustrated by Paul Gauguin, and *Hulter til bulter* (1979; Helter Skelter); Sidsel Mørck (1937–), with *Erta Berta sukkererta* (1978); Erta Berta Sugar Pea); and Jan-Magnus Bruheim (1914–88), who published many poetry books in the 1970s.

The 1980s have been referred to as a new golden age of Norwegian children's literature. We see a move away from social realism in the direction of fantasy and experimentation, the tone is less revolutionary, and the focus is once more on the individual. Beginning in the late 1970s, children's books were included for the first time in the government book-purchasing plan, whereby one thousand copies of each new title (after the year 1988, fifteen hundred copies) are bought by the state and distributed to libraries. As has always been the case in Norwegian children's literature, many authors of literature for adults also write children's books, including Torill Brekke, Einar Økland, Mari Osmundsen, Paal-Helge Haugen, Ragnar Hovland, and Arild Nyquist.

Einar Økland (1940–), Ragnar Hovland (1952–), and Torvald Sund (1952–) represent nynorsk literature of the 1970s and 1980s, which has tended to be more formally progressive than the bokmål literature of the time. Økland and Hovland both rejected the traditional form of the novel and began experimenting with form and genre, and Sund used fantasy and fable to address issues concerning the Sami population of northern Norway.

Of bokmål authors, Arild Nyquist (1937–) is one of the most imaginative, applying nonsense and humor in his treatment of everyday problems: *Snekkerne kommer* (1978; The Carpenters Are Coming), *Da onkel Krokodille og fetter Bamse drog til byen* (1978; When Uncle Crocodile and Cousin Teddy Bear Went to Town), and *Flyvende fru Rosenkrantz* (1983; Flying Mrs. Rosenkrantz) are three of many titles.

Two other leading children's writers of the 1980s are Torill Thorstad Hauger (1943–) and Rune Belsvik (1956–). Hauger has concentrated on historical fiction, particularly the viking period, but also immigration to America. Her book *Den store Chicago-reisen* (1988; The Great Chicago Journey), coauthored with Odd S. Lovoll, won an international prize and is currently being translated into several languages. Belsvik won the International Fiction Contest for his book *Den som kysser i vinden, blæs ikkje bort aleine* (1987; Whoever Kisses in the Wind, Does Not Blow Away Alone; Eng. tr. *Kissing in the Wind*, 1989).

Books for children play an important part in the history of Norwegian literature. They have a long tradition that has remained healthy through the 1980s, and unlike adult literature, they have increased in sales and have been widely translated and sold abroad. Despite competition from television and other media, Norwegian children clearly continue to read books. Similarly, writing about children's literature has gradually become an important part of Norwegian literary criticism. A pioneer in the field was Sonja Hagemann (1898–1990), whose magisterial *Barnelitteratur i Norge* (1–3, 1965–74) inspired younger scholars such as Kari Skjønsberg, Tordis Ørjasæter, Else Breen, and Gunvor Risa. Since 1974 the annual bibliography of Norwegian literary criticism of the *Norsk litterær årbok* (Norwegian Literary Yearbook) has included a section devoted to Norwegian children's literature, since 1977 a Norwegian yearbook of children's literature (*Norsk årbok for barne- og ungdomslitteratur*) has been published, and in 1979 a national institute for Norwegian children's literature (Norsk institutt for barnelitteratur) was established. For scholars wishing to conduct studies in the history of Norwegian children's literature, the Norwegian College of Library Science has put out a great number of specialized retrospective bibliographies.

Norwegian Women Writers

Faith Ingwersen

9

Some modern scientists who have tried to determine what particular abilities are inherent in the sexes have stressed women's greater aptitude with language (ideas and the abstract?) than with the adventurous and their greater preoccupation with interrelationships than with competitive fields of activity. If females have such innate predilections, there is reason to expect them to be excellent speakers and writers. They would understand the interaction between the artist and the public, as well as the art of characterization in works of fiction. And yet it is exactly the use of language that many modern women authors have felt alienated from, whether it is grammar's stress on gender (in which the female finds herself encompassed by the male: "man"kind) or the artistry to tell a story that would win plaudits for both its subject matter and its style.

How has the art of language been wrested from its rightful—its inherent—owners? Why have women not used it to their overwhelming advantage? Have they tried? How successful have they been? Are they truly renewing language in meaningful ways? When they have written, who have they been, and have they chosen to write poetry, drama, or novels? Have they preferred realism, romanticism, or modernism—or have they largely ignored male notions of the *Zeitgeist*? Do women have that particular aptitude for language, or is it awarded them as a scientific second prize, with masculine curiosity and competitiveness winning the species's blue ribbon? Or has female expression been banned by religious tradition, so that women, like children, may be seen but not heard? And if heard, not listened to?

Camilla Collett, Norway's first great feminist writer, wrote in *Mod strømmen* (1879; Against the Current) that women themselves had to stand up against their systematized oppression. Whether this oppression took the form of rape, abuse, violence, or injustice, women had to have a sacred wrath and prosecute unhesitatingly that immorality for its humiliation of them—thereby defeating its system of useless segregation, freeing themselves from all bonds, and scorning any situation in which they might be treated with less dignity than they had warranted.

A three-volume history of Norwegian women authors has recently (1990) been completed (see bibliography). Its editors, perhaps voicing the majority opinion of Norwegian feminist/female/feminine critics, found it prudent and necessary for such a separate account to be made available to reeducate the public about women's contribution to Norwegian letters. The editors, who believe there is a risk of creating a female "ghetto," also maintain that the ways authors formulate their works artistically depend partially on gender-related experiences. Hence one may speak of a somewhat alternative women's culture, and a study of the female author's situation must take place in order to revaluate her works, which hitherto have usually been either neglected or misrepresented. The study of Norwegian women artists is one that records a good many tragedies and some successes. Among the tragedies was the realization, repeated in endless variations, that the long struggle had rarely led to a desired state of self-determined personal freedom, a sufficient access to education, or an achievement of creative recognition. Among the triumphs is an eloquent and sophisticated feminist criticism that has brought the history of women writers out into the open and has increased the possibilities for women's self-understanding and, thus, for the attainment of their desired goals.

If the position of Collett's women in the 1870s still has much in common with that of women more than one hundred years later, one wonders what role the female played in the many centuries leading up to the 1870s and what changes, positive or negative, can be traced in the views held of her from the early Nordic past. There are a good many supernatural female beings known from the Old Norse Eddas and sagas: protectors of the land (dísir) or of individuals (fylgjur); weavers of fate and waterers of the world tree, Yggdrasill (nornir); and warrior maidens who chose those to be slain in battle (valkyrjur). There were goddesses who were silently all-knowing or desirably beautiful or who possessed the means of eternal youth, such as the goddess of marriage (Frigg) or of love (Freyja) or fertility (the earth mother Nerthus), or the guardian of the apples of youth (Iðunn). There were giant women who personified old age (Elli) or death (Hel), and there was the (erotically betrayed) protector of the mead of poetic inspiration and wisdom (Gunnlǫd). In addition to such supernatural or magically endowed females, there were seers (vǫlur), like the sibyl of the "Vǫluspá," a famous poem in the *Elder Edda* (which often treated women's work and experiences and—linguistically related to *óðr*, "ode"?—meant "great-grandmother"). It has been proposed that that sibyl's ultimate sinking into the earth symbolizes the final passing of women's cultural control over poetic wisdom, though not before women had created what is possibly Scandinavia's oldest literary genre and one that brought them particular honor: the "lament" (*grátr*, as in the Eddic poem "Oddrúnargrátr"), which was akin to the "incitement" to revenge in blood feuds (*hvǫt*, as in the Eddic poem "Guðrúnarhvǫt"). Along with female oral historians were the Scandinavian court poets or skalds; there are a dozen women whose names and fame as bards have survived to the present day, and some of them are Norwegian. In Snorri Sturluson's *Heimskringla* is a verse of the skald Hildr Hrolfsdóttir (ca. 900; presumed ancestor of William the Conqueror), pleading her son's case to King Harald Fairhair; and there is "Sendibítr," the longest such verse, by one Jórunn with the nickname Skáldmær or "Poet Maiden" (ca. 925). Other skaldic verses are by the sorceress Queen Gunnhild (ca. 950), who wielded power after the death of her husband, King Eirik Bloodaxe. In Old Norse times the female, natural as well as supernatural, granted and guarded life and determined death, knowledge of the future and the past, and—indirectly—of poetry.

Christianity was introduced to Scandinavia around the year 1000, and in the Church's teaching of Augustinian views, women were considered to be not only weaker than men but also of less worth. They were thought to represent the body or nature, whereas men represented the mind or spirit. During the following centuries four-fifths of those accused of witchcraft were women, and after the Reformation came to Norway in 1537, the Lutheran Church, which did not emphasize the Virgin Mary, became even more energetic than the Catholic in ridding the world of evil women and seductresses. The thinking that lay behind such actions, as well as the actions themselves, became a part of Norwegian folklore and affected society's views of women. Folklore also transmitted a positive view of them: a recent (1978) collection in English of feminist folktales includes many Norwegian examples, and the very title of the anthology is *Tatterhood*, a translation of "Lurvehette," collected by Asbjørnsen and Moe in *Norske folkeeventyr* (1852; Eng. tr. *Norwegian Folk Tales*, 1982, and others). That tale embodies an attitude found in numerous Norwegian folktales.

Tatterhood ("Mophead") is a plucky, smart, humorous woman who is deemed ugly by others but who takes charge of her own destiny and, after repeatedly proving her mettle, wins the happiness that is expected in the magic tale. "Lurvehette" and other tales provide role models by having active and resourceful female protagonists, thus contradicting the general pattern in Stith Thompson's famous *Types of the Folktale* (1961), in which the male character is assumed to be the protagonist and the female is relegated to the subordinate role of "helper." A case in point is Asbjørnsen and Moe's tale "Mestermøy," which Thompson designates Type 313 ("The Girl as Helper in the Hero's Flight"), even though it is obviously the witty, resilient woman who is the protagonist, particularly in the second part of the story. Other determined female protagonists from Asbjørnsen and Moe's collection include the spunky princess in "Finnekongens datter" (The Finn King's Daughter) and the woman who married a bear in "Kvitebjørn kong Valemon" (White Bear King Valemon). Both are initially passive women who have assented to their roles, but who rebel against ignorance and, through a *felix culpa,* become active characters fighting successfully for their own happiness.

One type of folktale, the *skjemteeventyr,* or prose fabliau, offers texts that are uniquely fit to poke more or less good-humored fun at the other sex. If, in Asbjørnsen and Moe's collection, "Giske" and "Somme kjerringer er slike" (Some Wives Are That Way) reveal glee over the stupidity of women, such tales as "Høna tripper i berget" (The Hen Is Tripping in the Mountain) and "Mannen som skulle stelle hjemme" (The Man Who Was Going to Mind the House), which expose male incompetence, take exactly the opposite view of the genders. The rich *sagn,* or legend, tradition of Norway offers similarly outstanding examples of women who, even when realizing that they must fit into their new communities—those of their spouses—do shape their own lives. The young woman in "The Girl Who Was Taken" (in O. K. Ødegaard, *Gamal tru og gamal skjikk ifraa Valdres,* 1911) is rewarded for daring to break with the restrictive social norm in a static, isolated valley community. "Gift med en hulder" (*Norsk folkeminnelags skrifter* 21, 1930; Married to a *Hulder*) suggests that the *hulder* (wood siren) must conform to her husband's community, but the text nevertheless stresses that the presence of that particular "foreigner" in the valley not only improves it but even transforms the man she marries: she is clearly deemed to be the wise person in the tale.

Many of the folktales, then, reflect that successful search for identity which is the main theme of latter-day female *Bildungsromane.* And it should be noted that Camilla Collett, author of Norway's first attempt in that genre, paid homage to folk tradition and to its existential strength. In "Eventyrsara og hendes datter" (1860; Folktale Sara and Her Daughter; Eng. tr. "Storyteller Sara," 1984), Collett recalls not only Sara's bitter fate but also her dignity and unique abilities as a storyteller and, by doing so, conjures up an image of the long procession of female storytellers who conveyed their stories to Asbjørnsen and Moe. Asbjørnsen and Moe made folklore a legitimate frame of reference for creative spirits. If the tales and legends had not been known from other sources than books, however, they would hardly have become as powerful a source of inspiration and symbolism as they did in the nineteenth century. Entirely different frames of reference dominate in the works of women from the baroque period in Norwegian literature.

Dorothe Engelbretsdatter (1634–1716) was a minister's daughter who called herself the first female poet in the realm and who was the first Norwegian author ever to get a copyright. She competed in a genre—the hymn—of which the authors were ministers, and she learned to use the baroque machinery so well that she earned the praise of the Danish master hymnist Thomas Kingo. Her two famous collections were *Siælens sang-offer* (1678; Song Offering of the Soul) and *Taare-offer* (1685; Offering of Tears), which show a soul's humility and penitence before God. It should be noted that though she bowed to her colleagues, it was by virtue of their education, not their gender. In her other poetry or rhymed epistles, she wrote quite satirically of the "trousers crowd," who accused her of plagiarism. In spite of her great popularity with the public and Kingo, many of her works were eventually considered too proper, too personal—or too vulgar—to be anthologized.

During the Age of Enlightenment, despite its general stress on reason and the promotion of women's emancipation by such writers as Ludvig Holberg, higher education remained the privilege of men, but as the eighteenth century progressed, so did the general ability to read, following the introduction of mandatory confirmation (1736), the establishment of public schools (1739, 1741), and the growth of the urban book market. Although written literature quickly became the province of men, while the oral tradition-bearers remained women of the lower classes, Protestant ministers' wives made up a group—along with the wives of the country's thousand civil servants—from which many women writers eventually were to come.

Magdalene Sophie Buchholm (1758–1825), the "Sappho of the North," was the only female writer recognized by the establishment in the latter half of the eighteenth century. She wrote some prose as well as poetry in its many subgenres (*Poesier,* 1793, 1806)—ballads, odes, elegies, cantatas, and so on—in which she describes unrequited love but preaches morality, peace, and freedom, all within a bourgeois framework. Her writing, which was typical of the age, has since fallen in esteem.

In the last years of the 1700s and as a result of the increasing national literacy, many journals appeared, and closed dramatic societies for amateur productions flourished. Birgitte Kühle (1762–1832) was Norway's first female editor. Her *Provinzial-lecture* (1794; Provincial Reading) featured translations of articles from several languages. She also wrote the earliest prologue preserved from the Bergen Drama Society, a cantata published in the year 1800. Like Kühle, Christiane Koren (1764–1815) was Danish-born. Her plays—which were not performed, but read—stressed female friendship and women's particular ability to understand and direct personal relationships, especially that of their children: typically, she has since been referred to as "Mother Koren." Koren achieved added fame more than a hundred years later through the publication of her diaries, from a trip to revisit Copenhagen in 1802 (published first in 1945) and from time spent under the shadow of the Napoleonic Wars during the years 1808–10 (published in 1915).

The Age of Enlightenment gradually gave way to romanticism, with its emphasis on feeling, nature's aesthetic variety, and the genius of the individual. Indicative of this change from the reasoned to the heartfelt were two hymnists of note, one whose works were little noticed and the other whose hymns remained popular throughout the nineteenth century: the Enlightenment hymnist Dorothea Maria Moss (1778–1851) and the Haugean hymnist Berthe Canutte Aarflot (1795–1859). Moss, whose *Psalmer og religiøse digte til huuslig opbyggelse* (Hymns and Religious Poems for Household Edification) appeared in 1840, stressed a loving God, spoke of Christ only twice in sixty-two hymns, and emphasized the divine spark within each individual. In contrast, Aarflot, in such collections as *Troens frugt* (pre-1832; The Fruits of Belief) and *Sjelens morgen- og aftenoffer* (1846; The Soul's Morning and Evening Offering), spoke of her own religious crisis and acceptance of grace, and she advised others to avoid the roar of Satan, common sense (which would block one's recourse to Christ), and love of the world, and to become a Bride of Christ. For Moss, the human being was good; for Aarflot, the human being was sinful but saved through a joyful passion for Christ.

As belles lettres spread to a wider public through lending libraries and journals and appeared as private theatrical productions, the propriety of woman's increased reading of works of "sensibility" was broadly discussed, and there were warnings of the dangers it brought to her duties and her family's well-being. Romanticism owed much of its philosophy to Rousseau (especially to his *Émile*, 1762), and some of his ideas were expounded in H. J. Birch's *Billedgalleri for fruentimmer* (1–3, 1793–95; Picture Gallery for

Women). Birch advocated strictly curtailing the desires, education, initiative, and even concentration of girls from the age of seven or eight in order to devote them more fully to the service of the male sex. Thus, women's reading of the very literature that projected the romantic to them often seemed to society to threaten their fulfillment of its ideals of service.

Camilla Collett (1813–95), after working on Asbjørnsen and Moe's *Norske folkeeventyr* (1842–44), made her debut in 1843 with a short story. Her only novel, *Amtmandens døttre* (1854–55; reedited and republished in 1879 and 1892; Eng. tr. *The District Governor's Daughters*, 1992) was first published anonymously. Collett wrote for newspapers and journals but ended her more fictional writing with *I de lange nætter* (1862; During the Long Nights), an autobiographical work. From the late 1860s to her death in 1895, she published her battle manifestoes, which appeared collectively as *Fra de stummes lejr* (1877; From the Encampment of Mutes), *Mod strømmen* (1, 1879, and 2, 1885; Against the Current), and *Sidste blade*. *Erindringer og bekjendelser* (1868, 1872, 1873; Last Pages: Remembrances and Confessions). Those works consisted of letters, poems, sketches, essays, and newspaper articles.

Collett, the sister of Henrik Wergeland, had experienced the double standard in a Rousseauean upbringing. She did not feel that women were "naturally" meant to be men's servants. In her "realistic" novel—the first in Norway and one that predated the Danish critic Georg Brandes's demand for literary realism by twenty years—she described young women who were raised to lack independence and self-assurance and who, shockingly enough, were dissatisfied with their bourgeois position in life. She later argued that society could not afford to let women's abilities and contributions go to waste and that each woman had the duty to use those abilities and make those contributions of which she was capable. The age tended to view women as madonnas who lived their lives in religious devotion, general ignorance, or personal self-sacrifice, or as whores who threatened men's minds and souls through their unchecked (uncivilized) sexuality. In contrast, Collett helped to found a female critique, especially of popular romantic novels that idealized woman's "degradation" in love affairs with Byronic/demonic lovers. Collett demanded personal moral responsibility. Each individual had to stand against the systematic injustice to which she was subjected, but she had to act with her sisters—collectively—to achieve change within society: in the difficult art of being a "female" writer, Collett clearly had her work cut out for her.

Eleven other Norwegian woman writers made their debuts shortly after Collett's. Many used local color, folklore, and nature symbolism, in works that blended genres. They all wrote, often in the first person, of heroines who belonged to civil-service families and who went through a process of *Bildung* that conformed to the age's romantic masculine ideals for femininity: self-sacrificing humility and modesty. Sexual desire, with its pursuant tragedies, was rejected by nearly all in preference for Platonic relationships. Although marriage was the heroine's usual reward, her religious awakening, a motif that mirrored the Grundtvigian revival of the 1850s, was also stressed. The heroine, in her relationship to her father, might then be portrayed as idealistic and religious—that is, accepting of, and devoted to, paternalistic authority.

Marie Wexelsen (1832–1911), who grew up in Grundtvigian surroundings, wrote novels of religious crisis; they featured repentance and self-sacrifice. Two of the best-known are *Et levnetsløb fortalt i stille timer* (1866; A Life Story Told in Quiet Hours) and *Vesle-Kari eller de forældreløse* (1858; Little Kari, or The Orphaned). Marie Colban (1814–84) began as a translator in the 1840s. After becoming a widow, she left Norway for Paris, where she lived by her pen and moved in aristocratic circles, while extolling work and self-sacrifice. Her works include *Lærerinden. En skisse* (1869; The Teacher: A Sketch) and *Jeg Lever* (1877; I Live), which was somewhat autobiographical.

Hanna Winsnes (1789–1872) made her name unforgettable by giving good housekeeping advice (1845–77) on work and conduct for maids, housekeepers, and poor housewives, as well as providing entertainment in the form of stories for those readers. She tried to give women a self-assurance through knowledge and practical accomplishments that would bring a feeling of creativity into their lives and provide them with pleasure and pride in their work. In the universe she portrayed, good work, common sense, and moral conduct brought life's rewards.

Although Winsnes wrote *Smaa-digte* (1848; Little Poems) under her own name, two novels—*Grevens datter* (1841; The Count's Daughter) and *Det første skridt* (1844; The First Step)—as well as several stories were written under the pen name Hugo Schwar(t)z. In those prose works she combined an everyday realism in description and fine characterization with the romantic tradition's action and intrigue. Her novel *Grevens datter* reflected her interest in politics as well: it was banned in Denmark for judging the freedoms given by the Norwegian Constitution of 1814 to be greater than those enjoyed by the Danes.

Interest in political affairs and historic events has often been reflected in memoirs and diaries, but most have tended to describe, usually for relatives, the cultural past, family life, and an individual's course of life. In addition to

Mother Koren's diaries—treating not only the effects of the Napoleonic Wars on Denmark, the economic difficulties of farmers, and the deaths of two of her children, but everyday life in the capital as well—we are fortunate to have the so-called letters that Conradine Dunker (1780–1866) wrote to a younger brother to describe the past, particularly the years 1780–90. She wrote about the great and the small, and she did so as colorfully as if she were writing short stories. Her memoirs were written in 1852–55, with extracts published in a magazine in 1860 and in book form in 1871. A complete edition appeared as *Gamle Dage. Erindringer og tidsbilleder* (1909; Old Days: Remembrances and Pictures of the Age). Her contribution to the genre influenced those who followed. Gustava Kielland (1800–1889), who had married a minister, dictated her memoirs when she was past eighty (published in 1883 in *Skillings-magazin* [Penny Magazine]), but she is best known for having started the first chapter of the Women's Mission Society (Kvinnemisjonsforeningen) in Norway. Elise Aubert (1837–1909) was a minister's daughter who, during the last thirty years of her life, published stories, some of them reprinted posthumously in the two-volume work *Da bestemor var ung* (1910; When Grandmother Was Young), as well as several novels. Aubert is best remembered, however, for her volume of memoirs, *Fra de gamle prestegaarde* (1902, 1909; From the Old Rectories), in which she records the daily life of her parents, her fifteen siblings, and the many guests who visited the minister's home in the mountains during the 1850s. A Norwegian minister's home on Washington Prairie, Iowa, was described by Elisabeth Koren (1832–1918), who had emigrated to America in 1853. A complete edition of her diary was translated into English and published in 1955 as *The Diary of Elisabeth Koren, 1853–1855*. Similarly, many Norwegian actresses, such as Lucie Wolf (1833–1902), Marie Bull (1827–1912), Octavia Sperati (1847–1918), and Sophie Reimers (1853–1932), published their memoirs. Most did not appear in their entirety until the twentieth century.

One of the most prominent writers of the period was the Danish-born Magdalena Thoresen (1819–1903), who belonged to quite a different social sphere and who created fiction from her experiences. She published more than twenty-five titles, in addition to numerous articles, stories, and sketches. She gave readings on the lecture circuit, and her dramas received acclaim. Her poetry collection, *Digte af en dame* (1860; Poems by a Lady), was among the first to be considered modern, in the author's refusal either to harmonize opposites or to deny female sexuality, and her *Billeder fra Midnatsolens land* (1884–86; Pictures from the Land of the Midnight Sun) was praised by Alexander Kielland (for its content) and Knut Hamsun (for its style). In dramatic short tales of common life, she treated the various aspects of North Norway—its nature, history, and culture—and that work is often cited as her best. Thoresen wanted to write of the common people in an epic Dickensian way, but as a foreigner she could not always render the spoken idiom accurately.

Thoresen suffered many losses in her life and felt in many ways an outsider with regard to the class and country to which she had come to belong. Critics have identified her with the protagonist of one of her works, *Studenten* (The Student, originally published in *Fortællinger* [1862; Tales]). This character was the first in a long line of Norwegian students—which eventually included the heroes of Garborg's *Bondestudentar* and Hamsun's *Sult*—to find themselves alone, alienated, hungry, and without hope in the big city.

In 1869 Laura Kieler (1849–1932) published her answer to Henrik Ibsen's play *Brand: Brands døtre* (Brand's Daughters), in which Brand after many years comes to believe in a forgiving savior and dies surrounded by loving daughters. Ibsen's basic model for Nora in *Et dukkehjem* (1879), Kieler, who had found herself in an almost Nora-like situation, was also assumed to be guilty of fraud, lost custody of her child, was separated from her husband, and became a patient in a mental hospital. When many years later (1891) she confronted Ibsen about his subsequent treatment of her life story, he did nothing to alleviate the situation publicly but used some of their dialogue in *Når vi døde vågner* (1899). The "Nora" scandal was followed by another, brought about by Kieler's play *Mænd af ære* (1888, publ. 1890; Men of Honor), which deals with a woman who, seduced by a critic into a free-love relationship and then abandoned, commits suicide. Kieler was unable to get the play staged in Denmark, where it was thought to portray the critic Georg Brandes. Praised by Ibsen, it was accepted for the stage in Norway in 1889.

Kieler discussed both the social and political problems of the day: the 1850s Samic revolt (fictionally in 1881) and the movement in Denmark to regain southern Jutland (journalistically in the 1890s).

Some writers of a political bent emigrated from their native country. Elise Wærenskjold (1815–95) worked for the prohibition of alcohol and drunkenness and published a pamphlet in that cause in 1843. Up to 1847 she was involved in the publication of a journal called *Norge og America* (Norway and America), and after her arrival in Texas in 1851 she joined the antislavery movement. Her letters from 1851 through 1895 were published in 1961 as *The Lady with the Pen*.

One woman who preferred emigration to the treatment she received in her native land was Aasta Hansteen (1824–1908), painter, poet, cultural critic, and champion of Norway's second language, nynorsk. Hansteen had participated in the debate brought about by Georg Brandes's translation of John Stuart Mill's *The Subjection of Women* (1869), and she campaigned against the Church's teachings on women's "place" and wrote her own book, *Kvinden skabt i Guds billede* (1872–73, publ. 1878; Woman Created in God's Image). She was the first woman to speak publicly in Norway, but her lectures led to enough unpleasantness that she spent nine years in the United States (1880–89), where she found publishing difficult. On her return to Norway she became a contributor to *Nylænde* (New Land), the new journal of the Norwegian Society for Women's Rights (Norsk Kvinde-sagsforening).

In 1871, lecturing on the day's liberal and anticlerical French, German, and English literary movements, Georg Brandes had called for a new, realistic literature that would put problems under debate. In Scandinavia the literary realism and ensuing Zolaesque naturalism of the 1870s to the 1890s came to be known by Brandes's term, "the Modern Breakthrough." Problems especially debated by women were prohibition, peace, morality between the sexes, and women's rights. Mathilde Schjøtt (1844–1926), best known as a literary critic, wrote *Venindernes samtale om kvindernes underkuelse* (1871; The Conversation of Female Friends on the Subjection of Women), and Gina Krog (1847–1916), editor of *Nylænde* from its beginning in 1887 to her death in 1916, wrote with clearly reasoned arguments for women's suffrage, the moral equality of the sexes, women's education and independence, and their attainment of gainful employment. In 1882 the first woman in Norway passed the university entrance exam, and three years later the first coeducational high school in Norway—with female teachers—was founded by Ragna Nielsen (1845–1924). By 1890 Norway had lost to America one of its first women to have a doctor's degree (from Munich): the poet and critic Agnes Mathilde Wergeland (1857–1914), who became a professor at the University of Wyoming, the state that, as a territory, was the first place in the world to give women suffrage and the rights of full citizenship (1869).

Marriage came sometimes to be viewed as a form of prostitution, and prostitution itself, legalized in 1840, and the double standard it reflected (giving rise to venereal disease as well as sadism) were greatly debated after the publication and confiscation (1885–86) of Hans Jæger's novel *Fra Kristiania-bohêmen*, which demanded "public" houses of prostitution. Ibsen's *Et dukkehjem* (1879) had already aroused discussion of women's lack of legal economic independence, and in 1888 married women were given the right of monetary majority. Another debate related to sexual freedom mainly pitted those who felt that morals for women were too strict against those who felt that morals for men were too slack. Georg Brandes and his followers, such as Amalie Skram and the authors around Jæger, made up the former group, whereas the latter was represented by Bjørnstjerne Bjørnson, one of whose plays, *En hanske* (1883; Eng. tr. *A Gauntlet,* 1886), had given title to the feud: the "Gauntlet Strife." Among those taking part in the battle were Margrete Vullum (1846–1918), who advocated trial marriages, and Hanna Andresen Butenschøn (1851–1928), who pointed out the contradiction in having sexually "experienced" men and "pure" women.

Like Hanna Butenschøn, whose novels and dramas appeared under the name of Helene Dickmar, many writers of the period used pseudonyms. Antoinette Meyn (1827–1915) made her debut in 1875 and wrote under the pseudonyms Marie and Holger Birch. Bolette (Nissen) Gjør (1835–1909), under the name Margrethe, wrote children's books and "revivalist" novels. Benedicte Karoline Mathilde Agerup (1847–1907) wrote as Mathilde. As Waldemar Steen, the lyricist Wilhelmine Gulowsen (1848–99) wrote love poems from a first-person masculine perspective. Short-story writer and novelist Elisabeth Schøyen (1852–1936), who also wrote under the name Paul Agathon, was widely popular and well traveled. She managed to live by her writing, and her historical romances, which she considered educational, were sold from door to door. Those who wrote of the "ideal"—even if they treated the themes of seduction, illegitimacy, alcohol addiction, venereal disease, and murder—became known as writers not of "literature" but of "entertainment." An author whose extremely popular works were sold in installments from door to door was novelist, editor, and first female professional journalist Karen Sundt (1841–1924). Her eight-hundred-page works were often set within a historical frame, her love stories crossed class lines, and her plots were filled with mystery. Sundt, who was not acceptable to the critics but was much admired by the lower classes, was a Grundtvigian, a radical, and an educator of the public. She sought also to treat women's place in history, under the law, and in the workplace in *Kvinden i det private og offentlige liv. Et praktisk indlæg i kvindespørsmålet* (1890; Woman in Private and Public Life: A Practical Contribution to the Women's Question). In a contemporary novel, *Dagny* (1882), by Elise Aubert, the heroine manages to become self-supportive, as Aubert deemed any honorable young woman would. Not only should young women be educated and conscientious in their work, but the divisions between the classes, detrimental even to widows of the bourgeoisie, ought to be recognized as artificial.

An author who was not popular with the public but who set the most lasting mark on the literature of the 1880s and 1890s was Amalie Skram

(1846–1905). She grew up in Bergen, where her family experienced a good deal of economic hardship. At the age of seventeen she married a sea captain, spent ten years at sea, had children, divorced, entered a mental hospital, then in 1884 married again, moved to Copenhagen, had another child, again spent time in a mental hospital after a nervous breakdown, in 1899 again divorced—and wrote. She had begun writing in the 1870s. Her novel of life at sea, *To venner* (1887; Two Friends), is considered one of the best on the topic in Norwegian literature. Her debut novel, *Constance Ring* (1885; Eng. tr. 1988)—one of the so-called novels of marriage—treated alienation and a loss of identity on the part of the protagonist, whose dream of true love is destroyed by the reality of men's infidelity. Because it dealt with the double standard and female sexuality, the novel caused a scandal and had, finally, to be printed at the author's expense. The novel *Forraadt* (1892; Eng. tr. *Betrayed*, 1987) contains some autobiographical details from Skram's first marriage, but its point is that both husband and wife are "deceived" by expectations that cannot be realized. Skram wrote two novels about her stays in mental hospitals, the shocking *Professor Hieronimus* (1895; Eng. tr. 1899)—registering complaints about the head doctor's regime and his dictatorial treatment of (especially female) patients—and *Paa St. Jørgen* (1895; Eng. tr. *Under Observation* [*Professor Hieronimus* and *Paa St. Jørgen*], 1992). A naturalistic four-volume family novel, *Hellemyrsfolket* (The People of Hellemyr)—consisting of *Sjur Gabriel* (1887), *To venner* (1887), *S. G. Myre* (1890), and *Afkom* (1898; Offspring)—is considered her finest work. The novel treats a fisherman's family that falls further and further into destitution and drunkenness, their faith in heavenly Providence destroyed. When patriarchal power is gone, the family no longer has the strength to overcome adversity. The work, containing dialogue in rustic Norwegian, is illustrative of a degeneracy stemming not only from heredity and environment, which naturalism found so common, but also from individual free choice. Skram's truths, so hard to accept at the time, have secured at last some recognition of her accomplishments. The "novel of disillusionment" had other, less Darwinistic or Zolaesque adherents than Skram, among them Skram's close friend Drude Krog Janson (1846–1934). Janson, under the name Judith Keller, wrote *Mira. Et livsløb* (1897; Mira: The Course of a Life), in which she autobiographically mirrored—rather shockingly—her former married state to the Minneapolis Unitarian minister Kristofer Janson, himself a writer.

In 1888 the Danish critic and literary trendsetter Georg Brandes, introducing the philosophy of Friedrich Nietzsche, had spoken about an "Aristocratic Radicalism." He helped to set literature off in a new direction, one that stressed the individual and the subjective rather than the collective and the politically/tendentiously realistic. Women who had written in the previous decade now found themselves outside the mainstream. The "artistic" was stressed above all, and the debate on women's rights and women's roles was gladly abandoned by indignant male writers of the age—like Garborg—who had found it both tiring and tiresome. Women's literature had remained "too romantic" during realism's official stage, and their literature was too tendentious in its realism during the age of what came to be known in Norway as neoromanticism.

At the end of the 1890s the Swede Ellen Key, influenced by Strindberg, Max Nordau, and Nietzsche, voiced ideas that were to be particularly influential throughout the next thirty to forty years. In 1896 she published *Missbrukad kvinnokraft* (Women's Misused Strength) and *Naturenliga arbetsområden för kvinnan* (Natural Areas of Work for Women), and two years later *Kvinnopsykologi och kvinnlig logik* (Women's Psychology and Women's Logic). It has been pointed out that Key accepted a basic natural difference between men and women in which biological processes determined their spiritual characteristics. Therefore, they were thought "naturally" to have separate, but "equal," spheres of occupation and concern. Love and motherhood—in the concrete sense of caring for society's needs of consoling, helping, nursing, and educating others—made up women's domain, whereas the material and the intellectual—that is, spheres dealing with research, religion, government, freedom, humanity, and art—made up men's domain. Since each area demanded all one's strength, to ask woman, as the feminists did, to be men's equals in areas deemed to be under male purview was to ask them to be "superwomen." Women's failure to devote all their time and energy to developing loving, gentle feelings would lead to sexual brutality and to the undermining of society and the end of humanity. Feminists would arouse men's hatred of women and of one class for another. Key thought women should be responsible priestesses of love for the sake of humanity. As wives and mothers they might have some kind of part-time or extra work in the home (an idea that was agreeable to some industries with unorganized labor), but economic matters were to be left in the hands of men.

Laura Marholm (= Laura Mohr), an influential antifeminist German critic and author living in Sweden, claimed that women and "the masses" were alike and that institutions or tendencies (such as feminism) that enhanced their individualism ought to be leveled. Feminists were led by "old maids" who could not be rational, but only bitter and self-righteous, in their governance. In "real" women, a wildness still existed—and a longing to be "women," to forget themselves in order to raise a new generation of men.

Internationally, women of the age were already bringing to the fore, debating, and becoming divided over what are now considered modern problems, such as equal pay for equal work, the need for preventive measures to limit the number of children being born out of wedlock, the right of a woman to control her own body and reproduction through abortion, and the rights of the abused, the illegitimate, and the unborn, and so on. In Scandinavia the earlier feminists' attempts to raise men's morals were forgotten, but Key's and Marholm's "utopian" (or "un-" and "anti-") feminist ideas would eventually discredit numerous feminists whom they had helped to brand in the public mind as frigid puritans, prudish Victorians, or society-destroying, free-love radicals.

Strong women who cared for their families and the land—in keeping with some of Key's ideas—began to make their appearance in novels primarily reflecting rural life. Alvilde Prytz (1846–1922), who stressed the need for education, published poetry, essays, plays, short stories, and fourteen novels, of which *Gunvor Thorsdatter til Hærø* (1896; Eng. tr. *The Heart of the Northern Sea*, 1907) was the most widely read. Prytz wrote lyrically of nature and about women whose strength (based in love) seemed akin to that of the women of the sagas. They find that living up to their ideals is what gives life its meaning. Dikken Zwilgmeyer (1853–1913) has a similarly strong character in her novel *Emerentze* (1906), whose protagonist married for the chance to exercise her own abilities through power and property. Hulda Garborg (1862–1934) tended to view the home with children as having mythic/mystical importance and saw women as all-loving of their spouses and—like the earth—as being the strength of generations. Her four Hedemark books, beginning with *Mens dansen går* (1920; While the Dance Goes On), of a matriarchy similar to Prydz's and Zwilgmeyer's, all appeared in the 1920s. In 1904, however, she had written *Kvinden skabt af manden* (The Woman Created by Man), a widely discussed book on women's sexuality, prompted by Otto Weininger's *Geschlecht und Charakter* (1903; Eng. tr. *Sex and Character*, 1906), which recommends that women be eliminated as priestesses of the misery that is sexuality. Garborg, who wrote most of her books in nynorsk, should also be remembered for her work as a dramatist and theater director: she was one of the driving forces behind the establishment of a nynorsk theater in Oslo (Det Norske Teatret, 1912–).

Among the authors who can be said to employ the 1890s *Jugend* style—using the aesthetic, the fantastic, and the descriptive language of nature or symbols—was Ragnhild Jølsen (1875–1908). In *Rikka Gan* (1904), a farm is again used as a major symbol; the characters, with their farms, are bound together through the crises they are undergoing, crises that in

Jølsen's universe take the form of a battle between good and evil, affection and enslavement to eroticism. The problems of the artist can be glimpsed in Jølsen's work, and they seem even more pronounced in the work of Dagny Juel Przybyszewska (1867–1901), a muse of the artists' circles in Berlin and Krakow. She wrote thirteen poems (first published in 1875) and, from 1893 to 1897, four expressionistic plays heavily laden with the flower and bird symbols loved by the 1890s. Hers were dramas concerning the erotic triangle, the love of two women for the same man. One of the play's characters is killed, and the result is depression, isolation, and even madness. Nevertheless, power, which cannot remain innocent, is achieved through sexuality. Although *Synden* (1898; The Sin), *Når solen går ned* (1899; When the Sun Goes Down), and *Ravnegård* (1902; Ravenwood) all appeared in Czech or Polish editions, only *Den sterkere* (1896; The Stronger) appeared in Norwegian before 1978. The murder of Dagny Juel Przybyszewska and the early death of Ragnhild Jølsen marked an end to the literati's femmes fatales—women admired as physically and mentally stimulating, but whose talents were, or came to be, overlooked. In addition to Jølsen's work, the fictional strain of the fantastic continued in such novels as *Dengang*— (1912; Then—), by Regine Normann (1867–1939), and *Jomfruen* (1914), by Barbra Ring (1870–1955), both of whom use folklore and folk belief to write of a particular region. Normann wrote of Nordland and its social ills; Ring, a journalist and widely known children's author, wrote thirty-five works for adults and emphasized family traditions and roots in one's relationship to the earth.

Marriage between people who simply do not belong together and the resulting problems for their children are themes not only in Ring's work but in some of the writings—such as *Jenny* (1911; Eng. tr., 1921) and the trilogy on the Middle Ages *Kristin Lavransdatter* (1920–22; Eng. tr. 1923–27)— of Sigrid Undset (1882–1949), winner of the Nobel Prize in 1928 and Norway's most famous female writer. The artist Jenny leaves her fiancé for his father, leaves him as well, and—after she loses her baby—kills herself. The book was criticized by feminists, but for Undset, nature had determined sexual differences and, as in the Christian family, made women subject to men. Erotic love was dangerous because it was illusory; it was not born of responsibility but broke rules and caused suffering. "Motherliness" was, however, "life" itself; *De kloge jomfruer* (1918; The Wise Virgins) and *Ida Elisabeth* (1932; Eng. tr. 1933) were particularly illustrative of that theme. Undset's works have been translated into seventy languages.

The more liberal Nini Roll Anker (1873–1942), a friend of Undset's, wrote thirty longer works between 1909 and 1942. Among them were novels, short stories, and plays. A few of the novels were written under the name of Kåre P. Works by Anker included the themes of workers' unrest, divorce, pacifism, and religious sectarianism. Best known are *Det svake kjøn* (1915; The Weaker Sex) and the "Stampe" trilogy (1923–27), about a family in the legal profession from the 1840s to World War I. The latter began with *Huset i Søgaten* (1923; The House on Lake Street).

It was said by the critic Helene Lassen in 1914 that, with Jølsen and the advent of Normann, Anker, and Undset, there was no longer "ladies' literature"; thereafter there was only "literature" (see bibliography under Lassen). Several women writers in the 1920s did write in a general way about life in Norway's small hamlets and parishes, which were described as the centers of true Norwegian values. Ingeborg Møller (1878–1964), a regional and cultural historian of note, wrote trilogies in the 1920s and 1930s and in one of them treated a period from the 1740s up through the twentieth century. Gro Holm (1878–1951), who wrote in nynorsk, published three volumes on "the people of Løstøl." The works deal with the late 1800s and lives so difficult that they often lead to emigration. The novels of Åsta Holth (1904–), also in nynorsk, describe the hard life of the Finnish families living in the border area between Norway and Sweden. Drudgery was also a theme for Magnhild Haalke (1885–1984). Her trilogy about Gry (1936–41) concerns a woman whose endless tasks and oppressive mother have imposed on her a form of slavery. Gry, though a strong woman, is never able to leave the family farm. Ingeborg Refling Hagen (1895–1989) wrote expressionistic novels, such as *Loke saar havre* (1922; Loki Sows Oats), that often criticized her region's pervasive material and spiritual poverty. In her well-known poetry collection, *Jeg vil hem att* (1932; I Want to Go Home Again), however, she nevertheless treated the "emigrant of necessity's" longing to return.

More than forty collections of poetry by women appeared in the decade between 1929 and 1939, and once again—like Magdalena Thoresen and Dagny Juel Przybyszewska before them—female poets had to struggle to establish their own voices as poetic subjects rather than traditional objects of male consciousness. Well known as an opera and lieder singer and as a theater director and actress, Cally Monrad (1879–1950) made her debut in 1913 with *Digte* (Poems). With eight collections of poetry, she was the most productive female poet in the early part of the century. She showed her versatility in *Con amore* (1924), which contains reflective *rimbrev* (letters in rhyme) as well as passionate love poetry. "Zinken Hopp" (Signe Marie Brochmann, 1905–87) published six collections of poetry between 1929 and 1938. She was superb in her sense of rhyme and rhythm and wrote anecdotally, humorously, and ironically—in the international style of light verse.

Of continued renown are two nynorsk poets. Aslaug Vaa (1889–1965) wrote of a longing for both independence and togetherness. She made her debut with *Nord i leite* (1934; In the North) and by the war's end had published six more collections. Vaa is not only one of Norway's major women lyricists, but also a dramatist of note. Halldis Moren Vesaas (1907–) began with *Harpe og dolk* (1929; Harp and Dagger). She, too, had written six more collections by the war's end. Confident of her personal and sexual identity, she added a new dimension to the content of Norwegian poetry: love's "we" and the expectant and creative joy of childbearing give poetry its voice. The bokmål poet Inger Hagerup (1905–85), who debuted with *Jeg gikk meg vill i skogene* (1939; I Lost My Way in the Woods), wrote of the "unheard" language spoken in a woman's heart and thereby created a line that was to become the title of an anthology of critical studies of women writers: *Et annet språk* (1977; Another Language).

With a somewhat wider presentation of Sigmund Freud's theories into Norway in the mid-1920s, several writers at last found labels for the mental and emotional states they were describing. Borghild Krane (1906–), a psychiatrist herself, depicted, in *Følelsers forvirring* (1937; Confusion of Feelings), the loneliness and rejection of the homosexual and, in *Tre unge kvinner* (1938; Three Young Women), a young woman's prostitution of herself for money to use for her studies. Cora Sandel (Sara Fabricius, 1880–1974), who spent many years in France and Italy, knew and used the settings at home and abroad for her "Alberta" trilogy: *Alberte og Jacob* (1926; Eng. tr. *Alberta and Jacob,* 1962), *Alberte og friheten* (1931; Eng. tr. *Alberta and Freedom,* 1963), and *Bare Alberte* (1939; Eng. tr. *Alberta Alone,* 1965). Alberta grows up in the civil-servant milieu of Tromsø. In her home, joyless and needy, traditional thinking allows her brother an education, but not her. She goes to Paris, starts to write, and finds that she is pregnant. In the end, Alberta leaves her six-year-old son behind with his grandmother and goes off to resume writing. Sandel herself treated women whose experiences often seemed to circle back on themselves, leading nowhere. Their brief moments of happiness and their sometimes desperate plights were largely determined by their sex, but as Freudian theory suggests, Alberta's early experiences—particularly in her relationship with her mother—were also extremely formative. Among Sandel's other works are several short stories and a novel, *Kranes konditori* (1945; Eng. tr. *Krane's Café,* 1968), realistically depicting the workings of a narrow-minded society.

The amount of literature published in Norway diminished during the war years, and in 1945 a great number of writers had manuscripts ready for publication. Among the new names was short-story writer and novelist Torborg Nedreaas (1906–87), whose *Bak skapet står øksen* (1945; The Ax Is Behind the Cupboard) is a collection of tales of everyday life during the German occupation, tales that show compassion for women of the lower classes or in a position of weakness. Perhaps Nedreaas's best-known work is the "Herdis" trilogy: *Trylleglasset* (1950; The Magic Prism), *Musikk fra en blå brønn* (1960; Eng. tr. *Music from a Blue Well*, 1988), and *Ved neste nymåne* (1971; By the Next New Moon). The novels/short stories bring the young Herdis face to face with society's disturbing demands. Nedreaas's Herdis is to the immediate postwar era what Alberta was to the period between the wars.

Ebba Haslund (1917–), a prominent feminist, is the author of twelve novels, a stage play, two collections of short stories, six children's books, and four radio plays. In *Drømmen om Nadja* (1956; The Dream of Nadja), she portrayed a young woman's sexual problems (induced by trauma during puberty). Later works have questioned the guiding family values in the modern state and have tried to expose the price one pays to live up to gender roles. In the novel *Torso* (1952), by Solveig Christov (1918–84), the meta-literary preface describes "living on the edge." Her novels deal, often allegorically, with the tensions of personal and international responsibility and guilt, and difficult ethical choices. Bergljot Hobæk Haff (1925–)—author of *Raset* (1956; The Landslide), *Heksen* (1974; The Witch), and other novels—writes about witches, whores, and wise women and has described her works as modern myths, recounted in a taut, dramatic-poetic formal language that contains elements of absurd humor. While Christov and Haff were projecting speculations about life into an abstract future, Vera Henriksen (1927–) projected hers into a distant past. *Sølvhammeren* (1961; The Silver Hammer) was the first work in a trilogy from the time of St. Olav and encompassed the country's battle between Christianity and paganism and the heroine's struggle with guilt and repentance. Ragnhild Magerøy (1920–), whose first book, *Gunhild,* appeared in 1957, is also known for her historical novels and for her realistic treatment of a woman's sexual conflicts. She shares this last quality with the poet Marie Takvam (1926–), who writes in nynorsk, semiautobiographically and in traditionally rhymed verse. In addition to drama and novels, and essays on subjects of interest to women, she has published poetry on social and political problems. Less political, more personal, and darkly intense is the poetry of Gunvor Hofmo (1921–), who has published seventeen collections since 1946.

During the late 1960s women again began to question the validity of gender roles. International student protest and the hippie movement, as well as the sexual revolution made possible by new birth-control methods, raised women's consciousness concerning the roles they were to play in the new era. Small new women's groups, mostly from the middle class or institutions of higher education, began to form in protest against the possibility of Norway's joining the European Community (EC), and by 1972 they had established Kvinnefronten (The Women's Front). Those women expressed their concerns not only in demonstrations and meetings but also in newspapers, journals, and books, and as they sought and assumed leading roles, the Key-Marholm ideal of women's willing subjugation to men at last seemed to give way.

Vigdis Stokkelien (1934–), who did not belong to the academic middle class, was one of the first women in Norway to become a naval officer. Her experiences from the sea figure in her novels and short stories about social and political issues. In *Båten under solseilet* (1982; The Boat beneath the Awning), she tells her readers what it means for a woman to hold a traditionally male job. Bjørg Vik (1935–), since her debut in 1963, has written numerous short stories, some plays, and one novel, and she has been active in the feminist movement. Vik's cast of characters is wide; her protagonists are of all ages, from various classes, and of both sexes. She often focuses on the devastating demands that societal or sexual roles cause one person to place on another or to try to shoulder alone; in doing so, she explores the problems of freedom and personal development in the face of commitment. Among her best-known works are *Kvinneakvariet* (1972; Eng. tr. *An Aquarium of Women,* 1987) and *En håndfull lengsel* (1979; A Handful of Longing; Eng. tr. *Out of Season,* 1983).

Two social critics are Karin Sveen (1949–) and Tove Nilsen (1952–). Sveen has published several poetry collections, a volume of short stories, and the modern fairy tale *Utbryterdronninga* (1982; Queen of the Breakout). Her themes concern working-class women in postwar Norway, mother-daughter relationships, the effect of class discrimination, and the challenging of oppression. Nilsen, from Oslo's east side, has portrayed its working-class milieu in novels and short stories about unemployment, delinquency, and attitudes toward abortion and homosexuality.

Among several other writers making their debuts in the 1970s, Kari Bøge (1950–) writes in her "Viviann" tetralogy (1974–88) of a woman's view of herself, her needs, and her demands. Liv Køltzov (1945–) has dealt with the conditions that limit women's lives. *Historien om Eli* (1975; The Story of Eli) is a novel of self-discovery told in a terse, everyday style. In 1981 Herbjørg Wassmo (1942–) published the first volume of her "Tora" trilogy, *Huset med den blinde glassveranda* (Eng. tr. *The House with the Blind Glass Windows,* 1987), concerning the child of a now-dead soldier of the German occupation forces in Norway. Although sexually abused by her stepfather, Tora sustains herself through fantasies. Her ultimately tragic story is continued in *Det stumme rommet* (1983; The Mute Room) and *Hudløs himmel* (1986; Sensitive Sky). For this last novel, Wassmo won the Nordic Council's literary prize. In Wassmo's massive novel *Dinas bok* (1989; Dina's Book), which is also innovative in form, she created a new female ideal, a woman strangely androgynous and both frightening and appealing. Professor, poet, short-story writer, and novelist Sissel Lie (1942–) writes, often metaliterarily and with immediacy, intensity, and urgency, of the nature of the erotic—the "weretiger"—in the twenty-three wryly ironic stories that make up *Tigersmil* (1986; Smile of the Tiger).

Two women authors whose works in theme and composition illustrate the questions raised at the beginning of this chapter are Cecilie Løveid (1951–) and Karin Moe (1945–). Løveid, who has published six works of prose, in *Sug* (1979; Suck; Eng. tr. *Sea Swell*, 1986), a title that alludes to both longing and nurturing, experiments with a combination of prose and poetry that defies genre definition. In expressionistic language it depicts its protagonist's struggle for self-realization. *Måkespisere* (1983; Eng. tr. *Seagull Eaters*, 1989) is a collection of works for radio and theater in which dramatic dialogue is added to the poetry/prose combination. Although Løveid's fragmented texts, filled with eroticism, humor, irony, dreams, unexpected associations, and elements of the absurd, are usually held together by character development, *Fanget villrose* (1977; Captured Wild Rose) depends on the unity of style and theme. Moe, writing in nynorsk, combines poetry with prose, and a linguistic playfulness with "fémininité's" politics and humor. Inspired by French feminist theory, she called her first book *Kjønnskrift* (1980; the word means "Sexscript" or "Gendersymbol" but has overtones of "Skjønnskrift" = Calligraphy or "Aestheticwriting.") Since gender and writing stand in an intimate relationship to each other, Moe tries to use a specifically female language to express special feminist concerns. The title of her third and fourth books pun with those concerns: the first with word gender, *Kyka* (1984; Cockette [feminine form of *kuk* = cock]), and the second with connotations, *Mordatter* (1985; "Motherdaughter" or "Murderagain," depending on how the word is divided). When the subtitle, *Opp(dikt) fra datterskapet* [Released (Lies) from Daughterhood, or The Daughter Closest], is added, one almost expects an algebraic relationship.

Like most literature, Norwegian women's literature is about love and about power—but in this case, the attaining of power over oneself, in the form of either self-control or the control of one's own selfhood. The goal is to achieve the self-assurance that is the love of self. Lacking such control, women of the past have seemingly always tried to express their need and dissatisfaction in two forms (for which one might rashly appropriate the descriptive terms from Old Norse mentioned earlier): the lament or the incitement. One could ascribe to them a broader distinction. What might be called the lament tries mournfully to accept the status quo, that is, the "separate but equal" status, which usually means a subjugation of the one to the other. The incitement wants things to be changed, wrongs to be righted—for oneself and one's entire sisterhood—and it demands "full integration" into the dominant power structure. To what degree the numerous poets and prose writers generally reflect one or the other of these stances—and it is undoubtedly a matter of expediency or of education—remains to be investigated. The many memoirists of an earlier time have given way to novelists writing fictionalized autobiographies (often in the form of trilogies) about the development of a young female (who may now be from the lower classes). Her life is a struggle against an entrapment by biological needs or by society's gender roles. Her strength must usually lie in some form of self-denial—whether giving up the love of a weak man, the care of a child, the approbation of the family, or even a longed-for position in society.

If one may judge from the examples of Løveid and Moe, women authors now "want it all": love and freedom expressed in a combination of genres, of the realistic and the absurd, and in a language that refuses to be pinned down but must be carefully listened to, a language that requires the reader's full attention and creative cooperation. In Norwegian literature, such cooperation has existed before—and should today—between authors and other members of the literary establishment. The poet/novelist Eva Jensen (1955–), in *Teori nok for eit kort liv. Roman-roman* (1987; Theory Enough for a Short Life: Novel-Novel), a work in nynorsk, has declared that one attempts to understand oneself and life through language and that the poet's calling of things by another name can furnish control over them and make them comprehensible, important, or even beautiful. The poet may have "theory" but needs "method," since reality can affect poetry in painful and dangerous ways. Each person is defined by what she does, but—one might "metaphorically" warn—though one dances for a refreshing rain, it may be radioactive. A great many women authors and critics have tried through language to refresh and renew the perception of women, and the writers and critics of the 1970s and 1980s have at last found ways and means to make their mark on the collective consciousness. If they have succeeded in modifying the literary environment—and not merely in isolating women's writing in a non-contaminating addendum to the study of literature—it will not be necessary again to "rediscover" either women's ever-recurring battles for self-determination or their many literary contributions. Whatever may be said about women's special facility with language, women's literature of the future may depict fewer of life's martyrs and many more of its conquering heroines, unless—as seems possible—women writers will always be not only too optimistic in their realism, but also too pessimistic in their idealism to fit fully into whatever fashion happens to be current.

Bibliography

ABBREVIATIONS

Edda: *Edda*. Oslo, 1914–.
FFC: *Folklore Fellows Communications*. Helsinki, 1910–.
NLÅ: *Norsk litterær årbok*. Oslo, 1966–.
Norseman: *Norwegian Literature*. Oslo, 1990–. Special issues of *The Norseman*.
NTW: *News from the Top of the World*. Oslo: Information Office for Norwegian Literature Abroad (NORLA), 1988–.
RNL: *Norway. Review of National Literatures* 12. Ed. Sverre Lyngstad. New York: Griffon House, 1983.
Scan: *Scandinavica*. Norwich, England, 1962–.
SR: *Scandinavian Review* (until 1975, *American-Scandinavian Review*). New York, 1913–.
SS: *Scandinavian Studies*. Madison, Wis., 1911–.
WITS: *Wisconsin Introductions to Scandinavia*. Madison: University of Wisconsin Dept. of Scandinavian Studies, 1981–.
WLT: *World Literature Today* (formerly *Books Abroad*). Norman, Okla., 1927–.

General References

NATIONAL BIBLIOGRAPHY

RETROSPECTIVE
Dahl, Willy. *Nytt norsk forfatterleksikon*. Oslo: Gyldendal, 1971.
Grønland, Erling. *Norway in English*. Oslo: Norwegian Universities Press, 1961.
Halvorsen, J. B. *Norsk forfatter-lexikon 1814–1880*. 6 vols. Oslo: 1885–1908.
Hoberman, John. "Bibliographical Spectrum." RNL 185–207.

Kvamme, Janet. *Index Nordicus: A Cumulative Index to English-Language Periodicals on Scandinavian Studies.* Boston: G. K. Hall, 1980.

Næss, Harald. *Norwegian Literary Bibliography 1956–1970.* Oslo: Universitetsforlaget, 1976.

Ng, Maria, and Michael Batts, comps. *Scandinavian Literature in English Translation.* Vancouver: Canadian Association of University Teachers of German, 1978.

Øksnevad, Reidar. *Norsk litteraturhistorisk bibliografi 1900–1945* and *Norsk litteraturhistorisk bibliogafi 1946–1955.* Oslo: Gyldendal, 1951 and 1958.

Pettersen, Hjalmar. *Bibliotheca Norvegica.* 4 vols. Oslo: 1899–1924.

Sather, Leland B. *Norway.* World Bibliographical Series no. 67. Oxford: Clio Press, 1986.

CURRENT

Norsk bokfortegnelse. Utarbeidet ved Universitetsbiblioteket i Oslo. Norske avdeling. 1814–.

"Bibliografi over norsk litteraturforsking." *NLÅ* (1966–).

LITERATURE IN ENGLISH TRANSLATION

Forestier, Auber, and Rasmus B. Anderson, eds. *The Norway Music Album.* Boston: Oliver Ditson, 1881. [Translations of folk songs and art songs from Bjerregaard to Bjørnson.]

Hanson, Katherine, ed. *An Everyday Story: Norwegian Women's Fiction.* Seattle: Seal Press, 1984. [Collett to Karin Moe.]

McFarlane, James, ed. *Slaves of Love and Other Norwegian Short Stories.* Oxford: Oxford University Press, 1982. [Bjørnson to Solstad.]

Ørbeck, Anders, ed. *Norway's Best Stories.* New York: American-Scandinavian Foundation, 1927. [Bjørnson to Undset.]

Stork, C. W., ed. *Anthology of Norwegian Lyrics.* Princeton, N.J.: American-Scandinavian Foundation, 1942. [Welhaven to Grieg.]

LITERARY HISTORY

Beyer, Edvard, ed. *Norges litteraturhistorie.* 6 vols. Oslo: Cappelen, 1974–75.

Beyer, Harald. *A History of Norwegian Literature.* Trans. and ed. Einar Haugen. New York: American-Scandinavian Foundation, 1956.

Beyer, Harald, and Beyer, Edvard. *Norsk litteraturhistorie.* Oslo: Aschehoug, 1978.

Brøndsted, Mogens, ed. *Nordens litteratur.* 2 vols. Oslo: Gyldendal, 1972.

Howitt, William, and Howitt, Mary. *The Literature and Romance of Northern Europe.* 2 vols. London: Colburn, 1852.

Lyngstad, Sverre, ed. *Norway. RNL.*

McFarlane, James. *Ibsen and the Temper of Norwegian Literature.* London: Oxford University Press, 1960.

HISTORY AND CIVILIZATION

Derry, T. K. *A History of Modern Norway.* Oxford: Oxford University Press, 1973.
Larsen, Karen. *A History of Norway.* Princeton, N.J.: American-Scandinavian Foundation, 1948.
Nordstrom, Byron, ed. *The Dictionary of Scandinavian History.* Westport, Conn.: Greenwood Press, 1986.
Popperwell, Ronald. *Norway.* Nations of the Modern World. London: Ernest Benn, 1972.

Chapter Bibliographies

CHAPTER 1: OLD NORWEGIAN LITERATURE

GENERAL

Bekker-Nielsen, Hans. *Old Norse-Icelandic Studies: A Select Bibliography.* Toronto Medieval Bibliographies 1. Toronto: University of Toronto Press, 1967.
Clover, Carol, and John Lindow. *Old Norse-Icelandic Literature: A Critical Guide.* Islandica 45. Ithaca, N.Y., and London: Cornell University Press, 1985.
Foote, Peter, and David M. Wilson. *The Viking Achievement: The Society and Culture of Early Medieval Scandinavia.* London: Sidgwick and Jackson, 1970.
Haugen, Einar. *The Scandinavian Languages: An Introduction to Their History.* London: Faber and Faber, 1976.
Kalinke, Marianne E., and P. M. Mitchell. *Bibliography of Old Norse-Icelandic Romances.* Islandica 44. Ithaca, N.Y., and London: Cornell University Press, 1985.
Kristjánsson, Jónas. *Eddas and Sagas: Iceland's Medieval Literature.* Trans. Peter Foote. Reykjavík: Hið Íslenska bókmenntafélag, 1988.
Lindow, John, Lars Lönnroth, and Gerd Wolfagang Weber, eds. *Structure and Meaning in Old Norse Literature: New Approaches to Textual Analysis and Literary Criticism.* The Viking Collection: Studies in Northern Civilization, vol. 3. Odense: Odense University Press, 1986.

ANTHOLOGIZED SOURCES

Krause, Wolfgang, with contributions by Herbert Jankuhn. *Die Runeninschriften im älteren Futhark.* Abhandlungen der Akademie der Wissenschaften in Göttingen, Phil.-hist. Kl., 3d ser., no. 65. Göttingen: Vandenhoeck and Ruprecht, 1966.
Monumenta historica Norvegiae: Latinske kildeskrifter til Norges historie i middelalderen. Ed. Gustav Storm. Christiania: Kildeskriftfondet, 1880; rpt. Oslo: Kjeldeskriftfondet, 1973.
Norges innskrifter med de yngre runer. 6 vols. to date. Oslo: Kjeldeskriftfondet, 1941–60, 1980–.

LITERATURE IN ENGLISH TRANSLATION

Corpus Poeticum Boreale. Ed. and trans. S. Vigfússon and F. York Powell. 2 vols. Oxford: Oxford University Press, 1883.

Duggals leiÞsla. Ed. and trans. Peter Cahill. Stofnun Árna Magnússonar a Íslandi, Rit, 25. Reykjavík: Stofnun Árna Magnússonar, 1983.

The Earliest Norwegian Laws, Being the Gulathing Law and the Frostathing Law. Trans. Laurence M. Larson. New York: Columbia University Press, 1935.

Erex Saga and Ívens Saga. Trans. Foster W. Blaisdell and Marianne E. Kalinke. Lincoln and London: University of Nebraska Press, 1977.

Fragments of the Saga of Magnus, Hacon's Son. In *The Saga of Hacon and a Fragment of the Saga of Magnus, with Appendices*. Trans. G. W. Dasent. Icelandic Sagas, vol. 4; Rerum Britannicarum medii aevi scriptores [88:4]. London: Rolls, 1894, pp. 374–87.

Karlamagnús Saga: The Saga of Charlemagne and His Heroes. 3 vols. Trans. Constance B. Hieatt. Mediaeval Sources in Translation 13, 17, 25. Toronto: Pontifical Institute of Mediaeval Studies, 1975–80.

The King's Mirror (Speculum Regale—Konungs skuggsjá). Trans. Laurence M. Larson. Scandinavian Monographs 3. New York: American-Scandinavian Foundation, 1917; rpt. New York: Twayne, 1973.

Poems of the Vikings: The Elder Edda. Trans. Patricia Terry. Indianapolis and New York: Bobbs-Merrill, 1969.

The Poetic Edda. Trans. Lee M. Hollander. 2d rev. ed. Austin and London: University of Texas Press, 1962.

Saga HeiÞreks konungs ins vitra; The Saga of King Heidrek the Wise. Ed. and trans. Christopher Tolkien. London: Nelson, 1960.

The Saga of Hacon, Hacon's Son. In *The Saga of Hacon and a Fragment of the Saga of Magnus, with Appendices*. Trans. G. W. Dasent. Icelandic Sagas, vol. 4; Rerum Britannicarum medii aevi scriptores [88:4]. London: Rolls, 1894, pp. 1–373.

The Saga of the Volsungs: The Norse Epic of Sigurd the Dragon Slayer. Trans. Jesse L. Byock. Berkeley: University of California Press, 1990.

The Saga of Thidrek of Bern. Trans. Edward R. Haymes. Garland Library of Medieval Literature 56 B. New York and London: Garland, 1988.

The Saga of Tristram and Ísönd. Trans. Paul Schach. Lincoln: University of Nebraska Press, 1973.

The Skalds: A Selection of Their Poems. By Lee M. Hollander. 2d ed. Ann Arbor: University of Michigan Press, 1968.

Strengleikar: An Old Norse Translation of Twenty-One Old French Lais. Ed. and trans. Robert Cook and Mattias Tveitane. Norrøne tekster 3. Oslo: Kjeldeskriftfondet, 1979.

Sturluson, Snorri. *Heimskringla: History of the Kings of Norway*. Trans. Lee M. Hollander. Austin: University of Texas Press for the American-Scandinavian Foundation, 1964.

Sverrissaga: The Saga of King Sverri of Norway. Trans. John Sephton. Northern Library 4. London: Nutt, 1899.

MONOGRAPHS AND ARTICLES

Bagge, Sverre. The Political Thought of The King's Mirror. Mediaeval Scandinavia Supplements 3. Odense: Odense University Press, 1987.

Dyvik, Helge, Karin Fjellhammer Seim, et al. The Bryggen Papers, Supplementary Series 2 ["A Review of the Runic Material," "Runic Inscriptions in Latin," "Addenda runica latina"]. Oslo, Bergen, and Tromsø: Norwegian Universities Press, 1988.

Elliot, Ralph W. V. Runes: An Introduction. 2d ed. Manchester: Manchester University Press; New York: St. Martin's Press, 1989.

Frank, Roberta. Old Norse Court Poetry: The Dróttkvætt Stanza. Islandica 42. Ithaca, N.Y., and London: Cornell University Press, 1978.

Hallberg, Peter. Old Icelandic Poetry: Eddic Lay and Skaldic Verse. Trans. Paul Schach and Sonja Lindgrenson. Lincoln and London: University of Nebraska Press, 1975.

Halvorsen, Eyvind Fjeld. The Norse Version of the Chanson de Roland. Bibliotheca Arnamagnæana, vol. 19. Copenhagen: Munksgaard, 1959.

Kalinke, Marianne E., and P. M. Mitchell. Bibliography of Old Norse-Icelandic Romances. Islandica 44. Ithaca, N.Y., and London: Cornell University Press, 1985.

Knirk, James E. Oratory in the Kings' Sagas. Oslo, Bergen, and Tromsø: Universitetsforlaget, 1981.

Leach, Henry Goddard. Angevin Britain and Scandinavia. Harvard Studies in Comparative Literature 6. Cambridge, Mass.: Harvard University Press; London: Oxford University Press, 1921.

Turville-Petre, E. O. Gabriel. Myth and Religion of the North: The Religion of Ancient Scandinavia. London: Weidenfeld and Nicolson; New York: Holt, Rinehart & Winston, 1964.

――――. Origins of Icelandic Literature. Oxford: Clarendon Press, 1953; rpt. 1967.

――――. Scaldic Poetry. Oxford: Clarendon Press, 1976.

Whaley, Diana. Heimskringla: An Introduction. Viking Society for Northern Research, Text Series, vol. 8. London: Viking Society for Northern Research, University College London, 1991.

CHAPTER 2: ORAL TRADITION, HUMANISM, AND THE BAROQUE

GENERAL

Jorgensen, Theodore. Norwegian Literature in Medieval and Early Modern Times. Northfield, Minn.: St. Olaf College Norwegian Institute, 1952.

Propp, Vladimir. Morphology of the Folktale. Austin: University of Texas Press, 1968, 1984.

LITERATURE IN ENGLISH TRANSLATION

Christiansen, Reidar Th., ed. *Folktales of Norway*. Trans. Pat Shaw Iversen. Chicago: University of Chicago Press, 1964.

Jorgensen, Theodore, ed. and trans. *The Trumpet of Nordland and Other Masterpieces of Norwegian Poetry from the Period 1250–1700*. Northfield, Minn.: St. Olaf College Press, 1954.

Kvideland, Reimund, and Henning K. Sehmsdorf, eds. *Scandinavian Folk Belief and Legend*. Minneapolis: University of Minnesota Press, 1988.

Rossel, Sven H., ed. *Scandinavian Ballads*. WITS II, 2, 1982.

MONOGRAPHS AND ARTICLES

Barnes, Michael. *Draumkvede: An Edition and Study*. Studia Norvegica 16. Oslo: Universitetsforlaget, 1974.

Christiansen, Reidar Th. *The Migratory Legends: A Proposed List of Types with a Systematic Catalogue of the Norwegian Variants*. FFC 175. Helsinki, 1958.

Entwistle, W. J. *European Balladry*. Oxford: Clarendon Press, 1939, 1951.

Friese, Wilhelm. "Scandinavian Baroque Literature: A Synthetic View." *Scandinavica* 4 (1965): 89–105.

Hodne, Bjarne. *Personalhistoriske sagn. En studie i kildeverdi*. Oslo: Universitetsforlaget, 1984.

Hodne, Ørnulf. *The Types of the Norwegian Folktale*. Oslo: Universitetsforlaget, 1984.

Holbek, Bengt. "Nordic Research in Popular Prose Narrative." *Studia Fennica* 27 (1983): 145–76.

Honko, Lauri. "Memorates and the Study of Folk Beliefs." *Journal of the Folklore Institute* 1 (1965): 5–19.

Johnsson, Bengt R., Svale Solheim, and Eva Danielsen, eds. *The Types of Medieval Scandinavian Ballad*. Oslo: Universitetsforlaget, 1970.

Kvalbein, Laila Akslen. *Feminin barokk: Dorothe Engelbretsdotters liv og diktning*. Oslo: Universitetsforlaget, 1970.

Kvideland, Reimund, and Henning K. Sehmsdorf, with Elizabeth Simpson. *Nordic Folklore: Recent Studies*. Bloomington: University of Indiana Press, 1989.

Liestøl, Knut. *Draumkvæde: A Norwegian Visionary Poem from the Middle Ages*. Oslo: Aschehoug, 1946.

———. *The Origin of the Icelandic Family Sagas*. Oslo: Institutt for sammenlignende kulturforskning, 1930.

Lüthi, Max. *The European Folk Tale: Form and Nature*. Trans. John D. Niles. Philadelphia: Institute for the Study of Human Issues, 1982.

Midbøe, Hans. *Petter Dass*. Oslo: Gyldendal, 1947.

Olrik, Axel. "Epic Laws of Folk Narrative." In *The Study of Folklore*. Ed. Alan Dundes. Englewood Cliffs, N.J.: Prentice Hall, 1965, pp. 129–41.

Pentikäinen, Juha. *The Nordic Dead-Child Tradition. Nordic Dead-Child Beings: A Study in Comparative Religion*. FFC 202. Helsinki, 1968.

Roberts, Warren E. *Norwegian Folktale Studies*. Studia Norvegica 13. Oslo: Universitetsforlaget, 1965.

Strömbäck, Dag. "Some Notes on the Nix in Older Nordic Tradition." In *Nordic Literature and Folklore Studies: Essays in Honor of F. L. Utley*. Ed. Jerome Mandel and Bruce Rosenberg. New Brunswick: Rutgers University Press, 1970, pp. 245–56.

———, ed. *Leading Folklorists of the North: Biographical Studies*. Oslo: Universitetsforlaget, 1971.

Sydow, Carl Wilhelm von. "Folktale Studies and Philology: Some Points of View." In *The Study of Folklore*. Ed. Alan Dundes. Englewood Cliffs, N.J.: Prentice Hall, 1965, pp. 219–42.

———. *Selected Papers on Folklore*. Copenhagen: Roskilde og Bagger, 1948.

Thompson, Stith. *The Folktale*. New York: Holt, Rinehart and Winston, 1946. 3d ed. Berkeley: University of California Press, 1970.

CHAPTER 3: HOLBERG AND THE AGE OF ENLIGHTENMENT

GENERAL

Beyer, Edvard, and Morten Moi. *Norsk litteraturkritikks historie. Vol. 1: 1770–1848.* Oslo: Universitetsforlaget, 1990.

Beyer, Harald. *A History of Norwegian Literature*. New York: American Scandinavian Foundation, 1956, pp. 91–116.

Howitt, William, and Howitt, Mary. *The Literature and Romance of Northern Europe*. Vol. 1. London: Colburn, 1852, pp. 343–443.

Semmingsen, Ingrid, Nina Karin Monsen, Stephan Tschudi-Madsen, and Yngvar Ustvedt, eds. *Fra forfall til ny vekst*. Vol. 3 of *Norges kulturhistorie*. 8 vols. Oslo: Aschehoug, 1983.

Venås, Kjell. *Den fyrste morgonblånen: Tekster på norsk frå dansketida*. Oslo: Novus, 1990.

LITERATURE IN ENGLISH TRANSLATION

Holberg, Ludvig. *Erasmus Montanus*. Trans. Petter Næss. wits II, 4, 1989.

———. *Jeppe of the Hill and Other Comedies*. Trans. Sven H. Rossel and Gerald S. Argetsinger. Carbondale: Southern Illinois University Press, 1990.

———. *The Journey of Niels Klim to the World Underground*. Ed. James I. McNab, Jr. Lincoln: University of Nebraska Press, 1960. [Based on original translation of 1742.]

———. *Memoirs*. Ed. Stewart E. Frazer. Leiden: Brill, 1970. [Original ed., London, 1827.]

———. *Peder Paars*. Trans. Bergliot Stromsoe. Lincoln: University of Nebraska Press, 1962.

———. *Selected Essays*. Trans. P. M. Mitchell. Lawrence: University of Kansas Press, 1955.

————. *Seven One-Act Plays.* Trans. Henry Alexander. Princeton, N.J.: American Scandinavian Foundation, 1950.

MONOGRAPHS AND ARTICLES

Argetsinger, Gerald. *Ludvig Holberg's Comedies.* Carbondale: Southern Illinois University Press, 1983.

Billeskov Jansen, F. J. *Ludvig Holberg.* New York: Twayne, 1974.

Campbell, Oscar J. *The Comedies of Holberg.* Cambridge, Mass.: Harvard University Press, 1914.

Jones, James F. "Adventures in a Strange Paradise: Utopia in *Nicolai Klimii Iter Subterraneum.*" *Orbis litterarum* 35 (1980): 193–205.

Naess, Harald. "Peter Harboe Frimann and the Hornelen Affair." *SS* 38 (1966): 26–35.

Parente, James A. "Holberg and Ibsen: A Reassessment." *Scan* 22 (1983): 23–32.

CHAPTER 4: NORWEGIAN LITERATURE 1800–1860

GENERAL

Aarnes, Sigurd Aa. *Æsthetisk Lutheraner og andre studier i norsk romantikk.* Oslo: Universitetsforlaget, 1968.

Beyer, Edvard, and Morten Moi. *Norsk litteraturkritikks historie. Vol. 1: 1770–1848.* Oslo: Universitetsforlaget, 1990.

Burchardt, C. B. *Norwegian Life and Literature: English Accounts and Views Especially in the Nineteenth Century.* Oxford: Oxford University Press, 1920.

Gosse, Edmund W. "Norwegian Poetry since 1814." In his *Studies in the Literature of Northern Europe.* London: Kegan Paul, 1879, pp. 1–37.

Semmingsen, Ingrid, Nina Karin Monsen, Stephan Tschudi-Madsen, and Yngvar Ustvedt, eds. *Det gjenfødte Norge.* Vol. 4 of *Norges kulturhistorie.* Oslo: Aschehoug, 1983.

Skard, Sigmund. *Classical Tradition in Norway: An Introduction with Bibliography.* Oslo: Universitetsforlaget, 1980.

Tysdahl, Bjørn. "Sir Walter Scott and the Beginnings of Norwegian Fiction." In *Scott and His Influence: The Papers of the Aberdeen Scott Conference, 1982.* Ed. J. H. Alexander and David Hewitt. Aberdeen: Association for Literary Studies, 1983, pp. 475–84.

LITERATURE IN ENGLISH TRANSLATION

Norwegian Folk Tales. Compiled by Peter Christen Asbjørnsen and Jørgen Moe. Trans. Pat Shaw and Carl Norman. New York: Pantheon Books, 1982.

Wergeland, Henrik. *Poems.* Trans. G. M. Gathorne-Hardy, Jethro Bithell, and Illit Grøndahl. 2d ed. Oslo: Gyldendal, 1960.

MONOGRAPHS AND ARTICLES
Aasen, Ivar
Walton, Stephen. *Farewell the Spirit Craven: Ivar Aasen and National Romanticism.*
Oslo: Det Norske samlaget, 1987.

Collett, Camilla
Steen, Ellisiv. *Diktning og virkelighet* and *Den lange strid.* Oslo: Aschehoug, 1947 and
1954.

Hansen, Mauritz
Tysdahl, Bjørn J. *Mauritz Hansens fortellerkunst.* Oslo: Aschehoug, 1987.

Moe, Jørgen
Hodne, Ørnulf. *Jørgen Moe. Folkeminnesamler—dikter—prest.* Oslo: Universitetsforlaget, 1982.

Vinje, Aasmund
Haarberg, Jon. *Vinje på vrangen.* Oslo: Universitetsforlaget, 1985.

Welhaven, Johan Sebastian
Andersen-Næss, Reidar. *J. S. Welhaven: Mennesket og dikteren.* Oslo: Gyldendal,
1959.

Wergeland, Henrik
Abrahamsen, Samuel. "Wergeland and Article 2 of the Norwegian Constitution." *SS*
38 (1966): 102–23.
Gathorne-Hardy, G. M. "Introduction." *Poems.* By Henrik Wergeland. Oslo: Gyl-
dendal, 1960, pp. xi–xlv.
Krogvik, Kjell. "Approach to Whitman through Wergeland." In *Walt Whitman
Abroad.* Ed. G. W. Allen. Syracuse: Syracuse University Press, 1955, pp. 137–43.

CHAPTER 5: NORWEGIAN LITERATURE 1860–1910

GENERAL
Budd, John, comp. *Eight Scandinavian Novelists: Criticism and Reviews in English.*
Westport, Conn.: Greenwood Press, 1981.
Downs, Brian. *Modern Norwegian Literature 1860–1918.* Cambridge: Cambridge
University Press, 1966.
Egge, Peter. *Minner.* 4 vols. Oslo: Gyldendal, 1948–55.
Rossel, Sven H. *A History of Scandinavian Literature 1870–1910.* Minneapolis: Uni-
versity of Minnesota Press, 1982.

LITERATURE IN ENGLISH TRANSLATION
Slaves of Love. Ed. James McFarlane. London: Oxford University Press, 1982. [Short
stories 1850–1975.]
Short Stories from Norway 1850–1900. WITS II, 3, 1986. [Short stories 1850–1900.]

The Novels of Bjørnstjerne Bjørnson. Ed. Edmund Gosse. 13 vols. New York: Macmillan, 1895–1909.

Plays by Bjørnstjerne Bjørnson. Trans. Edwin Björkman. 2 vols. London: Duckworth, 1914.

Poems and Songs by Bjørnstjerne Bjørnson. Trans. Arthur Hubbel Palmer. New York: American Scandinavian Foundation, 1915.

Hamsun, Knut. *Night Roamers and Other Stories.* Trans. Tiina Nunnally. Seattle: Fjord Press, 1991.

———. *Selected Letters.* Eds. James McFarlane and Harald Næss. Norwich, England: Norvik Press, 1990.

The Oxford Ibsen. Ed. James McFarlane. 8 vols. London: Oxford University Press, 1960–77.

Ibsen. Trans. Rolf Fjelde. New York: New American Library, 1978. [Major prose plays.]

Ibsen's Poems. Trans. John Northam. Oslo: Norwegian University Press, 1986.

Ibsen: Letters and Speeches. Trans. Evert Sprinchorn. New York: Hill and Wang, 1964.

Lie, Jonas. *The Seer and Other Norwegian Stories.* Trans. Brian Morton and Richard Trevor. London: Forest Books, 1990.

Poems from the Norwegian of Sigbjørn Obstfelder. Trans. Paul Selver. Oxford: Oxford University Press, 1920.

MONOGRAPHS AND ARTICLES

Andersen, Tryggve
Schiff, Timothy. *Scenarios of Modernist Disintegration: Tryggve Andersen's Prose Fiction.* Westport, Conn.: Greenwood Press, 1985.

Bjørnson, Bjørnstjerne
Larson, Harald. *Bjørnstjerne Bjørnson: A Study in Norwegian Nationalism.* New York: King's Croom Press, 1944.
Noreng, Harald. "Bjørnson Research: A Survey." *Scan* 4 (1965): 1–15.
Payne, William M. *Bjørnstjerne Bjørnson, 1832–1910.* Chicago: McClurg, 1910.

Garborg, Arne
Larsen, Hanna Astrup. "Arne Garborg." *SR* 12 (1924): 275–83.
Sjåvik, Jan. "Hulda Bergersen, Arne Garborg, and the Rhetoric of *Hjå ho mor.*" *SS* 55 (1983): 134–48.

Hamsun, Knut
McFarlane, James. "The Whisper of the Blood: A Study of Knut Hamsun's Early Novels." *PMLA* 71 (1956): 563–94.
Naess, Harald. *Knut Hamsun.* Boston: Twayne, 1984.

Ibsen, Henrik
Downs, Brian W. *A Study of Six Plays by Ibsen.* Cambridge: Cambridge University Press, 1950.

Koht, Halvdan. *Life of Ibsen*. New York: Benjamin Blom, 1971.

McFarlane, James. *Ibsen and Meaning: Studies, Essays, and Prefaces*. Norwich, England: Norvik Press, 1989.

Meyer, Michael. *Ibsen: A Biography*. New York: Doubleday, 1971.

Northam, John. *Ibsen's Dramatic Method*. London: Faber and Faber, 1953.

Valency, Maurice. *The Flower and the Castle*. New York: Grosset and Dunlap, 1963.

Weigand, Hermann. *The Modern Ibsen*. New York: Henry Holt, 1925.

Kielland, Alexander

Brown, James. "Charles Dickens and Norwegian *Belles-Lettres* in the Nineteenth Century." *Edda* 1970: 65–84.

Lie, Jonas

Gustafson, Alrik. *Six Scandinavian Novelists*. New York: American Scandinavian Foundation, 1940.

Lyngstad, Sverre. *Jonas Lie*. Boston: Twayne. 1977.

Obstfelder, Sigbjørn

Norseng, Mary Kay. *Sigbjørn Obstfelder*. Boston: Twayne, 1982.

Vogt, Nils

Elster, Kristian. "Three Lyrical Poets of Norway." *SR* 13(1925): 653–63.

CHAPTER 6: NORWEGIAN LITERATURE 1910–1950

GENERAL

Aarnes, Asbjørn. *Perspektiver og profiler i norsk poesi*. Oslo: Solum, 1989.

Birkeland, Bjarte, and Stein Ugelvik Larsen, eds. *Nazismen og norsk litteratur*. Bergen: Universitetsforlaget, 1975.

Dahl, Willy. *Tid og tekst 1884–1935*. Vol. 2 of *Norges litteratur*. Oslo: Aschehoug, 1984.

Egge, Peter. *Minner*. 4 vols. Oslo: Gyldendal, 1948–55.

Engelstad, Irene, and Janneken Øverland, eds. *Frihet til å skrive: Artikler om kvinnelitteratur fra Amalie Skram til Cecilie Løveid*. Oslo: Pax, 1981.

Heggelund, Kjell, Simon Skjønsberg, and Helge Vold, eds. *Fra Herman Wildenvey til Tarjei Vesaas*. Vol. 3 of *Forfatternes litteraturhistorie*. Oslo: Gyldendal, 1981.

———. *Fra Aksel Sandemose til Sigurd Evensmo*. Vol. 4 of *Forfatternes litteraturhistorie*. Oslo: Gyldendal, 1981.

Hoel, Sigurd. *Tanker om norsk diktning*. Oslo: Gyldendal, 1955.

Houm, Philip. *Norsk litteratur efter 1900*. Stockholm: Forum, 1951.

Imerslund, Knut, ed. *Norsk litteraturkritikk 1914–1945*. Oslo: Gyldendal, 1970.

Larsen, Alf. *I kunstens tjeneste. Essays*. Oslo: Dreyer, 1960.

Mæhle, Leif. *Frå bygda til verda: Studiar i nynorsk 1900-talsdikting*. Oslo: Det Norske samlaget, 1967.

Øverland, Arnulf. *I beundring og forargelse*. Oslo: Aschehoug, 1954.

Rønning, Helge, ed. *Sosialisme og litteratur*. Oslo: Pax, 1975.

LITERATURE IN ENGLISH TRANSLATION

Allwood, Inga Wilhelmsen, ed. "Modern Norwegian Poems." In *A Twentieth-Century Nordic Anthology*. Ed. Martin S. Allwood. Oslo: Gyldendal, 1950, pp. 109–88. [Poems by Bull, Nilsen, Ørjasæter, Wildenvey, Øverland, Grieg, Reiss-Andersen, Boyson, Hagerup, Vesaas, Gill, and others.]

Hanson, Katherine, ed. *An Everyday Story: Norwegian Women's Fiction*. Seattle: Seal Press, 1983. [Short stories by Anker, Undset, Sandel, Hagen.]

Herring, Robert, ed. "Norwegian Writing." *Life and Letters and the London Mercury* 65 (1950): 83–170. [Prose and poetry by Sandel, Hoel, Vesaas, Øverland, Reiss-Andersen, Hagen, Grieg and others.]

Jacobsen, Rolf. *The Silence Afterwards: Selected Poems of Rolf Jacobsen*. Trans. and ed. Roger Greenwald. Foreword by Poul Borum. Princeton, N.J.: Princeton University Press, 1982.

———. *Twenty Poems*. Trans. Robert Bly. Madison, Minn.: Seventies Press, 1977.

König, Fritz, ed. "Norwegian issue I: 'Nynorsk.'" *Micromegas* 4, 3 (1971): 1–54. [Poems by Aukrust, Nygard, Ørjasæter, Vaa, Vesaas, and others.]

McFarlane, James, ed. *Slaves of Love and Other Norwegian Short Stories*. Oxford: Oxford University Press, 1982. [Short stories by Duun, Uppdal, Falkberget, Sandel, Braaten, Omre, Øverland, Hoel, Vesaas, Sandemose.]

Sandel, Cora. *Selected Short Stories*. Trans. Barbara Wilson. Seattle: Seal Press, 1985.

———. *The Silken Thread: Stories and Sketches*. Trans. and intro. Elizabeth Rokkan. London: Peter Owen, 1986.

Sandemose, Aksel. *Ross Dane*. Trans. Christopher Hale. Manitoba: Gunnars and Campbell, 1989.

Vesaas, Halldis Moren. *Selected Poems*. Trans. O. Thompson and R. Wakefield. Fredonia: White Pine Press, 1989.

Vesaas, Tarjei. *30 Poems*. Trans. Kenneth Chapman. Oslo: Universitetsforlaget, 1971.

MONOGRAPHS AND ARTICLES

Duun, Olav

Birkeland, Bjarte. "Olav Duun." *Scan* 10 (1971): 112–21.

Naess, Harald. "Olav Duun Abroad." In *Grenzerfahrung—Grenzüberschreitung*. Ed. Leonie Marx and Herbert Knust. Heidelberg: Carl Winter Universitätsverlag, 1989, pp. 193–99.

Voss, James. "Olav Duun's *Menneske og maktene*: Form, Vision, and Contemporary Significance." *SS* 52 (1980): 361–80.

Hoel, Sigurd

Lyngstad, Sverre. *Sigurd Hoel's Fiction: Cultural Criticism and Tragic Vision*. Westport, Conn.: Greenwood Press, 1984.

Sandemose, Aksel

Birn, Randi. *Aksel Sandemose—Exile in Search of a Home*. Westport, Conn.: Greenwood Press, 1984.

Holmesland, Hilde. "The Undivided Self." *NTW* 2 (1988): 54–61.

Undset, Sigrid
Winsnes, A. H. *Sigrid Undset.* New York: Sheed and Ward, 1953.

Vesaas, Tarjei
Chapman, Kenneth. *Tarjei Vesaas.* New York: Twayne, 1969.
Hermundsgård, Frode. *Child of Earth: Tarjei Vesaas and Scandinavian Primitivism.* New York: Greenwood Press, 1989.

CHAPTER 7: NORWEGIAN LITERATURE SINCE 1950

GENERAL

Contemporary Norwegian Prose Writers. Oslo: Norwegian University Press, [1985].
Dahl, Willy. *Fra 40-tall til 70-tall.* Oslo: Gyldendal, 1973.
Garton, Janet. "New Directions in Norwegian Literature." In *RNL*, pp. 163–84.
Masat, Andras. "Modernism, Realism, and Some Other Terms: The Conception and Praxis of the Writer in Norwegian Prose During the Past Twenty Years." *New Comparison* 4 (1987): 151–63.
Naess, Harald. "From Hoel to Haavardsholm." *Literary Review* 12 (1968–69): 133–48.
Nettum, Rolf Nyboe, ed. *I diktningens brennpunkt. Studier i norsk romankunst 1945–1980.* Oslo: Aschehoug, 1982.
Rottem, Øystein. "Generasjoner og epoker: Litteraturhistoriske refleksjoner omkring 1960- og 1970-åra." *NLÅ* 1983: 169–88.
Ystad, Vigdis. "Recent Trends in Norwegian Literary Criticism." *SS* 57 (1985): 32–44.

LITERATURE IN ENGLISH TRANSLATION

Fulton, Robin, ed. "Five Norwegian Poets: Tarjei Vesaas, Rolf Jacobsen, Olav Hauge, Gunvor Hofmo, Stein Mehren." *Lines Review* (Loanhead, Midlothian) 55–56 (1976): 3–87.
Garton, Janet, and Henning Sehmsdorf. *New Norwegian Plays.* Norwich, England: Norvik Press, 1990. [Plays by Vik, Cappelen, Hoem, Løveid.]
Hanson, Katherine, ed. *An Everyday Story: Norwegian Women's Fiction.* Seattle: Seal Press, 1984.
Hauge, Olav H. *Selected Poems.* Trans. Robin Fulton. Fredonia, N.Y.: White Pine Press, 1990.
Johanssen, Terje, ed. *Twenty Contemporary Norwegian Poets.* Oslo: Universitetsforlaget, 1984.
McFarlane, James, ed. *Slaves of Love and Other Norwegian Short Stories.* Oxford: Oxford University Press, 1982.
"Modern Norwegian Writing." *Stand* (Newcastle upon Tyne) 23, 3 (1982): 4–52.
Naess, Harald, ed. "Norwegian Literature since World War II." *Literary Review* 12 (1968–69): 132–276.

Rokkan, Elizabeth, and Ingrid Weatherhead, eds. *View from the Window: Norwegian Short Stories*. Oslo: Norwegian University Press, 1986.

MONOGRAPHS AND ARTICLES

Mawby, Janet [Janet Garton]. "The Norwegian Novel Today." *Scan* 14 (1975): 101–13.

Økland, Einar. "A New Golden Age for Norway." *Times Literary Supplement* 10 (Sept. 1971): 1077–78.

Askildsen, Kjell

Thon, Jahn. "In the Eye of the Storm All Is Still." *NTW* 1 (1988): 42–46.

Bjørneboe, Jens

Garton, Janet. *Jens Bjørneboe: Prophet without Honor*. Westport, Conn.: Greenwood Press, 1985.

Wandrup, Fredrik. "Jens Bjørneboe: The Cry that Fell Silent." *NTW* 1 (1988): 3–7.

Borgen, Johan

Birn, Randi. *Johan Borgen*. New York: Twayne, 1974.

Brantenberg, Gerd

Moberg, Verne. "A Norwegian Women's Fantasy: Gerd Brantenberg's *Egalias døtre* as *kvinneskelig* Utopia." *SS* 57 (1985): 325–32.

Cappelen, Peder W.

Sehmsdorf, Henning K. "The Allegory of a New Beginning: Peder W. Cappelen's *Hvittenland*." *Selecta* 2 (1981): 97–102.

Carling, Finn

Muinzer, Louis A. "Finn Carling: A Man of Letters." *Norseman* 1991: 48–50.

Dahl, Tor Edvin

Hale, Frederick. "Tor Edvin Dahl and the Poverty of Norwegian Prosperity." *WLT* 57 (1983): 13–17.

Faldbakken, Knut

Lessing, Doris. "A Tragedy in Sultry Yellow Light." *Norseman* 1991: 85–87.

Norseng, Mary Kay. "The Crippled Children: A Study of the Underlying Myth in Knut Faldbakken's Fiction." *Scan* 22 (1983): 48–66.

Peterson, Ronald E. "Knut Faldbakken: A Norwegian Contemporary." *SR* 73 (1985): 80–85.

Fløgstad, Kjartan

Freihow, Halfdan W. "Literature as Pretext." *NTW* 1 (1988): 34–35. [On Fløgstad's *Det 7. klima*.]

Haavardsholm, Espen

Fristoe, James A. "Espen Haavardsholm's *Zink* and the Norwegian Literary Class Struggle." *SS* 57 (1985): 60–71.

Hauge, Alfred
Kongslien, Ingeborg R. "Fiction as Interpretation of the Emigrant Experience: The Novels of Johan Bojer, O. E. Rølvaag, Vilhelm Moberg and Alfred Hauge." *American Studies in Scandinavia* 18 (1986): 83–92.
Sjåvik, Jan. "Alfred Hauge's Utstein Monastery Cycle." *WLT* 56 (1982): 54–57.

Hauge, Olav H.
Johansen, Knut. "Beneath the Crag." *NTW* 1 (1988): 12–16.
Stegane, Idar, ed. *Dikt og artiklar om dikt. Til Olav H. Hauge på 70-års dagen*. Oslo: Noregs boklag, 1978.

Haugen, Paal Helge
Gulliksen, Øyvind. "American Resonances in the Poetry of Paal-Helge Haugen." *SS* 57 (1985): 286–309.
Langås, Unni. "The World Made Visible." *NTW* 2 (1989): 6–11.

Hoem, Edvard
Mork, Geir. *Eit romanprosjekt i samanbrot*. Oslo: Det Norske Samlaget, 1984.

Johannesen, Georg
Grøgaard, Johan Fredrik, Kjell Heggelund, Jan Erik Vold, and Einar Økland, eds. *En bok om Georg Johannesen*. Oslo: Gyldendal, 1981.
Mishler, William. "A Reading of Georg Johannesen's *Ars Moriendi*." *Scan* 28 (1989): 161–83.

Løveid, Cecilie
Smidt, Jofrid Karner. "'One Day We Will Find a Path that Has Heart.'" *NTW* 1 (1988): 8–11.

Mehren, Stein
Andersen, Per Thomas. *Stein Mehren—en logos-dikter*. Oslo: Aschehoug, 1982.
———. "'This Darkness So Inexhaustibly Full of Light.'" *NTW* 2 (1989): 26–33.
Bellquist, John Eric. "On Self and World in Stein Mehren's Early Poetry." *Perspectives on Contemporary Literature* 12 (1986): 78–86.
Naess, Harald. "Stein Mehren: Dialectic Poet of Light and Dreams." *WLT* 47 (1973): 66–70.

Mykle, Agnar
Ystaas, Torunn. *Mannsrolle og kvinnesyn hjå Agnar Mykle*. Oslo: Gyldendal, 1977.

Prøysen, Alf
Vestheim, Geir. *Ei bok om Alf Prøysen*. Oslo: Det Norske Samlaget, 1980.

Skouen, Arne
Skjønsberg, Simen, ed. *Hverdag og visjon. En antologi om Arne Skouen*. Oslo: Aschehoug, 1973.

Solstad, Dag
Bache-Wiig, Harald. "'I've Got to Get out of Here.'" *NTW* 2 (1989): 12–17.

Finslo, Yngve. "Rubbing History the Wrong Way." In *The Nordic Mind: Current Trends in Scandinavian Litarary Criticism*. Ed. Frank Egholm Andersen and John Weinstock. Lanham, Md.: University Press of America, 1986, pp. 207–20.

Kittang, Atle. *Allegory, Intertextuality and Irony in Dag Solstad*. Minneapolis: Center for Nordic Studies, 1989.

Sjåvik, Jan. "Language and Myth in Dag Solstad's *Arild Asnes, 1970*." *Pacific Coast Philology* 18 (1983): 30–36.

Vold, Jan Erik

Grøgaard, Johan Fredrik. *Jan Erik Vold, 50*. Oslo: Gyldendal, 1989.

Wassmo, Herbjørg

Isaacson, Lanae. "Fantasy, Imagination, and Reality: Herbjørg Wassmo's *Huset med den blinde glassveranda*." *Scan* 25 (1986): 177–89.

Norseng, Mary Kay. "A Child's Liberation of Space: Herbjørg Wassmo's *Huset med den blinde glassveranda*." *SS* 58 (1988): 48–66.

CHAPTER 8: NORWEGIAN CHILDREN'S LITERATURE

Breen, Else. *Slike skrev de: Verdi og virkelighet i barnebøker 1968–1983*. Oslo: Aschehoug, 1988. [English summary.]

Hagemann, Sonja. *Barnelitteratur i Norge*. 3 vols. Oslo: Aschehoug, 1965–74. [English summary.]

Norsk årbok for barne- og ungdomslitteratur. Ed. Audun Thorsen. Oslo: Lunde, 1977–.

Ørjasæter, Tordis. "Barne- og ungdomslitteraturen fram til vår egen tid." In *Den norske barnelitteraturen gjennom 200 år*. Ed. Tordis Ørjasæter, Halldis Leirpoll, Jo Lie, Gunvor Risa, and Einar Økland. Oslo: Cappelen, 1981, pp. 212–324.

Risa, Gunvor. "Eldre barnelitteratur." In *Den norske barnelitteraturen gjennom 200 år*. Ed. Tordis Ørjasæter, Halldis Leirpoll, Jo Lie, Gunvor Risa, and Einar Økland. Oslo: Cappelen, 1981, pp. 135–211.

Skjønsberg, Kari. *Kjønnsroller og miljø i barnelitteraturen*. Oslo: Universitetsforlaget, 1972. [English summary.]

Vold, Karin Beate. "Contemporary Norwegian Writing for Children: Vitality, National Identity, International Recognition." *NTW* 2 (1989): 40–53.

CHAPTER 9: NORWEGIAN WOMEN WRITERS

Other pertinent works are cited according to period in the other chapter bibliographies

GENERAL

Aasen, Elisabeth. *Kvinners spor i skrift. Supplement til norsk litteraturhistorie*. Oslo: Det Norske samlaget, 1986.

Bonnevie, Mai Bente, et al. *Et annet språk. Analyser av norsk kvinnelitteratur.* Oslo: Pax, 1977.

Engelstad, Irene, and Janneken Øverland. *Frihet til å skrive. Artikler om kvinnelitteratur fra Amalie Skram til Cecilie Løveid.* Oslo: Pax, 1981.

Engelstad, Irene, Jorunn Hareide, Irene Iversen, Torill Steinfeld, and Janneken Øverland, eds. *Norsk kvinnelitteraturhistorie.* 3 vols. Oslo: Pax, 1988–90.

Garton, Janet. *Norwegian Women Writers, 1850–1990.* London: Athlone Press, 1992.

Kress, Helga. "Icelandic Writers." In *Women's Studies Encyclopedia. Vol. 2: Literature, Arts, and Learning.* Ed. Helen Tierney. New York: Greenwood Press, 1990, pp. 165–68.

Kvinnenes kulturhistorie. 2 vols. Oslo: Universitetsforlaget, 1985.

Lassen, Helene. "Kvinnelige forfattere." In *Norske kvinder. En oversigt over deres stilling og livsvilkaar i hundredaaret 1814–1914.* Ed. Fredrikke Mørck. Christiania: Berg og Høgh, 1914, pp. 293–305.

Levin, Hjördis. *Testiklarnas herravälde: Sexualmoralens historia.* Värnamo: Akademilitteratur, 1986.

Norseng, Mary Kay. "Norwegian Writers." In *Women's Studies Encyclopedia. Vol. 2: Literature, Arts, and Learning.* Ed. Helen Tierney. New York: Greenwood Press, 1990, pp. 227–30.

Palmvig, Lis, ed. *Lysthuse. Kvindelitteraturhistorier.* Charlottenlund: Rosinante, 1985.

Rasmussen, Janet E. "Dreams and Discontent: The Female Voice in Norwegian Literature." In *RNL,* pp. 123–40.

———, comp. "Kvinner og norsk litteratur. En bibliografi over forskning 1955–1980." In *Gjennom kvinneøyne,* vol. 2. Ed. Åse Hiorth Lervik. Oslo: Universitetsforlaget, 1982, pp. 203–45.

Zuck, Virpi, Niels Ingwersen, and Harald Naess, eds. *Dictionary of Scandinavian Literature.* New York: Greenwood Press, 1990.

LITERATURE IN ENGLISH TRANSLATION

Claréus, Ingrid, ed. *Scandinavian Women Writers: An Anthology from the 1880s to the 1980s.* Contributions to Women's Studies 95. New York: Greenwood Press, 1989.

Hansen, Katherine, ed. *An Everyday Story: Norwegian Women's Fiction.* Seattle: Seal Press, 1984.

Rokkan, Elizabeth, and Ingrid Weatherhead, eds. *View from the Window: Norwegian Short Stories.* Oslo: Norwegian University Press, 1986.

MONOGRAPHS AND ARTICLES

Bredsdorff, Elias. *Den store nordiske krig om seksualmoralen.* Copenhagen: Gyldendal, 1973.

Clover, Carol. "Hildigunnr's Lament." *Structure and Meaning in Old Norse Litera-*

ture: New Approaches to Textual Analysis and Literary Criticism. Odense: Odense University Press, 1986, pp. 141–83.

Iversen, Irene. "Kvinnelige kritikere og etableringen av en kvinneoffentlighet i 1880 -åra." *Norskrift* 38 (1983): 1–83.

Rasmussen, Janet. "Feminist Criticism and Women's Literature in Norway: A Status Report." *Edda* 80 (1980): 45–52.

Sehmsdorf, Henning. "AT 711 'The Beautiful and the Ugly Twin': The Tale and Its Sociocultural Context." *SS* 61 (1989): 339–352.

Collett, Camilla
Rasmussen, Janet. "The Byronic Lover in Scandinavian Fiction." *Pacific Northwest Council on Foreign Languages: Proceedings* (Corvallis, Ore.) 29 (1978) and 30 (1979): 119–23.

Haff, Bergljot Hobæk
Lange-Nielsen, Sissel. "Angst and Appetite for Life." *Norseman* 1990: 16–18.

Janson, Drude Krog
Røssbø, Sigrun. "Drude Krog Janson, Norwegian-American and Norwegian Writer." In *Seminar on Norwegian-American Literature and History, Høvikodden 1984: Proceedings.* Oslo: NAHA-Norway, 1986, pp. 49–60.

Ostenso, Martha
Buckley, Joan N. "Martha Ostenso: Norwegian-American Immigrant Novelist." *Norwegian-American Studies* (Northfield, Minn.) 28 (1979): 69–81.

Przybyszewska, Dagny Juel
Norseng, Mary Kay. *Dagny: Dagny Juel Przybyszewska—The Woman and the Myth.* Seattle: University of Washington Press, 1991.

Sandel, Cora
Zuck, Virpi. "Cora Sandel: A Norwegian Feminist." *Edda* 1981: 23–33.

Skram, Amalie
Rasmussen, Janet. "Amalie Skram as Literary Critic." *Edda* 1981: 1–11.

Undset, Sigrid
Brunsdale, Mitzi. *Sigrid Undset, Chronicler of Norway.* Oxford and New York: St. Martins Press, 1988.

The Contributors

Faith Ingwersen, who received her doctorate in comparative literature from the University of Chicago, is a former editor of the scholarly journal *Scandinavian Studies*. Her publications include *Martin A. Hansen* (Twayne, 1976) and *Quests for a Promised Land: The Works of Martin Andersen Nexø* (Greenwood, 1984), both coauthored by Niels Ingwersen.

James E. Knirk is senior curator of the Runic Archive at the University Museum of National Antiquities, Oslo, Norway. He has published *Oratory in the Kings' Sagas* (Universitetsforlaget, 1981) and articles on runic inscriptions, sagas, and Old Icelandic manuscripts. He is the editor of the series *Norges innskrifter med de yngre runer*.

James McFarlane is a former pro-vice-chancellor and dean of European studies at the University of East Anglia, Norwich, England. His many publications include translations and critical works, such as the eight-volume *Oxford Ibsen* (1960–77), *Ibsen and the Temper of Norwegian Literature* (Oxford University Press, 1960), *Modernism* (with Malcolm Bradbury) (Penguin, 1976), *Knut Hamsun: Selected Letters* (with Harald Naess), and *Ibsen and Meaning* (both Norvik Press, 1990). He served as editor of the journal *Scandinavica* from 1975 to 1990.

William Mishler is associate professor of Scandinavian studies at the University of Minnesota. His publications include articles on Hamsun, Borgen, Bjørneboe, and Georg Johannesen, as well as many translations, including (with Roger Greenwald) Paal Helge Haugen's *Stone Fences*, which won the Richard Wilbur Prize for the best poetry translation of 1986.

Harald S. Naess is former Torger Thompson Professor of Scandinavian Studies at the University of Wisconsin. He is the author and editor of books on Norwegian literature and Norwegian-American immigrant studies, including *Hamsun og*

Amerika (Gyldendal, 1969), *Americana-Norvegica III* (with Sigmund Skard; Universitetsforlaget, 1971), *Knut Hamsun* (Twayne, 1984), and *Knut Hamsun: Selected Letters* (with James McFarlane; Norvik Press, 1990).

Margaret Hayford O'Leary, who received her doctorate from the University of Wisconsin, is assistant professor of Norwegian at Saint Olaf College and secretary of the Norwegian Teachers' Association of North America. She is the author of *Norsk i sammenheng* (with Frankie Shackelford; McGraw-Hill, 1993) and has published articles on Norwegian women writers.

Jan Sjåvik, with a doctorate in Germanic languages and literature from Harvard University, is associate professor of Scandinavian languages and literature at the University of Washington. He has published articles on Hamsun, Garborg, Alfred Hauge, and Dag Solstad and a book about Garborg's Christiania novels (Aschehoug, 1985).

Kathleen Stokker, who received her doctorate from the University of Wisconsin, is professor of Norwegian and director of Scandinavian studies at Luther College. She has published articles on Norwegian folklore as well as elementary and intermediate language texts, including (with Odd Haddal) *Norsk, nordmenn og Norge* (University of Wisconsin Press, 1981).

Index

Index

Index

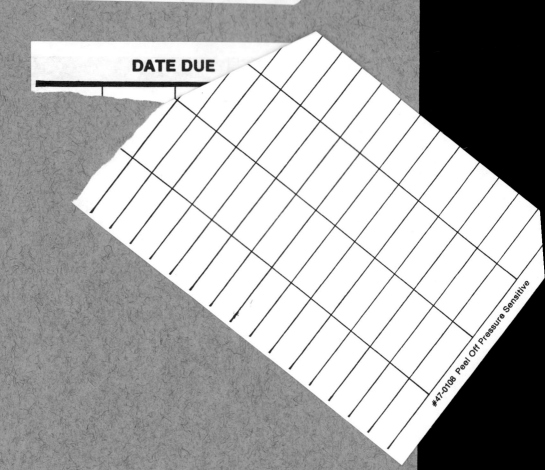

DATE DUE

#47-0108 Peel Off Pressure Sensitive